BURIED TREASURES

Also by Richard Melzer

Fred Harvey Houses of the Southwest

When We Were Young in the West: True Stories of Childhood (editor)

Valencia County, New Mexico:
History Through the Photographer's Lens (with Margaret Espinosa McDonald)

Breakdown: How the Secret of the Atomic Bomb Was Stolen During World War II

Coming of Age in the Great Depression: The Civilian Conservation Corps Experience in New Mexico

From Where I Stand: Contrasting Views of New Mexico History (editor)

Ernie Pyle in the American Southwest

Heroes of the Rio Abajo (editor)

Madrid Revisited: Life and Labor in a New Mexico Coal Mining Camp in the Years of the Great Depression

Buried Treasures
Famous and Unusual Gravesites in New Mexico History

Richard Melzer, Ph.D

SANTA FE

Book designed by Vicki Ahl

© 2007 by Richard Melzer, Ph.D. All rights reserved.

No part of this book may be reproduced in any form or by any electronic or mechanical means including information storage and retrieval systems without permission in writing from the publisher, except by a reviewer who may quote brief passages in a review.

Sunstone books may be purchased for educational, business, or sales promotional use. For information please write: Special Markets Department, Sunstone Press, P.O. Box 2321, Santa Fe, New Mexico 87504-2321.

Library of Congress Cataloging-in-Publication Data

Melzer, Richard.
  Buried treasures : famous and unusual gravesites in New Mexico history / Richard Melzer.
    p. cm.
  Includes index.
  ISBN 978-0-86534-531-7 (softcover : alk. paper)
 1. Sepulchral monuments--New Mexico. 2. Sepulchral monuments--New Mexico--Pictorial works. 3. Cemeteries--New Mexico. 4. New Mexico--Biography. 5. Historic sites--New Mexico. 6. New Mexico--History, Local. 7. New Mexico--History, Local--Pictorial works. 8. Registers of births, etc.--New Mexico. 9. New Mexico--Genealogy. I. Title.

F797.M45 2007
978.9--dc22

2007002180

WWW.SUNSTONEPRESS.COM
SUNSTONE PRESS / POST OFFICE BOX 2321 / SANTA FE, NM 87504-2321 /USA
(505) 988-4418 / ORDERS ONLY (800) 243-5644 / FAX (505) 988-1025

To all those who generously shared directions over thousands of miles of travel and through centuries of researched history, especially
Elizabeth Kelley to the far west,
David N. Lotz to the far east,
Marjorie Day to the far south, and
Nelson Van Valen to the far north.

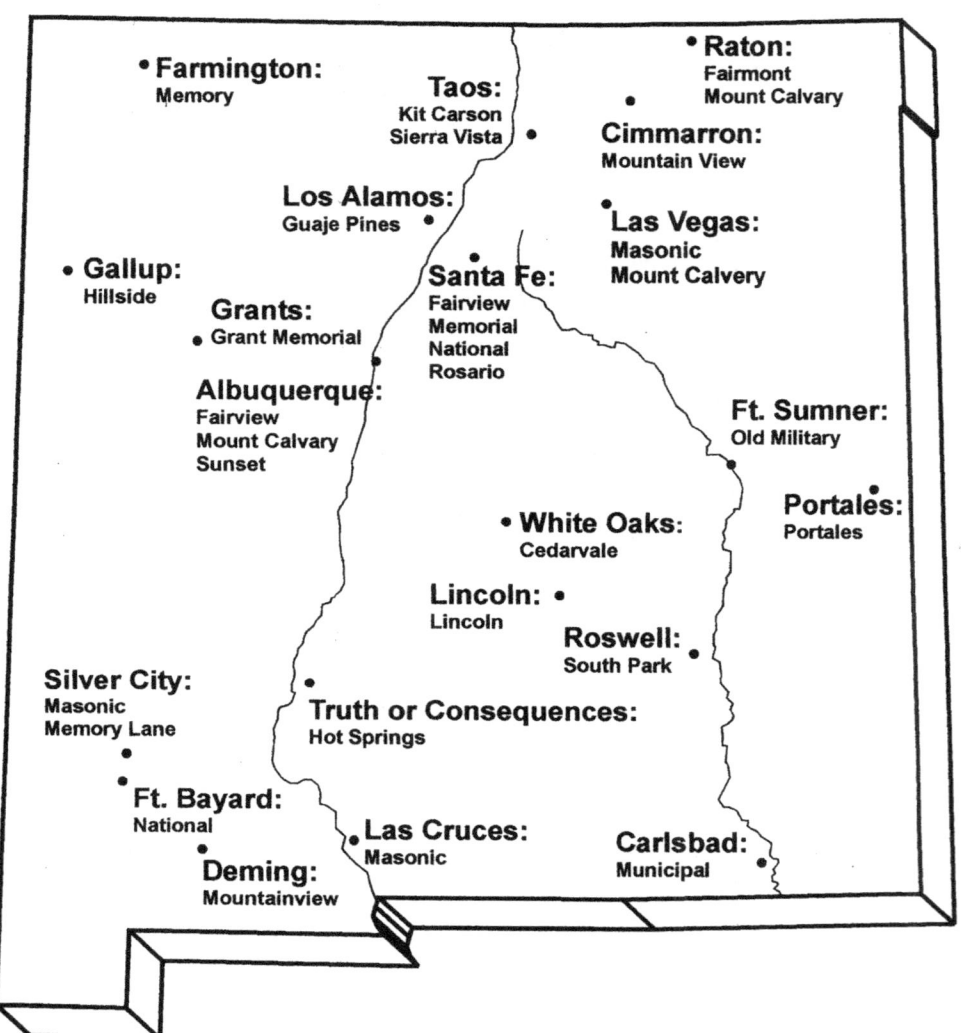

Thirty of the Historically Most Important Cemeteries in New Mexico.
Courtesy of Jill Chapman.

Contents

Acknowledgements 9
1. Not Forgotten? 13
2. Artists, Performers, and Directors 29
3. Authors and Composers 63
4. Cultural Preservationists 81
5. Business Leaders 97
6. Educational Leaders 119
7. Sung and Unsung Heroes 131
8. Lawmen, Criminals, and Victims of Crime 153
9. Political, Diplomatic, and Judicial Leaders 195
10. Religious Leaders 237
11. Scientists and Medical Personnel 251
12. Wartime Leaders and Victims to the End of the Indian Wars in New Mexico, 1886 261
13. Wartime Leaders and Victims Since the Spanish-American War, 1898 . . . 295
14. Unusual Graves 329

Appendix D: Famous New Mexicans Interred in Public Cemeteries in New Mexico 347

Appendix B: Famous New Mexicans Interred in Public Cemeteries in Other States and Countries 361

Appendix C: Famous New Mexicans Who Have Been Cremated 371

Appendix D: Famous New Mexicans Who Originally Came to New Mexico to Recover Their Health or to Accompany Someone Else Who Was Ill 375

Endnotes 379
Suggested Readings 459
Index 463

Acknowledgements

As with all travelers through time and space, I could not have found my way without the help of countless men and women who generously shared their knowledge with a person who was, for many, a complete stranger, but often, with time, became a friend.

Many of these trail guides were fellow students of the past, including Don E. Alberts, Dorothy Cave Aldrich, Linda Aldrich, Stephen J. Andrews, Cecilia Jensen Bell, Nancy R. Bartlit, Maisha Baton, John O. Baxter, Dorothy Simpson Beimer, Cecilia Jensen Bell, John P. Bloom, James Boeck, Robert E. Brennan, David L. Caffey, Sharon Callahan, Sharon DeBartolo Carmack, Mary Jean Straw Cook, Daniel Davis, Glenna Dean, Elvis E. Fleming, Manuel Garcia, Nasario García, Mark L. Gardner, Robert Hart, Robert L. Hart, Thomas Hedglen, Rick Hendricks, Janaloo Hill, Stan Hordes, Heidi Huckabee (and her able young students in Roswell), Jon Hunner, Chris Judson, Robert Julyan, Elizabeth Kelley, John Kessell, Catherine Lavender, Carleen Lazzell, Robert Lenberg, Jack Loeffler, Eleanor Love, E.A. Mares, Melissa Simpson Masterson, Sandra K. Mathews, Margaret Espinosa McDonald, Marian Meyer, Craig Newbill, Jenna Newell, Sally Noe, Frederick Nolan, Ana Pacheco, Gerald G. Raun, Ollie Reed, Jr., Sue Richardson, Nancy Robertson, Ray Sadler, Charlie Sanchez, Jr., Virginia Sanchez, Nancy E. Shockley, Francisco Sisneros, Jim Snyder, Sharon Snyder, Gail T. South, Jake Spidle, Diana Stein, John Taylor, Jerry Thompson, Robert J. Tórrez, David Townsend, Samuel Truett, Jerry Ueckert, Nelson Van Valen, Marta Weigle, Michael Welsh, Robert R. White, Jeanne Whitehouse, John P. Wilson, Christopher Ziegler, and Stephen Zimmer.

Other trail guides were archivists, librarians, and curators, including LesLee Alexander of the Shalam Colony and Oahspe Mystery Museum, Nathan Augustine of the Desert Caballeros Western Museum of Wickenburg, Arizona, Susan Berry of the Silver City Museum, D. Ray Blakeley of the Herzstein Memorial Museum in Clayton, Bill Boehm and Dennis Daily of the Archives and Special Collections Department at the New Mexico State University Library, Ed Boles, the Historic Preservation Planner for the City of Albuquerque; Nancy Brown-Martinez of the Center for Southwest Research at Zimmerman Library at the University of New Mexico, Marilyn Clark of the Menual History Library at the Menaul School in Albuquerque, George K. Combs of the Special Collections Department at the Alexandria, Virginia, Public Library, Irisha Corral at the

"There is nothing that we can do that is more American than getting in a car and striking out across country.... This is the way we enter history. Get in a car and find the country and ourselves."
—William Least Heat-Moon[1]

Donnelly Library at Highlands University, Louise Dano of the Joseph R. Skeen Library at New Mexico Tech in Socorro, Marjorie Day of the Thomas Branigan Memorial Library, Deanna Einspahr of the Randall Davey Audubon Center in Santa Fe, Dody Fugate of the Laboratory of Anthropology in Santa Fe; Gigi Gallisini of the Telephone Pioneers Museum in Albuquerque, Terry Gugliotta, University Archivist at the University of New Mexico, Margo Gutierrez at the University of Texas in Austin, Texas, Tomás Jaehn of the Fray Angélico Chávez Historical Library at the Museum of New Mexico in Santa Fe, Beth Lander of the Mercer Museum in Doylestown, Pennsylvania, LaRena Miller of the Geronimo Springs Museum in Truth or Consequences, New Mexico, Linda K. Lewis of Zimmerman Library at the University of New Mexico, Felicia Lujan of the New Mexico State Records Center and Archives in Santa Fe, Peggy McBride at the New Mexico Health Historical Collections at the University of New Mexico School of Medicine, Barbara McCandless of the Amon Carter Museum in Ft. Worth, Texas, Paul Merrill at the Ramah Museum in Ramah, New Mexico, Claire Munzenrider at the Museum of New Mexico in Santa Fe, Louise Moye of the Ruck County Public Library in Henderson, Texas, Nita Murphy at the Taos Historical Museum, Marina Ochoa at the Archives of the Archdiocese of Santa Fe, Arthur L. Olivas in the photo Archives at the Palace of the Governors in Santa Fe, Wendy Quintana at the Thomas C. Donnelly Library at New Mexico Highlands University in Las Vegas, New Mexico, Al Regensberg of the New Mexico State Records Center and Archives in Santa Fe, Allan Renga of the San Diego Aerospace Museum; Cameron Saffell of the New Mexico Farm and Ranch Heritage Museum in Las Cruces, Katherine Scott Sturdevant at the Pueblo, Colorado, Public Library, Barbara Thomas at the Billy the Kid Museum in Hico, Texas, Amy Verheide in the Photo Archives at the Palace of the Governors in Santa Fe, Richard "Chip" Ware at the University of New Mexico's Jonson Gallery, Kris A. White of Pima Community College in Tucson, and Esther N. Shir, Stephanie West, and Judy Marquez of the library at my home institution, the University of New Mexico-Valencia Campus.

Still other guides were helpful sextons and members of cemetery staffs, including Bob Baca and his staff at Rosario Cemetery in Santa Fe, Judy Bennett at the Masonic Cemetery in Las Cruces, William B. DeBoer, Jr., at the Colorado Springs Cemetery in Colorado Springs, Colorado, Jerry L. Ibarra and Angeleen V. Saiz at the Fairview Cemetery in Albuquerque, Paul F. Layer, Jr., and Sue Eifert at Sunset Memorial Park in Albuquerque, Dennis Martinez at the Kit Carson Cemetery in Taos, Henry Perea at the San Clemente Catholic Cemetery in Los Lunas, and Freida Robinson at the Ft. Bliss National Cemetery in El Paso.

Unable to travel to all the places to take all the photographs for this extensive study, I relied on a whole army of fellow cemetery photographers, including Ralph Beckwith, Thomas Broderick, Gary Chrisman, Steven B. Corley, Marty Davis, Richard R. Dean, Samuel L. Gauny, JoAnne Gosen, Andy Gregg, Scott Groll, Joan and Jack Gundolfi, Jim Harris, Shirley Hurd, Sam

Jackson, Kathryn Jones, Chris Kent, Gene Kirby, Steven Klein, Kent Kool, Beth Lander, Cindy Long, Elaine Lucarini, Kevin McKinney, J. Donald Morfe, Ronald R. Paul, Christopher A. Ratzel, Mary Robinson, Martin Skubinna, Mike Stevenson, Ken Taylor, Jim Thomas, Stew Thornley, Gina Marie Torres, Bill Walker, and Patricia Young. Special thanks to David N. Lotz who not only shared many of his existing photos, but also took many new ones and helped to track down the location of some of the most elusive gravesites included in this work.

Family members of famous New Mexicans were similarly helpful. They included Norman Bakos, Shirley Boles, Jim Brito, Michael Campbell, Sue Walsh Campbell, Jack Carmichael, Ed Chacon, Ted Chacon, Virginia Chacón, Kathleen D. Church, Francis Conway, Richard R. Dean, Frederick H. Fornoff, Zonnie Gorman, Wanda McLaughlin Hughes, Michael Hurd, Bill Jette, Karen Kilgore, Harrison Lapahie, Jr., Richard and Cindy Long, Margaret Espinosa McDonald, Oscar Medders, Lloyd Miles, Nadine Milford, Kenneth Mills, Bill Parks, Clara Parsons, Harry Parsons, Ashley D. Pond IV, Jonathan Porter, Carol Hurd Rogers, the Reverend Ned Ross, Ernest Sansome, Benny Sisneros, Martín Sisneros, Berry Spradley, Janet Steele, Josephine Waconda, Gene Walsh, Barbara Waters, and James Williams II.

Perhaps my best travel guide was a person I never met, no less traveled with. An anonymous author, who signed his work Quentin, wrote a rare, but valuable manuscript entitled, *Eternal New Mexicans: A Guide to the Final Resting Places of 350 Noteworthy Persons of the Land of Enchantment*.[2] The mysterious Quentin described burial sites across New Mexico, giving exacting instructions on how to find not only whole cemeteries, but also specific, often hard-to-find gravesites. Forty-eight of the gravesites photographed and included in this book were found with Quentin's able assistance.

Special thanks to Richard F. Madden, M.D., who not only has monitored this historian's health over many years, but has also generously lent his expertise to review all medical references in the text. Jill Chapman, Susan Jackson, and Mary Robinson shared their remarkable computer expertise at key junctures in the project.

Finally, there is my wife, Rena, who somehow understood my passion for this rather morbid project, sent me on my way on countless jaunts, and always greeted me with unwavering affection on my return. If we "get in a car [to] find the country and ourselves," as William Least Heat-Moon suggests, then we come home to find the happiness, love, and subsidence we need to live and work another day.

Mea Culpa

The author takes full responsibility for any unintended wandering from the always-preferred path of truth and accuracy.

—Richard Melzer
Belen, New Mexico

1

Not Forgotten?

"...we exist as long as somebody remembers us."
—*Carlos Ruiz Zafón[1]*

Large numbers of the living are fascinated by the resting places of the dead. Rather than think of cemeteries as dark, foreboding places, many visitors seek their serene surroundings for moments of quiet solitude and reflection. Health enthusiasts enjoy their peaceful walking paths. Historians search for evidence about everything from obscure local events to global crises. Genealogists look for important pieces in their families' historical puzzles. Artists admire the art and architecture and sometimes capture the beauty of cemeteries on canvas or on film. Authors use cemeteries for the settings of poignant fictional moments. Tourists include cemeteries on their itineraries to add a bit of mystery to their travel plans.[2]

Most visitors simply wander up and down rows of headstones, reading epitaphs and imagining the countless stories buried with those now gone. Epitaphs are usually heart-felt and sincere, but one has been of particular interest to me over the years. Time and again I have seen the words "gone but not forgotten" engraved on headstones, causing me to wonder if that noble vow was truly kept and, if so, by whom and for just how long. If not forgotten, what is remembered about a person and the life he or she lived? Are memories about a life more truth, fiction, a mixture of the two, or, most likely, whatever each generation, with its unique historical perspective, chooses to remember or believe about the dead?[3]

I am most likely to ponder these questions when I discover the headstones of famous New Mexicans. Despite the impressive size of their funerals or the number of friends, relatives, and admirers who may have mourned their passing, even the most celebrated of our predecessors seem destined to oblivion within two or three generations of their deaths. Sadly, most famous lives are like comets that draw awe and admiration as they speed across the sky, only to disappear quickly in the vast expanse of history. Few are remembered even when streets, parks, buildings, or whole towns are named in their honor. Clear proof of the public's collective amnesia is the fact that few today can recall where our most prominent New Mexicans are buried, no less when they died or what caused their demise.

To help us to better remember our most noteworthy citizens, I set out to discover the present locations of their human remains and, when feasible, to photograph their elaborate or, more often, humble, unassuming gravestones.

My quest began over a decade ago. After visiting more than 150 cemeteries (see Appendixes A and B) and covering thousands of miles of roads in my faithful Corolla (now convinced it must be an SUV), it is time to share my research in book form. Despite minor inconveniences (such as extreme temperatures and strong winds) and some harrowing moments (I have developed an aversion to narrow mountain roads), the journey has been intriguing, interesting, and often emotionally moving. At the conclusion of my journey, I can assert that I have probably stood closer to a greater number of famous New Mexicans than any single person in New Mexico history. I have uttered a silent prayer of acknowledgement—if not always appreciation—at gravesites across the state and, at times, across the nation.

My graveyard meanderings grew in intrigue when I came across not only famous, but also unusual gravesites. Reflecting New Mexico's celebrated diversity, many gravesites were unusual based on the cultural traditions of various ethnic, racial, and religious groups.[4] Reflecting New Mexico's widespread poverty, other gravesites were unusual based on their inexpensive, often innovative materials, ranging from old bed frames to porcelain bathtubs. And, reflecting the wit and humor of New Mexicans in good times and in bad, many gravestones were unique based on their often-comical epitaphs, icons, or designs. In an effort to balance the more somber tone of chapters 2 to 13, devoted to famous gravesites, I offer photos of more unusual, culturally diverse gravesites in chapter 14.

Combined, these chapters form a composite image of New Mexico, filled with heroes, villains, tradition, humor, poverty, and wealth. Cemeteries in towns like Tombstone, Arizona, are little more than crass commercial enterprises, while cemeteries in other states appear like well-manicured parks compared to the variety and seeming disarray of many cemeteries in New Mexico.[5] Of course these are the very qualities that give New Mexico a unique sense of place, making it an ideal land in which to live—and eventually rest—through the ages.

Who are included among the famous?

Determining who should be included among the famous in New Mexico history was a daunting task. After much thought, I decided to employ the broadest criteria. One therefore qualified for inclusion as among the most prominent if (1) he or she was born or died in New Mexico and became famous here or elsewhere or (2) he or she was born or died elsewhere, but participated in at least one major event in New Mexico's past.

As might be expected in a state of great diversity, the deceased whose gravesites appear in this volume include people of all ethnicities, races, religions, genders, ages, occupations, interests, and regions of New Mexico. (There are even a few noble animals that deserve recognition, if not equal status to humans.)

Whole groups, as well as deserving individuals, are represented, including the famous Buffalo Soldiers, the brave recipients of the Medal of Honor, the efficient Harvey Girls, the victims of Pancho Villa's 1916 raid on Columbus, the intrepid Navajo Code Talkers, and the long-suffering soldiers of the Bataan Death

March.[6] Although space does not allow the inclusion of all deceased members of these worthy groups, small samples have been gleaned to represent the many who served so admirably and well, often in the face of great adversity.

The book as a whole is divided into eleven broad categories of noteworthiness: artists, performers, and directors; authors and composers; cultural preservationists; business leaders; educational leaders; sung and unsung heroes; lawmen, criminals, and victims of crime; political, diplomatic, and judicial leaders; religious leaders; scientists and medical personnel; and wartime leaders and victims (to the end of the Indian wars in New Mexico in 1886 and since the Spanish-American War in 1898). Of course many persons cannot be pigeonholed into just one category. Multi-talented individuals like Carl Gorman and Fray Angélico Chávez are therefore listed in one category and cross-listed in one or more others.

In what eras did they live?

Photographing famous headstones requires the existence of identifiable gravesites. This statement sounds obvious enough until one realizes that several cultural groups preferred not to identify the location of their dead with physical markers during much, if not all, of their histories. This was especially true of many Native American tribes and most early Spanish settlers in New Mexico.[7]

As Martina Will de Chaparro has explained in her exceptional study of death and burial practices in colonial New Mexico, most early Catholics preferred to be buried beneath church floors. There was, in fact, a "hierarchy of sacred space" with places nearer the altar considered more holy, and hence more expensive to occupy, while spaces nearer the door were considered spiritually less desirable, and hence less expensive to claim. Without church diagrams to remind later generations where earlier parishioners had been buried, graves were regularly disturbed when later burials took place. The remains of as many as thirteen colonists "mixed without distinction" were discovered in a single grave in the Santuario de Guadalupe in Santa Fe.[8] A U.S. Army expedition of 1853 discovered "a great many human bones, which now lie scattered about," on the church floor at Gran Quivira, the mischief of treasure hunters who had pursued an old tale that Spanish gold or silver was buried somewhere in the mission. Nearly a century later, Civilian Conservation Corps workers unearthed forty-one human remains (including an adult with a child wrapped in its arms) while assisting archaeologists in the old Spanish mission church at Quarai.[9] An early twentieth century photo of archeologist Alfred V. Kidder at the Pecos Pueblo mission church shows Kidder beside a gruesome collection of human bones excavated from beneath the mission's floor.[10]

Not even the graves of the most powerful colonial leaders buried in New Mexico can be readily identified. In the best example of this kind, E. Boyd asserted that Don Diego de Vargas, the reconqueror of New Mexico following the Pueblo Revolt of 1680, was probably buried beneath the floor of a chapel located on the southeast corner of the Palace of the Governors in Santa Fe when he died in April 1704. But with remodeling and the loss or destruction of the first book of burial records in Santa Fe, we cannot be sure where Vargas's body lies today. In Boyd's opinion, it is quite possible that Vargas's remains may now lie beneath the pavement at the busy northwest corner of Santa Fe's Washington and Palace Avenues, where the old palace chapel once stood.[11] Others, led by John Kessell, believe that Vargas's body was probably moved from the old chapel to a respected place near the altar when the parish church was built a short distance from the palace between 1714 and 1717.[12]

Efforts to identify specific gravesites hardly improved with time in the colonial era. Boyd believed that with the exception of two Franciscan graves "there is not one identified grave of any person of the eighteenth century in New Mexico."[13] A third exception has been discovered at the St. Augustine Catholic Church in Isleta where Fray Juan José Padilla died and was buried near the sanctuary's main altar in February 1756.[14]

1. A sign on the corner of Washington and Palace Avenues identifies the possible site of Don Diego de Vargas's grave in Santa Fe's first chapel. Unless otherwise stated, all photos in this book were taken by the author and are part of his private collection.

Indoor burials were banned by royal decree in 1787, but the practice persisted for spiritual reasons and for fear of the desecration of outdoor graves by wild animals. Ideas and values changed slowly. Eventually, new attitudes regarding death and modern concerns for health and sanitation led a majority of Hispanics to request outside burials. By the mid nineteenth century Hispanics regularly used carved wooden and, increasingly, stone markers to demarcate and decorate their exterior graves, thus leaving far more reliable evidence of their gravesite locations.[15]

The use of more durable markers to identify the location of the deceased was a religious and cultural practice reinforced by New Mexico's ever increasing Anglo population in the nineteenth century. Anglos brought new woodworking tools, paint, iron, and, eventually, granite stone—essential items for the construction of more lasting grave markers. Once built into New Mexico after 1879, the railroad delivered large quantities of these industrial goods, making grave markers increasingly accessible and, for some, increasingly affordable. By 1905 the demand for accessible, affordable gravestones was so great in New Mexico and across the United States that Sears, Roebuck produced a special tombstone catalog, with marble tombstone markers ranging in price from as low as $4.88 to as high as $173.30. Inscribed letters cost an extra six cents each.[16]

The historical period covered in this book thus emphasizes the years since the mid-nineteenth century when more lasting, identifiable headstones were erected in the exterior graveyards of New Mexico. Largely intact, despite the ravages of time, the elements, and shameful acts of vandalism, these headstones are the earliest of the 345 famous markers photographed, included here, and hopefully preserved to help future generations remember the central figures of our long past.

Accompanying Data

Each famous New Mexican included in this volume is memorialized with the help of eight vital statistics: the deceased person's name(s), source(s) of notoriety, birth date, place of birth, date of death (and age), place of death, cause of death, and current resting place. Similar notations are offered for New Mexican leaders not photographed for various reasons, from lack of space to missing remains.

- *Name(s)*

    Every effort has been made to accurately provide each famous New Mexican's complete name, including first name, middle name(s), nickname(s), surname(s), original names (if later changed), maiden name (if married), pen name(s) (if authors), stage name(s) (if actors), and sundry aliases (if outlaws). As notorious badmen, Billy the Kid and "Bronco Bill" Walters vie for the record number of aliases and the dubious distinction of the best outlaw monikers.[17]

- *Notoriety*

    Each famous New Mexican's notoriety is described briefly, focusing on his or her most noteworthy deeds. These summaries are offered at the risk of neglecting other achievements that would undoubtedly be included if this work were a complete dictionary or encyclopedia of prominent New Mexicans—a much-needed endeavor far beyond the more modest scope of this work.

- *Birth Dates and Places*

    Each famous New Mexican's birth date has been recorded, although some birth months, days, and even years were either undocumented or reported differently at different times by different historians, later descendants, or even the subjects themselves. Confusion was especially possible if a person was born on the frontier where opportunities for record keeping, beyond the inside covers of family Bibles, were often rare and sometimes impossible, given a general lack of literacy and, frequently, scarce writing materials.

    At least some observers were candidly honest about this lack of vital information. In the case of Billy Gunter of Estancia, a question mark was prudently placed in lieu of his birth year because no one could recall this information after Billy had passed on, if Billy had ever known it himself.

- *Death Dates (Ages) and Places*

    Accuracy in reporting death dates and places is more likely than accuracy in reporting birth dates and places, if only because our most noteworthy historical figures were usually so well-known by the time of their respective deaths that their passing (down to the hour and minute of the day) was often noted in the press and in other public records by the early twentieth century. Difficulties still arose, especially because New Mexico has the dubious distinction of being one of the last two states in the nation to create a Department of Public Health. New Mexico and Georgia only created their departments of public health and

2. Estancia Cemetery, Estancia, New Mexico

began keeping death registration records in 1919, in the wake of the Spanish flu epidemic of the previous year. Even today, death records are closed to the general public for fifty years, meaning that the most recent accessible records are already fifty years old.[18]

Mistakes in newspaper reporting, on death certificates, and on gravestones themselves are woefully common. According to one estimate, death certificates are erroneous in one way or another twenty-nine percent of the time nationwide, with the death certificates of minorities most likely to suffer such unfortunate mistakes.[19] Errors were discovered on the headstones of at least twenty-two famous New Mexicans, from Sadie Orchard, a nineteenth century madam, to William McDonald, our first state governor.

- *Cause of Death*

Cause of death is noted, especially if it was well known, as with notorious murders, or if it was tragic, as with most accidents. Of course determining the cause of many deaths was problematic in earlier periods of history when medical and forensic science was less advanced and when determining cause of death was often uncertain or simply wrong, based on what we now know in retrospect. At other times, cause of death was intentionally omitted or even changed, given circumstances that were socially or culturally taboo in the past. For these and other reasons, "unstated natural causes" is often the best conclusion we can draw from admittedly incomplete contemporary sources.[20]

Although New Mexico has experienced more than its share of violence and is known for such violent characters as Billy the Kid and Clay Allison, the vast majority of famous New Mexicans succumbed to natural, rather than violent, causes of death. This was even true of famous lawmen. While a predictably high fifty-five percent of the criminals included in Chapter 8 (Lawmen, Criminal, and Victims of Crime) died in acts of violence, sixty-five percent of the lawmen listed in the same chapter died peaceably "with their boots on" of such common maladies as cirrhosis of the liver (as with Elfego Baca, aged eighty) and "heart ailment" (as with Prohibition agent Howard S. Beacham, also in his eightieth year).

- *Resting Place*

Current, rather than "final" resting places are noted, if only because many of our most famous New Mexicans have been laid to rest in various places over time. In fact, according to an author who has followed the "posthumous adventures" of famous individuals from around the world, "research shows that the more notable a person was during life, the less likely it is that he or she will be allowed to rest in peace" in death.[21]

In New Mexico history the long list of transient remains includes Zebulin Pike, Charles Bent, Kit Carson, Pat Garrett, Adolph Bandelier, and D.H. Lawrence. Reinterments were the result of such different circumstances as the abandonment of old cemeteries (as with most military forts in New Mexico by the 1890s), efforts to unite deceased family members (as with Pat Garrett), and attempts to bring the deceased home to New Mexico after they were initially buried elsewhere (as with Kit Carson, Adolph Bandelier, and D.H. Lawrence).

Billy the Kid's gravestone—by far the most famous and most frequently visited in New Mexico—provides an example of yet another problem in photographing headstones: they are sometimes stolen! In Billy the Kid's case, his gravestone was stolen not once but twice (including for a twenty-five year period), leading to the placing of iron bars not only around but also over his present marker. With entry into Billy's current "prison cell" only possible by unlocking a large, heavy-duty padlock, the often elusive outlaw is far better guarded in death than he ever was in life.

Causing more confusion, older, decaying gravestones have sometimes been replaced with newer, more durable stones by descendants or later admirers. While well intended, this practice has led to the loss of some valuable historical artifacts, the loss of accurate historical information, or, sometimes, the perpetuation of original mistakes. Billy the Kid's mother provides the best example of the latter problem. When Catherine Antrim died from tuberculosis in 1874 her gravesite in Silver City was marked by a wooden cross. Moved to a new cemetery northeast of town in 1882, her gravesite was marked with a headboard that claimed that Mrs. Kathrine Antrim had died on September 8 (rather than September 16), 1874, at the age of forty-five. Weather-beaten and decayed by 1947, the old headboard was replaced by a granite headstone donated by a Silver City funeral home. Fortunately, the wooden slab was saved and placed on display at the state historical museum in Lincoln. Unfortunately, while the generous makers of Mrs. Antrim's new granite stone corrected her date of death (if only by not mentioning a specific month or day), they never corrected the misspelling of her given name.[22]

Resting places are increasingly difficult to trace with the growing popularity of cremations. Some cremains have been buried in cemeteries with traditional ceremonies and headstones. But others have been scattered in less traditional locations, usually over places with special meaning in the deceased person's life, including mountains (as with Ansel Adams), ranches (as with Georgia O'Keeffe), cultural ruins (as with Adolph Bandelier), or the sea (as with J. Robert Oppenheimer). Other ashes have been kept in urns or wall niches located in the homes of close friends or relatives or in (hopefully) secure public places (as with Edgar Lee Hewett, Raymond Jonson, Charles Lummis, and John Gaw Meem).[23] (See Appendix C.)

Photographing resting places is also difficult when some remains have never been discovered, no less interred, as a result of tragedy or foul play. The most famous example of this kind involved the sad case of Albert J. and Henry Fountain, whose bodies were never recovered after this father and son pair mysteriously disappeared en route to their home in Mesilla in April 1896. In some cases, like the Fountains', the missing persons are remembered with a cenotaph, or commemorative headstone. More than fifty cenotaphs have been erected in a designated section of the Santa Fe National Cemetery to honor servicemen whose bodies have never been recovered. Unfortunately,

3. National Cemetery, Santa Fe, New Mexico

as in the case of Captain Maximiliano Luna (who drowned in November 1900 while attempting to cross a flooded river in the Philippines) not even a stone exists to honor many of those whose earthly remains have never been found, no less properly buried.

At least two famous New Mexicans were buried in gravesites that are known, but have gone unmarked. John Braden, one of the bravest, most selfless heroes in all of New Mexico history, lies buried in an unmarked grave in the old section of Albuquerque's Fairview Cemetery. Doc Noss, famous for his rumored gold mine at Victorio Peak, lies in an unmarked grave at the Masonic Cemetery in Las Cruces.

Locating other gravesites has been difficult because a surprisingly large number of gravesites and whole cemeteries have been lost, moved, or forgotten. As a ranch girl who grew to maturity on the violent frontier, Agnes Morley Cleaveland remembered accompanying a young friend to an isolated place where two men had been attacked by raiding Indians and had been buried where they'd died near the Datil Divide. "[T]here was little to see—just two grave-shaped mounds of loose rock with rough wooden crosses at their heads." After imagining the violence that had occurred at the scene, Agnes and her friend mournfully "mounted our ponies and rode away in silence."[24] Already obscure in the 1880s, the location of these gravesites has been lost forever in the passing years.

The same fate almost befell a small cemetery discovered near Alma, New Mexico, by archaeologist Richard Eiseler, as reported in the *Silver City Enterprise*. Eiseler found five gravestones enclosed within a dilapidated fence in 1933. According to three of these headstones, Charles Moore was "murdered at Lovejoy" in 1880, Edward W. Lyon, an Englishman, was "killed by Apaches" in 1885, and L. Flanagan was "murdered at Mogollon" in 1899.[25]

Other New Mexicans have opted to be buried on their private land in remote sections of the state. James E. Cree was buried in one such isolated site. A Scottish nobleman who created the large Pitchfork VV Ranch in the late nineteenth century, Cree's "lonely fenced grave" was located on a hillside on his former ranch between Capitan and Ruidoso. According to a 1939 article in the *Lincoln County News*, Cree's grave was "the only reminder of the power that the Pitchfork VV cattle brand once carried in historic Lincoln County."[26] Far to the north, crosses marking the graves of several local ranchers can still be seen on the Ciero de los Difuntos (Mesa of the Dead) towering high above the surrounding plains.

Robert Julyan, the well-traveled author of *The Place Names of New Mexico*, tells of finding similarly isolated, often mysterious gravesites on now-abandoned homesteads, distant ranches, and long-deserted rural communities.[27] Julyan knew of one such gravesite on "a featureless plain in the uninhabited badlands northeast of Socorro" only because he had seen the word "Grave" on an old U.S. Geological Survey fifteen-minute topographic map. Julyan recalls:

[I had to] derive latitude-longitude coordinates from the map and then use a Global Positioning System (GPS) device to take me there.... [When] my GPS unit said, "You're here, at the grave," I replied, "You must be wrong. There's nothing here." But as...I began looking closer, I noticed a dry stick pointing upward at an unnatural angle, and then the barest suggestion of an enclosure.... Someone had been buried here.

Julyan pondered how someone had come to be buried "on an anonymous treeless flat in uninhabited wilderness." He concluded, "there's an extra poignancy to a grave not only unmarked but also isolated from all others." Julyan was, undoubtedly, the last person to ever visit that solitary grave before "time and weather will have toppled the dry stick and erased all trace of the faint enclosure."[28] Whoever was buried at this desolate spot may or may not have requested such a site for his final resting place. Most would not. According to an old cowboy ballad entitled, "Bury Me Not On the Lone Prairie":

> It matters not, I've been told
> Where the body lays when the heart is cold.
> But grant, oh grant this wish for me
> An' bury me not on the lone prairie.[29]

Countless travelers died on trails to and through New Mexico. Most were buried in unmarked graves (for fear their remains might be disturbed) like dead sailors cast into the sea and lost beneath the waves with nothing more to mark the sad end of their earthly journeys. A young man and nineteen-year-old Sister Alphonsa Thompson thus died of cholera on their trip west on the Santa Fe Trail in 1867. Sister Blandina Segale reported that all efforts to find their common resting place proved fruitless within months of their deaths.[30] José Gurulé's caravan experienced even greater losses from cholera on a return trip from Kansas City that same year. José later recalled that he and his fellow laborers "left one of their number behind under a mound of dirt" at almost every stop they made.[31] These travelers' remains were lost forever, as were the remains of Antonio José Chávez, a Santa Fe Trail merchant who was abducted, robbed and murdered by outlaws who "unceremoniously [tossed his body] into a deep gully...where it was left exposed to the elements and predators" in 1843. A tall stone marker was erected along the trail near the scene of the most famous crime committed on the Santa Fe Trail, but even this physical reminder of Chávez's demise had vanished by the turn of the century.[32]

Travelers also met their deaths during Indian attacks, especially in southern New Mexico. Cooke's Canyon on the Butterfield Trail was so feared for its Apache ambushes that it was known as the "four miles of death." Evidence of as many as a hundred and fifty graves can be found along this treacherous stretch, making it the most dangerous part of the Butterfield Trail's 2,975 miles.[33] The city of Las Cruces is said to have been named for the multiple crosses that marked the graves of travelers killed by Apaches near the south end of the Jornada del Muerto, or infamous Journey of the Dead Man, on the Camino Real. The Jornada del Muerto, and specifically its campsite known as Aleman, refers to a seventeenth century German who died on this perilous route, perhaps from Indian attack.[34]

Navajo captives perished by the hundreds during the U.S. Army's campaign of submission and on the treacherous Long Walk trail of 1863-64. As many as twenty-five percent of the Navajo men, women, and children who began the forced march succumbed to starvation, disease, or rifle fire if they were unable to maintain the grueling pace in harsh winter weather conditions. No gravestones were placed to mark their remains along the long route to Bosque Redondo in the Pecos River Valley.[35] A monument to them and to those who survived the march but died in captivity at Bosque Redondo was dedicated at the Fort Sumner State Monument on June 4, 2005.[36] While a large crowd attended the dedication, "many Navajos will not venture to Bosque Redondo, considering it a slaughterhouse and a graveyard filled with too much pain."[37]

U.S. soldiers also dreaded death and burial in remote parts of New Mexico, especially if they were killed in combat and their comrades were too rushed in retreat to lay protective stones atop quickly-dug graves. Pointing out one such neglected gravesite during the U.S.-Mexican War, a disheartened soldier told his colleague, "*I'm sure the wolves has (sic) eaten that volunteer's body!*"[38] The gravesites of Buffalo Soldiers killed at the Battle of Las Animas Canyon on September 18, 1879, were not identified for over a hundred years. Their graves were so remote that it required "a good, heavy-duty, four-wheel drive vehicle with fourteen-inch or more clearance, and an experienced driver" to reach the field cemetery when it was finally dedicated with full military honors on June 14, 1997.[39]

Many soldiers were buried in graves inscribed "unknown" because military records were poor, lost, or destroyed. The late nineteenth century removal of hundreds of bodies from post cemeteries and battlefield graves to the newly created National Cemetery in Santa Fe caused many identities to be tragically lost. In fact, the first bodies buried at the National Cemetery belonged to unidentified Union soldiers from the Battle of Glorieta who had first been buried near the battlefield in 1862 and reinterred in 1867 before finding a final resting place in Santa Fe. At least 495 tombstones in the National Cemetery are currently marked "unknown," covering row after row in the eastern portion of the property.[40] As many as fourteen unknown soldiers were buried in the same gravesite; forty-six men were buried in a single row of ten adjacent gravesites. The situation in Santa Fe was hardly unique. When Fort Union's post cemetery was closed in 1891, 286 bodies were moved to the Fort Leavenworth National Cemetery by May 1892. Of these 286, 146, or fifty-one percent of the total, were listed as unknown.[41] The only marker that remains at Fort Union's closed cemetery (now on

4. National Cemetery, Santa Fe, New Mexico

private ranch land) reportedly belonged to a laundress, although her name, like the names of so many soldiers, is long forgotten.[42]

As hard as it is to imagine, whole cemeteries have suffered similar fates. Some graveyards, like the Our Lady of the Immaculate Conception Church cemetery, located by the Alameda plaza from 1710 to 1903, fell victim to a series of devastating floods over the years. The northwest Albuquerque graveyard was only found when heavy equipment crews unearthed the *camposanto* during road and utility projects. Legally required archeological excavations followed, although most of the damage done was irreversible.[43]

Cemeteries in Santa Fe, Socorro, Bernalillo, Las Cruces, and Belen have been moved to make way for such modern conveniences as parking lots, wider roads, office buildings, private homes, and at least one mobile home park.[44] Despite Manuel Armijo and José Leandro Perea's considerable power and wealth in life, their remains in Socorro and Bernalillo (respectively) now lie buried without markers beneath enormous asphalt slabs in church parking lots. When former New Mexico state historian Myra Ellen Jenkins first visited Santa Fe, she found the old San Miguel Church cemetery and "spent three or four hours poling through and reading the inscriptions [on headstones]." Jenkins later moved to Santa Fe, but could not find the ancient cemetery she had once explored "until finally it was apparent what [had] happened: it was gone, torn down for the PERA [Public Employment Retirement Association] Building." A part of the cemetery had even been bulldozed for a playing field. Some old gravestones from San Miguel were used to construct a walkway at a Santa Fe home.[45]

Mass graves, dug during natural calamities (like the Spanish flu epidemic) or violent conflicts (like Indian attacks or the Civil War), were often left unmarked and consequently lost for years or, regretfully, forever. No trace remains of the mass grave used to bury twenty-one Tomé residents killed on a single day, presumably during an Indian attack, in 1777.[46] Twenty-six Confederate soldiers who died in a makeshift hospital in Socorro after the February 21, 1862, Battle of Valverde were buried in a cemetery whose location on the west side of town has long since been forgotten.[47] The mass grave of thirty-one Confederate soldiers killed at the March 28, 1862, Battle of Glorieta Pass was not discovered until 1987 when a local resident uncovered it on his property while digging a foundation with a backhoe.[48]

Some cemeteries were sold to private individuals with the understanding that all efforts would be made to remove buried bodies before the land was utilized for new purposes. In 1892, for example, Jesuit priests at San Felipe Neri Church in Albuquerque sold an old cemetery to a farmer named John Mann with the agreement "that he would transport any bones he found to a common grave in the new cemetery" located elsewhere in town. Father Thomas J. Steele, S.J., writes that all went well until Mann began to level the land "and bones began to appear—hundreds of bones, wagonloads of bones, two tons of bones in all." Parishioners with ancestors buried in the field protested, but "faced with a fait accompli and [with] several Jesuits tightly wrapped in their own righteousness, there was little more the people could do."⁴⁹

Finally, the identification of specific gravesites in potter's fields can be especially difficult. With few—if any—known friends or relatives to purchase durable stones, gravesite locations in potter's fields have often been forgotten or confused with others over time. Often anonymous in life, the poor were thus doomed to anonymity in death as well. Such was the apparent fate of George Jones, one of Sierra County's oldest prospectors when he died of natural causes in Hillsboro on December 31, 1926. According to his obituary that appeared in the *Sierra County Advocate* two weeks later, Jones "had no known relatives… and, like many others of his class, lived…in the expectation of 'striking it rich,' a dream that was never realized and he died a pauper." Dead outlaws were often treated as paupers, for social as well as economic reasons. When killed by vigilantes, criminals there were usually disposed of in shallow, unmarked graves, as happened to two "bad actors" who dared to disrupt the peace on a Sunday morning in White Oaks in 1880.⁵⁰

Men, women, and children buried in institutional cemeteries often suffered the same treatment as those unfortunate enough to have left this world as paupers. Institutional residents succumbed and were buried at the insane asylum in Las Vegas, the old State Tuberculosis Sanatorium north of Socorro, the old Indian School in Northwest Albuquerque, the old State Hospital and Training School in Los Lunas, and the original territorial (and later state) prison in Santa Fe.⁵¹

Access to certain gravesites is not always possible, especially if sites are located in cemeteries normally closed to the general public, including those on private land, military bases, testing grounds, Indian reservations, and plots adjacent to *moradas,* or Penitente chapels.⁵² It is essential to respect these restrictions. Indeed, it is essential to respect all cemetery rules and etiquette based on local customs, religious beliefs, and security interests.

At the risk of undoubtedly preaching to the choir, I offer several essential thoughts to remember when visiting cemeteries in New Mexico—or anywhere in the world.

- *Do not trespass or take photographs on private, military, restricted government, or Indian reservation land without permission, preferably in writing.*

Access to cemeteries on Indian reservations is especially restricted for spiritual and cultural reasons. Restrictions have also been necessary because intrusive individuals, archeologists, and museum collectors have long pilfered Indian remains and sacred objects in the exalted name of history and science. Others have invaded Indian cemeteries motivated by sordid profits alone. In one such raid, Clotilde Grossetete, a late nineteenth century homesteader living near Apache Creek in western New Mexico, dug up "ancient Indian burial sites in search of fine specimens of prehistoric pottery that the early inhabitants usually interred with their dead." Collecting over two thousand pots and, in the process, disturbing countless gravesites, Grossetete had her finds packed in barrels and hauled to Socorro for shipment and eventual sale in San Francisco. In a perfect example of poetic justice, every pot in the ill-gotten shipment had been shattered by the time the barrels were opened at their destination in California.[53]

Legislation to stop the raiding of ancient burial sites was finally passed in New Mexico in 1989. Largely in response to the scandalous bulldozing of Mimbres burial sites in southwestern New Mexico and the publication of Tony Hillerman's best-selling novel, *A Thief of Time*, the state legislature passed laws making the disturbance of marked or unmarked burial grounds a felony punishable by a fine of five thousand dollars or eighteen months imprisonment or both.[54]

The 1990 Native American Graves Protection and Repatriation Act has helped tribes locate and reclaim at least some of the bodies shamelessly removed from Indian land over the years. On May 22, 1999, the remains of almost two thousand Native Americans were returned from the Peabody Museum of Archaeology and Ethnology on the Harvard University campus, where they had been taken between 1915 and 1929, to the Pecos National Historical Park for reburial. Six hundred Native Americans greeted the truck carrying their ancestors' remains in the largest single act of Indian repatriation in U.S. history.[55] But there is still much to be done, and the damage in historical trauma can never be completely reversed. By 2000 only ten percent of the estimated 200,000 remains still kept in public collections were accurately accounted for in this ongoing national tragedy.[56]

In the spirit of the Native American Graves Protection and Repatriation Act and with deep respect for native privacy, no photos of Indian gravesites on restricted reservation land have been included on the following pages. Famous Native Americans are listed and described, but only gravestones found in public, non-reservation cemeteries are documented with photographs here.

- *Find, read, and obey each cemetery's rules.* They are usually posted near the property's entrance or are available in the cemetery's office.
- *Drive slowly, turning off car radios and stereos.*
- *Do not walk on gravesites.* This is not only a gesture of respect for the dead, but also a cautionary practice for the living. Old sites have been known to cave in, causing falls and possible bodily harm, not to mention great shock to an unsuspecting visitor's fragile nervous system!
- *Do not remove anything, be it flowers, gravestones, pieces of gravestones, soil, or sundry "souvenirs," from cemetery grounds.* We should think of visiting cemeteries much as we think of visiting traditional museums filled with valuable artifacts displayed for us to see and admire, but not to use, disturb, or confiscate.
- *Do not take pets to cemeteries and, conversely, leave the wildlife at cemeteries alone.* Amazingly, a cemetery in eastern New

5. Fort Sumner Cemetery, Fort Sumner, New Mexico

6. San José Cemetery, Albuquerque, New Mexico

Mexico found it necessary to post a sign at its entrance to warn visitors against *hunting* on the premises!

- *Do not leave trash or vandalize cemeteries.* Despite the efforts of conscientious groups and individuals, like Father Clarence Galli in Corrales, who have spent countless hours cleaning and restoring local cemeteries, problems still exist.[57] Jazz great Lemon Jefferson went so far as to have the title of his popular song engraved on his Wortham, Texas, gravestone: "See that my grave is kept clean."[58] One cemetery in Albuquerque's south valley has even installed twenty-four hour surveillance cameras to help prevent vandalism. In Los Lunas, the old San Clemente church cemetery was so damaged by vandalism and the rattling of nearby trains that the parish priest had the broken pieces of old headstones cleared with a bulldozer and buried in a trench in 1978. Only a grotto with a bronze plaque listing the names of the 103 men, women, and children who were buried in the *camposanto* remains.[59]

Such extreme measures should not be necessary. But vandalism persists, especially on Halloween nights. As Taos County sheriff Anselmo Valerio reported after Halloween in 1968, "unknown malicious spirits" had overturned gravestones and had thrown many markers into the road adjoining a northern New Mexico cemetery.[60] Park Supervisor Julian Jaramillo had "some descriptive words" to say about similar vandalism at the Kit Carson Cemetery in Taos that same year.[61]

- *Do not intrude by walking, talking, using cell phones, or taking photographs during funerals or while people are visiting their deceased loved ones' graves.*

- *Grave rubbings should be done carefully and only after receiving at least rudimentary training.* Good sources on this skill include *Your Guide to Cemetery Research,* by Sharon Debartolo Carmack, and various web-sites, especially those made available by the Association of Gravestone Studies.[62]

If common decency does not motivate graveyard visitors to follow these few rules, warning signs at the entrance of several community cemeteries threaten rather severe penalties for the disrespectful. At Chilili visitors are greeted with a sign that warns that "vandals will face court action." No. 7

Anecdotes Regarding Final Days or Funerals

Anecdotes regarding the final days or funerals of prominent figures in New Mexico history are often compelling, moving, and instructive. These brief, but poignant anecdotes can teach us many lessons about death as the last stage of life. Each story reminds us that regardless of one's fame, fortune, or status in life, we each face the final phase of our lives alone, usually in our most fragile, vulnerable condition. Even when troubled by great pain and discomfort, most famous New Mexicans met this last stage with dignity and courage, much as they had lived most

7. Tomé Catholic Cemetery, Tomé, New Mexico

of their natural lives. As a collector of hundreds of last words from around the world has put it, these deathbed utterances can "open a window through which we feel we can catch a glimpse…of the entire life that preceded it."[63]

Other anecdotes point out certain ironies, especially in what is remembered about the deceased, as compared to how they actually lived much of their earthly lives. Laudatory newspaper obituaries for individuals like John Kinney and "Lottie Deno" Thurmond reflect the remarkable success of those with somewhat sordid pasts to reform or otherwise reinvent their lives in old age and onto death.[64]

Finally, there are anecdotes about confusion regarding funeral arrangements and burials even when the deceased left exacting instructions as to his or her wishes. We are reminded of Kit Carson's final wish to be buried in Taos—only to be first buried in Colorado!

Buried Treasures

New Mexico's cemeteries are much like remote desert islands where historical treasures await those who are patient enough to discover, appreciate, preserve, and hopefully respect what others have long forgotten or overlooked. With few monuments to honor famous New Mexicans, gravestones are often the only public reminders left to assure that the lives of noteworthy New Mexicans are not doomed to obscurity on the larger map of human history.

2
ARTISTS, PERFORMERS, AND DIRECTORS

Taos Society of Artists

The most famous artistic organization in New Mexico history, the Taos Society of Artists (TSA), was founded in July 1915 as a rather formal organization (with a constitution, by-laws, annual meetings, annual dues—a dollar—and a new membership application process) by an elite group of artists with high standards and noble goals. According to Article III of the TSA's constitution:

> This Society is formed for educational purposes, to develop a high standard of art among its members, and to aid in the diffusion of taste for art in general. To promote and stimulate the practical expressions of art—to preserve and promote the native art.
>
> To facilitate bringing before the public through exhibitions and other means, tangible results of the work of its members—to promote, maintain and preserve high standards of excellence in painting, and to encourage sculpture, architecture, applied arts, music, literature, ethnology, and archaeology, solely as its pertains to New Mexico and the States adjoining.

Starting with six members, the TSA eventually expanded to eleven active members, including Catharine Carter Critcher, the group's only female participant. The TSA's annual exhibit tour stopped at cities across the United States and overseas. By a unanimous vote, the TSA disbanded in March 1927 after a dozen years of remarkable success.[3]

Most former TSA members remained close for the balance of their natural lives. Five were also close after death, having been buried within yards of each other on the south end of the Sierra Vista Cemetery in Taos. The five were Oscar Berninghaus, Irving Couse, Buck Dunton, Victor Higgins, and Bert Geer Phillips.

"Art is the flowering of humanity. It embellishes life and reveals timelessly the nature of the plant on which it grew."
—Will Shuster[1]

"Art is the great, lasting, self-revealing activity of life. Through it, we transmit our spiritual power through the ages."
—Edgar L. Hewett[2]

Original Six Members (in alphabetical order)

Oscar Edmund "Bernie" Berninghaus
Award-winning Southwest painter, illustrator, muralist, and lithographer; a founding member of the Taos Society of Artists, July 1915; New Deal artist[4]
Date of Birth: October 2, 1874
Place of Birth: St. Louis, Missouri
Date of Death (age): April 27, 1952 (77)
Place of Death: Taos, New Mexico
Cause of Death: heart attack
Resting Place: Sierra Vista Cemetery, Taos, New Mexico[5]

Four days prior to Berninghaus's death, his friend, Bill James, visited the artist and later recalled that Berninghaus:

> was working on an enormous painting when I arrived, and he met me at the door, brushes and maulstick in his hand, spruce and spry as any youngster, and said: "Come on, Bill, sit down awhile and we'll have a talk." We talked about politics and taxes mostly. He told me about his trip back East…and said how happy he was to be home, that he would never leave Taos again, that he wanted to live here and no place else, wanted to die here, and no place else. And now he's gone, his brushes and maulstick, palette and paints laid down forever.[6]

Indian, Anglo, and Hispanic friends and admirers attended Berninghaus's funeral services, held in his Taos studio. Local businesses closed during the hours of his services as a sign of respect for the popular artist.[7] No. 8

Ernest Leonard "Blumy" Blumenschein
With Bert Geer Phillips, co-founder of the Taos art colony, after first visiting Taos (with a broken wheel) on September 3, 1898; a founding, albeit contentious, member of the Taos Society of Artists, July 1915; resigned, 1923; member of The New Mexico Painters; New Deal artist; University of New Mexico honorary degree recipient, 1947
Date of Birth: May 26, 1874
Place of Birth: Pittsburgh, Pennsylvania
Date of Death (age): June 6, 1960 (86)
Place of Death: a local hospital, Albuquerque, New Mexico
Cause of Death: arteriosclerosis of the brain
Resting Place: cremated[8]

Eanger Irving "Green Mountain" Couse[9]
First arrived in Taos in 1909; a founding member and the first president of the Taos Society of Artists, July 1915; best known for his romantic paintings of Native

8.

Americans and for his calendar illustrations for the Santa Fe Railroad, 1916-38
Date of Birth: September 3, 1866
Place of Birth: Saginaw, Michigan
Date of Death (age): April 26, 1936 (69)
Place of Death: a local hospital, Albuquerque, New Mexico
Cause of Death: pneumonia
Resting Place: Sierra Vista Cemetery, Taos, New Mexico[10]

According to an eyewitness at Couse's funeral:

> We gathered in the beautiful garden [at his house] to say good-bye. As the faithful Indians dressed in bright colored shirts, beaded moccasins and yellow buckskin trousers, before the body of the great artist from his studio, there seemed to hover over us a weird solemnity, an utter stillness, a closeness to God. [The Indians'] devotion was further demonstrated by their walking beside the body, covering the entire distance from [his] studio to the cemetery on foot. Stoically they stood over the grave until the last of us had departed, then in their simple way they offered up prayers, not audibly, but in the devotional language of their hearts....[11] No. 9

9.

William Herbert "Buck" Dunton
A founding member of the Taos Society of Artists, July 1915; noted for his cowboy paintings; resigned from the TSA, 1922; New Deal artist
Date of Birth: August 28, 1878
Place of Birth: Augusta, Maine
Date of Death (age): 10:15 p.m., March 18, 1936 (57)
Place of Death: Taos, New Mexico
Cause of Death: prostate, stomach, and lung cancer
Resting Place: Sierra Vista Cemetery, Taos, New Mexico[12] No. 10

10.

Bert Geer Phillips
With Ernest Blumenschein, co-founder of the Taos art colony, after first visiting Taos, September 3, 1898; one of six founding members of the Taos Society of Artists, July 1915; first Forest Ranger assigned to the Carson National Forest; New Deal artist
Date of Birth: July 15, 1868
Place of Birth: Hudson, New York
Date of Death (age): June 16, 1956 (87)
Place of Death: San Diego, California
Cause of Death: stroke
Resting Place: Sierra Vista Cemetery, Taos, New Mexico[13]
No. 11

11.

Joseph Henry Sharp
Legendary Taos painter of Pueblo Indians and Penitente Brothers; known as the "father of the Taos art colony" because he had suggested to Bert Geer Phillips and Ernest Blumenschein that they visit Taos in 1898 after he had first visited the area in 1893; a permanent resident of Taos from 1912-52; a founding member of the Taos Society of Artists, July 1915; probably the most monetarily successful member of the Taos Society of Artists; a street in Albuquerque was named in his honor
Date of Birth: September 27, 1859
Place of Birth: Bridgeport, Ohio
Date of Death (age): August 29, 1953 (93)
Place of Death: at his home in Pasadena, California (after closing his Taos home and studio in 1952)
Cause of Death: unstated natural causes after a long illness
Resting Place: cremated with ashes buried in the Mountain View Mausoleum, Mountain View Cemetery, Altadena, California

Near the end of his life, a reporter asked Sharp, "Of all the things you've seen and all the things you've done, what is it that you regret most?" Deaf since childhood, Sharp answered, "I never heard the beat of the drum and the whoop of the dance."

As his end drew near, Sharp commented that there were too many candles on his birthday cake for one man to blow out. He wrote that he felt "on the downgrade [with] no brakes."[14]

Later Members of the Taos Society of Artists (in alphabetical order)

Kenneth Miller Adams
Acclaimed painter and muralist; arrived in Taos in 1924; last person to join the Taos Society of Artists, July 12, 1926; Visiting Professor of Art, University of New Mexico, 1938-63; New Deal artist probably most famous for his controversial murals in Zimmerman Library at the University of New Mexico, although they were originally created to reflect "the spirit of democracy" and "the three races [Hispanic, Native American, and Anglo] as socially equal"[15]
Date of Birth: August 6, 1897
Place of Birth: Topeka, Kansas
Date of Death (age): June 27, 1966 (68)
Place of Death: Presbyterian Hospital, Albuquerque, New Mexico
Cause of Death: unstated natural causes
Resting Place: cremated[1]

Catharine Carter Critcher
First arrived in New Mexico in 1922; first and only woman elected to join the Taos Society of Artists; unanimously elected on July 12, 1924; painted New Mexico Hispanic and Indian subjects
Date of Birth: September 13, 1868

Place of Birth: Westmoreland County, Virginia
Date of Death (age): June 11, 1964 (95)
Place of Death: a nursing home in Blackstone, Virginia
Cause of Death: unstated natural causes
Resting Place: Ivy Hill Cemetery, Alexandria, Virginia[17]

Ernest Martin Hennings
First arrived in Taos in 1917, living there for most of each year as of 1921; landscape artist whose Indian paintings were used to help promote the Southwest on Santa Fe Railroad calendars; elected to the Taos Society of Artists, July 12, 1924; New Deal artist
Date of Birth: February 5, 1886
Place of Birth: Pennsgrove, New Jersey
Date of Death (age): May 19, 1956 (70)
Place of Death: at his home in Taos, New Mexico
Cause of Death: heart attack
Resting Place: Memorial Park Cemetery, Evanston, Illinois[18]

William Victor Higgins
Landscape painter and muralist; elected to the Taos Society of Artists, July 15, 1917; member of The New Mexico Painters; New Deal artist who painted the largest of ten murals in the new Taos County courthouse; ran for mayor of Taos, losing by a slim margin
Date of Birth: June 28, 1884
Place of Birth: Shelbyville, Indiana
Date of Death (age): 4:30 a.m., August 23, 1949 (65)
Place of Death: Holy Cross Hospital, Taos, New Mexico
Cause of Death: heart attack
Resting Place: Sierra Vista Cemetery, Taos, New Mexico

On a summer evening in 1949, Higgins had just finished a good steak dinner at the home of his Taos artist friend, Thomas Benrino. Higgins reportedly leaned back in his chair, lit a cigar, and suffered a fatal heart attack. Efforts to save him at Holy Cross Hospital failed, and he was pronounced dead the following morning.

Higgins was buried in the same cemetery that he had used as a scene in one of his prize-winning landscapes.[19] No. 12

12.

Walter Ufer
First artist elected to the Taos Society of Artists after the Original Six, July 15, 1917; member of The New Mexico Painters; famous for his landscapes and Indian paintings, especially using his Taos Pueblo model, Jim Mirabal; New Deal artist
Date of Birth: July 2, 1876
Place of Birth: Louisville, Kentucky
Date of Death (age): 12:30 p.m., August 2, 1936 (60)

Place of Death: St. Vincent Hospital, Santa Fe, New Mexico
Cause of Death: appendicitis
Resting Place: cremated with his ashes taken by his old friend, Bob Abbott, and his close friend and favorite model, Jim Mirabal, to a place east of Taos where the two men scattered the ashes to the winds, to blow over the Taos valley, as per Ufer's request[20]

Los Cinco Pintores of Santa Fe (in alphabetical order)

The famous Cinco Pintores (Five Painters) included Jozef Bakos, Fremont F. Ellis, Walter Mruk, Willard Nash, and Will Shuster. As neighbors on Santa Fe's Camino del Monte Sol (previously known as Telegraph Road), these young artists were far less organized—and apparently more fun-loving—than those in the TSA. They were, nevertheless, successful in exhibiting their work together, starting in December 1921, when their average age was only twenty-six years old. Building their adobe homes on what is known as Cinco Pintores Hill, their fellow artists in the Santa Fe art colony facetiously called them "the five little nuts in five adobe huts." Their close friendship continued, although their artistic alliance ended by 1926.[21]

Decades later, Bakos recalled the economic reality of his famous group. "No one made a living from painting in those days. Will Shuster did ironwork, Walter Mruk was a forest ranger, Fremont Ellis did sign work, and I made furniture and carved doors. Willard Nash was being sponsored by someone in Detroit, and the other artists enviously eyed the steak bones he left on his plate."[22]

13.

Jozef Gabryel Bakos
Said to be Los Cinco Pintores' organizer; member of The New Mexico Painters; subjects included as many as thirty registered bulls; New Deal artist; art studio teacher at Santa Fe High School; his "adobe hut" was located at 576 Camino del Monte Sol
Date of Birth: September 23, 1891
Place of Birth: Buffalo, New York
Date of Death (age): about 1:00 p.m., April 25, 1977 (85)
Place of Death: St. Vincent Hospital, Santa Fe, New Mexico
Cause of Death: Parkinson's disease
Resting Place: Rosario Cemetery, Santa Fe, New Mexico[23]

A year before his death, Bakos told a reporter, "[Joseph] Conrad said that life is short and art is long. Personally, I think the greatest art is the art of living."[24] No. 13

Fremont F. Ellis
Arrived in Santa Fe in 1919; last surviving member of Los Cinco Pintores; painter of some two thousand paintings in his sixty-year career; New Deal artist; a street in Albuquerque was named in his honor
Date of Birth: October 7, 1897
Place of Birth: Virginia City, Montana

Date of Death (age): January 12, 1985 (87)
Place of Death: St. Vincent Hospital, Santa Fe, New Mexico
Cause of Death: heart failure
Resting Place: Rosario Cemetery, Santa Fe, New Mexico[25] No. 14

14. Although some sources give Ellis's date of birth as October 7, the date on his gravestone is October 2.

Wladyslaw "Walter" Mruk (sometimes spelled Murk)
Modernist painter; member of Los Cinco Pintores, 1921-26, and The New Mexico Painters, 1924-26; political cartoonist for the *Santa Fe New Mexican*
Date of Birth: June 12, 1895
Place of Birth: Buffalo, New York
Date of Death (age): December 31, 1941 (46)
Place of Death: Buffalo, New York
Cause of Death: pneumonia contracted while working as a night watchman
Resting Place: St. Stanislaus Cemetery, Cheektowaga, New York[26]

Willard Aver Nash
Moved to Santa Fe in 1920; Santa Fe's most noted modernist; member of Los Cinco Pintores, 1921-26; New Deal artist
Date of Birth: March 29, 1898
Place of Birth: Philadelphia, Pennsylvania
Date of Death (age): 2:30 p.m., September 2, 1942 (44)
Place of Death: Presbyterian Hospital, Albuquerque, New Mexico
Cause of Death: chronic pulmonary tuberculosis
Resting Place: cremated with ashes scattered over Sunmount, the rounded mountain near his home[27]

A *Santa Fe New Mexican* editorial of September 4, 1942, read:

The Cinco Pintores were but three today.[28] Willard Nash died Wednesday, [September 2].

From the Camino del Monte Sol studios of the Cinco Pintores came remarkable canvasses, and a remarkable determination to keep Santa Fe as they discovered it.

It has been the voice of the Camino brush wielders that cries out the loudest when the old world charm that attracted them to the ancient village has been threatened. They have revolted often and violently with words, oil paint, letters, pamphlets, and sometimes their fists to keep the village from becoming another Strawberry Point, Iowa.

Their adversaries included mayors, newspapers, governors, the village population, Chautauquas, and on one occasion the Daughters of the American Revolution.

The result is the Santa Fe of today which we, and which just about everybody else, think is pretty much all right.

Santa Fe owes much to the Cinco Pintores. May their spirit carry on forever.

William Howard "Will" or "Shus" Shuster, Jr.

15.

U.S. Army Lieutenant in World War I; recovered TB healthseeker; modernist Santa Fe artist; member of Los Cinco Pintores, 1921-26; co-creator, with Gus Baumann, of Zozobra, the Santa Fe Fiesta's figure of gloom; New Deal artist

Date of Birth: November 26, 1893
Place of Birth: Philadelphia, Pennsylvania
Date of Death (age): evening, February 9, 1969 (75)
Place of Death: Veterans Hospital, Albuquerque, New Mexico
Cause of Death: acute emphysema
Resting Place: National Cemetery, Santa Fe, New Mexico

When Shuster's doctor told him that he had tuberculosis, the physician reportedly said the young man "could stay in Philadelphia and maybe live a year or go to a high, dry climate in the West where he had a good chance of dying of snake bite, old age, or bad whiskey." Shuster took the second option, moving to Santa Fe in 1920 and living to the age of 75.[29]

On his last evening alive, Shuster visited with his forty-eight year old son, Don. Don told him about his day flying planes. Suddenly, Shuster began coughing uncontrollably and his heart stopped. Efforts to revive him were unsuccessful. He was pronounced dead that Sunday night.[30] No. 15

The New Mexico Painters (in alphabetical order)

Eight famous Taos and Santa Fe artists organized themselves as The New Mexico Painters on June 6, 1923, largely in reaction to the TSA's reluctance to admit modernist painters as members. Said to represent the "Progressive or Radical Conservative Element in art today," the eight included Ernest Blumenschein, Victor Higgins, and Walter Ufer of the TSA plus Frank Applegate, Jozef Bakos, Gus Baumann, William Penhallow Henderson, and B.J.O. Nordfeldt. The group's membership increased to twelve by 1924 with the addition of John Sloan, Randall Davey, Walter Mruk, and Theodore Soelen. The Painters created an "agreement" which stated that they were to meet once a year, have only one officer (a secretary chosen alphabetically), pay ten dollar dues, and hold regular exhibitions. The Painters' first exhibition was held in New York in October 1923. The organization lasted about three years.[31]

Gustave "Gus" Baumann

Acclaimed painter, sculptor, and puppet maker; co-creator, with Will Shuster, of Zozobra, the Santa Fe Fiesta's figure of gloom; a founding member of The New Mexico Painters; a founding member of the Old Santa Fe Association, 1926; New Deal artist; restored La Conquistadora, the famous statue of the Virgin Mary at St. Francis Cathedral in Santa Fe

Date of Birth: June 27, 1881
Place of Birth: Magdeburg, Germany

Date of Death (age): October 8, 1971 (90)
Place of Death: at his home at 409 Camino de las Animas, Santa Fe, New Mexico
Cause of Death: unstated natural causes
Resting Place: cremated with ashes buried beside an aspen tree in the forest off the road to the Santa Fe ski basin by his daughter Ann, Peggy Pond Church, and Ann Fermer[32]

Randall Vernon Davey
Member of the famous Ashcan School; best known for his Western and race track scenes; member of The New Mexico Painters, 1924-26; New Deal artist
Date of Birth: May 24, 1887
Place of Birth: East Orange, New Jersey
Date of Death (age): about noon, November 7, 1964 (77)
Place of Death: near Baker, California
Cause of Death: car accident in his Jaguar on a trip to Los Angeles from Santa Fe; highway patrol officers estimated that he was traveling over ninety miles per hour
Resting Place: buried alongside his wife, Isabel Holt Davey, with a headstone for their infant child (not actually buried there) in the orchard of his Upper Canyon Road home in Santa Fe, New Mexico; his home and surrounding property is now the Randall Davey Audubon Center[33]

16.

Davey once told his friend John Sloan:

> Living out here in New Mexico I can see the political manipulations in the art world back east, and I know that if I chose to I could have more success with my work if I wanted to play their game. If I lived in a big city I could clean up on portraits. But I prefer to live here and paint for myself, and get along with teaching, now and then a portrait commission, and what little comes in from raising chickens. I am almost willing to get along on the chickens. I would rather take two days off a week and make an honest living. That way I can feel free.[34] No. 16

William Penhallow "Whippie" Henderson
Southwest painter, illustrator, muralist, furniture maker, preservationist, and architect; co-owner of the Pueblo-Spanish Building Company; first Anglo resident of Camino del Monte Sol, arriving in Santa Fe in 1916 after marrying poet Alice Corbin Henderson, October 14, 1905; designed the Elizabeth and Martha White compound (now the School of American Research) and the current Wheelwright Museum in Santa Fe; a founding member of The New Mexico Painters; New Deal artist who painted six murals in Santa Fe's Federal Courthouse
Date of Birth: June 4, 1877
Place of Birth: Medford, Massachusetts

17.

Date of Death (age): 8:30 a.m., October 15, 1943 (66)
Place of Death: at his home in Tesuque, New Mexico
Cause of Death: heart attack
Resting Place: Fairview Cemetery, Santa Fe, New Mexico[35] No. 17

Bror Julius Olsson (B.J.O.) "Nordy" Nordfeldt
First arrived in Santa Fe in 1919; artist of paintings, etchings, and lithographs featuring the Southwestern landscape and Hispanic culture; a founding member of The New Mexico Painters, 1923-26; New Deal artist
Date of Birth: April 13, 1878
Place of Birth: Tullstorp, Sweden
Date of Death (age): April 21, 1955 (77)
Place of Death: Henderson Memorial Hospital, Henderson, Texas
Cause of Death: stroke
Resting Place: Restland Memorial Park Cemetery, Dallas, Texas[36]

According to the 1920 U.S. census, Nordfeldt became a naturalized U.S. citizen in 1896, when he was eighteen years old. The 1920 census listed his occupation as "artist at home."[37]

John French Sloan
New York artist; one of eight Eastern painters of the famous Ashcan school; painted each summer in Santa Fe, 1920-50; joined The New Mexico Painters, 1924-26; a popular, respected, and extremely influential member of the Santa Fe art colony; a U.S. postage stamp was issued in his honor
Date of Birth: August 2, 1871
Place of Birth: Lock Haven, Pennsylvania
Date of Death (age): September 7, 1951 (80)
Place of Death: Hanover, New Hampshire (the only summer he had spent away from Santa Fe since he first arrived in 1920)
Cause of Death: complications following an operation to remove a tumor
Resting Place: cremated with his ashes mixed with those of his first wife Dolly and scattered from a mountain near his birthplace by his second wife, Helen, January 20, 1952

Sloan wrote that in New Mexico the "ground is not covered with green mold as it is elsewhere. The piñon trees dot the surface of hills and mesas with exciting textures…. Because the air is so clear you feel the reality of things in the distance."[38]

In the hospital on the day of his death, John Sloan told his wife Helen, "I'm so tired." Worried that he had to paint the next day, Helen assured him that he did not. "It's a fight, isn't it?" he said and fell asleep. He died before midnight that evening.[39]

Within days after Sloan's death, his friend Witter Bynner wrote a poem, "Farewell, Dear John":

> Farewell, Dear John, who led us all with strength,
> With laughter, with indomitable pride:
> Which means for us that in the final length
> And breadth of spirit it is we who died
> Unless we feel goodbye with more than tears,
> Feel life, not death, from you, and use our years.[40]

Additional Members of the Santa Fe Art Colony *(in alphabetical order)*

Gerald Cassidy; originally Ira Diamond Cassidy; original Irish family name, O'Cassidy
Arrived in Santa Fe with his author wife, Ina Sizer Cassidy, in 1912; recovered TB healthseeker; celebrated Southwest artist; New Deal artist
Date of Birth: November 10, 1869
Place of Birth: Covington, Kentucky
Date of Death (age): 11: 45 a.m., February 12, 1934 (64)
Place of Death: at his studio in his home at 924 Canyon Road, Santa Fe, New Mexico
Cause of Death: turpentine and carbon monoxide fumes from an improperly installed heater in his studio
Resting Place: Fairview Cemetery, Santa Fe, New Mexico[41] No. 18

18. The writing on Cassidy's stone is a replica of the artist's personal signature.

Orrin Sheldon Parsons
Recovered healthseeker; portrait artist whose subjects included President William McKinley and Susan B. Anthony; Santa Fe landscape artist; New Deal artist
Date of Birth: April 3, 1866
Place of Birth: Newark, New York
Date of Death (age): 7:00 p.m., September 24, 1943 (77)
Place of Death: St. Joseph Hospital, Albuquerque, New Mexico
Cause of Death: heart attack with asthmatic complications
Resting Place: cremated[42]

According to the *Santa Fe New Mexican:*

> Parsons was as much Santa Fe as any figure in the artists' colony. His flamboyantly brimmed Stetson, his immaculately kept white goatee and his flawless dress made him a person whom strangers turned to watch in admiration. But apart from his presence, he was a painter who stood on his own and whose work is in the museums and palaces as far away as India. "Sheldon Parsons carried New Mexico to the world," Mrs. George Van Stone, former curator of the Art Museum for twenty years, said.[43]

Olive Rush
Santa Fe artist famous for her large fresco murals as well as for her sensitive watercolors of animals; New Deal artist
Date of Birth: June 10, 1873
Place of Birth: Fairmount, Indiana
Date of Death (age): August 20, 1966 (93)
Place of Death: St. Vincent Hospital, Santa Fe, New Mexico
Cause of Death: unstated natural causes
Resting Place: cremated with her cremains buried in the family plot in Park Cemetery, Fairmount, Indiana

Near the end of her life, Rush told a reporter that "As I grow older in art and life, I do not find merely expressing myself worthwhile, just as imitating nature seems trivial, but I paint when I feel the necessity of transmitting some strong emotion that I experience. Only this and the ability to 'put it over' is a worthy thing."[44]

A devoted Quaker, Rush willed her Santa Fe home at 630 Canyon Road to the Religious Society of Friends to be used as a Quaker meeting house.[45]

Carlos "The Skipper" Vierra

19.

Recovered TB healthseeker, arriving in Santa Fe in 1904; Santa Fe art colony painter, photographer, and architect; advocate for preserving and restoring adobe-style architecture; said to be Santa Fe's first resident artist
Date of Birth: October 3, 1876
Place of Birth: Moss Landing, California
Date of Death (age): 11:55 p.m., December 19, 1937 (61)
Place of Death: Santa Fe, New Mexico
Cause of Death: pneumonia
Resting Place: Fairview Cemetery, Santa Fe, New Mexico[46]

According to a Santa Fe editorial that appeared ten days after his death, Carlos Vierra had been "Born to the sea, [but] he investigated the entire world, a lifelong, roving search for a completely satisfying place in which to live. He found what he wanted in the mountains of New Mexico." Over many years, "He trained himself to become the leading student of the pure style of Santa Fe architecture. His brush worked in harmony with the piñons and the atmosphere of canyons and hills. His mind and his fingers were attuned to the nature of adobe bricks and mud walls.... It is not possible to think of New Mexico, its ancient culture and its real values, its intimate personality and the breadth of its scene, without remembering him."[47] No. 19

Artists From Across New Mexico (in alphabetical order)

The Honorable Lady Dorothy Eugenie "The Brett" Brett; Lady Brett
Legendary Taos artist; first arrived in Taos with friends D.H. and Frieda Lawrence, as guests of Mabel Dodge Luhan, in April 1924

Date of Birth: November 10, 1883
Place of Birth: London, England
Date of Death (age): August 27, 1977 (93)
Place of Death: Holy Cross Hospital, Taos, New Mexico
Cause of Death: congestive heart failure
Resting Place: cremated

According to her will, "the urn which will contain my ashes shall be taken and deposited at the Pink Rocks of the Del Monte Ranch." Despite complications that delayed the fulfillment of her wishes, Lady Brett's British biographer, Sean Hignett, asserted that by 1983 her ashes were "scattered where she wished them to be, on the Red Rocks below Mount Lobo. But the mountain was not happy about it. When the scatterer returned to his car, all four tyres [tires] had mysteriously gone flat."[48]

Andrew Dasburg
Pioneer modernist painter; exhibited at the famous 1913 Armory Show; University of New Mexico honorary degree recipient, 1958
Date of Birth: May 4, 1887
Place of Birth: Paris, France
Date of Death (age): August 13, 1979 (92)
Place of Death: at his home in Talpa, New Mexico
Cause of Death: unstated natural causes probably related to Addison's disease
Resting Place: cremated

Near the end of his life, Dasburg told a reporter, "What I want to arrive at is a quality of serenity in my paintings, a quality of serenity arrived at through a harmonization of opposites, of dualities. Maybe this has something to do with age."[49]

After enjoying a radio replay of a Taos Music Festival concert, he mentioned his beloved late wife, Marina Wister, and reportedly said, "I think I want to go." He died the next day.[50]

Henriette Wyeth "Bini" Hurd
Acclaimed Southwest artist from the famous Wyeth family of artists; most noted for her portraits, including paintings of the actress Helen Hayes, the author Paul Horgan, and First Lady Pat Nixon; a street in Albuquerque was named in her honor
Date of Birth: October 22, 1907
Place of Birth: Wilmington, Delaware
Date of Death (age): April 3, 1997 (89)
Place of Death: 3:30 a.m., Eastern New Mexico Medical Center, Roswell, New Mexico
Cause of Death: unstated natural causes
Resting Place: private plot beside her husband, Peter Hurd, overlooking their beloved Sentinel Ranch, San Patricio, New Mexico[51] No. 20

20.

21.

Peter Howard "Pete" Hurd; originally Harold Hurd, Jr.
Award-winning Southwest artist of murals, illustrations, and paintings; New Deal artist; December 18, 1970, was proclaimed "Peter Hurd Day" in New Mexico; alum and strong supporter of the New Mexico Military Institute; University of New Mexico honorary degree recipient, 1975; a street in Albuquerque was named in his honor
Date of Birth: February 22, 1904
Place of Birth: Roswell, New Mexico
Date of Death (age): July 9, 1984 (80)
Place of Death: St. Mary's Hospital, Roswell, New Mexico
Cause of Death: complications caused by pneumonia after several years suffering from Alzheimer's disease
Resting Place: cremated with ashes partly scattered and partly buried on a private plot on his beloved Sentinel Ranch, San Patricio, New Mexico[52]

Commissioned to paint President Lyndon Johnson's official portrait, LBJ declared that the finished painting was "the ugliest thing I ever saw," to which Hurd replied that he only painted what he saw! After Johnson had died, Hurd claimed that he was the only person to ever get the president to sit still for more than ten minutes. Hurd also mimicked the former president's famous Texas accent, saying, "Pore ol' Lyn'on! He's up there with them angels, now; they're paintin' 'im up there [now]!" Hurd had returned the $60,000 commission he had received for doing Johnson's portrait.[53] No. 21

22.

Carl Raymond Jonson[54]
Modern artist; arrived in Santa Fe in 1924; founder of the Transcendental Painting Group, 1938; New Deal artist; University of New Mexico artist-in-residence; his house (designed by John Gaw Meem) was both his home and an art gallery on the UNM campus, 1949-82; the house remains a campus art gallery today; University of New Mexico honorary degree recipient, 1971
Date of Birth: July 18, 1891
Place of Birth: near Chariton, Iowa
Date of Death (age): May 10, 1982 (90)
Place of Death: at his home in Albuquerque, New Mexico
Cause of Death: unstated natural causes
Resting Place: cremated, with his ashes stored in a vault in Jonson Gallery, University of New Mexico, Albuquerque, New Mexico

Jonson had originally wished to be cremated with his ashes scattered on a New Mexico mountain. It was only toward the end of his life that he decided that his ashes would be stored in a vault along with the ashes of his wife, his brother, and his sister-in-law at Jonson Gallery.[55] No. 22

Oliver LaGrone
First came to New Mexico when his sister was diagnosed with tuberculosis in 1931; graduated from the University of New Mexico, 1938; New Deal artist; noted Black sculptor, poet, teacher, and civil rights advocate; a scholarship was named in his honor
Date of Birth: December 9, 1906
Place of Birth: McAlester, Oklahoma Territory
Date of Death (age): October 15, 1995 (88)
Place of Death: probably Detroit, Michigan
Cause of Death: unstated natural causes
Resting Place: unknown[56]

Georgia Totto O'Keeffe
Most famous woman painter of the twentieth century; first arrived in New Mexico in 1929; her *Bear Lake, New Mexico* (1930), which hangs in the Green Room, is part of the White House's permanent collection; spent many summers painting at Ghost Ranch, New Mexico, permanently moving to Abiquiu, New Mexico, in 1950; most famous for her paintings of animal skulls, flowers, and doorways; University of New Mexico honorary degree recipient, 1964; a street and an elementary school in Albuquerque were named in her honor; a U.S. postage stamp was issued in her honor; the Georgia O'Keeffe Museum, opened on July 17, 1997, in Santa Fe, was the first art museum in the United States dedicated to the art of a major woman artist
Date of Birth: November 15, 1887
Place of Birth: Sun Prairie, Wisconsin
Date of Death (age): 12:20 p.m., March 6, 1986 (98)
Place of Death: St. Vincent Hospital, Santa Fe, New Mexico
Cause of Death: not disclosed at family's request[57]
Resting Place: cremated with her ashes scattered over Ghost Ranch, New Mexico[58]
According to one of her biographers:

> O'Keeffe liked to say that she would live to be a hundred. When she passed her ninetieth birthday, she upped the figure to 125. She would admit no fear of death. She once said, "When I think of death, I only regret that I will not be able to see this beautiful country anymore, unless the Indians are right and my spirit will walk here after I'm gone."[59]

At her request, no funeral or memorial service was held when she died. Instead, her friend, Juan Hamilton, took her ashes north of her home in Abiquiu to the top of Pedernal. "Pausing until the wind was blowing to the north, he threw the ashes so they would be scattered over her beloved Ghost Ranch."[60]

Other Artists include:
Bill Mauldin (Chapter 13: Wartime Leaders and Victims Since the Spanish-American War, 1898)

E. Boyd (Chapter 4: Cultural Preservationists)
Kenneth Chapman (Chapter 4: Cultural Preservationists)
Fray Angélico Chávez (Chapter 4: Cultural Preservationists)
John Ehrlichman (Chapter 8: Lawmen, Criminals, and Victims of Crime)
Ernest Thompson Seton (Chapter 7: Sung and Unsung Heroes)

Native American Artists (in alphabetical order)

Helen Quintana Cordova
Creator of the Pueblo storyteller figure, originally a male (inspired by her grandfather, Santiago Quintana) with five children on his lap, 1964
Date of Birth: June 17, 1915
Place of Birth: Cochiti Pueblo, New Mexico
Date of Death (age): July 24, 1994 (79)
Cause of Death: unstated natural causes after a lengthy illness
Place of Death: Santa Fe Indian Hospital, Santa Fe, New Mexico
Resting Place: Cochiti Pueblo Cemetery, Cochiti Pueblo, New Mexico; not accessible to the general public

Shortly before her death, Cordova said:

> I don't know why people go for my work the way they do. Maybe it's because to me they aren't just pretty things that I make for money. All my potteries come out of my heart. They're my little people. I talk to them and they're singing. If you're listening, you can hear them.[61]

Rudolph Carl "R.C." Gorman
Most popular Navajo painter and sculptor of the twentieth century; described as the Picasso of Native American artists; son of artist and Navajo Code Talker, Carl Gorman; a scholarship was named in his honor
Date of Birth: July 26, 1931
Place of Birth: Chinle, Arizona
Date of Death (age): 12:20 p.m., November 3, 2005 (74)
Place of Death: University of New Mexico Hospital, Albuquerque, New Mexico
Cause of Death: bacterial infection resulting in multiple complications, including pneumonia, blood clots, kidney failure, and a coma
Resting Place: his private land in Las Colonias near Taos, New Mexico

A Navajo medicine man came to the hospital shortly before Gorman's death to perform the Blessing Way ceremony, a traditional blessing given "to ensure peace, harmony, and protection on a journey." Upon Gorman's death, New Mexico Governor Bill Richardson ordered flags across New Mexico to be flown at half-staff.[62] According to the *Albuquerque Journal* of November 8, 2005, "Gorman, whose traditional Navajo headband became his trademark, was buried in a handmade cedar casket with his headbands sewn into a lining."

Allan Haozous (Pulling Roots) Houser
World famous Chiricahua Apache sculptor; New Deal artist; a founding instructor at the Institute of American Arts, Santa Fe, New Mexico; received the National Medal of the Arts, the country's highest award in art, 1992; Native American flutist
Date of Birth: June 30, 1914
Place of Birth: Apache, Oklahoma
Date of Death (age): August 22, 1994 (80)
Place of Death: at his home in Santa Fe, New Mexico
Cause of Death: colon cancer
Resting Place: Memorial Garden Cemetery, Santa Fe, New Mexico

23.

Houser said of his art, "I've been doing experiments all the time. It's what keeps you alive. I'd get bored if I did the same thing all the time. That's why I'm known as someone who is versatile, who keeps coming up with new things." He added that "In my work, this is what I strive for—this dignity, this goodness that is in man. I hope I am getting it across. If I am, then I am doing what I have always wanted."[63]

An amphitheater at his studio south of Santa Fe had been built so that Houser "would be able to entertain his friends and family with his other talent, playing his Native American flute. This was the site of his memorial service with over five hundred attending and [where his] son, Bob Haozous, played the Native American flute in his memory."[64] No. 23

Lucy Martin Lewis
Award-winning Acoma potter famous for her revival of Mimbres black-on-white pottery designs; lived most of her life at Acoma, but taught at the Idyllwild School of Music and the Arts, Idyllwild, California
Date of Birth: date unknown, although she celebrated November 2; year unknown, although it was estimated to be about 1899
Place of Birth: Acoma Pueblo, New Mexico
Date of Death (age): March 12, 1992 (about 93)
Place of Death: McCartys, New Mexico
Cause of Death: unstated natural causes
Resting Place: unknown[65]

Julian "Po-ea-no" (Herd of Animals) Martinez
With his wife, Maria Martinez, became famous for their black-on-black pueblo pottery style; New Deal artist
Date of Birth: 1897
Place of Birth: San Ildefonso Pueblo, New Mexico
Date of Death (age): evening, March 5, 1943 (about 46)
Place of Death: near San Ildefonso Pueblo, New Mexico
Cause of Death: unstated natural causes

Resting Place: In accordance with his pueblo's tradition, Julian's body was buried in a secret location on the San Ildefonso Pueblo. Not even his wife, María, knew of its location. Also, in accordance with tradition, all of his personal belongings, including his notebook of pottery designs, were burned at the time of his death.[66]

Maria Antonia Montoya "Puvika" (Flower Leaf) or "Poveka" (Pond Lily) Martinez[67]

Pueblo Indian potter, internationally known for her black-on-black pottery, with her work on display in museums around the world and some of her pottery selling for $15,000 each at the time of her death; New Deal artist

Date of Birth: 1881, 1883, 1885, 1886, or 1887

Place of Birth: San Ildefonso Pueblo, New Mexico

Date of Death (age): July 20, 1980 (between 93 and 99)

Place of Death: at her home in San Ildefonso Pueblo, New Mexico

Cause of Death: unstated natural causes following a hospital stay of several weeks

Resting Place: San Ildefonso Catholic Cemetery, San Ildefonso Pueblo, New Mexico; not accessible to the general public

Sadly, because so many tourists disturbed her resting place and those buried near her, her gravestone has been removed and her gravesite is now unmarked.[68]

Maria Margarita "Margaret" "Corn Blossom" Tafoya

Award-winning matriarch of Santa Clara Pueblo potters

Date of Birth: August 13, 1904

Place of Birth: Santa Clara Pueblo, New Mexico

Date of Death (age): February 25, 2001 (96)

Place of Death: at her home in Santa Clara Pueblo, New Mexico

Cause of Death: unstated natural causes

Resting Place: unknown

Margaret Tafoya always prayed to Mother Clay before making her pottery. She never talked of "when I die," but rather "if I die."[69]

Quincy Tahoma

Navajo shepherd; one of the most successful artists of Dorothy Dunn's Studio, Santa Fe Indian School; accomplished sandpainter and painter known for his brilliant colors depicting traditional Indian activities; World War II veteran

Date of Birth: 1920

Place of Birth: Tuba City, Arizona

Date of Death (age): November 11, 1956 (about 36)

Place of Death: Santa Fe, New Mexico

Cause of Death: complications resulting from alcoholism

Resting Place: unknown[70]

Pablita "Tse Tsan" (Golden Dawn) Velarde

One of the most successful artists of Dorothy Dunn's Studio, Santa Fe Indian School; one of the first female Indian painters; employed by the Works Progress

Administration to paint murals and paintings of pueblo life at Bandelier National Monument, 1939-43; mother of famed artist Helen Hardin (1951-92); recipient of more than fifty honors and awards at the state and national levels; University of New Mexico honorary degree recipient, 1978
Date of Birth: 1912; naming day, September 22, 1915
Place of Birth: Santa Clara Pueblo, New Mexico
Date of Death (age): January 10, 2006 (about 94)
Place of Death: at her home in Albuquerque, New Mexico
Cause of Death: pneumonia
Resting Place: Santa Clara Pueblo, New Mexico; not accessible to the general public

    Velarde once wrote that "Each year I take three bouquets of flowers on Memorial Day to the graveyard at Santa Clara. I plant one on my daughter Helen's grave. But there is no grave marker for my mother. No one remembers where she was buried. I don't even remember her funeral. I was two and a half years old when she died of TB…. So as I plant two bouquets of flowers on my father's grave, I whisper, 'Dad, please give one to Mom from me.'"[71]

Other Native American Artists include:
Carl Nelson Gorman (Chapter 13: Wartime Leaders and Victims Since the Spanish-American War, 1898)

Hispanic Artists (in alphabetical order)

José Rafael Aragón
Known as "The Father of New Mexico *Santero* Art"; proficient at not only painting *retablos* (religious paintings), but also carving *bultos* (religious sculptures); famous for signing his works, while other *santeros* did not
Date of Birth: 1796
Place of Birth: Santa Fe, New Mexico
Date of Death (age): 1862 (about 66)
Place of Death: Córdova, New Mexico
Cause of Death: unstated natural causes
Resting Place: originally in the San Antonio Cemetery, Córdova, New Mexico, but later moved to Our Lady of Mount Carmel Chapel, Santa Cruz, New Mexico[72] No. 24

24.

Patrocinio Barela[73]
Ranch hand and itinerant laborer; wood carver who worked for the Works Progress Administration's Federal Art Project, 1936-39, and its Art Administration's Project to 1943
Date of Birth: October 14, 1902
Place of Birth: Bisbee, Arizona
Date of Death (age): October 24, 1964 (62)
Place of Death: in his workshop in Cañon, New Mexico
Cause of Death: killed in a fire
Resting Place: Nuestra Señora de Dolores Cemetery, Cañon, New Mexico[73] No. 25

25.

Luis Alfonso Jimémez, Jr.
Award-winning controversial creator of large, bold, raw, colorful sculptures of subjects from immigrant workers crossing the Rio Grande to a mourning Aztec warrior displayed in public spaces from the Smithsonian in Washington, D.C., to the National Hispanic Cultural Center in Albuquerque; former artist in the Roswell Artist in Residence Program, Roswell, New Mexico, 1972-73; considered by many to be the most important Chicano artist in the United States
Date of Birth: July 30, 1940
Place of Birth: El Paso, Texas
Date of Death (age): about noon, June 13, 2006 (65)
Place of Death: Lincoln County Medical Center, Ruidoso, New Mexico
Cause of Death: pinned under a piece of his thirty-two-foot high fiberglass sculpture, *Mustang*, at his Hondo, New Mexico, studio, severing his femoral artery in what the police described as an "industrial accident"
Resting Place: his chosen location in El Jardin de los Angeles (the Garden of the Angels), a box canyon in the Sacramento Mountains, about a mile from his studio in Hondo, New Mexico. His eighteen-and twenty-year-old sons dug their father's grave on land where he had hunted, hiked, and raised his children.

Susan Jimémez, Luis's estranged wife, asserted that, "Luis died in battle, the battle of creating."

At his funeral service in his studio, Jimémez's plain metal casket was placed atop a paint-spattered workbench that once belonged to his father, an illegal Mexican immigrant. Following the funeral service, Jimémez's friends loaded his coffin in his work truck and brought him to his gravesite.

José Dolores López
A Penitente Brotherhood leader; prize-winning furniture maker and *santero* who developed the Córdova wood carving style, featuring unpainted aspen and juniper wood with elaborately carved geometric designs; his sons George (1900-96) and Ricardo (1902-2000) and about thirty-three male and female members of the family carried on the tradition; New Deal artist
Date of Birth: 1868
Place of Birth: Córdova, New Mexico
Date of Death (age): May 17, 1937 (about 69)
Place of Death: Córdova, New Mexico
Cause of Death: unstated natural causes
Resting Place: San Antonio Church Cemetery, Córdova, New Mexico[75] No. 26

Pedro "Pete" López Cervántez
New Deal artist; muralist and landscape painter
Date of Birth: 1914
Place of Birth: Wilcox, Arizona
Date of Death (age): July 1987 (about 72)
Place of Death: Clovis, New Mexico

26. José Dolores López's gravestone is to the right of the San Antonio Church doors.

Cause of Death: unstated natural causes
Resting Place: Bovina Cemetery, Bovina, Texas[76] No. 26

Esquípula Romero de Romero
Albuquerque sign painter and owner of the Romero Outdoor Advertising Company, 1904-26; internationally known landscape and portrait artist; New Deal artist; traveled the world, especially Latin America, 1936-63; worked with Mexican muralist Diego Rivera and other famous artists of his generation; known for his Van Dyke beard and Basque beret; designed the Bernalillo County medallion
Date of Birth: December 3, 1889
Place of Birth: Cabezón, New Mexico
Date of Death (age): April 21, 1975 (85)
Place of Death: in a nursing home in Albuquerque, New Mexico
Cause of Death: unstated natural causes
Resting Place: cremated with his ashes scattered over the Sandia Mountains east of Albuquerque, New Mexico[77]

27.

Leo Salazar
Taos-area *santero*, nephew of famed woodcarver, Patrocinio Barela; won the Masters Lifetime Achievement Award at the 1990 Spanish Market where he had exhibited his work since the early 1970s
Date of Birth: May 20, 1933
Place of Birth: unknown
Date of Death (age): February 7, 1991 (57)
Place of Death: unknown
Cause of Death: unstated natural causes
Resting Place: Nuestra Señora de Dolores Cemetery, Cañon, New Mexico[78] No. 27

Horacio E. Valdez
Member of the Penitente Brotherhood and one of the most popular *santero* artists at the annual Spanish Market in Santa Fe; created more than two hundred crucifixes in his eighteen-year career; known as "the *santeros'* *santero*"
Date of Birth: July 13, 1929
Place of Birth: Dixon, New Mexico
Date of Death (age): having just returned from Sunday mass and having retired for a mid-day nap, August 16, 1992 (63)
Place of Death: Apodaca, New Mexico
Cause of Death: unstated natural causes
Resting Place: Father Cooper's Cemetery, Dixon, New Mexico[79]

     Shortly before his death, Valdez spoke about his work, saying, "It seems like I get closer to God when I'm carving. I pray a little bit and think

28. Horacio E. Valdez's gravestone is in the bottom left-hand corner of this photo.

good thoughts, and pray a little more that the carving will come out right. I find joy in working because I realize that I am working with God and God is working with me."[80] No. 28

Other Hispanic Artists include:
Fray Angélico Chávez (Chapter 4: Cultural Preservationists)
Carlos Vierra (this chapter)

Architects and Builders (in alphabetical order)

Mary Elizabeth Jane Colter

29. Photo courtesy of Stew Thornley.

Architect and interior designer, especially for many Harvey Houses, including the Indian Building at the Alvarado in Albuquerque and, with John Gaw Meen, the remodeled La Fonda in Santa Fe
Date of Birth: April 4, 1869
Place of Birth: Pittsburgh, Pennsylvania
Date of Death (age): January 8, 1958 (88)
Place of Death: Santa Fe, New Mexico
Cause of Death: unstated natural causes
Resting Place: Oakland Cemetery, St. Paul, Minnesota[81]

Learning of the closing or destruction of many of the Harvey Houses she had designed, Colter declared in May 1953, "There's such a thing as living too long."[82] No. 29

John Gaw Meem IV

First arrived in Santa Fe in 1920; recovered TB healthseeker; famous Pueblo Revival Style architect; designed such famous structures as the Laboratory of Anthropology in Santa Fe, several buildings on the Church of the Holy Faith grounds in Santa Fe, Fuller Lodge at the Los Alamos Ranch School, the Albuquerque Little Theatre, many buildings at the University of New Mexico, and numerous private homes; a leader of the Old Santa Fe Association and the Committee for the Preservation and Restoration of New Mexico Mission Churches; University of New Mexico honorary degree recipient, 1960; a street in Santa Fe was named in his honor
Date of Birth: November 17, 1894
Place of Birth: Pelotas, Brazil
Date of Death (age): August 4, 1983 (88)
Place of Death: St. Vincent Hospital, Santa Fe, New Mexico
Cause of Death: cancer
Resting Place: cremated with his and his wife's cremains (added upon her death in 1990) placed in a niche in the wall east of the altar in Santa Fe's Church of the Holy Faith, the Episcopal church he had helped design and they had attended for decades[83]

At Meem's memorial service held at St. John's College on November 6, 1983, fellow architect Van Dorn Hooker claimed that Meem's success as an architect was his ability to communicate with his clients. He always assumed responsibility for the mistakes of his office. He inspired loyalty from his employees and his associates. He was very generous to educational and religious causes, and to the profession of architecture. He was my friend. And I might add that he was, in every sense of the word, a gentleman.[84] No. 30

30. The niche with the Meems' cremains is to the far right of the altar.

Isaac Hamilton Rapp
Creator of the Santa Fe style of architecture with many famous works, including the New Mexico Territorial Capitol, the New Mexico Territorial Executive Mansion, the Museum of Fine Arts in Santa Fe, the New Mexico Building at the Louisiana Purchase Centennial Exposition in St. Louis, the New Mexico Building at the California–Pacific Exposition in San Diego, the Sunmount Sanatorium in Santa Fe, and La Fonda in Santa Fe
Date of Birth: 1854
Place of Birth: Orange County, New Jersey
Date of Death (age): 10:30 p.m., March 27, 1933 (about 79)
Place of Death: at his home in Trinidad, Colorado
Cause of Death: unstated natural causes
Resting Place: Masonic Cemetery, Trinidad, Colorado[85]

François-Jean "Frenchy" or "Frank" Rochas
French carpenter who built the so-called Miracle Staircase in the Loretto Chapel, Santa Fe, New Mexico, probably between October 1880 and April 1881; recluse Dog Canyon rancher
Date of Birth: September 22, 1843
Place of Birth: Vif, Isère Department, France
Date of Death: December 26, 1894 (51)
Place of Death: at his home in Dog Canyon, Otero County, New Mexico
Cause of Death: bullet wound to the chest; listed as a suicide by the local coroner, but actually murdered in his isolated cabin; although no one was ever charged with the crime, Oliver Lee, a controversial, reportedly jealous neighbor, was suspected[86]
Resting Place: Our Lady de la Luz Cemetery, La Luz, New Mexico[87]

31. "Frenchy" Rochas's coffin and plot reportedly cost $13.80.[90] The words at the foot of his gravestone read: "Gunned down at his rock cabin in Dog Canyon."

People told Rochas that he was crazy to try to live in Dog Canyon alone, saying, "You've got no business living out there all by yourself. Them Apaches will take your hair—they've got a regular road in that canyon; and if the Injuns don't scalp you, there's white men that will." Rochas reportedly responded by laughing and saying, "I don't hurt anybody, and nobody hurts me."[88]

Three days before his death, Rochas wrote to a fellow Frenchman living in Santa Fe, saying, "As for me, it is always the same thing. I am just the same, except for a few gray hairs. I feel well except for this miserable catarrh in the head and also in the stomach. Well, some day one will die, and that will relieve us of all these maladies."[89] This unmailed letter was found on the table in Rochas's small cabin when his dead body was discovered days later by a cowhand. No. 31

Katherine "Kate" Stinson-Otero

Famed early woman pilot; only the fourth woman in the United States to obtain a pilot's license, 1912; known as "The Flying Schoolgirl"; first female airmail pilot; first woman to fly solo at night; first woman to fly the loop-the-loop maneuver; flying instructor; denied a chance to enlist as a pilot in World War I, she drove Red Cross ambulance cars in Europe; recovered TB healthseeker; noted Southwest architect

Date of Birth: February 14, 1896
Place of Birth: Birmingham, Alabama
Date of Death (age): July 8, 1977 (81)
Place of Death: Santa Fe, New Mexico
Cause of Death: unstated natural causes
Resting Place: cremated with her ashes buried at the National Cemetery, Santa Fe, New Mexico[91] No. 32

Other Architects and Builders include:
Carlos Vierra (this chapter)
William P. Henderson (this chapter)
Victor Westphall (Chapter 7: Sung and Unsung Heroes)

Photographers *(in alphabetical order)*

Ansel Easton Adams
Sierra Club director, 1936-70; wildlife and wilderness photographer, best known in New Mexico for his October 31, 1941, photo, *Moonrise, Hernandez, New Mexico*, a print of which sold for over $71,000 in 1989; recipient of the Medal of Freedom, the nation's highest civilian honor, 1980
Date of Birth: February 20, 1902
Place of Birth: San Francisco, California
Date of Death (age): April 22, 1984 (82)
Place of Death: Carmel, California
Cause of Death: heart disease
Resting Place: cremated with his ashes scattered off a cliff in his beloved Yosemite National Park, California[92]

Adams wrote, "I cannot command the creative impulse on demand. I never know in advance precisely what I will photograph. I go out into the world and hope I will come across something that imperatively interests me. I am addicted to the found object. I have no doubt that I will continue to make photographs till my last breath."[93]

When asked what he would like as his epitaph, Adams reportedly replied, "He lived for better or for worse, but he's dead for good."[94]

32. Katherine Stinson-Otero was buried at the National Cemetery with her husband, Major Miguel A. Otero, Jr., a World War I veteran. She had assisted in the war by helping to train early pilots. Although sources often give her year of birth as 1896, the year on her gravestone is 1891.

An 11,760-feet high peak on the southeast boundary of Yosemite National Park was named in Adams's honor on the first anniversary of his death. Dedication ceremonies were held on August 24, 1985.[95]

Edward Sheriff "Shadow Catcher" Curtis
Western photographer and author, most noted for his photographs of Western tribes; his monumental *North American Indian* (1907-30), a twenty-volume collection of over forty thousand photographs, included Volume 1 on the Navajo and Apache in New Mexico (1907)
Date of Birth: February 16, 1868
Place of Birth: Whitewater, Wisconsin
Date of Death (age): October 19, 1952 (84)
Place of Death: at his daughter's home in Whittier, California
Cause of Death: heart attack
Resting Place: Forest Lawn Memorial Park, Glendale, California[96]

The wording on Curtis's gravestone simply reads: "Edward S. Curtis. Beloved Father. 1868-1952."

Laura Gilpin
Southwest photographer, most famous for her portraits of Native Americans, her landscapes, and her books, especially her last, *The Enduring Navajo* (1968); Farm Security Administration (FSA) photographer; University of New Mexico honorary degree recipient, 1970
Date of Birth: April 22, 1891
Place of Birth: Austin Bluffs, Colorado
Date of Death (age): November 30, 1979 (88)
Place of Death: St. Vincent Hospital, Santa Fe, New Mexico
Cause of Death: congestive heart failure and complications
Resting Place: cremated with most of her ashes buried at her mother's gravesite, Evergreen Cemetery, Colorado Springs, Colorado, and the rest of her ashes reportedly scattered along Canyon de Chelly[97]

At age 76 Gilpin wrote her publisher, "It's a good thing that I am so busy getting ready for exhibitions or I would be lost with nothing to do." A friend said that months before Gilpin's death, "A film crew was here from Amon Carter Museum to do a documentary on Laura. Even though she was in a wheelchair, they managed to get her into a plane. And Laura happily photographed."[98]

At memorial services held at the School of American Research in Santa Fe, a Native American admirer quoted a chant from the Navajo Nightway ceremonial:

> In Beauty (happily) I walk
> With Beauty before me I walk
> With Beauty behind me I walk
> With Beauty above me I walk
> With Beauty all around me I walk
> It is finished in Beauty.[99] No. 33

33. Laura Gilpin's inscription simply states her name, dates, and occupation, "Photographer."

Dorothea Lange; originally Dorothea Margaretta Nutzhorn[100]
Photographer most famous for her Farm Security Administration (FSA) photos of victims of the Great Depression and her photos of Japanese-Americans interned in relocation camps during World War II; a U.S. postage stamp was issued in her honor
Date of Birth: May 25, 1895
Place of Birth: Hoboken, New Jersey
Date of Death (age): early morning, October 11, 1965 (70)
Place of Death: French Hospital, Berkeley, California
Cause of Death: cancer of the esophagus
Resting Place: cremated with ashes scattered over the Pacific Ocean

Near the end of Lange's life, an old friend visited her at home. "It was a bad day for Dorothea, and she was unable to get up. She lay in bed while he talked quietly to her. Suddenly she said, 'I just photographed you.' He knew what she meant. Unable to hold a camera, she still had been observing him as if she were photographing.... 'To live a visual life is an enormous undertaking,' Dorothea said. 'I've only touched it, just touched it.'" She died before dawn a few days later.

When her family put her ashes in the water near her Pacific coast cabin at Steep Ravine, California, the ashes floated away rather than sank. Her son, John, recalls that "We started to laugh. You couldn't keep her down. It was a bittersweet reminder. Even now she would not go peacefully."[101]

Russell Werner Lee
Trained as a chemical engineer, he became one of the most successful, prolific photographers of the twentieth century; most famous for his photos for the Farm Security Administration (FSA), 1936-42, as featured in books like William Wroth, ed., *Russell Lee's FSA photographs of Chamisal and Peñasco, New Mexico* (1985)
Date of Birth: July 21, 1903
Place of Birth: Ottawa, Illinois
Date of Death (age): August 28, 1986 (83)
Place of Death: Austin, Texas
Cause of Death: unstated natural causes
Resting Place: unknown[102]

Eliot Furness Porter
Southwest nature photographer, especially of birds, who pioneered the use of color in nature photographs; produced almost two dozen books of photography; University of New Mexico honorary degree recipient, 1987
Date of Birth: December 6, 1901
Place of Birth: Winnetka, Illinois
Date of Death (age): November 2, 1990 (88)
Place of Death: St. Vincent Hospital, Santa Fe, New Mexico
Cause of Death: cardiac arrest, a complication of amyotrophic lateral sclerosis (ALS), commonly known as Lou Gehrig's disease
Resting Place: Great Spruce Head Island, Maine

Three years prior to his death, when he was diagnosed with Lou Gehrig's disease, Eliot Porter told his assistant, who was pregnant at the time, "I have Lou Gehrig's disease. You're pregnant. We have a lot of work to do. We'd better get started." The product of their final effort, *Nature's Chaos* (1990), was published (with text by James Gleick) just before Porter's death.[103]

Other photographers include:
Frank Applegate (Chapter 4: Cultural Preservationists)
Kenneth Chapman (Chapter 4: Cultural Preservationists)
Charles F. Lummis (Chapter 4: Cultural Preservationists)
Carlos Vierra (this chapter)

Performers and Directors *(in alphabetical order)*

Bruce Cabot, originally Jacques Etienne de Pelissier Bujac, Jr.
Movie actor; played important roles in thirty-four films, including *King Kong* (1933), *The Last of the Mohicans* (1936), and *The Green Berets* (1968)
Date of Birth: April 21, 1904
Place of Birth: Carlsbad, New Mexico
Date of Death (age): May 3, 1972 (68)
Place of Death: Motion Picture Country Home and Hospital, Hollywood Hills, California
Cause of Death: lung and throat cancer
Resting Place: Carlsbad Municipal Cemetery, Carlsbad, New Mexico

34. Photo courtesy of David N. Lotz.

Cabot was "killed" many times in his thirty-eight-year acting career, 1933-71. Often playing the villain's role, he was drowned in a river fight *(Last of the Mohicans)*, took a bullet in the chest *(Angel and the Badmen)*, and was shot by British agents *(Diamonds Are Forever)*.[104] No. 34

John Wallace "Captain Jack" "Genius in Buckskin" Crawford
Shortly before his death, Captain Jack told a reporter in Brooklyn, "I am simply Jack Crawford, boy, soldier, rustic poet, scout, [and] bad actor."[105]
Date of Birth: March 4, 1847
Place of Birth: Carndonagh, County Donegal, Northern Ireland
Date of Death (age): 3:00 a.m., February 28, 1917 (69)
Place of Death: at his home in Brooklyn, New York
Cause of Death: Bright's disease, pneumonia, and asthma
Resting Place: National Cemetery, Brooklyn, New York

When his doctors gave up on him, Captain Jack dismissed them, declaring, "I'll try Christian Science. I am not ready to give up yet."[106]

A large delegation of veterans attended his funeral on March 2, 1917. An American flag was buried with his remains in Brooklyn's National Cemetery.[107] No. 35

35. Photo courtesy of Steven Klein.

John O'Hea Crosby
Los Alamos Boys Ranch Student, 1940-41; recovered healthseeker; World War II veteran, 1944-46; founder of the Santa Fe Opera, with the opening of its first opera, Puccini's "Madame Butterfly," on July 3, 1957, on a seventy-six acre ranch seven miles north of Santa Fe; general director of the Santa Fe Opera, 1957-2000, during which 114 operas were performed; longest serving general director of an American opera company; University of New Mexico honorary degree recipient, 1967; recipient of the National Medal of Arts, 1991
Date of Birth: July 12, 1926
Place of Birth: Bronxville, New York
Date of Death (age): December 15, 2002 (76)
Place of Death: Eisenhower Memorial Hospital, Rancho Mirage, California
Cause of Death: complications from surgery
Resting Place: National Cemetery, Santa Fe, New Mexico

Crosby once declared, "Our brief moment upon this earth should be full and happy, and, hand-in-hand with music, it can be."[108]

John Denver; originally Henry John Dutschendorf, Jr.
Popular folk singer and environmentalist
Date of Birth: December 31, 1943
Place of Birth: Roswell, New Mexico
Date of Death (age): October 12, 1997 (53)
Place of Death: Monterey Bay, about a hundred yards off the coast of Pacific Grove, California
Cause of Death: multiple blunt force trauma after crashing in a one-engine fiberglass experimental plane
Resting Place: cremated with ashes scattered

Denver's body was so badly damaged in his fatal crash that his identity could only be confirmed with fingerprint records sent from his home in Colorado.[109]

Ralph Livingstone Edwards
Radio and television host who challenged any town in the country to change its name to the name of his popular radio show, "Truth or Consequences"; the citizens of Hot Springs, New Mexico, voted to accept this challenge by a vote of 1,294 to 295 in 1950; true to his word, Edwards broadcast his show from Truth or Consequences on April 1, 1950, and returned to the town every year until 1999; the annual Ralph Edwards Fiesta is held in his honor on the first weekend of May in Truth or Consequences; a riverside park and a room in the Geronimo Springs Museum in Truth or Consequences were named in his honor; a bronze bust of Edwards was dedicated before the Ralph Edwards Civic Center Auditorium on his last visit to Truth or Consequences, 1999
Date of Birth: June 13, 1913
Place of Birth: Merino, Colorado
Date of Death (age): 9:13 a.m., November 16, 2005 (92)

Place of Death: at his home in West Hollywood, California
Cause of Death: heart failure
Resting Place: Forest Lawn Memorial Park, Glendale, California

On December 1, 2005, the day of Edwards's funeral in California, Truth or Consequences's radio station KCHS re-broadcast the Truth or Consequences radio game show broadcast from the town, with Edwards as its host, on April 1, 1950. Town residents also gathered in the Ralph Edwards Room at the Geronimo Springs Museum to sign a guest book that was later sent to Edwards's family.[110]

The epitaph on the stone above Edwards's graves reads: "Time Flies, Sun Rises, Shadows Fall. Let Time Go By, Love is Forever, Over All. Ralph and Barbara Edwards."

Eileen Evelyn Greer Garson Fogelson
Award-winning screen actress; patron of the arts, especially at the College of Santa Fe where the Greer Garson Theater and the Greer Garson Communications Center and Studio were named in her honor; owner of the Forked Lightning Ranch near Pecos, New Mexico, much of which is now part of the Pecos National Monument
Date of Birth: September 29, 1904
Place of Birth: London, England
Date of Death (age): April 6, 1996 (91)
Place of Death: Dallas, Texas
Cause of Death: congestive heart failure
Resting Place: Hillcrest Memorial Park, Dallas, Texas[111]

According to a press release issued within hours after Garson's death: "Until the last few days, when she became very critical, she was very lucid and very bright. It was very peaceful."[112] No. 36

36. Greer Garson's stone is inscribed: "Greer Garson Fogelson, 1904–1996; Dignified Lady of Grace and Beauty, Her Wit, Charm, and Talent Thrilled the World and Touched All Who Knew Her." **Photo courtesy of Thomas Murrell.**

William "Bill" Hanna
Cartoonist; creator, with Joseph Barbera, of such cartoon characters as Yogi Bear, Tom and Jerry, the Flintstones, and the Jetsons; winner of eight Academy Awards
Date of Birth: July 14, 1910
Place of Birth: Melrose, New Mexico
Date of Death (age): March 22, 2001 (90)
Place of Death: North Hollywood, California
Cause of Death: unstated natural causes
Resting Place: Ascension Cemetery, Lake Forest, California

Hanna's gravestone is quite simple, without icons of the cartoon characters he helped to create.[113]

Charles Hardin "Buddy" Holly; originally Holley[114]
Lead guitar player and singer of the Crickets, an early rock 'n' roll band that recorded its first songs in Norman Petty's studio at 1313 West 7th Street, Clovis, New Mexico,

37. Buddy Holly's original gravestone was stolen. Its replacement includes images of hollies and the Fender Stratocaster guitar Holly played. Thousands of fans have visited his gravesite, often leaving items, including nickels, pennies, red carnations, plastic crickets (for his band, "The Crickets"), black horn-rim glasses (like those Holly wore), and guitar picks so that his "music lives on."
Photo courtesy of David N. Lotz.

from January to April 1956; his eight-foot, six-inch bronze statue, located in front of the Lubbock Memorial Civic Stadium in downtown Lubbock, was unveiled on September 5, 1980; a U.S. postage stamp was issued in his honor
Date of Birth: September 7, 1936 (Labor Day)
Place of Birth: Lubbock, Texas
Date of Death: 1:05 a.m., February 3, 1959 (22)
Place of Death: a farm field eight miles from Mason City, Iowa
Cause of Death: multiple injuries sustained during a terrible crash in a small Beechcraft Bonanza plane, named the *American Pie*, shortly after takeoff in cold, snowy weather
Resting Place: Lubbock City Cemetery, Lubbock, Texas

Holly usually drove buses from one performance to the next, but decided to rent a small plane for his February 1959 trip to Fargo, North Dakota, with fellow performers, Richie Valens, and J.P. Richardson, better known as "The Big Bopper," and their pilot, Roger Peterson.

Holly was mourned by millions of his fans and immortalized in Don McLean's 1971 song, *American Pie*, in which McLean recalled hearing of Holly's death:

> A long, long time ago,
> I can still remember how that music used to make me smile.
> And I knew if I had my chance
> That I could make those people dance,
> And maybe they'd be happy for a while.
>
> But February made me shiver
> With every paper I'd deliver.
> Bad news on the doorstep.
> I couldn't take one more step.
>
> So, bye bye, Miss American Pie
> Drove my Chevy to the levy
> But the levy was dry
> And them good old boys were drinkin' whiskey and rye, singin'
> This'll be the day that I die.
> This'll be the day that I die.

In a 1990 auction, Holly's guitar sold for $242,000. His trademark eyeglasses went for $45,100.[115] No. 37

Herbert "Herbie" Mann; originally Herbert Solomon
Top jazz flutist; performed on as many as a hundred record albums; lived in Santa Fe, New Mexico, 1989-2003

Date of Birth: April 16, 1930
Place of Birth: Brooklyn, New York
Date of Death (age): July 1, 2003 (73)
Place of Death: at his home in Pecos, New Mexico
Cause of Death: prostate cancer
Resting Place: cremated

  Mann discovered he had inoperable prostate cancer in November 1997. To urge men to get Prostate Specific Antigen (PSA) blood tests on a regular basis, Mann organized the Herbie Mann Prostate Cancer Awareness Music Foundation (www.herbiemannpcamf.com).

  Herbie Mann's last performance was on May 3, 2003, less than two months prior to his death. Although extremely weak, he played at the New Orleans Jazz and Heritage Festival, receiving a five minute standing ovation. Active to the end, he also completed a final project with alto saxophonist Phil Woods just weeks before his death.[116]

Roger Dean Miller
Country music singer and resident of Santa Fe, most famous for his 1965 song, *King of the Road*; inducted posthumously in the Country Music Hall of Fame, 1995
Date of Birth: January 2, 1936
Place of Birth: Fort Worth, Texas
Date of Death (age): October 25, 1992 (56)
Place of Death: Los Angeles, California
Cause of Death: throat cancer
Resting Place: cremated[117]

Thomas Hezekiah "Tom" Mix
Cowboy silent film star of the early twentieth century; his seventeen or more movies shot in New Mexico included *Local Color, The Tenderfoot's Triumph*, and *The Girl, the Villain, and the Dog* (all in 1915); starred in films with his famous horses, Tony, Tony II, and Old Blue
Date of Birth: January 6, 1880
Place of Birth: Mix Run, Pennsylvania
Date of Death (age): October 12, 1940 (60)
Place of Death: a road outside Tucson, Arizona
Cause of Death: accident while speeding in his custom-made roadster; swerved and braked to avoid a road crew, causing a metal suitcase in the back of the car to fling forward, striking Mix in the back of his head; a monument with the figure of a riderless horse marks the place on the road where Mix rode his last wild ride
Resting Place: Forest Lawn Memorial Park, Glendale, California[118]

  Tom Mix was so popular in Las Vegas, New Mexico, while his film company worked there that the local newspaper claimed that the town suffered from "the Mix Craze…. One merchant is featuring Mix cravats, while…Murphy's soda dispenser has threatened to get a brand new Mix-ed drink."[119]

Mix once wrote a poem entitled, "My Wish For You:"

May you brand your largest calf crop.
May your range grass never fail.
May your water holes stay open.
May you ride an easy trail.

May you never reach for leather
Nor your saddle horse go lame.
May you drop your loop on critters
With your old unerring aim.

May your stack of chips grow taller.
May your shootin' e'er stay true.
May good luck plumb snow you under
Is always my wish for you.[120]

James Douglas "Jim" Morrison
Lead singer and lyricist for the rock 'n' roll band, The Doors; lived in New Mexico in the late 1940s where he reportedly experienced a life-changing event after witnessing a terrible car crash between Albuquerque and Santa Fe in 1947; the crash was featured in The Doors' early hit song, *The End* (1967)
Date of Birth: December 8, 1943
Place of Birth: Melbourne, Florida
Date of Death (age): July 3, 1971 (27)
Place of Death: a bathtub, Paris, France
Cause of Death: heart failure under mysterious circumstances
Resting Place: Cimetière du Père Lachaise, Paris, France
According to newspaper reports:

38. A German fan lays a memento on Jim Morrison's grave.
Photo courtesy of David N. Lotz.

No tomb in France has caused more trouble than the one under a tall tree in Division No. 6 of the Père Lachaise cemetery in northeastern Paris. The headstone is a dark, squat block of granite, inset with a graffiti-marred plaque bearing the name of the deceased…. His grave became the site of drug parties, Black Masses, and trysts with prostitutes. In 1991, on the twentieth anniversary of the rock star's death, thousands of unruly fans rioted at Père Lachaise, and the skull-busting CRS, an elite unit of the French police, had to be called in….. A guard is constantly on hand to keep an eye on crowds that can swell to three hundred during peak hours. [A] TV camera also keeps watch, in case reinforcements have to be called in.[121] No. 38

Kathryn Kennedy O'Connor

First arrived in New Mexico in July 1927; recovered TB healthseeker; founder and first director of the Albuquerque Little Theatre, 1930, first at the KiMo Theater and, after 1936, at the Little Theatre building, a Works Project Administration Project designed by John Gaw Meem, at 224 San Pasquale SW, Albuquerque, New Mexico, retiring in 1961 after thirty years and 207 theatrical productions

Date of Birth: 1894
Place of Birth: Cortland, New York
Date of Death (age): November 16, 1965 (about 71)
Place of Death: Albuquerque, New Mexico
Cause of Death: unstated natural causes
Resting Place: Mount Calvary Catholic Cemetery, Albuquerque, New Mexico[122]
No. 39

39. The words along the top of Kathryn's gravestone read "Last Curtain."

Vivian Vance; originally Vivian Roberta Jones

Albuquerque Little Theatre actress, 1930-32; movie and stage star of the 1930s and 1940s; USO entertainer during World War II; played the character Ethel Mertz in Lucille Ball and Desi Arnaz's popular comic television show, *I Love Lucy*, for which she was the first woman to win an Emmy Award for Best Supporting Actor, 1954

Date of Birth: July 26, 1909
Place of Birth: Cherryvale, Kansas
Date of Death (age): August 17, 1979 (70)
Place of Death: Belvedere, California
Cause of Death: cancer
Resting Place: cremated

Best known as Ethel Mertz in the long-running television show, *I Love Lucy*, Vance believed that "When I die there will be people who send Ethel Mertz flowers."[123]

Other Performers include:
Frank Applegate (Chapter 4: Cultural Preservationists)
Elizabeth Garrett (Chapter 3: Authors and Composers)
Janaloo Hill Hough (Chapter 4: Cultural Preservationists)

3

AUTHORS AND COMPOSERS

Authors *(in alphabetical order)*

Edward Paul "Ed" Abbey
Southwest author of nineteen books, including *The Brave Cowboy* (1956) and *Fire On the Mountain* (1962) set in New Mexico; ardent environmentalist
Date of Birth: January 29, 1927
Place of Birth: Home, Pennsylvania
Date of Death: sunrise, March 14, 1989 (62)
Place of Death: in his writing cabin outside his home in Oracle, Arizona
Cause of Death: bleeding esophageal varices
Resting Place: Cabeza Prieta Wilderness, Arizona[2]

Writing in *The Fool's Progress: An Honest Novel*, published a year before his death, Abbey asserted that "Life is a dog and then you die. No, no, life is a joyous dance through daffodils beneath cerulean blue skies. And then? I forget what happens next."[3]

Douglas Peacock, a former Vietnam medic and close friend, stayed with Abbey through the author's last night, "later calling it the bravest dying that he had ever seen, and remembering that Abbey's last smile passed over his face when Peacock told him the illegal [federally owned] site in the desert where he planned to bury him."[4]

True to his word, Peacock, Jack Loeffler, and two other friends buried Abbey in the Cabeza Prieta Wilderness of southwest Arizona. According to Abbey's most recent biographer, the site "offered a striking view of some of the area's most beautiful mountains and rolling desert terrain."[5] It was the kind of natural beauty that Abbey had fought so hard to preserve. The four men marked the spot with a basalt boulder and a marker that read:

> Edward Paul Abbey
> 1927–1989
> No Comment

Great efforts have been made to keep Abbey's burial site a secret. So far, these efforts have been successful.

It is [the author's] privilege to help man endure by lifting his heart, by reminding him of the courage and honor and hope and pride and compassion and pity and sacrifice which have been the glory of his past.
—*William Faulkner*
American novelist
(1897–1962)[1]

Ruth Barbara Laughlin Alexander

40.

Southwest novelist and observer; a founding member of the Old Santa Fe Association, 1926; most famous for her epic novel, *The Wind Leaves No Shadow* (1948)
Date of Birth: May 14, 1889
Place of Birth: Santa Fe, New Mexico
Date of Death (age): July 30, 1962 (73)
Place of Death: St. Vincent Hospital, Santa Fe, New Mexico
Cause of Death: "a sudden illness"
Resting Place: Fairview Cemetery, Santa Fe, New Mexico[6]
No. 40

Mary Hunter Austin

41. View from the location of the concrete vault holding Mary Austin's ashes on Mount Picacho, New Mexico.
Photo courtesy of Kathryn Jones.

Moved to Santa Fe in 1923; cultural preservationist and activist; Southwest author of thirty-four books; probably best known for her *Land of Little Rain* (1903) and her autobiography, *Earth Horizon* (1932); co-founder (with Frank Applegate) of the Spanish Colonial Arts Society, 1925, and the Indian Arts Fund; University of New Mexico honorary degree recipient, 1933
Date of Birth: September 9, 1868
Place of Birth: Carlinville, Illinois
Date of Death (age): August 13, 1934 (65)
Place of Death: in her famous adobe home, Casa Querida (Beloved House), at 439 Camino del Monte Sol, Santa Fe, New Mexico
Cause of Death: heart attack
Resting Place: cremated with her ashes buried in a concrete vault on Mount Picacho, New Mexico[7]
According to the *Santa Fe New Mexican* on the day following Austin's death:

> With amazing industry she had just completed the late Frank Applegate's unfinished and ambitious work on Spanish [colonial arts] and the material had been sent [to] the publisher; she had left with her attorney, Francis C. Wilson, instructions as to her estate and her funeral; [had] made a public appearance which was a beautiful farewell and [had] slipped out of the world in sleep.[8]

With Austin's death, her Casa Querida became an art center. It now houses Santa Fe's prestigious Gerald Peters Gallery. No. 41

Squire Omar Barker; penname Dan Scott; often signed his books with his ranch brand, The Lazy SOB (his initials)

Cowboy poet and author of some two thousand poems, fifteen hundred short

stories and novelettes, about twelve hundred non-fictional articles, and five books, including *Cowboy Poetry Classic Rhymes* (latest edition, 1998); known as the "Sage of Sapello" and the "Poet Lariat of New Mexico"; winner of three Western Writers of America Spur Awards; elected to the National Cowboy Hall of Fame, 1978; conservationist Elliott S. Barker's brother
Date of Birth: June 16, 1894
Place of Birth: near Beulah, New Mexico
Date of Death (age): April 1, 1985 (90)
Place of Death: at his home in Las Vegas, New Mexico
Cause of Death: unstated natural causes
Resting Place: National Cemetery, Santa Fe, New Mexico

In 1956, when asked to write a short autobiographical sketch, Barker responded with a typical cowboy poem:

> Barker born one Junish morn in 1894
> Started ridin' horses at about the age of four.
> Raised among the cowfolks of New Mexico, and then
> Started writin' yarns and verse about the horseback men.
>
> Forest ranger, soldier, and one time legislator,
> Spanish teacher for a while, but mostly a narrator
> Of cowboy stories in a hundred mags, almost,
> Including Ranch Romances and the well known Sat Eve Post.
>
> His wife is Elsa Barker, also in the writin' biz.
> Their home is in Las Vegas—New Mexico, that is.

Shortly before his death, and after three years of suffering from a terrible illness, Barker had asked his brother, "Why can't I die?" On the day of his death, his wife, Elsa, had rolled him in his wheelchair to their living room and went about housecleaning. When she returned, he had died peacefully.[9]

Harold Witter "Hal" Bynner
Lyric poet; author of more than twenty books; popular host of Santa Fe artists and authors in his famous house at 342 Buena Vista, Santa Fe, New Mexico; University of New Mexico honorary degree recipient, 1962
Date of Birth: August 10, 1881
Place of Birth: Brooklyn, New York
Date of Death (age): June 1, 1968 (86)
Place of Death: at his home in Santa Fe, New Mexico
Cause of Death: unstated natural causes
Resting Place: cremated with ashes buried with the ashes of his long-time companion, Robert Hunt, beneath the carved stone

42.

image of a weeping dog in the garden at the house Hunt had restored and where they had planned to live on Atalaya Hill, Santa Fe, New Mexico. The house is currently used as the president's house for St. John's College.

After suffering a severe stroke in 1965, Bynner lived "under constant care. All but the very closest of friends were discouraged from visiting and a doctor's sign on the door warned that visits were limited to one minute. [It was a] sadly ironic ending for this most gregarious of men."[10]

In the last verse of his poem, "In a Mexican Hospital," Bynner had written:

> Tomorrow again it will rain
> And tomorrow it will shine,
> And so may the world be rid of pain
> Like mine.[11] No. 42

Perlina Barnum Sizer "Ina" Cassidy

43.

Arrived in Santa Fe with her artist husband, Gerald Cassidy, in 1912; author; director of New Mexico's Federal Writers Project, October 15, 1935-39; chair of the Old Santa Fe Association; wrote a regular column, entitled "Art and Artists," for the *New Mexico Magazine*, 1931-60

Date of Birth: March 4, 1869
Place of Birth: Sizer's Ranch, Bent County, Colorado
Date of Death (age): September 9, 1965 (96)
Place of Death: Santa Fe, New Mexico
Cause of Death: unstated natural causes
Resting Place: cremated with ashes buried at Fairview Cemetery, Santa Fe, New Mexico[12]

According to a commemorative editorial in the *Santa Fe New Mexican*, "No one has done more than Miss Cassidy in boosting Santa Fe and Northern New Mexico."[13] No. 43

Willa Silbert Cather

Novelist; winner of the Pulitzer Prize, 1922; most famous in New Mexico for her controversial historical novel, *Death Comes for the Archbishop* (1927)
Date of Birth: December 7, 1876
Place of Birth: Winchester, Virginia
Date of Death (age): 4:30 p.m., April, 24, 1947 (70)
Place of Death: at her home in New York City, New York
Cause of Death: cerebral hemorrhage
Resting Place: Old Burying Ground, Jaffery, New Hampshire[14]

Edith Lewis, Cather's long-time companion, wrote that Cather

> was never more herself than on the last morning of her life.... Her spirit was high, her grasp of reality as firm as always. And she had kept that warmth of heart, that youthful, fiery generosity which life so often burns

out. She was a little tired that morning; full of winning courtesy to those around her; fearless, serene—with the childlike simplicity which had always accompanied her greatness; giving and receiving happiness.[15]

Edith Lewis died twenty-five years after her friend, on August 11, 1972. They were buried side-by-side. No. 44

Margaret "Peggy" Pond Church
Author and poet, most noted for *The House at Otowi Bridge: The Story of Edith Warner and Los Alamos* (1959); known as "The First Lady of New Mexico Poetry"; founder of the Los Alamos Ranch School Ashley Pond's daughter; married to Fermor S. Church of the Ranch School faculty, 1924
Date of Birth: December 1, 1903
Place of Birth: Watrous, New Mexico
Date of Death (age): October 23, 1986 (82)
Place of Death: Santa Fe, New Mexico
Cause of Death: As a member of the Hemlock Society and with the quality of her life declining, she took her own life.
Resting Place: cremated with ashes scattered near Garcia Canyon, east of Los Alamos, a favorite hiking and picnic site for her and her husband, Fermor, whose ashes were also scattered there[16]

44. The epitaph on her grave reads: "Willa Cather, December 7, 1876-April 24, 1947; The Truth and Charity of Her Great Spirit Will Live On in the Work Which Is Her Enduring Gift to Her Country and All Its People; '….that is happiness: to be dissolved into something complete and great.'" From Willa Cather, *My Ántonia* (1918) Photo courtesy of Joan and Jack Gundolfi.

About a year prior to her death, Church wrote a poem entitled, "Last Night the Moon":

> Last night the moon—
> light suddenly
> flooding through my window
> escaping a net
> of dark clouds.
>
> Over and over
> our thoughts came to the brink
> of death. An abyss
> we could not cross with our blind words.
>
> "What do you think will happen
> to you after you die?"
>
> "I think that's none of my business,"
> I said quickly
> and wondered why they all laughed sharply
> as at a child who does not know
> what he is saying.

> I thought they might have understood better,
> the Zen teacher and his students,
> that attention to *one* life
> at a time
> is all that we are asked.
>
> Would they have asked a river
> what it thinks will happen
> after it meets the sea?[17]

In a parting letter to family and friends, Church quoted a verse from another of her poems:

> Oh never fear death for me
> for I have looked at the earth and loved it.
> I have been part of earth's beauty
> in moments beyond the edge of living.[18]

Ann Nolan Clark; pseudonym Marie Dunn
Indian educator and author of Indian children's books, many of them bilingual; winner of the Newbery Medal, 1953
Date of Birth: December 5, 1896
Place of Birth: Las Vegas, New Mexico
Date of Death (age): the day before her ninety-ninth birthday, December 4, 1995 (98)
Place of Death: Tucson, Arizona
Cause of Death: unstated natural causes
Resting Place: unknown[19]

Agnes Morley Cleaveland
Rancher and author, most famous for her autobiographical *No Life For a Lady* (1941)
Date of Birth: June 26, 1874
Place of Birth: Cimarron, New Mexico
Date of Death (age): March 8, 1958 (83)
Place of Death: at her home on the Cleaveland Ranch, New Mexico
Cause of Death: kidney infection and other complications
Resting Place: cremated with ashes scattered over her Datil ranch, New Mexico[20]

Morley wrote that as a young girl her family and their neighbors heard that raiding Apaches were dangerously near. Gathering at a ranch, the adults stayed up all night, planning what to do if the Indians attacked. From an adjoining room, Agnes heard the men deciding who among them would kill the children, rather than have them taken by the raiders. A neighbor, Jim Wheeler, was chosen to shoot Agnes. The Indians did not attack, but years later Agnes recalled:

with daylight came a new world to a child benumbed in spirit and in body, a world wherein life itself loomed as a blessing so great that nothing ever seemed very important by contrast. I rode…home a quite different person from the one who had passed over that trail a few hours before.[21]

As an adult, Agnes was often asked her opinion about events in the past. In a letter to the editor of the *Albuquerque Tribune* in 1949 she stated, "Us old-timers plumb admire to tell present day John J. Tenderfoot what he likes to hear. He doesn't believe us when we tell the truth. We are an amiable lot. Anything to oblige."[22]

Two months before her death, Agnes was seriously ill in an Albuquerque hospital but insisted that she be allowed to return to her ranch to die. Cared for by two nurses, she returned to the ranch and died on March 8, 1958.

Brian Boru "Bee Bee" Dunne
Santa Fe journalist; most noted for his long-running *Santa Fe New Mexican* column, "Village Gossip"
Date of Birth: July 13, 1878
Place of Birth: Salt Lake City, Utah
Date of Death (age): 12:10 a.m., December 31, 1962 (84)
Place of Death: St. Vincent Hospital, Santa Fe, New Mexico
Cause of Death: apparent stroke
Resting Place: Rosario Cemetery, Santa Fe, New Mexico[23]

45.

Dunne was famous as a fixture in the La Fonda Hotel lobby where he gathered much of the information for his regular newspaper column. Unfortunately, Dunne was also known for his drinking habits. The author John L. Sinclair told a story about how Dunne finally quit drinking. According to Sinclair, Dunne

was at La Fonda as usual, and had ordered his champagne from a barmaid known as La Lulu…. La Lulu took Bee Bee's order, and then looked at him, and he looked at her. "I'm sorry that I'm not going to be seeing you much longer," she told him, "because you're going to die, and soon. You drink too much." Bee Bee told me that the way she looked at him affected him so much that he never touched liquor again after that; he knew that he was at the end of the line.[24]

Dunne was famous for his "flat-topped, very broad-brimmed brown hat—not quite a cowboy hat, more like a southern-planter hat with a concha [sic] belt around the crown," which he wore all the time. Over the years many people asked Dunne if they could inherit his hat when he died. According to author Richard Bradford, "A thousand people had asked him, [and] he'd agreed a thousand times. When he did die, a thousand people turned up at his house…so they could get his hat." Bradford suspected that it might have been buried with Dunne, but it actually went to Robert McKinney, the owner of the *Santa Fe New Mexican*.[25] No. 45

Erna Mary Fergusson
Co-founder and operator of the Koshare Tours company, 1921-27; trainer of the famous "couriers" of the Southwestern Indian Detours; Southwest author most noted for the first published New Mexico cookbook, *Mexican Cookbook* (1934) and her *New Mexico, A Pageant of Three Peoples* (1951); known as New Mexico's "First Lady of Letters"; merchant Franz Huning's granddaughter, Congressman H.B. Fergusson's daughter, and author Harvey Fergusson's sister; University of New Mexico honorary degree recipient, 1943; a branch library of the Albuquerque Public Library was named in her honor
Date of Birth: January 10, 1888
Place of Birth: Huning Castle, Albuquerque, New Mexico
Date of Death (age): 3:00 a.m., July 30, 1964 (76)
Place of Death: at her home in northwest Albuquerque, New Mexico
Cause of Death: cancer
Resting Place: cremated with ashes scattered over Albuquerque's West Mesa[26]

Fergusson was writing a biography of Clyde and Carrie Tingley (entitled "The Tingleys of New Mexico") when she died. Her unfinished manuscript can be found in the Center for Southwest Research at Zimmerman Library, University of New Mexico, Albuquerque, New Mexico.[27]

According to her friend Lawrence Clark Powell, Erna kept a diary by which to remember her days:

> "4:30: Awoke depressed about finances. 11:00: Baby squirrels on the step. 3:00: Jittery. 6:00: A still gray sad day. 11:30: Lights out." And another day: "Too weary to write. Rain. Smell of autumn. Pain getting beyond endurance. Nembutal."

Erna persisted in penciling these brief notes. They became harder to decipher, until her last entry on the day before she died was only a scrawl.[28]

Harvey Fergusson; penname Mark West
Southwest author probably most remembered for his *Conquest of Don Pedro* (1954); Hollywood screenwriter; merchant Franz Huning's grandson, Congressman H.B. Fergusson's son, and author Erna Fergusson's brother
Date of Birth: January 28, 1890
Place of Birth: Albuquerque, New Mexico
Date of Death (age): about 2:30 p.m., August 27, 1971 (81)
Place of Death: unstated hospital, Berkeley, California
Cause of Death: heart attack
Resting Place: cremated[29]

According to his biographer, Robert F. Gish, Fergusson's health was so poor near the end of his life that "it was a wonder he was able to write anything. One [of his last diary entries] during this period seems to sum up how he felt: 'My life is an ordeal by pain and fatigue.' Life had always been an ordeal for him—but without the pain and fatigue of old age."[30] His 1971 observation that life had become "an ordeal by pain and fatigue" was ominously similar to his sister Erna's 1964 note near the end of her life: "Pain getting beyond endurance."[31]

Alice R. Corbin Henderson
TB healthseeker who first arrived in Santa Fe in 1916; Santa Fe poet and an art colony leader; married artist William Penhallow Henderson, October 14, 1905; co-founder (with Harriet Monroe) of the prestigious *Poetry* magazine in Chicago, October 1912; editor-in-chief of the Works Progress Administration Federal Writers Project's *New Mexico: A Guide to the Colorful State* (1937), although her role as editor was never mentioned in the final publication
Date of Birth: April 16, 1881
Place of Birth: St. Louis, Missouri
Date of Death (age): July 18, 1949 (68)
Place of Death: Tesuque, New Mexico
Cause of Death: heart failure
Resting Place: Fairview Cemetery, Santa Fe, New Mexico (see Chapter 2, No. 17 for the gravestone she shares with her husband, William P. Henderson)[32]

Thanks largely to Oliver LaFarge and Witter Bynner, a special issue of the *New Mexico Quarterly Review* was published to celebrate Alice Corbin Henderson's achievements, especially as a poet and as a friend to the arts (and of many artists and authors) in New Mexico. The project was kept a secret from her, but, with delays, there was doubt if it would be published before her death. "Fortunately, the magazine appeared in ample time for her to know the concrete appreciation of her efforts....[by] writers whom she had encouraged during their more trying periods."[33]

Paul George Vincent O'Shaughnessy "Plito" Horgan
Arrived in New Mexico with his parents, 1915; World War II Army officer; Southwest novelist and historian; most noted for his two Pulitzer Prize winning works, *Great River: The Rio Grande in American History* (1955) and *Lamy of Santa Fe: His Life and Times* (1975); winner of a Western Writers of America Spur Award, 1976; received nineteen honorary degrees, including one from the University of New Mexico, 1963; Paul Horgan Library at the New Mexico Military Institute, where he served as librarian, 1926-42, was named in his honor in 1970
Date of Birth: August 1, 1903
Place of Birth: Buffalo, New York
Date of Death (age): March 8, 1995 (91)
Place of Death: Middletown, Connecticut
Cause of Death: cardiac arrest
Resting Place: United German and French Grounds, Mount Calvary Cemetery, Cheektowaga, New York

46. March 7, the date of death on Paul Horgan's stone, is incorrect.
Photo courtesy of Patricia Young.

Writing in the *New York Times Book Review* in 1989, historian David

McCullough said of Horgan, "With the exception of Wallace Stegner, no living American has so distinguished himself in both fiction and history. The difference is his luminous imagination."[34] No. 46

Walter Willard "Spud" Johnson; his serious and comical pen names included Walter Mallon and Bud Villiers
Taos poet, journalist, cultural preservationist, anti-billboard campaigner, and editor of the satirical magazine, *Laughing Horse*, April 10, 1922-39; long-time author of "The Horse Fly" column for the *Taos News* and "The Gadfly" column for the *Santa Fe New Mexican*
Date of Birth: June 3, 1897
Place of Birth: Illinois
Date of Death (age): evening, November 4, 1968 (71)
Place of Death: St. Vincent Hospital, Santa Fe, New Mexico
Cause of Death: unstated natural causes
Resting Place: body willed to the University of New Mexico's School of Medicine[35]

Johnson once wrote an (unpublished) poem entitled, "Autobiography":
> One of my dreams is very old
> And never has been or will be told—
> But three of them have long been sold
> And ten have caught their death of cold.[36]

47.

Oliver Hazard Perry LaFarge
World War II officer; Southwest author of twenty-one books; most famous for his Pulitzer Prize winning novel, *Laughing Boy* (1929), and his defense of Indian rights and culture
Date of Birth: December 19, 1901
Place of Birth: New York City, New York
Date of Death (age): 2:15 p.m., August 2, 1963 (61)
Place of Death: Bataan Memorial Hospital, Albuquerque, New Mexico
Cause of Death: heart failure following chest surgery
Resting Place: National Cemetery, Santa Fe, New Mexico

LaFarge's six pallbearers, representing the Indian and artists' cultures, included three Pueblo Indians, led by Taos Pueblo Governor Manuel Lujan, and three white friends, led by Will Shuster.[37] No. 47

Louis L'Amour (originally Louis Dearborn LaMoore)
Western novelist and poet; in his early years a boxer, circus roustabout, sailor, and soldier; author of over a hundred novels (with seven set in New Mexico), which were translated into a dozen languages and sold more than 225,000,000 copies; winner of a Western Writers of America Spur Award, 1969; only novelist to receive both the Congressional Gold Medal and the Presidential Medal of Freedom, 1984
Date of Birth: March 22, 1908
Place of Birth: Jamestown, North Dakota

Date of Death (age): June 10, 1988 (80)
Place of Death: at his home in Los Angeles, California
Cause of Death: lung cancer
Resting Place: Forest Lawn Memorial Park, Glendale, California[38]

David Herbert "D.H." "Lorenzo" Lawrence; pseudonym Lawrence H. Davidson
Poet and novelist, most famous for his supposedly scandalous novel, *Lady Chatterly's Lover* (1928); suffered from TB; first visited Taos, New Mexico, with his wife Frieda, at Mabel Dodge Luhan's invitation, on his thirty-seventh birthday, September 11, 1922
Date of Birth: September 11, 1885
Place of Birth: Eastwood, England
Date of Death (age): March 2, 1930 (44)
Place of Death: Ad Astra Sanatorium, Vence, France
Cause of Death: pleurisy
Resting Place: buried in a cemetery at Vence, France, but exhumed and cremated, with his ashes brought to his Kiowa Ranch, San Cristobal, New Mexico, in 1935

48. Interior of D.H. Lawrence's shrine, Kiowa Ranch, New Mexico

Weeks before his death, Lawrence wrote from France to his friend, Lady Dorothy Brett, in Taos, "I want so much to get well enough to be able to start for New Mexico.... [B]y the end of March, surely, I shall be well enough again—I pray the gods."[39]

Lawrence never did return to New Mexico. Slowly dying, he stayed at a rented villa and then a sanatorium in Vence. He suffered terribly on his last day. To his wife, Frieda, he said, "Hold me, hold me. I don't know where I am. I don't know where my hands are…where am I?" Given morphine, he uttered, "I am better now." Frieda recalled:

> He was breathing more peacefully, and then suddenly there were gaps in the breathing. The moment came when the thread of life tore in his heaving chest, his face changed, his cheeks and jaw sank, and death had taken hold of him…. Death was there, Lawrence was dead. So simple.
>
> Then we buried him, very simply, like a bird we put him away, a few of us who loved him. We put flowers into his grave and all I said was: "Good-bye, Lorenzo," as his friends and I put lots and lots of mimosa on his coffin. Then he was covered over with earth while the sun came out on to his small grave in the little cemetery of Vence which looks over the Mediterranean that he cared so much for.[40]

According to the interpretive sign located outside the D.H. Lawrence Memorial:

> After Lawrence died, Frieda returned to [Kiowa] Ranch accompanied by Angelo Ravagli, her Italian lover and third husband [1950-56]. In 1934,

she had [a] memorial built for Lawrence [at their ranch]. The following year Frieda had his body exhumed, cremated, and the ashes brought to Taos. Her plan was to have the ashes housed in an urn in the memorial, but [Lady] Brett and Mabel Dodge Luhan wanted to scatter the ashes over the ranch. (While Lawrence was alive the three women had often competed for his attention.) In response, Frieda dumped the ashes into a wheelbarrow containing wet cement and exclaimed, "now let's see them steal this!" The cement was used to make the memorial's altar. There are other stories concerning the whereabouts of Lawrence's ashes, but this one is the most widely accepted.[41]

Lawrence's shrine on Kiowa Ranch was dedicated in 1935 with many friends (but not Mabel or Brett) present to hear a Shakespearean actress read Lawrence's poetry and listen to the San Cristobal Orchestra perform.[42]

Many authors have since visited the shrine in search of creative inspiration.[43] No. 48

Emma Maria Frieda Johanna Freiin von Richothofen Lawrence Ravagli

Married D.H. Lawrence, 1914; wrote of her life with Lawrence in her memoirs, *Not I, But the Wind* (1934)

Date of Birth: August 11, 1879
Place of Birth: a suburb of Metz, France
Date of Death (age): her birthday, August 11, 1956 (77)
Cause of Death: stroke suffered three days before her death
Place of Death: El Prado, New Mexico
Resting Place: outside the entrance to D.H. Lawrence's shrine on their Kiowa Ranch, San Cristobal, New Mexico[44]

According to Frieda's biographer, "She had asked for a small, plain, wooden cross, but Angelo [Ravagli, her third husband, from 1950-56,] was afraid people would think he was being mean, so he had a tombstone made."[45] No. 49

49. Frieda Lawrence's gravestone is to the left of the shrine's entrance.

Eugene Manlove "Gene" Rhodes

Working cowboy; acclaimed Southwest author, perhaps best known for his articles about the West in the *Saturday Evening Post* and for his novel, *The Proud Sheriff* (1935); Rhodes Pass, Rhodes Canyon, and Rhodes Spring in Socorro County, New Mexico, were named in his honor

Date of Birth: January 19, 1869
Place of Birth: Techumseh, Nebraska
Date of Death (age): June 27, 1934 (65)
Place of Death: Pacific Beach, California
Cause of Death: "heart trouble"
Resting Place: As Rhodes requested, he was buried at the summit of

a pass in the San Andres Mountains on the Charles Hardin ranch, not far from his own small ranch, now part of the highly restrictive White Sands Missile Range, New Mexico. The Tularosa Basin Historical Society has offered an annual tour of the site for many years.

Rhodes once wrote that, despite "hard times.... I recommend this planet as a good place to spend a lifetime."

After his death, Rhodes's remains were taken by train to New Mexico, arriving on June 30, 1934, accompanied by his widow, May, and several close friends. His neighbors dug his grave at the site he had chosen and his body was transported to the isolated spot in a mountain wagon. At his gravesite, a simple wooden cross was erected with the words "Pasó por aquí" (the title of his most famous short story) penciled in. Later, a group of his friends and admirers, including Will Keleher, E. Dana Johnson, and Alice Corbin Henderson, raised funds to replace the wooden cross with a more permanent gravestone. The new stone was dedicated in May 1941.[46]

50. Photo courtesy of the Palace of the Governors (MNM/DCA), Santa Fe, New Mexico, neg. no. 128705.

Rhodes's self-authored epitaph reads:
> Now hushed at last the murmur of his mirth,
> Here he lies quiet in the quiet earth.
> When the last trumpet sounds on land and sea
> He will arise then, chatting cheerfully,
> And, blandly interrupting Gabriel,
> He will go sauntering down the road to hell.
> He will pause loitering at the infernal gate,
> Advising Satan on affairs of state,
> Complaining loudly that the roads are bad
> And bragging what a jolly grave he had![47] No. 50

John Leslie Sinclair

Author of a dozen fictional and non-fictional books; most noted for *In Time of Harvest* (1943); winner of a Western Writers of America Spur Award, 1978

Date of Birth: December 6, 1902

Place of Birth: Brooklyn, New York

Date of Death (age): December 17, 1993 (91)

Place of Death: in a nursing home in Albuquerque, New Mexico

Cause of Death: unstated natural causes

Resting Place: cremated with his ashes scattered over "my beloved New Mexico," in his words

On his ninetieth birthday, Sinclair said "he didn't want to scar up the New Mexico landscape with his grave. He said he wanted his ashes scattered in the empty mesa country down the road from [his] rock cabin" on the Santa Ana Indian reservation.[48]

Philip "Phil" Stevenson; pen name Lauris Lawrence
Controversial radical author and playwright, especially known for his multi-volume epic, *The Seed*, about the violent, prolonged Gallup coal strike of 1933
Date of Birth: 1897
Place of Birth: probably New York State
Date of Death (age): September 28, 1965 (about 68)
Place of Death: while vacationing at Alma-Ata, Kazakstan, Soviet Union
Cause of Death: unstated natural causes
Resting Place: unknown[49]

Sabine Reyes Ulibarri

51.

University of New Mexico Professor of Romance Languages for forty-two years; poet and author of fifteen books on New Mexico's Hispanic culture, many in bilingual form, including *Tierra Amarilla: Stories of New Mexico/ Cuentos de Nuevo Mexico* (1993); strong advocate of bilingual education; University of New Mexico honorary degree recipient, 1999
Date of Birth: September 21, 1919
Place of Birth: Tierra Amarilla, New Mexico
Date of Death (age): January 4, 2003 (83)
Place of Death: Albuquerque, New Mexico
Cause of Death: cancer
Resting Place: Mount Calvary Cemetery, Albuquerque, New Mexico[50] No. 51

Susan Arnold Elston Wallace
Wife of Governor Lew Wallace, married May 6, 1852; author of many articles and six books, including the controversial *Land of the Pueblos* (1888) about New Mexico
Date of Birth: Christmas, December 25, 1830
Place of Birth: Montgomery County, Indiana
Date of Death (age): 6:00 p.m., October 1, 1907 (76)
Place of Death: Crawfordsville, Indiana
Cause of Death: unstated natural causes
Resting Place: Oak Hill Cemetery, Crawfordsville, Indiana

Two years after Lew Wallace's death on February 15, 1905, Susan wrote to a relative, "The life of my life is gone. I am now seventy-six years old and my heart is a tired hour glass." She joined her husband in death within months after writing these fateful words.[51]

Frank Waters
Editor of (Taos) *El Crepusculo*, 1949-51; Southwest author of twenty-three books; most noted for his influential *The Man Who Killed the Deer* (1942); strong proponent of Indian rights; University of New Mexico honorary degree recipient, 1978
Date of Birth: July 25, 1902

Place of Birth: Colorado Springs, Colorado
Date of Death (age): June 3, 1995 (92)
Place of Death: at his home in Arroyo Seco, New Mexico
Cause of Death: unstated natural causes; had suffered from emphysema since 1993
Resting Place: cremated with ashes buried at various places on his property in Arroyo Seco, New Mexico[52]

"In a 1941 letter to [Mabel Dodge] Luhan that accompanied the manuscript for *The Man Who Killed the Deer*, Waters described a universal human value that might be applied to his life's inspiration: 'We all break away. We look outward and inward, and finally see ourselves. And what prompts us, and ever keeps us on the track of self-fulfillment, is that peculiar thing we call conscience which turns us back, or the intuition which illumines the forward step. It might just as well be called a deer.'"[53] No. 52

52.

Other Authors include:
Clinton P. Anderson (Chapter 9: Political, Diplomatic, and Judicial Leaders)
Yogi Bhajan (Chapter 10: Religious Leaders)
Ross R. Calvin (Chapter 10: Religious Leaders)
Fray Angélico Chávez (Chapter 4: Cultural Preservationists)
Jack Crawford (Chapter 2: Artists, Performers, and Directors)
John Ehrlichman (Chapter 8: Lawmen, Criminals, and Victims of Crime)
George Fitzpatrick (Chapter 5: Business Leaders)
Janaloo Hill Hough (Chapter 4: Cultural Preservationists)
Oliver LaGrange (Chapter 2: Artists, Performers, and Directors)
Charles F. Lummis (Chapter 4: Cultural Preservationists)
Ernie Mills (Chapter 7: Sung and Unsung Heroes)
John Ballou Newbrough (Chapter 10: Religious Leaders)
Nina Otero-Warren (Chapter 7: Sung and Unsung Heroes)
Ernie Pyle (Chapter 13: Wartime Leaders and Victims Since the Spanish-American War, 1898)
Ernest Thompson Seton (Chapter 7: Sung and Unsung Heroes)
Charlie Siringo (Chapter 8: Lawmen, Criminals, and Victims of Crime)
N. Howard Thorp (Chapter 4: Cultural Preservationists)
Benjamin J. Vijoen (Chapter 13: Wartime Leaders and Victims Since the Spanish-American War, 1898)
Lew Wallace (Chapter 9: Political, Diplomatic, and Judicial Leaders)

Composers *(in alphabetical order)*

Elizabeth Garrett
Known as "New Mexico's First Lady of Song" for writing New Mexico's first state song, *O' Fair New Mexico*, composed in 1915, becoming the official state song in 1917; music teacher, soprano, and later a member of the Board of Regents at the

53.

New Mexico School for the Visually Handicapped where she composed the school's anthem; Pat Garrett's daughter
Date of Birth: October 9, 1884 or 1885
Place of Birth: Eagle Creek, Lincoln County, New Mexico
Date of Death (age): 10:20 p.m., October 16, 1947 (62 or 63)
Place of Death: Roswell, New Mexico
Cause of Death: striking her forehead on the sidewalk when she fell, while accompanied by her seeing-eye dog, Teene
Resting Place: South Park Cemetery, Roswell, New Mexico (the only member of the Garrett family not buried in the Masonic Cemetery, Las Cruces, New Mexico)[54]

The first verse and chorus of Elizabeth's *O' Fair New Mexico*:

Under a sky of azure,	O, Fair New Mexico
Where balmy breezes blow,	We love, we love you so,
Kissed by the golden sunshine	Our hearts with pride o'erflow,
Is Nuevo Mejico.	No matter where we go.
Land of the Montezuma,	O, Fair New Mexico,
With fiery hearts aglow,	We love, we love you so,
Land of deeds historic,	The grandest state to know
Is Nuevo Mejico.	New Mexico.

Elizabeth said that "My father tried to bring peace and harmony to our country with his guns. I would like to do my part with my music." Apparently, she achieved her goal. On hearing of her death, Governor Thomas J. Mabry said, "New Mexico has lost a great and lovable character.... She touched deeply the hearts of [all New Mexicans] with her music and [her] charm."[55] No. 53

Norman Eugene "Clovis Man" Petty
Internationally known songwriter and record producer whose Norman Petty Studios were located at 1313 West 7th Street in Clovis, New Mexico; a "father of rock 'n' roll", who wrote for and recorded Buddy Holly and the Crickets, Roy Orbison, Waylon Jennings, and Jimmy Gilmer and the Fireballs; created Clovis's first FM radio station, KTQM-FM, 1963
Date of Birth: May 25, 1927
Place of Birth: Clovis, New Mexico
Date of Death (age): August 15,1984 (57); August 15 was Buddy Holly's wedding anniversary
Place of Death: at a hospital in Lubbock, Texas
Cause of Death: leukemia perhaps "engendered by years of inhaling toxic fumes from the carbon tetrachloride he used to clean his studio equipment"

54.

Resting Place: Mission Garden of Memories Cemetery, Clovis, New Mexico[56]
No. 54

Other Composers include:
John Denver (Chapter 2: Artists, Performers, and Directors)
Buddy Holly (Chapter 2: Artists, Performers, and Directors)
Herbie Mann (Chapter 2: Artists, Performers, and Directors)
Roger Miller (Chapter 2: Artists, Performers, and Directors)
Jim Morrison (Chapter 2: Artists, Performers, and Directors)
John Donald Robb (Chapter 4: Cultural Preservationists)
N. Howard Thorp (Chapter 4: Cultural Preservationists)

4

Cultural Preservationists

Cultural Preservationists (in alphabetical order)

Frank Guy Applegate
Cultural preservationist; co-founder (with Mary Austin) of the Spanish Colonial Arts Society, 1925; a founding member of the Old Santa Fe Association, 1926; first known Anglo *santero*; actor; member of The New Mexico Painters
Date of Birth: February 9, 1881
Place of Birth: Eminence, Illinois
Date of Death (age): about midnight, February 12, 1931 (50)
Place of Death: at his home in Santa Fe, New Mexico
Cause of Death: heart failure, despite his otherwise good health
Resting Place: Fairview Cemetery, Santa Fe, New Mexico

On the morning of his death, Applegate, accompanied by fellow artist William Penhallow Henderson, tore down what they considered to be offensive looking billboards near Santa Fe. In the afternoon, Applegate had a long conversation with Philip "Ted" Stevenson, the playwright and novelist, who was directing a play Applegate was acting in. That evening, Applegate participated in the play's rehearsals until about 11:00 p.m., when he returned home. About midnight, his wife, Alta, found him slumped over in an easy chair in front of their fireplace. Ironically, *The Monkey's Paw*, in which he was performing, was a highly emotional play about death.[2]

Unfortunately, Applegate's headstone at Fairview Cemetery in Santa Fe is badly pitted, making a good photo impossible to obtain.

Adolph Francois Alphonse "Dolph" Bandelier
First arrived in New Mexico on August 23, 1880; renowned pioneer anthropologist, archeologist, ethnographer, historian, archivist, novelist, explorer, geographer, and scientist; Bandelier National Monument was named in his honor when it was created on February 11, 1916; a street in Los Alamos, a street in Santa Fe, and an elementary school in Albuquerque are also named in his honor
Date of Birth: August 6, 1840
Place of Birth: Bern, Switzerland
Date of Death (age): March 18, 1914 (73)
Place of Death: Seville, Spain
Cause of Death: probably heart disease and chronic bronchitis

"These are old, old trails over which we have walked in the Southwest in order to bring the experiences of the past into the life of today."
—Edgar Lee Hewett[1]

Resting Place: cremated with ashes scattered in Frijoles Canyon, New Mexico

Bandelier was buried in the San Fernando Cemetery in Seville, Spain, for sixty-three years. His remains were transported to Santa Fe, arriving on March 3, 1977, thanks to the efforts of leaders at the School of American Research. Requests to bury the body and erect a large headstone in his honor at Bandelier National Monument were repeatedly rejected by monument officials. It was finally decided to cremate the remains, although it reportedly caused quite a stir when someone from the School of American Research arrived at a crematorium and simply asked how much a cremation would cost; the police were called to investigate where this body had suddenly come from. Despite such complications, the remains were cremated on October 16, 1980 (the hundredth anniversary of Bandelier's first visit to Frijoles Canyon), with his ashes scattered near the north wall of the canyon, between the visitors' center and the ruins of Tyuonyi pueblo, as his wife, Fanny, had always wanted. A plaque in Bandelier's honor was also erected on the patio wall of the Bandelier National Monument's Visitors Center.[3] The plaque reads: "Adolph F. Bandelier Archaeologist, Archivist, Historian Born in Bern, Switzerland August 6, 1840. Died in Seville, Spain, March 18, 1914. A Great American Scholar." No. 55

55. Frijoles Canyon, Bandelier National Monument, New Mexico

Elizabeth Boyd; also E. Boyd White and, most often, E. Boyd
First arrived in New Mexico in 1929; curator of Spanish art for the Museum of New Mexico, 1951-74; respected author of *Popular Art of Spanish New Mexico*, twelve years in the making and published in May 1974, just four months prior to her death; artist, archeologist
Date of Birth: September 23, 1903
Place of Birth: Philadelphia, Pennsylvania
Date of Death (age): September 30, 1974 (71)
Place of Death: St. Vincent Hospital, Santa Fe, New Mexico
Cause of Death: cancer
Resting Place: cremated with ashes scattered in the hills surrounding Cerro Gordo Park, Santa Fe, New Mexico

At Boyd's funeral service in the San Miguel mission church she helped restore, Fray Angélico Chávez told the overflow crowd, "We ask the *santos* that she restored to receive her in their company" in heaven.[4]

Bainbridge Bunting
University of New Mexico Professor of Art, 1948-80; scholar of adobe architecture, perhaps best known for his *Early Architecture in New Mexico* (1976)
Date of Birth: November 23, 1913
Place of Birth: Kansas City, Missouri
Date of Death (age): February 13, 1981 (67)
Place of Death: Beverly, Massachusetts
Cause of Death: unstated natural causes

Resting Place: with respect to Bunting's wishes, his body was donated to the Harvard Medical School

At the time of his death Bunting was living in Beverly, Massachusetts, preparing to teach a course on American architecture at the Massachusetts Institute of Technology (MIT).[5]

Fabiola Cabeza de Baca (also C de Baca) Gilbert
Taught homemaking in rural New Mexico communities for thirty years; most famous for her autobiographical *We Fed Them Cactus* (1954) and for her many efforts to preserve Hispanic culture, as reflected in her *Historic Cookery* (1939) and *The Good Life: New Mexico Traditions and Food* (1949)
Date of Birth: May 16, 1894
Place of Birth: near Las Vegas, New Mexico
Date of Death (age): October 14, 1991 (97)
Place of Death: Albuquerque, New Mexico
Cause of Death: unstated natural causes
Resting Place: Newkirk Cemetery, Newkirk, New Mexico[6] No. 56

56. The words at the top of Fabiola Cabeza de Baca's gravestone read: "Beloved Aunt, Educator, and Writer."

Kenneth Milton "Chap" Chapman
Recovered TB healthseeker; writer, teacher, archaeologist, anthropologist, curator, administrator, author, and artist whose painting of the Kearny Expedition of 1846 was used as the image on a three-cent postage stamp, 1946; University of New Mexico honorary degree recipient, 1952
Date of Birth: July 13, 1875
Place of Birth: Ligonier, Indiana
Date of Death (age): February 24, 1968 (92)
Cause of Death: unstated natural causes
Place of Death: St. Vincent Hospital, Santa Fe, New Mexico
Resting Place: cremated with ashes scattered in the foothills in Santa Fe, not far from the School of American Research's Laboratory of Anthropology

When asked what he considered to be the high point of his long, diverse career, Chapman answered without hesitation, "Coming to New Mexico."[7]

Florence May Hawley Ellis
Esteemed archeologist associated with the University of New Mexico, 1935-1971; the Florence Hawley Ellis Museum at the Ghost Ranch Conference Center, Abiquiu, New Mexico, where Ellis led many archaeology excavations, was named in her honor; University of New Mexico honorary degree recipient, 1988
Date of Birth: September 17, 1906
Place of Birth: Cananea, Sonora, Mexico
Date of Death (age): April 6, 1991 (84)
Place of Death: at her home in Albuquerque, New Mexico
Cause of Death: unstated natural causes
Resting Place: cremated with ashes scattered over Ghost Ranch, New Mexico[8]

57. The plaque next to Hewett's remains reads: "Edgar Lee Hewett, 1865–1946. Organizer and First Director of the School of American Research and the Museum of New Mexico. Leader and Inspirator of Youth. Wise Counselor and True Friend of the Indian. Humanist, Educator, Author, Scientist, and Outstanding American."

58.

Edgar Lee Hewett

Archeologist; first president of the New Mexico Normal School (now New Mexico Highlands University), 1898-1903; instrumental in persuading Congress to enact the Antiquities Act, 1906; a founder and first Director of the Museum of New Mexico, 1909; first Director of the School of American Archeology (renamed the School of American Research, 1917); Director of Exhibits at San Diego's Panama-California Exposition, 1915-17; Director of New Mexico's exhibit at the Panama-California Exposition, 1915-17; executive of the Santa Fe Fiesta, helping to create the Southwest Indian Fair, 1922; a founder of the Santa Fe Archaeological Society; Professor of Archeology and Anthropology at the University of New Mexico and the University of Southern California; a founder of the University of New Mexico Press; University of New Mexico honorary degree recipient, 1934; the Historical Society of New Mexico's award for outstanding public service was named in his honor

Date of Birth: November 23, 1865
Place of Birth: Warren County, Illinois
Date of Death (age): December 31, 1946 (81)
Place of Death: Presbyterian Hospital, Albuquerque, New Mexico
Cause of Death: stroke and uremic poisoning
Resting Place: cremated with his ashes placed in a niche in a wall of the interior courtyard at the Museum of Fine Arts, Santa Fe, New Mexico[9]

Near the end of his life, Hewett wrote:

> If I wrote an autobiography…it would read about as follows: For fifteen years I was a country farm boy, working for elementary knowledge as best I could. For five years I did my best to get a high school and college education. For twenty years I was a teacher, student, executive, amateur archaeologist and explorer. The rest of the time has been divided between the excavation trenches, the classroom, pushing forward toward horizons of the world and writing up results.[10] No. 57

Cleofas Martinez Jaramillo

Founder of La Sociedad Folklórica, 1935; author, most noted for her *Romance of a Little Village Girl* (1955); mother of Angelina Jaramillo, the victim of one of Santa Fe's most famous murders, committed on November 15, 1931

Date of Birth: December 6, 1878
Place of Birth: Arroyo Hondo, New Mexico
Date of Death (age): November 30, 1956 (77)
Place of Death: El Paso, Texas
Cause of Death: unstated natural causes
Resting Place: Rosario Cemetery, Santa Fe, New Mexico[11] No. 58

Alfred Vincent "Ted" Kidder, Sr.

First arrived in New Mexico in 1907 to participate in Edgar Hewett's first archaeological field school; chief archeologist at Pecos Pueblo, 1915-29; organized the first Pecos Conference of August 1927 which developed the "Pecos Classification" of pre-Columbian periods of Native American culture; author of *An Introduction to the Study of Southwestern Archaeology with a Preliminary Account of the Excavations at Pecos* (1924); the foremost American archeologist of his generation; University of New Mexico honorary degree recipient, 1934

Date of Birth: October 25, 1885
Place of Birth: Marquette, Michigan
Date of Death (age): June 11, 1963 (77)
Place of Death: Cambridge, Massachusetts
Cause of Death: unstated natural causes
Resting Place: Pecos National Monument, Pecos, New Mexico; out of respect for the wishes of the Kidder family, park rangers at the National Monument do not reveal Kidder's gravesite[12]

Clyde Kay Maben Kluckhohn

Cultural anthropologist, famous for his studies of Navajo culture; University of New Mexico professor, 1932-34; Harvard University professor, 1935-60; Curator of Southwestern American Ethnology, Peabody Museum, 1935-60; author of prize-winning books, including *The Navajo* (1946) and *Mirror for Man* (1949); University of New Mexico honorary degree recipient, 1949

Date of Birth: January 11, 1905
Place of Birth: LeMars, Iowa
Date of Death (age): July 29, 1960 (55)
Place of Death: St. Vincent Hospital, Santa Fe, New Mexico
Cause of Death: unstated natural causes
Resting Place: cremated with his ashes scattered over Ramah, New Mexico, by plane[13]

Charles Fletcher "Lum" Lummis

Southwest traveler, editor, photographer, and author; first arrived in New Mexico, 1884, returning as a healthseeker, 1888; most noted for *A Tramp Across the Continent* (1892) and *Land of Poco Tiempo* (1893); chief librarian, Los Angeles Public Library, 1905-10; founder of the Southwest Museum, Los Angeles, California, 1907; Lummis Canyon at the Bandelier National Monument was named in his honor

Date of Birth: March 1, 1859
Place of Birth: Lynn, Massachusetts
Date of Death (age): November 25, 1928 (69)
Cause of Death: cancer
Place of Death: Los Angeles, California

59. The plaque next to Lummis's remains reads: "Charles Fletcher Lummis, March 1, 1859, to November 25, 1928. He founded the Southwest Museum. He built this house. He saved four missions. He studied and recorded Spanish America. 'He tried his best to do his share.'"

Resting Place: cremated in his favorite Indian blankets, with his ashes placed in a niche in a wall of the courtyard at El Alisal, the unique house he had built over several years[14]

According to his *Los Angeles Times* obituary, Lummis had been told in February 1928 that he

> suffered from an incurable malady, and cancer experts could promise him no more than another year of life. With this knowledge [and his usual great energy,] Lummis decided that there was yet another achievement with which to round out his eventful life. He wished to complete his life's poems and publish them, and sheer strength of will bent him to the task. He worked at top speed,...prepared the manuscript,...submitted it to his publishers, and it was accepted on October 28, [a month before his death]. Usually a book taken at this late date is published the following spring, but knowing Dr. Lummis's condition, his publishers hastened the work of bringing the volume out. Thus *Bronco Pegasus*...was returned from the bindery on [November 8] and...a copy was sent to him by air mail.[15] No. 59

Harry Percival "Doc" Mera, Jr.

Medical doctor; arrived in New Mexico in 1905; U.S. Army Captain in World War I; brother of Dr. Frank E. Mera; created the New Mexico State flag (featuring the Zia symbol), winning a twenty-five dollar competition for the best design, with the original sateen flag sown by his wife, Reba, 1925, replacing the original state flag designed by Ralph Emerson Twitchell in 1915; an original founder of the Pueblo Pottery Fund (later known as the Indian Arts Fund), 1923; left medicine to become the first curator of archaeology at the Laboratory of Anthropology, 1929; wrote three archaeological books, including *Style Trends of Pueblo Pottery, 1500-1840* (1939)

60.

Date of Birth: October 16, 1875
Place of Birth: Potstown, Pennsylvania
Date of Death (age): April 15, 1951 (75)
Cause of Death: heart failure
Place of Death: St. Vincent Hospital, Santa Fe, New Mexico
Resting Place: Fairview Cemetery, Santa Fe, New Mexico[16]
No. 60

Alfonso Alex "Al" Ortiz

Renowned Native American anthropologist; Indian activist; founder and president of the Kiva Club, the first Native American organization at the University of New Mexico; University of New Mexico professor, 1974-97; most noted for his *The Tewa World: Space, Time, Being and Becoming a Pueblo Society* (1969); member of the National Advisory Council of the National Indian Youth Council, 1972-90; president of the Association of American Indian Affairs, 1973-88; the Alfonso Ortiz Center for Intercultural Studies at the University of New Mexico was named in his honor

Date of Birth: April 30, 1939
Place of Birth: San Juan Pueblo, New Mexico
Date of Death (age): evening, January 27, 1997 (57)
Place of Death: at his home in Santa Fe, New Mexico
Cause of Death: heart disease
Resting Place: cremated with his ashes scattered on a sacred mountain near his native San Juan Pueblo[17]

Elsie Worthington Clews Parsons
Ethnologist trained by Franz Boas at Columbia University; President of the American Anthropological Association, the American Ethnological Society, and the American Folklore Society; author of twenty-one books based on her annual field trips around the world, including New Mexico; most noted for her two-volume *Pueblo Indian Religion* (1939)
Date of Birth: November 27, 1874
Place of Birth: New York City, New York
Date of Death (age): December 19, 1941 (67)
Place of Death: at a hospital in New York City, New York
Cause of Death: kidney failure following an emergency appendectomy
Resting Place: cremated with ashes left at crematorium[18]

Shortly before her death, Parsons wrote to her daughter with the following instructions regarding her death: "If convenient, cremation (ashes left at crematory), otherwise, if not convenient, burial, but not in a cemetery and without gravestone. No funeral and no religious service whatsoever. Relatives requested not to wear mourning [clothes]."[19]

John Donald Robb
Attorney, composer, University of New Mexico Dean of Fine Arts, 1947-1957, and ethno-musicologist who collected nearly three thousand traditional folk songs and dances; best known for his work, *Hispanic Folk Songs of New Mexico* (1954); served on the Board of Regents at New Mexico Highlands University, 1966-72, where he had earlier taught; University of New Mexico honorary degree recipient, 1986
Date of Birth: June 12, 1892
Place of Birth: Minneapolis, Minnesota
Date of Death (age): January 6, 1989 (96)
Place of Death: Albuquerque, New Mexico
Cause of Death: unstated natural causes
Resting Place: cremated[20]

Nathan Howard "Jack" "Cowboy Jack" Thorp
Collector of cowboy songs, most noted for his collection, *Songs of the Cowboys* (1908, 1921); cowboy poet and songwriter, most famous for his ballad, "Little Joe the Wrangler" (1898), written on the trail from Chimney Lake, New Mexico, to Higgins, Texas
Date of Birth: June 10, 1867

61.

Place of Birth: New York City, New York
Date of Death (age): 6:00 p.m., June 4, 1940 (72)
Place of Death: at his home near Alameda, New Mexico
Cause of Death: cardiac hypertrophy
Resting Place: Fairview Cemetery, Santa Fe, New Mexico[21]

"Little Joe the Wrangler" was about the death of a much-admired young cowhand, killed while gallantly attempting to stop a stampede on his horse, Rocket. In the wake of a stampede:

At last we got them milling and kinda quieted down,
And the extra guard back to the wagon went;
But there was one a-missing' and we knew it at a glance,
'Twas our little Texas stray, poor Wrangling Joe.

The next morning just at daybreak, we found where Rocket fell,
Down in a washout twenty feet below'
And beneath the horse, mashed to a pulp,—his spur had wrung the knell,—
Was our little Texas stray, poor Wrangling Joe.[22]

Cowboy Jack never made any money from his "Little Joe the Wrangler" and sold his *Songs of the Cowboys* for only fifty cents each. Today, a clean copy of the collection sells for more than $2,000 in rare bookstores.[23] No. 61

Other Cultural Preservationists include:
Ruth Laughlin Alexander (Chapter 3: Authors and Composers)
Mary Austin (Chapter 3: Authors and Composers)
Gus Baumann (Chapter 2: Artists, Performers, and Directors)
Ina Cassidy (Chapter 3: Authors and Composers)
Tibo J. Chavez, Sr. (Chapter 9: Political, Diplomatic, and Judicial Leaders)
Ann Nolan Clark (Chapter 3: Authors and Composers)
Louise Holland Coe (Chapter 9: Political, Diplomatic, and Judicial Leaders)
Dorothy Dunn Kramer (Chapter 6: Educational Leaders)
Erna Fergusson (Chapter 3: Authors and Composers)
Carl N. Gorman (chapter 13: Wartime Leaders and Victims Since the Spanish-American War, 1898
Spud Johnson (Chapter 3: Authors and Composers)
Concha Ortiz y Pino de Kleven (Chapter 9: Political, Diplomatic, and Judicial Leaders)
Oliver LaFarge (Chapter 3: Authors and Composers)
John Gaw Meem (Chapter 2: Artists, Performers, and Directors)
Frank Mera (Chapter 11: Scientists and Medical Personnel)
John R. McFie (Chapter 9: Political, Diplomatic, and Judicial Leaders)
Frank V. Ortiz (Chapter 9: Political, Diplomatic, and Judicial Leaders)
Ernest Thompson Seton (Chapter 7: Sung and Unsung Heroes)
Joseph Henry Sharp (Chapter 2: Artists, Performers, and Directors)

Fred Sisneros (Chapter 7: Sung and Unsung Heroes)
Frank Springer (Chapter 6: Educational Leaders)
William Tight (Chapter 6: Educational Leaders)
Sabine R. Ulibarri (Chapter 3: Authors and Composers)
Carlos Vierra (Chapter 2: Artists, Performers, and Directors)

Historians (in alphabetical order)

Fray Angélico Chávez, O.F.M.; originally Manuel Ezequiel Chávez; pseudonyms include F. Chambers Ayers, Ann Jellicoe, and Monica Lloyd

Received the Franciscan habit, August 15, 1929; first native-born New Mexican to be ordained as a Franciscan priest in New Mexico, May 6, 1937; Army chaplain during World War II and the Korean War; noted artist, poet, genealogist, and historian; perhaps most noted for his *Origins of New Mexico Families* (1953) and *La Conquistadora: The Autobiography of an Ancient Statue* (1954); inducted by the King and Queen of Spain as an Official de la Orden de Isabel la Católica, 1972; the Fray Angélico Chávez Library and Photographic Archives at the Museum of New Mexico, Santa Fe, New Mexico, was named in his honor; his statue greets visitors at the library's entrance; University of New Mexico honorary degree recipient, 1947 and 1974

62.

Date of Birth: April 10, 1910
Place of Birth: Wagon Mound, New Mexico
Date of Death (age): March 18, 1996 (85)
Place of Death: Horizon Healthcare Nursing Center, Santa Fe, New Mexico
Cause of Death: complications stemming from a brain hemorrhage
Resting Place: Rosario Cemetery, Santa Fe, New Mexico[24]

Near the end of his life, Fray Angélico often lamented, "I don't remember anything anymore." His good friend, Archdiocese of Santa Fe archivist Marina Ochoa, would respond by "sneakily put[ting] in a question about something that I really needed the answer to and he always had the answer." After his death, the *Santa Fe New Mexican* asserted that "Perhaps no other person has done more to preserve and restore New Mexico history."[25] No. 62

Antonio Gilberto Espinosa

Descendent of Captain Marcelo Espinosa, an original Spanish pioneer who arrived in New Mexico with Don Juan de Oñate in 1598; Albuquerque attorney, 1921-81; member of the Museum of New Mexico's Board of Regents; secretary of the 1940 Cuatro Centennial Celebration; historian; lecturer; author; translator of Gaspar Pérez de Villagrá's *Historia de la Nueva Mexico* (1933); received numerous honors and awards, including the Bishop Lamy Medal from the Archdiocese of Santa Fe; the Historical Society of New Mexico's Gilberto Espinosa Prize was named in his honor
Date of Birth: December 11, 1897

63.

Place of Birth: Del Norte, Colorado
Date of Death (age): August 3, 1983 (85)
Place of Death: at his home in Albuquerque, New Mexico
Cause of Death: unstated natural causes
Resting Place: cremated with his ashes buried at Mount Calvary Cemetery, Albuquerque, New Mexico[26] No. 63

Janaloo Hill Hough
Actress, dancer, model, teacher, historian, author of five books, playwright, rancher; along with her parents, Frank and Rita Hill, and her husband, Manny Hough, historical preservationist of Shakespeare, New Mexico, despite a fire that destroyed much of the ghost town on April 10, 1997
Date of Birth: 1939
Place of Birth: Santa Fe, New Mexico
Date of Death (age): May 26, 2005 (65)
Place of Death: at her home in Shakespeare, New Mexico
Cause of Death: cancer
Resting Place: cremated with her ashes buried on a hill overlooking Shakespeare, beside her parents' graves[27]

According to Janaloo's husband, Manny, "She had been battling cancer for five years and she knew she was losing the fight, and this is where she wanted to die. Within a few days of dying, she was doing some writing and entertaining visitors."[28]

Janaloo's memories of her mother's death and funeral in May 1985 might well have applied to her own:

> [We] had her body cremated. Practical as always about such things, [Rita] remembered the great difficulties we had digging a grave in our family cemetery for [my father] Frank [in 1970]. Little holes for small boxes are much easier to dig and the whole thing was so much more economical. Rita wanted money spent where it would do more good than on the trappings of a formal burial.[29]

In Janaloo's case, she had requested that donations be made to the Shakespeare Ghost Town, Inc. Even in death she was determined to preserve Shakespeare for history.

Myra Ellen "Dr. J" Jenkins
New Mexico State Senior Archivist and Historian, 1967-80; ardent preserver of traditional cultural and original historical documents; the Historical Society of New Mexico's Myra Ellen Jenkins Graduate Prize was named in her honor
Date of Birth: September 26, 1916
Place of Birth: Elizabeth, California
Date of Death (age): June 22, 1993 (76)

Place of Death: Santa Fe, New Mexico
Cause of Death: unstated natural causes
Resting Place: Fairmont Cemetery, Denver, Colorado
      In 1992 she told a reporter that she was just a "fuddy-duddy, footnote happy historian." When asked if she was busy in retirement, she said, "I don't have a problem keeping interested. I have so doggone many interests, I can't keep up with them."[30] No. 64

64.
Photo courtesy of David N. Lotz.

William Aloysius "Will" Keleher
Lawyer and historian; most famous for his works on late nineteenth century New Mexico, including his *Fabulous Frontier* (1945); University of New Mexico honorary degree recipient, 1946 and 1968; a street in Albuquerque was named in his honor
Date of Birth: November 7, 1886
Place of Birth: Lawrence, Kansas
Date of Death (age): December 18, 1972 (86)
Place of Death: St. Joseph Hospital, Albuquerque, New Mexico
Cause of Death: respiratory complications
Resting Place: Santa Barbara Cemetery, Albuquerque, New Mexico[31]
No. 65

65.

Gaspar Pérez de Villagrá
Spanish captain and legal officer of Don Juan de Oñate's conquest of New Mexico, 1595-1601; author of the epic poem (in thirty-four *cantos*) chronicling the Spanish conquest, *Historia de la Nueva México* (1610), the first published history of New Mexico
Date of Birth: probably 1555
Place of Birth: Puebla de Los Angeles, New Spain
Date of Death (age): 1620 (about 65)
Place of Death: en route from Spain to Guatemala
Cause of Death: unstated natural causes
Resting Place: unknown[32]

Benjamin Maurice "Ben" Read
Important Republican Party leader; a founder of the New Mexico Bar Association; superintendent of Santa Fe schools, 1875-80; author of the *Illustrated History of New Mexico* (1912) and the widely-used *Popular Elementary History of New Mexico* (1914); a street in Santa Fe was named in his honor
Date of Birth: September 20, 1853
Place of Birth: Las Cruces, New Mexico
Date of Death (age): about 3:00 a.m., September 15, 1927 (73)
Place of Death: at his home in Santa Fe, New Mexico
Cause of Death: heart failure
Resting Place: Rosario Cemetery, Santa Fe, New Mexico

66. The birth date on Read's gravestone is incorrect.

67.

Days before his death, Read rode through the streets of Santa Fe on a float in the Santa Fe Fiesta dressed as King Ferdinand. Already ill, he had fainted while getting down from the float. By coincidence, Mrs. L. Bradford Prince, who had ridden on a similar float in the role of Queen Isabella a few years earlier, also died shortly after the fiesta had ended.[33] No. 66

Frances Vinton "Papa" Scholes
World War I veteran; arrived in Albuquerque as a healthseeker, 1924; University of New Mexico Professor of History, 1925-62; Dean of the UNM Graduate School, 1946-49; UNM Academic Vice President, 1949-56; dean of New Mexico historians of the Spanish colonial era; UNM honorary degree recipient, 1972; UNM's administration building was named in his honor
Date of Birth: January 26, 1897
Place of Birth: Bradford, Illinois
Date of Death (age): February 11, 1979 (82)
Place of Death: a local hospital, Albuquerque, New Mexico
Cause of Death: lung cancer
Resting Place: National Cemetery, Santa Fe, New Mexico[34]

As an editorial in the *Albuquerque Journal* asserted, Frances Scholes was noted for his many administrative contributions to the University of New Mexico, but he was "most comfortable, and is best remembered, in the role for which his native talents and training qualified him: as a superb historian, scholar, and teacher."[35] No. 67

Ralph Emerson Twitchell
Lawyer and historian; President of the New Mexico Bar Association, 1898-99; Mayor of Santa Fe; District Attorney of Santa Fe County; most noted for his five-volume *Leading Facts of New Mexican History* (1911-17); President of the Historical Society of New Mexico; designed New Mexico's first state flag, in use from 1915 to 1925 when it was replaced by the current flag
Date of Birth: November 29, 1859
Place of Birth: Ann Arbor, Michigan
Date of Death (age): 5:45 a.m., August 26, 1925 (65)
Place of Death: Clara Barton Hospital, Los Angeles, California
Cause of Death: paralytic stroke and heart failure
Resting Place: Fairview Cemetery, Santa Fe, New Mexico

68.

Shortly after his father's death, Twitchell's son declared, "Had he only submitted to treatment and controlled his temper and quit fighting everything and everybody, he would have been on his feet today."[36]

His last wish, to be buried below the Cross of the Martyrs in Santa Fe, was unanimously approved by the Santa Fe city council, but he was temporarily buried at Fairview Cemetery until a site below the cross could be identified. His funeral at Fairview was one the largest in Santa Fe history, with leading members of both major political parties present and a line of cars stretching half a mile. His temporary burial site at Fairview has become permanent and his last wish has not been fulfilled.[37] No. 68

Other Historians include:
J. Francisco Chaves (Chapter 9: Political, Diplomatic, and Judicial Leaders)
Tibo J. Chavez, Sr. (Chapter 9: Political, Diplomatic, and Judicial Leaders)
George Curry (Chapter 9: Political, Diplomatic, and Judicial Leaders)
Paul Horgan (Chapter 3: Authors and Composers)
E. Bradford Prince (Chapter 9: Political, Diplomatic, and Judicial Leaders)
Victor Westphall (Chapter 7: Sung and Unsung Heroes)

Patrons of the Arts *(in alphabetical order)*

Mabel Ganson Evans Dodge Sterne Luhan
Patroness of the arts and hostess for many leading artists, authors, and intellectuals, including D.H. Lawrence, Paul Strand, Andrew Dasburg, Nicolai Fechin, Ansel Adams, John Marin, Edmund Wilson, Mary Austin, Willa Cather, Dorothy Brett, Georgia O'Keeffe, Robinson Jeffers, Thomas Wolfe, Leo Stein, Witter Bynner, Thorton Wilder, Carl Jung, and John Collier, in her nine-guest room estate, Los Gallos, in Taos; also known for her many contributions, including land and the original building for Holy Cross Hospital (where she died), the bandstand in Taos plaza, and signed copies of books by internationally famous authors to the Harwood Foundation in Taos; such an imposing figure in Taos that a street was named in her honor, and she was sometimes referred to as the "Empress of Mabel Town"; married Tony Lujan of Taos Pueblo in April 1923
Date of Birth: February 26, 1879
Place of Birth: Buffalo, New York
Date of Death (age): August 13, 1962 (83)
Place of Death: Holy Cross Hospital, Taos, New Mexico
Cause of Death: coronary thrombosis
Resting Place: Kit Carson Cemetery, Taos, New Mexico[38]

69.

One afternoon in the summer of 1953 a representative of the Kit Carson Park Foundation came to visit Mabel with "wonderful news." The foundation's board of directors had just voted Mabel the "wonderful honor of being buried in the Kit Carson Cemetery nice and close to Kit Carson. [Mabel] was so appalled that she didn't say anything for a while—then she got up and walked across the room and stood in front of the woman's chair, her hands on her hips. 'I think I want you to leave,' she said glaring at her." Calling her lawyer, Mabel declared that she would never be buried at the cemetery that bears Carson's name. 'I hate Kit Carson,'" she said. Instead, Mabel wanted to be buried in the garden of her famous estate. Her son, John Evans, opposed this idea, claiming that "the house would be harder to sell" if someone was buried in its garden.

Mabel finally conceded to being buried in the Kit Carson Cemetery, but only at the extreme southwest corner, far from Carson's grave (near the northwest corner) and beside Ralph Meyers's, Mabel's friend, a Taos merchant, and reportedly the inspiration for a favored character in Frank Waters's *The Man Who Killed the Deer*. Mabel was the last person to be buried in the cemetery.[39]

Mabel's old friend, Dorothy Brett, attended Mabel's funeral and painted a picture of the memorable scene. According to Emily Hahn, who once owned the painting, the picture shows:

> A closed coffin with a sheaf of gladioli [sic] lying on it.... Four white-clad figures stand in mourning attitudes. Seated in a row of chairs facing the coffin, their backs to the spectator, we see the members of Mabel's household.... [In] profile we can clearly see John Evans, Mabel's son, Spud Johnson, and an aged Tony, bespectacled, with gray braids. Brett in blouse and blue Levi's stands to one side, facing the party. It is a bright [painting], full of flowers and fun.[40]

Mabel's ex-daughter-in-law, Alice Rossin, recalled the funeral and Tony's presence there:

> Tony had been very quiet through everything, then suddenly he started to talk, looking up at the sky. He said the sun had gone out[;] he said lots of other things. We were all staggered, because usually he didn't talk much at all. We tried to calm him down, and that worked to some extent, but through the rest of the proceedings he was apt to say to people, "Where's Mabel?" or "We can't start without Mabel." It was awful, poor old thing.[41]

Tony died on January 27, 1963, less than half a year after Mabel's demise.

Since her death Mabel's famous house, Los Gallos, has been used as a conference center and as a bed and breakfast. Workers and guests claim they have seen the image of a woman in a white dress and have smelled the distinct smell of cinnamon in various parts of the building, including the kitchen, the old library, in bedrooms, and on the stairs. Mabel was fond of wearing white dresses and enjoyed the smell of cinnamon throughout her house. Some have also heard the sound of a male voice singing Native American songs.[42] No. 69

Mary Millicent Abigail Rogers; also known as Mary Huddleston Rogers
Art collector and wealthy heir to the Standard Oil fortune; famous for her failed marriages to an Austrian count, an Argentine millionaire, and an American broker; moved to Taos in 1947; her art collection became the basis of the Millicent Rogers Museum following her death; a street in Taos was named in her honor
Date of Birth: February 1, 1902
Place of Birth: New York
Date of Death (age): 7:15 a.m., January 1, 1953 (50)
Place of Death: St. Joseph Hospital, Albuquerque, New Mexico
Cause of Death: massive stroke and fall in the bathroom of her home in Taos; died following surgery at St. Joseph Hospital
Resting Place: Sierra Vista Cemetery, Taos, New Mexico[43]

According to newspaper reports, Rogers was buried "in a simple but colorful ceremony…. The services were attended mainly by Spanish-language neighbors of Mrs. Rogers and by an unusual number of Indians from nearby Taos pueblo in colorful blankets and leggings. Since she came here…to live a quiet life, Mrs. Rogers became interested in Indian affairs and made many friends among the tribesmen."[44] No. 70

Other Patrons of the Arts include:
Greer Garson (Chapter 2: Artists, Performers, and Directors)

70.

5
Business Leaders

Merchants and Travelers on the Santa Fe Trail (in alphabetical order)

Manuel Alvarez
A prominent Santa Fe merchant, fur trapper, author; U.S. Consul in Santa Fe, 1836-41
Date of Birth: 1794
Place of Birth: Abelgas, Spain
Date of Death (age): July 5, 1856 (about 62)
Place of Death: Santa Fe, New Mexico
Cause of Death: "after a short illness"[2]
Resting Place: most likely buried outside the north wall of the Parroquia, Santa Fe's main church, or in Monterrey, Mexico[3]

William Becknell
Established the Santa Fe Trail as the major commercial route connecting the United States and Mexico, first arriving in Santa Fe on November 16, 1821; long known as "The Father of the Santa Fe Trail"
Date of Birth: 1787
Place of Birth: Amherst County, Virginia
Date of Death (age): April 25, 1856 (about 69)
Place of Death: Red River County, Texas
Cause of Death: unstated natural causes
Resting Place: under a grove of trees in a cattle pasture about five miles from Clarksville, Texas

For almost a hundred years, Becknell's grave was left unmarked. In 1957 the State of Texas erected a large gray granite stone in his memory.[4] No. 71

George Bent
Brother of Charles, William, John, and Robert Bent, with Cerán St. Vrain, the main builders and operators of Bent's Fort
Date of Birth: April 15, 1814
Place of Birth: St. Louis, Missouri
Date of Death (age): October 23, 1847 (33)
Place of Death: Bent's Fort, Colorado

"It is somewhat tangled, but it is a way to make money."
—Damaso Robledo, 1846[1]

71. The epitaph on Becknell's grave reads: "William Becknell. Born in Virginia 1797. Pioneered the Santa Fe Trail. Served in the Army of the Republic of Texas. Died 1865." Both dates are incorrect.
Photo courtesy of Jim H. Thomas.

Cause of Death: apparently malaria
Resting Place: originally in the fort's graveyard, a short distance from the northeast bastion; later exhumed to be buried with his brothers, Robert and John, at Bellefontaine Cemetery, St. Louis, Missouri[5]

William Wells Bent
Brother of Charles, John, George, and Robert Bent; main builder and operator of Bent's Fort on the Mountain Branch of the Santa Fe Trail
Date of Birth: May 23, 1809
Place of Birth: St. Louis, Missouri
Date of Death (age): May 19, 1869 (59)
Place of Death: a ranch near Fort Lyon, Colorado
Cause of Death: pneumonia
Resting Place: Las Animas Cemetery, Las Animas, Colorado

    A few days after his death, the *Pueblo Chieftain* "paid its respects with a proper obituary and estimated that he left a fortune of between $150,000 and $200,000. Concerning the other things he had left to the plains and the mountains, things that had made such cities and such newspapers possible, the account had little to say."[6] No. 72

72.

Antonio José Chávez
Santa Fe Trail merchant; most famous murder victim in the trail's long history
Date of Birth: about 1814
Place of Birth: probably Los Padillas, New Mexico
Date of Death (age): between April 7 and April 10, 1843 (about 29)
Place of Death: near the Owl Creek crossing on the Santa Fe Trail
Cause of Death: robbed of $11,000 in gold and furs and murdered by John McDonald, David McDonald, Joseph Brown, Thomas Towson, and William Mason[7]
Resting Place: Chávez's body was "tossed unceremoniously into a deep gully of Owl Creek where it was left exposed to the elements and predators." Friends or relatives later erected a tall stone marker near the site of Chávez's murder, but the marker had vanished by the end of the nineteenth century.[8]

José Felipe Chávez; "El Millonario" (The Millionaire) Don Felipe
Santa Fe Trail merchant, sheep rancher, businessman with interests in real estate, mining, and stocks and bonds; philanthropist; second only to José Leandro Perea in wealth in New Mexico by 1870
Date of Birth: 1835
Place of Birth: Los Padillas, New Mexico
Date of Death (age): April 11, 1905 (about 70)
Place of Death: at his home in Belen, New Mexico
Cause of Death: cerebral hemorrhage
Resting Place: Our Lady of Belen Catholic Cemetery, Belen, New Mexico

    Not long before his death, Don Felipe's house was robbed. As a result, "the old gentleman remained suspicious of strangers," according to the *Albuquerque Morning Journal*. One day a doctor and a companion from Albuquerque "went to Belen on a duck hunting trip. Having a few minutes to spare, they decided to call on Mr. Chávez. Both [men] were in hunting costumes and carrying shotguns. They knocked at the door, but there was no response. Repeated knocking brought Mr. Chávez to his window. Seeing [the men] armed, he promptly declined to admit them, saying that he cared to see no strangers and they failed to pay their proposed visit."[9]

73.

Near death, Don Felipe summoned Dr. William D. Radcliffe, one of the only physicians in the Belen area, and asked him to move into El Millonario's home to provide round-the-clock care. Dr. Radcliffe agreed. Even with constant medical attention, Don Felipe died within a few weeks.

Don Felipe's funeral was well attended and included an out-of-town band brought to Belen in a special railroad car to perform the funeral march.

Thinking that he would have an enclosed, permanent resting place, Chávez had had a marble mausoleum built for himself and his family in a commanding location in front of Our Lady of Belen Catholic Church. The structure, designed by architect Angelo de Tullio and built of red sandstone and white Carrara marble (cut to order in Italian quarries), featured three full-sized figures, stained glass windows, an iron fence, and a music box imported from Paris.

Unfortunately, despite all his wealth and plans, Chávez's resting place was not permanent and, in the long run, not enclosed. His impressive mausoleum was moved when the Our Lady of Belen's church entrance was widened in 1946. Later, in 1973, the mausoleum was dismantled when the church cemetery was moved behind a new church building. Today only a wall made of the original marble remains, marking the burial place of Chávez, his wife Josefa (who had died in January 1898), his daughter Manuela (who died in June 1920), and a popular parish priest, the Reverend Juan Picard (who died in December 1918).[10] No. 73

Josiah Gregg
Recovered TB healthseeker; traveler and merchant on the Santa Fe Trail, first arriving in Santa Fe in 1831; Western explorer who opened a new route to Santa Fe from Van Buren, Arkansas, 1839; most noted for his memoirs of life on the Santa Fe Trail, *Commerce of the Prairies* (1844)
Date of Birth: July 19, 1806
Place of Birth: Overton County, Tennessee
Date of Death (age): February 25, 1850 (43)
Place of Death: near Clearlake, California
Cause of Death: Exhausted and starving, he died when he fell from his horse while exploring a new trail into northern California.
Resting Place: buried where he died in the wilderness near Clearlake, California[11]

Franz "Frank" Huning

Arrived in Albuquerque, 1852; Santa Fe Trail merchant; instrumental in bringing the railroad to Albuquerque, developing the Huning-Highland addition of Albuquerque, and creating the New Mexico territorial fair; owner of the famous fourteen-room Huning Castle on Railroad (later Central) Avenue in Albuquerque (built in 1883; demolished in 1955); father of Congressman H.B. Fergusson; grandfather of authors Erna and Harvey Fergusson; a street in Albuquerque was named in his honor

Date of Birth: October 26, 1827
Place of Birth: Hanover Province, Germany
Date of Death (age): November 4, 1905 (78)
Place of Death: Huning Castle, Albuquerque, New Mexico
Cause of Death: unstated natural causes
Resting Place: cremated with his ashes buried at Fairview Cemetery, Albuquerque, New Mexico

According to Harvey Fergusson, Huning's grandson:

> When he was about seventy his flour mill was destroyed by fire. It was a rankhackle wooden structure and burned like a torch while the whole city [of Albuquerque] turned out to watch.... The next day my grandfather remarked quietly that now [that] the mill was gone he would not stay much longer. Shortly afterwards he took to his bed with a chronic ailment which had troubled him for years. He never got up again but was a long time dying—an ordeal he endured with great patience and equanimity.... It was the tragedy of the pioneers that in doing their work they destroyed the world they loved.[12]

On his death bed Huning reportedly "said a serene goodbye to those around him, turned his face to the wall and died."[13]

Always a German *Freidenker* (freethinker) and atheist, Huning left instructions in his will that

> I direct that my remains be cremated, the ashes put into an urn and deposited alongside my children, Lina and Elly. And I strictly forbid any and all religious nonsense. If any Old Timer should be handy, he may make a speech, but not mix up any cant with it.[14] No. 74

74.

James Wiley "Don Santiago" Magoffin

Santa Fe Trail merchant; said to have bribed Mexican Governor Manuel Armijo with at least $30,000 (funded by the U.S. government) to not resist the American invasion of New Mexico, 1846; a founding father of El Paso, Texas; brother of fellow merchant Samuel Magoffin; Susan Magoffin's brother-in-law

Date of Birth: 1799
Place of Birth: Harrodsburg, Kentucky
Date of Death (age): September 27, 1868 (about 69)

Place of Death: San Antonio, Texas
Cause of Death: dropsy
Resting Place: Dwyer family vault on a ranch owned by Joseph Dwyer, his son-in-law, near San Antonio, Texas[15]

Susan H. "Doña Susanita" Shelby Magoffin
Early Anglo woman traveler on the Santa Fe Trail, 1846; most famous for her published journal, *Down the Santa Fe Trail and into Mexico* (1926); married Santa Fe Trail merchant Samuel Magoffin (1801-88), on November 25, 1845; James Wiley Magoffin's sister-in-law
Date of Birth: July 30, 1827
Place of Birth: Arcadia, Kentucky
Date of Death (age): October 25, 1855 (28)
Place of Death: St. Louis, Missouri
Cause of Death: With ongoing poor health caused by the rigors of her trip to Mexico, Susan died soon after the birth of her second daughter, also named Susan.
Resting Place: Bellefontaine Cemetery, St. Louis, Missouri[16] No. 75

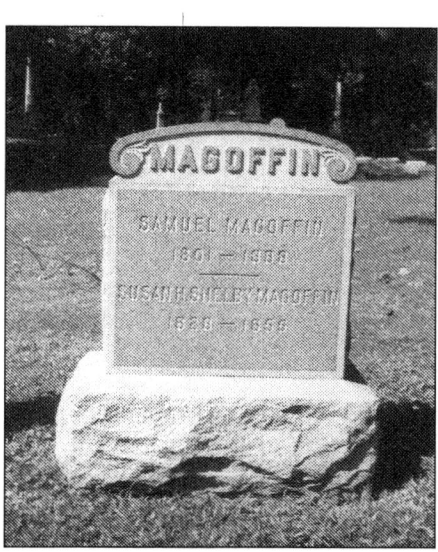

75. Susan lies buried with her husband, Samuel, referred to in her famous journal as "*mi alma* (my soul)." Although sources often give Susan's year of birth as 1827, the year on her gravestone is 1828.

José Leandro Perea
Merchant, banker, and sheep rancher; reportedly the richest man in post-Civil War New Mexico
Date of Birth: about 1820
Place of Birth: Bernalillo, New Mexico
Date of Death (age): April 2, 1883 (about 63)
Place of Death: Bernalillo, New Mexico
Cause of Death: unstated natural causes
Resting Place: cemetery in front of Our Lady of Sorrows Catholic Church, Bernalillo, New Mexico; now a paved parking lot[17] No. 76

Marion (or Marian) Sloan "Mother Marion" Russell
Traveler on the Santa Fe Trail; most famous for her published memoirs, *Land of Enchantment* (1954)
Date of Birth: January 26, 1845
Place of Birth: Peoria, Illinois
Date of Death (age): Christmas, December 25, 1936 (91)
Place of Death: Trinidad, Colorado
Cause of Death: injuries suffered in an auto accident
Resting Place: Stonewall Cemetery, Stonewall, Colorado[18]

Like other frontier women, Marion Russell experienced the tragic deaths of many loved ones. In stirring terms she described the death of her infant daughter at Fort Bascom, New Mexico:

> One August morning I thought she was sleeping too long. I went and lifted her from her cradle. It was a long, long time before I could realize

76. Our Lady of Sorrows Catholic Church, Bernalillo, New Mexico

that I held in my arms a little, dead baby. I stood and held her, saying nothing until [my husband] Richard came and took her from me.... We did not stay much longer in Fort Bascom for Richard [an officer in the U.S. Army] was ordered to report to Fort Union [but] I think of Fort Bascom tenderly, for a little grave is there where Hattie Eliza is sleeping.[19]

After leaving the military, Marion's husband Richard was killed in the Maxwell Land Grant controversy. Marion recalled:

The five days that he lay suffering lie open on my heart today.... The hours that I spent by his bedside were long, hideous hours.... The messenger we had sent for a doctor had been intercepted by [Richard's enemies]. There was nothing we could do. Five hundred armed men followed my husband's body to the little cemetery [in southern Colorado]. I stood dry-eyed and heard the "dust to dust" spoken. The angry thoughts and smarting pain are gone, replaced by the growing knowledge that vengeance belongs to God.[20]

77. Marion lies buried beside her husband, Richard Russell. Her date of birth, as listed on her gravestone, is incorrect.

Years after Marion's death, historian Marc Simmons, who had urged the University of New Mexico Press to issue a new paperback edition of *Land of Enchantment*,

visited the graves of Marian and Richard Russell, located in a pioneer cemetery.... I had a copy of the freshly minted *Land of Enchantment* under my arm, and I placed it briefly on her tombstone. I figured that if Marian's spirit was lurking about, she would be pleased to learn that her book was back in print and available to a new generation of readers.[21] No. 77

Cerán de Hault de Lassusde St. Vrain; called Black Beard by the Indians
Beaver trapper; co-owner of Bent, St. Vrain & Co., a freighting and commercial venture centered in Taos and Bent's Fort in southern Colorado, founded in 1830; volunteer in the suppression of the Revolt of 1847 and in the Civil War in New Mexico; the Curry County settlement of Saint Vrain may well have been named in his honor
Date of Birth: May 5, 1802
Place of Birth: St. Louis County, Missouri
Date of Death (age): 6:00 p.m., October 28, 1870 (68)
Place of Death: Mora, New Mexico
Cause of Death: apoplexy
Resting Place: private cemetery outside Mora, New Mexico

An estimated two thousand persons attended St. Vrain's funeral on October 30, 1870, with Masonic rites and full military honors. According to the *Santa Fe Daily New Mexican*, "The service was very impressive and the surroundings of a highly romantic character; nothing equal to it was ever seen in New Mexico."[22] No. 78

78. Photo by Charles Bennett, courtesy Palace of the Governors (MNM/DCA), neg. no. 139597.

Solomon Spiegelberg
First Jewish merchant to arrive in New Mexico, 1846; one of seven brothers and Santa Fe business partners, including Levi (arriving in 1848), Elias (arriving in 1850), Emanual (arriving in 1853), Lehman (arriving in 1857), Willi (arriving in 1861), and Abraham; left the Territory by 1854, due to poor health; the brothers operated one of Santa Fe's main mercantile stores, located on the south side of the plaza, and the Second National Bank of Santa Fe
Date of Birth: 1826
Place of Birth: Hanover, Germany
Date of Death (age): March 1898 (about 72)
Place of Death: Meran, Austria
Cause of Death: unstated natural causes
Resting Place: unknown[23]

Richens Lacy "Uncle Dick" Wootton
Fur trapper, Indian fighter, Indian trader, buffalo rancher, sheep driver to California, operator of a twenty-seven mile toll road at Raton Pass on the Mountain Branch of the Santa Fe Trail, 1866-1879
Date of Birth: May 6, 1816
Place of Birth: Mecklenburg County, Virginia
Date of Death (age): August 22, 1893 (77)
Place of Death: unknown
Cause of Death: unstated natural causes
Resting Place: Trinidad Catholic Cemetery, Trinidad, Colorado[24] No. 79

79. Wootton's first name, as shown on his gravestone, is incorrect.

Other Merchants and Workers on the Santa Fe Trail include:
Manuel Alvarez (Chapter 9: Political, Diplomatic, and Judicial Leaders)
Manuel Armijo (Chapter 9: Political, Diplomatic, and Judicial Leaders)
Francis X. Aubry (Chapter 7: Sung and Unsung Heroes)
Charles Bent (Chapter 9: Political, Diplomatic, and Judicial Leaders)
Henry Connelly (Chapter 9: Political, Diplomatic, and Judicial Leaders)
Charles L. Fraker (Chapter 14: Unusual Graves)

Farmers and Ranchers (in alphabetical order)

Frank Bond
Arrived in New Mexico in 1883; sheep rancher, owner of a large mercantile business based in Española (and later in Albuquerque); vast land owner
Date of Birth: February 13, 1863
Place of Birth: Argenteull County, Quebec Province, Canada
Date of Death (age): June 21, 1945 (82)
Place of Death: a hospital in Pasadena, California
Cause of Death: heart ailment
Resting Place: Fairview Cemetery, Albuquerque, New Mexico[25] No. 80

80.

81. Photo courtesy of David N. Lotz.

82. Stephen Dorsey's smaller gravestone, in front of the tall Dorsey family stone, includes the words: "Lieut. Colonel, Union Army, 1861-1865; United States Senator, 1873-1878." Photo courtesy of David N. Lotz.

John Simpson Chisum; original name was Chisholm

Pecos Valley rancher known as New Mexico's "Cattle King," with his 130-mile long South Spring Ranch opened in 1873; by 1875 his hundred cowboys ran eighty thousand head of cattle on the ranch; famous for his Jinglebob cattle earmark; sided with the Tunstall-McSween faction in the Lincoln County War, 1878-81; founder of the Chisum Trails for cattle drives in Texas and New Mexico; the community of Chisum, New Mexico, was named in his honor; a large statue of Chisum stands near the center of town in Roswell, New Mexico

Date of Birth: August 15, 1824

Place of Birth: Jardeman, Tennessee

Date of Death (age): December 22, 1884 (60)

Place of Death: Eureka Springs, Arkansas

Cause of Death: post-operative complications following the July 1884 surgical removal of a large tumor under his right ear

Resting Place: buried on Christmas Day, 1884, in his family plot, Paris, Texas[26]

According to the *White Oaks Golden Era* newspaper of January 1, 1885, "Mr. Chisum was one of the pioneers…of Lincoln County, having come here at a very early day, and had been identified with its history ever since. Eccentric in many ways, gruff in manner, yet he was always a warm friend, and no man ever looked closer after the pleasure and comfort of the men under his employee…."[27] No. 81

Stephen Wallace Dorsey

Union officer in the Civil War; New Mexico cattle baron; member of the infamous Santa Fe Ring; U.S. Senator, Arkansas, 1873-78; implicated in the national Star Route scandal; builder and owner of the famous ten-thousand square foot, thirty-six room Dorsey Mansion (built 1878-86) east of Springer, New Mexico, with its indoor bathroom (perhaps the first in New Mexico), nine bedrooms, a swimming pool (with three islands), a gazebo, a dining room (that could seat fifty guests), and the carved faces of Dorsey, his wife, his brother, and his great political enemy, James Blaine (in the form of a gargoyle) in the building's high tower

Date of Birth: February 28, 1842

Place of Birth: Benson, Vermont

Date of Death (age): March 20, 1916 (74)

Place of Death: Los Angeles, California

Cause of Death: unstated natural causes

Resting Place: Fairmont Cemetery, Denver, Colorado

A New Mexico state historical marker is located near the Dorsey Mansion on US 56, mile marker 23.7.[28] No. 82

Charles Goodnight

Former Texas Ranger; with Oliver Loving, founder of the Goodnight-Loving Trail, first leaving Texas to blaze the new trail with eighteen men and two thousand head of cattle on June 6, 1866; Goodnight, Texas, was named in his

honor; a U.S. postage stamp was issued in his honor
Date of Birth: March 5, 1836
Place of Birth: Macoupin County, Illinois
Date of Death (age): December 12, 1929 (93)
Place of Death: Goodnight, Texas
Cause of Death: unstated natural causes
Resting Place: Goodnight Cemetery, Goodnight, Texas

A New Mexico state historical marker was placed on US 380, west of Roswell, to honor the partners who established the Goodnight-Loving Trail from Texas to Wyoming.[29]

Cowboy handkerchiefs tied to the fence in front of Goodnight's grave are believed to represent gifts left by recent visitors. A stone near Goodnight's marker is dedicated to him and his wife, Mary Ann Dyer Goodnight. It reads: "Together they conquered a new land and performed a duty to man and God. He was a trail blazer and Indian scout. She was a quiet home-loving woman. Together they built a home in the Palo Duro Canyon [Texas] in 1876. They developed the cattle industry. They fathered higher education and civic enterprise. To them the [Texas] Panhandle pays reverent and grateful tribute." No. 83

83. Photo courtesy of David N. Lotz.

James Lawrence "Santiago" "Don Santiago" Hubbell
Albuquerque merchant, freighter, sheep rancher, and farmer; Civil War Union Captain in New Mexico; a street in Albuquerque was named in his honor
Date of Birth: May 26, 1824
Place of Birth: Connecticut
Date of Death (age): 2:00 p.m., February 5, 1885 (60)
Place of Death: at his home in Pajarito, New Mexico
Cause of Death: stroke
Resting Place: Fairview Cemetery, Albuquerque, New Mexico[30] No. 84

Oliver Loving
Texas rancher; with Charles Goodnight, founder of the Goodnight-Loving Trail, first leaving Texas to blaze the new trail with eighteen men and two thousand head of cattle on June 6, 1866; led four cattle drives into New Mexico; known as the "Dean of Texas Trail Drivers"; Loving, New Mexico, Loving Bend on the Pecos River, and Loving, Texas, were named in his honor
Date of Birth: December 4, 1812
Place of Birth: Hopkins County, Kentucky
Date of Death (age): September 25, 1867 (54)
Place of Death: Fort Sumner, New Mexico
Cause of Death: gangrene after he was wounded in an Indian attack at Loving Bend on the Pecos River
Resting Place: Greenwood Cemetery, Weatherford, Texas

84.

85. Oliver Loving's age at death is incorrect on his gravestone.
Photo courtesy of David N. Lotz.

Although his last wish was to be buried in Texas, Loving was first buried in Fort Sumner, New Mexico. His wish was finally fulfilled when he was reburied, with Masonic honors, in Weatherford, Texas, on March 4, 1868.[31] No. 85

Other Farmers and Ranchers include:
Elliott Speer Barker (Chapter 7: Sung and Unsung Heroes)
Thomas F. Bolack (Chapter 9: Political, Diplomatic, and Judicial Leaders)
Everett Bowman (Chapter 7: Sung and Unsung Heroes)
John Burroughs (Chapter 9: Political, Diplomatic, and Judicial Leaders)
José Felipe Chávez (this chapter)
Agnes Morley Cleaveland (Chapter 3: Authors and Composers)
Frank Coe (Chapter 8: Lawmen, Criminals, and Victims of Crime)
Albert B. Fall (Chapter 9: Political, Diplomatic, and Judicial Leaders)
Pat Garrett (Chapter 8: Lawmen, Criminals, and Victims of Crime)
Greer Garson (Chapter 2: Artists, Performers, and Directors)
James Gililland (Chapter 8: Lawmen, Criminals, and Victims of Crime)
James Fielding Hinkle (Chapter 9: Political, Diplomatic, and Judicial Leaders)
Janaloo Hill Hough (Chapter 4: Cultural Preservationists)
Charles Kennedy (Chapter 8: Lawmen, Criminals, and Victims of Crime)
Concha Ortiz y Pino de Kleven (Chapter 9: Political, Diplomatic, and Judicial Leaders)
Henry Lambert (this chapter)
Oliver Lee (Chapter 8: Lawmen, Criminals, and Victims of Crime)
Solomon Luna (Chapter 9: Political, Diplomatic, and Judicial Leaders)
Tranquilino Luna (Chapter 9: Political, Diplomatic, and Judicial Leaders)
Georgia Lee Witt Lusk (Chapter 9: Political, Diplomatic, and Judicial Leaders)
Thomas J. Maeston (Chapter 12: Wartime Leaders and Victims to the End of the Indian Wars in New Mexico, 1886)
Patricio "Paddy" Martinez (this chapter)
Billy Mathews (Chapter 8: Lawmen, Criminals, and Victims of Crime)
George McJunkin (Chapter 7: Sung and Unsung Heroes)
Bernice Walsh McLaughlin (Chapter 7: Sung and Unsung Heroes)
Susan McSween (Chapter 8: Lawmen, Criminals, and Victims of Crime)
Maud Medders (Chapter 13: Wartime Leaders and Victims Since the Spanish-American War, 1898)
Lawrence G. Murphy (Chapter 8: Lawmen, Criminals, and Victims of Crime)
Mariano Sabino Otero (Chapter 9: Political, Diplomatic, and Judicial Leaders)
Francisco Perea (Chapter 9: Political, Diplomatic, and Judicial Leaders)
José Leandro Perea (this chapter)
Eugene Manlove Rhodes (Chapter 3: Authors and Composers)
Trinidad Romero (Chapter 9: Political, Diplomatic, and Judicial Leaders)
William Logan Rynerson (Chapter 12: Wartime Leaders and Victims to the End of the Indian Wars in New Mexico, 1886)

Albert G. Simms (Chapter 9: Political, Diplomatic, and Judicial Leaders)
Charlie Siringo (Chapter 8: Lawmen, Criminals, and Victims of Crime)
Joe Skeen (Chapter 9: Political, Diplomatic, and Judicial Leaders)
Ebin Stanley (Chapter 12: Wartime Leaders and Victims to the End of the Indian Wars in New Mexico, 1886)
Montague Stevens (Chapter 7: Sung and Unsung Heroes)
Ray Sutton (Chapter 8: Lawmen, Criminals, and Victims of Crime)
John Henry Tunstall (Chapter 8: Lawmen, Criminals, and Victims of Crime)
Benjamin J. Viljoen (Chapter 13: Wartime Leaders and Victims Since the Spanish-American War, 1898)
Harvey Whitehill (Chapter 8: Lawmen, Criminals, and Victims of Crime)

Land Owners and Developers *(in alphabetical order)*

Charles "Carlos" Beaubien
Taos merchant; with Guadalupe Miranda, recipient of the Beaubien-Miranda Land Grant, later known as the Maxwell Land Grant when acquired by his son-in-law, Lucien Maxwell
Date of Birth: October 22, 1800
Place of Birth: Three Rivers, Canada
Date of Death (age): February 10, 1864 (63)
Place of Death: Taos, New Mexico
Cause of Death: unstated natural causes
Resting Place: under what is now the parking lot of the former site of Our Lady of Guadalupe Church close to Ranchitos Road, Taos, New Mexico[32]

Charles Bishop Eddy
Pecos River Valley land, water, and railroad developer; founder of several towns, including Carlsbad (originally Eddy) and Alamogordo, New Mexico; founder of the El Paso and Northeastern Railroad and the El Paso and Rock Island Railroad; Eddy County was named in his honor when it was created in 1889
Date of Birth: 1857
Place of Birth: Milford, New York
Date of Death (age): April 13, 1931 (about 74)
Place of Death: St. Vincent Hospital, New York City, New York
Cause of Death: unstated natural causes following a recent operation
Resting Place: Milford Cemetery, Milford, New York[33]

    Learning of Eddy's death in New York, Judge W.A. Hawkins, Eddy's old friend and associate, recalled the last time he saw the developer "several years ago in New York. I invited him to come to La Luz to live and die between two railroads he built. He told me that was a great wish of his."[34] Charles Eddy never fulfilled his "great wish."

James John "J.J." Hagerman
Pecos River Valley land and railroad developer; father of Territorial Governor Herbert J. Hagerman; Hagerman, New Mexico, was named in his honor shortly after it was founded in 1895; Hagerman Barracks at the New Mexico Military Institute was named in his honor because Hagerman donated the school's campus grounds in Roswell
Date of Birth: March 23, 1839
Place of Birth: Port Hope, Ontario, Canada
Date of Death (age): September 15, 1909 (70)
Place of Death: Milan, Italy
Cause of Death: stroke of apoplexy
Resting Place: unknown cemetery, Milwaukee, Wisconsin[35]

Hagerman's son, Percy, asserted that "while no one can deny that his gigantic efforts resulted in great good to the [Pecos River] valley and to New Mexico in general, it is equally undeniable that he would have been better off personally if he had let the whole business alone."[36]

Joseph Calloway "Captain" "J.C." Lea
Civil War Confederate officer; arrived in New Mexico in 1876; land developer; known as the "Father of Roswell"; rancher; known as the "Father of the New Mexico Military Institute," originally Goss Military Institute, 1891; Lea Hall at NMMI was named in his honor; first mayor of Roswell, 1903-04; Lea County was also named in his honor when it was created in 1917
Date of Birth: November 8, 1841
Place of Birth: Cleveland, Tennessee
Date of Death (age): February 4, 1904 (62)
Place of Death: Roswell, New Mexico
Cause of Death: pneumonia
Resting Place: South Park Cemetery, Roswell, New Mexico[37]
No. 86

86.

Lucien Bonaparte Maxwell
Fur trapper and trader; banker; owner of the largest land grant in New Mexico history, measuring more than 1,700,000 acres in northern New Mexico and southern Colorado; banker; railroad developer; the Colfax County community of Maxwell City (now Maxwell) was named in his honor in 1890
Date of Birth: September 14, 1818
Place of Birth: Kaskaskia, Illinois
Date of Death (age): July 25, 1875 (56)
Place of Death: Fort Sumner, New Mexico
Cause of Death: uremic poisoning
Resting Place: Old Military Cemetery, Fort Sumner, New Mexico[38]

Despite his great wealth and power in life, Maxwell's gravesite went unmarked for nearly seventy-five years until a group of historians from Colorado and New Mexico had a stone monument erected in the Old Military Cemetery on May 29, 1949.[39]

A map of the Maxwell Land Grant (complete with a scale to measure the grant's controversial size) is inscribed on Lucien's headstone. Below the map is the epitaph: "A native of Kaskaskia, Illinois. A fur trader and trapper who by industry, good fortune and trading became sole owner in 1864 of the largest single tract of land owned by any one individual in the United States. Maxwell founded the First National Bank of Santa Fe, New Mexico, and invested $250,000 to help build the Texas Pacific Railroad. Dynamic, Charitable, Lavish. One of the great builders of the American West. Died in quiet retirement, July 25, 1875, at Fort Sumner, New Mexico. Born September 14, 1818." No. 87

87.

Other Land Owners and Developers include:
Thomas B. Catron (Chapter 9: Political, Diplomatic, and Judicial Leaders)
"Shoeless Jerry" Simpson (Chapter 9: Political, Diplomatic, and Judicial Leaders)

Hotel & Restaurant Owners, Operators, and Workers *(in alphabetical order)*

Mary Watt Dodson Donoho
Reportedly the first Anglo woman to travel the Santa Fe Trail, 1833; with her husband, William (1798-1845), operated the Exchange Hotel, Santa Fe, 1833-37
Date of Birth: November 24, 1807
Place of Birth: western Tennessee
Date of Death (age): January 12, 1880 (72)
Place of Death: Clarksville, Texas
Cause of Death: unstated natural causes
Resting Place: Clarksville Cemetery, Clarksville, Texas

For many years Susan Shelby Magoffin had been considered to be the first Anglo woman to travel the Santa Fe Trail, arriving in Santa Fe on August 31, 1846. By the early 1990s new historical evidence proved that this distinction belonged to Mary Donoho, who arrived in the capital city in 1833.

According to Mary Donoho's obituary, "Her death was painless and without previous illness. Complaining of a difficulty in getting her breath, to the question of her son, 'What can I do for you?' [t]here was no response and she quietly without a struggle passed away."[40] No. 88

88. Traditionally, a gravestone with two pillars or columns symbolizes a passageway into the next life.[41]
Photo courtesy of Jim H. Thomas.

89. It is ironic that after spending two-thirds of her life in the quiet isolation of Frijoles Canyon, Frey's gravesite is adjacent to Menaul Boulevard, one of the busiest streets in Albuquerque and in all of New Mexico. She was buried there to be next to her son's and mother's graves.

Evelyn Lenora Cecil Frey

Guest ranch and Park Service lodge operator in Frijoles Canyon, New Mexico; served such famous guests as Willa Cather, Erna Fergusson, Charles Lummis, Will Rogers, William Allen White, and key Manhattan Project personnel during World War II

Date of Birth: February 12 or 18 (as given on her headstone), 1892

Place of Birth: Vanderwoort, Arkansas

Date of Death (age): September 11, 1988 (96)

Place of Death: Bandelier, New Mexico

Cause of Death: unstated natural causes

Resting Place: Sunset Cemetery, Albuquerque, New Mexico

Frey once said, "In all, it has been a very happy experience to help people enjoy what we had here, mostly the scenery, the food, the horses, and the nice little trips that they did take up…. And that has always been my pleasure, to do a little along that line."[42] No. 89

Frederick Henry "Fred" Harvey

English-born restaurateur who founded and operated the famous Harvey House restaurants, with their equally famous Harvey Girls and high "Harvey Standard," along the Santa Fe Railway from 1876 until his death in 1901; there were eight Harvey House restaurants and eight Harvey Hotels in New Mexico

Date of Birth: June 27, 1835

Place of Birth: London, England

Date of Death (age): February 9, 1901 (65)

Place of Death: Leavenworth, Kansas

Cause of Death: intestinal cancer

Resting Place: Mount Muncie Cemetery, Lansing, Kansas

In a last bit of business advice, Fred Harvey reportedly told his sons, "Don't cut the ham too thin."[43]

At Harvey's funeral, Elbert Hubbard, a popular author, read the eulogy:

Fred Harvey is dead, but his spirit still lives. The standard of excellence he set can never go back. He has been a civilizer and benefactor. He has added to the physical, mental, and spiritual welfare of millions. No sermon can equal a Fred Harvey example—no poet can better a Fred Harvey precept. Fred Harvey simply kept faith with the public. He gave pretty nearly a perfect service.[44]

90. Photo courtesy of Ralph Beckwith.

In a final act of generosity, Harvey stipulated in his will that every Harvey employee at the time of his death would receive a lifetime pension equal to his or her salary at the time of retirement.[45] No. 90

Opal K. Sells Hill

Exceptionally dedicated Harvey Girl who worked in eight western states, including at New Mexico's La Fonda and Alvarado hotels, over forty-three years before retiring at age 69
Date of Birth: 1900
Place of Birth: Hall County, Texas
Date of Death (age): May 18, 1987 (about 87)
Place of Death: a local hospital, Albuquerque, New Mexico
Cause of Death: unstated natural causes
Resting Place: Fairview Cemetery, Albuquerque, New Mexico[46]

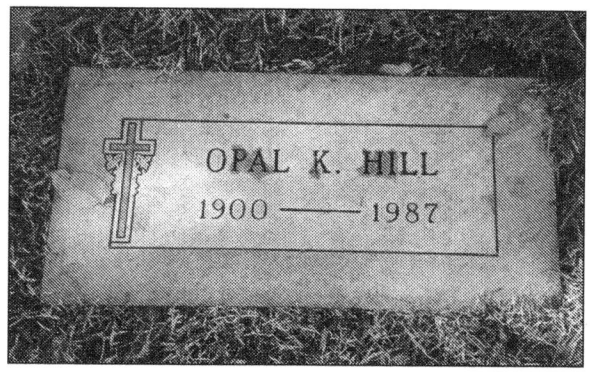

91.

After witnessing the razing of Albuquerque's Alvarado Harvey House in early 1970, Opal said:

> There were quite a lot of us old-timers watching. They had gutted the hotel and sold all of the fine furniture and art work.... People felt very badly about it being torn down. It was like watching our own home being destroyed. That's how Harvey Houses were to employees and railroad people...very special places.[47]

No. 91

Conrad Nicholson "Connie" Hilton

At twenty-four, the youngest member of the first New Mexico state legislature; hotel magnate who, at the time of his death, owned 125 hotels throughout the world and was reportedly worth $100 million; opened the ten-story Albuquerque Hilton (later La Posada de Albuquerque), long the city's tallest building, 1939; a street in Albuquerque was named in his honor
Date of Birth: December 25, 1887
Place of Birth: San Antonio, New Mexico
Date of Death (age): January 3, 1979 (91)
Place of Death: Santa Monica, California
Cause of Death: unstated natural causes
Resting Place: Calvary Hills Cemetery, Dallas, Texas

92. The epitaph on Conrad Hilton's gravestone (directly in front of the larger family stone) reads: "Charity is a supreme virtue and the great channel through which the mercy of God is passed on to mankind. Christmas is forever."
Photo courtesy of David N. Lotz.

On his deathbed, Hilton was asked if he had any last words of wisdom, to which the elderly innkeeper reportedly replied, "Leave the shower curtain on the inside of the tub."[48]

According to an editorial in the *Albuquerque Journal*, "Although his name flashes conspicuously throughout the world as a beacon of welcome, he never permitted himself to forget his New Mexico roots, his immigrant parentage or the rural New Mexico culture so deeply woven into his sparkling personality."[49]

No. 92

93.

Henry (or Henri) Lambert
Arrived in the United States from France in 1861; arrived in New Mexico, May 1868; served as General Ulysses S. Grant's cook; owned and operated Cimarron's famous St. James Hotel after 1876; rancher
Date of Birth: October 28, 1838
Place of Birth: Nantes, France
Date of Death (age): January 24, 1913 (74)
Place of Death: at his home in Cimarron, New Mexico
Cause of Death: stroke
Resting Place: Mountain View Cemetery, Cimarron, New Mexico[50] No. 93

Other Hotel and Restaurant Owners, Operators, and Workers include:
Howard Beacham (Chapter 8: Lawmen, Criminals, and Victims of Crime)
Charles F. Lambert (Chapter 8: Lawmen, Criminals, and Victims of Crime)
Sadie Orchard (Chapter 8: Lawmen, Criminals, and Victims of Crime)
Ebin Stanley (Chapter 12: Wartime Leaders and Victims to the End of the Indian Wars in New Mexico, 1886)
Lucy "Mother" Whiteside (Chapter 11: Scientists and Medical Personnel)

Media Owners, Publishers, and Editors (in alphabetical order)

94.

George Michael Fitzpatrick
Author; editor of the *New Mexico Magazine*, 1935-69
Date of Birth: May 19, 1904
Place of Birth: Erie, Pennsylvania
Date of Death (age): February 24, 1983 (78)
Place of Death: Albuquerque, New Mexico
Cause of Death: heart attack
Resting Place: Memorial Gardens, Santa Fe, New Mexico
"Many referred to him as Mr. New Mexico for no other person held so many anecdotes in his head or so many letters in his files."[51] No. 94

Max Eugene Frost
Ardently Republican publisher and editor of the *Santa Fe Daily New Mexican*, long considered the main source of propaganda for the Republican Party and the Santa Fe Ring; a Master, 33rd degree Mason
Date of Birth: January 1, 1852
Place of Birth: Vienna, Austria (although he claimed New Orleans, Louisiana)
Date of Death (age): October 13, 1909 (57)
Place of Death: Taos County, New Mexico
Cause of Death: "after a long illness"
Resting Place: Fairview Cemetery, Santa Fe, New Mexico[52] No. 95

Edward Dana (E. Dana) Johnson

After working for the *Albuquerque Journal* and the *Albuquerque Herald*, he became the editor of the *Santa Fe New Mexican* in 1913, serving in this capacity for nearly twenty-five years.

Date of Birth: June 15, 1879

Place of Birth: Parkersburg, West Virginia

Date of Death (age): December 10, 1937 (58)

Place of Death: Las Encinas Sanatorium, Pasadena, California

Cause of Death: heart attack

Resting Place: Fairview Cemetery, Santa Fe, New Mexico

Years before his death, Johnson wrote his own obituary in which he described himself as a "Permanently amateur golfer, enthusiastic but unsuccessful fisher and hunter…; Old Santa Fe nut; hobby is old Spanish customs, architecture, folklore, songs; member of Gene Rhodes cult…. Occasional short stories have accidentally gotten into magazines."[53] No. 96

Carlton Cole "Carl" Magee

Controversial editor of the *Albuquerque Journal*, *Magee's Independent*, the *New Mexico State Tribune*, and the *Oklahoma News*; responsible for breaking the Teapot Dome scandal involving New Mexico's Albert B. Fall, then serving as the U.S. Secretary of the Interior; inventor of the parking meter, 1931

Date of Birth: 1873

Place of Birth: Iowa

Date of Death (age): February 4, 1946 (about 73)

Place of Death: Oklahoma City, Oklahoma

Cause of Death: pneumonia

Resting Place: Rose Hill Memorial Park, Tulsa, Oklahoma[54]

95.

96.

Involved in one of many controversial issues, Magee reportedly said, "Gentlemen, this fight isn't going to be any good if I have to worry about what's going to happen to me personally. I'm trying an experiment here in truth-telling, and I don't want to spoil it by worrying about myself."[55]

Despite this statement, Magee had good cause to worry about his wellbeing: he was sentenced to jail for contempt of court in 1923 (later pardoned by Governor James F. Hinkle), was attacked by D.H. Leahy (the judge who had sentenced him to jail), and was acquitted for the killing of John B. Lasseter (a bystander at the attack scene).

William Henry "Billy" Manderfield

Owner of the pro-Republican, Santa Fe Ring-dominated *Santa Fe New Mexican*, 1863-81

Date of Birth: June 16, 1841

Place of Birth: Berks County, Pennsylvania

97. The Manderfield mausoleum is the largest mausoleum at Rosario Cemetery and perhaps the entire state.

Date of Death (age): December 3, 1888 (47)
Place of Death: Santa Fe, New Mexico
Cause of Death: unstated natural causes
Resting Place: Manderfield Mausoleum, Rosario Cemetery, Santa Fe, New Mexico[56] No. 97

Other Media Owners, Publishers, and Editors include:
Clinton P. Anderson (Chapter 9: Political, Diplomatic, and Judicial Leaders)
Kirby Benedict (Chapter 9: Political, Diplomatic, and Judicial Leaders)
John Burroughs (Chapter 9: Political, Diplomatic, and Judicial Leaders)
Ezequiel C de Baca (Chapter 9: Political, Diplomatic, and Judicial Leaders)
Charles P. Clever (Chapter 9: Political, Diplomatic, and Judicial Leaders)
Bronson M. Cutting (Chapter 9: Political, Diplomatic, and Judicial Leaders)
Albert B. Fall (Chapter 9: Political, Diplomatic, and Judicial Leaders)
Albert Jennings Fountain (Chapter 8: Lawmen, Criminals, and Victims of Crime)
Spud Johnson (Chapter 3: Authors and Composers)
George Kendall (Chapter 12: Wartime Leaders and Victims to the End of the Indian Wars in New Mexico, 1886)
Oscar P. "O.P." McMains (Chapter 8: Lawmen, Criminals, and Victims of Crime)
John E. Miles (Chapter 9: Political, Diplomatic, and Judicial Leaders)
Nestor Montoya (Chapter 9: Political, Diplomatic, and Judicial Leaders)
Norman Petty (Chapter 2: Artists, Performers, and Directors)
Charles G. Sage (Chapter 13: Wartime Leaders and Victims Since the Spanish-American War, 1898)
Frank Springer (Chapter 6: Educational Leaders)
William Bell Walton (Chapter 9: Political, Diplomatic, and Judicial Leaders)
Richard Weightman (Chapter 9: Political, Diplomatic, and Judicial Leaders)

Other Businessmen (in alphabetical order)

John Harris "Long John" "Juan Largo" Dunn
Taos mail carrier, 1906-38; taxi driver; toll bridge operator on the Rio Grande; gambler
Date of Birth: 1857
Place of Birth: Victoria, Texas
Date of Death (age): May 22, 1953 (about 96)
Place of Death: Taos, New Mexico
Cause of Death: "an illness of the kidneys"
Resting Place: Kit Carson Cemetery, Taos, New Mexico

A few months before his death, Dunn and an old friend "took to the road" over much of the area that Dunn had traveled

98. The death date on John Dunn's stone is incorrect.

in his earlier years, including Eagle Nest, Elizabethtown, and Red River. Stopping at the Rio Grande Gorge where Dunn "had built the bridge of his dreams....John got out and stood a minute and said, 'It shore was hard, but it shore was fun.'" He might have been referring to the bridge, but then he might have been referring to his adventure-filled life overall.[57] No. 98

Charles "Tio Carlos" Ilfeld

Arrived in New Mexico in 1865, with five dollars in his pocket, at the age of eighteen; Taos, Las Vegas, and Albuquerque merchant who created the most successful mercantile empire in the New Mexico Territory; the San Miguel County community of Ilfeld was named to honor the Ilfeld family; a street in Albuquerque was also named to honor the family, although it is misspelled as Ilfield

Date of Birth: April 19, 1847

Place of Birth: Homburg vor de Hohe, Germany

Date of Death (age): 2:15 p.m., January 3, 1929 (81)

Place of Death: Las Vegas, New Mexico

Cause of Death: stroke

Resting Place: Masonic Cemetery, Las Vegas, New Mexico[58] No. 99

99.

Patricio "Paddy" "Pat" "Julián" Martinez

Sheep owner and businessman; first discoverer of uranium deposits on Haystack Mountain west of Grants, New Mexico, 1951

Date of Birth: June 3, 1878

Place of Birth: Pine Dale, New Mexico

Date of Death (age): August 26, 1969 (91)

Place of Death: a hospital in Grants, New Mexico

Cause of Death: unstated natural causes

Resting Place: Grants Memorial Park Cemetery, Grants, New Mexico[59]

100.

After uncovering a "yellow rock" while horseback riding on Santa Fe Railway property, Martinez brought his find to Grants where he was told "there is no uranium in this country." Later, he took the rock to a friend in Bluewater and asked the friend to help him file a claim. The man helped, but insisted, "Pat, you are getting crazy—there's no uranium in this country." Hearing of his claim, people in Grants "laughed and said, 'Here comes the uranium king.'" Only an investigation by railroad mining engineer Tom Evans proved that Martinez was right all along.[60]

It is curious that Martinez's death was not announced in the *Grants Beacon*, although his friend Tom Evans's death on almost the same day was reported in a page one article. A photo of Evans and Martinez near the Haystack Mountain uranium mine appeared beside the announcement of Evans's passing.[61] No. 100

101. Like the elaborate Staab Mansion in Santa Fe, the Staab family headstone dominates its surroundings at Santa Fe's Fairview Cemetery.

Abraham Staab
Along with his brother Zodoc Staab (1835-84) one of Santa Fe's most successful businessmen with diverse interests, especially in commerce, real estate, and banking; long rumored to have helped finance construction of St. Francis Cathedral in exchange for Archbishop Jean B. Lamy agreeing to have a tetragrammaton inscribed in Hebrew letters above the cathedral's doors;[62] a street in Santa Fe was named in the Staab family's honor
Date of Birth: February 27, 1839
Place of Birth: Lüdge, Westphalia, Germany
Date of Death (age): January 4, 1913 (73)
Place of Death: Pasadena, California
Cause of Death: heart attack
Resting Place: Fairview Cemetery, Santa Fe, New Mexico[63]

Going to Pasadena with his son, he told friends, "I wish to escape the very cold weather [of northern New Mexico] at my time of life. I guess a man can take a vacation in California." He died shortly after arriving.[64] No. 101

Other Businessmen and Women include:
Ben Abruzzo (Chapter 7: Sung and Unsung Heroes)
Clinton P. Anderson (Chapter 9: Political, Diplomatic, and Judicial Leaders)
Maxie Anderson (Chapter 7: Sung and Unsung Heroes)
William "Bull" Andrews (Chapter 9: Political, Diplomatic, and Judicial Leaders)
María Gertrudes Barceló (Chapter 8: Lawmen, Criminals, and Victims of Crime)
Thomas F. Bolack (Chapter 9: Political, Diplomatic, and Judicial Leaders)
Charles P. Clever (Chapter 9: Political, Diplomatic, and Judicial Leaders)
Frank Coe (Chapter 8: Lawmen, Criminals, and Victims of Crime)
James T. Dean (Chapter 13: Wartime Leaders and Victims Since the Spanish-American War, 1898)
Alexander Grzelachowski (Chapter 12: Wartime Leaders and Victims to the End of the Indian Wars in New Mexico, 1886)
Andrew W. Hockenhull (Chapter 9: Political, Diplomatic, and Judicial Leaders)
Antonio Joseph (Chapter 9: Political, Diplomatic, and Judicial Leaders)
John Kinney (Chapter 8: Lawmen, Criminals, and Victims of Crime)
Thomas J. Maeston (Chapter 12: Wartime Leaders and Victims to the End of the Indian Wars in New Mexico, 1886)
Francisco Manzanares (Chapter 9: Political, Diplomatic, and Judicial Leaders)
Alexander McSween (Chapter 8: Lawmen, Criminals, and Victims of Crime)
David Meriwether (Chapter 9: Political, Diplomatic, and Judicial Leaders)
Frederick Mueller (Chapter 13: Wartime Leaders and Victims Since the Spanish-American War, 1898)
Lawrence G. Murphy (Chapter 8: Lawmen, Criminals, and Victims of Crime)
Mariano Sabino Otero (Chapter 9: Political, Diplomatic, and Judicial Leaders)

Miguel A. Otero, Sr. (Chapter 9: Political, Diplomatic, and Judicial Leaders)
Francisco Perea (Chapter 9: Political, Diplomatic, and Judicial Leaders)
Norman Petty (Chapter 2: Artists, Performers, and Directors)
Samuel Ravel (Chapter 13: Wartime Leaders and Victims Since the Spanish-American War, 1898)
Trinidad Romero (Chapter 9: Political, Diplomatic, and Judicial Leaders)
Esquípula Romero de Romero (Chapter 2: Artists, Performers, and Directors)
Harold Runnels (Chapter 9: Political, Diplomatic, and Judicial Leaders)
Arthur Seligman (Chapter 9: Political, Diplomatic, and Judicial Leaders)
"Shoeless Jerry" Simpson (Chapter 9: Political, Diplomatic, and Judicial Leaders)
John Henry Tunstall (Chapter 8: Lawmen, Criminals, and Victims of Crime)
William Walton (Chapter 9: Political, Diplomatic, and Judicial Leaders)
Victor Westphall (Chapter 7: Sung and Unsung Heroes)
Richard Wetherill (Chapter 8: Lawmen, Criminals, and Victims of Crime)
Joseph E. Wheeler (Chapter 10: Religious Leaders)

6

*E*DUCATIONAL LEADERS

The province [of New Mexico] does not count, nor has it ever counted upon to date, the kinds of public [educational] facilities enjoyed by other Spanish provinces.... In the capital itself, it has not been possible to fund a teacher for the general instruction of the community.
—Don Pedro Baptista Pino (about 1752-1829) from his report to the Spanish Cortes, 1810[1]

A uniform system of free public schools sufficient for the education of, and open to, all the children of school age in the state shall be established and maintained.
—Article XII, Section 1
New Mexico State
Constitution of 1910

Early Superintendents of Public Schools

Amado Chaves
New Mexico's first Superintendent of Public Schools, 1891-97 and 1904-05; known as New Mexico's "Father of Rural Education"; Mayor of Santa Fe, 1901-03; the small community of Amado near his ranch in Valencia (now Cibola) County was named in his honor; son of Indian fighter and Civil War hero Manuel Chaves
Date of Birth: April 14, 1851
Place of Birth: Santa Fe, New Mexico
Date of Death (age): 7:00 p.m., December 30, 1930 (79)
Place of Death: at his home in Santa Fe, New Mexico
Cause of Death: tuberculosis
Resting Place: Fairview Cemetery, Santa Fe, New Mexico[2] No. 102

Other Early Territorial, State, and County Superintendents of Public Schools include:[3]
J. Francisco Chavez (Chapter 9: Political, Diplomatic, and Judicial Leaders)
Hiram Hadley (this chapter)
Georgia Lusk (Chapter 9: Political, Diplomatic, and Judicial Leaders)
Nina Otero-Warren (Chapter 7: Sung and Unsung Heroes)
Benjamin M. Read (Chapter 4: Cultural Preservationists)

School Founders and Leaders *(in alphabetical order by institution)*

Los Alamos Ranch School, Los Alamos, New Mexico (in chronological order of service)

Ashley Pond, Jr.
Founder of the Los Alamos Ranch School, 1917; renowned poet Peggy Pond Church's father; Ashley Pond, a pond in central Los Alamos, was named in his honor

102.

Date of Birth: July 6, 1872
Place of Birth: Detroit, Michigan
Date of Death (age): June 21, 1933 (60)
Place of Death: Pasadena, California
Cause of Death: influenza, encephalitis sub acute, and encephalomalacia
Resting Place: cremated with ashes sent to Detroit, Michigan, for burial[4]

Albert James "A.J." Connell

103.

U.S. Forest Service Ranger; Director of the Los Alamos Ranch School, 1917-1942; leader of the Ranch School's famous Boy Scout Troop 22
Date of Birth: March 17, 1882
Place of Birth: Bronx, New York City, New York
Date of Death (age): February 11, 1944 (61)
Place of Death: St. Vincent Hospital, Santa Fe, New Mexico
Cause of Death: complications following viral pneumonia
Resting Place: Mount Calvary Cemetery, Albuquerque, New Mexico[5] No. 103

New Mexico College of Agriculture and Mechanic Arts (New Mexico A&M; New Mexico State University as of 1960), Las Cruces, New Mexico (in alphabetical order)

Ralph Willis Goddard

104.

New Mexico A&M Professor of Electrical Engineering, 1914-29; Dean of Engineering, 1920-29; radio pioneer; founder of the KOB radio station, first licensed as 5XD, 1919, and first broadcast as KOB on April 5, 1922, on the New Mexico A&M campus and known as the "Voice of the Great Southwest" and, for a period, the most powerful college radio station in the United States; president of the New Mexico Association for the Advancement of Science; Goddard Hall on the New Mexico A&M campus was named in his honor, 1934
Date of Birth: April 20, 1887
Place of Birth: Waltham, Massachusetts
Date of Death (age): 5:08 p.m., New Year's Eve, December 31, 1929 (42)
Place of Death: in the transmitter generating room of the KOB radio station, New Mexico A&M, Las Cruces, New Mexico
Cause of Death: electrocuted by twelve thousand volts of electricity as he prepared the radio station for its evening broadcast; did not recover, despite heroic efforts at resuscitation by a student radio operator, firemen, and Goddard's seventeen-year-old son, Kenneth
Resting Place: Masonic Cemetery, Las Cruces, New Mexico[6]

Days before Goddard's death Professor Hugh Milton, came by the KOB station and urged his friend to "slow down some, Dean. You look mighty tired." Goddard replied, "Yes, well, I'll probably be getting out from under the station pretty soon, and then I can settle down to being an old middle-aged man."[7]

Ironically, Dean Goddard had just lectured in El Paso, Texas, on the dangers of electricity the night before his death. After his death, a memorial service, held at Hadley Hall, was broadcast over KOB. An estimated fifteen hundred friends, relatives, and admirers attended his funeral.[8] No. 104

Hiram Hadley
First president of Las Cruces College, 1888-89; first President of the New Mexico Agricultural College, November 1889-June 30, 1894; Vice President of the University of New Mexico, 1894-98; Territorial Superintendent of Instruction, 1905-07; Hadley Hall, the main administration building on the New Mexico State University campus, and two streets in Las Cruces were named in his honor
Date of Birth: March 17, 1833
Place of Birth: Wilmington, Ohio
Date of Death (age): December 3, 1922 (89)
Place of Death: Christian Church Hospital, Kansas City, Missouri
Cause of Death: unstated natural causes
Resting Place: Masonic Cemetery, Las Cruces, New Mexico

105.

In October 1920, in one of his last speeches to the student body of New Mexico A&M, Hadley declared that there were three "great movements" in the recent moral progress of the world: womens suffrage, Prohibition, and world peace. He asserted that the first two had been accomplished, while the third was "sure to come." He identified a fourth movement, anti-tobacco, as inevitable because, in his words, tobacco was "useless, offensive, and wasteful."[9] No. 105

Also see:
Fabian Garcia (Chapter 11: Scientists and Medical Personnel)
John R. McFie (Chapter 9: Political, Diplomatic, and Judicial Leaders)
L. Bradford Prince (Chapter 9: Political, Diplomatic, and Judicial Leaders)
Edmund G. Ross (Chapter 9: Political, Diplomatic, and Judicial Leaders)

New Mexico Highlands University (formerly the New Mexico Normal School), Las Vegas, New Mexico (in chronological order of service)

Frank Springer
Arrived in New Mexico in 1873; key attorney for the Maxwell Land Grant Company in the Colfax County War; newspaper editor of the *Cimarron News and Press*; rancher; paleontologist; member of the state Constitutional Convention of 1889; key supporter of the creation of the Museum of Art, Santa Fe, New Mexico; a founder of the New Mexico Normal School (today's Highlands University), Las Vegas, New

106.

Mexico, and president of the school's first Board of Regents, 1898-1903; the school's first building was renamed in his honor, 1919; Springer Lake and the nearby town of Springer, New Mexico, were also named in his honor

Date of Birth: June 17, 1848

Place of Birth: Wapello, Iowa

Date of Death (age): 2:00 p.m., September 22, 1927 (79)

Place of Death: at his daughter's home in Overbrook, Pennsylvania

Cause of Death: chronic myocarditis

Resting Place: cremated with his ashes buried at the Masonic Cemetery, Las Vegas, New Mexico

According to his obituary in the *Santa Fe New Mexican*, Springer remained busy to his final days, spending "such time as he could leave bed working on his last volume. In fact, much of the proof was read while he was confined to bed, his indomitable will keeping him busy to the end."[10] No. 106

Thomas Claude "Tom" Donnelly

Professor of Government, New Mexico Western College, 1931-1933, and the University of New Mexico, 1935-1952; longest serving President in New Mexico Highlands University's history, 1952-1970; New Mexico Highlands University's Donnelly Library, completed in 1966, was named in his honor

Date of Birth: April 1, 1905

Place of Birth: Rock Castle, West Virginia

Date of Death (age): April 12, 1980 (75)

Place of Death: Lovelace Hospital, Albuquerque, New Mexico

Cause of Death: cancer

Resting Place: cremated[11]

Francisco "Frank" Angel, Jr.

Decorated World War II B-24 pilot; Nambe, New Mexico, elementary school teacher; University of New Mexico professor; President of New Mexico Highlands University (August 1971-August 1975), becoming the first Hispanic to serve as the president of a public university in the United States; University of New Mexico honorary degree recipient, 1982

Date of Birth: 1914

Place of Birth: Las Vegas, New Mexico

Date of Death (age): May 29, 2005 (about 91)

Place of Death: Porto Alegre, Brazil

Cause of Death: unstated natural causes

Resting Place: cremated with half his ashes scattered in Brazil and half scattered near the Gallinas River in New Mexico[12]

Also see:
Edgar L. Hewett (Chapter 4: Cultural Preservationists)
John Donald Robb (Chapter 4: Cultural Preservationists)

New Mexico Institute of Mining and Technology (New Mexico Tech) (originally the New Mexico School of Mines), Socorro, New Mexico

Everly John "E.J." "Jack" Workman
University of New Mexico Department of Physics chair, 1936-46; established the New Mexico Proving Ground (later part of Kirtland Air Force Base) for the testing of critical weapons (especially the important radio proximity fuse) during World War II; worked in conjunction with the Manhattan Project during World War II; President of New Mexico Tech, 1946-64; brought UNM's Research and Development Division to New Mexico Tech; responsible for expanding Tech's enrollment, undergraduate and graduate programs, scientific research, and physical plant; helped to create the High School Science Fair program in New Mexico; University of New Mexico honorary degree recipient, 1964; Workman Center at New Mexico Tech was named in his honor
Date of Birth: July 2, 1899
Place of Birth: Loudenville, Ohio
Date of Death (age): December 27, 1982 (83)
Place of Death: Santa Barbara, California
Cause of Death: unstated natural causes
Resting Place: cremated with ashes scattered over the New Mexico Tech golf course, which he had had built to assist in the recruitment and retention of good faculty, staff, and students. An avid golfer, Workman had designed the course's first nine holes in 1953 and had had nine more holes added in 1964.[13]

Also see:
Edmund G. Ross (Chapter 9: Political, Diplomatic, and Judicial Leaders)

New Mexico Military Institute (originally Goss Military Institute), Roswell, New Mexico

Robert Stewart Goss
Founder and commandant of the Goss Military Institute, Roswell, New Mexico, 1891-93
Date of Birth: August 2, 1860
Place of Birth: Nicholasville, Kentucky
Date of Death (age): May 22, 1941 (80)
Place of Death: at his home in Boulder, Colorado
Cause of Death: unstated natural causes
Resting Place: Green Mountain Cemetery, Boulder, Colorado[14]

Also see:

James J. Hagerman (Chapter 5: Business Leaders)
Paul Horgan (Chapter 3: Authors and Composers)
Peter Hurd (Chapter 2: Artists, Performers, and Directors)
Joseph C. Lea (Chapter 5: Business Leaders)
John C. Morgan (Chapter 13: Wartime Leaders and Victims Since the Spanish-American War, 1898)

Sandia Prep School, Albuquerque, New Mexico

Ruth Hanna McCormick Simms

107. The large rock at the top of Ruth's grave was moved, on her request, from the site in the Sandia Mountains where her twenty-one-year-old son, John Medill McCormick, was killed in a lightning storm while climbing a trail on June 22, 1938. John is buried to Ruth's right, her husband, Albert Gallatin Simms, is buried to her left.[16]

Daughter of powerful Republican leader Senator Marcus Alonzo "Mark" Hanna (1837-1904) of Ohio; Republican U.S. Congress woman from Illinois, 1929-1931, serving as the first woman elected to the U.S. House of Representatives; married former U.S. Congressman from New Mexico Albert G. Simms on March 9, 1932; president of the Albuquerque Little Theatre, 1937; founder of Sandia School, 1932, a private day and boarding school for girls, which later became Sandia Prep; founder of Manzano Day School, 1938, originally housed in the Huning Castle; the new maternity wing of the Presbyterian Hospital, Albuquerque, New Mexico, was named in her honor in 1947; Albert G. Simms gave a statue, called the Desert Maiden, to the New Mexico Institute of Mining and Technology in her memory

Date of Birth: March 27, 1880
Place of Birth: Cleveland, Ohio
Date of Death (age): New Year's Eve, December 31, 1944 (64)
Place of Death: Billings Memorial Hospital, Chicago, Illinois
Cause of Death: ruptured pancreas
Resting Place: Fairview Cemetery, Albuquerque, New Mexico

Ruth's daughter, "Bazy," recalled that in late 1944, "None of us admitted Mother was dying. She had a wonderful nurse, Miss Heinz, who came in at night and said not to be afraid. Mother answered, 'I was never afraid in my life.' But it also bespeaks the frame of mind she was in[;] she didn't have a lot to live for. She had a bad marriage, and no more work to do."[15] No. 107

The words engraved on her gravestone read:

> Build these more stately mansions, O my soul.
> As the swift seasons roll!
> Leave thy low vaulted past!
> Let each new temple nobler than the last
> Shut thee from heaven with a dome more vast
> Till thou at length art free
> Leaving thine outgrown shell by life's unresting sea!

University of New Mexico, Albuquerque, New Mexico (in chronological order of service)

William George "Billy" Tight
President of the University of New Mexico, 1901-09, responsible for introducing Pueblo Revival Style architecture to the university with architect E.B. Christy; Tight Grove, guarded by a statue of a lobo, on the UNM campus was named in his honor
Date of Birth: March 19, 1865
Place of Birth: Granville, Ohio
Date of Death (age): January 15, 1910 (44)
Place of Death: in a hospital, Glendale, California
Cause of Death: acute stomach disorder and blood poisoning
Resting Place: cremated with his ashes placed in a small urn and sent from California to his hometown of Granville, Ohio, via Albuquerque

The day after Tight's death, his widow sent a brief telegram to his successor as president of the University of New Mexico. It read: "Billy passed away last night. There was nothing to save him. Mabel Tight." A memorial stone on the east side of UNM's Hodgin Hall, which had been remodeled with Pueblo Revival Style architecture, reads, "His monument stands before you."[17]

James Fulton Zimmerman
President of the University of New Mexico, 1927-44; responsible for much of the academic growth of the university and its physical expansion using Pueblo Revival Style architecture, largely financed with New Deal funding in the 1930s; the university's main library was named in his honor upon its completion in 1938; a street in Albuquerque is also named in his honor
Date of Birth: September 11, 1887
Place of Birth: Glen Allen, Missouri
Date of Death (age): October 20, 1944 (57)
Place of Death: Albuquerque, New Mexico[18]
Cause of Death: coronary thrombosis
Resting Place: Fairview Cemetery, Albuquerque, New Mexico

108.

On hearing of President Zimmerman's death, Edgar Lee Hewett wrote: "Some of us have been privileged to witness the building of the University from the nondescript plant that he took over, into a campus of distinction among the universities of the United States. It was a distinguished achievement for any man, yet he claimed no credit for it."[19] No. 108

Thomas Lafayette "Tom" Popejoy
University of New Mexico football star famous for his field goal that defeated previously undefeated rival University of Arizona in 1924; state director of the National Youth Administration (NYA), 1935-39; first native New Mexican to serve as the President of the University of New Mexico, 1948-68; more than half of the

university's ninety buildings were built while he was president; UNM honorary degree recipient, 1969
Date of Birth: December 2, 1902
Place of Birth: Raton, New Mexico
Date of Death (age): October 24, 1975 (72)
Place of Death: Bernalillo County Medical Center, Albuquerque, New Mexico
Cause of Death: a prolonged, unstated natural illness
Resting Place: cremated[20]

In one of the great understatements of New Mexico history, one of Popejoy's undergraduate professors at the University of New Mexico wrote in 1925 that "Tom Popejoy shows considerable promise."[21]

When asked if he'd like the university's new football field named after him, Popejoy replied that he'd rather have the new concert hall as his memorial. A good choice, Popejoy Hall opened in the fall of 1966.[22]

Also see:
Bernard S. Rodey (Chapter 9: Political, Diplomatic, and Judicial Leaders)
Edmund G. Ross (Chapter 9: Political, Diplomatic, and Judicial Leaders)
E.J. Workman (this chapter)

Western New Mexico University (formerly the New Mexico Normal School and the New Mexico State Teachers College), Silver City, New Mexico

See:
Thomas Donnelly (this chapter)
William G. Ritch (Chapter 9: Political, Diplomatic, and Judicial Leaders)

Other School Founders and Presidents include:
Sister Mary Katharine Drexel (Chapter 10: Religious Leaders)
Emily Jane Harwood (Chapter 10: Religious Leaders)
Thomas Harwood (Chapter 10: Religious Leaders)
James A. Menaul (Chapter 10: Religious Leaders)
John B. Newbrough (Chapter 10: Religious Leaders)

Deans, Teachers, Coaches, and Librarians *(in alphabetical order)*

109.

Julia Duncan Brown Asplund
Suffragette; first librarian at the University of New Mexico; chair of the New Mexico Library Commission from its inception to 1954; first woman to serve on the University of New Mexico's Board of Regents, 1921-23
Date of Birth: October 6, 1875
Place of Birth: Palmyra, Missouri
Date of Death (age): July 26, 1958 (82)
Place of Death: Pasadena, California

Cause of Death: unstated natural causes
Resting Place: Fairview Cemetery, Santa Fe, New Mexico[23] No. 109

Roy William "Old Iron Head" Johnson
World War I and II veteran; first University of New Mexico Athletic Director, 1920; coached all sports, but particularly football (1920-30), basketball (1920-40), and track and field (1922-59), retiring in 1959; first football coach in the country whose team traveled to an away game via airplane, playing Occidental College in Rose Bowl Stadium, 1929; Johnson Gym on the UNM campus was named in his honor, 1957
Date of Birth: September 6, 1892
Place of Birth: Grand Rapids, Michigan
Date of Death (age): September 20, 1989 (97)
Place of Death: Albuquerque Manor Nursing Home, Albuquerque, New Mexico
Cause of Death: unstated natural causes
Resting Place: National Cemetery, Santa Fe, New Mexico[24] No. 110

110.

Robert Lee "Bob" King
University of New Mexico head basketball coach, 1962-72; with a 175-89 record, he was considered the "Founder of UNM Basketball"; coach when UNM opened its new 14,831-seat University Arena, better known as The Pit, on December 1, 1966; named UNM's All Star Coach on the hundredth anniversary of UNM basketball, 2003; The Pit's center court is known as Bob King Court
Date of Birth: August 24, 1923
Place of Birth: Gravity, Iowa
Date of Death (age): December 10, 2004 (81)
Place of Death: Veterans Hospital, Albuquerque, New Mexico
Cause of Death: unstated natural causes
Resting Place: National Cemetery, Santa Fe, New Mexico[25] No. 111

111. The icon on Coach King's gravestone represents the Mormon Angel Moroni.

Dorothy Dunn Kramer
Taught at Santo Domingo Pueblo Day School, 1928-30; founder of the Santa Fe Indian School's famous Studio, September 1932 (which developed into the Institute of American Indian Arts in Santa Fe) where she taught (1932-37) and influenced many young Indian artists, including Harrison Begay, Joe Hilario Herrera, Allan Houser, Quincy Tahoma, and Pablita Velarde; author of *American Indian Paintings of the Southwest and Plains* (1968)
Date of Birth: December 2, 1903
Place of Birth: Potowatomi County, Kansas
Date of Death (age): July 5, 1992 (88)
Place of Death: Mountain View, California
Cause of Death: Alzheimer's disease

112. Harriet S. Carpenter and Francis M. Dunn were Dorothy Dumm Kramer's sisters.
Photo courtesy of JoAnne Gosen.

Resting Place: cremated with ashes placed in an Indian pot made by her daughter and buried in San Gorgonio Memorial Park, Banning, California

Geronima Cruz Montoya, one of Kramer's students at The Studio, said, "She did a lot for us. She made us realize how important our own Indian ways were because we had been made to feel ashamed of them. She gave us something to be proud of."[26] No. 112

George Isidore Sánchez y Sánchez

Educational reformer, civil rights activist; president of the League of United Latin American Citizens (LULAC); Professor of Latin American Studies at the University of Texas, 1940-72; author, most noted for his book, *Forgotten People: A Study of New Mexicans* (1940); known as the "father of the movement for quality education for Mexican-Americans"; University of New Mexico honorary degree recipient, 1967; an Austin elementary school, a Houston high school (with ninety-six percent Hispanic student enrollment), and the College of Education at the University of Texas were named in his honor.[27]

Date of Birth: October 4, 1906
Place of Birth: Barelas, New Mexico
Date of Death (age): April 5, 1972 (65)
Place of Death: Austin, Texas
Cause of Death: unstated natural causes
Resting Place: cremated with ashes buried at Forest Oaks Cemetery, Austin, Texas

Other Educators include:
John Baker (Chapter 7: Sung and Unsung Heroes)
Jozef Bakos (Chapter 2: Artists, Performers, and Directors)
Frank Boyer (Chapter 7: Sung and Unsung Heroes)
Bainbridge Bunting (Chapter 4: Cultural Preservationists)
Fabiola Cabeza de Baca Gilbert (Chapter 4: Cultural Preservationists)
Kenneth Chapman (Chapter 4: Cultural Preservationists)
Ann Nolan Clark (Chapter 3: Authors and Composers)
Louise Holland Coe (Chapter 9: Political, Diplomatic, and Judicial Leaders)
Catharine Carter Critcher (Chapter 2: Artists, Performers, and Directors)
Florence Ellis (Chapter 4: Cultural Preservationists)
Richard P. Feynman (Chapter 11: Scientists and Medical Personnel)
Klaus Fuchs (Chapter 11: Scientists and Medical Personnel)
Robert Goddard (Chapter 11: Scientists and Medical Personnel)
Carl Gorman (Chapter 2: Artists, Performers, and Directors)
Ted Hall (Chapter 11: Scientists and Medical Personnel)
Janaloo Hill Hough (Chapter 4: Cultural Preservationists)
Allan Houser (Chapter 2: Artists, Performers, and Directors)
A.A. Jones (Chapter 9: Political, Diplomatic, and Judicial Leaders)

Carl Raymond Jonson (Chapter 2: Artists, Performers, and Directors)
Alfred V. Kidder (Chapter 4: Cultural Preservationists)
Concha Ortiz y Pino de Kleven (Chapter 9: Political, Diplomatic, and Judicial Leaders)
Clyde Kluckhohn (Chapter 4: Cultural Preservationists)
Oliver LaGrone (Chapter 2: Artists, Performers, and Directors)
Lucy Lewis (Chapter 2: Artists, Performers, and Directors)
Georgia Lusk (Chapter 9: Political, Diplomatic, and Judicial Leaders)
Roy Nakayama (Chapter 11: Scientists and Medical Personnel)
Alfonso Ortiz (Chapter 4: Cultural Preservationists)
Nina Otero-Warren (Chapter 7: Sung and Unsung Heroes)
Frances V. Scholes (Chapter 4: Cultural Preservationists)
Sister Blandina Segale (Chapter 10: Religious Leaders)
Ernest Thompson Seton (Chapter 7: Sung and Unsung Heroes)
Katherine Stinson-Otero (Chapter 2: Artists, Performers, and Directors)
Clyde Tombaugh (Chapter 11: Scientists and Medical Personnel)
Miguel Trujillo (Chapter 7: Sung and Unsung Heroes)
Sabine R. Ulibarri (Chapter 3: Authors and Composers)
Annie Dodge Wauneka (Chapter 11: Scientists and Medical Personnel)
Clara Belle Williams (Chapter 7: Sung and Unsung Heroes)

7
Sung and Unsung Heroes

Men and Women who Performed Acts of Heroism (in alphabetical order)

John Braden
Teamster, wagon master, stage driver, and former Indian scout who bravely rescued onlookers from a runaway fireworks wagon on October 16, during the 1896 Territorial Fair parade in Albuquerque, New Mexico; a monument to his bravery was dedicated in Robinson Park on Railroad (later Central) Avenue in Albuquerque on November 14, 1897, just over a year after his supreme sacrifice
Date of Birth: about 1828
Place of Birth: Allegheny County, Pennsylvania
Date of Death (age): 2:15 p.m., October 17, 1896 (about 68; some say as old as 74)
Place of Death: Railroad (now Central) Avenue, Albuquerque, New Mexico
Cause of Death: severe burns over his entire body
Resting Place: unmarked grave, Fairview Cemetery, Albuquerque, New Mexico, although money had been raised to give Braden a "hero's funeral" and he was buried with "full honors"

Three days after Braden's heroic sacrifice, the *Albuquerque Daily Citizen* published an anonymously written poem, entitled "To Be A Hero":

>A gala night, a mighty throng
>In thousands pass the street along.
>To hail the pageant, bright and gay,
>In honor of our Natal Day....
>
>But sudden on the evening air
>Flames up a lurid, blinding flare,
>Followed by the thundering, awful shock,
>That makes the startled city rock!
>
>Glad joy is turned to shuddering fear!
>The wings of Death are rustling near!
>Two maddened horses rushing on,

If all heroics are in war then we are destined to a terrible future. But heroics are also in people's efforts to help improve our lives. There are millions who turn from cynicism and give us hope and faith in the potential goodness of people.
—Arthur Kopecky[1]

A flaming wreck behind them drawn,
Came sweeping in their fiery path,
Like the lost angel in his wrath,
Adown the densely crowded street!

But, see! Upon the flaming seat,
Enveloped in a sheet of flames,
His burning hands upon the reins,
Thoughtless of self, where duty needs,
A brave man guides the furious steeds.

To save himself in this fell hour
He scorns, as with his failing power
He strives to check the awful pace
That in another moment's space
Must through the surging human tide
Scatter death and destruction wide!

But now the danger safely past,
The hero, overcome at last,
Falls burned and helpless from his seat,
While Death's cold hands stretch out to greet
His glorious deed, and soon in peace,
He from his sufferings finds release....[2]

Laurel Blair Salton Clark
Naval medical doctor; NASA flight surgeon astronaut aboard the STS-107 Space Shuttle Columbia (January 16 to February 1, 2003); spent two years of her childhood in Albuquerque, New Mexico, attending Hodgin Elementary School and Monroe Middle School
Date of Birth: March 10, 1961
Place of Birth: Ames, Iowa
Date of Death (age): about 7:00 a.m., February 1, 2003 (41)
Place of Death: air space over Texas
Cause of Death: explosion aboard the Columbia during reentry, along with six fellow crew members, sixteen minutes before their scheduled landing in Florida[3]
Resting Place: body never recovered; a monument to the seven space shuttle astronauts was dedicated at Arlington National Cemetery a year after the explosion that took their lives; Challenger Garden at the Space Hall of Fame in Alamogordo, New Mexico, was named in the crew's honor

Six weeks before the Columbia's launch, Clark, her husband, Jon, and their young son, Iain, were flying in a small plane from their home in Houston to Albuquerque to spend Christmas with Laurel's family, who still live in New Mexico.

According to a newspaper account:

> The plane hit strong turbulence over West Texas and, for the first time ever, Laurel got airsick. Jon Clark [the pilot] was trying to land when the plane got caught in a downdraft. In a flash, the stall warning went off and the craft was sucked down, careened off the runway and smashed into an embankment. The plane was damaged beyond repair. But the Clarks walked away.

Young Iain was so shaken up by the incident that he had great fears about his mother's launch on January 16, 2003. Jon Clark always wondered if his son had had a premonition of the disaster to come.[4]

Ernest Thomas "Ernie" Mills
Journalist and radio political commentator; played a key role in negotiations with inmate leaders, helping to save many lives during the thirty-six-hour Santa Fe prison riot, February 2-3, 1980
Date of Birth: December 29, 1926
Place of Birth: Pittsburgh, Pennsylvania
Date of Death (age): February 27, 2003 (76)
Place of Death: St. Vincent Hospital, Santa Fe, New Mexico
Cause of Death: pneumonia
Resting Place: cremated

Prepared earlier, Mills's last broadcast aired on the day he died, ending with his trademark sendoff, "Don't say we didn't tell you."[5]

Sarah J. "Sallie" Rooke
Crippled elderly telephone operator who stayed at her switchboard during the devastating Folsom flood of August 27, 1908, to warn and save forty families; perished, with sixteen others in the disaster
Date of Birth: about 1840
Place of Birth: perhaps Preston, Iowa (her last residence before moving to Folsom in 1905)
Date of Death (age): about midnight, August 27, 1908 (about 68)
Place of Death: Folsom, New Mexico
Cause of Death: killed in flood
Resting Place: her body (identified by the curvature of the spine that had left her crippled) was found several miles downstream on a ranch, February 4, 1909

A granite monument with a bronze plaque was dedicated in Sallie Rooke's memory in the Folsom Cemetery on May 15, 1926. The monument was purchased with ten-cent contributions from 4,334 workers of the Mountain States

113.

Telephone Company. Many of the residents whose lives she helped save were present at the dedication ceremonies. The Reverend Hamilton closed the ceremony with the words, "Our lives are not worth much, after all, if they are not used for the good of others."

Others killed in the 1908 flood were:

Mrs. Cox	Mrs. Dan B. Wenger
Theler Cox	Dan Wheeler
Lucy Creighton	Infant Son Wheeler
Demetrio Guerin	Lula Cox Wheeler
Mrs. Demetrio Guerin	Thomas W. Wheeler
Antonio Salas	Vera Wheeler
Daisy Wenger	Walter Wheeler
Dan Wenger	Willie Cox Wheeler[6]

The inscription on her monument reads:

> In Honored Memory of
> Sarah J. Rooke
> Telephone Operator
> Who Perished in the Flood Waters
> Of the Dry Cimarron at Folsom, New Mexico
> August 27, 1908
> While at her switchboard warning
> Others of their danger.
> With heroic devotion she glorified
> Her calling by sacrificing her own
> Life that others might live.
> "Greater love hath no one than this."
> Erected by her fellow workers.

A large display honoring Sarah's courage is located in the Telephone Pioneer Museum, Albuquerque, New Mexico. No. 113

Others Who Performed Acts of Heroism include:
Tamara Long Archuleta (Chapter 13: Wartime Leaders and Victims Since the Spanish-American War, 1898)
Phil Chacon (Chapter 8: Lawmen, Criminals, and Victims of Crime)
Manuel Chaves (Chapter 12: Wartime Leaders and Victims to the End of the Indian Wars in New Mexico, 1886)
James Cooney (Chapter 14: Unusual Graves)
Lawrence Martin Jenco (Chapter 10: Religious Leaders)
Maud Medders (Chapter 13: Wartime Leaders and Victims Since the Spanish-American War, 1898)
Susie Parks Kendrick (Chapter 13: Wartime Leaders and Victims Since the Spanish-American War, 1898)

Smith Henry Simpson (Chapter 12: Wartime Leaders and Victims to the End of the Indian Wars in New Mexico, 1886)
John Paul Stapp (Chapter 11: Scientists and Medical Personnel)
Medal of Honor winners (Chapter 12: Wartime Leaders and Victims to the End of the Indian Wars in New Mexico, 1886, and Chapter 13: Wartime Leaders and Victims Since the Spanish-American War, 1898)

Advocates of Important or Controversial Issues (in alphabetical order)

Elliott Speer Barker

Rancher, conservationist, professional guide and hunter, U.S. Forest Service employee who worked for the legendary conservationist, Aldo Leopold; New Mexico's first Game Warden, April 1, 1931-53; adopted a rescued bear cub who became known as Smokey Bear; author of nine books, including his autobiography, *Western Life and Adventures, 1889-1970* (1970); recipient of many awards, including Conservationist of the Year, the Leopold Conservation Award, and the Western Writers of America Spur Award; a 5,415-acre wildlife area for the preservation of deer, elk, bear, and turkey was named in his honor, as was a trail in the Carson National Forest; Mount Barker in the Sangre de Cristo Mountains was named in the Barker family's honor; author S.O. Barker's brother

114.

Date of Birth: Christmas Day, December 25, 1886
Place of Birth: Moran, Texas
Date of Death (age): April 3, 1988 (101)
Place of Death: La Residencia Nursing Home, Santa Fe, New Mexico
Cause of Death: "just old age," according to his wife, Ethel
Resting Place: Memorial Garden Cemetery, Santa Fe, New Mexico

Barker was still leading pack trips into the New Mexico mountains when he was eighty-four. Writing on Barker's hundredth birthday, Stan Steiner asserted that although Barker had won many honors, "His life has been its own reward. At the ageless age of one hundred, he has more fire burning in his eyes than men half his age."[7] According to Barker's son, Roy, "He tried to write even after we put him in a nursing home."[8] No. 114

William Ware "Mack" Brazel

Foreman of the J.B. Foster sheep ranch, thirty miles southeast of Corona, New Mexico; delivered the news to Roswell after discovering debris at what some believed to be a UFO crash site, June 14, 1947
Date of Birth: 1899
Place of Birth: unknown
Date of Death (age): October 1, 1963 (about 64)
Place of Death: Tularosa, New Mexico
Cause of Death: heart attack
Resting Place: Tularosa Cemetery, Tularosa, New Mexico[9] No. 115

115.

Ralph Johnson Bunche

Spent two years of his childhood in Albuquerque with his healthseeker mother, father, and uncle, 1915-17; civil rights leader; Howard University and Harvard scholar; United Nations peacemaker, receiving the Nobel Peace Prize, 1950, the first black person ever awarded the prize; received the Medal of Freedom from President John F. Kennedy, 1963; a U.S. postage stamp was issued in his honor in 1982

Date of Birth: August 7, 1904
Place of Birth: Detroit, Michigan
Date of Death (age): 12:40 a.m., December 9, 1971 (67)
Place of Death: New York City, New York
Cause of Death: complications from kidney malfunction, diabetes, and heart disease
Resting Place: Woodlawn Cemetery, Bronx, New York[10]

Shortly before his death, Bunche wrote a personal note in which he hoped not to have

> an agonizing death, so as to be able to pass on with my characteristic smile on my lips. That would be entirely appropriate for me as I have always looked on life—and myself—with considerable amusement. Is a smiling corpse possible? Can the undertaker preserve it without it appearing macabre?[11]

Juan R. "Johnny" Chacón

Labor leader of Local 890 of the Mine, Mill and Smelter Workers Union and the leading man in *Salt of the Earth*, the classic radical movie based on his and his fellow workers' roles in the longest labor strike in New Mexico history, in the copper mines of Hanover, New Mexico, October 1950-January 1952 (fifteen months); his wife, Virginia Chacón, and many other women also played important roles in both the actual strike and in the movie

Date of Birth: November 8, 1919
Place of Birth: Dwyer, New Mexico
Date of Death: February 16, 1985 (65)
Place of Death: Deming, New Mexico
Cause of Death: unstated natural causes
Resting Place: San José Catholic Cemetery, Dwyer, New Mexico[12] No. 116

116. The symbol under Juan Chacón's name represents the United Steelworkers of America Union, Local 890. The image to the left is of "Saint Joseph, the Worker."

John Collier

U.S. Commissioner of Indian Affairs, 1933-45; responsible for many Indian reforms, especially during the New Deal era; author of the influential *Indians of America* (1947)

Date of Birth: May 4, 1884
Place of Birth: Atlanta, Georgia
Date of Death (age): May 8, 1968 (84)

Place of Death: Holy Cross Hospital, Taos, New Mexico
Cause of Death: lung ailment
Resting Place: Descanso Cemetery, Ranchos de Taos, New Mexico No. 117

Irma Flores Gonzales
Hispanic civil rights activist and leader; president of the Colegio César Chávez, 1979-85; board member of the National Council of La Raza for nearly three decades and chairwoman, 1995-97; received the Mujer Award from the National Hispana Leadership Institute, 1996; Governor Bill Richardson declared December 30, 2004, "Irma Flores Gonzales Day" in New Mexico
Date of Birth: 1942
Place of Birth: El Paso, Texas
Date of Death (age): (Christmas Eve) December 24, 2004 (about 62)
Place of Death: Albuquerque, New Mexico
Cause of Death: cancer
Resting Place: cremated

Praised as an Hispanic leader, Irma Flores Gonzales was also admired for her long, brave battle against cancer.[14]

117. The words on John Collier's headstone, "Come lovely and soothing death," are from the poem, "Memories of President Lincoln," by Walt Whitman.[13]

Walter G. Haut
U.S. Army Lieutenant, World War II; Roswell Army Air Base (later renamed Walker Air Force Base, 1948) public information officer who released news of a possible UFO landing near Corona, New Mexico, in June 1947; a founder of the International UFO Museum and Research Center, Roswell, New Mexico, 1991; known as "Mr. UFO," with this nickname even on his New Mexico state license; inducted into the New Mexico Tourism Hall of Fame, 2002
Date of Birth: June 3, 1922
Place of Birth: Chicago, Illinois
Date of Death (age): December 15, 2005 (83)
Place of Death: at his home in Roswell, New Mexico
Cause of Death: unstated natural causes
Resting Place: South Park Cemetery, Roswell, New Mexico[15]

Alice Faye Kent Hoppes
President of Albuquerque's chapter of the National Association for the Advancement of Colored People (NAACP), 1984-96; Director of the New Mexico State Office of African-American Affairs; played key role in creating the African-American Pavilion at the New Mexico State Fair and in establishing Martin Luther King, Jr., Day as a New Mexico state holiday
Date of Birth: May 20, 1939
Place of Birth: Tucumcari, New Mexico
Date of Death (age): October 21, 2003 (64)
Place of Death: Albuquerque, New Mexico

118. The epitaph on Alice Hoppes's gravestone reads: "Well done, good and faithful servant. Enter into the joy of thy Lord." Matthew 25: 21

Cause of Death: cancer
Resting Place: Sunset Memorial Cemetery, Albuquerque, New Mexico

One of the first black children to integrate Tucumcari's public schools, Alice raised her hand and strongly objected when a white teacher used the word "nigger" in class. Alice was suspended, but she proudly noted that her teacher never used that hated racial slur in her presence again.[16] No. 118

Clinton E. "Clint" Jencks; "El Palomino"[17]
U.S. Army Air Force veteran, World War II; a union organizer for the Mine, Mill and Smelter Worker Union and an actor who played Frank Barnes, a character based on his real-life role, in *Salt of the Earth*, the classic radical movie based on the longest labor strike in New Mexico history, in the copper mines of Hanover, New Mexico, October 1950-January 1952 (fifteen months); his first wife, Virginia Jencks, and many other women also played important roles in both the actual strike and in the movie rendition; blacklisted; found guilty of breaking a provision of the Taft-Hartley Act, but vindicated in a Supreme Court decision of June 3, 1957; Professor of Economics, San Diego State University, 1964-88
Date of Birth: March 1, 1918
Place of Birth: Colorado Springs, Colorado
Date of Death (age): December 14, 2005 (87)
Place of Death: at his home in San Diego, California
Cause of Death: unstated natural causes
Resting Place: cremated[18]

Aldo Leopold
Renowned conservationist with the U.S. Forest Service, 1909-33; known as the "Father of the National Forest Wilderness System" and famous for his highly influential *Sand Creek Almanac* (1949); the Aldo Leopold Wilderness in the Black Range of southwestern New Mexico was named in his honor, as was the prestigious Leopold Conservation Award

119.

Date of Birth: January 11, 1887
Place of Birth: Burlington, Iowa
Date of Death (age): April 21, 1948 (61)
Place of Death: near Baraboo, Wisconsin
Cause of Death: heart attack after fighting a fire that threatened a mink ranch near his summer home
Resting Place: Aspen Grove Cemetery, Burlington, Iowa[19] No. 119

George McJunkin
Highly respected black ranch foreman of the XYZ Ranch; most famous for his role in discovering ten-thousand-year-old Folsom Ice Age Man after finding enormous animal bones in Wild Horse Arroyo on the Crowfoot Ranch in the aftermath of the August 27, 1908, Folsom, New Mexico, flood; Carl Schwachheim found a man-made spear point between the ribs of bones from the same site, August 2, 1927;

for years, McJunkin was not given credit for this important archeological find[20]
Date of Birth: January 9, 1856
Place of Birth: Rogers Prairie, Texas
Date of Death (age): January 21, 1922 (66)
Place of Death: Folsom, New Mexico
Cause of Death: unstated natural causes
Resting Place: Folsom Cemetery, Folsom, New Mexico

120.

George McJunkin was never the same after his cabin at Stuyvesant Springs Ranch, New Mexico, was struck by lightning and burned to the ground in the early 1920s with many of his belongings inside, including his fiddle, his guitar, his books, and his telescope. At least the mysterious large animal bones that he had discovered after the terrible Folsom flood of 1908 were not present and were preserved. McJunkin "had always made a joke about lightning. 'It never strikes a black man,' he used to say." But it did in this case. George moved to a back room in the hotel in Folsom and died shortly thereafter. Fellow cowboys used their lariats to lower McJunkin's coffin into his grave in the local cemetery outside of town.[21] No. 120

Milton Ernest "Doc" Noss; Milton Starr[22]
Claimed to have discovered a fabulous hidden treasure at Victorio Peak, New Mexico, while deer hunting with four friends in November 1937; with his wife, Ova "Babe" Beckworth Noss, he reportedly uncovered 350 gold bars at Victorio Peak between 1937 and 1949
Date of Birth: July 3, 1905
Place of Birth: Talogo, Oklahoma
Date of Death (age): 3:00 p.m., March 5, 1949 (43)
Place of Death: Hatch, New Mexico
Cause of Death: shot in the head by Charles Ryan, who was tried in Las Cruces and acquitted with a verdict of justifiable homicide, May 26, 1949[23]
Resting Place: unmarked grave, Masonic Cemetery, Las Cruces, New Mexico. Leaders of the Victorio Peak Project plan to place a large limestone rock taken from Victorio Peak to mark Noss's gravesite in Las Cruces.[24]

It was rumored that Noss went so far as to hide some of the gold he had recovered from Victorio Peak in false graves. Despite all the wealth he claimed to have found from 1937 to 1949, Doc Noss died with only $2.16 in his pocket.

Maria Adelina Emilia "Nina" Otero-Warren
Womens suffrage leader; cultural preservationist; author, most noted for her *Old Spain in Our Southwest* (1936); first woman to run for Congress from New Mexico, 1922; Santa Fe County School Superintendent; New Mexico State Director of Literacy Education, 1937; Puerto Rico Director of Adult Literacy, 1941;

121.

strong advocate for bilingual education; Congressional Delegate Miguel Otero, Sr.'s niece; Republican Party leader Solomon Luna's niece; Governor Miguel Otero, Jr.'s cousin; Congressional Delegate Marinao Sabino Otero's cousin

Date of Birth: October 23, 1881
Place of Birth: La Constancia, New Mexico
Date of Death (age): morning, January 3, 1965 (83)
Place of Death: at her home in Santa Fe, New Mexico
Cause of Death: unstated natural causes
Resting Place: Rosario Cemetery, Santa Fe, New Mexico[25]

"As [Nina] was preparing for mass on Sunday morning, January 3, 1965, she complained...that she felt ill. She asked for brandy and managed to drink it before collapsing. She was gone before [Dr.] Bergere [Kenney, her nephew and family physician,] could get to [her side at] the Big House, but 'she died happy,' Jack [Kenney, another nephew,] said. 'A quick and painless death after a long and fruitful life—and a good brandy—was all she could have wanted.'"[26] No. 121

John Albert Prather
Arrived in southern New Mexico as a child with his family in 1883; rancher known as the "Mule King"; most famous for his determined resistance to the U.S. government's planned expansion of the McGregor Missile Range onto his ranch property, 1956-57; Edward Abbey's novel, *Fire on the Mountain* (1962), was largely based on Prather's struggle with government authorities[27]

Date of Birth: November 21, 1873
Place of Birth: Van Zandt County, Texas
Date of Death (age): 8:00 a.m., February 12, 1965 (91)
Place of Death: in his last caregiver Daisy Speers's home in Alamogordo, New Mexico
Cause of Death: unstated natural causes after being incapacitated by two strokes and a recent case of pneumonia
Resting Place: as he requested, on his Prather Ranch, McGregor Missile Range, New Mexico

When confronted by U.S. Army's demands that he leave his family's ranch so that the land could be used as part of an expanded missile range, Prather defiantly replied, "If they come after me, they better bring a box."

In 1963, Prather became seriously ill, but refused to go to a hospital, saying "If I've got to die, I want to die on my ranch, right here in front of my fireplace." His son-in-law had to literally carry him to a car to transport him to the hospital in Alamogordo, where he was treated for pneumonia.[28]

Later, while a resident in a private rest home in Alamogordo, Prather insisted that he be allowed to keep a rifle by his bed. His nurse made sure the weapon was not loaded.

According to press reports, on his last morning Prather awoke

122. To protect his last bit of land on earth, John Prather's gravesite is largely surrounded by cacti.

in apparent good health and spirits...and breakfasted on oatmeal, apple juice, and his usual raw egg. About the time he finished breakfast, Mrs.

Speers was called to the telephone to answer a query from a Prather relative concerning the aged rancher's health, but moments later was summoned back to his bedside by the maid who had detected a change in Prather's condition. Mrs. Speers immediately attempted emergency treatment, but the old fighter had expired.[29]

Prather was buried on a site he had selected on the property he had fought so hard to protect, symbolically still standing guard over the land he had defiantly protected. He never accepted a hundred thousand dollar check the government had offered him as compensation for this cherished ranch.[30] No. 122

Miguel H. Trujillo

Indian educator; World War II U.S. Marine veteran; instrumental in winning Native American voting rights in New Mexico, 1948; father of Michael H. Trujillo, the first Native American to graduate from the UNM School of Medicine, 1974, and Josephine Waconda, the first Native American woman to hold the rank of admiral in the Commissioned Corps of the Public Health Service

Date of Birth: April 30, 1904

Place of Birth: Isleta Pueblo, New Mexico

Date of Death (age): August 27, 1989 (85)

Place of Death: Rainbow Nursing Home, Laguna Pueblo, New Mexico

Cause of Death: after a long illness, starting with a stroke in 1980

Resting Place: National Cemetery, Santa Fe, New Mexico[31]

Fifteen years after Miguel Trujillo's death, San Ildefonso Pueblo and the All Indian Pueblo Council produced an impressive poster commemorating his struggle to win voting rights for New Mexico Indians and to encourage Indians to exercise their suffrage.[32] No. 123

123.

Clara Belle Drisdale Williams

New Mexico State University's first black graduate, 1937; taught at Las Cruces's segregated Booker T. Washington School for twenty-seven years; honorary doctorate recipient from New Mexico State University, 1980; the Clara Belle Williams Awards Ceremony, to honor exceptional black students, has been held at New Mexico State University each year since 1987; Clara Belle Williams Day was celebrated at New Mexico State University on February 13, 2005, when the university's English Department building was officially renamed Clara Belle Williams Hall; a street on the NMSU campus is also named in her honor

Date of Birth: October 21, 1885, the daughter of sharecroppers

Place of Birth: Plum, Texas

Date of Death (age): July 3, 1994 (108)

Place of Death: Chicago, Illinois

Cause of Death: unstated natural causes

Resting Place: Chicago, Illinois

Clara Belle Williams's grandson, Dr. James Williams II, says that his grandmother loved to grow flowers. More than a decade after her death, many of her flowers, like her contributions in life, still thrive.[33]

Other Advocates of Important or Controversial Issues include:
Pablo Abeita (Chapter 9: Political, Diplomatic, and Judicial Leaders)
Mary Austin (Chapter 3: Authors and Composers)
Wendell Chino (Chapter 9: Political, Diplomatic, and Judicial Leaders)

124. Above Frank Boyer's name is the word "Father" and a Masonic symbol. Below his name are the words "Devoted Husband."

Elizabeth Garrett (Chapter 3: Authors and Composers)
Alice Corbin Henderson (Chapter 3: Authors and Composers)
William Penhallow Henderson (Chapter 2: Artists, Performers, and Directors)
Janaloo Hill Hough (Chapter 4: Cultural Preservationists)
Oliver LaFarge (Chapter 3: Authors and Composers)
Oliver LaGrone (Chapter 2: Artists, Performers, and Directors)
Tony Lujan (Chapter 9: Political, Diplomatic, and Judicial Leaders)
Patricio "Paddy" Martinez (Chapter 5: Business Leaders)
Frank Waters (Chapter 3: Authors and Composers)

Providers of Long-Term Community Service *(in alphabetical order)*

Francis Marion "Frank" Boyer
Founder of Blackdom, an all-black community in eastern New Mexico incorporated on December 5, 1911, and Vado, an all-black community south of Las Cruces, New Mexico, in 1920; teacher
Date of Birth: July 11, 1871
Place of Birth: Macon, Georgia
Date of Death (age): 1949 (about 78)
Place of Death: probably Vado, New Mexico
Cause of Death: unstated natural causes
Resting Place: Vado Cemetery, Vado, New Mexico[34] No. 124

Addison D. "Add" "Old Negro Ad" Jones
Highly respected southeastern New Mexico black cowhand at the LFD, Four Lakes, and Yellow House ranches of the Littlefield Cattle Company; his funeral records state that his occupation was "Cow Puncher"
Date of Birth: 1845
Place of Birth: Gonzales, Texas
Date of Death (age): 11:20 p.m., March 24, 1926 (about 81)
Place of Death: Roswell, New Mexico
Cause of Death: interstitial nephritis
Resting Place: segregated black section of South Park Cemetery, Roswell, New Mexico[35]

125. The spelling of Addison Jones's first name and his date of birth are incorrect.

According to one admirer, "There was never a Littlefield horse too rough for Add; never a Littlefield trail too long for him to ride. He rode until he was so crippled with rheumatism that he could not get on a horse; and then, like a man whose work is well done, he lay down on his bed and died."[36] No. 125

Ernest Thompson Seton; pen names Ernest Seton-Thompson and Ernest E. Thompson; nicknamed "The Chief" and "Black Wolf"
Naturalist, artist, illustrator, author, lecturer, and founder of the Boy Scouts of America, 1910; created the College of Indian Wisdom on 2,500 acres of his property known as Seton Village east of Santa Fe, 1932; retired to his thirty-two room, 6,900 square foot Seton Castle, the unique home he built near the College of Indian Wisdom campus
Date of Birth: August 14, 1860
Place of Birth: South Sheilds, Durham, England
Date of Death (age): October 23, 1946 (86)
Place of Death: at his home, Seton Castle, east of Santa Fe, New Mexico
Cause of Death: "circulatory failure"
Resting Place: cremated with ashes scattered over High Cone, northeast of Seton Castle, on August 14, 1960[37]

Seton completed his forty-second book, gave his final lecture (about the Indians of New Mexico) on his eighty-sixth birthday at the University of New Mexico), and was planning an ambitious ten-thousand-mile lecture tour when he died in the fall of 1946.[38]

Federico "Don Federico" "Fred" Sisneros
National Parks Service's oldest ranger who devoted his life to the care of the San Gregorio de Abó Mission ruins, for which he received several awards, including the Park Service's Superior Service Award, 1981; worked to the day he died
Date of Birth: March 17, 1894
Place of Birth: Abó, New Mexico
Date of Death (age): March 13, 1988 (93)
Place of Death: Presbyterian Hospital, Albuquerque, New Mexico
Cause of Death: heart attack
Resting Place: about ten yards east of the San Gregorio de Abó Mission ruins

126.

Prior to his death, Sisneros had requested that he be buried under a juniper tree beside the ruins he had cared for for so long. In appreciation for his many years of dedicated service, the Park Service granted this special permission.[39] No. 126

Carrie Wooster Tingley
Recovered TB healthseeker who first arrived in New Mexico in 1911; First Lady and advocate for the ill, especially crippled children; Carrie Tingley Hospital for Crippled Children was built and named in her honor during her husband Clyde Tingley's second term as governor, 1937-39

127. Clyde Tingley's grave is directly to the left (west) of Carrie's.

Date of Birth: May 20, 1877
Place of Birth: Bowling Green, Ohio
Date of Death (age): 1:22 p.m., November 7, 1961 (84)
Place of Death: at her famous home at 1523 Silver SE, Albuquerque, New Mexico
Cause of Death: leukemia and a stroke
Resting Place: Fairview Cemetery, Albuquerque, New Mexico

Carrie was popular for her love of the color purple, elaborate hats, antiques, movies, and many charities, especially those helping children at the Carrie Tingley Hospital for Crippled Children in Hot Springs (renamed Truth or Consequences), New Mexico (transferred to Albuquerque in 1981). Her will left $75,000 to her church, the First Congregational of Albuquerque, and $75,000 to St. Anthony's Home for Boys.[40] No. 127

Victor Walter Westphall

World War II Naval veteran; home builder; historian best known for his *Thomas Benton Catron and His Era* (1973) and *Mercedes Reales* (1983); president of the Historical Society of New Mexico; founder and director of the Vietnam Veterans National Memorial on U.S. 64, dedicated May 1971, to honor all Vietnam veterans, including his son, twenty-eight-year-old Marine First Lt. Victor David Westphall III, who was killed on patrol in Vietnam, May 22, 1968[41]

Date of Birth: October 13, 1913
Place of Birth: Fort Atkinson, Wisconsin
Date of Death (age): July 22, 2003 (89)

128. The Memorial Chapel at the Vietnam Veterans National Memorial is seen to the west of Dr. Westphall's grave. In November 2005, the Memorial became a New Mexico State Park.

Place of Death: in his apartment at the Vietnam Veterans National Memorial, Angel Fire, New Mexico
Cause of Death: arteriosclerotic cardiovascular disease
Resting Place: beside the Vietnam Veterans National Memorial, Angel Fire, New Mexico

Dr. Westphall combined his three greatest interests—building, history, and family—in creating a monument to his fallen son and to all those who died for their country in Vietnam. The monument, designed by Santa Fe architect Ted Luna and completed in 1971, was the first and, for many years, the only memorial dedicated to U.S. soldiers of the Vietnam era.[42]

At the age of eighty-one Dr. Westphall went to the site in Vietnam where his son was killed to leave soil brought from Angel Fire. In a gesture of peace and cooperation, he took soil from the site in Vietnam back to the monument he had built in northern New Mexico.

According his second son, Walter:

Although his hearing and eyesight had become poor and he was increasingly frail and in great pain from arthritis and other ailments,....he could not bear to leave the Memorial and would not give up his duties, including greeting veterans and other visitors. He performed those and other duties up until the day before his death. Up until the end, he demonstrated why he deserved to be regarded as a prime example of the "greatest generation."[43] No. 128

James Larkin "Jim" White
Carlsbad Caverns explorer and the caverns' Chief Ranger, 1924-29; opened the caverns to tourism
Date of Birth: July 11, 1882
Place of Birth: Mason County, Texas
Date of Death (age): April 26, 1946 (63)
Place of Death: a hospital in Carlsbad, New Mexico
Cause of Death: coronary thrombosis
Resting Place: Carlsbad Municipal Cemetery, Carlsbad, New Mexico

129. Jim White was buried beside his wife, Fannie. Below his name and dates are the words "The Discoverer of Carlsbad Caverns."

Two days before White's death he told a *Carlsbad Current-Argus* reporter that he felt well, but not quite ready to ride a horse to California, as he had done at the age of twenty-six in 1908.

By the day of his death, 2,589,800 people had visited Carlsbad Caverns.[44] No. 129

Other Providers of Long-Term Community Service include:
all educational leaders (Chapter 6: Educational Leaders)
all lawmen (Chapter 8: Lawmen, Criminals, and Victims of Crime)
all medical personnel (Chapter 11: Scientists and Medical Personnel)
all patrons of the arts (Chapter 4: Cultural Preservationists)
all religious leaders (Chapter 10: Religious Leaders)
Gus Baumann (Chapter 2: Artists, Performers, and Directors)
Ina Cassidy (Chapter 3: Authors and Composers)
Bill Mauldin (Chapter 13: Wartime Leaders and Victims Since the Spanish-American War, 1898)
Dorothy McKibbin (Chapter 13: Wartime Leaders and Victims Since the Spanish-American War, 1898)
Navajo Code Talkers (Chapter 13: Wartime Leaders and Victims Since the Spanish-American War, 1898)
Kathryn O'Connor (Chapter 2: Artists, Performers, and Directors)
Louis R. Rocco (Chapter 13: Wartime Leaders and Victims Since the Spanish-American War, 1898)
Will Shuster (Chapter 2: Artists, Performers, and Directors)

Record Holders (in alphabetical order)

Benjamin L. "Ben" Abruzzo

Real estate developer; developer of the Sandia ski basin and the Sandia Peak tram (opened May 7, 1966); with Maxie Anderson and Larry Newman, the first to fly a manned balloon, the Double Eagle II, across the Atlantic Ocean, August 12-17, 1978; with three others, the first to fly a manned balloon, the Double Eagle V, across the Pacific Ocean, November 9-12, 1981; the Albuquerque International Balloon Museum was named in his and Maxie Anderson's honor, with ground breaking ceremonies held on October 11, 2002, and its opening during the Albuquerque Balloon Fiesta on October 1, 2005

Date of Birth: June 9, 1930

Place of Birth: Rockfort, Illinois

Date of Death (age): 10:14 a.m., February 11, 1985 (54)

Place of Death: Albuquerque, New Mexico

Cause of Death: plane crash two minutes after takeoff from Albuquerque's Coronado Airport; his wife, Patty, and four family friends also died in the crash

Resting Place: Gate of Heaven Cemetery, Albuquerque, New Mexico[45] No. 130

130. Ben and Patty Abruzzo's profiles appear on this unique headstone. The words on their stone read, "Strength" and "Love." The Sandia Peak tram, which they developed, is to the east, in clear site of their gravesite.

Max Leroy "Maxie" Anderson

Chief Executive Officer of Ranchers Exploration and Development Corporation; with Ben Abruzzo and Larry Newman, the first to cross the Atlantic Ocean in a manned balloon, the Double Eagle II, August 12-17, 1978; the Albuquerque International Balloon Museum was named in his and Ben Abruzzo's honor, with ground breaking ceremonies on October 11, 2002, and its opening during the Albuquerque Balloon Fiesta on October 1, 2005

Date of Birth: September 10, 1934

Place of Birth: Sayre, Oklahoma

Date of Death (age): June 27, 1983 (48)

Place of Death: in a Bavarian forest near Schweinfurt, Germany

Cause of Death: balloon crash while attempting to avoid crossing into Communist East Germany

Resting Place: Sunset Memorial Cemetery, Albuquerque, New Mexico[46] No. 131

131. The epitaph on Maxie Anderson's gravestone is quoted from Dean Alfange's creed. It reads: "I do not choose to be a common man. It is my right to be uncommon—if I can. I seek opportunity—not security. I want to take the calculated risk; to dream and to build, to fail and to succeed, to refuse to barter incentive for a dole. I prefer the challenges of life to the guaranteed existence, the thrill of fulfillment to the stale calm of utopia."

Francis Xavier Aubry

Famous freighter and captain on the Santa Fe Trail; set the record for the fastest trip on the trail three times, including fourteen days (in December 1847 to January 1848), eight days and ten hours (in May 1848), and, finally, in five days and twenty-two hours, riding a total six horses (in September 1848); known as the "Skimmer of the Plains"; explored a potential railroad route from New Mexico to California

Date of Birth: December 3, 1824
Place of Birth: Maskinongé, Quebec Province, Canada
Date of Death (age): August 18, 1854 (29)
Place of Death: Mercure Brothers Store, Santa Fe, New Mexico
Cause of Death: killed with a Bowie knife by Richard H. Weightman, who was tried for murder in Santa Fe on September 20-21, 1854, and acquitted on grounds of justifiable homicide because Aubry reportedly drew and shot his pistol first
Resting Place: in the Parroquia, the parish church in Santa Fe, New Mexico

Aubry's large, expensive funeral was "graced by the presence of hundreds of persons, great and small, who admired and respected him. It was a tragic and ignoble end for a man who had courted danger all his life and whose marvelous exploits were accomplished on sheer nerve and grit."[47]

Arthur Cornelius "Art" Goebel, Jr.
Early aviator; winner of the $25,000 Dole Prize for flying the first flight from California to Oahu, Hawaii, about 2,400 miles, in twenty-six hours and seventeen minutes, August 16-17, 1927, two hours faster than the second-place finisher; a street in Belen, New Mexico, was named in his family's honor
Date of Birth: October 19, 1895
Place of Birth: Belen, New Mexico
Date of Death (age): 1:10 p.m., December 3, 1973 (78)
Place of Death: Veterans Hospital, Wadsworth, California
Cause of Death: pneumonia and myelofibrosis
Resting Place: Forrest Lawn Memorial Park, Glendale, California[48]

Charles Francis Walsh
Early aviator credited with building the first practical airplane in California; received Pilot's License No. 1, issued by the Aero Club of California, August 8, 1911; flew the first plane in New Mexico history, at the Territorial Fair, from 4:10 to 4:25 p.m. on October 11, 1911, in his single-propeller Curtis Model "D" biplane; set world record by carrying a passenger, Raymond Stamm, over five thousand feet above sea level (Albuquerque's altitude); flew at the Colfax County Fair in Raton, New Mexico, and at similar events across the United States and into Canada and Cuba from May 1911 till his death in October 1912; a replica of his plane hangs from a high ceiling at the Albuquerque Sunport International Airport
Date of Birth: October 27, 1877
Place of Birth: Mission Valley, California
Date of Death (age): late afternoon, October 3, 1912 (34)
Place of Death: State Fair, Trenton, New Jersey
Cause of Death: before a crowd of 65,000, Walsh crashed from an altitude of two thousand feet while attempting a spiral descent; an attending doctor confirmed that every bone in his body was broken in the fall
Resting Place: Calvary Memorial Pioneer Cemetery, San Diego, California

The Democratic presidential candidate, Woodrow Wilson, was scheduled to fly as a passenger in Walsh's plane later on the day of the pilot's fatal crash.

The train carrying Walsh's remains en route from Trenton to burial in San Diego stopped in Albuquerque for a brief, poignant moment.[49]

Other Record Holders include:
Katherine Stinson-Otero (Chapter 2: Artists, Performers, and Directors)

Athletes (in alphabetical order)

John Willard "Coach John" Baker
Champion long-distance runner, immortalized in William Buchanan's *A Shining Season* (1978); Physical Education teacher at Albuquerque's Aspen Elementary School (renamed in his honor, May 16, 1971) and coach of the champion Duke City Dashers Track Club, which he co-founded in 1967

132.

Date of Birth: June 29, 1944
Place of Birth: Springfield, Missouri
Date of Death (age): about 7:00 a.m., November 26, 1970 (26)
Place of Death: Presbyterian Hospital, Albuquerque, New Mexico
Cause of Death: testicular cancer
Resting Place: crypt, Gate of Heaven Cemetery, Albuquerque, New Mexico

On Thanksgiving Day, 1970, Baker turned to his mother from his bed at Presbyterian Hospital and said, "'I can't fight any longer. I'm sorry I've been so much trouble.' With a final sigh, John Baker closed his eyes forever." The star athlete's gallant eighteen month struggle with cancer had ended.[50] No. 132

Everett Bowman
Rodeo champion, 1923-44; world champion calf roper, 1929, 1935, 1937; world champion steer wrestler, 1930, 1933, 1935, 1938; world champion steer roper, 1937; president of the Cowboys Turtle Association (now the Rodeo Cowboys Association), 1936-45; inducted into the National Cowboy Hall of Fame, 1979, and the Pro Rodeo Hall of Fame; known as a "cowboy's cowboy"; ranked as the sixth best athlete in New Mexico history by *Sports Illustrated Magazine*; Arizona lawman and rancher; the rodeo arena in Wickenburg, Arizona, was named in his honor, 1978
Date of Birth: July 12, 1899
Place of Birth: Hope, New Mexico
Date of Death (age): morning of October 25, 1971 (72)
Place of Death: between Boulder City, Nevada, and Wickenburg, Arizona
Cause of Death: as a result of poor visibility, crashed in his private plane
Resting Place: Safford Union Cemetery, Safford, Arizona

Bowman, who wore his boots and spurs everywhere he went, died with his boots and spurs on when his Cessna 172 crashed.[51]

Robert Anderson "Wild Horse" Crosby
Known as the "King of the Cowboys" after winning the Roosevelt Trophy as the best all-around cowboy in 1925, 1927, and 1928
Date of Birth: February 27, 1897
Place of Birth: Midland, Texas
Date of Death (age): 3:15 p.m., October 20, 1947 (50)
Place of Death: on a road twenty miles north of Roswell, New Mexico
Cause of Death: head and chest injuries resulting from a jeep accident
Resting Place: South Park Cemetery, Roswell, New Mexico

     As a world champion rodeo cowboy, Crosby was often heard to say, "Ah was born on a hoss and Ah want to die on a hoss." He did not die on his famous rodeo horse Jellybean, but at the time of his death he undoubtedly wore the same battered black felt cowboy hat he had worn for over twenty years.[52] No. 133

133. The image at the bottom of Crosby's gravestone is of a lasso, his cowboy tool.

John Arthur "Jack" "Papa Jack" Johnson
Controversial black heavy weight boxer; world champion, 1908-15; won eighty of his 114 fights (forty-five by knockouts), 1897-1928; defeated Jim "Fireman" Flynn (whose original name was Andrew Chiariglione) in Las Vegas, New Mexico, July 4, 1912
Date of Birth: March 31, 1878
Place of Birth: Galveston, Texas
Date of Death (age): 6:10 p.m., June 10, 1946 (68)
Place of Death: St. Agnes Hospital, Raleigh, North Carolina
Cause of Death: internal injuries after he lost control of his Lincoln Zephyr automobile on a road about twenty miles north of Raleigh, North Carolina, crashing into a light pole shortly after hearing a racial dispute in a Raleigh diner
Resting Place: Graceland Cemetery, Chicago, Illinois

     Known for his rather reckless driving, Johnson once said, "I drive fast, but I'm more careful than slowpoke drivers."[53] No. 134

134. Photo courtesy of Stew Thornley.

Benjamin Vernon "Ben" Lilly
Legendary hunter of bears, bobcats, and mountain lions in the mountains of southwestern New Mexico; a street in Silver City was named in his honor
Date of Birth: December 31, 1856
Place of Birth: Wilcox County, Alabama
Date of Death (age): 6:50 p.m., December 17, 1936 (79)
Place of Death: County Farm on Big Dry Creek, Grant County, New Mexico
Cause of Death: "old age"
Resting Place: Memory Lane Cemetery, Silver City, New Mexico[54]

135. Ben Lilly's small marker was donated by the Town Country Garden Club. The inscription on Lilly's headstone includes the words: "Lover of the Great Outdoors."

136. The epitaph at the bottom of "Miz Mac's" gravestone reads: "I will lift up mine eyes unto the hills from whence cometh my help. Psalm 121:1"

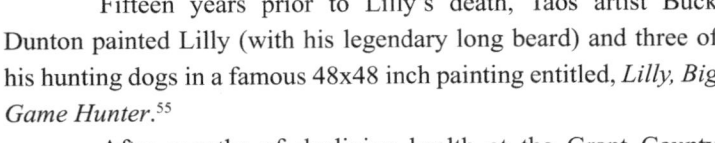

137.

Fifteen years prior to Lilly's death, Taos artist Buck Dunton painted Lilly (with his legendary long beard) and three of his hunting dogs in a famous 48x48 inch painting entitled, *Lilly, Big Game Hunter*.[55]

After months of declining health at the Grant County Farm, two hours before he died, Ben reportedly declared, "I'll be better off."

At his funeral his daughters were shocked to discover that someone had shaved off Ben's legendary long beard.[56] No. 135

Bernice Walsh "Miz Mac" McLaughlin
World Champion horse jumper, clearing 6'2" on her horse Smokey, April 1911; rancher; chosen Top New Mexico Homemaker, 1959; inducted into the National Cowgirl Hall of Fame, 1977
Date of Birth: November 27, 1891
Place of Birth: Alberta, Canada
Date of Death (age): July 10, 1985 (93)
Place of Death: Union County General Hospital, Clayton, New Mexico
Cause of Death: unstated natural causes
Resting Place: Clayton Cemetery, Clayton, New Mexico[57]

Miz Mac's daughter recalls that her mother was busy to the end of her life. Days before she entered the hospital, Miz Mac insisted on picking cherries from the cherry trees on her ranch, twenty-five miles north of Clayton. Even in the Union County General Hospital, Miz Mac asked that her son-in-law drive his stagecoach by her hospital window so she could see the horses before he displayed them in a local parade. She was a devoted horse woman to the very end.[58] No. 136

Montague Farquhar Sheffields Stevens
English owner of the WS, SU, and NH ranches in southwest New Mexico; famed grizzly bear hunter, said to have killed eighteen grizzlies, despite the loss of an arm, as described in his book, *Meet Mr. Grizzly* (1943)
Date of Birth: December 10, 1859
Place of Birth: Madras, India
Date of Death (age): December 16, 1953 (94)
Place of Death: Albuquerque, New Mexico
Cause of Death: unstated natural causes
Resting Place: Fairview Cemetery, Albuquerque, New Mexico[59]
No. 137

Jeremy Henry "Jerry" Unser, Jr.
Albuquerque High School sports hero and 1951 alumnus; began racing when he was only fourteen years old; served in the U.S. Navy during the Korean War; won the stock car division championship at the annual Pike's Peak race, 1956 and 1957; national stock car champion, 1957; Formula One race car driver; competed in the 1958 Indianapolis 500 race; member of the famous Unser race car driving family; brother Bobby won the Indy 500 in 1968, 1975, and 1981; brother Al, Sr., won in 1970, 1971, 1978, and 1987; nephew Al, Jr., won in 1992 and 1994; son Johnny ran at Indy in 1996-2000; Albuquerque's Unser Boulevard was named in the family's honor; the Unser Racing Museum was dedicated in Albuquerque on September 15, 2005

138.

Date of Birth: November 15, 1932
Place of Birth: Colorado Springs, Colorado
Date of Death (age): 8:15 a.m., May 17, 1959 (26)
Place of Death: Robert Long Hospital, Indianapolis, Indiana
Cause of Death: burn injuries sustained in a racing accident while practicing for the Indianapolis 500 on May 2, 1959; his vehicle, a Kuzma racing car, burst into flames when it hit a retaining wall after he came out of the fourth (northwest) turn at the Indianapolis Speedway, going approximately 133 miles per hour; Unser's third crash within about a year
Resting Place: Sunset Cemetery, Albuquerque, New Mexico[60]

As a result of Unser's death, racing officials required all drivers to wear fire-resistant driving suits when racing, both in practice and in actual competition.

According to Sunset Cemetery officials, there was talk of burying Jerry in one of his race cars. Only logistics made this novel idea impossible.[61] No. 138

Other Athletes and Coaches include:
Roy Johnson (Chapter 6: Educational Leaders)
Bob King (Chapter 6: Educational Leaders)
Tom Popejoy (Chapter 6: Educational Leaders)
Robert Scott (Chapter 13: Wartime Leaders and Victims Since the Spanish-American War, 1898)

8

LAWMEN, CRIMINALS, AND VICTIMS OF CRIME

Lawmen (in alphabetical order)

Elfego Baca

Socorro County lawman, most famous for surviving a thirty-three-hour shoot-out with an estimated eighty Texas gunmen at Frisco, New Mexico, October 29-31, 1884; Albuquerque attorney and private detective; a street in Albuquerque was named in his honor

Date of Birth: February 10, 1865, reportedly after his mother, Juanita, had just competed in "Las Iglesias," a game similar to today's softball

Place of Birth: an athletic field, Socorro, New Mexico

Date of Death (age): 9:15 p.m., August 27, 1945 (80)

Place of Death: at his home at 1501 North Third Street, Albuquerque, New Mexico

Cause of Death: cirrhosis of the liver

Resting Place: Sunset Memorial Cemetery, Albuquerque, New Mexico

According to his wife, Elfego—one of the most feared men in his prime—died peacefully in his living room while awaiting a radio address by Senator Clinton P. Anderson, whom he respected greatly.[1] No. 139

Sierra County hasn't had a killing in ten years —rough men in a rough country, all armed.
—Eugene Manlove Rhodes
The Proud Sheriff (1935)

139.

Charles Littlepage "Charlie" Ballard

Roswell deputy sheriff and city marshal; helped subdue the High Five Gang led by "Black Jack" Christian; arrested George Musgraves for the murder of George Parker; Rough Rider in the Spanish-American War, 1898

Date of Birth: October 11, 1866

Place of Birth: Hays County, Texas

Date of Death (age): April 16, 1950 (83)

Place of Death: at his home in Duncan, Arizona

Cause of Death: unstated natural causes

Resting Place: Evergreen Cemetery, El Paso, Texas[2] No. 140

140.

141.

Howard S. Beacham

First arrived in Alamogordo, January 1, 1907; owned and operated the Alamogordo Hotel, 1913-17; Otero County sheriff, 1921-23, 1935-39; ardent, effective Prohibition agent, 1924-33; arrested George "Machine-Gun" Kelly, 1933; later a municipal judge and justice of the peace

Date of Birth: January 27 or 28 (as given on his headstone), 1883
Place of Birth: Baltimore, Maryland
Date of Death (age): March 9, 1963 (80)
Place of Death: Gerald Champion Memorial Hospital, Alamogordo, New Mexico
Cause of Death: "heart ailment compounded by an asthmatic condition"
Resting Place: Monte Vista Cemetery, Alamogordo, New Mexico[3] No. 141

142.

Frederick "Fred" Fornoff

Albuquerque city marshal; Rough Rider in the Spanish-American War, 1898; Captain in the New Mexico Mounted Police; played key roles in many cases, including the investigation of Pat Garrett's murder, 1908, and the halting of Jack Johnson's prize fight in Las Vegas, New Mexico, 1912

Date of Birth: February 23, 1859
Place of Birth: Baltimore, Maryland
Date of Death (age): November 26, 1935 (76)
Place of Death: Veterans Hospital, Fort Sheridan, Wyoming
Cause of Death: unstated natural causes
Resting Place: National Cemetery, Santa Fe, New Mexico[4] No. 142

Patrick Floyd Jarvis "Pat" "Juan Largo" Garrett

Buffalo hunter; rancher; Texas Ranger; arrived in New Mexico, 1878; elected Sheriff of Lincoln County, November 2, 1880; killed Billy the Kid in Fort Sumner, July 14, 1881; Doña Ana County Sheriff, 1896-1902; U.S. Collector of Customs, El Paso, Texas, 1902-06; collaborated in the writing of *The Authentic Life of Billy the Kid, The Noted Desperado of the Southwest* (1882)

Date of Birth: June 5, 1850
Place of Birth: Chambers County, Alabama
Date of Death (age): February 29, 1908 (Leap Year Day) (57)
Place of Death: on the road near Alameda Arroyo, four miles outside Las Cruces, New Mexico
Cause of Death: shot by Wayne Brazel over disputed rights to a goat ranch; claiming self-defense, Brazel was acquitted within fifteen minutes after a one-day trial, April 19, 1909
Resting Place: originally buried in Las Cruces's IOOF Cemetery; reinterred in 1957 across the street in the Masonic Cemetery with his wife, Apolinaria, and nine other members of his family[5]

According to his daughter Elizabeth, Garrett believed that in shooting Billy the Kid "it was the Kid or me." Elizabeth felt that her father had "almost a parental feeling toward the Kid and deplored the fact that the killing was the only course to pursue in dealing with the young bandit."[6]

Garrett had predicted that he would "die with his boots on," and he did. He was so tall that no appropriate casket was available in Las Cruces, so a special one had to be ordered from El Paso. At his funeral on March 5, 1908, his family used the same eulogy the famous agnostic orator Robert G. Ingersoll (1833-99) had read at the service for his dead brother on May 31, 1879. Garrett had long admired Ingersoll and had identified this eulogy as his favorite.[7] No. 143

143.

Charles Fred Lambert
Owner of the St. James Hotel, Cimarron, New Mexico; legendary New Mexico Mounted Police officer
Date of Birth: January 23, 1887
Place of Birth: Cimarron, New Mexico
Date of Death (age): February 3, 1971 (84)
Place of Death: Raton, New Mexico
Cause of Death: unstated natural causes
Resting Place: Mountain View Cemetery, Cimarron, New Mexico
　　Lambert was the last surviving member of the New Mexico Mounted Police when he died in 1971.[8] No. 144

144.

George Adolphus "Old Scarbrow" Scarborough
Deputy U.S. Marshal; famous for killing John Henry Selman (the killer of outlaw John Wesley Hardin), April 6, 1896, and helping to capture train robber William "Bronco Bill" Walters, 1898
Date of Birth: October 2, 1859
Place of Birth: Natchitoches Parish, Louisiana
Date of Death (age): April 6, 1900 (40)
Place of Death: Deming, New Mexico
Cause of Death: wounds suffered in an ambush by outlaws
Resting Place: Mountain View Cemetery, Deming, New Mexico[9] No. 145

Charles Angelo "Charlie" Siringo
Cowboy; Pinkerton detective (known as "The Cowboy Detective"), 1886-1907; Santa Fe area rancher, 1907-1922; New Mexico Ranger, 1916-1918; author, probably best known for *A Texas Cowboy* (1885), said to be the first autobiography of a working cowboy, and *Cowboy Detective* (1912); three streets in Santa Fe were named in his honor
Date of Birth: February 7, 1855
Place of Birth: Matagorda County, Texas
Date of Death (age): October 18, 1928 (73)
Place of Death: Altadena, California
Cause of Death: heart attack

145. Although sources often give George Scarborough's date of death as April 6, the date on his gravestone is April 5.

146. Photo courtesy of Scott Groll.

Resting Place: Inglewood Park Cemetery, Inglewood, California

Unable to attend Siringo's funeral in California, friends Will Rogers and Bill Hart sent a telegram from New York that read: "Another American plainsman has taken the long trail. May flowers always grow over his grave."[10] No. 146

Harvey Howard Whitehill
Union soldier in the Civil War in New Mexico, 1861-62; early Silver City community leader; miner; rancher; Sheriff of Grant County, New Mexico, during most of the period 1875-91; said to have arrested more outlaws than any other lawman in New Mexico territorial history; the first lawman to arrest Billy the Kid; said to be the inspiration for Sheriff Breckenridge "Brick" Garvey in Archibald Clavering Gunter's popular Western novel, *Miss Nobody of Nowhere* (1890)
Date of Birth: September 2, 1837
Place of Birth: Wooster, Ohio
Date of Death (age): September 7, 1906 (69)
Place of Death: Deming, New Mexico
Cause of Death: Bright's disease
Resting Place: Masonic Cemetery, Silver City, New Mexico[11]

L. Edison "Bobcat" Wilson, Sr.
Gallup's Deputy Sheriff; shot during a riot while accompanying defendants from the Gallup courthouse to jail on April 4, 1935; Sheriff Mack Carmichael and Ignacio Velarde were killed and at least five others were injured; the ten men accused of the riot were tried in a nine-day October 7-16, 1935, trial, leading to second-degree murder convictions for three and not guilty verdicts for the remaining seven; a main character in Gary L. Stuart's *The Gallup 14: A Novel* (2000), based on the riot and the trial that followed
Date of Birth: July 6, 1907
Place of Birth: unknown
Date of Death (age): October 21, 1993 (86)
Place of Death: probably Gallup, New Mexico
Cause of Death: unstated natural causes
Resting Place: Hillcrest Cemetery, Gallup, New Mexico[12] No. 147

147.

Charles B. Winstead
FBI agent who fired two of the three bullets that killed John Dillinger outside the Biograph Theatre in Chicago, Illinois, at 10:30 p.m. on July 22, 1934; FBI agent assigned to Albuquerque, 1940-1943; intelligence and security officer, Manhattan Project in Los Alamos during World War II
Date of Birth: May 25, 1891

Place of Birth: Sherman, Texas
Date of Death (age): August 3, 1973 (82)
Place of Death: Veterans Hospital, Albuquerque, New Mexico
Cause of Death: unstated natural causes
Resting Place: cremated[13]

Other Lawmen include:
Everett Bowman (Chapter 7: Sung and Unsung Heroes)
Frank C. Brito (Chapter 13: Wartime Leaders and Victims Since the Spanish-American War, 1898)
John M. Campbell (Chapter 9: Political, Diplomatic, and Judicial Leaders)
Mack Carmichael (this chapter)
Phil Chacon (this chapter)
Edward A. Clary (Chapter 13: Wartime Leaders and Victims Since the Spanish-American War, 1898)
Albert Jennings Fountain (this chapter)
Benigno Cárdenas Hernández (Chapter 9: Political, Diplomatic, and Judicial Leaders)
Maximiliano Luna (Chapter 13: Wartime Leaders and Victims Since the Spanish-American War, 1898)
Tranquilino Luna (Chapter 9: Political, Diplomatic, and Judicial Leaders)
Edwin Mechem (Chapter 9: Political, Diplomatic, and Judicial Leaders)
Trinidad Romero (Chapter 9: Political, Diplomatic, and Judicial Leaders)
David "Dirty Dave" Rudebaugh (this chapter)
Ray Sutton (this chapter)

Infamous (or Suspected) Criminals *(in alphabetical order)*

148. A second stone, at the foot of Allison's grave, is inscribed with the words: "He never killed a man that did not need killing."

> Let sixteen gamblers come handle my coffin
> Let sixteen cowboys come sing me a song.
> Take me to the graveyard and lay the sod o'er me,
> For I'm a poor cowboy and I know I've done wrong.
> —"The Cowboy's Lament"[14]

Robert Clay Allison
Confederate soldier; gunslinger; a key player in the Colfax County War, 1875-78; accused of killing at least four men between 1870 and 1876
Date of Birth: September 2, 1840
Place of Birth: Waynesboro, Tennessee
Date of Death (age): July 3, 1887 (46)
Place of Death: Pope's Crossing near Pecos, Texas
Cause of Death: injuries sustained from a fall off his wagon
Resting Place: originally buried in the old Pecos cemetery;[15] reburied on August 28, 1975, at the first and only gravesite on the grounds of the West of the Pecos

Museum, Pecos, Texas. As one author has observed, "Allison is perhaps the only gunfighter who has an entire cemetery to himself."[16]

When Clay Allison was reburied in 1975, the few eyewitnesses at the scene discovered Allison's skeleton still intact with his wool suit relatively well-preserved. After burial in his new gravesite adjacent to the West of the Pecos Museum, the Reverend Ray Powell performed a recommittal service "in good taste and very solemn," in his words.[17] No. 148

Apache Kid; Ma-si; Haskay-Bay-Nay-Ntayl, meaning Tall, Brave, and Will Come to a Mysterious End
At the age of eighteen, among those captured and exiled with Geronimo, 1886; feared Chiricahua Apache killer and horse thief, known to victimize white settlers as well as fellow Indians; the reward for his capture reached six thousand dollars; Apache Kid Wilderness in the San Mateo Mountains was named for him when it was created in 1980
Date of Birth: 1868
Place of Birth: probably White Mountain, Arizona Territory
Date of Death (age): 1907 (about 39)
Place of Death: San Mateo Mountains in southern New Mexico
Cause of Death: shot by a posse led by Billy Keene
Resting Place: body left where he was shot, but Keene reportedly removed the Kid's head, reduced it to a skull in an iron kettle of boiling water, and presented it to hunters visiting the area from Chicago[18]

Jesse Wayne Brazel
Suspected of killing Pat Garrett on February 29, 1908, over disputed rights to a goat ranch; claiming self-defense, Brazel was acquitted within fifteen minutes after a one-day trial, April 19, 1909
Date of Birth: December 31, 1876
Place of Birth: Greenwood City, Kansas
Date of Death (age): unknown
Place of Death: probably South America, where he supposedly fled sometime after 1914
Cause of Death: unknown, although some suggest that he was killed by the Butch Cassidy Gang
Resting Place: probably South America[19]

William T. "Black Jack" "Will" "202" (because of his large size) Christian; also known as Ed Williams
Leader of the High Five Gang, famous for robbing stores, banks, post offices, stagecoaches, and trains in Arizona and New Mexico
Date of Birth: 1871
Place of Birth: north Texas
Date of Death (age): April 28, 1897 (about 26)

Place of Death: ambushed by lawmen at his hideout in eastern Arizona in what is now known as Black Jack Canyon
Cause of Death: shot in the hip and died of the wound within hours
Resting Place: his body was reportedly placed on public display and was then buried in an unknown location[20]

John Daniel Ehrlichman
President Richard M. Nixon's chief domestic policy advisor, 1969-73; found guilty in 1975 of conspiracy, perjury, and obstruction of justice for his role in the Watergate scandal; served eighteen months (October 1976 to April 1978) in the Swift Trail federal minimum security prison in southeastern Arizona; lived in Santa Fe as an author, artist, and commentator before and after serving his prison term; his memoirs, written while he lived in Santa Fe, were entitled, *Witness to Power: The Nixon Years* (1982)
Date of Birth: March 20, 1925
Place of Birth: Tacoma, Washington
Date of Death (age): February 14, 1999 (73)
Place of Death: at his home in Atlanta, Georgia
Cause of Death: complications from diabetes
Resting Place: cremated[21]

 Moving into a hundred-year-old house on Montoya Circle in Santa Fe, Ehrlichman said he came to New Mexico to finish his first book, *The Company* (1976). "I didn't know a soul here," he said. "I knew I needed a place where nobody would have a claim on my time. Santa Fe was a place I had visited many times before, and it just seemed ideal."[22]

Robert Newton "Bob" Ford
Forever known as Jesse James's assassin; killed James on April 3, 1882, to collect a five thousand dollar reward; instead, convicted of James's murder and sentenced to hang, but was pardoned by Missouri Governor Tom Crittenden; briefly co-owned the Bank Saloon in West Las Vegas, New Mexico, and another such establishment in Cerillos, New Mexico; also served as a an unpopular policeman in Las Vegas, New Mexico, 1885
Date of Birth: December 8, 1861
Place of Birth: Missouri
Date of Death (age): June 8, 1892 (30)
Place of Death: his Exchange Saloon, Creede, Colorado
Cause of Death: shot by Edward O'Kelley, the man Ford had accused of stealing a diamond ring and pistol whipping him in Pueblo, Colorado
Resting Place: originally buried at the Sunnyside Cemetery, Creede, Colorado, but soon transferred by his widow to the Richmond City Cemetery, Richmond, Missouri[23]

149. The birth year on Bob Ford's gravestone is incorrect.
Photo courtesy of Bill Walker.

 Bob Ford's murder of Jesse James is remembered in the cowboy song,

Jesse James:

> Jesse James was a lad that killed a-many a man;
> He robbed the Danville train,
> But that dirty little coward that shot Mr. Howard
> Has laid poor Jesse in his grave.[24] No. 149

Joel A. Fowler
Saloonkeeper, rancher, and murderer accused of killing twenty-six or more men; known in the press as "The Human Exterminator"
Date of Birth: 1849
Place of Birth: either Indiana or Mississippi
Date of Death (age): January 22, 1884 (about 35)
Place of Death: Socorro, New Mexico
Cause of Death: lynched from a cottonwood tree down Death Alley by the Socorro Committee of Safety; the committee's last known victim
Resting Place: his last request was that his body be shipped to an uncle in Fort Worth, Texas; cemetery unknown[25]

According to the *Las Vegas Optic*, as the mob escorted Fowler to his hanging he "loudly called on Heaven to protect him, [to which] some wag in the crowd called out: 'It's a cold night for angels, Joel. Better call on someone nearer town.' [Fowler] then protested that the law-abiding citizens should protect him. The same voice [in the crowd] replied: 'You are in the hands of the law-abiding citizens, Mr. Fowler, and they will see that you get your just deserts.'"[26]

Fowler's publicly displayed hung body was said to have been viewed by as many as three thousand people the following day. A coroner's jury issued a formal, rather droll ruling which read: "Deceased came to his death at the hands of a mob of unknown persons, who placed a rope around his neck and hanged him until he was dead."[27]

James Robert "Jim" Gililland

150.

Southern New Mexico rancher tried and acquitted, with Oliver Lee, for the February 1, 1896, murder of Albert J. Fountain and his son, Henry
Date of Birth: March 22, 1874
Place of Birth: Brown County, Texas
Date of Death (age): August 8, 1946 (72)
Place of Death: Hot Springs (renamed Truth or Consequences), New Mexico
Cause of Death: coronary thrombosis
Resting Place: Tularosa Cemetery, Tularosa, New Mexico[28]

Attorney historian William A. Keleher interviewed Gililland shortly before Gililland's death to make one last attempt to learn what had become of Albert Fountain and his son. According to Keleher, Gililland was "polite, courteous, and responsive up to a certain point, [but] skirted and evaded all efforts" to reveal what he might have known about the mysterious events of February 1, 1896.

A week after his death, the *Sierra County Advocate* wrote that "James Robert Gililland was as typical a pioneer western cowman as any author of scenario, song or story could ask for."[29] No. 150

John Henry "Doc" Holliday
Dentist, gambler, gunfighter, and thief; briefly owned a saloon in East Las Vegas, New Mexico, in 1879; a survivor of the famous gunfight at the OK Corral, Tombstone, Arizona, October 26, 1881
Date of Birth: August 14, 1851
Place of Birth: Valdosta, Georgia
Date of Death (age): November 8, 1887 (36)
Place of Death: Glenwood Springs, Colorado
Cause of Death: pulmonary tuberculosis (the disease that had caused him to leave his native Georgia and head west in the early 1870s)
Resting Place: Linwood Cemetery, Glenwood Springs, Colorado

After fifty-seven days of delirium in the fall of 1887, Doc awoke and asked for a glass of whiskey. Drinking it and glancing at his naked feet, he reportedly said, "This is funny," because he always thought he'd die with his boots on. He died shortly thereafter.[30] No. 151

151. The back of "Doc" Holliday's tombstone reads: "John Henry Holliday, D.D. Born Valdosta, Georgia, in 1852 [sic]. Graduate of Baltimore Dental School in 1872 at the Age of 20. One of the Great Gamblers and the Speediest Man with a Gun in the West. He Lost His Biggest Bet When He Died November 8, 1887, in a Glenwood Springs, Colorado, Sanitarium with Tuberculosis Instead of Being Cut Down by a Bullet."
Photo courtesy of David N. Lotz.

Edward Lee Howard; KGB Codename: Robert
Only U.S. CIA agent to defect to the Soviet Union during the Cold War; despite tight FBI surveillance, he defected from his home in Santa Fe, New Mexico, September 21, 1985
Date of Birth: October 27, 1951
Place of Birth: Alamogordo, New Mexico
Date of Death (age): July 12, 2002 (50)
Place of Death: his home in Moscow, Russia
Cause of Death: reportedly from a broken neck suffered in a fall; reliable sources in the American intelligence community suspect foul play at the hands of the KGB
Resting Place: cremated

According to Howard's family and friends, he wanted his body to be disposed of without "noise or hullabaloo."[31]

Charles Kennedy
Arrived in New Mexico about 1865; rancher; "innkeeper" at the mouth of the Fernandez Canyon at the foot of Palo Flechado Pass in northern New Mexico; mass murderer
Date of Birth: unknown

Place of Birth: unknown
Date of Death (age): shortly after 11:00 p.m., October 7, 1870 (unknown)
Cause of Death: lynched by vigilantes
Place of Death: Elizabethtown, New Mexico
Resting Place: unknown (body disposed of by a lynch mob)

Accused of killing many of the guests at his isolated roadside inn, Charles Kennedy was lynched by "parties unknown" either from a rafter in a slaughterhouse, from a pole in front of the Elizabethtown courthouse, from a beef-skinning windlass in a corral, or by being dragged on the ground with a rope around his neck. Just prior to his death, he reportedly confessed to killing twenty-one men, but admitted that he would have been happier if he had succeeded in killing four more of his enemies. Once dead, Kennedy's skull was supposedly either unceremoniously placed on a fence post in Cimarron, sent back East for scientific examination, or both.[32]

Samuel W. "Sam" Ketchum
Train robber and member of the "Black Jack" Ketchum Gang that robbed post offices, banks, and trains in Arizona and New Mexico; outlaw Thomas "Black Jack" Ketchum's older brother
Date of Birth: January 4, 1854
Place of Birth: Caldwell County, Texas
Date of Death (age): July 24, 1899 (45)
Place of Death: in his cell four days after his arrival in the New Mexico Territorial Prison, Santa Fe, New Mexico
Cause of Death: died from wounds and blood poisoning after a shootout with a posse near Folsom, New Mexico; refused to have his badly injured arm amputated, although the prison physician, Dr. M.F. Desmarais, had warned him that without the operation he would surely die
Resting Place: the old territorial prison cemetery; a cenotaph was placed at the Odd Fellows Cemetery, Santa Fe, New Mexico[33]

152. Sam Ketchum's isolated cenotaph was purchased by a descendent, Berry Spradley of Spring, Texas, and researcher Samuel L. Gauny of Ruidoso, New Mexico, about fifteen years ago. Spradley chose the words engraved on Ketchum's stone: "Cowboy, Husband, Father, and Outlaw. Shot and captured by posse. Brother of Thomas E. "Black Jack" Ketchum." The stone is sometimes decorated with the items that filled Sam's life: dice, a liquor bottle, and bullets. Ketchum's actual gravesite is probably under what is now Cerrillos Road.[35]

When Sam Ketchum died, his brother Berry Ketchum was notified at his home in Tom Green County, Texas. Accompanied by his friend, Sheriff G.W. Shield, Berry came to Santa Fe to attend to Sam's funeral, calling the news a "terrible shock." According to the *Santa Fe New Mexican*:

> The scene when Mr. Ketchum first saw his brother's body was very affecting. Mr. Ketchum had neither seen nor heard of his brother for many years and had hoped that perhaps the report of death was false after all. But when he saw the body he was convinced, and tears stood in the eye of the strong man.[34] No. 152

Thomas Edward "Black Jack" Ketchum; also known as George Stevens[36]
Train robber and notorious leader of the "Black Jack" Ketchum Gang that robbed post

offices, banks, and trains in Arizona and New Mexico; captured after unsuccessfully attempting to single-handedly rob a train outside Folsom, New Mexico, on August 16, 1899; wounded, he was captured the following day; Sam Ketchum's younger outlaw brother

Date of Birth: October 31, 1863

Place of Birth: San Saba County, Texas

Date of Death (age): 1:21 p.m., April 26, 1901 (37)

Place of Death: Clayton, New Mexico; a plaque on the current Union County sheriff's office reads: "Against this wall Thomas Edward "Black Jack" Ketchum swung into eternity, April 26, 1901. Desperado. Train Robber. 'A good cowboy that went wrong.'"

Cause of Death: decapitated when hanged for train robbery[37]

On the day of Black Jack's execution, the *Santa Fe New Mexican* reported:

> Ketchum passed a quiet night, ate a [good] breakfast, took a bath, and put on a new suit of clothes this morning. Twenty deputies were on guard last night. A priest from Trinidad was with him from midnight till dawn.... Ketchum made the strange request that he be buried face downward.
>
> Upon awakening this morning he...asked Sheriff Salome Garcia to hurry up with the hanging so he could get to hell in time for dinner. At 11:30 [a.m.] Ketchum asked for music. A violin and guitar were sent for.
>
> Ketchum talked over an hour with visitors, cooler than anyone who met him. He declared that death is preferable to imprisonment. Ketchum told of the robberies in which he was [accused], but declared he never killed a man, and only shot three. He said he is not Black Jack and that the bandit still lived. Ketchum refused to give the names of friends still at liberty.
>
> [At 1:17 p.m. Ketchum climbed the scaffold, looking] very pale..., but showed no fear. A priest stood at his side. [Standing over the trap door, Ketchum asked for a black hood and shook hands with Sheriff Garcia and several deputies.] He declined to make a speech and merely muttered:... "please dig my grave very deep," and finally, "All right, hurry up." [His final words were, "Let 'er go, boys, let 'er go."] Nerve did not fail him.
>
> [Sheriff Garcia cut the rope at 1:21 p.m., but when] the body dropped through the trap the half inch rope severed his head as cleanly as if a knife had cut it.... He alighted on his feet and his headless trunk stood for an instant upright, then swayed, then fell, and great streams of blood spurted out from the severed neck. The head, remaining in the black cap, rolled to one side and the rope, released, flew high in the air. No physician was needed to tell that life was extinct.
>
> He retained his nerve to the last and died game, like he said he would. He failed to make the speech [he had] promised, but included all

153. The words on Black Jack's new gravestone were chosen by Berry Spradley who writes that he "tried to find words that left a bit of hope for his soul."[43] The quotation is taken from Shakespeare's Hamlet, Act 3, Scene 3, in which Hamlet asserts, "And how his audit stands who knows save heaven." At the base of Black Jack's headstone is a second stone that reads: "Tom and brother Sam chose the outlaw trail and paid the ultimate price. Sam was shot by a posse and is buried in Santa Fe. Tom was hung in Clayton and is buried here." An anonymous admirer left flowers on Black Jack's grave for many years.

he had to say in his statement to his lawyer, [John R. Guyer]. He said he would advise all the boys not to steal sheep, cattle, or horses, but if they must steal, to rob a bank or a railroad train.[38]

Resting Place: originally in Clayton's old cemetery

Sheriff Garcia deliberately left Black Jack's original grave unmarked, causing later visitors to complain that they could not find the outlaw's gravesite.[39] As a result:

In 1933 the owner of [Clayton's new] cemetery, by permission, moved the body.... The disinterment was made on the afternoon of Sunday, September 10. It was a beautiful day and fully fifteen hundred curious citizens and strangers from every direction gathered for the occasion. It took two hours of careful work before workmen...struck the [outlaw's pine board box]. Meanwhile, Mr. H.H. Errett, of Clayton, mounted on a truck nearby, told the story of Black Jack's history. When the top of the coffin was removed, the remains of the outlaw were found in a remarkable state of preservation after over thirty-two years. His black hair and long thick mustache had turned a maroon red. His black suit still covered his body, but it [had] turned to a red-gray color. After having been viewed by the public, the remains were transferred to a new grave in the [new] cemetery where it [is still] today.[40]

Black Jack's new grave remained without a gravestone until the fall of 1987 when the Union County Historical Society arranged for the laying of a stone with the cooperation of Berry Spradley, Ketchum's great grand-nephew.[41]

After celebrating Dinosaur Days as a tourist attraction since 1989, the town of Clayton began celebrating the Black Jack Ketchum Festival in 2001, the centennial of Ketchum's death. As part of the festivities, Black Jack's capture was re-enacted at 11:00 a.m. on Saturday, June 2, 2001. After a break for lunch, his dramatic hanging was re-enacted, sans its decapitation, at 1:00 p.m. that same day.[42]
No. 153

Oliver Milton Lee, Jr.
Arrived in New Mexico in 1884; powerful owner of a million-acre ranch; accused, with Jim Gililland, of the murder of Albert J. Fountain and his son, Henry, February 1, 1896, but acquitted after seven minutes of jury deliberation in a famous trial held in Hillsboro from May 25 to June 13, 1899; also suspected in the December 26, 1894, death of "Frenchy" Rochas; Eugene Manlove Rhodes estimated that Lee was responsible for a total of eight deaths; New Mexico state legislator, 1918-32; Oliver Lee Memorial State Park on Lee's former ranch (with its rebuilt original ranch house) was named in his memory when it opened in 1979
Date of Birth: October 31, 1865

Place of Birth: Buffalo Gap, Texas
Date of Death (age): 9:10 p.m., December 15, 1941 (76)
Place of Death: Rousseau Hospital, Alamogordo, New Mexico
Cause of Death: paralytic stroke
Resting Place: Monte Vista Cemetery, Alamogordo, New Mexico[44] No. 154

154.

Marino Leyba

Known as the "Sandia Mountains' Desperado" for terrorizing local residents and travelers in the 1880s; suspected in the murder of a thirty-year-old U.S. geological surveyor, Colonel Charles Potter, in mid-October 1880; convicted of assault with intent to kill Pat Garrett, and served four years in the federal prison in Fort Leavenworth, Kansas, 1882-86
Date of Birth: July 25, 1857
Place of Birth: on the Rio Puerco, New Mexico
Date of Death (age): about 9:00 a.m., March 29, 1887 (29)
Place of Death: on the road southwest of Golden, New Mexico; a three-foot high wooden cross marked the location of his death until the 1950s[45]
Cause of Death: killed in a shootout with deputies Joaquin Montoya and Carlos Jacome
Resting Place: potter's field, Santa Fe, New Mexico

     Deputies Montoya and Jacome transported Leyba's body by wagon, stopping in Golden and other communities so that all could confirm that the bandit who had terrorized the region for so long was in fact dead. Once in Santa Fe, the body was placed on a table in the local jail where an estimated two thousand people passed by to see the notorious outlaw's remains.[46]

David "Dirty Dave" Rudebaugh

Las Vegas, New Mexico, policeman; murderer and thief who rode with Billy the Kid's gang in the lower Pecos River Valley; captured, along with Billy the Kid and two others by Pat Garrett on December 24, 1880
Date of Birth: July 1854
Place of Birth: unknown
Date of Death (age): February 18, 1886 (31)
Place of Death: Parral, Mexico
Cause of Death: decapitated by mob angered by Rudebaugh's killing of two card players in a Parral cantina, among other nefarious deeds
Resting Place: mob stuck his head on a pole and reportedly paraded it around the town plaza; final destination unknown[47]

Vicente Silva

Notorious leader of the Forty Thieves outlaw gang, controlled from his Imperial Saloon, south of the plaza in Las Vegas, New Mexico

Date of Birth: 1845
Place of Birth: near Albuquerque, New Mexico
Date of Death (age): May 18, 1893 (about 48)
Place of Death: camp in mountains outside Las Vegas, New Mexico
Cause of Death: shot by Antonio Valdez, one of Silva's Forty Thieves
Resting Place: Silva's gang robbed their dead leader's money belt and hastily disposed of his body in an arroyo; the body was later reburied in an unmarked grave in Las Vegas's potter's field[48]

William Rogers "Russian Bill" Tettenborn; also known as Feador Telfin, Bill Littenborn, William Tatenbaum, and Waldemar Tethenborn
Russian immigrant who aspired to be a Western outlaw; arrived in Shakespeare from St. Louis, Missouri, in 1878

155. Russian Bill's and Sandy King's headstone was erected by the John T. Muir Ranch

Date of Birth: unknown
Place of Birth: probably Russia, based on his accent
Date of Death (age): January 1, 1881 (unknown)
Place of Death: the rafters of the Grant House, Shakespeare, New Mexico
Cause of Death: lynched (along with Sandy King, also known as Jefferson King) by vigilantes for horse stealing
Resting Place: Shakespeare Cemetery, Shakespeare, New Mexico

Russian Bill's and Sandy King's bodies still hung from Shakespeare's Great House's rafters when startled stagecoach passengers arrived to rest from their travels the morning after the two men were lynched.

Later, when a Russian woman wrote to ask about her missing son, Shakespeare's sarcastic postmaster supposedly replied, "Dear Madam—I'm sorry to report that your son has died of throat trouble."[49] No. 155

William H. "Bronco Bill" Walters (Inmate No. 1282, New Mexico Penitentiary); also known as Broncho Bill Williams, J.C. Brown, Walter Brown, William Brown, W.C. "Bill" Brown, William Raper, Billy Swingle, and Kid Swingle
Outlaw, best known as a notorious train robber and the leader of a gang consisting of Bill "Kid" Johnson, Jim Burnett, and Daniel M. "Red" Pipkin
Date of Birth: 1869
Place of Birth: Austin, Texas
Date of Death (age): 2:00 p.m., June 16, 1921 (about 52)
Place of Death: Diamond A Ranch, Hachita, New Mexico
Cause of Death: broken neck suffered from an accidental fall off a windmill
Resting Place: Hachita Cemetery, Hachita, New Mexico[50]

156.

"Bronco Bill" lived for four hours after his fatal fall. Carried to a ranch house and placed in a bed, he asked the cowboys gathered around him to "Go bring the boy to me." The cowboys knew that Bill meant young Jethro S. Vaught, Jr., whom Bill had grown fond of since they'd met about 1919, after Walters's release from the state penitentiary in 1917. All suspected that Bill wanted to finally disclose where he had hidden the money he and Kid Johnson had stolen in their most famous train robbery, south of Belen in 1898. If that was Bill's intent, he failed, dying before Jethro could be found and brought to his bedside.[51] No. 156

John Joshua "J.J." Webb; also known as Sam King
A formerly respected businessman in Dodge City, Kansas, who came to Las Vegas, New Mexico, and became known as a member of Las Vegas's notorious Dodge City Gang; convicted of the murder of Michael Kelliher, March 10, 1880; escaped from jail, April 2, 1880
Date of Birth: February 14, 1847
Place of Birth: Jackson, Iowa
Date of Death (age): April 12, 1882 (35)
Place of Death: Winslow, Arkansas
Cause of Death: smallpox
Resting Place: probably Winslow, Arkansas[52]

Milton J. Yarberry; alias John Armstrong[53]
Albuquerque's first town marshal, albeit with a dubious past, in 1881; accused of killing an innocent bystander on an Albuquerque street in June 1881
Date of Birth: about 1844
Place of Birth: Walnut Ridge, Arkansas
Date of Death: 3:00 p.m., February 9, 1883 (about 39)
Place of Death: Albuquerque, New Mexico
Cause of Death: lynched by vigilantes for the June 1881 killing of Charles Campbell
Resting Place: Santa Barbara Cemetery, Albuquerque, New Mexico

With a black cap already drawn over his head prior to execution, Yarberry called out, "Gentlemen, you are hanging an innocent man."[54] Following his hanging, his body was lowered into a plain wooden coffin, the noose still around Yarberry's neck. He was the only peace officer legally or illegally executed in New Mexico territorial history.[55] No. 157

157. **For unknown reasons Yarberry's headstone (with his name misspelled) was removed from the Santa Barbara Cemetery and was kept in the San Felipe de Neri Church museum in Old Town Albuquerque for several years. It has since disappeared, so that only this image, taken by photojournalist Andy Gregg, remains.[56]**
Photo courtesy of Andy Gregg.

Other Infamous (or Suspected) Criminals include:
William Bonney (this chapter)
"Pancho" Griego (this chapter)
John Kinney (this chapter)
Ebin Stanley (Chapter 12: Wartime Leaders and Victims to the End of the Indian Wars in New Mexico, 1886)

Femmes Fatales and Other Notorious Women (in alphabetical order)

Paula Angel; alias Paula Martin
Tried and convicted of killing her two-timing lover, Juan Miguel Martín, on March 23, 1861; sentenced to be hanged by Judge Kirby Benedict, March 28, 1861; the first and only woman legally hanged in New Mexico history
Date of Birth: about 1834
Place of Birth: probably Loma Parda, New Mexico
Date of Death (age): shortly after noon, April 26, 1861 (about 27)
Place of Death: a large cottonwood tree a mile northwest of Las Vegas, New Mexico
Cause of Death: hanged twice (after the first attempt failed) by Sheriff Antonio Herrera
Resting Place: said to be a "special corner of the church yard," Las Vegas, New Mexico[57]

Paula's brother, Juan Angel, composed a *corrido* (ballad) in her honor. Much of the ballad consisted of Paula's imagined farewell to her family, friends, and familiar places. Its words included:

> Year 1861, how many pains and torments you have brought me, and today you hand me over to death! Have pity on me, everyone….

> I had honorable parents, whom I can never deny; as a disobedient daughter, I failed them. Heed my example, how I lost my grace….

> Let the bells ring sadly. Farewell, honorable priest. Farewell, unfortunate town. Farewell, infamous jail. Today I die from your rigor, O most inhuman fortune….

> Farewell, everyone. I have already left this world. O good Christian women, I was born to be unhappy; ask the bells to ring twice as sad for me.[58]

María Gertrudes "Doña Tules" "La Tules" Barceló
Powerful, controversial gambling hall operator of the Mexican and early U.S. territorial eras; central character in Ruth Laughlin Alexander's epic novel, *The Wind Leaves No Shadow* (1948)
Date of Birth: between 1800 and 1811
Place of Birth: probably Sonora, Mexico
Date of Death (age): January 15, 1852 (between 41 and 52)
Place of Death: at her home in Santa Fe, New Mexico
Cause of Death: many believe tuberculosis
Resting Place: beneath the floor of the Parroquia before St. Francis Cathedral was built over the old parish church, beside her granddaughter[59]

Doña Tules was buried in an elaborate ceremony that she had planned, largely in defiance of the local upper class that had always shunned her. Nearly all the citizens of Santa Fe attended the funeral on January 17, 1852. It reportedly cost $160, a small fortune in the mid nineteenth century.[60]

Mildred Clark "Madame Millie" Cusey; originally named Willette Angela Fantetti
Most famous madam of twentieth century New Mexico
Date of Birth: February 28, 1906
Place of Birth: a farm in Kentucky
Date of Death (age): November 8, 1993 (87)
Place of Death: Pinos Altos, New Mexico
Cause of Death: unstated natural causes; the "cause of death" question was left blank in her funeral home records
Resting Place: National Cemetery, Fort Bayard, New Mexico[61]

After a very active, controversial life, Madame Millie was said to be "up and lively" until two days before her death. She was buried with her husband, James Wendell Cusey, a Naval veteran of World War II, who had died on February 20, 1991.[62] No. 158

158.

Sarah Jane Creech "Sadie" Orchard
Arrived in New Mexico in 1886; Kingston and Hillsboro madame and, later, a stagecoach driver and innkeeper of the Ocean Grove Hotel in Hillsboro; perhaps most famous for once riding Lady Gadivia-style down the main street of Hillsboro to win a bet; Prohibition bootlegger; "Sadie" Orchard Day is now held in her honor
Date of Birth: August 1861 (as she told a census taker in 1900)
Place of Birth: London, England
Date of Death (age): 5:00 a.m., April 3, 1943 (81)
Place of Death: at her home "in the weather-beaten and deteriorated remains of her old hotel," Hillsboro, New Mexico[63]
Cause of Death: paralysis
Resting Place: Hot Springs Cemetery, Hot Springs (later renamed Truth or Consequences), New Mexico[64]

Near the end of her life, Sadie laughingly told an interviewer, "I'm a product of the 'Old West' and you know in those days we didn't have much chance to practice the niceties of high society."[65]

Sadie was buried in Hot Springs, rather than in her hometown of Hillsboro, because "Friends in charge of funeral arrangements said they were unable to have interment in Hillsboro cemetery since there is no longer anyone available for digging graves in the rocky hillside cemetery, where blasting is always necessary to make the excavations."[66]

Once Sadie's few possessions were sold off and funeral expenses were paid, only forty-five dollars remained.[67] No. 159

159. The inscribed date of Sadie's birth is incorrect.

160. Lottie's simple headstone is located a few feet behind her husband Frank's stone, just as Lottie had placed herself in the lookout chair slightly to the left behind Frank as he gambled in their early years.[72]

Charlotte J. Thompkins "Lottie" Thurmond; "Lottie Deno" "Angel of San Antonio" "Mystic Maud" "Aunt Lottie"

Red-haired female gambler known as the "Faro Queen" of Silver City; retired from gambling and moved to Deming in 1881; thought to be the inspiration for the Faro Nell character in Alfred Henry Lewis's popular Wolfville books, especially *Faro Nell and Her Friends* (1913), the Miss Kitty character in the *Gunsmoke* television series, and the Laura Denbo character in the movie *Gunfight at the O.K. Corral* (1957)

Date of Birth: April 21, 1844
Place of Birth: Warsau, Kentucky
Date of Death (age): 11:45 a.m., February 9, 1934 (89)
Place of Death: Deming, New Mexico
Cause of Death: "uremia and old age"[68]
Resting Place: Mountain View Cemetery, Deming, New Mexico[69]

Lottie Deno was famous for many near-death moments in her earlier gambling days, including one experience at a gambling hall called the Bee Hive in Fort Griffin, Texas, where she was dealing faro. Two gamblers, Smokey Joe and Monte Bill, killed each other in a gunfight, but Lottie never flinched. When the local sheriff declared that he and most others would have run for cover, she reportedly replied, "Then, Sheriff, you have never known a desperate woman. Besides, who was going to watch the pot?"[70]

Lottie Deno's obituary in the *Deming Graphic* never mentioned her gambling days in Texas and New Mexico prior to moving to Deming in 1881. Instead, the obituary noted her help in building the local Episcopal Church, her teaching Sunday School classes in the church, and her being a charter member of the Golden Gossip Club. The newspaper also noted the Revered William Sickels's graveside praise of her "wonderful devoted life, living only to make friends."[71] No. 160

Famous Adult Victims of Crime (in alphabetical order)

161. Photo courtesy of Jack Carmichael.

Mack Rubert Carmichael

Gallup's Deputy Sheriff, 1931-35, and Sheriff, January 1, 1935, to April 4, 1935
Date of Birth: December 16, 1896
Place of Birth: Higgins, Texas
Date of Death: April 4, 1935 (38)
Place of Death: alley behind the old post office, Gallup, New Mexico
Cause of Death: shot in the chest, face, and neck during a riot while accompanying defendants from the Gallup courthouse to jail; Ignacio Velarde, 38, was also killed, and at least five others were injured; the ten men accused of the riot were tried in a nine-day October 7-16, 1935, trial, leading to second-degree murder convictions for three and not guilty verdicts for the remaining seven

Resting Place: Higgins Cemetery, Higgins, Texas[73]

    Referred to by Gallup's mayor as "our martyr," Carmichael's funeral service was held in Gallup's Masonic Temple while all town businesses remained closed a day after the courthouse riot. Following the services, his remains were placed on board Santa Fe Railroad train No. 22 at 9:45 p.m. to be transported to his hometown of Higgins, Texas, for burial.[74] No. 161

Philip Horace "Phil" Chacon
U.S. Navy veteran; award-winning Albuquerque policeman and Community Relations Officer, 1973-80; had twice before captured burglary suspects during his off-duty hours; an Albuquerque police sub-station, a park, and a school library were named in this esteemed officer's honor
Date of Birth: May 22, 1944
Place of Birth: Albuquerque, New Mexico
Date of Death (age): September 10, 1980 (36)
Place of Death: at the southeast corner of the intersection of East Central Avenue and Wyoming Boulevard, Albuquerque, New Mexico
Cause of Death: shot by a suspected robber after an off-duty pursuit on his motorcycle; three men were tried for his slaying, but no one was ever convicted of the crime
Resting Place: Mount Calvary Cemetery, Albuquerque, New Mexico

162.

    Family members say that Phil never liked his middle name until he read about another Horace, Horace Mann, who once said, "Only a life lived for others is a life worthwhile." Phil like that ideal, living it to his dying day.

    On the twenty-fifth anniversary of Phil's death, his brother, Ted Chacon, and the Albuquerque Police Department celebrated Phil's life and achievements by placing a wreath near the spot where this hero was killed. The wreath bore the words "Phil 25" and included the image of a motorcycle like Chacon's. That same day, a mass was said and policemen fired a twenty-one gun salute and played taps at Phil's gravesite.[75] No. 162

Francisco "Frank" Chávez
A Democratic Party leader and former sheriff of Santa Fe County
Date of Birth: about 1851
Place of Birth: probably Santa Fe County, New Mexico
Date of Death (age): shortly after 10:00 p.m., May 29, 1892 (about 41)
Place of Death: en route home, near the Guadalupe Street bridge, Santa Fe, New Mexico
Cause of Death: assassinated, reportedly by agents of the Santa Fe Ring, which Chávez had opposed
Resting Place: Rosario Cemetery, Santa Fe, New Mexico

    The *Santa Fe New Mexican* reported that Chávez was killed as "The moon had gone down, the wind was blowing a stiff breeze, and the night was dark." Shot at least three times, an eyewitness recalled his last words: "The brutes have murdered me."[76]

Nearly three thousand people attended Chávez's funeral at St. Francis Cathedral, making it the largest funeral in Santa Fe since Bishop Jean B. Lamy's four years earlier. An estimated thousand mourners followed the body to Rosario Cemetery in fifty-one carriages or on foot. Organizations, including the Catholic Knights of America, the Frank Chávez Young Men's Democratic Club, and the city fire department led the procession.[77]

Reward money equaling $3,450 was quickly raised, with contributions from the territorial government ($200) and from many individuals, including Governor L. Bradford Prince ($100), Max Frost ($100), and Ralph Twitchell ($100), several of whom were identified with the Santa Fe Ring.[78]

Exactly three years after Chávez's assassination, Francisco Gonzales y Borrego, Antonio Gonzales y Borrego, Patricio Valencia, and "Chino" Alarid were found guilty of the crime in a highly publicized, thirty-seven day trial. On April 2, 1897, the four men were executed on a large scaffold within three blocks of where Chávez had been killed.[79]

Chávez's gravesite is no longer marked with a gravestone.

Melanie Milford Cravens
Wife and mother
Date of Birth: January 1, 1961
Place of Birth: Culver City, California
Date of Death (age): between 9:30 and 10:00 p.m., Christmas Eve, December 24, 1992 (31)
Place of Death: I-40, near 98th Street, en route to her mother's home in Albuquerque's Westgate Heights to go Christmas caroling
Cause of Death: killed, along with her three daughters, nine-year-old Kandyce (May 18, 1983-December 24, 1992), eight-year-old Erin L. (September 24, 1984-December 24, 1992), and five-year-old Kacee D. Woodard (February 9, 1987-December 24, 1992), in a head-on car crash with a truck traveling over ninety miles per hour in the wrong lane
Resting Place: Sunset Cemetery, Albuquerque, New Mexico[80]

An estimated 2,500 people packed the Victory Love Fellowship Chapel (seating capacity, eighteen hundred) for Melanie and her daughters' funeral. Led by the Reverend Rob Carman, the funeral was "transformed from a tragic goodbye into a vibrant crusade for DWI reform in New Mexico."[81] A funeral procession "of massive proportions" traveled to Sunset Cemetery in what Chester French Smith, president of French Mortuary, described as "the biggest funeral to ever have taken place in Albuquerque."[82]

Melanie was buried beside her three daughters. Only Melanie's husband,

163. At the top of their shared gravestone are the words: "Four Mighty Women of God." Below Kandyce's name are the words: "She was hope." Below Erin's name are the words: "She was love." And below Kacee's name are the words: "She was faith."

Paul Cravens, and the driver of the other vehicle, Gordon House, survived.

As a result of this tragedy, Melanie's mother, Nadine Milford, became an influential leader in the movement to prevent drunk driving. As Milford declared within days of the tragedy, "These girls are not going to die in vain. This story will be told over and over until something is done about DWI."[83] Milford's work as the chair of New Mexico's Mothers Against Drunk Driving (MADD) has led to the passage of tougher drunk driving laws in the state, although the problem persists and much is left to be done. No. 163

Albert Jennings Fountain
Member of the California Column; Indian fighter, lawyer, newspaper editor, play producer, agricultural college advocate, and a Doña Ana County Republican leader
Date of Birth: October 23, 1838
Place of Birth: Staten Island, New York
Date of Death (age): probably February 1, 1896, the date of his disappearance (57)
Place of Death: probably near Chalk Hill on the road home to Mesilla, New Mexico, although his body (along with his youngest son, Henry's) was never found
Cause of Death: murdered
Resting Place: a memorial headstone for Fountain and his son was placed in the Masonic Cemetery, Las Cruces, New Mexico[84]

As a controversial figure, Fountain's life had been threatened several times before his disappearance. His family was also threatened. In 1892 an assassin had fired a shot through Albert J. Fountain, Jr.'s bedroom window where the intended victim, his wife, and their infant son slept. According to a local newspaper, "Nothing but a miracle has prevented the person who fired the shot from being a murderer." Outraged, the senior Fountain offered a hundred-dollar reward for information that might lead to the conviction of those involved in the crime.[85]

Four years later, meeting Saturnino Barela, a mail carrier, on the road to Las Cruces, Fountain said that he saw three riders in the distance. Fountain told Barela that the riders had been traveling near him and his young son, Henry, "for miles. I am afraid they are going to attack us." When Barela suggested that the Fountains travel back to Luna's Well with him, Fountain opted to travel on since eight-year-old Henry had a cold and needed his mother's care. "I'll push along," said the father, "and take my chances." Albert and Henry Fountain were never seen again.

Oliver Lee and James Gililland were accused of the crime, but both were acquitted in June 1899. Years later, a lawman named Bob Lewis claimed that Sam Ketchum had told him that he had witnessed Tom "Black Jack" Ketchum kill the Fountains.[86]

A New Mexico state historical marker was placed on US 70 near where the Fountains were last seen alive.[87] No. 164

164.

Arthur Rockfort Manby; "Old Man Manby"

Englishman who arrived in New Mexico in 1889; involved in many questionable business schemes; Manby Hot Springs in Taos County were named in his memory

Date of Birth: July 14, 1859

Place of Birth: Morecambe, England

Date of Death (age): June 30, 1929 (69)

Place of Death: in his home in Taos, New Mexico

Cause of Death: doctors first concluded that he had died of natural causes, probably paresis, probably due to a massive stroke; a second death certificate claimed that he had been killed and decapitated.[88] His decapitated body was found in his double-locked house on July 3, 1929. Some speculated that his remains had been attacked by his five fierce guard dogs, also found in his house.

Resting Place: first buried in his garden, but exhumed on August 21, 1929, so that his cause of death could be investigated by three doctors; finally buried outside the entrance to the Kit Carson Cemetery, Taos, New Mexico[89]

165. The lettering on Manby's gravestone reads: "Arthur R. Manby. Born 1860, England. Died 1929, Taos. He planted the trees in this park and on Pueblo Road." The inscribed birth date is incorrect.

Within weeks of Manby's death, some accused him of perpetrating a hoax to avoid paying a twelve thousand dollar court judgement. According to this theory, "the body found...in Manby's home...was that of another man [procured from a local cemetery,] dressed in Manby's clothes and mutilated so that identification would be impossible." Although Manby's nephew called these charges "absolutely ridiculous," many believed that the "wealthy recluse" was quite capable of such outlandish behavior.[90]

Authors, including S.S. Van Dyne and Marquis W. Childs, became interested in Manby's classic "locked room" mystery within weeks of its occurrence. Childs asserted that there were "more interesting points in this Manby mystery than in perhaps any other murder story that has been published in decades."[91]

The Manby mystery has remained of interest to Taosenos for years.[92] A play by Steve Parks, entitled "Manby," played to packed houses in Taos in July and September 1977.[93] No. 165

166. In Ray Sutton's honor, his family placed a memorial headstone in the Clayton Cemetery, Clayton, New Mexico.

Raymond "Ray" Sutton, Sr.

Arrived in New Mexico in 1915; rancher; Sheriff of Union County, 1916-20; federal prohibition agent, 1920-33

Date of Birth: 1873

Place of Birth: Woodward County, Oklahoma

Date of Death (age): probably on August 30, 1930, three days after his abduction (about 57)

Place of Death: probably on the road to Dawson, New Mexico

Cause of Death: probably foul play; although a hundred-man posse was unable to find his remains

Resting Place: unknown

Sutton's disappearance while on duty as a prohibition agent remains one of the greatest unsolved mysteries in New Mexico history. The unworkable prohibition amendment was finally repealed four months following Sutton's tragic disappearance.[94] No. 166

Richard "Anasazi" Wetherill
Rancher, Indian trader, archeologist
Date of Birth: June 12, 1858
Place of Birth: Chester County, Pennsylvania
Date of Death (age): June 22, 1910 (52)
Place of Death: near his trading post, Rincon del Camino, Chaco Canyon, New Mexico
Cause of Death: shot and killed in an ambush by Chis-chilling-begay
Resting Place: buried near Pueblo Bonito in Chaco Canyon, New Mexico

Chis-chilling-begay was found guilty of manslaughter on June 8, 1912, and was sentenced to five to ten years in the state penitentiary in Santa Fe. He served less than three years of his sentence. Released on June 11, 1915, he lived to 1950, or until about his eightieth birthday.

Wetherill was not as rich as many believed. He died with $74.23 in the bank and about ten thousand dollars in largely uncollected debts. His widow, Marietta Palmer Wetherill, lived the rest of her life as what she called a "gypsy," finally moving to Albuquerque, where she died at the age of seventy-seven in 1954. Cremated, her ashes were buried in Richard's remote grave near Pueblo Bonito.[95] No. 167

167. Richard Wetherill's last name is incorrectly spelled "Wetherell" on his isolated gravestone. This can be seen in the larger version of this photograph on the cover of this book. **Photo courtesy of Kris White.**

Other Famous Adult Victims of Crime include:
Giovanni Maria "The Hermit" Augustini (Chapter 10: Religious Leaders)
James Bell (this chapter)
J. Francisco Chaves (Chapter 9: Political, Diplomatic, and Judicial Leaders)
Antonio José Chávez (Chapter 5: Business Leaders)
Milton E. "Doc" Noss (Chapter 7: Sung and Unsung Heroes)
François-Jean "Frenchy" Rochas (Chapter 2: Artists, Performers, and Directors)
John P. Slough (Chapter 12: Wartime Leaders and Victims to the End of the Indian Wars in New Mexico, 1886)
L. Edison "Bobcat" Wilson (this chapter)

Famous Young Victims of Crime *(in alphabetical order)*

Kaitlyn Clare "Kait" Arquette
1989 graduate of Albuquerque's Highland High School; she had planned to attend the University of New Mexico and become a doctor; daughter of famous children's literature author Lois Arquette (pen name, Lois Duncan)
Date of Birth: September 18, 1970
Place of Birth: Albuquerque, New Mexico

168.

Date of Death (age): July 17, 1989 (18)
Place of Death: her Ford Tempo car, on Lomas Boulevard near Broadway, Albuquerque, New Mexico
Cause of Death: shot in head in what police ruled was a random drive-by shooting, a conclusion contested by the Arquette family
Resting Place: Sunset Cemetery, Albuquerque, New Mexico

At Kait's memorial service, Dr. Harry Vanderpool asserted that in death Kait had helped to preserve life when her family donated six of her organs to five donor recipients, including a thirty-six-year-old man who received her lungs and heart.

The Arquette family continues to search for their daughter's killer. Lois Duncan has written a book on the mystery, entitled *Who Killed My Daughter?* (1992), and has appeared on many crime solving TV shows, including "Unsolved Mysteries."

Anyone with information about the case is urged to contact the Arquettes at Post Office Box 27187, Albuquerque, New Mexico 87125, or Cold Case Detective Don Roberts at (505) 768-2436. The family is offering a $25,000 reward.

The words on Kait's gravestone read:

> Warm Summer Sun, Shine Kindly Here.
> Warm Southern Wind, Blow Softly Here.
> Green Sod Above, Lie Light, Lie Light.
> Good Night, Dear Heart, Good Night,
> Good Night.

These words are quoted from Mark Twain's eulogy to his daughter Olivia Susan "Susy" Clemens (March 19, 1872-August 18, 1896), who had also died suddenly (of spinal meningitis) at a young age (24), having lived her short life with a parent (Twain) who was also a famous author. The quote appears on Susy's headstone in the family plot at Woodlawn Cemetery, in Elmira, New York. The words are from a poem by Robert Richardson.[96] No. 168

Ovida "Cricket" Coogler

Five-foot, two-inch waitress at the DeLuxe Café, Las Cruces, New Mexico, whose disappearance, rape, and murder led to charges of political corruption and police brutality, although her murder was never solved
Date of Birth: November 9, 1930
Place of Birth: Washington County, Florida
Date of Death (age): probably March 31, 1949, when she was reported missing (18)
Place of Death: remote shallow gravesite twelve miles south of Las Cruces, discovered by four rabbit hunters on Easter Sunday, 1949

Cause of Death: according to her death certificate, "violent death of which the nature is unknown"
Resting Place: Masonic Cemetery, Las Cruces, New Mexico[97]

Almost everything about Coogler's murder remains a mystery, including the lack of an autopsy, a question mark used to answer the question "cause of death" on her death certificate, and the presence of quicklime (that destroyed possible forensic evidence) in her coffin when it was exhumed for reexamination. As R.A. Durio, a member of the Doña Ana grand jury said, "It is hard to say what happened, but you could…tell someone was covering up something…. You can't make anyone tell you anything. You can get them under oath, and they'll still lie to you."[98] No. 169

169.

Dena Lynn Gore

Four-foot, nine inch, ninety-eight pound nine-year-old Artesia girl abducted, raped, and murdered by thirty-year-old Terry Douglas Clark, who had been convicted in June 1985 of kidnapping and raping a six-year-old Roswell girl on October 8, 1984, and had been sentenced to serve a total of twenty-four years, but had been released on fifty thousand dollar bail pending appeal of his earlier conviction; Clark murdered Dena Lynn within months of being released on bail
Date of Birth: October 12, 1976
Place of Birth: unknown
Date of Death (age): abducted July 17; body discovered July 22, 1986, after a search carried out by more than 120 volunteers (9)
Place of Death: Squaw Canyon Ranch (where Clark was employed as a ranch hand), sixty miles northwest of Artesia
Cause of Death: shot three times in the back of the head
Resting Place: Cedarvale Cemetery, White Oaks, New Mexico (beside her aunt, Joyce Ray, who had also died a tragic death, the victim of a car accident in El Paso, Texas, when she was only fifteen years old)

As funeral services for Dena Lynn were held in Artesia on July 25, 1986, protest rallies were staged beginning that Friday and lasting through the weekend in Roswell, the Chaves County seat. An estimated five hundred protesters gathered outside the county courthouse, carrying placards with angry messages criticizing Clark, the judge who had released him on bail, and Clark's public defender. A candlelight vigil was held on Sunday night, with an equally large crowd present.[99]

As a result of these protests, as well as a petition with the signatures of some twenty thousand citizens from across New Mexico, the state legislature passed legislation to prevent those convicted of certain felonies, especially rape, from being set free on bail while they appealed their cases. As stated on Dena Lynn's gravestone,

170. On the back of Dena Lynn's gravestone are the words: "This child's death made attempted changes in the laws of the state of New Mexico [possible] and to this child was given a beautiful memorial from all concerned citizens."

171.

her death was not in vain as it helped focus attention on a glaring problem in the state's legal system. The new law, enacted in 1988, is appropriately called the "Dena Lynn Gore Law."

Clark pleaded guilty to all charges and was sentenced to be executed on May 7, 1987. After fourteen years on death row and a second trial held in 1996, he became the first person to be executed in New Mexico in forty-one years. His execution by lethal injection took place at 7:00 p.m. on November 6, 2001. He was declared dead at 7:12 p.m.[100] No. 170

Angelina Eloisa Biatriz "Angie" Jaramillo
Venceslao Jaramillo and Cleofas Martinez Jaramillo's teenage daughter; the victim of one of the most famous murder mysteries in Santa Fe history
Date of Birth: October 6, 1913
Place of Birth: Santa Fe, New Mexico
Date of Death (age): 11:30 p.m., November 15, 1931 (18)
Place of Death: at her home in Santa Fe, New Mexico
Cause of Death: stabbed over her left ear
Resting Place: Rosario Cemetery, Santa Fe, New Mexico[101]

For Angelina's funeral at St. Francis Cathedral, "Every seat was filled. Friends and relatives from throughout the region and beyond had come to pay their respects. The entire student body at Loretto Academy [where she had been a student] tearfully said good-bye.... Carried into the cathedral by eight of her classmates dressed in white caps and gowns, Angelina was later borne on their shoulders as the crowd of mourners accompanied her [body] to the Rosario Cemetery."[102]

Thomas Johnson was captured in Albuquerque and found guilty of the murder, although his conviction has since been questioned. Johnson died in the electric chair in the New Mexico State Penitentiary on July 21, 1933, the first of seven men to be executed in this manner between 1933 and 1956. The electric chair was replaced by the gas chamber as the legal means of execution in New Mexico by 1960. No. 171

Samuel Alexander "Sam" Steel, Jr.
Highly admired, popular New Mexico A&M student scheduled to be the new college's first graduate in May 1893; Judge John R. McFie's nephew
Date of Birth: 1876
Place of Birth: Ireland
Date of Death (age): about 7:00 p.m., March 9, 1893 (about 17)
Place of Death: Mesilla Park, New Mexico
Cause of Death: held-up and murdered by John A. Roper, an intoxicated cowhand, while Sam delivered the evening milk from his family's dairy farm. Although Roper was found guilty of the crime and was sentenced to be hanged on April 18, 1893, he was released on appeal to a higher court.
Resting Place: Odd Fellows Cemetery, Las Cruces, New Mexico[103]

The Mesilla and Las Cruces communities were outraged by young Sam's murder. According to the local press, the crime was "one of the most cold-blooded murders ever perpetrated, and the greatest indignation and consternation exists…for it is felt that if such a thing can happen to a quiet inoffensive lad like Sam Steel, then no one's life is safe."¹⁰⁴

Describing Sam's funeral, the *Rio Grande Republican* reported:

> The grief at the loss of so promising a young citizen and the indignation at the cowardly murder brought out the largest number of mourners and followers that ever attended a funeral in [Las Cruces]. The church was literally crowded and not even standing room was left. All the faculty and students of the college attended in a body and we counted over forty carriages in the cortege.¹⁰⁵

Speaking at the funeral service, New Mexico A&M president Hiram Hadley said, "It is rather more than forty years since I consecrated my life to the work of education. In that period I have had under my care many brilliant youths, a large number of whom now fill exalted positions in their chosen callings, but taken, all in all, I have never known the superior, if the equal, of Samuel Steel."¹⁰⁶

Knowing of Sam's interest in entomology, A&M professors C.H. Tyler Townsend and T.D.A. Cockerell, named the Bergrothia steelii insect in his honor.

NMSU granted Sam an honorary Bachelors degree on May 15, 1998, 105 years after his death. A Sam Steel Society was created for alumni and friends of New Mexico State University's College of Agriculture and Home Economics; a campus road, named Sam Steel Way, was dedicated in November 1995.¹⁰⁷ No. 172

172.

Other Famous Young Victims of Crime include:
Henry Fountain (this chapter)
Kandyce Cravens (this chapter)
Erin L. Cravens (this chapter)
"Charley" McComas (Chapter 12: Wartime Leaders and Victims of War to the End of the Indian Wars in New Mexico, 1886)
Kacee D. Woodard (this chapter)

Colfax County War Participants, 1875-78 *(in alphabetical order)*
The Colfax County War was a period of prolonged frontier violence mainly between the Maxwell Land Grant and Railroad Company (associated with the Santa Fe Ring), which had purchased the 1,714,764.93-acre (2,679 square mile) land grant in 1870, and squatters who had settled on land they considered public domain.¹⁰⁸

Juan Francisco "Pancho" Griego
Monte dealer at the St. James Hotel where he shot four U.S. soldiers on May 30, 1875; notorious gunman for the Santa Fe Ring in the Colfax County War
Date of Birth: about 1837
Place of Birth: probably Santa Fe, New Mexico

173.

Date of Death (age): November 1, 1875 (about 38)
Place of Death: St. James Hotel, Cimarron, New Mexico
Cause of Death: killed in a shootout with Clay Allison
Resting Place: originally buried in Cimarron, but reinterred in Rosario Cemetery, Santa Fe, New Mexico, on March 4, 1877

Four days after his death, the *Santa Fe New Mexican* declared that Griego "had killed a great many men, and was considered as a dangerous man; few regret his loss."[109] No. 173

Oscar P. "O.P." McMains

Methodist minister, newspaper owner, territorial legislator, and active member of the Colfax County Anti-Grant Association; traveled to Washington, D.C., fourteen times to unsuccessfully plead the grant settlers' case from 1881 to 1896
Date of Birth: 1840
Place of Birth: Milford, Ohio
Date of Death (age): shortly after midnight, April 15, 1899 (about 59)
Place of Death: at his home in Stonewall, Colorado
Cause of Death: unstated natural causes
Resting Place: Stonewall Cemetery, Stonewall, Colorado

On his deathbed, McMains reportedly uttered his last words, telling friends, "Goodbye, goodbye, I can do no more."[110]

William Raymond Morley, Sr.

Railroad engineer and developer who surveyed the first railroad route into New Mexico via the Raton Pass, February 1878; a key leader of the anti-grant company faction in the Colfax County War; author Agnes Morley Cleaveland's father
Date of Birth: September 15, 1846
Place of Birth: Hampton County, Massachusetts
Date of Death (age): January 3, 1883 (36)
Place of Death: Santa Rosalia, Mexico
Cause of Death: allegedly accidentally shot with rifle[111]
Resting Place: originally in the Masonic Cemetery, Las Vegas, New Mexico, but, after vandalism to his large, impressive monument, moved by his grandson, Norman Cleaveland, to a private plot about two miles west of Datil, New Mexico, 107 years later, in October 1990

Realizing that he'd been shot, Morley told his companions, "I am a dead man.... Boys, I am sorry this has happened."[112]

When Morley's remains and monument were moved to Datil, about forty friends and relatives attended the ceremony. The Reverend Jake Snyder told the small crowd, "I don't know, of course, but I think the Morleys would want to be here." Looking around him at the beautiful countryside, Snyder added, "I think heaven must be a lot like this."[113] No. 174

174. Morley's monument in its original location in the Masonic Cemetery in Las Vegas. The monument, made of a rare Italian marble, includes a bronze plaque, which reads: "Wm. Raymond Morley. Born Sept. 15, 1846. Died Jan. 3, 1883. In whom were combined courage, loyalty, love and honor; every manly virtue and all noble qualities of heart. This monument is erected by his friends."[114] Photo courtesy of the New Mexico State University Library, Archives and Special Collections, #RG2001-03, Audrey Alpers Collection.

Franklin J. Tolby
Methodist minister and a key figure in the anti-grant company faction in the Colfax County War; Tolby Creek and Tolby Peak, near the scene of his murder, were named in his honor
Date of Birth: September 26, 1841
Place of Birth: White County, Indiana
Date of Death (age): September 14, 1875 (33)
Place of Death: Cimarron Canyon, near Clear Creek, outside Cimarron, New Mexico
Cause of Death: assassinated, supposedly on orders from the Santa Fe Ring, after he had criticized the ring's illegal activities in a national news story
Resting Place: Mountain View Cemetery, Cimarron, New Mexico No. 175

Other Colfax County War Participants include:
Robert Clay Allison (this chapter)
Samuel B. Axtell (Chapter 9: Political, Diplomatic, and Judicial Leaders)
Frank W. Springer (Chapter 6: Educational Leaders)

175. Franklin J. Tolby's original headstone is now displayed in a rather precarious location along the main floor hall in the St. James Hotel in Cimarron. Masons had replaced the stone with a new marker in the Mountain View Cemetery in the 1930s.[115]

Lincoln County War Participants, 1878-81
    The Lincoln County War was caused by a struggle for the political and economic dominance of Lincoln County. Warring factions were led by Lawrence G. Murphy, associated with the Santa Fe Ring, and newcomer John Tunstall, associated with a group that became known as the Regulators. According to a contemporary source, of the thirty graves dug in the town of Lincoln during a five-month period at the start of the war in 1878, only one person died of natural causes.[116]

The Regulators, their Families, and Imposters (in alphabetical order)
    The original Regulators, organized on March 1, 1878, were William Bonney, Charlie Bowdre, Dick Brewer, Henry Brown, Jim French, Frank McNab, John Middleton, Doc Scurlock, Sam Smith, and Fred Waite. Later members included George W. Coe, Ignacio Gonzales, John Scroggins, and "Dirty" Steve Stephens.

Catherine Antrim
Billy the Kid's mother; Catherine McCarty, came to New Mexico as a TB healthseeker by 1873; married William Henry Harrison "Bill" Antrim, Billy the Kid's step-father, in Santa Fe, March 1, 1873
Date of Birth: 1829
Place of Birth: Ireland
Date of Death (age): September 16, 1874 (about 45)
Place of Death: at her cabin on Main Street, Silver City, New Mexico
Cause of Death: tuberculosis
Resting Place: Memory Lane Cemetery, Silver City, New Mexico[117]
    Described as a "jolly Irish lady, full of fun and mischief," Catherine nevertheless suffered terribly from tuberculosis, from which she sought relief by

176. Catherine's original marker, now displayed at the Lincoln Courthouse Museum, Lincoln, New Mexico. Notice that her name (Kathrine) and date of death (September 8) were incorrect.

moving from New York to New Mexico with her two sons, Joseph and Billy. Despite treatments of warm sulfur water baths and confinement in bed for at least four months, her condition worsened in the fall of 1874. "As she lay in bed gasping for breath and coughing up crimson, Catherine realized she was dying.... [H]er only concern was for the well-being of her two boys. As a last request, she asked Clara Truesday, her nurse, to look after them" in what she referred to as "wild country."[118] Catherine could not have known that her younger son Henry (soon known as Billy the Kid) was about to make this "wild country" far wilder over the next seven years.

Catherine's modest funeral was held at her house at 2:00 p.m. on the day following her death. According to a woman from Silver City, a small express wagon was used to take Catherine's body to Silver City's original cemetery. "There was no undertaker.... They just got her body ready and fixed a box and...took her out."[119]

Catherine was later reinterred in the Memory Lane Cemetery, Silver City's newer graveyard.

Catherine's original grave marker, made of wood, was replaced with the present granite headstone by Sidney H. Curtis and S. Ernest Pollock (owners of a Silver City funeral home) in 1947. With no local museum to which to donate the original marker in 1950, the wooden piece was taken to the Lincoln Courthouse Museum in Lincoln, New Mexico, where it remains on display today.[120]

Silver City's Town and Country Garden Club requested that the New Mexico State Highway Department place an historical marker near the entrance to the Memory Lane Cemetery. Critics opposed such a marker, claiming that it would help draw attention to Catherine when her only contribution to history "was to inflict a predatory killer on society." Thanks to the efforts of historian Marc Simmons and others, calmer heads prevailed and a marker was installed and dedicated by 1984.[121] No. 176, No. 177

177. Catherine's new marker in Memory Lane Cemetery, Silver City, New Mexico. Notice that her first name is spelled incorrectly, as it was on her original wooden marker now in Lincoln.

William Henry "Billy the Kid" Bonney; also known as Henry McCarty, Henry Antrim, and Kid Antrim

Most famous gunslinger in New Mexico history, killing as many as twenty-one men, including Sheriff William Brady on April 1, 1878; key figure in the John Henry Tunstall faction in the Lincoln County War; Billy the Kid Spring, reportedly a Billy the Kid hideout, was named in his memory

Date of Birth: November 20, 1859

Place of Birth: probably 70 Allen Street, New York City, New York

Date of Death (age): about midnight, July 14, 1881 (21)

Place of Death: main bedroom of Pete Maxwell's house in Fort Sumner, New Mexico

Cause of Death: shot just above his heart by Sheriff Pat Garrett

Resting Place: Old Military Cemetery, Fort Sumner, New Mexico[122]

Found guilty on April 9, 1881, in a Las Cruces trial for the killing of Sheriff

William Brady, Billy the Kid's execution date was set for May 13, 1881. In the most famous escape in New Mexico history, the young outlaw broke out of the Lincoln County jail in Lincoln on April 28, 1881, killing jailers Jimmy Bell and Bob Olinger. Learning of his escape, the *Las Cruces Gazette* of May 13, 1881, wrote, "Billy the Kid was to have had his neck stretched here today. But since he has taken French leave from the Lincoln County jail, the matinee has been indefinitely postponed."[123]

Finally tracked down at Pete Maxwell's house in Fort Sumner, Billy the Kid was shot and killed by Lincoln County Sheriff Pat Garrett. Reportedly, his last words, uttered as he entered Maxwell's darkened bedroom, were, "*¿Quien es? ¿Quien es?*" ("Who is it? Who is it?")[124]

A coroner's jury examined Billy's body and decided that Garrett's act was "justifiable homicide and we are of the opinion that the gratitude of the whole community is owed to said Garrett for his deed." A wake followed, with Billy's remains placed on a workbench in a carpenter's shop, "the women placing lighted candles around it according to their ideas of properly conducting a 'wake' for the dead." Billy the Kid was buried on the afternoon of July 15, 1881, in the Old Military Cemetery at Fort Sumner. According to historian Frederick Nolan, "Practically the whole population attended the funeral, although who conducted the service—there was no priest—is not known for certain. After the burial a rough wooden cross was erected and the crowd dispersed."[125]

Newspapers in cities as distant as Los Angeles in the West and Boston in the East reported the news of Billy's demise.[126]

Controversy and legend have followed Billy in death, much as they had followed the outlaw in life. According to one story, local residents "cut off fingers and carried them away as trophies or souvenirs," a notion that a contemporary called "absurd, as the thought of such a thing never entered our minds, and, besides, we were not that kind of people."[127]

In another ugly rumor, a reporter for the *Las Vegas Daily Optic* claimed that Billy's body had been taken from Fort Sumner five days after his death. Brought to Las Vegas, New Mexico, the body was supposedly "slipped quietly into the private office of a practical 'sawbones,' who, by dint of diligent labor and careful watching to prevent detection, boiled and scraped the skin off the 'pate' so as to separate the skull." The skeleton was then "'fixed up'—hung together by wires and varnished with shellac to make it presentable," while the rest of the body was "covered in the dirt in a corral."[128]

Although this news story was undoubtedly a hoax, within two weeks of its publication a female admirer from Oakland, California, went so far as to write to the *Optic* and ask for one of Billy's body parts, specifically his severed finger. The newspaper's editor reported that he replied to the California woman's inquiry with a "sorrowful letter, full of touching condolence, and broke the news gently that we had just sold our relic of her lover for $150 cash." This follow-up story was probably just as fanciful as the original.[129]

Stories also began to circulate about Billy's grave marker. In one such tale,

178. Billy the Kid's footstone, erected in 1940 and stolen twice, 1950-76 and February 1981. Along the top of the stone are the words, "Truth and History." Above his name is the inscription, "21 Men," referring to the twenty-one men Billy the Kid reportedly killed in his twenty-one years of life. Below his name, given simply as "Billy the Kid," are his dates, including the incorrect birth date of November 23, 1860, which would have made him only twenty years old at the time of his death on July 14, 1881. Below Billy's dates are the words: "The Boy Bandit King. He died as he had lived."

179. Billy the Kid's gravestone, erected in 1931 on the fiftieth anniversary of his death. The stone is inscribed with the words: "PALS. Tom O'Folliard, died December 1880. William H. Bonney, alias Billy the Kid, died July 1881. Charlie Bowdre, died December 1880." Notice the chips along the edges of the headstone, the handiwork of intrusive souvenir hunters within months of its erection, according to the *Fort Sumner Leader* of October 14, 1932.

army soldiers of the late nineteenth century "took target practice at the [original] plain wooden marker."[130] In another tale, a local "person removed the marker from the site and took it home as one might [honor] the relics of a saint."[131]

Meanwhile, soldiers interred in the Old Military Cemetery were moved to the National Cemetery in Santa Fe by 1906. Some Fort Sumner pioneers believe that Billy's remains and those of his fellow outlaws may have been unintentionally removed to the National Cemetery. In the words of one old-timer, "Wouldn't it be ironic if those...desperados now rest in Santa Fe as 'Unknown Soldiers' with American flags over them?"[132]

In September 1904, a flood swept through the Old Military Cemetery, covering the area in four feet of water and carrying away or moving many grave markers, including Billy's.[133] For years, only a small metal marker marked the spot where tourists came to pay their respects in increasing numbers by the 1920s.[134] It was not until 1930 that the De Baca County Chamber of Commerce procured a stone marker to designate what they considered to be the location of Billy's grave. Reportedly, three of Billy's surviving pallbearers were asked to individually locate the outlaw's grave, but picked three different places in the cemetery. Billy's stone was placed in the middle of the three places. Knowing that Billy's friends, Tom O'Folliard and Charlie Bowdre, had been buried near Billy, the word "PALS" was placed at the top of the stone. Some say that King Vidor, the movie producer who made the first major Billy the Kid movie (starring Robert Taylor), donated the funds for the Kid's headstone, which was probably erected in 1931 for the fiftieth anniversary of Billy's death.[135]

In 1938 controversy arose when the Old Military Cemetery was sold to a private individual for back taxes. Townspeople were understandably nervous when they noticed that "a plow has chiseled an ugly ditch across the sacred plot... dangerously close" to several gravesites. The situation was said to have "rocked Fort Sumner to its very foundation" before it was finally resolved and the cemetery's grounds were again protected.[136]

A second marker, or footstone, was placed in 1940. A much smaller stone, it has been vulnerable to theft over the years. First taken in 1950, it was discovered under a boxcar in Granbury, Texas, twenty-six years later, in 1976. It was reset in the Old Military Cemetery to the accompanying music of bagpipes. Taken again in early February 1981, the stone was recovered on February 12, 1981, in Huntington Beach, California. Governor Bruce King sent De Baca County Sheriff "Big John" McBride to California to retrieve the stone and transport it home safely. The stone was reset in another formal ceremony held at the Old Military Cemetery on May 30, 1981. Jarvis Garrett, Pat Garrett's son, attended the ceremony during the centennial celebration of Billy the Kid's death, although the *De Baca County News* described Billy as no more than "a cold blooded murderer [who] got the justice he deserved."[137]

By 1982 Billy's footstone was anchored down with iron shackles and "a huge steel cage, with bars an inch thick, now cover[ing] the [entire] grave." Seeing the shackles and cage for the first time in the fall of 1982 historian Marc Simmons commented that "The next thief will need a bulldozer" to disturb Billy's famous stones.[138]

In 1962 a New Mexico District Court judge refused a request to rebury Billy in Lincoln, stating that the "lapse of time and natural causes" made it impossible to accurately locate the outlaw's body. Charlie Bowdre's relatives concurred with this decision, saying that Charlie's remains might be disturbed in the process of moving Billy's.[139] In 1981, the same year in which Billy the Kid's headstone was returned from California, the Fort Sumner village council refused a request to unearth Billy's remains to verify their identity.[140]

With all this confusion (moving bodies to the National Cemetery, the loss of Billy's wooden marker in the 1904 flood, the nearby burials of O'Folliard and Bowdre, and the stealing of his footstone in 1950 and 1981) it would be difficult—if not impossible—to find the exact location of Billy's remains. A body may yet be exhumed at Fort Sumner, but who is to say that it is actually Billy's, a soldier's, or one of his pal's?[141]

180. Billy the Kid's gravesite poorly secured behind a chain-and-link fence, probably in the 1950s or 1960s. Photo courtesy of the Palace of the Governors (MNM/DCA), Santa Fe, New Mexico, neg. no. 183299.

Despite this confusion, in May 2003 three southeastern New Mexico lawmen sought legal permission to compare Billy's DNA to his mother's in an attempt to end the seemingly endless dispute about Billy's identity and final resting place.[142] These efforts drew national attention, with press coverage in roughly two thousand newspapers, including the *New York Times*.[143] Faced with considerable opposition, the three officers finally dropped their request to exhume and test Billy's remains by September 2004.[144]

Glad to see the case dropped, given the value of Billy's grave as a tourist attraction, Fort Sumner Mayor Raymond López told the press, "Our main purpose was to keep Billy the Kid underground, and I think we succeeded."[145] A small contingent, led by historian Frederick Nolan, celebrated by traveling to the Old Military Cemetery and placing a bouquet of flowers on Billy's grave. Apparently not everyone was pleased with this turn of events. Three days later someone cut through three padlocks to enter Billy's fenced-in grave and remove the newly placed flowers.

In the most recent twist in the long history of the Kid's identity, the *Albuquerque Journal* of November 6, 2005, reported that DNA testing has been performed on John Miller, who claimed to be the outlaw, as well as on blood stains from a bench said to have come from the Maxwell house where Billy was shot.

Billy's grave is by far the most famous, most frequently visited gravesite in New Mexico.[146] As early as April 11, 1930, the *Fort Sumner Leader* reported that the local chamber of commerce had "markers erected on the highway, directing tourists [and their money!] through the Valley roads to the cemetery." Tourists regularly leave flowers and toss coins onto the grave. However, the site also continues to be the most controversial grave in the state, producing seemingly endless commentary in both the print and electronic media. An hour-long History Channel special, co-produced by historian Paul Hutton, aired on April 26, 2004. In Hutton's respected opinion, "Billy the Kid is buried in the

181. Billy the Kid's gravesite, more securely protected behind and below iron bars by the 2000s.

grave at Fort Sumner, unless someone dug him up in the intervening years [since 1881]."

In recent years, an annual Billy the Kid Tombstone Race has been held in Fort Sumner with up to $2,000 in prizes offered each June. In one version of the race, male contestants carry an eighty pound stone (about the weight of Billy's headstone) a distance of twenty-five yards, clearing two hurdles en route. In the women's race, contestants carry a twenty pound stone over the same distance, sans hurdles.[147] No. 178, No. 179, No. 180, No. 181

Richard M. "Dick" Brewer

Foreman of John Henry Tunstall's horse and cattle ranch who witnessed Tunstall's February 18, 1878, killing; gunman in the Lincoln County War
Date of Birth: February 19, 1850
Place of Birth: St. Albans, Vermont
Date of Death (age): April 4, 1878 (28)
Place of Death: Blazer's Mill, New Mexico
Cause of Death: shot by Andrew "Buckshot" Roberts at the Blazer's Mill battle of the Lincoln County War
Resting Place: Blazer Cemetery, Mescalero, New Mexico

Brewer's marble stone was placed at his gravesite by his descendants. Ironically, Brewer is buried next to Buckshot Roberts, the man who killed him.[148]

Alexander Anderson "Mac" McSween

Arrived in Lincoln, New Mexico, in March 1875; John Henry Tunstall's lawyer, business partner, and ally; a key figure in the Lincoln County War
Date of Birth: between February and May 1843
Place of Birth: Prince Edward Island, Canada
Date of Death (age): about 9:00 p.m., July 19, 1878 (35)
Place of Death: at his burning house in Lincoln, New Mexico
Cause of Death: shot five times at the Battle of Lincoln
Resting Place: Although a cross is displayed behind his and Tunstall's store, McSween was buried in a lot he had planned to use as a site for a future church, east of his store in Lincoln. (See No. 186.) McSween's frugal wife, Susan, reportedly thought it was a waste of money to erect a marker over her husband's grave.[149]

As McSween was surrounded by his enemies and his house burned, the lawyer reportedly called out, "I shall surrender." But then McSween changed his mind, crying out, "I shall never surrender." Both sides opened fire, shooting blindly and at close range, leaving McSween and two others dead within moments.[150] No. 182

182. Alexander McSween's memorial cross behind his and John Tunstall's store, beside a memorial cross for Tunstall.

Susanna Ellen Hummer (or Homer) Barber "Susan" "Sue" McSween

Married on August 23, 1873, in Atchison, Kansas, to Alexander McSween, John Henry Tunstall's lawyer, business partner, and ally in the Lincoln County War;

married George B. Barber on June 20, 1880, but divorced him on grounds of abandonment, October 16, 1891; rancher, known as the "Cattle Queen of Lincoln County"
Date of Birth: December 30, 1845
Place of Birth: Tyrone, Pennsylvania
Date of Death (age): 8:00 p.m., January 3, 1931 (85)
Place of Death: at her home in White Oaks, New Mexico
Cause of Death: influenza
Resting Place: Cedarvale Cemetery, White Oaks, New Mexico[151]

183. McSween is spelled incorrectly on Susan's gravestone.

According to an 1892 article about Susan, written in the *New York Commercial Advertiser*, "Near the town of White Oaks, New Mexico, lives one of the most remarkable women of this remarkable age.... A woman who can run a ranch, build a house, manage a mine and engineer a successful [project] deserves a prominent place in the ranks of women of genius."[152]

In 1930 MGM produced a highly fictionalized movie version of Billy the Kid's life. The press reported that Susan "was taken to Carrizozo a few days before her death to see the new movie and was thoroughly incensed...because of the liberties that the author of the screen version took with the historical facts."[153] Newspapers did not speculate if Susan's reaction to the movie had any impact on her health and rapid decline. No. 183

John Miller
Claimed to be Billy the Kid
Date of Birth: December 1850
Place of Birth: Fort Sill, Oklahoma
Date of Death (age): 6:30 p.m., November 7, 1937 (86)
Place of Death: Arizona Pioneers' Home in Prescott, Arizona
Cause of Death: unstated natural causes
Resting Place: unmarked grave at the Arizona Pioneers' Home Cemetery, Prescott, Arizona

Miller's stories about his life as Billy the Kid were told only privately, and his obituary in the *Prescott Evening Courier* never mentioned the claim. Instead, his obituary stated that Miller "was not a man to make up stories about himself [so] consequently what he had told [people] has been taken as the truth."[154] His body has nevertheless been exhumed so his DNA can be examined by a Texas-based laboratory, according to the *Albuquerque Journal* of November 6, 2005.

Ollie Partridge "Brushy Bill" Roberts; "Kid Roberts" "Rattlesnake Bill" "Hugo Kid" "Billy the Kid"
Claimed to be Billy the Kid; sought a full pardon from Governor Thomas Mabry, but, after a famous interview with Roberts at the Governor's Mansion in Santa Fe on November 29, 1950, Mabry rejected Roberts's claim and refused to grant a pardon

184. The names William Henry, rather than Ollie Partridge, probably appear on Roberts's gravestone because Roberts claimed to be Billy the Kid and William Henry were William Henry Bonney's given names. Photo courtesy of Ray Weathers

Date of Birth: December 31, 1859
Place of Birth: Buffalo Gap, Texas
Date of Death (age): 1:00 p.m., December 27, 1950 (90)
Place of Death: standing in front of the local newspaper office in Hico, Texas
Cause of Death: heart attack en route to deliver a package for his wife
Resting Place: Oakwood Cemetery, Hamilton, Texas[155]

Reportedly, Roberts's first headstone gave December 31, 1868, as his date of birth, making him only twelve when Billy the Kid faced Pat Garrett in Fort Sumner in July 1881. This original stone was later replaced, with a new birth date, December 31, 1859, making him twenty-one in 1881.

On March 1, 1989, the television series "Unsolved Mysteries" featured Brushy Bill's contention that he was Billy the Kid. Lincoln County residents reacted to the show with comments like "poorly done," "lousy," and "fraudulent."[156]

Even computers have been used to compare photos of Billy the Kid and Brushy Bill in an effort to finally answer the question of their true identities.[157]

Hico, Texas, Roberts's hometown, celebrates Brushy Bill's claim with a Billy the Kid Museum and an annual Billy the Kid Day each spring.[158] No. 184

John Henry Tunstall

English rancher who arrived in Lincoln, New Mexico, on November 6, 1876, and soon challenged the economic and political domination of Lawrence G. Murphy, leading to the Lincoln County War; Tunstall Canyon was named in his honor
Date of Birth: March 6, 1853
Place of Birth: London, England
Date of Death (age): about 5:30 p.m., February 18, 1878 (24)
Place of Death: Tunstall Canyon about ten miles from Lincoln, New Mexico, as he rode with four of his men, including Billy the Kid, en route from his ranch to town[159]
Cause of Death: killed by Sheriff William Brady's posse at the onset of the Lincoln County War
Resting Place: Although a cross is displayed behind his Lincoln store in his memory, he was buried in a lot that Alexander McSween had planned to use as a site for a future church, east of the store the two had owned. George and Frank Coe, Dick Brewer, and Billy the Kid served as pallbearers at Tunstall's funeral. A large crowd of Anglos and Hispanics attended, with the services translated from English into Spanish.[160]

185. John Tunstall's memorial cross behind his and Alexander McSween's store, beside a second memorial cross placed for McSween.

Although Alexander McSween had written to Tunstall's family about procuring a headstone in St. Louis, Missouri, nothing came of this suggestion. Historian Frederick Nolan believes that the epitaph for such a headstone would have read much like the "death card" Tunstall's family received in far-off London:

In Remembrance of
John Henry Tunstall
The Only Beloved Son of
John Partridge and Emily Tunstall
Who Died February 18, 1878,
In Lincoln County, New Mexico.
Aged 24 Years.

"Weep ye not for the dead, neither bemoan him: but weep sore for him that goeth away: for he shall return no more, nor see his native country."[161]
No. 185, No. 186

186. The suspected site of Tunstall and McSween's real graves, east of their store in Lincoln.

Richard Bonney "Uncle Dick" Williams
Claimed on his deathbed that he was the real Billy the Kid
Date of Birth: 1860
Place of Birth: unknown
Date of Death (age): 1934 (about 74)
Place of Death: Barton, New Mexico
Cause of Death: unstated natural causes
Resting Place: Mountain Valley Cemetery, Edgewood, New Mexico

187. Richard Williams's original headstone read "William Bonney."[163]

Moving to the Edgewood area with his wife in about 1918, Williams was said to be a quiet, well-liked man who was a good shot and had a fondness for horseracing. He nevertheless avoided all picture taking and always traveled in his wagon with an Indian blanket across his lap to cover the rifle or pistol he kept with him at all times.

Just prior to his death, Williams called two friends, Orville Guest and Pete Reeves, to his bedside and declared, "I am William Bonney, who was known as Billy the Kid." Williams made his friends swear to keep the news secret until he had died.[162] No. 187

The Lawrence G. Murphy Faction (in alphabetical order)

William Brady
Indian fighter, 1851-61; Civil War Union officer with the New Mexico Volunteers, 1861-66; Sheriff of Lincoln County, 1876-78
Date of Birth: August 16, 1829
Place of Birth: Cavan, Ireland
Date of Death (age): about 10:00 a.m., April 1, 1878 (48)
Place of Death: Lincoln, New Mexico
Cause of Death: ambushed and killed (along with George W. Hindman) by Billy the Kid and at least five others outside the Tunstall Store, Lincoln, New Mexico

188.

189. James Dolan's gravestone incorrectly gives his birth date as May 2, 1848, the day he was baptized.

Resting Place: originally in the Lincoln Cemetery, but later moved by his family to his private ranch east of town[164] No. 188

James Joseph "Jimmy" Dolan

Union Army soldier in the Civil War and after, 1863-69; Lawrence G. Murphy's business associate and close ally in the Lincoln County War; Lincoln County treasurer, 1884-88

Date of Birth: April 22, 1848

Place of Birth: Loughrea, County Galway, Ireland

Date of Death (age): February 26, 1898 (49)

Place of Death: at his Flying H Ranch on the Feliz River, New Mexico

Cause of Death: cerebral hemorrhage

Resting Place: buried at the Spring Ranch below Fritz cemetery near the Rio Bonito, New Mexico

Ironically, Dolan eventually acquired John Henry Tunstall's ranch, making it his home and naming it the Flying H.[165]

The epitaph at the base of his headstone reads:

> Thy gentle voice now is hushed.
> Thy warm true heart is stilled.
> God in his wisdom has recalled
> The boon his love had given. No. 189

John William Young Kinney

U.S. Army cavalryman, 1867-73; arrived in New Mexico 1868; gunman for the Lawrence G. Murphy faction in the Lincoln County War; leader of the Kinney Gang of cattle rustlers; known in New Mexico as the "King of the Rustlers"; found guilty of the February 6, 1883, murder of Frank Emmons; sentenced to seven years in prison, but served less than three; Arizona businessman

Date of Birth: August 31, 1847 or 1848 or 1853

Place of Birth: Hampshire, Massachusetts

Date of Death (age): August 25 or 28, 1919 (65, 70, or 71)

Place of Death: Prescott, Arizona

Cause of Death: Bright's disease (glomerulonephritis)

Resting Place: IOOF Cemetery, Prescott, Arizona[167]

After peacefully living the last twenty years of his life in Prescott, Arizona, Kinney's obituary in the *Prescott Journal-Miner* was laudatory in the extreme, claiming that in his early days Kinney "was known in the Southwest as one of the most daring and courageous in the annals of men who were sacrificing and unflinching [in their efforts] to preserve law and order"![168] No. 190

Jacob Basil "Billy" Mathews

Union Army soldier in the Civil War; arrived in New Mexico in 1867; deputy sheriff in charge of the posse that shot John Henry Tunstall (on February 18,

190. Photo courtesy of David N. Lotz.

1878), starting the Lincoln County War; present at the April 1, 1878, murder of Sheriff William Brady and at the July 1878 Battle of Lincoln; later a well-known rancher and farmer

Date of Birth: May 5, 1847

Place of Birth: near Woodbury, Tennessee

Date of Death (age): June 3, 1904 (57)

Place of Death: Roswell, New Mexico

Cause of Death: pneumonia

Resting Place: South Park, Roswell, New Mexico[169]

According to the *Roswell Daily Record*, all were saddened to hear of Mathews's death "not because he had been a popular official, not because he had been a brave soldier in war, and a man who in the early days of the Territory had been a terror to the evil doers, but [because] he was honored and respected for his own innate qualities of manhood that won everybody to him…. No more popular man has ever lived or died in Chaves County."[170] No. 191

191.

Lawrence Gustave Murphy

Kit Carson's Quartermaster in the Union Army during the Civil War; dominant political and economic leader of Lincoln County prior to the Lincoln County War; had strong ties to the Santa Fe Ring; owner of the L.G. Murphy and Company mercantile store in Lincoln and the Bar W Ranch in Lincoln County

Date of Birth: 1831

Place of Birth: Wexford, Ireland

Date of Death (age): 7:00 a.m., October 20, 1878 (about 47)

Place of Death: St. Vincent Hospital, Santa Fe, New Mexico

Cause of Death: effects of alcoholism and cancer of the bowels

Resting Place: originally in the old Masonic and Odd Fellows Cemetery, Santa Fe, New Mexico; later in the National Cemetery, Santa Fe, New Mexico

In 1927 Frank Coe told an interviewer that the sisters at St. Vincent Hospital "would not let [Murphy] have whiskey and that cut his living off. He died in a short time and everybody rejoiced in it."

Heavily in debt to Thomas Catron and the First National Bank of Santa Fe when he died, Murphy's estate sold his Bar W Ranch to British investors for $225,000.[166] No. 192

192.

George Warden "Dad" Peppin

U.S. Army California Column volunteer in the Civil War, 1861-64; stonemason; present at the April 1, 1878, murder of Sheriff William Brady; successor to Sheriff William Brady and leader of the Murphy-Dolan faction at the five-day Battle of Lincoln, July 15-20, 1878, during the Lincoln County War

Date of Birth: October 1841

Place of Birth: Mountville, Vermont

Date of Death (age): September 18, 1904 (62)
Place of Death: at his home in Lincoln, New Mexico
Cause of Death: "bowel trouble"
Resting Place: Lincoln Cemetery, Lincoln, New Mexico[171] No. 193

Andrew L. "Buckshot" Roberts; also known as Bill Williams; also known as Jesse Andrews
Member of the Murphy-Dolan faction in the Lincoln County War
Date of Birth: unknown
Place of Birth: unknown
Date of Death (age): April 5, 1878 (unknown)
Place of Death: Blazer's Mill, New Mexico
Cause of Death: killed in the Battle of Blazer's Mill
Resting Place: Blazer Cemetery, Mescalero, New Mexico

Shortly after killing Dick Brewer in the Battle of Blazer's Mill, Roberts was also killed; ironically Roberts and Brewer are buried side-by-side at the top of a heavily-shaded hill.[172]

Other Key Lincoln County War Participants *(in alphabetical order)*

193.

Frank Warner Angel
Lawyer; author of a voluminous, controversial federal report on troubles in Lincoln County, which led to the dismissal of Governor Samuel Axtell and the appointment of Governor Lew Wallace in 1878
Date of Birth: May 28, 1845
Place of Birth: Watertown, New York
Date of Death (age): 5:30 a.m., March 15, 1906 (60)
Place of Death: at his home in Jersey City, New Jersey
Cause of Death: a stroke
Resting Place: unknown[173]

James W. "J.W." "Long Bell" "Jimmy" Bell
Deputy sheriff killed by Billy the Kid during Billy's infamous Lincoln County courthouse escape, April 28, 1881
Date of Birth: 1853
Place of Birth: unknown
Date of Death (age): April 28, 1881 (about 28)
Place of Death: Lincoln County Courthouse, Lincoln, New Mexico
Cause of Death: shot
Resting Place: Cedarvale Cemetery, White Oaks, New Mexico

Billy the Kid killed two guards when he escaped from the Lincoln County courthouse: James Bell, whom Billy said he regretted killing, and Ameridth Robert B. "Bob" Olinger (April 1850-April 28, 1881), whom he did not.[174]

194. James Bell's new headstone was paid for by the New Mexico Sheriffs and Police Association.

Stone markers indicate the location of the two guards' deaths outside the courthouse, Bell to the south and Olinger (incorrectly identified as Robert M. Olinger) to the east.

On Saturday morning, July 19, 2003, Lincoln County Sheriff Tom Sullivan led a group of a hundred or more local residents, many in period costumes, to dedicate a new headstone at Bell's gravesite. A priest said a few words, and someone played "Rock of Ages" on an old hand-cranked organ. A wake and mock gunfight followed at the nearby No Scum Allowed Saloon in White Oaks. No. 194

Nathan Augustus Monroe Dudley
Union Army officer in the Civil War; controversial Army officer at several New Mexico forts, perhaps most noted for his lack of action after his arrival with four officers, twenty-four white infantrymen, and eleven Buffalo Soldiers on July 19, 1878, at the Battle of Lincoln, July 15-20, 1878
Date of Birth: August 20, 1825
Place of Birth: Lexington, Massachusetts
Date of Death (age): April 29, 1910 (84)
Place of Death: Roxbury, Massachusetts
Cause of Death: unstated natural causes
Resting Place: National Cemetery, Arlington, Virginia[175] No. 195

195. Photo courtesy of David N. Lotz.

Peter Menard "Pete" "Pedro" Maxwell
Lucien Maxwell's oldest son; owner of the Fort Sumner house where Sheriff Pat Garrett shot Billy the Kid, July 14, 1881; present in the house's darkened bedroom where Billy was shot
Date of Birth: April 27, 1848
Place of Birth: Taos, New Mexico
Date of Death (age): June 21, 1898 (50)
Place of Death: Fort Sumner, New Mexico
Cause of Death: unstated natural causes
Resting Place: Old Military Cemetery, Fort Sumner, New Mexico[176]

Historian Frederick Nolan notes that "According to local [Fort Sumner] tradition, after [Pete's] ignominious flight from the bedroom [after] the Kid was killed, [Maxwell] was always referred to as 'Don Chootme' [Don't Shoot Me]."[177] No. 196

Other Key Players in the Lincoln County War include:
Samuel B. Axtell (Chapter 9: Political, Diplomatic, and Judicial Leaders)
John Chisum (Chapter 5: Business Leaders)
Pat Garrett (this chapter)
William Logan Rynerson (Chapter 12: Wartime Leaders and Victims to the End of the Indian Wars in New Mexico, 1886)
Lew Wallace (Chapter 9: Political, Diplomatic, and Judicial Leaders)

196. The epitaph at the foot of Pete Maxwell's grave reads: "No pains, no griefs, no anxious tears can reach our loved one sleeping here." Maxwell is buried several yards south of Billy the Kid's grave.

POLITICAL, DIPLOMATIC, AND JUDICIAL LEADERS

9

Spanish Colonial Governors *(in chronological order by term of service)*[2]

Don Juan de Oñate y Salazar
Spanish conqueror and settler of New Mexico, 1598, as chronicled in Gaspar Pérez de Villagrá's *Historia de la Nueva México* (1610); Spanish Governor and Captain-General of New Mexico, 1598-August 24, 1607; found guilty of abusing his authority as governor; largely absolved of all charges by King Felipe IV, August 11, 1623; appointed to the Military Order of Santiago, 1625; two streets in Albuquerque, a street in Santa Fe, an elementary school in Albuquerque, and a high school in Las Cruces were named in his honor
Date of Birth: 1552
Place of Birth: Zacatecas, New Spain
Date of Death (age): on or about June 3, 1626 (about 74)
Place of Death: in a mine he was inspecting in Guadalcanal, Spain
Cause of Death: unstated natural causes
Resting Place: probably within the main Catholic church, Guadalcanal, Spain[3]

    An impressive twelve-foot high bronze equestrian statue of Oñate stands in Alcalde, New Mexico. On January 7, 1998, at the beginning of the four hundredth anniversary of Oñate's conquest of New Mexico, someone removed the statue's right foot, apparently in protest over the governor's removal of the right feet of twenty-four Acoma warriors following the Acoma Revolt of 1598-99. The incident at Alcalde was only the first salvo in a year-old debate regarding Oñate's controversial role in New Mexico history.[4]

Don Diego José de Vargas Zapata Luján Ponce de León y Contreras
Spanish re-conqueror of New Mexico, 1692-93; Spanish Governor and Captain-General of New Mexico, 1692-97 and 1703-04; four streets in Albuquerque and two streets, a mall, and a middle school in Santa Fe were named in his honor
Date of Birth: November 8, 1643
Place of Birth: Madrid, Spain
Date of Death (age): about 5:00 p.m., April 8, 1704 (60)
Place of Death: Fernando Durán y Chaves's house in Bernalillo, New Mexico
Cause of Death: probably dysentery

"How many people come to [a politician's] funeral will depend a great deal more on the weather that day than what he'd done."
—A political leader's observation shared with Bruce King, Governor of New Mexico, 1971–75, 1979–83, 1991–95[1]

Resting Place: probably the now-destroyed chapel in the Palace of the Governors, Santa Fe, New Mexico. A photo of the sign indicating the probable location of the chapel in which Vargas was buried is included in Chapter 1, No. 1.

On his deathbed in Bernalillo, Vargas dictated his will, including his desire to lie in state before the main altar of the main church in Santa Fe for nine days. His casket was to be surrounded by no less than a hundred candles.[5]

The annual Santa Fe Fiesta celebrates Vargas's re-conquest of New Mexico.

Juan Bautista de Anza the Younger
Spanish explorer; Spanish Governor and Captain-General of New Mexico, 1778-87; defeated and established peace with the Comanches, 1786; a street in Albuquerque was named in his honor
Date of Birth: July 7, 1736
Place of Birth: Cuquiárachi, Sonora, New Spain
Date of Death (age): December 19, 1788 (52)
Place of Death: Arizpe, Sonora, New Spain
Cause of Death: unstated natural causes
Resting Place: Nuestra Señora de la Asuncion Church, Arizpe, Sonora, New Spain[6]

Mexican Era Leaders (in chronological order by term of service)[7]

Manuel Armijo
Controversial Mexican Governor of New Mexico, 1827-29, 1837-44, and 1845-46, including during the U.S. conquest of New Mexico, 1846; leader of counter-revolutionary forces in the Revolt of 1837; a street in Santa Fe was named in the Armijo family's honor
Date of Birth: 1790
Place of Birth: Plaza de San Antonio, New Mexico
Date of Death (age): December 9, 1853 (about 63)
Place of Death: at his home in Lemitar, New Mexico
Cause of Death: unstated natural causes
Resting Place: buried either in the church or about six feet to the left of the entrance to the San Miguel Catholic Church, Socorro, New Mexico

Four days after Armijo's death, Dr. Henry Connelly proposed the following resolution to his fellow members of the Territorial Council in Santa Fe:

Resolved, That this Council has heard with profound regret of the death of our distinguished citizen, General Armijo, who expired on the ninth day of this month.

Resolved, That this Council offer the most sincere condolence to the family and friends of General Armijo and to

197.

the Territory for the loss of one of its greatest benefactors.

Resolved, That in respect to the memory and distinguished services of General Armijo this Council now adjourns until 10 o'clock tomorrow.[8]
No. 197

Albino Pérez
Controversial Mexican governor of New Mexico, 1835-37, including during the Revolt of 1837
Date of Birth: unknown
Place of Birth: probably Mexico City, Mexico
Date of Death (age): August 9, 1837 (unknown)
Place of Death: near today's Agua Fria Road, Santa Fe, New Mexico
Cause of Death: killed and beheaded by rebels in the Revolt of 1837
Resting Place: Santa Fe "city graveyard"[9]

According to Santa Fe Trail merchant Josiah Gregg, who was present in Santa Fe at the time, Pérez was "chased back to the suburbs of the city, and savagely put to death [by rebel soldiers]. His body was then stripped and shockingly mangled; his head was carried as a trophy to the camp of the insurgents, who made a foot-ball of it among themselves." Other [government] leaders were mutilated, tortured, and killed by the rebels, with their "bodies…for several days exposed to the beasts and birds of prey."[10]

In the early twentieth century the Sunshine (now the Stephen Watts Kearny) Chapter of the Daughters of the American Revolution erected a monument in Pérez's honor on Agua Fria Street, Santa Fe, where he had been brutally killed. A large rock, the monument has since been moved to the interior courtyard at the Palace of the Governors, Santa Fe, New Mexico.[11]

José Angel Gonzalez
Rebel governor of New Mexico during the ill-fated Revolt of 1837
Date of Birth: April 14, 1799 (baptismal date)
Place of Birth: San Francisco del Rancho, New Mexico
Date of Death (age): January 27, 1838 (38)
Place of Death: Santa Cruz, New Mexico
Cause of Death: executed for his role in the revolt
Resting Place: probably Santa Cruz, New Mexico

After Gonzalez respectfully greeted the leader of the counter revolution of 1837, General Manuel Armijo, Armijo reportedly declared, "Confess yourself, my friend, for I am going to have you shot." Once Padre Antonio José Martínez had heard the undoubtedly stunned rebel governor's confession, Gonzalez was shot five times, as ordered by General Armijo, who then assumed the governorship of New Mexico for the second of three times in his career.[12]

According to one historian, "The rise and fall of José Gonzalez was so rapid that almost no biographical details were recorded."[13]

Other Mexican Era Leaders include:
Donaciano Vigil (this chapter)

U.S. Territorial Governors *(in chronological order by term of service)*

Charles Bent
Co-owner of Bent, St. Vrain and Company, a freighting and commercial venture, founded in 1830; a founder of Bent's Fort on the Mountain Branch of the Santa Fe Trail; brother of George, William, John, and Robert Bent; first U.S. civilian governor of New Mexico, 1846-47; an Albuquerque elementary school, a street in Albuquerque, and the street where his home was located in Taos were named in his honor
Date of Birth: November 11, 1799
Place of Birth: Charleston, Virginia (now West Virginia)
Date of Death (age): dawn, January 19, 1847 (47)
Place of Death: at his home in Taos, New Mexico
Cause of Death: scalped and killed by rebels in the Revolt of 1847
Resting Place: buried four times: first in a secret location in Taos (so the rebels could not find him); then on February 13, 1847, at the old post cemetery at Fort Marcy in Santa Fe; next, in 1864, at the Masonic Cemetery in Santa Fe; finally, in 1895, in the National Cemetery, Santa Fe, New Mexico[14]

A contemporary observer reported that Bent's remains may have been disturbed yet another time when Bent's grave and the grave of another victim of the Revolt of 1847 were opened "in order to deposit in them…the scalps of the dead, which had been recovered from the Indians" within four months after their murders.[15] No. 198

198. The inscription on Governor Bent's headstone reads: "He was the first American governor of New Mexico and was killed by the Indians in the massacre of Taos in 1847. He was a man of kind and gentle manners; of true benevolence of heart; of untarnished probity and lofty carriage. He laid down his life to save those dearth to him than life itself."

Donaciano Vigil
Indian fighter; trusted government official under both Mexican and U.S. rule; military secretary to Governor Manuel Armijo; U.S. secretary of the Territory three times in the period 1846- March 1851; acting governor of New Mexico after Charles Bent's assassination in the Revolt of 1847, 1848-49; strong early supporter of education in New Mexico; a street in Santa Fe and another in Taos were named in his honor
Date of Birth: September 6, 1802
Place of Birth: Santa Fe, New Mexico
Date of Death (age): 6:45 a.m., August 11, 1877 (74)
Place of Death: at his son's home in Santa Fe, New Mexico
Cause of Death: hernia and asthma
Resting Place: Rosario Cemetery, Santa Fe, New Mexico[16]

Vigil's adobe house in Santa Fe's Barrio de Guadalupe, not far from the plaza, was restored in the 1960s and 1970s and is now listed on both the state and national registries of historic buildings.[17]

James Silas Calhoun

U.S. Army Colonel in the U.S.-Mexican War; first U.S. Indian agent west of the Mississippi, 1849; first Territorial Governor of New Mexico following the Compromise of 1850, 1851-52, after New Mexico became a U.S. Territory, 1850; a street in Albuquerque was named in his honor
Date of Birth: 1802
Place of Birth: Georgia
Date of Death (age): July 2, 1852 (about 50)
Place of Death: on the plains near Independence, Missouri
Cause of Death: scurvy
Resting Place: Union Cemetery, Kansas City, Missouri

199. Photo courtesy of Bill Walker.

Gravely ill at Fort Union on a trip to Washington, D.C., Calhoun had army carpenters build his coffin so that he could take it on the trail in case he died en route east. Calhoun died of his illness shortly before reaching Independence, Missouri.[18]
No. 199

William Carr Lane

Physician; first mayor of St. Louis, Missouri, 1823-29 and 1837-40; Whig Territorial Governor of New Mexico, 1852-53
Date of Birth: December 1, 1789
Place of Birth: near Brownsville, Pennsylvania
Date of Death (age): January 6, 1863 (73) (exactly forty-nine years prior to New Mexico statehood)
Place of Death: St. Louis, Missouri
Cause of Death: "congestion of the brain," according to cemetery records; probably a stroke
Resting Place: Bellefontaine Cemetery, St. Louis, Missouri[19]

David Wood Meriwether

Democratic Territorial Governor of New Mexico, 1853-57; a street in Albuquerque was named in his honor
Date of Birth: October 30, 1800
Place of Birth: Louisa County, Virginia
Date of Death (age): April 4, 1893 (92)
Place of Death: on his farm near Louisville, Kentucky
Cause of Death: unstated natural causes
Resting Place: Cave Hill Cemetery, Louisville, Kentucky[20]

William Watts Hart Davis

U.S. Attorney General of New Mexico, 1853-56; interim Territorial Governor, 1856-57; probably most famous for his culturally biased observations of New Mexico and New Mexicans in *El Gringo or New Mexico and Her People* (1857)
Date of Birth: July 27, 1820

200. Photo courtesy of Beth Lander

Place of Birth: Davisville, Pennsylvania
Date of Death (age): December 26, 1910 (90)
Place of Death: Doylestown, Pennsylvania
Cause of Death: unstated natural causes
Resting Place: Doylestown Cemetery, Doylestown, Pennsylvania[21] No. 200

Abraham Rencher
U.S. Congressman from North Carolina, 1829-39, 1841-43; Minister to Portugal, 1843-47; Democratic Territorial Governor of New Mexico, 1857-61
Date of Birth: August 12, 1798
Place of Birth: Raleigh, North Carolina
Date of Death (age): July 6, 1883 (84)
Place of Death: Chapel Hill, North Carolina
Cause of Death: unstated natural causes
Resting Place: St. Bartholomew's Episcopal Churchyard, Pittsboro, North Carolina[22]

William Frederick Milton Arny
Early Republican Party leader in New Mexico; Territorial Secretary; interim Republican Territorial governor, 1862-63 and 1866; federal Indian agent; a street in Santa Fe was named in his honor
Date of Birth: March 6, 1813
Place of Birth: Washington, D.C.
Date of Death (age): between 5:00 and 6:00 p.m., September 18, 1881 (68)
Place of Death: Topeka, Kansas
Cause of Death: attacked during robbery
Resting Place: National Cemetery, Santa Fe, New Mexico[23]

Already ill, Arny was en route to his home in Santa Fe when he died in Kansas, apparently after being attacked. In the stark words of a telegram sent to his wife, "Arny is dead. We are preparing his body for removal. He was robbed Tuesday night, and there is no money on his person. Send directions." The former governor's demise was overshadowed by national news of President James A. Garfield's shooting on July 2, 1881, and death two and a half months later, on the day following Arny's own.[24] No. 201

201. Apparently, Arny was buried under a military headstone because he served as an interim Territorial governor during the Civil War.

Henry Connelly
First arrived in New Mexico in 1824; married a wealthy Peralta widow, Dolores Perea, in 1849; physician, merchant, and Republican Territorial Governor of New Mexico during the Civil War and shortly after, 1861-66; his Peralta hacienda suffered $30,000 worth of damages in the Battle of Peralta, April 15, 1862
Date of Birth: 1800
Place of Birth: Nelson (now Spencer) County, Kentucky
Date of Death (age): August 12, 1866 (about 66)
Place of Death: at his house in Santa Fe, New Mexico

Cause of Death: an accidental overdose of opiate medicine used to induce sleep, less than a month after leaving political office on July 16, 1866
Resting Place: near the side altar, Rosario Cemetery Chapel, Santa Fe, New Mexico; Bishop Jean B. Lamy conducted Connelly's funeral service[25] No. 202

Robert Byington Mitchell
Civil War Union Brigadier General; Republican Territorial Governor of New Mexico, 1866-69
Date of Birth: April 4, 1823
Place of Birth: Mansfield, Ohio
Date of Death (age): January 26, 1882 (58)
Place of Death: Washington, D.C.
Cause of Death: unstated natural causes
Resting Place: National Cemetery, Arlington, Virginia[26]

William Anderson Pile[27]
Civil War Union Brevet Major General; U.S. Congressman from Missouri, 1867-69; Republican Territorial Governor of New Mexico, 1869-71, most famous for discarding valuable documents from the Palace of the Governors in what is sometimes known as "the blunder of 1870"; U.S. Minister to Venezuela, 1871-74; mayor of Monrovia, California, 1888-89
Date of Birth: February 11, 1829
Place of Birth: Indianapolis, Indiana
Date of Death (age): July 7, 1889 (60)
Place of Death: Monrovia, California
Cause of Death: unstated natural causes
Resting Place: Live Oak Memorial Park, Monrovia, California
     Although Pile was the mayor of Monrovia when he died, no gravestone marked his gravesite in Monrovia's town cemetery for over a hundred years. On May 27, 1996, Pile's great nephew, Forrest Pyle, honored his ancestor by placing a headstone and leading a ceremony in his memory at Live Oak Memorial Park.[28] No. 203

Marsh Giddings
Member of the Michigan State Constitutional Convention; Republican Territorial Governor of New Mexico, 1871-75; a street in Albuquerque was named in his honor
Date of Birth: November 19, 1816
Place of Birth: Sherman, Connecticut
Date of Death (age): 3:15 p.m., June 3, 1875 (58)
Place of Death: Palace of the Governors, Santa Fe, New Mexico
Cause of Death: unstated natural causes "after a protracted illness" of nearly three months
Resting Place: Mountain Home Cemetery, Kalamazoo, Michigan[29]

202.

203. The words above Pile's name read: "Chaplain, General, Congressman, Governor, Ambassador, Mayor."

204.

William Gillett Ritch
Civil War Union Lieutenant; recovered healthseeker; Territorial Secretary of New Mexico, 1873-85; acting Republican Territorial Governor, 1875; member of the Board of Regents of the New Mexico Normal School, Silver City, New Mexico; president of the Historical Society of New Mexico, 1880; added the Latin phrase "Crescit Eundo" ("Grows as it goes") to the territorial seal, 1882
Date of Birth: May 4, 1830
Place of Birth: Ulster County, New York
Date of Death (age): September 14, 1904 (74)
Place of Death: Engle, New Mexico
Cause of Death: unstated natural causes
Resting Place: National Cemetery, Santa Fe, New Mexico[30] No. 204

Samuel Beach Axtell
Democratic Territorial Governor of Utah, 1874-75, and of New Mexico, 1875-78, including at the outset of the Lincoln County War in 1878; Chief Justice of the New Mexico Supreme Court, 1882-May 25, 1885
Date of Birth: October 14, 1819
Place of Birth: near Columbus, Ohio
Date of Death (age): 5:00 p.m., August 6, 1891 (71)
Place of Death: at his daughter's home in Morristown, New Jersey
Cause of Death: unstated natural causes
Resting Place: First Presbyterian Church Cemetery, Morristown, New Jersey[31]

205. Photo courtesy of Oak Hill Cemetery.

Lewis "Lew" Wallace
Civil War Union General; Territorial Governor of New Mexico, 1878-81, during much of the Lincoln County War; author of the twenty-thousand-word epic novel, *Ben Hur, A Tale of the Christ* (1880), largely written in New Mexico; U.S. Minister to Turkey; his statue, representing his home state of Indiana, was placed in the National Statuary Hall of Congress in Washington, D.C., 1910; the Lew Wallace School in Albuquerque, the Lew Wallace Building in Santa Fe, the Lew Wallace Room in the Palace of the Governors in Santa Fe, Lew Wallace Peak in Taos County, two streets in Albuquerque, and a street in Santa Fe were named in his honor; a street in Santa Fe is even named Ben Hur Drive
Date of Birth: April 10, 1827
Place of Birth: Brookville, Indiana
Date of Death (age): 9:10 p.m., February 15, 1905 (77)
Place of Death: Crawfordsville, Indiana
Cause of Death: stomach cancer
Resting Place: Oak Hill Cemetery, Crawfordsville, Indiana[32]

Near the end of his life Lew Wallace spoke out on various issues, including his opposition to a Congressional bill that would have combined the territories of New Mexico and Arizona as a single new state. "I love the people of

New Mexico," he wrote. "I lived with them two and a half years as their Governor, and I know their condition and their needs."³³

Wallace died a short time later. Noting his passing, the Crawfordsville, Indiana, newspaper declared, "He fought the good fight and died, as he had lived, without fear."³⁴

Among other items placed with Wallace's body in his coffin was the final sheet of his unfinished autobiography. The last words he had written, in describing his participation in the Civil War Battle of Monocacy, also described his life in general: "I betook myself to action."³⁵ Wallace's "'do-something' responsiveness" was praised by nearly all who knew him in the war, in New Mexico, and since.³⁶ No. 205

Lionel Allen Sheldon
Civil War Union General; Republican Territorial Governor of New Mexico, 1881-85
Date of Birth: August 30, 1831
Place of Birth: Worcester, New York
Date of Death (age): January 17, 1917 (85)
Place of Death: Pasadena, California
Cause of Death: unstated natural causes
Resting Place: cremated³⁷

Edmund Gibson Ross
Newspaperman; Civil War Union Major; as a Republican U.S. Senator from Kansas, 1867-71, he cast the controversial deciding vote for acquittal in the impeachment trial of President Andrew Johnson, May 16, 1868; Territorial Governor of New Mexico, 1885-89; signed legislation establishing the University of New Mexico, the New Mexico Agricultural College (now New Mexico State University), the New Mexico School of Mines (now the New Mexico Institute of Mining and Technology), and the New Mexico Insane Asylum, February 28, 1889; Secretary of the U.S. Bureau of Immigration, 1894-96
Date of Birth: December 7, 1826
Place of Birth: Ashland, Ohio
Date of Death (age): May 8, 1907 (80)
Place of Death: Albuquerque, New Mexico
Cause of Death: pneumonia
Resting Place: Fairview Cemetery, Albuquerque, New Mexico

At the conclusion of his brief autobiography, Ross described himself as "by turns [a] printer, farmer, gentleman at leisure, author, philosopher, [and] tramp—but never a SOREHEAD."

Ross once declared, "I will be a bigger man dead than I have been alive."³⁸ Ross's prediction was not to be. Although justly praised for his courage in casting the deciding vote in Andrew Johnson's impeachment trial, a chapter on Ross in John F. Kennedy's *Profiles in Courage* asserts that "In a lonely grave, forgotten and unknown, lies 'the man who saved a

206. Edmund G. Ross's grave is within blocks of the University of New Mexico, whose creation he signed into law in 1889.

207.

President' and who as a result may have preserved for ourselves and posterity Constitutional government in the United States."[39] No. 206

LeBaron Bradford Prince
Chief Justice of the New Mexico Supreme Court, 1878-82; Republican Territorial Governor of New Mexico, 1889-93; author; historian; strong proponent for New Mexico statehood; President of the Historical Society of New Mexico, 1883; President of the New Mexico A&M Board of Regents; a street in Santa Fe was named in his honor
Date of Birth: July 3, 1840
Place of Birth: Flushing, New York
Date of Death (age): December 8, 1922 (82)
Place of Death: Flushing Hospital, Flushing, New York
Cause of Death: respiratory ailment
Resting Place: St. George's Cemetery, Flushing, New York[40]

William Taylor Thornton
Mayor of Santa Fe, 1891; Democratic Territorial Governor of New Mexico, 1893-97; a street in Albuquerque was named in his honor
Date of Birth: February 9, 1843
Place of Birth: Calhoun, Missouri
Date of Death (age): 8:30 p.m., March 16, 1916 (73)
Place of Death: at his sister-in-law's home in Santa Fe, New Mexico
Cause of Death: influenza
Resting Place: Fairview Cemetery, Santa Fe, New Mexico[41] No. 207

Miguel Antonio "Gillie" Otero II
Republican; longest serving U.S. Territorial Governor, 1897-1906; first and only Hispanic governor of territorial New Mexico; Congressional Delegate Miguel Antonio Otero, Sr.'s son; Congressional Delegate Mariano Otero's cousin; woman suffrage leader Nina Otero-Warren's cousin; strong advocate for New Mexico statehood; a street in Santa Fe was named in his honor; a street in Santa Fe and Otero County, New Mexico, were named in the Otero family's honor
Date of Birth: October 17, 1859
Place of Birth: St. Louis, Missouri
Date of Death (age): about 7:30 a.m., August 7, 1944 (84)
Place of Death: at his home at 354 East Palace Avenue, Santa Fe, New Mexico
Cause of Death: blood clot
Resting Place: Fairview Cemetery, Santa Fe, New Mexico[42]

208. Given their political animosity during much of their lives, it is ironic that Governor Otero's grave is located so near to Thomas Catron's mausoleum at Fairview Cemetery in Santa Fe.

The former governor spent his last evening with his son, Major M.A. Otero, talking about the progress of World War II and "commenting wittily on the political situation." The next morning his son was told that Otero was sleeping quietly. A half hour later he was gone.[43] No. 208

Herbert James Hagerman

U.S. diplomat in Russia; Republican Territorial Governor of New Mexico, 1906-07; son of businessman J.J. Hagerman; a street in Albuquerque was named in his honor

Date of Birth: December 15, 1871

Place of Birth: Milwaukee, Wisconsin

Date of Death (age): 11:50 p.m., January 28, 1935 (63)

Place of Death: St. Vincent Hospital, Santa Fe, New Mexico

Cause of Death: intestinal obstruction

Resting Place: cremated with his ashes interred beside his parents' gravesites in an unspecified cemetery in Milwaukee, Wisconsin[44]

George Curry

Rough Rider Captain in the Spanish-American War, 1898; governor of various provinces of the Philippine Islands, 1901-07; Republican Territorial Governor of New Mexico, 1907-10; U.S. Congressman, 1912-13; first New Mexico State Historian, 1945-47; Curry County was named in his honor when it was created in 1909;[45] a street in Albuquerque was also named in his honor

Date of Birth: April 3, 1861

Place of Birth: Greenwood Plantation, West Feliciana Parish, Louisiana

Date of Death (age): Thanksgiving Day, November 27, 1947 (86)

Place of Death: Veterans Hospital, Albuquerque, New Mexico

Cause of Death: complications from a kidney ailment and old age

Resting Place: National Cemetery, Santa Fe, New Mexico

209.

Curry was wrongly declared to be dead three times before his actual death in 1947. On the first occasion, he was confused with an English visitor who had mistakenly taken Curry's vest from the hotel where both men were staying in Trinidad, Colorado, in 1885. The Englishman was robbed and murdered, but it was assumed that he was Curry when envelopes addressed to Curry were found in the dead man's vest pocket.

Later, in 1902, while Curry served with the Army in the Philippines, most of his unit were killed in battle and it was thought that Curry had perished as well. Hearing of this mistake, Curry's old Rough Rider friend, Teddy Roosevelt, sent him a telegram, saying, "Hearty congratulations on your miraculous escape. Keep a stiff upper lip: I am with you. Theodore."

Thirty years later the Associated Press announced that Curry had died in Hillsboro, New Mexico. The *Albuquerque Journal* printed the story on April 12, 1932. The state went into mourning, and flags were flown at half-staff in Santa Fe before the mistake was finally realized. Hearing of his own demise, Curry declared, "There is virtually no basis whatever for the report of my death."[46] Displaying less of a sense of humor about the incident, Curry's son went so far as to sue the *Journal* for damages, but lost the case when the New Mexico Supreme Court decided that the newspaper was not liable.[47]

Eight months prior to his actual death, reporter Mary Nell Taeger interviewed the former governor in his home in Lincoln, New Mexico. Taeger concluded:

> Visiting with…this gracious old gentleman, whom you cannot realize is eighty-six years old because of his brilliant mind, was a rare privilege…. Anyone who cares to visit with him and hear tales of old from his own lips can find him in his home at the courthouse in Lincoln. That is after he gets through doing all the visiting he has planned for the next two weeks up and down the valley.[48]

Alert to the end, Curry sat for a portrait painted by Sam Smith a month before his death on Thanksgiving Day, 1947. His pallbearers were fellow veterans from the Spanish-American War and the Philippines.[49] No. 209

William Joseph Mills
Republican Chief Justice of the New Mexico Supreme Court, 1898-1910; last Territorial Governor of New Mexico, 1910-12
Date of Birth: January 11, 1849
Place of Birth: Yazoo City, Mississippi
Date of Death (age): 10:20 p.m., Christmas Eve, December 24, 1915 (66)
Place of Death: at his home in East Las Vegas, New Mexico
Cause of Death: pneumonia
Resting Place: Masonic Cemetery, Las Vegas, New Mexico[50] No. 210

Congressional Delegates of the U.S. Territorial Period *(in chronological order by term of service)*

Richard Hanson Weightman
Captain in the U.S.-Mexican War; Santa Fe newspaper editor; Democratic Congressional Delegate, 1851-53; Indian agent; Confederate Colonel during the Civil War
Date of Birth: December 28, 1816
Place of Birth: Washington, D.C.
Date of Death (age): August 10, 1861 (44)
Place of Death: Wilson's Creek near Republic, Missouri
Cause of Death: killed in the Civil War Battle of Wilson's Creek
Resting Place: originally buried at the Wilson's Creek Battlefield; later interment at the National Cemetery, Springfield, Missouri[51]

José Manuel Gallegos
Controversial Albuquerque parish priest; long-time member of the Territorial legislature; Democratic Congressional Delegate, 1853-57 and 1871-73; Superintendent of Indian Affairs for New Mexico, 1868
Date of Birth: October 30, 1815

Place of Birth: Abiquiu, New Mexico
Date of Death (age): about 7:30 a.m., April 21, 1875 (59)
Place of Death: at his home in Santa Fe, New Mexico
Cause of Death: stroke and paralysis
Resting Place: Rosario Cemetery, Santa Fe, New Mexico[52]

Writing in the Santa Fe burial register, Father Augustine Truchard noted that on April 22, 1875, he had buried "José Manuel Gallegos in the private cemetery of Nuestra Señora del Rosario." A French priest and one of Archbishop Jean Baptiste Lamy's allies in his confrontation with local Hispanic priests, Father Truchard failed to mention that the deceased had ever been a priest. Accusing Gallegos of "trying to do all the mischief he can," Lamy had suspended Gallegos from the priesthood by 1852.[53] No. 211

211. At the bottom of Padre Gallegos's gravestone are the Latin words, *"Requiescat en Pace!* [May He Rest in Peace!]"

Miguel Antonio Otero, Sr.
Merchant, banker, farmer; Democratic Congressional Delegate, 1857-61; Governor Miguel Antonio Otero, Jr.'s father; woman suffrage leader Nina Otero-Warren's uncle; Congressional Delegate Mariano Sabino Otero's uncle; Otero County, Colorado, was named in his honor; La Junta, Colorado, celebrates Miguel Otero Fiesta Day in June of each year; the now-abandoned Colfax County community of Otero was also named in his honor; a street in Albuquerque was named in his family's honor
Date of Birth: June 21, 1829
Place of Birth: Valencia, New Mexico
Date of Death (age): May 30, 1882 (52)
Place of Death: Las Vegas, New Mexico
Cause of Death: pneumonia
Resting Place: Riverside Cemetery, Denver, Colorado[54]

John Sebrie Watts
Associate Justice, 1851-54, and Chief Justice of the Supreme Court, New Mexico, 1868-69; Republican Congressional Delegate, 1861-63
Date of Birth: January 19, 1816
Place of Birth: Boone County, Kentucky
Date of Death (age): June 11, 1876 (60)
Place of Death: Bloomington, Indiana
Cause of Death: unstated natural causes
Resting Place: Rose Hill Cemetery, Bloomington, Indiana[55]

Francisco Perea
Civil War Union officer; Republican Congressional Delegate, 1863-65; was sitting near his friend Abraham Lincoln on the evening that the President was assassinated in Ford's Theater in Washington, D.C., April 14, 1865; businessman
Date of Birth: January 9, 1830
Place of Birth: Los Padillas, New Mexico

212. Chaves's surname is incorrectly spelled with a "z."

Date of Death (age): May 21, 1913 (83)
Place of Death: Albuquerque, New Mexico
Cause of Death: unstated natural causes
Resting Place: Fairview Cemetery, Albuquerque, New Mexico[56]

José Francisco (J. Francisco) Chaves
Indian fighter; Civil War Union officer; Republican Congressional Delegate, 1865-67 and 1869-71; Superintendent of Public Instruction, 1901-04; Territorial Historian, 1903-04; Chaves County in eastern New Mexico was named in his honor when it was created in 1889
Date of Birth: June 27, 1833
Place of Birth: Los Padillas, New Mexico
Date of Death (age): November 26, 1904 (71)
Place of Death: at a ranch in Pino Wells, New Mexico
Cause of Death: assassinated
Resting Place: National Cemetery, Santa Fe, New Mexico

Despite a $25,000 reward offered by the territorial legislature, Chaves's killer was never found, no less convicted and punished for his crime.[57] No. 212

Charles P. Clever
Santa Fe merchant; publisher of the *Santa Fe Gazette* and the *Santa Fe New Mexican*; Territorial Attorney General, 1862-67; Democratic Congressional Delegate, 1867-69
Date of Birth: February 23, 1830
Place of Birth: Cologne, Prussia
Date of Death (age): July 8, 1874 (44)
Place of Death: Tomé, New Mexico
Cause of Death: unstated natural causes
Resting Place: National Cemetery, Santa Fe, New Mexico[58]

213. The inscription on Stephen Elkins's gravestone reads: "Served his country as scholar and statesman. Member of State Legislature; District Attorney; Territorial District Attorney; Member of the 43rd and 44th Congress Representing New Mexico; Member of Republican National Committee; Secretary of War under President Benjamin Harrison; U.S. Senator from 1894 Until His Death."
Photo courtesy of Steve B. Corley.

Stephen Benton "Smooth Steve" Elkins
Civil War Union officer; U.S. District Attorney, 1870-73; Republican Congressional Delegate, 1873-77, most famous for his Elkins's Handshake in Congress, which doomed New Mexico's chances for statehood, 1875; reportedly a leader of the Santa Fe Ring; U.S. Secretary of War, 1891-93; U.S. Senator from West Virginia, 1895-1911; two now-abandoned communities (one in Colfax County and the other in Eddy County) were probably named in his honor; Elkins, West Virginia, was named in his honor
Date of Birth: September 26, 1841
Place of Birth: New Lexington, Ohio
Date of Death (age): midnight, January 4, 1911 (69)
Place of Death: Washington, D.C.
Cause of Death: blood poisoning
Resting Place: Maplewood Cemetery, Elkins, West Virginia[59]

Elkins died almost one year prior to when New Mexico finally gained its statehood on January 6, 1912. No. 213

Trinidad Romero
Republican Congressional Delegate, 1877-79; mercantile merchant; stock rancher; U.S. Marshall, 1889-93
Date of Birth: June 14, 1835
Place of Birth: Golden, New Mexico
Date of Death (age): about 6:00 p.m., August 28, 1918 (83)
Place of Death: at his home in Wagon Mound, New Mexico
Cause of Death: unstated natural causes
Resting Place: Mount Calvary Catholic Cemetery, Las Vegas, New Mexico[60] No. 214

214. The death date on Trinidad Romero's headstone is incorrect.

Mariano Sabino Otero
Republican Congressional Delegate, 1879-81; rancher; banker; Congressional Delegate Miguel Antonio Otero, Sr.'s nephew; Governor Miguel Antonio Otero, Jr.'s cousin; woman suffrage leader Nina Otero-Warren's cousin
Date of Birth: August 29, 1844
Place of Birth: Peralta, New Mexico
Date of Death (age): 4:00 a.m., February 1, 1904 (59)
Place of Death: Albuquerque, New Mexico
Cause of Death: apoplexy
Resting Place: Santa Barbara Cemetery, Albuquerque, New Mexico[61]

Tranquilino Luna
Stock rancher; Republican U.S. Congressional Delegate, 1881-84; Sheriff of Valencia County, 1888-92; Republican Party leader Solomon Luna's brother; Rough Rider Maximiliano Luna's father; woman's suffrage leader Nina Otero-Warren's uncle; Los Lunas, New Mexico, was named in the Luna family's honor
Date of Birth: February 25, 1849
Place of Birth: Los Lunas, New Mexico
Date of Death (age): November 20, 1892 (43)
Place of Death: Peralta, New Mexico
Cause of Death: dysentery
Resting Place: San Clemente Catholic Cemetery, Los Lunas, New Mexico
    After years of vandalism and decay, the headstones at the old San Clemente Catholic Cemetery were removed in 1978. A large marker in the center of the cemetery now lists the 103 persons buried there, including Tranquilino Luna.[62] No. 215

215. A statue of Christ stands atop the grotto at what remains of the original San Clemente Catholic Cemetery.

Francisco Antonio Manzanares
Merchant; Democratic Congressional Delegate, 1884-85
Date of Birth: January 25, 1843
Place of Birth: Abiquiu, New Mexico
Date of Death (age): September 17, 1904 (61)
Place of Death: Las Vegas, New Mexico
Cause of Death: Bright's disease
Resting Place: Mount Calvary Catholic Cemetery, Las Vegas, New Mexico[63]

Antonio Joseph
Mercantile business owner; Democratic Congressional Delegate, 1885-95
Date of Birth: August 25, 1846
Place of Birth: Taos, New Mexico
Date of Death (age): April 19, 1910 (63)
Place of Death: at his home in Ojo Caliente, New Mexico
Cause of Death: unstated natural causes
Resting Place: Fairview Cemetery, Santa Fe, New Mexico[64]

Harvey Butler "H.B." Fergusson
Democratic Congressional Delegate, 1897-99; Democratic Party leader at the New Mexico State Constitutional Convention, 1910; U.S. Congressman, 1913-15; William Jennings Bryan's secretary; father of authors Erna and Harvey Fergusson; son-in-law of Franz Huning
Date of Birth: September 9, 1848
Place of Birth: Pickensville, Alabama
Date of Death (age): June 10, 1915 (66)
Place of Death: Albuquerque, New Mexico
Cause of Death: according to the press, a stroke; according to his death certificate, suicide by hanging
Resting Place: cremated in Los Angeles, California

According to various sources, Fergusson's suicide was caused by financial problems, his bad marriage, and/or depression.

Hearing of Fergusson's death, William Jennings Bryan sent a Western Union Telegram to Fergusson's widow, saying:

> I am distressed to learn of the death of your husband. For twenty years we have been in cordial and sympathetic cooperation in the field of politics. I counted him among the most useful men of our party as well as among my personal friends.[65]

Francisco "Pedro" Perea
Wealthy sheep rancher; banker; Republican Congressional Delegate, 1899-1901
Date of Birth: April 22, 1852
Place of Birth: Bernalillo, New Mexico
Date of Death: 4:30 a.m., January 11, 1906 (53)
Place of Death: at his home in Bernalillo, New Mexico
Cause of Death: stomach ailment
Resting Place: Our Lady of Sorrows Catholic Cemetery, Bernalillo, New Mexico[66]

Bernard Shandon Rodey
Arrived in New Mexico in 1881; Republican Congressional Delegate, 1901-05; such a strong advocate for New Mexico statehood that Governor Miguel Otero called him Bernard "Statehood" Rodey; instrumental in the creation of the University of New

Mexico, where Rodey Theatre commemorates his name; founder of the Rodey law firm, now one of the largest law firm's in New Mexico; the southwestern New Mexico community of Rodey was renamed in his honor in 1904
Date of Birth: March 1, 1856
Place of Birth: County Mayo, Ireland
Date of Death (age): 9:00 a.m., March 10, 1927 (71)
Place of Death: St. Joseph Sanatorium, Albuquerque, New Mexico
Cause of Death: vascular heart disease
Resting Place: Fairview Cemetery, Albuquerque, New Mexico[67] No. 216

216. Bernard S. Rodey's headstone gives March 3 as the date of his birth, although this may have been the date of his baptism. At the bottom of Rodey's stone are words by the first century A.D. Roman poet, Marcus Manilius: "There is no death. The stars go down to rise up on some other shore."

William Henry "Bull" Andrews
Arrived in New Mexico in 1900; president of the Santa Fe Central Railway; Republican Congressional Delegate, March 4, 1905-January 7, 1912; New Mexico's last Congressional Delegate prior to statehood, 1912
Date of Birth: January 14, 1852
Place of Birth: Youngsville, Pennsylvania
Date of Death (age): January 16, 1919 (67)
Place of Death: Carlsbad, New Mexico
Cause of Death: influenza and pneumonia
Resting Place: Woodlawn Cemetery, Titusville, Pennsylvania[68]

Other Congressional Delegates include:
Thomas B. Catron, 1895-97 (this chapter)

Leaders of the Fifty-Day New Mexico State Constitutional Convention, October 3-November 21, 1910[69]

Solomon "King Saul" Luna
Largest sheep rancher in the New Mexico Territory by 1900; Republican leader and the dominant figure at the New Mexico State Constitutional Convention, 1910; Congressional Delegate Tranquilino Luna's brother; woman's suffrage leader Nina Otero-Warren's uncle; Rough Rider Maximiliano Luna's uncle; Luna County was named in his honor when it was created in 1901; a street in Albuquerque was also named in his honor; Los Lunas, New Mexico, was named in the Luna family's honor
Date of Birth: October 18, 1858
Place of Birth: Los Lunas, New Mexico
Date of Death (age): August 30, 1912 (53)
Place of Death: a sheep ranch in western Socorro County, New Mexico
Cause of Death: accidentally drowned in a sheep dipping vat
Resting Place: Santa Barbara Cemetery, Albuquerque, New Mexico

While accepted as accidental by most, some believed that Luna's death was caused by foul play. Luna family members and their allies in the press dismissed the latter interpretation as nothing more than politically motivated "ugly" rumors when these stories began to circulate in 1914.[70] No. 217

217. Traditionally, a gravestone in the shape of an obelisk symbolizes eternal life.[71] For many years Luna's obelisk was the tallest gravestone at the Santa Barbara Cemetery. It is now second to the Candelaria family's obelisk.

Other Members of the New Mexico State Constitutional Convention of 1910 include:
H.O. Bursum, Sr. (this chapter)
Thomas Catron (this chapter)
Albert B. Fall (this chapter)
H.B. Fergusson (this chapter)
Washington E. Lindsey (this chapter)
Thomas J. Mabry (this chapter)
William McDonald (this chapter)
Nestor Montoya (this chapter)
William Walton (this chapter)

State Governors *(in chronological order by term of service)*

William Calhoun McDonald

Democratic leader; member of the New Mexico State Constitutional Convention, 1910; New Mexico's first State Governor, January 15, 1912-17; the small southeastern New Mexico community of McDonald was named in his honor
Date of Birth: July 25, 1858
Place of Birth: Jordonville, New York
Date of Death (age): April 11, 1918 (59)
   Place of Death: El Paso, Texas
   Cause of Death: Bright's disease
   Resting Place: Cedarvale Cemetery, White Oaks, New Mexico[72] No. 218

218. On top of William McDonald's headstone are the words: "First State Governor of New Mexico, 1911-1915." Both dates are incorrect.

Ezequiel C de Baca; also Cabeza de Baca

Associate editor of *La Voz del Pueblo*; New Mexico's first state Lieutenant Governor, 1913-17; Democratic State Governor of New Mexico for forty-nine days, January to February 1917; first New Mexico state governor to die in office; de Baca County was named in his honor within days after his death
Date of Birth: November 1, 1864
Place of Birth: Las Vegas, New Mexico
Date of Death (age): shortly before 4:00 p.m., February 18, 1917 (52)
   Place of Death: St. Vincent Hospital, Santa Fe, New Mexico
   Cause of Death: pernicious anemia
   Resting Place: Mount Calvary Catholic Cemetery, Las Vegas, New Mexico

     Ill during his campaign for governor, C de Baca had gone to a hospital in California immediately after his election in hopes of recovering. Returning to Santa Fe on December 30, 1916, he went straight to St. Vincent Hospital where he took the oath of office as governor in his hospital room on January 1, 1917, with fourteen persons present. While in the hospital, "He greeted visitors with his customary courtesy, assuring them that although he regretted having to act as governor from a sickbed, he had faith in his doctors and Almighty God and hoped for improvement." Despite blood transfusions from brothers, sisters, and other relatives, he never recovered. C de Baca died in St. Vincent's and never served as

219. The inscription near the base of C de Baca's headstone reads: "They never sought in vain that sought the Lord aright." The phrase is from Robert Burns's poem, "The Cotter's Saturday Night" (1785).

New Mexico's chief executive in the Governor's Mansion. Only his remains entered the mansion for a religious service after his death. His corpse, accompanied by a procession that included his successor and five former living governors, was later brought to Las Vegas for burial.[73] No. 219

Washington Ellsworth Lindsey
Mayor of Portales, New Mexico, 1909-10; member of the New Mexico State Constitutional Convention, 1910; Republican State Governor of New Mexico, 1917-19, during all of World War I; a park and school in Portales were named in his honor; Lindsey's statue, dedicated in 1999, stands before the Roosevelt County Courthouse in Portales
Date of Birth: December 20, 1862
Place of Birth: Armstrong, Ohio
Date of Death (age): 8:30 a.m., April 5, 1926 (63)
Place of Death: Portales, New Mexico
Cause of Death: suicide, shooting himself in the heart with an automatic pistol after having been despondent and in poor health for several months
Resting Place: Portales Cemetery, Portales, New Mexico

220.

To his end, Lindsey's favorite quote was from Robert Burns: "I don't give a damn for any damn man that don't give a damn about me."[74] No. 220

Octaviano Ambrosio Larrazolo, Sr.
Republican State Governor of New Mexico, 1919-21; first and only Mexican-born U.S. territorial or state governor of New Mexico; U.S. Senator, 1928-29; first Hispanic senator in the U.S. Senate
Date of Birth: December 7, 1859
Place of Birth: El Valle de Allende, Chihuahua, Mexico
Date of Death (age): 7:15 p.m., April 7, 1930 (70)
Place of Death: at his home in Albuquerque, New Mexico
Cause of Death: cirrhosis of the liver
Resting Place: Santa Barbara Cemetery, Albuquerque, New Mexico[75]

221.

"Hearing of [Larrazolo's failing health following a severe stroke, his] old friend, Father C.M. Garde of El Paso...came to visit him. The visit was very short, as Larrazolo [once the greatest orator in New Mexico] could hardly talk. Garde said of him, 'Larrazolo looked upon death as the key to his Father's home.' Larrazolo, ever conscious of his life [as an attorney] in the courts of justice, told the priest, 'Father, I am ready for the summons.'"[76] No. 221

Merritt Cramer Mechem
Recovered healthseeker; Territorial Supreme Court Judge, 1909-12; District Court Judge, 1912-20; Republican State Governor of New Mexico, 1921-23; Governor Ed

222.

Mechem's uncle; a street in Albuquerque was named in his honor
Date of Birth: October 10, 1870
Place of Birth: Ottawa, Kansas
Date of Death (age): May 24, 1946 (75)
Place of Death: St. Joseph Hospital, Albuquerque, New Mexico
Cause of Death: pneumonia
Resting Place: Mount Calvary Cemetery, Albuquerque, New Mexico[77] No. 222

James Fielding Hinkle

Arrived in New Mexico in 1885; Mayor of Roswell, New Mexico, 1904-06; Democratic State Governor of New Mexico, 1923-25; known as the "Cowboy Governor" because he had been the manager of the large C.A. Bar Cattle Company in Lincoln County and because many ranchers had given him their strong political support; a street in Albuquerque was named in his honor
Date of Birth: October 20, 1864
Place of Birth: Franklin County, Missouri
Date of Death (age): 3:10 p.m., March 26, 1951 (86)
Place of Death: at his home in Roswell, New Mexico
Cause of Death: pneumonia, leading to heart complications
Resting Place: South Park Cemetery, Roswell, New Mexico[78] No. 223

223. Governor Hinkle was buried beside his wife, Lillie Roberts Hinkle. Their vertical joint gravestone is to the left of the carved image of an angel.

Soledad Chávez de Chacón

First Hispanic woman elected to a statewide office in New Mexico when she was elected Secretary of State, 1922; lifelong Democrat; first woman (acting) governor of New Mexico when Lieutenant Governor José A. Baca died in May 1924 and Governor James Hinkle traveled out of state, June 21 to July 5, 1924; identified simply as a "housewife" on her death certificate
Date of Birth: August 11, 1892
Place of Birth: Albuquerque, New Mexico
Date of Death (age): 8:35 a.m., August 4, 1936 (43)
Place of Death: Women's and Children's Hospital, Albuquerque, New Mexico
Cause of Death: peritonitis, following major surgery
Resting Place: Mount Calvary Cemetery, Albuquerque, New Mexico[79]

Not all New Mexicans were pleased with the news that Soledad Chávez de Chacón was serving as the acting governor of the state in 1924. Shortly after she assumed office, the editor of the *Alamogordo News* asserted, "there are few women adapted to such a job. The gentle sex did not [evolve] to that end, and were [sic] evidently not designed by the Creator as dominant.... The woman who is adapted for a large political office is apt to be mannish and lacking in many feminine qualities...."[80] No. 224

224.

Arthur Thomas Hannett

Mayor of Gallup, 1918; Democratic State Governor of New Mexico, 1925-27; a street in Albuquerque was named in his honor

Date of Birth: February 17, 1884

Place of Birth: Lyons, New York

Date of Death (age): March 18, 1966 (82)

Place of Death: Presbyterian Hospital, Albuquerque, New Mexico

Cause of Death: following surgery

Resting Place: Fairview Cemetery, Albuquerque, New Mexico[81]

225.

Hannett claimed that he arrived in Gallup in 1911 with nothing more than a typewriter, three law books, and eight dollars. In the last paragraph of his autobiography, he wrote, "I have had a full and turbulent career and as I approach the end I join with William Shakespeare who said, 'With mirth and laughter let old wrinkles come. Let my liver rather heat with wine than cool with mortifying groans!'"[82] No. 225

Richard Charles "Picnic Dick" Dillon

Republican State Governor of New Mexico, 1927-31; first state governor to serve two terms; known as "Picnic Dick" because he enjoyed picnics with lots of friends, games, and singing during his "neighborly campaigns" for office; the now-abandoned northeastern New Mexico community of Dillon was named in his honor

Date of Birth: June 24, 1877

Place of Birth: St. Louis, Missouri

Date of Death (age): January 4, 1966 (88)

Place of Death: in a hospital in Albuquerque, New Mexico

Cause of Death: following exploratory surgery for a pancreas ailment

Resting Place: Fairview Cemetery, Albuquerque, New Mexico[83] No. 226

226.

Arthur Seligman

Mayor of Santa Fe, 1910-12; president of the First National Bank of Santa Fe, 1924-33; Democratic State Governor, 1931-33; second state governor to die in office (Ezequiel C de Baca had been the first in 1917); a street in Albuquerque was named in his honor

Date of Birth: June 14, 1871

Place of Birth: Santa Fe, New Mexico

Date of Death (age): September 25, 1933 (62)

Place of Death: Albuquerque, New Mexico

Cause of Death: heart attack, perhaps as a result of stress after three threats to kidnap his granddaughter and an aborted attempt to rob the First National Bank of Santa Fe five weeks before his death

Resting Place: Fairview Cemetery, Santa Fe, New Mexico

227.

After Seligman returned from a weekend trip to Eagle Nest Lake with his wife, the governor left for Albuquerque on Monday, September 25, 1933, to deliver a speech. "He left Santa Fe in good health. By noon he was dead. Just after his speech he had had a sudden and unexpected heart attack."[84] No. 227

Andrew Walter Hockenhull

Republican State Governor of New Mexico, 1933-35, serving out Arthur Seligman's term when Governor Seligman died in office, September 25, 1933; attorney; president of the Clovis National Bank, 1926-46; contributed more than $250,000 to non-denominational mission work in Sonora, Mexico

Date of Birth: January 16, 1877
Place of Birth: Bolivar, Missouri
Date of Death (age): June 20, 1974 (97)
Place of Death: Retirement Ranch Nursing Home, Clovis, New Mexico
Cause of Death: unstated natural causes
Resting Place: Mission Garden of Memories Cemetery, Clovis, New Mexico[85]

On his ninety-fourth birthday, Hockenhull attributed his long life to the fact that he never worried and always put his faith in the Lord. As a result, he was seldom sick and seldom went to the doctor. He told a reporter that he had only spent ten dollars on doctor bills in 1970 (his ninety-third year), "and that was for a flu shot."[86] No. 228

228. At the base of Andrew Hockenhull's gravestone are words that reflected not only his career, but also his strong beliefs: "Pioneer, Lawyer, Banker, Farmer, Missionary. God will provide. 'The step of a good man is ordered by the Lord and he delighteth in his way though he fall he shall not be utterly lost.' Psalm 37:23-24."

Clyde Kendle "Buster" Tingley

Colorful Albuquerque alderman (1916-17), city commission member (1922-35 and 1939-55), and powerful, four-time ex-officio mayor (chairman of the city commission), June 1925-December 1934, October 1939-April 1946, August 1947-January 1948, and October 1951-April 1954; twice Democratic State Governor of New Mexico, 1935-37 and 1937-39; responsible for bringing many New Deal projects to New Mexico; Tingley Beach, Tingley Field, Tingley Drive, and Tingley Coliseum in Albuquerque, New Mexico, were named in his honor

Date of Birth: January 5, 1881
Place of Birth: on a farm near London, Ohio
Date of Death (age): 4:05 a.m., Christmas Eve, December 24, 1960 (79)
Place of Death: Bataan Memorial Hospital, Albuquerque, New Mexico
Cause of Death: "heart ailment" after entering the hospital suffering from diabetes and a "kidney condition" on December 12, 1960
Resting Place: Fairview Cemetery, Albuquerque, New Mexico

229. Governor Tingley's gravestone is directly to the left (west) of his wife Carrie Tingley's.

Tingley was famous for his colorful comments and political humor, especially regarding his political opponents. Once, while the ex-officio mayor of Albuquerque, he showed a friend around town, pointing out the ways he hoped to improve the community. Impressed, the friend said, "Clyde, someday the people are going to canonize you for this." Tingley replied, "They…..are trying to do that right now."[87] No. 229

John Esten Miles
Publisher of the Santa Fe *New Mexico Democrat* and the *Las Vegas Independent*; Democratic State Governor of New Mexico, 1939-43, at the outset of World War II; U.S. Congressman, 1949-51; long known as New Mexico's "Mr. Democrat"; a street in Santa Fe was named in his honor
Date of Birth: July 28, 1884
Place of Birth: Murfreesboro, Tennessee
Date of Death (age): about 9:00 a.m., October 7, 1971 (87)
Place of Death: Four Seasons Rest Home, Santa Fe, New Mexico
Cause of Death: unstated natural causes
Resting Place: Memorial Gardens, Santa Fe, New Mexico[88] No. 230

230.

John Joseph "Old Port" Dempsey
Democratic State Governor of New Mexico, 1943-47, during much of World War II; U.S. Congressman, 1935-41 and 1951-59; a street in Albuquerque and one in Santa Fe were named in his honor
Date of Birth: June 22, 1879
Place of Birth: Whitehaven, Pennsylvania
Date of Death (age): March 11, 1958 (78)
Place of Death: George Washington University Hospital, Washington, D.C.
Cause of Death: complications from a viral infection
Resting Place: Rosario Cemetery, Santa Fe, New Mexico

Representative Dempsey had just filed for reelection on March 4, 1958, a week before his death.[89] No. 231

231.

Thomas Jewett Mabry
At twenty-five, the youngest member of the 1910 New Mexico State Constitutional Convention; New Mexico Supreme Court Justice, 1939-46; Democratic State Governor of New Mexico, 1947-51; a street in Albuquerque was named in his honor
Date of Birth: October 17, 1884
Place of Birth: Cunningham, Kentucky
Date of Death (age): December 23, 1962 (78)
Place of Death: San Francisco, California
Cause of Death: anemia
Resting Place: Fairview Cemetery, Albuquerque, New Mexico

Mabry had had a close call with death in 1912 when the passenger train he was riding collided head-on with another

232.

train going full speed near El Reno, Oklahoma. One passenger was killed in the wreck, forty were injured, and both engines were "reduced to scrap iron." Somehow Mabry escaped unharmed.[90] No. 232

233.

Edwin Leard "Big Ed" (6'2") "Honest Ed" Mechem
FBI agent during World War II; Republican State Governor of New Mexico, 1951-55, 1957-59, and 1961-62; U.S. Senator, 1962-65; U.S. District Court Judge, 1982-2002; Governor Merritt C. Mechem's nephew
Date of Birth: July 2, 1912
Place of Birth: Alamogordo, New Mexico
Date of Death (age): November 27, 2002 (90)
Place of Death: at his home in Albuquerque, New Mexico
Cause of Death: congestive heart failure
Resting Place: Fairview Cemetery, Albuquerque, New Mexico

Mechem once said that "He didn't mind dying—he just didn't want to be there when it happened."[91] No. 233

234.

John Field Simms, Jr.
Democratic State Governor of New Mexico, 1955-57; at thirty-eight, the youngest New Mexico state governor to date; son of New Mexico Supreme Court Justice John Field Simms, Sr.; nephew of New Mexico's U.S. Congressman Albert Simms; a street in Albuquerque was named in the Simms family's honor
Date of Birth: December 18, 1916
Place of Birth: Albuquerque, New Mexico
Date of Death (age): April 11, 1975 (58)
Place of Death: St. Joseph Hospital, Albuquerque, New Mexico
Cause of Death: probably an intestinal disorder
Resting Place: Fairview Cemetery, Albuquerque, New Mexico[92]

According to an *Albuquerque Journal* editorial that appeared a day after his death, Simms was "equally at ease with his hard-working neighbors, his hired hands, presidents, heads of state, financiers, and industrial tycoons.... There was no segment of human society that did not greet him with sincere and hearty welcome."[93] No. 234

John Burroughs
Peanut farmer; radio station owner; Eastern New Mexico College football broadcaster; Democratic State Governor of New Mexico, 1959-61
Date of Birth: April 7, 1907
Place of Birth: Robert Lee, Texas
Date of Death (age): May 21, 1978 (71)
Place of Death: Dallas, Texas
Cause of Death: lung infection

Resting Place: Portales Cemetery, Portales, New Mexico[94]

In the peanut processing business, Burroughs was dubbed the "peanut politician," to which he said that many men ended their careers in the "nut house," but he had been the first to progress from the "nut house" to the state house.[95] No. 235

Thomas Felix "Tom" Bolack
Owner of the B-Square Ranch, located between Farmington and Bloomfield; oilman; owner of Albuquerque's minor league baseball team; big game hunter; Mayor of Farmington, 1952-54; Republican State Lieutenant Governor of New Mexico, 1961-62; Governor of New Mexico, December 1962; dedicated conservationist; the Tom Bolack Museum of Fish and Wildlife in Farmington, a street in Albuquerque and the Secretory Physiology Laboratory at Lovelace Memorial Hospital were named in his honor
Date of Birth: May 18, 1918
Place of Birth: Burden, Kansas
Date of Death (age): 1:27 p.m., May 20, 1998 (80)
Place of Death: San Juan Regional Medical Center, Farmington, New Mexico
Cause of Death: heart attack
Resting Place: cremated with most of his ashes scattered over his B-Square Ranch by his son, Tommy, who mixed them with sixteen fireworks and fired them off over the ranch on the Fourth of July, 1999.

235.

According to Tommy Bolack, his father "wanted his remains spread on the ranch; he just didn't say how. He loved fireworks. He would have wanted to go out this way, I believe." The rest of Bolack's ashes are kept in a blue urn on a table in the ranch's meeting room. Tommy said, "He's still part of the meetings in one way or another."[96]

John Moren "Jack" Campbell
Arrived in Albuquerque in 1940; FBI agent; World War II Marine Corps officer; lawyer, businessman, legislator; Democratic State Governor of New Mexico, 1963-67; best known as the driving force behind the construction of the Rio Grande Gorge Bridge, the John M. Campbell Highway, and New Mexico's uniquely designed state capitol, the circular Roundhouse
Date of Birth: September 10, 1916
Place of Birth: Hutchinson, Kansas
Date of Death (age): June 14, 1999 (82)
Place of Death: Ponce de Leon Retirement Home, Santa Fe, New Mexico
Cause of Death: probably complications from a liver ailment
Resting Place: cremated with ashes scattered in the Pecos Wilderness, New Mexico

In a eulogy at his father's funeral service, Michael Campbell said that of all his honors, Governor Campbell was most proud of a trophy given to him from the New Mexico Game and Fish Department for catching the largest brook trout ever caught in the state. He was so fond of fishing that he often said, "If there ain't no fishin' in heaven, I ain't goin' there."[97]

U.S. Senators *(in chronological order by term of service)*

236.

Thomas Benton "Tom" Catron
Confederate officer in the Civil War; U.S. District Attorney in New Mexico, 1869-72; reportedly the leader of the corrupt Santa Fe Ring; largest landowner in New Mexico by the early twentieth century, with most of his land acquired as compensation in land grant legal cases; U.S. Congressional Delegate, 1895-97; a leader at the New Mexico State Constitutional Convention, 1910; Republican U.S. Senator, 1913-17; Catron County, New Mexico's largest county in square miles, was named in his honor when it was created in 1921, the year of Catron's death; streets in Santa Fe and Albuquerque were also named in his honor

Date of Birth: October 6, 1840
Place of Birth: Lexington, Missouri
Date of Death (age): 8:00 a.m., May 15, 1921 (80)
Cause of Death: cirrhosis of the liver and bronchitis
Place of Death: at his home in Santa Fe, New Mexico
Resting Place: Catron Mausoleum, Fairview Cemetery, Santa Fe, New Mexico[98]

Following Catron's death, one of his friends said that Catron, "most of his life, was regarded as a stern, aggressive man. I feel sure now [that] this character was donned by him as a suit of armor for business or political success. The last two years he came out of it, and everyone around him found the senator a kind hearted, genial man. Unlike most patients suffering with a painful, deadly malady, he never showed a peevish moment. He was as jolly a good fellow in sickness as he had been rather stern and severe many times in health."[99]

Presenting Catron's eulogy at the Scottish Rite cathedral in Santa Fe, George W. Prichard said, "Thomas Benton Catron had his faults. Who has not? But they were the faults of the gladiator. He punished his enemies while the combat was on, but like the true fighter, he laid aside his weapon when the battle was over."[100] No. 236

237.

Albert Bacon Fall
Owner of the Three Rivers Ranch in southern New Mexico; Territorial District Court Judge, 1893-95; Captain in the First Territorial Infantry during the Spanish-American War, 1898; a Republican leader at the New Mexico State Constitutional Convention, 1910; Republican U.S. Senator, 1913-21; owner of the *Mesilla Independent Democrat* in the early 1890s and the *Albuquerque Morning Journal*, 1918-20; U.S. Secretary of the Interior, 1921-24; most famous for his controversial role in the Teapot Dome scandal, which led to his 1929 conviction for taking a bribe; became the first former U.S. cabinet member to

be convicted of a felony; sentenced to a year in prison and a $100,000 fine
Date of Birth: November 26, 1861
Place of Birth: Frankfort, Kentucky
Date of Death (age): 4:30 p. m., November 30, 1944 (83)
Place of Death: Hotel Dieu Catholic Hospital, El Paso, Texas, where he had been a patient since 1942
Cause of Death: "senility, chronic arthritis, arteriosclerosis"[101]
Resting Place: Evergreen Cemetery, El Paso, Texas[102]

In 1938, after his conviction for taking a bribe and having served just less than a year in the New Mexico State Penitentiary, Fall told a reporter, "I haven't long to live. I've paid my debt to society. I owe it nothing." Although plagued with illnesses and public shame, Fall lived another six years.[103]

According to historian C.L. Sonnichsen, "When [Fall's] time came, he went quickly. His heart stopped while he was reading his paper. There was an impressive Catholic funeral attended by big and little people from all over the Southwest. Many kind and charitable words were said, but all who came were conscious of a glory departed—a great opportunity missed—a triumph turned into tragedy. So much given! So much accomplished! So little at the end!"[104] No. 237

238. Photo courtesy of David N. Lotz.

Andrieus Aristieus "A.A." Jones
Principal of the Las Vegas, New Mexico, public schools, 1885-87; Mayor of Las Vegas, 1893-94; Republican U.S. Senator, 1917-27
Date of Birth: May 16, 1862
Place of Birth: near Union City, Tennessee
Date of Death (age): 11:15 p.m., December 20, 1927 (65)
Place of Death: at his Meridian Mansion apartment in Washington, D.C.
Cause of Death: heart attack
Resting Place: Masonic Cemetery, Las Vegas, New Mexico[105] No. 238

Holm Olaf "H.O." Bursum, Sr.
Recovered healthseeker who moved to New Mexico in 1881; a leader at the New Mexico State Constitutional Convention, 1910; Republican U.S. Senator, 1921-March 3, 1925; sponsor of the controversial Bursum Bill regarding Pueblo Indian lands, 1922; a street in Socorro, the western New Mexico settlement of Bursum, and the Bursum Road (NM 159) were named in his honor
Date of Birth: February 10, 1867
Place of Birth: Fort Dodge, Iowa
Date of Death (age): August 7, 1953 (86)
Place of Death: a hospital in Colorado Springs, Colorado
Cause of Death: unstated natural causes
Resting Place: Socorro Protestant Cemetery, Socorro, New Mexico[106]
No. 239

239.

240.

Sam Gilbert Bratton

Arrived in New Mexico in 1915; New Mexico Supreme Court Justice, 1923-24; Democratic U.S. Senator, March 4, 1925-June 24, 1933; Judge in the U.S. Court of Appeals, 1933-61; University of New Mexico honorary degree recipient, 1954

Date of Birth: August 19, 1888

Place of Birth: Kosse, Texas

Date of Death (age): about 3:00 p.m.; September 22, 1963 (75)

Place of Death: Albuquerque, New Mexico

Cause of Death: heart attack

Resting Place: Fairview Cemetery, Albuquerque, New Mexico

The Sunday of his death, Bratton had attended morning church services as usual and had then retired for a nap. When he failed to respond to efforts to awaken him, he was taken to the nearby Bataan Methodist Memorial Hospital where he was pronounced dead.[107] No. 240

241. Senator Cutting's gravestone is in the foreground, beside his parents' gravestones. The inscription under his name and dates reads: "Son of William Bayard Cutting and Olivia Peyton Murray. United States Senator from New Mexico. Light and understanding and wisdom was found in him. And the common people heard him gladly." The latter verses are from the Bible, Daniel 5:11 and Mark 12:37, respectively. Photo courtesy of Ken Taylor.

Bronson Murray Cutting

Arrived in Santa Fe as a TB healthseeker, 1910; wealthy owner of the *Santa Fe New Mexican* and *El Nuevo Mexicano*; World War I U.S. Army officer; Republican/Progressive U.S. Senator, 1927-May 6, 1935; Cutting Hall on the Northern New Mexico Community College's El Rito Campus was named in his honor

Date of Birth: June 23, 1888

Place of Birth: New York City, New York

Date of Death (age): 3:30 a.m., May 6, 1935 (46)

Place of Death: south of Kirksville, Missouri

Cause of Death: severe head injuries suffered in a 3:30 a.m. plane crash

Resting Place: Greenwood Cemetery, Brooklyn, New York

Cutting had planned to remain in Santa Fe for several more days in the spring of 1935, but decided to return to Washington, D.C., when he learned of new developments in the Senate on the Bonus Bill, an issue in which he had particular interest, given his strong ties to the American Legion as a World War I veteran.

After dining with friends at his home in Santa Fe, Cutting left for the airport in Albuquerque. His friends, Jesus Baca, H.H. Dorman, Herman Baca, and B.B. Dunne, said that as the senator climbed on board the plane "he never appeared more genial or in better health." One of his last comments was about Dennis Chavez's challenge to his electoral victory on November 6, 1934. Cutting reportedly said, "The contest will not get anywhere. No possible showing he can make will overturn this majority of votes for me."

On his DC-2 Transcontinental and Western Airlines flight from Albuquerque to New York, Cutting apparently moved from his assigned seat in the rear of the plane to avoid the sound of a crying baby that prevented him from sleeping. Once asleep, the senator did not see the pilot's warning light to fasten his seat belt. In the ensuing crash, Cutting, two passengers, and the pilot and co-pilot were killed. All five were near the front of the plane. The remaining five passengers escaped with minor injuries. A survivor and a doctor who later viewed Cutting's body concluded that the senator "died without awakening or knowing what had happened." According to some reports, his body was so badly mangled in the crash that it could only be identified by a picture of his mother found in his wallet.[108]

Cutting had wanted to be buried in the Santa Fe National Cemetery, near his late friend, Lt. Antonio J. Luna, but his family's wishes prevailed, and he was buried in New York.[109]

Funeral services were held at the St. James Episcopal Church in New York City on May 10, 1935, with several honorary pallbearers, including E. Dana Johnson, Herman Baca, B.B. Dunne, and Miguel A. Otero, Jr. Among the estimated two thousand mourners were J.P. Morgan, Walter Lippmann, Nicholas Murray Butler, Colonel Edwin House, Norman Thomas, Alice Roosevelt Longworth, and many of Cutter's fellow members of Congress.[110]

A *corrido* (ballad) about Cutting's life and death was written within ten days after the crash that took his life.[111]

At a 1937 memorial service held at the University of New Mexico, Colonel J.D. Atwood declared that with trouble around the world in the 1930s, "If America has ever had cause to pray for Divine help—now is that time, and our prayer should be 'God give us men—men like Bronson Cutting.'"[112]

A bust in Santa Fe was dedicated in Cutting's honor on May 6, 1939, the fourth anniversary of his death. No. 241

Dionisio "Dennis" "El Senador" Chavez

Democratic U.S. Congressman, 1931-35; appointed U.S. Senator, May 11, 1935, following Senator Bronson Cutting's death; elected to the U.S. Senate, November 3, 1936, the first native born Hispanic to be elected to the Senate, serving until his death in 1962; most noted for his defense of minority rights which became the basis of the Civil Rights Act, 1964; a street in Albuquerque and the Dennis Chavez Elementary Schools in Los Chávez and Albuquerque, New Mexico, were named in his honor; a U.S. postage stamp was issued in his honor, 1991
Date of Birth: April 8, 1888
Place of Birth: Los Chávez, New Mexico
Date of Death (age): November 18, 1962 (74)
Place of Death: Washington, D.C.
Cause of Death: heart attack following an unsuccessful operation for throat cancer six months earlier, on May 28, 1961
Resting Place: Mount Calvary Cemetery, Albuquerque, New Mexico

According to an *Albuquerque Journal* editorial on the day after his death, "The senator's long and heroic fight for life, while enduring great suffering after he had been stricken with cancer, followed the pattern of his whole career in never yielding without a fight to the finish." Dr. William R. Lovelace, Sr., Chavez's

242. The inscription at the top of Senator Chavez's signature reads: "*Aqui yace en Santo Entierro* (Here in Holy Interment)." Below these words is an inscription of the seal of the U.S. Senate. And on the bottom half of the stone are the words: "Represented New Mexico four years in the House of Representatives and twenty-seven years in the United States Senate. A friend to all. He championed the poor. *Dejó este señor una vereda trazada que nunca se olvidará, lo hizo con la esperanza de que otros la sigan.* (This gentleman left a planned path that no one will forget, made with the hope that others will follow it.)"

personal physician, added that the senator's death was "one of the greatest losses New Mexico ever had. He had done so much for his town, his state, and his country. He will be greatly missed by everybody."[113]

Reflecting the great respect President John F. Kennedy had for Chavez, El Senador's body was flown from Washington, D.C., to Albuquerque on Air Force One, accompanied by his family, Vice President Lyndon B. Johnson (Chavez's longtime friend in the U.S. Senate), and a large delegation from the U.S. Congress.[114]

A thousand people crowded the Catholic Church for Chavez's funeral and about three times that number attended the graveside services at Mount Calvary Cemetery in Albuquerque. According to one report, there were many high-ranking officials present,

> But most of the crowd had no offices, no titles, no wealth. There were elderly women in black mantillas, younger women in simple black dresses, men whose Sunday suits needed pressing. They were the folk who had considered the senator their friend, had looked to him for aid when in trouble and had voted for him in election after election. They surged close around the grave, around the honor guard and past the military police who tried to hold them back. They showered the casket with their flowers as it was lowered into the grave. They crowded around the family after the graveside services, offering their sympathy to the senator's widow, his daughter and grandchildren…. [Vice President Johnson told the crowd,] "His voice was always the voice pleading for the underprivilged."[115]

A bronze statue of Chavez, by Felix W. de Weldon, was dedicated in the National Statutory Hall of Congress on March 31, 1966, with many dignitaries in attendance, including Vice President Hubert H. Humphrey and Chief Justice of the Supreme Court Earl Warren. Each state has two statues in the hall. Chavez's was New Mexico's sole statue until 2005 when it was joined by a statue of Popé, the Indian leader of the Pueblo Revolt of 1680.[116] No. 242

Carl Atwood "Smiling Carl" Hatch

Arrived in New Mexico in 1916; New Mexico District Court Judge, 1923-29; Democratic U.S. Senator, 1933-49; author of the Hatch Political Activities Act, an early campaign finance reform, 1939; U.S. District Court Judge, 1949-62

Date of Birth: November 27, 1889

Place of Birth: Kirwin, Kansas

Date of Death (age): 4:30 a.m., September 15, 1963 (73)

Place of Death: Bataan Memorial Hospital, Albuquerque, New Mexico

Cause of Death: chronic lung disease

Resting Place: Fairview Cemetery, Albuquerque, New Mexico[117]

243.

No. 243

Clinton Presba Anderson

Recovered TB healthseeker who arrived in New Mexico in 1917; Albuquerque newspaper reporter and editor, 1918-22; insurance company owner; New Mexico State Treasurer, 1934-35; New Deal official, 1934-38; managing director of the 1940 Cuatro Centennial Celebration; Democratic U.S. Congressman, 1941-45; U.S. Secretary of Agriculture, 1945-48; U.S. Senator, 1949-January 3, 1973; as a result of his work in support of the U.S. space program, he was inducted into the International Space Hall of Fame, Alamogordo, New Mexico, in 1977; a street in Albuquerque and a Southwest research room in Zimmerman Library at the University of New Mexico were named in his honor
Date of Birth: October 23, 1895
Place of Birth: Centerville, South Dakota
Date of Death (age): about 6:00 p.m., November 11, 1975 (80)
Place of Death: at his home in the south valley of Albuquerque, New Mexico
Cause of Death: a stroke
Resting Place: Fairview Cemetery, Albuquerque, New Mexico[118] No. 244

244.

Joseph Manuel "Little Joe" Montoya

Elected to the New Mexico State House of Representatives at the age of twenty-one in 1936; the youngest member of the State Senate at the age of twenty-nine in 1944; Lieutenant Governor, 1947-51 and 1955-57; Democratic U.S. Congressman, 1957-65; U.S. Senator, 1965-January 3, 1977; became nationally known as a member of the Senate Select Committee on Presidential Campaign Activities investigating the Watergate scandal that led to President Richard M. Nixon's resignation on August 9, 1974; stressing his humble origins, he was often called "the barefoot boy from Peña Blanca"; T-VI's campus in northeast Albuquerque was named in his honor when it opened on September 4, 1979, fifteen months following the senator's death; a street in Albuquerque was also named in his honor
Date of Birth: September 24, 1915
Place of Birth: Peña Blanca, New Mexico
Date of Death (age): 6:56 a.m., June 5, 1978 (62)
Place of Death: Washington, D.C.
Cause of Death: nodular regenerative hyperplasia, a rare liver disease
Resting Place: Rosario Cemetery, Santa Fe, New Mexico[119] No. 245

245.

Other U.S. Senators (in chronological order by term of service)
Octaviano Ambrosio Larrazolo (this chapter)
Edwin Mechem (this chapter)

U.S. Congressmen (in chronological order by term of service)

New Mexico's First Two U.S. Congressmen were:
H.B. Fergusson (this chapter)
George Curry (this chapter)

246. The gate to the Walton family plot.

William Bell "Billy" Walton
Attorney; editor of the *Deming Headlight*, 1891-1893; owner of the *Silver City Independent*, 1893-1934; member of the New Mexico State Constitutional Convention, 1910; Democratic U.S. Congressman, 1917-19
Date of Birth: January 23, 1871
Place of Birth: Altoona, Pennsylvania
Date of Death (age): 8:50 p.m., April 14, 1939 (68)
Place of Death: at his home in Silver City, New Mexico
Cause of Death: a "lingering illness" with a stroke ten days before his death
Resting Place: Masonic Cemetery, Silver City, New Mexico[120] No. 246

Benigno Cárdenas "B.C." Hernández
Sheriff of Rio Arriba County, 1904-06; Republican U.S. Congressman, 1915-17 and 1919-21; the northern New Mexico village of Hernández was renamed in his honor in 1920 after he had objected to its being called Alabam, the name of a local saloon
Date of Birth: February 13, 1862
Place of Birth: Taos, New Mexico
Date of Death (age): October 18, 1954 (92)
Place of Death: Los Angeles, California
Cause of Death: unstated natural causes
Resting Place: Inglewood Park Cemetery, Inglewood, California[121]

Nestor Montoya
Founder of the Spanish newspapers *La Voz del Pueblo*, 1888, and *La Bandera Americana*, 1901; member of the New Mexico State Constitutional Convention, 1910; Republican U.S. Congressman, 1921-23
Date of Birth: April 14, 1862
Place of Birth: Albuquerque, New Mexico
Date of Death (age): January 13, 1923 (60)
Place of Death: at his home in Washington, D.C.
Cause of Death: unstated natural causes
Resting Place: Santa Barbara Cemetery, Albuquerque, New Mexico[122]

John Francis "Uncle John" "Honest John" Morrow
Democratic U.S. Congressman, 1923-29
Date of Birth: April 19, 1865
Place of Birth: near Darlington, Wisconsin

Date of Death (age): 2:30 a.m., February 25, 1935 (69)
Place of Death: St. Vincent Hospital, Santa Fe, New Mexico
Cause of Death: complications from diabetes
Resting Place: Fairmont Cemetery, Raton, New Mexico[123]
No. 247

Albert Gallatin Simms
Arrived in Albuquerque, 1906; recovered TB healthseeker; Republican U.S. Congressman, 1929-31; one of the wealthiest men in New Mexico with interests in banking and real estate, although he described himself as "simply a rancher"; brother of New Mexico Supreme Court Justice John Field Simms; married U.S. Congresswoman Ruth Hanna McCormick, March 9, 1932; a street in Albuquerque was named in the Simms family's honor
Date of Birth: October 8, 1882
Place of Birth: Washington, Arkansas
Date of Death (age): December 29, 1964 (82)
Place of Death: at his six-hundred-acre Los Poblanas Ranch, New Mexico
Cause of Death: unstated natural causes
Resting Place: Fairview Cemetery, Albuquerque, New Mexico; beside his wife, Ruth Hanna McCormick (Chapter 6, No. 107)[124]

247.

Antonio Manuel "Tony" Fernandez
Democratic U.S. Congressman, 1943-56
Date of Birth: January 17, 1902
Place of Birth: Springer, New Mexico
Date of Death (age): 8:30 a.m., November 7, 1956 (54)
Place of Death: St. Joseph Hospital, Albuquerque, New Mexico
Cause of Death: stroke suffered while making a campaign speech on October 25, 1956, in Las Vegas, New Mexico
Resting Place: Rosario Cemetery, Santa Fe, New Mexico

248.

Although still in a coma following his stroke, Fernandez was reelected to Congress for an eighth consecutive term by the voters of New Mexico on Tuesday, November 6, 1956. He died the following day. He had been reluctant to seek reelection, telling friends that his preference was to serve as a judge in Santa Fe.[125] No. 248

Georgia Lee Witt Lusk
New Mexico State Superintendent of Public Schools, 1931-35, 1943-47, 1955-60; first New Mexico woman elected to the U.S. House of Representatives, November 5, 1946; Democratic U.S. Congresswoman, 1947-49; rancher

249.

Date of Birth: May 12, 1893
Place of Birth: Blue Spring Ranch near Carlsbad, New Mexico
Date of Death (age): January 5, 1971 (77)
Place of Death: St. Joseph Hospital, Albuquerque, New Mexico
Cause of Death: unstated natural causes
Resting Place: Sunset Gardens Memorial Park, Carlsbad, New Mexico[126] No. 249

Elver Stephen "Johnny" Walker
World War II U.S. Army veteran; New Mexico state legislator who introduced legislation that gave women the right to serve on New Mexico juries; State Land Commissioner; Democratic U.S. Congressman, 1965-67; won approval for the establishment of the Pecos National Monument; was instrumental in the passage of the Medicare Act, 1965
Date of Birth: June 18, 1911
Place of Birth: Fulton, Kentucky
Date of Death (age): October 8, 2000 (89)
Place of Death: Anna Kaseman Hospital, Albuquerque, New Mexico
Cause of Death: leukemia
Resting Place: cremated with ashes buried at the National Cemetery, Santa Fe, New Mexico[127]

Harold Lowell "Mud" Runnels
Businessman; Democratic U.S. Congressman, 1971-1980; a key supporter of the Waste Isolation Pilot Project (WIPP) near Carlsbad in his southern New Mexico Congressional district; the Harold Runnels Memorial Scholarship at New Mexico Tech is named in his honor
Date of Birth: March 17, 1924
Place of Birth: Dallas, Texas
Date of Death (age): 2:05 a.m., August 5, 1980 (56)
Place of Death: a hospital in New York City, New York
Cause of Death: chronic lung disease
Resting Place: Resthaven Memorial Gardens, Lovington, New Mexico[128] No. 250

250. The words along the top of Harold Runnels's gravestone read: "Dedicated Servant of his State and Country. A True American." Photo courtesy of Jim Harris.

Steven Harvey "Steve" Schiff
Bernalillo County District Attorney, 1980-88; Republican U.S. Congressman, 1989-98; officer in the New Mexico Air National Guard for twenty-two years; a U.S. Post Office in Albuquerque was named in his honor
Date of Birth: March 18, 1947
Place of Birth: Chicago, Illinois
Date of Death (age): March 25, 1998 (51)
Place of Death: Albuquerque, New Mexico
Cause of Death: squamous-cell skin cancer

Resting Place: Fairview Cemetery, Albuquerque, New Mexico[129] No. 251

Joseph Richard "Joe" Skeen
Sheep rancher; Republican U.S. Congressman, 1981-2002; first won election to Congress in a successful write-in campaign, only the third victory of its kind in U.S. history; longest serving Congressman from New Mexico; a key supporter of the Waste Isolation Pilot Plant (WIPP) that opened near Carlsbad in his southern New Mexico Congressional district in 1999; the Joseph R. Skeen Library on the New Mexico Tech campus was named in his honor
Date of Birth: June 30, 1927
Place of Birth: Roswell, New Mexico
Date of Death (age): 8:20 p.m., December 7, 2003 (76)
Place of Death: Eastern New Mexico Medical Center, Roswell, New Mexico
Cause of Death: complications from Parkinson's disease
Resting Place: at his family's Buckhorn Ranch in Picacho on the eastern edge of Lincoln County, New Mexico

251. Note the pebbles placed on the corners of Congressman Schiff's gravestone. It is a Jewish custom to leave a stone on a gravestone to indicate that people have visited the site. Clearly, the Congressman's gravesite is visited often. The inscription under his name reads: "Beloved husband, father, and public servant. Colonel (Ret.) USAFR NMANC District Attorney."

During Skeen's final days in a Roswell hospital, the New Mexico State Transportation Commission named U.S. Highway 70 from Roswell to Ruidoso, in the heart of his Congressional district, the Joe Skeen Highway.[130]

Diplomatic Leaders

Francis Vincent "Frank" Ortiz, Jr.
Served in the U.S. Army Air Force, 1944-46; U.S. Ambassador to Barbados and Grenada (1977-79), Guatemala (1979-80), Peru (1981), and Argentina (1983-86); served nearly forty years in the U.S. diplomatic service (1951-90) with other assignments in Ethiopia, Mexico, Panama, and Uruguay; one of the highest ranking Hispanics in the U.S. foreign service; instrumental in negotiating the Chamizal border agreement with Mexico, 1963; recipient of many honors, including a knighthood from the King of Spain; a founder of the Friends of the Palace of the Governors; active in other historical preservation and community-based organizations since his retirement in 1990; University of New Mexico honorary degree recipient, 1986
Date of Birth: March 14, 1926
Place of Birth: Santa Fe, New Mexico
Date of Death (age): February 27, 2005 (78)
Place of Death: at his home in Santa Fe, New Mexico
Cause of Death: cancer
Resting Place: Rosario Cemetery, Santa Fe, New Mexico[131]

As a boy of five his grandmother, Alcaria Ortiz, took young Frank to a neighbor's house to witness his first wake. "She wanted me to know very early that death was a part of life. I've never forgotten that."[132]

After retiring from the diplomatic corps in 1990, Ortiz and his wife visited Rosario Cemetery to check if there was room for their future graves. Finding his family plots "chock-a-block full," they made arrangements to be buried near the cemetery's old chapel. They "also went the slightly ghoulish lengths of choosing passages from the sacred scrip to be inscribed on our tombstones. Perhaps they serve well as an epitaph to [our] lives together." Ortiz's final choice was from Paul's letter to Timothy: "My life is already being poured away as a libation, and the time has come for me to be gone. I fought the good fight to the end; I have run the race to the finish; I have kept the faith." Describing the completion of his race, Ortiz finished his autobiography by noting, "I can imagine Grandmother Alcaria nodding in approval, saying, *'Bien, bien, hijo mío.* (Well done, my son.)'"[133]

Ortiz's headstone had not yet been erected by August 2005.

Other Diplomatic Leaders include:
Tibo J. Chavez, Sr. (this chapter)
Herbert James Hagerman (this chapter)
Patrick J. Hurley (Chapter 13: Wartime Leaders and Victims Since the Spanish-American War, 1898)
William A. Pile (this chapter)
Abraham Rencher (this chapter)
Lew Wallace (this chapter)

Other Political Leaders *(in alphabetical order)*

Louise Holland Coe

First woman elected to serve in the New Mexico State Senate, 1925-41; first woman to serve as President Pro-Tem of the New Mexico State Senate; President Pro-Tem of the New Mexico State Senate, 1929-41; first woman to serve as a Democratic Party candidate for the U.S. Congress, 1940; the community of Glencoe, New Mexico, was named in the Coe family's honor
Date of Birth: November 26, 1894
Place of Birth: Bartlett, Texas
Date of Death (age): March 13, 1985 (90)
Place of Death: Casa Maria Health Care Center, Roswell, New Mexico
Cause of Death: unstated natural causes
Resting Place: cremated with ashes buried at the private Coe Family Cemetery, Glencoe, New Mexico; not accessible to the general public[134] No. 252

252. On the back of Louise Coe's gravestone are the words: "University of New Mexico, Pioneer New Mexico Educator, First Woman New Mexico State Senator, 1925-41, President Pro-Tem, 1929-41, Strong Willed, Dogged Determination, World Traveler, Writer, Historian, Gracious Coe Ranch Hostess to Friends from Hondo to Singapore, Music, Flowers, A Dynamic, Colorful Spirit, *Salud!*"

María Concepción "Concha" Ortiz y Pino de Kleven

Honored as the "*Gran Dama* of New Mexico"; descendent of the Pino family that arrived with Don Diego de Vargas in his reconquest of New Mexico in the 1690s; founded a vocational school in Galisteo to teach traditional Hispanic crafts; a Democrat, elected to the New Mexico state legislature at age twenty-six, in 1936, serving three terms; the first woman in the United States to be chosen majority whip

in a state legislature, 1941; managed her family's 100,000-acre Agua Verde ranch, 1951-56; a leading advocate of women's rights, bilingual education, the rights of persons with mental and physical disabilities, and prisoner rehabilitation programs; appointed to national boards by five U.S. presidents; honored with dozens of awards for local, state, and national public service; a state building in Santa Fe was named in her honor in 2004
Date of Birth: May 20, 1910
Place of Birth: Galisteo, New Mexico
Date of Death (age): early morning, September 30, 2006 (96)
Place of Death: El Castillo Retirement Residences, Santa Fe, New Mexico
Cause of Death: pneumonia
Resting Place: Rosario Cemetery, Santa Fe, New Mexico

Jeremiah "Shoeless Jerry" Simpson
Colorful Populist politician; U.S. Congressman from Kansas, 1891-95 and 1897-99; Roswell business developer and civic leader, 1902-05
Date of Birth: March 31, 1842
Place of Birth: Prince Edward Island, Canada
Date of Death (age): 6:05 a.m., October 23, 1905 (63)
Place of Death: St. Francis Hospital, Wichita, Kansas
Cause of Death: aneurysm of the heart
Resting Place: Maple Grove Cemetery, Wichita, Kansas[136]

William Howard Taft
U.S. Secretary of War, 1904-08; Republican U.S. President (1909-13) who signed New Mexico's statehood bill at 1:35 p.m., January 6, 1912; Chief Justice of the U.S. Supreme Court, 1921-30; a U.S. postage stamp was issued in his honor
Date of Birth: September 15, 1857
Place of Birth: Cincinnati, Ohio
Date of Death (age): late in the afternoon, March 8, 1930 (72)
Place of Death: Washington, D.C.
Cause of Death: probably heart disease
Resting Place: National Cemetery, Arlington, Virginia[137] No. 253

253. Photo courtesy of Sam Jackson.

Other Political Leaders include:
Julia Asplund (Chapter 6: Educational Leaders)
Stephen Dorsey (Chapter 5: Business Leaders)
John Ehrlichman (Chapter 8: Lawmen, Criminals, and Victims of Crime)
Albert Jennings Fountain (Chapter 8: Lawmen, Criminals, and Victims of Crime)
Conrad Hilton (Chapter 5: Business Leaders)
Patrick J. Hurley (Chapter 13: Wartime Leaders and Victims Since the Spanish-American War, 1898)
Oliver Milton Lee, Jr. (Chapter 8: Lawmen, Criminals, and Victims of Crime)

W.H.H. Llewellyn (Chapter 13: Wartime Leaders and Victims Since the Spanish-American War, 1898)

Maximiliano Luna (Chapter 13: Military Leaders and Victims Since the Spanish-American War, 1898)

Ruth McCormick (Chapter 6: Educational Leaders)

O.P. McMains (Chapter 8: Lawmen, Criminals, and Victims of Crime)

Nina Otero-Warren (Chapter 7: Sung and Unsung Heroes)

Sterling Price (Chapter 12: Wartime Leaders and Victims to the End of the Indian Wars in New Mexico, 1886)

Benjamin M. Read (Chapter 4: Cultural Preservationists)

Theodore Roosevelt (Chapter 13: Wartime Leaders and Victims Since the Spanish-American War, 1898)

Frank Springer (Chapter 6: Educational Leaders)

Native American Political Leaders (in alphabetical order)

Pablo Abeita
Pueblo leader and defender of Native American rights; president of the All-Pueblo Council; famous for his refusal to honor Francisco Coronado at the Coronado Cuatro Centennial, 1940; known as the "Grand Old Man of Isleta Pueblo"
Date of Birth: February 10, 1871
Place of Birth: Isleta, New Mexico
Date of Death (age): December 17, 1940 (69)
Place of Death: Isleta, New Mexico
Cause of Death: heart attack
Resting Place: Isleta Catholic Cemetery, Isleta Pueblo, New Mexico; not accessible to the general public[138]

Wendell Chino
Mescalero Apache leader, 1955-98; first Mescalero president, reelected seventeen times; outspoken, nationally recognized defender of Native American rights
Date of Birth: December 27, 1923
Place of Birth: Mescalero Reservation, Mescalero, New Mexico
Date of Death (age): 1:28 p.m., November 4, 1998 (74)
Place of Death: Santa Monica-UCLA Medical Center, Santa Monica, California
Cause of Death: heart attack while undergoing a cardiac stress test
Resting Place: Mescalero Cemetery, Mescalero, New Mexico; not accessible to the general public

Famous for bringing economically lucrative businesses to the Mescalero Reservation, Chino once said that the Navajos make rugs, the Pueblos make pottery, and "the Mescaleros make money."

More than a thousand people attended Chino's funeral, held at a Mescalero gymnasium. Dignitaries, from then-governor Gary Johnson to Senator Pete Domenici, attended. One Native American speaker told the assembled mourners that Chino was now traveling in the Indian spirit world. Hearing the sound of a window-shaking winter wind and remembering Chino's famous sense of humor, the same speaker added, "Maybe he's clattering that window up there. Maybe he's telling us to cut it short."[139]

Henry Chee Dodge; Hastiin Adiits'a'ii (Man Who Interprets); Mister Interpreter

Navajo Long Walk survivor; official translator for the Navajo by the time he was twenty years old; last official chief of the Navajo nation; elected chairman of the first Navajo tribal council, 1923; Native American activist Annie Dodge Wauneka's father
Date of Birth: 1857
Place of Birth: Fort Defiance, Arizona
Date of Death (age): 6:00 a.m., January 7, 1947 (about 90)
Place of Death: Presbyterian Hospital, Ganado, Arizona
Cause of Death: unstated natural causes
Resting Place: Fort Defiance Cemetery, Fort Defiance, Arizona

A granite monument supported by dark red concrete slabs was installed at Dodge's gravesite in May 1949. In addition to his name and dates are the words, "The former Mister Interpreter here permanently lies in the Earth."[140]

Antonio "Tony" Lujan

Pueblo leader; married to Mabel Dodge Luhan, 1923-62, her fourth husband[141]
Date of Birth: January 2, 1879
Place of Birth: Taos Pueblo, New Mexico
Date of Death (age): about 1:30 a.m., January 27, 1963 (84); less than half a year after Mabel Dodge Luhan's death
Place of Death: Holy Cross Hospital, Taos, New Mexico
Cause of Death: fell down stairwell at night
Resting Place: Taos Pueblo Cemetery, Taos Pueblo, New Mexico; not accessible to the general public[142]

Frank Waters recalled that Taos Pueblo Indians had taken Tony's body to the pueblo for burial within hours after his death. Waters wrote that "According to custom, his body was wrapped in his red-and-blue Chief blanket. [A] large turquoise and silver ring…shone on his hand. His full-beaded turquoise moccasins had been put on his protruding bare feet. The body was now lashed with ropes and lowered into the grave. There was no coffin, no box. He was simply returned to his Mother Earth."[143]

Pedro Pino; originally Lai-iu-ah-tsai-lu[144]

Governor of Zuni Pueblo during most of the period 1830-78; met with President Chester A. Arthur in Washington, D.C., 1882
Date of Birth: about 1788
Place of Birth: Zuni Pueblo, New Mexico
Date of Death (age): about 1888 (about 100)
Place of Death: Zuni Pueblo, New Mexico

Cause of Death: "heart wore out"
Resting Place: on the Zuni Pueblo, New Mexico[145]

Jacob Viarrial
Vietnam War U.S. Navy veteran; Governor of Pojoaque Pueblo for more than twenty years, first elected in 1978 and continuously since 1985; worked for his pueblo's economic development, with controversial stands on Indian gaming and water usage, going so far as to close U.S. 84-285 in protest over gaming issues, 1996
Date of Birth: 1946
Place of Birth: Pojoaque Pueblo
Date of Death (age): June 26, 2004 (about 58)
Place of Death: hotel in Juárez, Mexico
Cause of Death: heart attack
Resting Place: Pojoaque Pueblo Cemetery, Pojoaque Pueblo, New Mexico[146]

Other Native American Political Leaders include:
Popé (Chapter 12: Wartime leaders and Victims to the End of the Indian Wars in New Mexico, 1886)
Annie Dodge Wauneka (Chapter 11: Scientists and Medical Personnel)

Judges (in alphaabetical order)

Kirby Benedict
Controversial U.S. Territorial judge, 1853-66; Chief Justice of the New Mexico Territorial Supreme Court, 1858-66; owner and editor of the *New Mexico Weekly Union*, 1873-74; accused of being intoxicated while serving on the bench; President of the Historical Society of New Mexico, 1865
Date of Birth: November 23, 1810
Place of Birth: Kent, Connecticut
Date of Death (age): February 27, 1874 (63)
Place of Death: at his home in Santa Fe, New Mexico
Cause of Death: heart attack
Resting Place: originally buried in the Masonic section of Rosario Cemetery until he and other Masons were reinterred at Santa Fe's Fairview Cemetery when it opened on Cerillos Road in 1884 or at the Santa Fe National Cemetery in 1895; in either case, his gravesite is currently unknown and, hence, unmarked

The *Santa Fe New Mexican* described Benedict's funeral as "very imposing" with services

> Conducted by the Masonic fraternity which was out in heavy force. The 8th cavalry band in their new and flashy uniforms led the procession, playing dirges to the grave. The music was very fine [although] the mud interfered with the comfort of the pedestrians. A very large concourse of our citizens were out and altogether the demonstration indicated a decidedly kindly feeling by the general community toward the deceased.[147]

Tibo Juan Chavez, Sr.

Descendent of the original Chavez Spanish family that arrived in New Mexico with Don Juan de Oñate in 1598; U.S. Foreign Service Officer, 1943-45; New Mexico State Senator, 1948-50 and 1956-74; introduced the Fair Employees Practices Act, 1949, the Cultural Properties Act, 1973, and the State Monuments Designation Act, 1973; Lieutenant Governor of New Mexico, 1950-54; State District Court Judge, 1979-91; one of the few New Mexican leaders to serve in all three branches of the state government; Hispanic cultural preservationist, folklorist, and expert on herbs and folk medicine; lecturer and author of historical books and articles, especially *New Mexican Folklore of the Rio Abajo* (1987); a scholarship at the University of New Mexico-Valencia Campus was named in his honor

Date of Birth: June 12, 1912
Place of Birth: Belen, New Mexico
Date of Death (age): November 25, 1991 (79)
Place of Death: a local hospital in Albuquerque, New Mexico
Cause of Death: cardiac pulmonary arrest
Resting Place: Our Lady of Belen Catholic Cemetery, Belen, New Mexico[148]

254. A collector of *dichos* (Spanish proverbs), Tibo Chavez's gravestone includes one of favorites: *"Haz bien y no mires a quien."* (Do well unto others and don't worry to whom.) His headstone also lists his many achievements: "Statesman, Historian, Author, Lecturer, Herbalist, Humanitarian, Husband, Father, Grandfather." A second stone, at the foot of his grave, reads: "A Descendant of the Original Chavez Family Who Came to New Mexico in 1598 with Juan de Oñate, First Governor of New Mexico."

    A local priest recalled his last visit with Judge Chavez in the hospital room where he died. An avid horseman, Chavez told the cleric, "Get a couple of horses and get me out of here so I can go home." Sadly, Chavez died without ever riding home again to Belen.[149]

    Hundreds attended the beloved judge's funeral, including Governor Bruce King. A riderless horse, with cowboy boots turned backwards, accompanied the hearse that carried Chavez's remains to his burial site in the Belen parish cemetery. As a final act, the judge's family sprinkled Indian cornmeal on his coffin, telling the gathered crowd that the cornmeal, delivered by an Indian friend, was meant to "help the [Chavez] family commune with the old folklorist's spirit."[150]
No. 254

John Robert McFie

Civil War U.S. Army veteran; co-founder of Las Cruces College, 1888; President of the first Board of Regents at New Mexico A&M (the college's first building was named in his honor, 1891); Territorial Supreme Court Justice, 1889-93 and 1897-1912, serving longer than any other Supreme Court justice in New Mexico's territorial history; a foremost sponsor of New Mexico archeological research

Date of Birth: October 9, 1848
Place of Birth: Randolph County, Illinois
Date of Death (age): July 19, 1930 (81)
Place of Death: Santa Fe, New Mexico
Cause of Death: unstated natural causes after a fifteen-month illness
Resting Place: National Cemetery, Santa Fe, New Mexico[151] No. 255

255.

256.

William Hayes Pope
Territorial Chief Justice, 1910-12, and the first U.S. District Court judge after statehood, 1912-16
Date of Birth: June 14, 1870
Place of Birth: Beaufort, South Carolina
Date of Death (age): 3:30 a.m., September 13, 1916 (46)
Place of Death: at his sister-in-law's home in Atlanta, Georgia
Cause of Death: pernicious anemia
Resting Place: Fairview Cemetery, Santa Fe, New Mexico

Pope had gone to Atlanta in mid 1916 to seek medical attention, but died at his sister-in-law's home in that city before he could recover.[152]
No. 256

Other Judges include:
Samuel Axtell (this chapter)
Howard S. Beacham (Chapter 8: Lawmen, Criminals, and Victims of Crime)
Sam Bratton (this chapter)
Albert B. Fall (this chapter)
Carl A. Hatch (this chapter)
Thomas J. Mabry (this chapter)
Edwin Mechem (this chapter)
Merritt C. Mechem (this chapter)
William J. Mills (this chapter)
L. Bradford Prince (this chapter)
John P. Slough (Chapter 12: Military Leaders and Victims to the End of the Indian Wars in New Mexico, 1886)
John S. Watts (this chapter)

Famous and Unusual Gravesites in New Mexico History 237

10

Religious Leaders

Archbishops of Santa Fe *(in chronological order by years of service)*

Jean Baptiste Lamy
First bishop, 1851-75, and first archbishop, 1875-85, of New Mexico; introduced many changes to the Catholic Church in New Mexico, including the recruitment of over 120 French priests and nuns to live and work in the region and the construction of the Romanesque St. Francis Cathedral in Santa Fe, October 1869-October 18, 1895; depicted as Archbishop Jean Marie Latour in Willa Cather's controversial novel, *Death Comes for the Archbishop* (1927); the railroad community of Lamy in Santa Fe County, New Mexico, was named in his honor; streets in Santa Fe and Albuquerque were also named in his honor
Date of Birth: October 11, 1814
Place of Birth: Lempdes, France
Date of Death (age): 7:45 a.m., February 13, 1888 (73)
Place of Death: Archbishop's House in Santa Fe, New Mexico
Cause of Death: pneumonia
Resting Place: the first of six archbishops buried in a stone crypt beneath the north side of the sanctuary in St. Francis Cathedral, Santa Fe, New Mexico[2]

False rumors of Lamy's death on one of his many trips down the Santa Fe Trail circulated in 1867. Reportedly, raiding Indians had killed and mutilated the bishop and his traveling companions. Requiem masses were already being said when Lamy and his caravan arrived safely in Trinidad, Colorado. Despite a terrible rain storm, church bells rang and hundreds gathered to welcome their religious leader home when he finally arrived in Santa Fe, tired but in good health, on August 15, 1867.[3]

Lamy's actual death occurred twenty-one years later.

Ill and taken home to his bedroom in Archbishop's House, Lamy asked his successor, Jean Baptiste Salpointe, to administer the last rites of the Catholic Church. Later he told his old friend, "Thank you. I was able to follow every word of the prayers you came to say for me. Keep praying for me, for I feel that I am going."[4] According to a newspaper report, "He passed away as he had lived, calmly and beautifully, a smile of Christian contentment encircling his noble face like a halo of glory."[5]

An estimated six thousand people viewed Lamy's body when it lay

*How beautiful on the mountains
Are the feet of those who bring good news,
Who proclaim peace,
Who bring good tidings,
Who proclaim salvation,
Who say to Zion,
"Your God reigns!"*
—*Isaiah 52:7*[1]

257.

in state at St. Francis Cathedral.⁶ According to the *Santa Fe New Mexican*, the day of his funeral

> was an impressive one in the extreme. The mourning multitude packed every space in the great edifice. The decorations were imposing. The altars were ablaze with resplendent draperies. Sadness was depicted in every countenance, and the thousands who on yesterday had elbowed their way through the aisles to kiss the soles of the Archbishop's purple sandals now pressed forward quite as eagerly to catch the voice of the eulogists, or buried their faces as the choir rendered the Te Deum. Fifty persons composed the choir. The obsequies began at 9 o'clock and lasted four hours. Most Reverend J.B. Salpointe, archbishop of Santa Fe, and Most Reverend Machebeuf, archbishop of Denver, were celebrants of the high mass.⁷ No. 257

Jean Baptiste Salpointe; originally Gilbert Salpointe
Bishop of Arizona, 1869-84; second Archbishop of Santa Fe, 1885-94; Salpointe Catholic High School in Tucson, Arizona, was named in his honor
Date of Birth: February 21, 22, or 25, 1825
Place of Birth: Saint Maurice de Poinstat, France
Date of Death (age): July 15, 1898 (73)
Place of Death: Tucson, Arizona
Cause of Death: unstated natural causes
Resting Place: originally by the altar at St. Augustine Church, Tucson, Arizona; moved in the 1960s to Holy Hope Catholic Cemetery, Tucson, Arizona⁸ No. 258

258. Photo courtesy of Kris White.

Placid Louis Chapelle
Third Archbishop of Santa Fe, 1895-97; Archbishop of New Orleans, Louisiana, 1897-1905
Date of Birth: August 28, 1842
Place of Birth: Runes, France
Date of Death (age): August 9, 1905 (62)
Place of Death: New Orleans, Louisiana
Cause of Death: yellow fever
Resting Place: below the sanctuary of St. Louis Cathedral, New Orleans, Louisiana⁹

Pierre (or Peter) Bourgade
First Bishop of Tucson, Arizona, 1897-99; fourth Archbishop of Santa Fe, 1899-1908
Date of Birth: October 17, 1845
Place of Birth: Vollore-Ville, Puy-dé- Dome, France
Date of Death (age): May 17, 1908 (62)

Place of Death: Chicago, Illinois
Cause of Death: rheumatic fever that degenerated into heart failure
Resting Place: crypt beneath the north side of the sanctuary in St. Francis Cathedral, Santa Fe, New Mexico[10] No. 257

Jean Baptiste Pitaval
Fifth and last of the French archbishops of New Mexico, 1909-18
Date of Birth: February 10, 1858
Place of Birth: Sant Genis-Terrenoire, France
Date of Death (age): May 23, 1928 (70)
Place of Death: St. Anthony Hospital, Denver, Colorado
Cause of Death: unstated natural causes after he was in poor health for the decade following his retirement
Resting Place: Mount Olive Cemetery, Denver, Colorado

      Realizing that his end was near, Pitaval selected the plot in the cemetery where he wanted to be buried as well as the wording on a simple granite cross he wanted erected over his grave, leaving only a blank for the date of his demise.[11]

Albert Thomas "Padre Alberto" Daeger, O.F.M.
Sixth Archbishop of Santa Fe, 1919-32; first and only Franciscan priest to serve as the Archbishop of Santa Fe
Date of Birth: March 5, 1872
Place of Birth: St. Ann, Indiana
Date of Death (age): 2:40 p.m., December 2, 1932 (60)
Place of Death: St. Vincent Hospital, Santa Fe, New Mexico
Cause of Death: fractured skull from a ten foot fall down the basement stairs in a Santa Fe, New Mexico, garage
Resting Place: crypt beneath the north side of the sanctuary in St. Francis Cathedral, Santa Fe, New Mexico[12] No. 257

Rudolph Aloysius Gerken
First Bishop of Amarillo, Texas, 1927-33; seventh Archbishop of Santa Fe, 1933-43
Date of Birth: March 7, 1887
Place of Birth: Dyersville, Iowa
Date of Death (age): 1:15 p.m., March 2, 1943 (55)
Place of Death: St. Vincent Hospital, Santa Fe, New Mexico
Cause of Death: cerebral thrombosis
Resting Place: crypt beneath the north side of the sanctuary in St. Francis Cathedral, Santa Fe, New Mexico[13] No. 257

Edwin Vincent Byrne
First Bishop of Ponce, Puerto Rico, 1925-29; Bishop of San Juan, Puerto Rico, 1929-43; eighth Archbishop of Santa Fe, 1943-63
Date of Birth: August 9, 1891

Place of Birth: Philadelphia, Pennsylvania
Date of Death (age): July 25, 1963 (71)
Place of Death: St. Vincent Hospital, Santa Fe, New Mexico
Cause of Death: complications following gall bladder surgery
Resting Place: crypt beneath the north side of the sanctuary in St. Francis Cathedral, Santa Fe, New Mexico[14] No. 257

James Peter Davis
Bishop of San Juan, Puerto Rico, 1943-60; first Archbishop of San Juan, Puerto Rico, 1960-1964; ninth Archbishop of Santa Fe, 1964-1974
Date of Birth: June 9, 1904
Place of Birth: Houghton, Michigan
Date of Death (age): March 4, 1988 (83)
Place of Death: St. Joseph Hospital, Albuquerque, New Mexico
Cause of Death: respiratory arrest
Resting Place: crypt beneath the north side of the sanctuary in St. Francis Cathedral, Santa Fe, New Mexico[15] No. 257

Catholic Brothers and Priests (in alphabetical order)
Although well over three hundred Franciscan missionaries served in New Mexico during the Spanish colonial era, the location of only three of their graves can be identified today. As noted in Chapter 1, the three Franciscans are Father Asencio de Zárate and Father Gerónimo de la Llana, now buried in St. Francis Cathedral in Santa Fe, and Fray Juan José Padilla, buried by the altar at the St. Augustine Catholic Church in Isleta. Since the end of Spanish rule, hundreds of other priests and missionaries have served in the region and have been buried in cemeteries across New Mexico. Large numbers of their graves can be found in special sections of Rosario Cemetery in Santa Fe and at Mount Calvary Cemetery in Albuquerque.

Mathias "Brother Mathias" Barrett
Founder of the Little Brothers of the Good Shepherd in Albuquerque, New Mexico, 1951; admired for his work among the poor, sometimes known as the "Mother Teresa of America"
Date of Birth: March 15, 1900
Place of Birth: Waterford, Ireland
Date of Death (age): August 12, 1990 (90)
Place of Death: St. Joseph Hospital on the West Mesa, Albuquerque, New Mexico
Cause of Death: complications following gall bladder surgery
Resting Place: behind the Little Brothers of the Good Shepherd Center, Albuquerque, New Mexico[16]

Over a decade after his death, Brother Mathais's annual St. Patrick's Day dinner still raised nearly $30,000 for the Good Shepherd Center, Albuquerque, New Mexico.[17] No. 259

259.

Albert "Father Albert" "Father Al" Braun, O.F.M.; originally John William Braun[18]

First Franciscan missionary to live and work full-time among the Mescalero Apache; principal builder of St. Joseph's Apache Mission Church in Mescalero, New Mexico, 1920-39; Civilian Conservation Corps chaplain; U.S. Army chaplain in World War I and World War II; captured with the surrender of Corregidor, May 6, 1942; Japanese Prisoner of War, 1942-45; received the Purple Heart (during World War I), two Silver Stars (one in World War I and one in World War II), and the Legion of Merit (in World War II)

Date of Birth: September 5, 1889
Place of Birth: Los Angeles, California
Date of Death (age): March 6, 1983 (93)
Place of Death: Phoenix, Arizona
Cause of Death: cancer
Resting Place: his crypt lies to the south side of the altar at St. Joseph's Mission Church, Mescalero, New Mexico[19]

According to his biographer, Dorothy Cave Aldrich, Father Albert never stopped helping others,

260.

> even in his last years, in a nursing home run by the Little Sisters of the Poor.... His leg had never recovered from a time when, as a POW, he had been forced to kneel on icy concrete for a day and a night. Finally the doctors insisted the leg must be amputated. Even then, minus the leg, partially deaf, and dying of cancer, he was a familiar sight racing about the streets in his wheelchair....seeking couples who needed marrying, children who needed baptizing, strangers who needed religious instruction, and—in election years—urging people to vote. He said Mass daily for the nursing home residents and the nuns up until five days before he died at the age of ninety-three.[20]

A restoration project, projected to cost two million dollars and take nine more years to complete, is currently underway at St. Joseph's Mission Church.[21] No. 260

Lawrence Martin "Father Marty" Jenco, O.S.M.

Member of the Servite Order who served in Yemen, Thailand, India, and Lebanon; Pastor at Our Lady of Belen Catholic Church, 1979-81; kidnapped while serving as the head of Catholic Relief Services and held hostage by radical Shiite Muslims in Beirut, Lebanon, January 8, 1985, to July 26, 1986, as described in his book, *Bound to Forgive: The Pilgrimage of Reconciliation of a Beirut Hostage* (1995)

Date of Birth: November 27, 1934
Place of Birth: Joliet, Illinois
Date of Death (age): July 19, 1996 (61)
Place of Death: St. Domitilla Church rectory, Hillside, Illinois
Cause of Death: pancreatic and lung cancer
Resting Place: Queen of Heaven Cemetery, Hillside, Illinois[22]

Joseph Projectus Machebeuf

French missionary in New Mexico, Arizona, Utah, and Colorado; Bishop Jean B. Lamy's Vicar General, 1851-68; first bishop (later archbishop) of Colorado, 1868-89; depicted as Father Vaillant in Willa Cather's controversial historical novel, *Death Comes for the Archbishop* (1927)

Date of Birth: August 11, 1812
Place of Birth: Riom, France
Date of Death (age): July 10, 1889 (76)
Place of Death: at his small room at St. Vincent Orphanage, Denver, Colorado
Cause of Death: unstated natural causes
Resting Place: Gallagher Chapel at Mount Olive Cemetery, Denver, Colorado

Mount Olive Cemetery had been a 440-acre farm purchased by Bishop Machebeuf and donated by him to the Catholic Church for use as a cemetery.[23]
No. 261

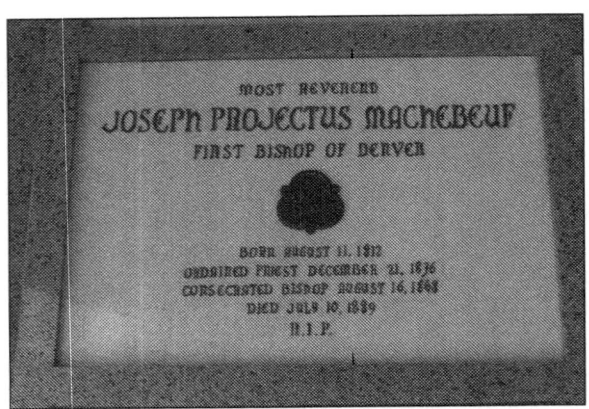

261. Photo courtesy of David N. Lotz.

Antonio José Martínez; Padre Martínez

Powerful Hispanic priest of the Rio Arriba, ordained February 10, 1822; ran a school in Taos at which as many as twenty future priests were first educated; published the first book in New Mexico, 1934; famous for his many differences with Archbishop Jean Baptiste Lamy; defrocked, 1854, and excommunicated, 1857; depicted and heavily criticized in Willa Cather's controversial historical novel, *Death Comes for the Archbishop* (1927); a street in Taos was named in his honor; his statue is in the Taos plaza

Date of Birth: January 17, 1793
Place of Birth: Abiquiu, New Mexico
Date of Death (age): 9:00 p.m., July 27, 1867 (74)
Place of Death: Taos, New Mexico
Cause of Death: unstated natural causes, perhaps related to a respiratory ailment
Resting Place: Kit Carson Cemetery, Taos, New Mexico

Reportedly, Padre Martínez's last words were: "Thy will be done." Because he supported and was supported by the Penitentes, local members of the Brotherhood of Our Father Jesus the Nazarene "gave him a burial service that would have honored a king." Originally buried in the Taos Catholic cemetery, he was later removed to the outskirts of a Protestant one, undoubtedly as a result of his 1857 excommunication.[24] Nos. 262, 263, 264

262. Padre Martínez's original gravestone. Photo courtesy of the Palace of the Governors (MNM/DCA), neg. no. 14816.

Jean Baptiste Rallière

Among 114 French priests recruited to serve in New Mexico by Bishop Jean Baptiste Lamy, first arriving in Santa Fe, New Mexico, with the bishop in 1856; served as the parish priest at Our Lady of the Immaculate Conception Church, Tomé, New Mexico, June 13, 1858, until his retirement on April 20, 1913, for a total of almost fifty-five years, causing him to be known as "El Padre Eterno" (The Eternal Priest); longest serving French priest recruited by Lamy; Superintendent of Schools, Valencia County, New Mexico, 1887-88

Date of Birth: April 30, 1854

Place of Birth: France

Date of Death (age): 9:00 p.m., July 18, 1915 (61)

Place of Death: Tomé, New Mexico

Cause of Death: unstated natural causes

Resting Place: to the left of the altar in Our Lady of the Immaculate Conception Church, Tomé, New Mexico

Symbolically, Father Rallière was buried in Tomé with the French chalice he had brought with him from his native France as a novice priest.[25]

263. Padre Martínez's gravestone in ruins after years of decay.

Other Catholic Priests and Brothers include:

Fray Angélico Chávez (Chapter 4: Cultural Preservationists)

Father José Manuel Gallegos (Chapter 9: Political, Diplomatic, and Judicial Leaders)

Fray Marcos de Niza (Chapter 12: Wartime Leaders and Victims to the End of the Indian Wars in New Mexico, 1886)

Father Alexander Grzelachowski (Chapter 12: Wartime Leaders and Victims to the End of the Indian Wars in New Mexico, 1886)

Catholic Nuns (in alphabetical order)

Sisters of various orders, including the Sisters of Charity and the Sisters of Loretto, began arriving in New Mexico in the mid-nineteenth century, thanks in large part to the recruiting efforts of Bishop Lamy. Many served admirably in Catholic schools, orphanages, and hospitals, the church's new social institutions in New Mexico. Space does not allow for more than a small sample of nuns, although, as with many priests, the gravesites of nuns are particularly prevalent in New Mexico's two largest Catholic cemeteries, Rosario in Santa Fe and Mount Calvary in Albuquerque.[26]

Katharine Mary Drexel; Sister Mary Katharine Drexel

Founder of the missionary order of the Sisters of the Blessed Sacrament for Indians and Colored People, February 1891, with over five hundred members serving in twenty-one states by 1955; founder of over a hundred mission schools for Indian and black children in the Southwest and the South, including St. Catherine's Convent and Boarding School, Santa Fe, New Mexico; second U.S. citizen to be canonized a Catholic saint, September 30, 2000

Date of Birth: November 26, 1858

Place of Birth: Philadelphia, Pennsylvania

Date of Death (age): March 3, 1955 (96)

Place of Death: at her convent in Cornwells Heights, Pennsylvania

Cause of Death: unstated natural causes

Resting Place: interred in the crypt of the Sisters of the Blessed Sacrament's motherhouse chapel, Benslem, Pennsylvania[27]

264. Padre Martínez's new gravestone erected by the Taos town government by the early 2000s. The epitaph is the same as on his original stone. Translated, it says: "The legislature of New Mexico called him the 'The honor of his country.' He served the spiritual needs of Taos as its parish priest for forty-two years." Photo courtesy of Mary Robinson.

265. Sister Catherine is buried beside nine other early Sisters of Charity as well as several brothers and priests. A nearby plaque reads: "In loving memory of our beloved pioneer Sisters of Charity of Cincinnati, Christian brothers, and priests who worked for the glory of God and the salvation of souls in Santa Fe and in Northern New Mexico."

Catherine Mallon; Sister Catherine
One of the original four Sisters of Charity who arrived in New Mexico in September 1865 to found St. Vincent Hospital in Santa Fe, January 1866; founder of St. Joseph Hospital, Albuquerque, New Mexico, and St. Raphel Hospital, Trinidad, Colorado
Date of Birth: 1846
Place of Birth: Ireland
Date of Death (age): 6:00 p.m., October 27, 1906 (about 60)
Place of Death: St. Vincent Hospital, Santa Fe, New Mexico
Cause of Death: heart disease
Resting Place: Rosario Cemetery, Santa Fe, New Mexico[28]

According to one biographer, this selfless nun "suffered from rheumatism, neuralgia, and pleurisy, and her long hours nursing the sick, the many dangerous begging trips to raise money for the hospital and orphanage in all kinds of weather only aggravated her condition and several times brought her near to death."[29]

Several months before her death, Sister Catherine had gone to the Sisters of Charity's motherhouse in Cincinnati for a retreat. She had almost decided to retire to the motherhouse when she "was seized by a yearning to return to Santa Fe." The trip back was difficult. On the morning of her death, she collapsed while saying her morning prayers. Knowing that the end was near, she "was thankful that the Lord had permitted her to die amid the scenes which were so fraught with hardships in her early days."[30]

The *Santa Fe New Mexican* described Sister Catherine's funeral:

Clad in the habit of the order to which she had belonged since girlhood with her rosary beads and vows clasped in her right hand, she looked natural even in death and her face wore an expression of extreme peaceful content. Six Sisters of Charity who had been associated with her in her work acted as the pallbearers.[31] No. 265

Rosaister "Rosa" Maria Segale; Sister Blandina
Early Sister of Charity who wrote of her Southwest adventures and work in her famous book, *At the End of the Santa Fe Trail* (1932); served at St. Vincent Hospital in Santa Fe, New Mexico, January 1877 to September 1882; taught school in Albuquerque, New Mexico, September 1882 to August 1889; mother superior of Our Lady of the Angels School in Albuquerque; a convent in Albuquerque is named in her honor
Date of Birth: January 23, 1850
Place of Birth: Cicagna, Italy
Date of Death (age): February 23, 1941 (91)
Place of Death: motherhouse of the Sisters of Charity, Cincinnati, Ohio
Cause of Death: unstated natural causes
Resting Place: motherhouse of the Sisters of Charity Cemetery, Cincinnati, Ohio

According to Sister Blandina's biographer:

> To [her fellow] Sisters [of Charity] who came into her room in the infirmary [at her motherhouse] she would say, "Child, pray that God may give me the grace to endure, to persevere." When terrific headaches would strike her, she would smile, "From my mother I have inherited these bad headaches. My mother's name was Malatesta, which means, 'bad head.' And all my life I have had this bad head."[32]

Religious Mystics *(in alphabetical order)*

Giovanni María "El Solitario" "The Hermit" Augustini; also Giovanni María de Agostini

Reclusive religious figure who lived in isolation northwest of Las Vegas, New Mexico, in a cave on Cerro Tecolote, better known as Hermit's Peak (named in his honor), 1863-67, and then east of Las Cruces in a cave in the Organ Mountains by 1869[33]

Date of Birth: 1800

Place of Birth: Sizzano, Italy

Date of Death (age): April 17, 1869 (the date in which his body was discovered) (about 69)

Place of Death: near La Cueva, New Mexico

Cause of Death: killed with a knife to his back, apparently while saying his prayers

Resting Place: San Albino Cemetery, Mesilla, New Mexico[34]

"The Hermit" told friends in Las Cruces that "I shall make a fire in front of my cave every Friday while I shall be alive. If the fire fails to appear, it will be because I have been killed. I shall bless you daily in my prayers."

His fire was seen every Friday night until Friday, April 16, 1869. Shepherds found his body the following day. Witnesses were amazed that although there were many "wild beasts in that region the body was in no way…molested by the beasts of the mountains."[35] Friends carried his body to the Church of San Albino in Mesilla, where he lay in state. Crowds came to see him and pray day and night.

Once buried in Mesilla, his grave was visited each All Saints Day by those who knew and admired him. For years, they smoothed and decorated the grave with flowers and evergreen sprigs.[36]

Back in Las Vegas, "[a]s late as 1965 annual pilgrimages were made to his cave by the Sociedad del Eremitano." A New Mexico state historical marker has been placed near the site of the now-famous cave.[37]

No. 266

266. Translated, the inscription on The Hermit's original cross, on the sandstone marker carved by Albert Jennings Fountain, and on the current cement stone reads: "Don Juan Maria Justiniano. Hermit of the old and the new world. He died April 17, 1869, at the age of sixty-nine years, having professed for forty-nine years. A rare life in this nineteenth century."[38]

Francis "The Healer" Schlatter
Mysterious, humble religious figure known to perform miracles in Colorado and New Mexico
Date of Birth: April 29, 1856
Place of Birth: Alsace-Lorraine, France
Date of Death (age): 1897 (about 41)
Place of Death: Chihuahua, Mexico
Cause of Death: probably hypothermia and starvation
Resting Place: grave marked with a cross under a pine tree in the Piedras Verdes River Valley near Nuevas Casas Grandes, Chihuahua, Mexico

"The Healer" spent several months with Ada Morley and her family on their ranch near Datil. He spent much of this time dictating a manuscript to Ada, later published as *The Life of the Harp in the Hand of the Harper*. A believer in Schlatter and his spiritual powers, Ada was not surprised when his grave was later discovered in Chihuahua, Mexico. "He told me to expect this," Ada told her daughter, Agnes. "He is not dead. He will return."[39]

When archeologist Edgar Lee Hewett found Schlatter's grave in Chihuahua in 1906 Hewett's Mexican guide told him of an experience he had had one morning when he was a boy:

> I saw a man lying under [a pine] tree, covered with a gray blanket. I supposed he was asleep. In the afternoon as I came down, I saw he was still there, and went over to see him. He was dead. Very much frightened, I ran all the way down to the village and told the *jefe político*. They sent an inquest up, decided that the man had died of starvation and freezing. It was then dead of winter, and there had been a great blizzard in the south. So they buried the man there under the tree.[40]

The villagers collected the man's belongings, including his large white horse, a fine western saddle, a copper rod, and a Bible inscribed with the name, Francis Schlatter.

Hewett, who had met Schlatter when the Healer lived in Denver, returned to Nuevas Casas Grandes in 1922 and asked more questions about the mysterious dead man found outside the village. All of his possessions were gone, save the copper rod.

Returning to Santa Fe where he now headed the Museum of New Mexico, Hewett soon received a strange package "bundled in gunny sacks and tied with scraps of rope." The archeologist was "bowled over" when, "on cutting away the cords and string and burlap, there emerged the copper rod of the great healer, Francis Schlatter." The people of Nuevas Casas Grandes had given Hewett the rod, perhaps in gratitude for his help in securing a school teacher for their children. The rod remains at the Museum of New Mexico.[41]

Protestant Ministers *(in alphabetical order)*

Ross R. Calvin
Recovered healthseeker; Episcopal minister in Silver City for fifteen years and in Clovis for another fifteen years; author, especially known for his *Sky Determines* (1934); University of New Mexico honorary degree recipient, 1953
Date of Birth: November 22, 1889
Place of Birth: Chrisman, Illinois
Date of Death (age): January 30, 1970 (80)
Place of Death: at a nursing home in Albuquerque, New Mexico
Cause of Death: unstated natural causes
Resting Place: Fairview Cemetery, Albuquerque, New Mexico[42] No. 267

267.

Emily Jane Duncan Harwood
Methodist teacher and missionary; wife of missionary, Thomas Harwood, arriving with him in New Mexico, 1869; missionary; founder, with her husband, of the Harwood Girls School in Albuquerque, 1887-1976
Date of Birth: April 19, 1842
Place of Birth: Folsom, New York
Date of Death (age): January 15, 1902 (59)
Place of Death: at her family home in Albuquerque, New Mexico
Cause of Death: unstated natural causes; she had earlier contracted malaria and nearly lost her eyesight
Resting Place: Fairview Cemetery, Albuquerque, New Mexico

268. Emily Harwood is buried beside her husband, Thomas.

While traveling by train near Chama, New Mexico, Harwood came close to death when a Pullman car jumped the track and overturned, killing several of her fellow passengers. Returning home, Harwood asserted to her students that "We ought always to live prepared for whatever may come." She added, "it is better sometimes to be poor, and not have much money, for if I had had plenty of money, I might have been in the Pullman instead of the chair-car, and might have been killed [too]."[43]

According to Harwood's biographer, "Hundreds came weeping to her funeral and more than a thousand letters of condolence from Mexicans, Americans, Catholics, and Protestants alike poured into the home of Mr. Harwood."[44] No. 268

Thomas Harwood
Civil War Union Army chaplain; arrived in New Mexico with his wife, Emily, 1869; Methodist missionary who traveled thousands of miles throughout the territory; founder of the Harwood Boys School in Albuquerque, 1887; author of *History of New Mexico Spanish and English Missions of the Methodist Episcopal Church from*

269.

1850 to 1910 (1910)
Date of Birth: October 16, 1829
Place of Birth: Caroline County, Maryland
Date of Death (age): December 31, 1916 (87)
Place of Death: Albuquerque, New Mexico
Cause of Death: cardiac asthma[45]
Resting Place: Fairview Cemetery, Albuquerque, New Mexico; buried beside his wife, Emily. No. 268

James Allen Menaul
Arrived in New Mexico, 1881; Presbyterian pastor and missionary; the Menaul School for Spanish American boys (originally an Indian school founded in 1881) was renamed in his honor, 1896; Menaul Boulevard in Albuquerque was also named in his honor
Date of Birth: December 30, 1842
Place of Birth: Tychany, Trone County, Ireland
Date of Death (age): 6:00 p.m., March 14, 1897 (54)
Place of Death: Albuquerque, New Mexico
Cause of Death: unstated natural causes
Resting Place: Fairview Cemetery, Albuquerque, New Mexico[46] No. 269

Other Protestant Ministers include:
John Chivington (Chapter 12: Wartime Leaders and Victims to the End of the Indian Wars in New Mexico, 1886)
O.P. McMains (Chapter 8: Lawmen, Criminals, and Victims of Crime)
Harry P. Stagg (Chapter 13: Wartime Leaders and Victims Since the Spanish-American War, 1898)
Franklin J. Tolby (Chapter 8: Lawmen, Criminals, and Victims of Crime)

A Church of Jesus Christ of Latter-Day Saints (Mormon) Leader

Joseph Edward Wheeler
Mormon pioneer, missionary, and businessman; polygamist who married Lucy Ann Bingham (by whom he had thirteen children) and her sister Harriet Adeltha Bingham (by whom he had fifteen children); by the time of his death, he had 343 descendents
Date of Birth: August 22, 1856
Place of Birth: Ogden, Utah
Date of Death (age): April 19, 1947 (90)
Place of Death: near Durango, Colorado
Cause of Death: unstated natural causes
Resting Place: Fruitland Cemetery, Fruitland, New Mexico[47]
No. 270

270. Harriet Adeltha Bingham's given name was spelled with one "t", not two, as shown on this gravestone.

Famous and Unusual Gravesites in New Mexico History

A Leading Jewish Rabbi

David D. Shor
U.S. Army Chaplain during World War II; served as the longest serving rabbi of Congregation Temple Albert, Albuquerque, New Mexico, October 1948-June 1978; known for his efforts to build bridges between Jewish, Christian, and other religious communities; New Mexico Human Rights Commission member, 1969

Date of Birth: April 2, 1913
Place of Birth: New Orleans, Louisiana
Date of Death (age): October 19, 1998 (85)
Place of Death: Albuquerque, New Mexico
Cause of Death: apparent heart attack
Resting Place: Congregation Albert Section, Fairview Cemetery, Albuquerque, New Mexico[48] No. 271

271.

A Sikh Leader

Harbhajan Singh Khalsa Jogiji; Yogi Bhajan; originally Harbhajan Singh Puri
Foremost Sikh leader and teacher of the Western world; author of thirty books; founder of a successful drug rehabilitation center; spiritual leader of Akal Security, Inc., based in Santa Cruz, New Mexico

Date of Birth: August 26, 1929
Place of Birth: India (in a region which is now part of Pakistan)
Date of Death (age): 9:05 p.m., October 6, 2004 (75)
Place of Death: at his home in Española, New Mexico
Cause of Death: complications due to heart failure
Resting Place: following Sikh tradition, his body was cremated, with last rites administered seventeen days after his death[49]

A Church Founder

John Ballou Newbrough; the Prophet Tae
Dentist, novelist, social reformer, investigator of the paranormal; author of *Oahspe,* a nearly thousand-page book first published in 1882 upon which the First Church of Tae was based; founder of the utopian, 1,490-acre Shalam Colony of "Faithists" and orphans, 1884, near Doña Ana, New Mexico; a New Mexico State Historical Marker indicates the location of the colony, which closed in 1907

Date of Birth: June 5, 1828
Place of Birth: Mohicanville, Ohio
Date of Death (age): April 22, 1891 (62)
Place of Death: Shalam Colony, near Doña Ana, New Mexico, north of Las Cruces

Cause of Death: pneumonia, after attending to ten children, his wife, and daughter who suffered from the flu

Resting Place: Masonic Cemetery, Las Cruces, New Mexico[50]

With Newbrough's sudden death people reportedly

huddled in frightened groups as strange noises, crashings, and swirling air currents filled the rooms. Floors and walls creaked and roared, dishes fell, and furniture 'walked' and toppled over. The whole fabric of Shalam [colony] shuddered as if in dire pain.[51]

Newbrough was originally buried near the temple he had built at the Shalam Colony. His daughter, Justine, later had his remains moved to the Masonic Cemetery in Las Cruces. Members of the Faithist community in Montrose, Colorado, erected a stone marker over Newbrough's grave in November 1952.[52]

The Shalam Colony and Oahspe Mystery Museum is now open to the public in Mesilla, New Mexico.[53] No. 272

272. The icons on John Newbrough's stone have unique meanings in the First Church of Tae. The symbol at the top represents Jehovih, the creator. The symbol on the bottom left represents Ses, or the spirit world. The symbol on the bottom right represents Es, or signs of the times (change). The symbol in the middle represents Kosmon, or the new age (the present). The inscribed day of death (April 23) is probably incorrect.[54]

11

SCIENTISTS AND MEDICAL PERSONNEL

Scientists *(in alphabetical order)*

Niels Henrik David Bohr
Danish physicist; winner of the Nobel Prize in Physics, 1922; a key Manhattan Project scientist at Los Alamos during World War II
Date of Birth: October 7, 1885
Place of Birth: Copenhagen, Denmark
Date of Death: November 18, 1962 (77)
Place of Death: Copenhagen, Denmark
Cause of Death: unstated natural causes
Resting Place: Assistens Cemetery, Copenhagen, Denmark[1]

"I am thrilled, and yet my mind trembles with fear at seeing what has not been seen before."
—*The Bhagavad-Gita, XI:45*

Norris Edward (or Edwin, as inscribed on his headstone) Bradbury
Director, Los Alamos National Labs, 1945-70; winner of the Atomic Energy Commission's Enrico Fermi Award, the commission's highest honor, among countless other tributes; University of New Mexico honorary degree recipient, 1953; the Bradbury Science Museum in Los Alamos was named in his honor when it opened on August 5, 1963
Date of Birth: May 30, 1909
Place of Birth: Santa Barbara, California
Date of Death (age): August 20, 1997 (88)
Place of Death: at his home in Los Alamos, New Mexico
Cause of Death: unstated natural causes after a long illness
Resting Place: Guaje Pines Cemetery, Los Alamos, New Mexico[2] No. 273

273.

Enrico Fermi
Winner of the Nobel Prize in Physics, 1938; directed the world's first controlled nuclear chain reaction beneath the sports stands at the University of Chicago, December 2, 1942; a key Manhattan Project scientist at Los Alamos during World War II; a U.S. postage stamp was issued in his honor on September 29, 2001, the hundredth anniversary of his birth
Date of Birth: September 29, 1901
Place of Birth: Rome, Italy

274. Photo courtesy of David N. Lotz.

Date of Death (age): November 28, 1954 (53)
Place of Death: Chicago, Illinois
Cause of Death: stomach cancer, believed by some to be caused by years of exposure to radiation
Resting Place: Oak Woods Cemetery, Chicago, Illinois[3] No. 274

Richard Phillips Feynman
A leading scientist in the Manhattan Project at Los Alamos during World War II; probably the only person to watch the atomic blast at Trinity Site with the naked eye, protected only by a truck windshield, which, he believed, would screen ultraviolet rays; winner of the Nobel Prize in Physics, 1965; a U.S. postage stamp was issued in his honor on May 4, 2005
Date of Birth: May 11, 1918
Place of Birth: Queens, New York
Date of Death (age): February 15, 1988 (69)
Place of Death: Los Angeles, California
Cause of Death: kidney failure and ruptured gastrointestinal ulcer
Resting Place: Mountain View Cemetery, Altadena, California

According to Feynman's obituary in the *New York Times*, "Much of what he accomplished [as a scientist] he would admit to not understanding. 'I can live with doubt and uncertainty,' he once said. 'I think it's much more interesting to live not knowing than to have answers which might be wrong.'"[4]

Emil Julius Klaus Fuchs
German emigrant physicist in the Manhattan Project at Los Alamos during World War II; confessed to passing secrets to the atomic bomb to a Soviet spy during World War II; found guilty of espionage, March 1, 1950, and sentenced in England to fourteen years imprisonment; served nine years in prison and was released, June 24, 1959; fled to East Germany where he taught and conducted research the rest of his life
Date of Birth: December 29, 1911
Place of Birth: Rüsselsheim, Germany
Date of Death (age): January 28, 1988 (76)
Place of Death: probably Dresden, East Germany
Cause of Death: unstated natural causes
Resting Place: not disclosed[5]

Fabian "Old Director" Garcia
Member of the first graduating class of New Mexico A&M, 1894; first Hispanic graduate of New Mexico A&M, 1894; Professor of Agriculture, New Mexico A&M; first Hispanic member of the New Mexico A&M faculty; researched and developed major New Mexico crops, including Chile No. 9, Yellow and White Grano onions, Acala cotton, and pecan as the first director of New Mexico A&M's Agricultural

Experiment Station, 1914-45; known as the father of the Mexican food industry in the United States; recipient of honorary degrees from New Mexico A&M and the University of New Mexico, 1943; enshrined in the national Hall of Fame for Horticultural Science, 2005; New Mexico State University's Fabian Garcia Science Center was named in his honor
Date of Birth: January 20, 1871
Place of Birth: Chihuahua, Mexico
Date of Death (age): August 6, 1948 (77)
Place of Death: McBride's Hospital, Las Cruces, New Mexico
Cause of Death: Parkinson's Disease
Resting Place: Masonic Cemetery, Las Cruces, New Mexico

Professor Garcia willed his entire estate to New Mexico A&M for the purpose of building a new dorm for poor Hispanic students as well as a scholarship, still known as the Fabian Garcia Multicultural Scholarship, for minority students. In his words, "I want to help poor boys, for I know their hardships."[6]

Robert Hutchings "Robbie" Goddard

Physicist and rocket scientist who launched the first liquid-fueled rocket in 1926 and continued his intensive research at his ranch in Roswell, New Mexico, 1930-42; known as the "Rocket Man"; Roswell's Goddard High School was named in his honor when it opened in 1965, as was the Robert H. Goddard Planetarium when it opened in Roswell in 1968; inducted into the International Space Hall of Fame, Alamogordo, New Mexico, in 1976; a U.S. postage stamp was issued in his honor
Date of Birth: October 5, 1882
Place of Birth: Worchester, Massachusetts
Date of Death (age): August 10, 1945 (62)
Place of Death: at his home in Worchester, Massachusetts
Cause of Death: throat cancer
Resting Place: Hope Cemetery, Worchester, Massachusetts[7]

275. Photo courtesy of Hope Cemetery.

Goddard lived just long enough to read of the American atomic bombs that were dropped on Japan on August 6 and 9, 1945, helping to end World War II. No longer able to speak, he simply gave a friend the V sign for victory.[8] No. 275

Theodore Alvin "Ted" Hall; originally Theodore Holtzberg

At eighteen, the youngest physicist in the Manhattan Project at Los Alamos during World War II; accused of passing the secrets to the atomic bomb to a Soviet spy in Albuquerque, 1945; never prosecuted for his espionage activities; lived out his life as an eminent research scientist in England
Date of Birth: October 20, 1925
Place of Birth: New York City, New York
Date of Death (age): November 1, 1999 (74)
Place of Death: Cambridge, England

Cause of Death: inoperable cancer of the kidney
Resting Place: not disclosed[9]

Shortly before his death, Hall said that when he was at Los Alamos he was "immature, inexperienced, and far too sure of myself. I am no longer that person—but I am by no means ashamed of him."[10]

Eric Randolph Jette
Metallurgist and a key Group Leader in the Manhattan Project at Los Alamos during World War II and after, 1944-56; husband of Eleanor Jette, author of *Inside Box 1663* (1977) about life in Los Alamos during the war

Date of Birth: September 30, 1897
Place of Birth: Lancaster, Pennsylvania
Date of Death (age): February 22, 1963 (65)
Cause of Death: cancer
Place of Death: St. Vincent Hospital, Santa Fe, New Mexico
Resting Place: cremated with remains buried at the Guaje Pines Cemetery, Los Alamos, New Mexico

The Atomic Energy Commission awarded Jette a citation for meritorious contributions to the American nuclear energy program on February 9, 1963, in the Santa Fe hospital where he lay ill days before his death. Los Alamos Lab director Norris Bradbury attended the ceremony.[11] No. 276

276.

Roy Nakayama
World War II U.S. Army veteran; New Mexico State University Professor of Horticulture, 1950-53, 1955-84; agricultural researcher whose work helped make chile a major cash crop in New Mexico with the development of such varieties as the "NuMex Big Jim" (1975) and the "NuMex R Naky" (1985); known to many as "Mr. Chile"; extensive research with pecans as well; chosen as one of the hundred most outstanding graduates of NMSU's College of Agriculture, 1988
Date of Birth: September 11, 1923
Place of Birth: at what had been the Children's House at the Shalam Colony, near Doña Ana, New Mexico, north of Las Cruces
Date of Death (age): July 11, 1988 (64)
Place of Death: Memorial General Hospital, Las Cruces, New Mexico
Cause of Death: unstated natural causes
Resting Place: cremated with his ashes scattered in his favorite places[12]

A year before his death, Nakayama told an interviewer that if Henry Ford "would have come out with a [single version of the] Model T and quit there, would we all be driving Model T's? You don't stop with what you have; you keep trying to improve."[13]

John Paul Stapp
U.S. Army colonel flight surgeon, 1942-70; veteran of World War II, the Korean War, and Vietnam; set the world record for ground speed, 632 MPH, enduring the

force of 40 Gs and braking to a stop in 1.4 seconds on a rocket-propelled sled known as Sonic Wind No. 1 at Holloman Air Force Base, New Mexico, on December 10, 1954; known as "the fastest man on earth"; founder of Holloman Air Force Base's Aeromedical Field Laboratory, 1953; inducted into the International Space Hall of Fame, Alamogordo, New Mexico, in 1979, where a memorial garden was named in his honor; received the National Medal of Technology from President George H.W. Bush, September 1991

Date of Birth: July 11, 1910

Place of Birth: Bahia, Brazil

Date of Death (age): November 13, 1999 (89)

Place of Death: at his home in Alamogordo, New Mexico

Cause of Death: unstated natural causes

Resting Place: cremated with ashes buried at Fort Bliss National Cemetery, El Paso, Texas[14]

277.

Surviving twenty-nine high-speed test rides, Stapp was asked what he thought about while waiting for each dangerous test to begin. Stapp replied, "First I look around at the mountains and at the bright skies and I don't think about anything. Then I say to myself, 'Paul, it's been a good life.'" Asked why he insisted on being the human guinea pig in the experiments he designed, Stapp said, "If there was a fatality, I didn't want it to be anybody but me."[15] No. 277

Edward Teller

Nuclear physicist instrumental in the development of the atomic bomb by 1945 and, with Stan Ulam, the hydrogen bomb by 1952; known as the "Father of the Hydrogen Bomb"; provided controversial testimony in J. Robert Oppenheimer's security hearings before the Atomic Energy Commission, April 1954; proponent of the controversial space-based defense system known as "Star Wars" in the 1980s; received the Presidential Medal of Freedom, the nation's highest civilian honor, 2003

Date of Birth: January 15, 1908

Place of Birth: Budapest, Hungary

Date of Death: 3:30 p.m., September 9, 2003 (95)

Place of Death: at his home on the Stanford University campus in Palo Alto, California

Cause of Death: unstated natural causes after suffering a stroke days earlier

Resting Place: not disclosed, although he had told friends that he would like to be buried in Israel

Teller wrote in his memoirs, "I deeply regret the deaths and injuries that resulted from the atomic bombings, but my best explanation of why I do not regret working on weapons is a question: What if we hadn't?"[16]

After receiving the Presidential Medal of Freedom less than two months before his death, Teller said, "In my long life I had to face some difficult decisions and found myself often in doubt whether I acted the right way. Thus the medal is a great blessing for me."[17]

278. A view of "A" Mountain looking east.[19]

Clyde William Tombaugh
New Mexico State University astronomer, 1955-73; discovered the planet Pluto, February 18, 1930, as well as several star clusters, a comet, and fourteen asteroids; an asteriod, 1604 Tombaugh 1, discovered in 1931, was named after him; recipient of the Royal Astronomical Society's Jackson-Gwilt Medal, 1931; probably the most respected astronomer to have reported seeing an Unidentified Flying Object (UFO), on August 20, 1949; inducted into the International Space Hall of Fame, Alamogordo, New Mexico, in 1980
Date of Birth: February 4, 1906
Place of Birth: near Streator, Illinois
Date of Death (age): January 17, 1997 (90)
Place of Death: at his home in Mesilla Park, New Mexico
Cause of Death: unstated natural causes
Resting Place: cremated with most of his ashes scattered over "A" Mountain (Tortugas Mountain) near NMSU where he had built two observatories and worked so long; some of his ashes sent aboard the $650,000,000 New Horizons space mission to Pluto, launched on January 19, 2006; a memorial window was placed in his honor at the Unitarian Church, Las Cruces, New Mexico

At Clyde Tombaugh's memorial service, held on the New Mexico State University campus, his daughter Annette read a poem she had written for him. In it she is a little girl and he tells her to fetch a star, to which she says, "Tis beyond my reach." And he replies, "Then I'll be your stairway to the sky."[18] No. 278

Stanislaw Marcin "Stan" Ulam
Los Alamos scientist and mathematician, 1944-67; along with Edward Teller, largely responsible for the development of the first hydrogen bomb by 1952; creator of the Monte-Carlo method of solving mathematical problems; University of New Mexico honorary degree recipient, 1969
Date of Birth: April 3, 1909
Place of Birth: Lwów, Poland
Date of Death (age): May 13, 1984 (75)
Place of Death: at his home in Santa Fe, New Mexico
Cause of Death: heart attack
Resting Place: cremated[20]

Like most great scientists, Ulam was awed by scientific discovery. He once said:

> In the span of my life great changes have taken place in the sciences.... Sometimes I feel that a more rational explanation for all that has happened during my lifetime is that I am still only thirteen years old, reading Jules Verne or H.G. Wells, and have fallen asleep.[21]

After Ulam's death, his widow recalled that "he used to say 'the best way to die is of a sudden heart attack or to be shot by a jealous husband.' He had the good fortune of succumbing to the first, though I believe he might had preferred the second."[22]

A memorial service was held at Fuller Lodge in Los Alamos. His widow asked that in lieu of flowers "donations should go to any of the nuclear disarmament causes."[23]

Werner Von Braun; originally Wernher Von Braun
A leader in the development of German and U.S. long-range ballistic missiles, including the V-2 (tested more than sixty times at White Sands Proving Ground, 1946-52); played a key role in early American space travel, including work on the Explorer I satellite and the Saturn 5 rocket; received nineteen honorary doctorate degrees; authored dozens of books and articles
Date of Birth: March 23, 1912
Place of Birth: Wirsitz, Germany
Date of Death (age): June 16, 1977 (65)
Place of Death: at a local hospital in Alexandria, Virginia
Cause of Death: colon cancer
Resting Place: Ivy Hill Cemetery, Alexandria, Virginia[24]

279. Photo courtesy of Martin Skubinna. Appropriately, Psalm 19:1 says, "The heavens declare the glory of God; the skies proclaim the work of his hands."

Von Braun kept his sense of humor to the end. When astronaut Neil Armstrong visited him in the hospital, he said, "Statistically, my prospects are very poor. But, you know how false statistics can be. By the prognosis of statisticians, you should be dead in space, and I should be in jail [for my work as a German weapons scientist] on earth!"[25] No. 279

Other Scientists include:
Ralph W. Goddard (Chapter 6: Educational Leaders)
J. Robert Oppenheimer (Chapter 13: Wartime Leaders and Victims Since the
　Spanish-American War, 1898)
Ernest Thompson Seton (Chapter 7: Sung and Unsung Heroes)
Frank Springer (Chapter 6: Educational Leaders)
E.J. Workman (Chapter 6: Educational Leaders)

Medical Personnel (in alphabetical order)

Carl Herman "Dr. G" Gellenthien
Arrived at the Valmora Sanatorium, in northeastern New Mexico, in November 1924; recovered TB healthseeker; long-time medical director of the Valmora Sanatorium; long-time country doctor; president of the New Mexico Medical Society, 1944-46; vice president of the American Medical Association, 1953 and 1954
Date of Birth: November 27, 1900
Place of Birth: Chicago, Illinois
Date of Death (age): December 24, 1989 (89)
Place of Death: unknown

280. This memorial plaque is stored in the administrator's office on the grounds of the former sanatorium, now the campus of Rancho Valmora, a school for troubled children ages twelve to eighteen.

Cause of Death: unstated natural causes

Resting Place: cremated, with his ashes scattered near Valmora, New Mexico

After surviving tuberculosis and other forms of poor health, Dr. G said, "The BOSS has been good to me. I wouldn't be here today if it hadn't been for Him. Today is a gift from God, a day I shouldn't have. But if I can help someone along the way, it is my way of telling God *thanks*."[26]

Dr. G and Alice Brown Gellenthien were married for forty-five years (1928-73). Her ashes were scattered on a mountain overlooking the Valmora valley. Dr. G visited the area often, placing a plaque there, which read: "Alice Brown Gellenthien, January 7, 1901-December 27, 1973. Unto almighty God I commend the soul of my beloved wife Alice and according to her wish I have spread her ashes upon the lands of Valmora which have been her cherished and only home on earth."[27] No. 280

281.

William Randolph "Uncle Doc" "Old Doc" Lovelace I

Arrived in Sunnyside, New Mexico, in 1906, moving to Fort Sumner in 1908 and to Albuquerque in 1913; recovered TB healthseeker; co-founder of the Lovelace Clinic (later the Lovelace Medical Center), 1922; space medicine pioneer William Randolph Lovelace II's uncle; a street in Albuquerque was named in his honor

Date of Birth: July 27, 1883

Place of Birth: Dry Fork, Missouri

Date of Death (age): December 4, 1968 (85)

Place of Death: Bataan Memorial Methodist Hospital, Albuquerque, New Mexico

Cause of Death: stroke

Resting Place: Fairview Cemetery, Albuquerque, New Mexico[28] No. 281

282.

William Randolph "Randy" Lovelace II

Moved to Albuquerque to join his uncle, Dr. William Randolph Lovelace I, 1946; space medicine pioneer; Director of Space Medicine for the National Aeronautics and Space Administration (NASA), 1964-65; surgeon at the Lovelace Medical Clinic; inducted into the International Space Hall of Fame, Alamogordo, New Mexico, in 1976

Date of Birth: December 30, 1907

Place of Birth: Springfield, Missouri

Date of Death (age): December 12, 1965 (57)

Place of Death: at the 11,000-foot Independence Pass east of Aspen, Colorado

Cause of Death: killed in a small private plane crash

Resting Place: Fairview Cemetery, Albuquerque, New Mexico

Dr. Lovelace was killed, along with his fifty-three-year-old wife, Mary, and twenty-three-year-old pilot, Milton Brown, en route from his Aspen home to Albuquerque. According to the men who discovered the plane wreckage on a snow covered pass, Brown probably survived the crash and "although he must have been suffering terrible pain, he placed the [Dr. and Mrs. Lovelaces'] bodies together, covered them, [and] then sat down by his shattered plane to die."[29] No. 282

Frank Eustace Mera
Recovered TB healthseeker in Colorado Springs, Colorado; arrived in Santa Fe in 1905; acquired Tent City (established in 1903), which became Sunmount Sanatorium, for the treatment of TB patients; physician who treated hundreds of TB patients, including talented "lungers" like Alice Colbin Henderson, Dorothy McKibbin, and John Gaw Meem who had come to Santa Fe to "chase the cure" and remained to make major contributions to the region; a founder and charter member of the Old Santa Fe Association since its creation, 1926; Dr. Harry P. Mera's brother
Date of Birth: March 1, 1879
Place of Birth: Mansfield, Ohio
Date of Death (age): early morning, August 19, 1970 (91)
Place of Death: Phoenix, Arizona
Cause of Death: unstated natural causes
Resting Place: Fairview Cemetery, Santa Fe, New Mexico[30]

283.

On Mera's ninetieth birthday, his friends presented him with a book gift with the citation:

> To Dr. Frank Mera,
> Some of us owe our lives to you, all of us are indebted to you for your wise counsel and loving friendship over the years. We, the undersigned, salute you on this, your ninetieth birthday.[31]

A world traveler who lived in Santa Fe during most of his life, Dr. Mera had only moved to the Phoenix area to live with his daughter three weeks prior to his death.[32] No. 283

Abraham Given Shortle
First arrived in Albuquerque, New Mexico, 1906; nationally known specialist in the treatment of TB; founder and operator of the Albuquerque Sanatorium on East Central Avenue (nicknamed Lunger Alley), Albuquerque, New Mexico, 1909-22; strong civic leader who helped in the creation of the city commission form of government, the Chamber of Commerce in Albuquerque, and the State Department of Public Health for New Mexico
Date of Birth: February 14, 1871
Place of Birth: Rockville, Indiana
Date of Death (age): 11:30 p.m., May 26, 1922 (51)

284.

Place of Death: Presbyterian Sanatorium, Albuquerque, New Mexico
Cause of Death: septicemia (blood poisoning) following surgery
Resting Place: Fairview Cemetery, Albuquerque, New Mexico[33] No. 284

Annie Dodge Wauneka
Navajo public health advocate, especially in the areas of tuberculosis, diabetes, infant deaths, and drug and alcohol abuse; advocate for Native American education; second woman to be elected to the Navajo Tribal Council, 1951, serving twenty-seven years; first Native American to receive the Presidential Medal of Freedom, 1963; designated by the Navajo Tribal Council as "Our Legendary Mother of the Navajo Nation," 1984; University of New Mexico honorary degree recipient, 1985; University of Arizona honorary degree recipient, 1996; chosen for the National Womens Hall of Fame, 2000; a junior college, a fellowship, and a scholarship have been named in her honor; daughter of Navajo chief Henry Chee Dodge
Date of Birth: April 10, 1910
Place of Birth: on the Navajo Reservation near Sawmill, Arizona
Date of Death (age): November 10, 1997 (87)
Place of Death: Flagstaff Medical Center, Flagstaff, Arizona
Cause of Death: Alzheimer's disease
Resting Place: private cemetery on the Round Tree Ranch, Arizona[34]

Lucy Jane Ross "Mother" Whiteside
Grants midwife who helped deliver more than 450 babies in her career; owner of the Whiteside Hotel and Café to 1952

285. Despite her extensive ties to Grants, Mother Whiteside was buried beneath a tree in Gallup's Hillcrest Cemetery to lay in rest beside her daughter.

Date of Birth: May 3, 1871
Place of Birth: Missouri
Date of Death (age): May 12, 1958 (87)
Place of Death: Glendale, California
Cause of Death: unstated natural causes
Resting Place: Hillcrest Cemetery, Gallup, New Mexico

The town of Grants honored Mother Whiteside by naming its public library the Mother Whiteside Memorial Library, dedicated on November 21, 1954. When asked how long she had lived in Grants, she replied that she'd been there so long that Mount Taylor was a little knoll when she first arrived.[35] No. 285

Other Medical Personnel include:
Laurel Clark (Chapter 7: Sung and Unsung Heroes)
Henry Connelly (Chapter 9: Political, Diplomatic, and Judicial Leaders)
John Henry "Doc" Holliday (Chapter 8: Lawmen, Criminals, and Victims of Crime)
William Carr Lane (Chapter 9: Political, Diplomatic, and Judicial Leaders)
Harry P. Mera (Chapter 4: Cultural Preservationist)
John Ballou Newbrough (Chapter 10: Religious Leaders)
Sister Blandina Segale (Chapter 10: Religious Leaders)
John Paul Stapp (this chapter)

12

WARTIME LEADERS AND VICTIMS TO THE END OF THE INDIAN WARS IN NEW MEXICO, 1886

Explorers *(in chronological order)*

Álvar Nuñez Cabeza de Vaca
Shipwrecked royal treasurer of the ill-fated Pánfilo de Naráez expedition to Florida who, with three other survivors, brought back news of suspected great wealth on the far northern frontier of New Spain after an eight-year journey of survival from Florida to New Spain, 1528-36; Spanish Governor of Paraguay, 1540-45
Date of Birth: about 1490
Place of Birth: Jerez, Spain
Date of Death (age): 1564 (about 74)
Place of Death: Seville, Spain
Cause of Death: unstated natural causes
Resting Place: probably the cathedral in Seville, Spain[1]

Estéban or Estevanico
Moorish black slave of the ill-fated Pánfilo de Naráez expedition to Florida who, with Álvar Nuñez Cabeza de Vaca and two other survivors, brought back news of suspected great wealth on the far northern frontier of New Spain after an eight-year journey of survival from Florida to New Spain, 1528-36; scout for the Fray Marcos de Niza expedition to New Mexico, 1539
Date of Birth: about 1510
Place of Birth: Azamor, Morocco
Date of Death (age): May 1539 (about 29)
Place of Death: Hawikuh (later known as Zuni Pueblo, New Mexico)
Cause of Death: killed by Zuni Indians
Resting Place: After Estéban's death an Indian informed the Spanish that the slave's "body was cut into a great many pieces, which were distributed among all the chiefs in order that they might know that he was surely dead."[2]

The muffled drum's sad roll has beat
  The soldier's last tattoo;
No more on life's parade shall meet
  That brave and fallen few.
On Fame's eternal camping-ground
  Their silent tents are spread,
And Glory guards, with solemn round,
  The bivouac of the dead.
—From "The Bivouac of the Dead"
  Theodore O'Hara (1820-67)
On a plaque at the entrance to the
  National Cemetery,
  Santa Fe, New Mexico

Fray Marcos de Niza
Franciscan leader of a Spanish expedition into the far northern frontier of New Spain, 1539, returning with news of the mythical Seven City of Cíbola in today's New Mexico; accompanied the Coronado expedition to New Mexico, 1540
Date of Birth: about 1495
Place of Birth: Nice, France
Date of Death (age): March 25, 1558 (about 63)
Place of Death: Mexico City, New Spain
Cause of Death: unstated natural causes
Resting Place: Convento Gulande de San Francisco, Mexico City, New Spain[3]

Francisco Vázquez de Coronado y Luján
Arrived in New Spain in 1535; Spanish Governor of Nueva Galicia, New Spain, 1538-44; Spanish explorer of New Mexico and the surrounding regions, 1540-42; a state monument near Bernalillo and as many as three streets in Albuquerque (plus a shopping mall and airport), two streets in Santa Fe, a street in Belen, and a street in Taos were named in his honor; a U.S. postage stamp was issued in his honor in 1940, the four hundredth anniversary of his exploration of New Mexico
Date of Birth: about 1510
Place of Birth: Salamanca, Spain
Date of Death (age): September 22, 1554 (about 44)
Place of Death: Mexico City, New Spain
Cause of Death: unstated natural causes; never fully recovered from injuries suffered when he fell from a horse at Tiguex on December 27, 1541
Resting Place: within the Church of Santo Domingo, Mexico City, New Spain[4]

Zebulon Montgomery Pike
U.S. Army Lieutenant ordered by the U.S. government to explore the Spanish Southwest, 1806-07; received amicably in Santa Fe by Spanish Governor Joaquin Real Alencaster; famous for his published report, *An Account of Expeditions to the Sources of the Arkansas, La Platte, and Pierre Juan Rivers* (1810); Brigadier General in the War of 1812
Date of Birth: January 5, 1779
Place of Birth: Lamberton, New Jersey
Date of Death (age): April 27, 1813 (34)
Place of Death: Toronto, Canada
Cause of Death: killed when a power magazine exploded, causing a rock to strike him in the chest at the Battle of York in the War of 1812
Resting Place: Military Cemetery, Sacketts Harbor, New York

    In a letter to his father shortly before he died, Pike wrote:

> I embark tomorrow in the fleet at Sacketts Harbor at the head of fifteen hundred choice troops, on a secret expedition. If success attends my steps, honor and glory await my name—if defeat, still shall it be said we died like brave men; and conferred honor even in death on the American name.[5]

There is some confusion about the fate of Pike's remains. Originally, he was buried in the cemetery outside Fort Tompkins, New York. In 1819 his body and all others at Fort Tompkins were moved to the new post cemetery at Madison Barracks, New York. Sadly, the post cemetery was not kept up and the wooden slab that marked Pike's grave deteriorated to the point that the exact location of Pike's body was forgotten.

Plagued by frequent floods at Madison Barracks cemetery, the 130 bodies at the cemetery were later moved to a new location east of Sacketts Harbor. Assuming that the remains in an uncovered iron casket must be Pike's, authorities opened the casket, allowing air to enter the chamber and causing the body to disintegrate. The grave was nevertheless marked with a gravestone at last.

In both the 1920s and 1940s groups in Colorado Springs, Colorado, attempted to have Pike's body removed to the peak that bears his name, with a large monument to honor his explorations. The people of Sacketts Harbor adamantly opposed this idea. According to their mayor in the late 1940s, "General Pike's been buried here for more than a century, and we mean to keep him here." So far the citizens of Sacketts Harbor have been successful in their efforts "to keep him here."[6] No. 286

286. Photo courtesy of Robert E. Brennan.

Other Explorers include:
Juan Bautista de Anza (Chapter 9: Political, Diplomatic, and Judicial Leaders)
Kit Carson (this chapter)
Philip St. George Cooke (this chapter)
Francisco Várquez de Coronado y Luján (this chapter)
Josiah Gregg (Chapter 5: Business Leaders)
Don Juan de Oñate y Salazar (Chapter 9: Political, Diplomatic, and Judicial Leaders)
Don Diego José de Vargas Zapata Luján Ponce de León y Contreras (Chapter 9: Political, Diplomatic, and Judicial Leaders)
Gaspar Pérez de Villagrá (Chapter 4: Cultural Preservationists)

The Texas-Santa Fe Expedition, 1841 (in alphabetical order)

In 1841 the Republic of Texas attempted to assert its claim to a large portion of New Mexico by launching a "commercial" expedition into its western neighbor's territory. The expedition failed for many reasons, from poor leadership to a disastrously poor knowledge of New Mexico geography. The invasion culminated in a mass surrender to Mexican Governor Manuel Armijo and a terrible death march down the Camino Real, causing ill feelings between Texans and New Mexicans for years to come.[7]

George Wilkins Kendall
Co-founder of the New Orleans *Picayune*, 1837; correspondent who accompanied the ill-fated Texas-Santa Fe Expedition of 1841, as described in his *Narrative of the Texan Santa Fe Expedition* (1844); considered the first modern war correspondent

for his in-person coverage of the U.S.-Mexican War, 1846-48; known as the father of sheep ranching in Texas; Kendall County, Texas, was named in his honor

Date of Birth: August 22, 1809
Place of Birth: Mt. Vernon, New Hampshire
Date of Death (age): 8:45 p.m., October 21, 1867 (58)
Place of Death: at his Post Oak Ranch, Kendall County, Texas
Cause of Death: pneumonia
Resting Place: Boerne City Cemetery, Boerne, Texas[8]

The epitaph on Kendall's gravestone reads: "Printer, Journalist, Author, Farmer, Eminent in All."[9]

Hugh McLeod

Officer in the Texas war for independence from Mexico, 1836; commander of the ill-fated Texas-Santa Fe Expedition of 1841; interred at Perote Prison, Mexico, until mid 1842; Confederate Civil War Colonel

Date of Birth: August 1, 1814
Place of Birth: New York City, New York
Date of Death (age): early morning, January 2, 1862 (47)
Place of Death: Dumfries, Virginia
Cause of Death: pneumonia
Resting Place: Texas State Cemetery, Austin, Texas[10] No. 287

287. The inscription on Hugh McLeod's gravestone reads: "Born in New York. Appointed from Georgia to West Point where he was graduated, 1835. Entered Army of Texas, 1836. First Adjutant General of Texas, 1840-41. Commander of Santa Fe Expedition, 1841. Represented Galveston in Second Legislature, 1847. Colonel 1st Regiment Texas Infantry, C.S.A. Died at Dumfries, Virginia, January 2, 1862. Erected by the State of Texas." Photo courtesy of David N. Lotz.

The U.S.-Mexican War, 1846-48 (in alphabetical order)

The United States declared war on Mexico on May 13, 1846. In the following months, the U.S. Army attacked Mexico in three major campaigns, including into New Mexico via the Santa Fe Trail. The U.S. Army of the West under Brigadier General Stephen Watts Kearny captured Santa Fe on August 18, 1846. After crushing the Revolt of 1847, U.S. forces occupied New Mexico and initially ruled the region under a body of laws known as the Kearny Code. The Treaty of Guadalupe-Hidalgo ended the war in 1848. New Mexico became a U.S. territory in 1850.[11]

Philip St. George Cooke

U.S. Army officer, 1827-73; escorted James Magoffin to his negotiations with Mexican Governor Manuel Armijo, leading to the U.S. capture of New Mexico during the U.S.-Mexican War, 1846; commander of the Mormon Battalion as they marched through New Mexico to California during the U.S.-Mexican War, creating an important new route through the Southwest; author of *The Conquest of New Mexico and California* (1878); Indian fighter; Civil War Brevet Major General; Confederate General J.E.B. Stuart's father-in-law; author of a standard U.S. cavalry tactics manual; sometimes called the "Father of the U.S. Cavalry"; Western explorer; Cookes Spring on the Butterfield Trail was named in his honor

Date of Birth: June 13, 1809
Place of Birth: Leesburg, Virginia

Date of Death (age): March 20, 1895 (85)
Place of Death: Detroit, Michigan
Cause of Death: unstated natural causes
Resting Place: Elmwood Cemetery, Detroit, Michigan[12]

Alexander William "Will" Doniphan
Commander of the First Regiment, Missouri Mounted Volunteers of the U.S. Army of the West that invaded and conquered New Mexico in the U.S.-Mexican War; commander of U.S. forces in the Battle of Brazito, the only battle of the U.S.-Mexican War fought in New Mexico, Christmas day, 1846; Union Colonel during the Civil War
Date of Birth: July 9, 1808
Place of Birth: Mason County, Kentucky
Date of Death (age): August 8, 1887 (79)
Place of Death: at his boarding house home in Richmond, Missouri
Cause of Death: unstated natural causes
Resting Place: Liberty Cemetery, Richmond, Missouri

On his seventy-fifth birthday, four years before his death, Doniphan wrote to a longtime friend, "Blessed is the man who having nothing to say, abstains from giving us wordy evidence of the fact, especially in writing. So farewell."[13]

The words on Doniphan's gravestone read: "Orator, Jurist, Statesman, Soldier, and a Christian."

A statue in Doniphan's honor was dedicated on July 29, 1918, on the courthouse square in Richmond, Missouri. In the words of historian Joseph G. Dawson III, "Armed with a dragoon's saber and standing ten feet tall atop a seven-foot-high red granite pedestal, a bronze Doniphan gazes to the southwest…toward Santa Fe and on to Chihuahua."[14]

Stephen Watts Kearny[15]
Commander of the Army of the West that invaded and conquered New Mexico for the United States in the U.S.-Mexican War, 1846; a U.S. postage stamp was issued in his honor in 1946, the hundredth anniversary of his conquest of New Mexico; Kearnys Gap in San Miguel County, a street in Santa Fe, and two streets in Albuquerque were named in his honor
Date of Birth: August 30, 1794
Place of Birth: Newark, New Jersey
Date of Death (age): October 31, 1848 (54)
Place of Death: at the country home of his old friend, Meriwether Lewis Clark, near St. Louis, Missouri
Cause of Death: yellow fever
Resting Place: originally buried at the private cemetery on the estate of Kearny's friend, Colonel John O'Fallon; reinterred in Bellefontaine Cemetery, St. Louis, Missouri

288. The birth year on Kearny's stone (1796) is incorrect. Photo courtesy of Bellefontaine Cemetery.

Weakened by yellow fever contracted in Veracruz, Mexico, during the U.S.-Mexican War, Kearny went to St. Louis, but his health did not improve. Two bits of news brightened his final days: his promotion to the rank of major general on September 7, 1848, and news of the birth of a boy to his wife, Mary. It was said that Kearny "smiled proudly when told of the news and died peacefully…, never having seen his child."[16]

Kearny's funeral was one of the largest in St. Louis, with a procession, led by a regiment of First Dragoons, that stretched for a mile. "Following the hearse was the General's favorite horse with boots reversed in the stirrups to symbolize a soldier's death."[17] No. 288

Sterling "Old Pap" Price
U.S. Congressman from Missouri, 1844-46; Commander of the 2nd Missouri Infantry in the U.S. Army of the West that invaded and conquered New Mexico in the U.S.-Mexican War, 1846; Governor of Missouri, 1853-57; Major General in the Confederate Army during the Civil War
Date of Birth: September 9, 1809
Place of Birth: Prince Edward County, Virginia
Date of Death (age): 2:12 a.m., September 29, 1867 (58)
Place of Death: St. Louis, Missouri
Cause of Death: unstated natural causes
Resting Place: Bellefontaine Cemetery, St. Louis, Missouri[18] No. 289

289. Photo courtesy of Bellefontaine Cemetery.

Other U.S.-Mexican War Soldiers, Officials, and Agents include:
Charles Bent (Chapter 9: Political, Diplomatic, and Judicial Leaders)
James Silas Calhoun (Chapter 9: Political, Diplomatic, and Judicial Leaders)
Edward R.S. Canby (this chapter)
James Henry Carleton (this chapter)
James Magoffin (Chapter 5: Business Leaders)
Cerán St. Vrain (Chapter 5: Business Leaders)
Henry H. Sibley (this chapter)
Donaciano Vigil (Chapter 9: Political, Diplomatic, and Judicial Leaders)
Richard Hanson Weightman (Chapter 9: Political, Diplomatic, and Judicial Leaders)

The Civil War, 1861-65

Confederate forces invaded New Mexico in both the summer of 1861 and, in a far larger campaign with grand plans to ultimately capture California and the entire Southwest, in early 1862. Under General Henry H. Sibley, the Confederate Army of New Mexico was finally turned back following its conclusive defeat at the Battle of Glorieta Pass on March 28, 1862.[19]

Union Soldiers and Officers (in alphabetical order)

Edward Richard Sprigg Canby
Commanding officer of Union forces in New Mexico during the Confederate invasion, 1861-62; Indian fighter; the only general officer killed in the Indian wars;

Canby, Oregon, Fort Canby, Washington, and Canby Road in Peralta, New Mexico, near the site of the Civil War Battle of Peralta, were named in his honor
Date of Birth: November 9, 1817
Place of Birth: Piatt's Landing, Maryland
Date of Death (age): Good Friday, April 11, 1873 (55)
Place of Death: eastern Oregon
Cause of Death: killed by Modoc Indians during peace talks
Resting Place: Crown Hill Cemetery, Indianapolis, Indiana[20]

Canby and his aides had gone unarmed to the peace talks, despite the warnings of a Modoc interpreter regarding a plot to kill the general. Hearing of this plot, Canby

290. Photo courtesy of Marty Davis.

declared that negotiations should continue because the Modocs "dare not do it" with so many U.S. soldiers surrounding their position.... When news of the slaying was reported, the public was outraged that such an important man had been killed while on a "mission of peace." General Canby was nationally known and extremely popular.[21]

Transported to San Francisco, Canby's body lay in state for two days, with flags flown at half-staff on all public buildings. Taken by train to Indianapolis, his body was buried at a funeral attended by several of Canby's fellow generals, including Phil Sheridan, William Tecumseh Sherman, and Lew Wallace. At Canby's funeral the Reverend J.H. Bayliss told those present, "We have ready applause for [General Canby's] brilliant deeds, and are not slow to admire genius; and yet the thing which most commands our profound and abiding reverence is not the flash of some brilliant achievement, but the steady, strong, broad progress of noble character."[22]

Following a clearly unfair trial, two Modocs, Schonchin John and Captain Jack, were found guilty of Canby's murder and hanged on October 3, 1873. When their bodies

were taken from the scaffold, an army surgeon cut off their heads for shipment to Washington, D.C., ...for craniology studies. For over a hundred years, the two men's skulls rested on shelves of the Army Medical Museum and later the Smithsonian Institution.[23] No. 290

James Henry Carleton
U.S.-Mexican War Army officer; Commander of the California Column during the Civil War; commander of U.S. Army troops in New Mexico, September 1862 to early 1867; most famous for ordering the defeat and removal of over eight thousand Mescalero Apache and Navajo Indians to the hellish Bosque Redondo reservation, 1863-68
Date of Birth: December 27, 1814
Place of Birth: Lubec, Maine

291. Photo courtesy of Ronald R. Paul.

292.

Date of Death (age): January 7, 1873 (58)
Place of Death: San Antonio, Texas
Cause of Death: pneumonia
Resting Place: Mount Auburn Cemetery, Cambridge, Massachusetts[24] No. 291

Rafael Chacon
Indian fighter; trader; stockman; Civil War Union Army officer
Date of Birth: April 22, 1833
Place of Birth: near Santa Fe, New Mexico
Date of Death (age): 2:30 a.m., July 23, 1925 (92)
Place of Death: at his home in Trinidad, Colorado
Cause of Death: lobar pneumonia
Resting Place: Trinidad Catholic Cemetery, Trinidad, Colorado

According to Chacon's biographer, "The old soldier was laid to rest in his army uniform, which he had loved so well and which distinguished his appearance in public on numerous occasions while he was a resident of Trinidad."[25] No. 292

Manuel Antonio "El Leoncito" (The Little Lion) Chaves
Indian fighter and U.S. Army officer who played a key role in the Union victory at the Civil War Battle of Glorieta Pass, March 28, 1862; father of educator Amado Chaves
Date of Birth: October 18, 1818
Place of Birth: Atrisco, New Mexico
Date of Death (age): late January 1889 (70)
Place of Death: San Mateo, New Mexico
Cause of Death: complications from old leg wounds, probably sustained in battle
Resting Place: buried (with two musket balls) in a hollowed log beneath the altar of his private chapel near his San Mateo hacienda. When the chapel was torn down, his remains were removed by his son, Amado, to the local San Mateo cemetery.[26]

John Milton "The Fighting Parson" Chivington
Ordained Methodist or Episcopal minister; First Colorado Volunteers (Colorado Column) Union officer at the Civil War Battle of Glorieta Pass, 1862; led U.S. forces at the Sand Creek Massacre, a surprise attack on a peaceful camp of Cheyenne, leaving at least two hundred men, women, and children dead, November 29, 1864
Date of Birth: January 27, 1821
Place of Birth: Warren County, Ohio
Date of Death (age): October 4, 1894 (73)
Place of Death: Denver, Colorado
Cause of Death: cancer

Resting Place: Fairmont Cemetery, Denver, Colorado

Two hours before Chivington's death, the Reverend Isaac Beardsley, a Methodist minister and friend, asked, "Colonel, how is it? Is Jesus precious to you?" With a smile, Chivington answered, "His presence dwells within. It's all around me. It fills the room."[27] No. 293

Louis Felsenthal
Arrived in Santa Fe in 1858; Union Army Captain at the Civil War Battle of Valverde, February 21, 1862
Date of Birth: November 5, 1832
Place of Birth: Iserlohn, Germany
Date of Death (age): 2:15. p.m., June 8, 1909 (76)
Place of Death: Branch National Home for Disabled Volunteer Soldiers, Santa Monica, California
Cause of Death: prostate cancer
Resting Place: National Cemetery, Los Angeles, California

293. Photo courtesy of David N. Lotz.

According to Felsenthal's biographer, the captain and many of his fellow veterans suffered deplorable, scandalous conditions at the soldiers' home in Santa Monica.[28]

James "Paddy" Graydon
Colorful Civil War Union Army soldier and spy; controversial Indian fighter
Date of Birth: early 1832
Place of Birth: Lisnakea, Northern Ireland
Date of Death (age): 2:00 p.m., November 9, 1862 (30)
Place of Death: post hospital, Fort Stanton, New Mexico
Cause of Death: Fatally shot in left lung during a shootout with army surgeon Dr. John Marmaduke Whitlock who accused Graydon of getting several Apache Indians drunk on whiskey and then shooting them in cold blood in what is known as the Gallinas Massacre of October 1862. In retaliation, Whitlock was killed by Graydon's shocked and angry troops.
Resting Place: originally at the post cemetery, Fort Stanton, New Mexico; twenty-four years later, his remains were interred in the National Cemetery, Santa Fe, New Mexico

Struck by a bullet near his heart, the wounded Graydon declared, "The son of a b—- has killed me." But Graydon did not die immediately. In fact, he was expected to fully recover in the Fort Stanton hospital when, three days after being shot, he suddenly lost his struggle with death.[29] No. 294

Alexander "Padre Polaco" "Don Alejandro" Grzelachowski
Polish priest who arrived in New Mexico with Bishop Lamy in 1851; U.S. Army chaplain who played a key role as a guide in the Civil War Battle of Glorieta Pass, March 28, 1862; Las Vegas and Puerto de Luna merchant after

294.

295. The epitaph on Alexander Grzelachowski's gravestone reads: "Padre Polaco (Polish Father), Priest, Military Guide, Merchant; Always a man of God; Solid Integrity."

leaving the priesthood in 1857
Date of Birth: 1824
Place of Birth: Gracina, Poland
Date of Death (age): May 24, 1896 (about 72)
Place of Death: near Puerto de Luna, New Mexico
Cause of Death: wagon accident when his team of horses bolted and his vehicle overturned
Resting Place: Nuestra Señora de El Refugio Cemetery, Puerto de Luna, New Mexico[30]

The Las Vegas press showered Don Alejandro with praise when it learned of his passing. The *Las Vegas Optic* declared, "There can be no question despite all creeds, as to his future rewards."[31] No. 295

Alexander "Alec" McRae

Civil War artillery officer in New Mexico who chose to help defend the Union, rather than join other members of his prominent North Carolina family in support of the Confederate cause; Fort McRae, New Mexico, was named in his honor, 1863
Date of Birth: September 4, 1829
Place of Birth: Fayetteville, South Carolina
Date of Death (age): shortly after 4:00 p.m., February 21, 1862 (32)
Cause of Death: fatal head wound received at the decisive moment in the Battle of Valverde when his Union battery unit was overrun in a Confederate charge
Resting Place: although originally interred at Fort Craig, near the Valverde battlefield, his remains were removed to the West Point Cemetery, U.S. Military Academy (where McRae had graduated), West Point, New York, on June 5, 1867

As the Confederates charged, a Texas officer (perhaps a former fellow officer in the Union army) reportedly shouted, "Surrender, McRae, we do not want to kill you," to which McRae replied, "Shoot the son-of-a-bitch!" They shot one another and, according to a romantic version of their deaths, both fell across the barrel of the same cannon.

A Southerner by birth, McRae was well respected by both sides. In fact, upon his death the Confederate commander, General Henry H. Sibley, wrote to McRae's father, John, that "the universal voice of this Army attests to the gallantry of your son. He fell valiently [sic] defending the Battery he commanded."[32]

Slightly a year after McRae's death, Fort McRae was established on the east side of the Rio Grande, northwest of

296. Alexander McRae's granite gravestone to the right is four stones from General George Armstrong Custer's larger one to the far left. Photo courtesy of Christopher A. Ratzel.

the present town of Truth or Consequences, and named in his honor on April 3, 1863. Many of the soldiers stationed at the fort were Buffalo Soldiers, the very men that McRae helped free from slavery by choosing to fight with the North against the South. The fort was abandoned on October 30, 1876, and dismantled in 1879. Its site is now largely covered by the waters of Elephant Butte Lake. The New

Mexico Hometown Heroes Committee dedicated a monument to the fort on the lake's western shore on April 5, 2003.³³ No. 296

William Logan Rynerson
Member of the California Column in the Civil War, 1862-66; rancher; lawyer; most famous for shooting Chief Justice John P. Slough on December 17, 1867; acquitted on grounds of self-defense; Lincoln County District Attorney identified with the Murphy-Dolan faction in the Lincoln County War, 1878-81; later an opponent of the Santa Fe Ring
Date of Birth: February 22, 1828
Place of Birth: Mercer County, Kentucky
Date of Death (age): September 26, 1893 (65)
Place of Death: Las Cruces, New Mexico
Cause of Death: unstated natural causes
Resting Place: Masonic Cemetery, Las Cruces, New Mexico³⁴

Smith Henry Simpson
Staunch Union supporter who in 1861, with other Union loyalists, including Kit Carson, Ceran St. Vrain, and Tom Boggs, raised the U.S. flag and nailed it to a tall tree pole in the Taos plaza after Confederate sympathizers had removed the Union banner. Simpson and his friends guarded the flag day and night. An American flag has flown over the plaza ever since. A post-Civil War Indian fighter; his ghost reportedly haunts his former home, now the Harwood Foundation in Taos. Simpson Peak in Taos County and a street in Taos were named in his honor.
Date of Birth: May 8, 1833
Place of Birth: Oyster Bay, New York
Date of Death: April 4, 1916 (82)
Place of Death: Taos, New Mexico
Cause of Death: unstated natural causes
Resting Place: Kit Carson Cemetery, Taos, New Mexico³⁵

According to one story that circulated in Taos, Smith Simpson was outraged when Father Joseph Giraud built a new Catholic church in 1911 and "ruthlessly exhumed the bones of a number of people who had been buried in the [old] church yard." Simpson went so far as to forbid his family from attending the newly constructed sanctuary. This may well have led to his and his wife's burial in the Protestant Kit Carson Cemetery rather than in the local *camposanto*.³⁶

On the hundredth anniversary of Kit Carson's death, Simpson's granddaughter, Margaret Berg, and Carson's eighty-year-old grandson, Charles Wood, raised the American flag over Taos plaza in a solemn patriotic ceremony.³⁷

Three years later, a tourist from California was outraged when he saw the American flag flying after sundown in the plaza, where there were "no lights on it, or even near it." John Loomis was so upset that he fired off letters to his Congressman in Washington, D.C., to Governor David Cargo in

297. The year of Simpson's birth inscribed on his gravestone is incorrect.

Santa Fe, and to the editor of the *Taos News*. The *News* responded by pointing out that Taos plaza was one of only fourteen places in the United States that had special government permission to fly the flag day and night, changing the flag twice a year in formal ceremonies. Taos resident Becina Steinke also responded by suggesting that Loomis should keep his "hands off" the "great tradition" established long ago by Smith Simpson and his friends.[38]

High spring winds and other inclement weather have threatened the flagpole and its honored flag, but both have survived, thanks to the diligence of the citizens of Taos.[39] No. 297

John Potts Slough
Civil War Union Army commander of the First Colorado Volunteers, also known as the Colorado Column, and post-war Chief Justice of the New Mexico Supreme Court, 1866-67
Date of Birth: February 1, 1829
Place of Birth: Cincinnati, Ohio
Date of Death (age): December 17, 1867 (38)
Place of Death: Santa Fe, New Mexico
Cause of Death: shot at the Exchange Hotel (today's La Fonda) by Captain William Logan Rynerson after calling Rynerson a "damned lying thief," a "coward," and a "son of a bitch"
Resting Place: Spring Grove Cemetery, Cincinnati, Ohio

When told he was not hurt badly, Slough declared, "Yes I am. Send for a doctor."[40]

Other Civil War Union Soldiers, Chaplains, and Officers include:
Thomas Boyne (this chapter)
William Brady (Chapter 8: Lawmen, Criminals, and Victims of Crime)
Kit Carson (this chapter)
J. Francisco Chaves (Chapter 9: Political, Diplomatic, and Judicial Leaders)
Philip St. George Cooke (this chapter)
Jimmy Dolan (Chapter 8: Lawmen, Criminals, and Victims of Crime)
Alexander William Doniphan (this chapter)
Stephen Dorsey (Chapter 5: Business Leaders)
Nathan A.M. Dudley (Chapter 8: Lawmen, Criminals, and Victims of Crime)
Stephen Elkins (Chapter 9: Political, Diplomatic, and Judicial Leaders)
Albert J. Fountain (Chapter 8: Lawmen, Criminals, and Victims of Crime)
Thomas Harwood (Chapter 10: Religious Leaders)
Santiago Hubbell (Chapter 5: Business Leaders)
Billy Mathews (Chapter 8: Lawmen, Criminals, and Victims of Crime)
John R. McFie (Chapter 9: Political, Diplomatic, and Judicial Leaders)
James McNally (this chapter)
Robert Byington Mitchell (Chapter 9: Political, Diplomatic, and Judicial Leaders)
Lawrence G. Murphy (Chapter 8: Lawmen, Criminals, and Victims of Crime)

298. At the bottom of John Baylor's decorative gravestone are words from Theodore O'Hara's poem, "The Bivouac of the Dead": "On fame's eternal camping ground their Silent tents are spread and Glory guards with Solemn round the Bivouac of the dead."
Photo courtesy of David N. Lotz.

George Peppin (Chapter 8: Lawmen, Criminals, and Victims of Crime)
Francisco Perea (Chapter 9: Political, Diplomatic, and Judicial Leaders)
William Pile (Chapter 9: Political, Diplomatic, and Judicial Leaders)
William G. Ritch (Chapter 9: Political, Diplomatic, and Judicial Leaders)
Edmund G. Ross (Chapter 9: Political, Diplomatic, and Judicial Leaders)
Cerán St. Vrain (Chapter 5: Business Leaders)
Thomas Shaw (this chapter)
Lionel Allen Sheldon (Chapter 9: Political, Diplomatic, and Judicial Leaders)
Lew Wallace (Chapter 9: Political, Diplomatic, and Judicial Leaders)
Harvey Whitehill (Chapter 8: Lawmen, Criminals, and Victims of Crime)

Confederate Soldiers and Officers (in alphabetical order)

John Robert Baylor
Commander of Confederate forces that captured Mesilla and Fort Fillmore, July 25-27, 1861; governor of the Confederate Territory of New Mexico; Indian fighter
Date of Birth: July 27, 1822
Place of Birth: Paris, Kentucky
Date of Death (age): February 6, 1894 (71)
Place of Death: Montell, Texas
Cause of Death: unstated natural causes after spending the last year of his life almost completely paralyzed
Resting Place: Ascension Montell Church Cemetery, Montell, Texas[41] No. 298

Thomas "Tom" Green
Texas independence fighter at the decisive Battle of San Jacinto, April 21, 1836; Indian fighter; Confederate commander in the South's victory at the Battle of Valverde, February 21, 1862; Tom Green County, Texas, was named in his honor, 1874
Date of Birth: June 8, 1814
Place of Birth: Buckingham County, Virginia
Date of Death (age): April 12, 1864 (49)
Place of Death: Blair's Landing on the Red River, Louisiana
Cause of Death: "decapitated while leading a drunken and suicidal attack on Federal gunboats"[42]
Resting Place: Oakwood Cemetery, Austin, Texas

Preparing his last charge at the Battle of Blair's Landing, Green placed "himself at the head of his men [and] told them he was going to show them how to fight." Unlike his famous charge at the Battle of Valverde, this attack proved unsuccessful and, for Green, fatal.

In addition to his smaller headstone at Oakwood Cemetery, the United Daughters of the Confederacy and surviving members of his brigade collected $1,200 to erect a twenty-five foot high monolith of Texas gray granite stone, dedicated on February 22, 1909.[43] No. 299

299. At the bottom of Tom Green's gravestone are the words: "A soldier in the Battle of San Jacinto and in the Indian wars of the Republic of Texas. A member of the 4th Congress of the Republic of Texas and an official in the 2nd, 3rd, 5th, 6th and 8th Congresses. Captain in Hays Regiment of Texas Rangers in the War Between the United States and Mexico. Clerk of the Supreme Court of Texas, 1841-1861. Brigadier General in the Army of the Confederate States. Fell in Battle at Blair's Landing, Louisiana, on April 12, 1864."
Photo courtesy of David N. Lotz.

Henry Hopkins Sibley

U.S. Army officer; Confederate commander of the Army of New Mexico that vainly attempted to invade the Territory in early 1862; Egyptian army officer, 1870-73; the now-abandoned community of Sibley in San Miguel County, New Mexico, may have been named in his honor

Date of Birth: May 25, 1816
Place of Birth: Natchitoches, Louisiana
Date of Death (age): 5:00 a.m., August 23, 1886 (70)
Place of Death: Fredericksburg, Virginia
Cause of Death: reportedly colic
Resting Place: Fredericksburg City Cemetery, Fredericksburg, Virginia (not the adjacent Confederate Cemetery)

Sibley was an inventor as well as a soldier in both the U.S. and the Confederate armies. Near the end of his life and nearly penniless, Sibley filed an affidavit stating, "I have been applying to several Congresses for relief and have never neglected or abandoned my claim against the [U.S.] Government for the use of my invention, known as the Sibley tent. My claim is a just one." Just or unjust, the former Confederate general's claim was ignored by the government in Washington. Sibley died eight months later.[44] No. 300

300. Sibley's grave went unmarked for seventy years, until 1956. Unfortunately, the date of his death is incorrect on his stone. **Photo courtesy of Jerry D. Thompson.**

Other Confederate Soldiers and Officers in the Civil War include:
Robert Clay Allison (Chapter 8: Lawmen, Criminals, and Victims of Crime)
Thomas B. Catron (Chapter 9: Political, Diplomatic, and Judicial Leaders)
J.C. Lea (Chapter 5: Business Leaders)
Thomas J. Maeston (this chapter)
Hugh McLeod (this chapter)
Sterling Price (this chapter)
Richard Hanson Weightman (Chapter 9: Political, Diplomatic, and Judicial Leaders)

Confederate Mass Grave

On June 23, 1987, Kip Siler was using a backhoe to dig a foundation on his property in Pecos, New Mexico, when he discovered a mass grave. Historians and archeologists were called in to examine the ten-foot by six-foot grave. Studying forensic evidence, experts concluded that the thirty-one bodies interred in the grave were Confederate (mostly Texan) casualties from the March 28, 1862, Civil War Battle of Glorieta Pass. Of the thirty-one bodies, one was identified as an officer's (Major John "Shrop" Shropshire) and two others could be identified as regular soldiers (J.S.L. Cotton and Ebineezer Hanna).[45]

The next question was what to do with the discovered remains. In May 1990 Major Shropshire's body was sent to Valley Forge, Kentucky, for burial near his parents' graves. But should the others be sent to Texas for burial, as argued by Texas Governor Bill Clements? Or should they be buried in New Mexico?

Authorities decided on the latter course. On Sunday, April 25, 1993, in a large formal ceremony with about fifty Civil War reenactors, several descendents of the deceased, and a crowd of between two and four hundred people, the twenty-eight Confederate casualties were buried in another mass grave in the northeast corner (Section K) of the National Cemetery in Santa Fe. Cotton and Hanna were buried in simple pine coffins in separate Confederate graves. Soil from Texas was thrown on the two coffins and on the mass grave before they were finally covered with New Mexico soil. Bagpipes played a rendition of "Dixie", and a bugler played taps.[46] As identified in Confederate records, the twenty-eight fallen men (plus three others killed at the battle, but "whose burial site remains known only to God," according to the plaque on the National Cemetery mass grave) were:

Farrier Joseph G.H. Able
Private Richard Alday
Private Reuben P. Bentley
Private William Booker
Private Edward T. Burrowes
Private Everett C. Foley
Private Christopher Gollmer
Corporal Benjamin G. Greely
Private August Habermann
Private Peter Hail
Private Jacob Henson
Private F.J. Hopkins
Private August Juhl
Corporal William Langston
Private James McCord
Private William McCormick

Blacksmith James Manus
Sergeant Stephen Marbach
Private John R. Martin
Sergeant John N. McKnight
Private Alexander Montgomery
Private William T. Parsons
Private Fritz Schaefer
Sergeant Otto Schroeder
Private E.R. Slaughter
Private James R. Stevens
Private Burton R. Stone
Private William Straughn
Bugler G.N. Taylor
Private Robert P. Walker
Sergeant Thomas D. Wilson
No. 301

301. J.S.L. Cotton and Ebineezer Hanna's graves are seen in the foreground, with the Confederate mass grave in the background to the left. Confederate gravestones are pointed at their tops, as compared to rounded Union stones. According to many Southerners, the points are to prevent "damn Yankees" from disrespectfully sitting on their rebel headstones![47]

In the rush of battle, other Confederate soldiers were buried in similar mass graves. Assigned to a burial detail following the Battle of Valverde, a Confederate private later recalled that "We dug a ditch four feet deep, wrapped forty of our boys in their blankets, and placed them in the earth without so much as marking the spot." A later resident of the area said that local farmers "would occasionally plow up a skull and other human bones when they prepared their fields for spring planting."[48]

Wounded Confederates from Valverde were transported to a makeshift hospital in Socorro where at least three officers and twenty-three men died between February 27 and April 20, 1862. The twenty-six bodies were buried at a now-forgotten military cemetery west of town. Despite efforts by several Socorro residents, no trace of these gravesites has ever been discovered.[49]

302.

303. The notice to the right of Carson's headstone reads: "Anyone defaceing [sic] this stone will be prosecuted to the full extent." Masons attempted to better protect Carson's grave by replacing the wooden fence seen here with an imposing iron fence 1908. Courtesy of the Palace of the Governors (MNM/DCA), Santa Fe, New Mexico, neg. no. 31479.

Indian War Fighters and Victims (in alphabetical order)

John Montgomery "Captain" Bullard

Arrived in New Mexico in 1866; early Silver City miner and a town founder; a main street in Silver City, Bullard Canyon in Grant County, and peaks in both Arizona and New Mexico were named in his honor[50]

Date of Birth: May 26, 1841

Place of Birth: Missouri

Date of Death (age): February 23, 1871 (29)

Place of Death: west of Bullard Peak, Arizona

Cause of Death: After defeating a band of about seventeen Apaches, Bullard was shot in the chest by a wounded Indian.

Resting Place: said to be the first burial in Memory Lane Cemetery, Silver City, New Mexico

An eyewitness to Bullard's death said that he "tore open his shirt, gazed a moment at his bleeding wound, and, without a word or a groan, fell back dead."[51]

Bullard's brother, a fellow prospector, left the area about 1885, declaring, "It is only a matter of time until the Indians get me [too] if I stay here."[52]

Bullard was originally buried at Silver City's old cemetery, between 10th and 12th Streets, in a funeral that was said to be the largest held in southwestern New Mexico to that time. An officer at the service declared that "Captain Bullard has given another valuable life to pave the way for civilization."[53]

Bullard was reinterred at Memory Lane Cemetery when it was opened about 1882. Old-timers say that his and other early gravesites were covered with pieces of old brick "to keep the burros from walking on the graves."[54] No. 302

Christopher Houston "Kit" Carson

Arrived in Santa Fe, 1824; recovered healthseeker; Mountain Man; guide for Western explorer John C. Frémont; Civil War officer; Indian agent; Indian fighter, most famous for his controversial scorched earth policy used in defeating the Navajo, 1863-64; led expedition of 325 troops and seventy-five Utes against Kiowas and Comanche warriors at Adobe Walls, November 25, 1864; an elementary school in Albuquerque, streets in Taos and Albuquerque, the small community of Carson in Taos County, Carson National Forest, Kit Carson Memorial State Park (with its Kit Carson Cemetery) in Taos, Kit Carsons Cave in McKinley County, Kit Carson Mesa in Colfax County, Kit Carsons Mound in Quay County, Carson City, Nevada, Kit Carson, Colorado, and the Fort Carson Military Reservation (with its Kit Carson Memorial Chapel and Fort Carson Military Cemetery), Colorado, were all named in his honor; a monument in Carson's honor was dedicated on Federal Place in

Santa Fe on Memorial Day, May 30, 1885; a U.S. postage stamp was issued in his honor, 1994

Date of Birth: December 24, 1809

Place of Birth: Madison County, Kentucky

Date of Death (age): 4:25 p.m., May 23, 1868 (58) one month after his beloved wife, Josefa, had died from complications in childbirth, April 27, 1868

Place of Death: surgeon's quarters at Fort Lyon, Colorado

Cause of Death: aortic aneurysm

Resting Place: originally buried at Fort Lyon, Colorado, but in 1869 reinterred, with his wife, in what became known as Kit Carson Cemetery, Taos, New Mexico[55]

304. Despite the Masons' iron fence, Carson's gravestone is often defaced, as shown here with swastikas. Kit Carson Cemetery supervisor Dennis Martinez and his staff regularly clean it up.

According to one version of Carson's death, "After several weeks on a limited diet, he had demanded a heavy dinner of his favorite buffalo steak and a bowl of coffee followed by a smoke, although he was warned it could be fatal." It was. "The old frontiersman died lying on buffalo robes on the floor of a house at Fort Lyon."[56] According to a second version, "While... reclining and smoking a pipe which had been given to him by General Frémont, he was stricken with a severe fit of coughing, expectorating a large quantity of blood, and holding the hand of his intimate friend, Aloys Scheurich, gasped, 'Good-bye, Compadre,' and died."[57] According to yet another version of Carson's death scene, his last words were, "Tell [Smith H.] Simpson and Tom Boggs that I wish to be buried at Taos."[58]

Once he was buried in Taos, a grave marker (made of stone quarried near Raton) was dedicated in December 1884. A crowd of twelve hundred attended, with speeches given in both Spanish and English.[59]

As a result of his controversial role in the defeat of the Navajos and Mescalero Apache Indians in the 1860s, Carson's gravestone has sometimes been vandalized with swastikas and other hateful symbols.[60] Outraged by such destructive acts, one Taosian wrote for many when he declared the vandalism to be "saddening, depressing, and disgusting."[61] In the aftermath of yet another such incident in 1998 Taos Pueblo Governor Ruben Romero asserted, "If you have a grievance about something, you should talk to people, not take it out on a grave."[62]

On the hundredth anniversary of Kit Carson's death, his eighty-year-old grandson, Charles Wood, and Smith Simpson's granddaughter, Margaret Berg, raised the American flag over Taos plaza in a solemn ceremony, just as their ancestors had proudly raised the flag to prove their loyalty to the Union during the Civil War. A special ceremony was also held at Carson's gravesite. A Kit Carson medallion was cast and sold at the event.[63] No. 303, No. 304

Charles Ware "Charley" McComas

Six-year-old boy kidnapped by Apache Indians after his parents, H.C. McComas and Juanita McComas, were killed in an attack on the road between Silver City and Lordsburg at about noon, March 28, 1883

305. Charley's parents', H.C. (November 9, 1831-March 28, 1883) and Juanita (March 4, 1846-March 28, 1883), gravestone, Evergreen Cemetery, Fort Scott, Kansas. Photo courtesy of Shirley Hurd.

Date of Birth: November 1876
Place of Birth: Fort Scott, Kansas
Date of Death (age): unknown
Place of Death: unknown
Cause of Death: unknown
Resting Place: unknown[64]

Despite a massive search, including the use of cardboard posters with Charley's image and the offer of a $1,000 reward, the boy was never found. However, reports of sightings of a tall, light-haired member of a small Apache war party in the 1920s led some to conclude that Charley not only survived, but perhaps became a leader among his captors. Marc Simmons, the foremost expert on this tragedy, concludes that this and "all the known Indian accounts that relate to Charley and his captivity contain confusing and conflicting details, leading us to believe that they must be regarded with skepticism and used with utmost caution."[65]

A New Mexico state historical marker was placed on US 90 near where the McComas family was ambushed.[66] No. 305

Thomas J. Maeston (also spelled Mastin)

A leading merchant, lawyer, rancher, and miner of Pinos Altos, New Mexico; Captain of the sixty-one member Arizona Scouts (or Guards) of the Confederate States of America in Pinos Altos, 1861
Date of Birth: September 13, 1839
Place of Birth: Aberdeen, Mississippi

306.

Date of Death (age): October 27, 1861 (22)
Place of Death: Pinos Altos, New Mexico
Cause of Death: severe wounds suffered in a battle defending Pinos Altos against attack by as many as four hundred Apaches led by Chief Cochise, September 27, 1861
Resting Place: Pinos Altos Cemetery, Pinos Altos, New Mexico

The day after Maeston's death, the residents of Pinos Altos gathered to mourn the passing of this "enterprising and invaluable citizen." All present resolved to "wear the usual badge of mourning, on the left arm, for thirty days."[67] No. 306

Other Indian War Fighters and Victims include:
John R. Baylor (this chapter)
William Brady (Chapter 8: Lawmen, Criminals, and Victims of Crime)
Edward R.S. Canby (this chapter)
James H. Carleton (this chapter)
Rafael Chacon (this chapter)
J. Francisco Chaves (Chapter 9: Political, Diplomatic, and Judicial Leaders)
Manuel Chaves (this chapter)

John Chivington (this chapter)
James Cooney (Chapter 14: Unusual Graves)
Jack Crawford (Chapter 2: Artists, Performers, and Directors)
Nathan A.M. Dudley (Chapter 8: Lawmen, Criminals, and Victims of Crime)
Albert J. Fountain (Chapter 8: Lawmen, Criminals, and Victims of Crime)
James "Paddy" Graydon (this chapter)
John Kinney (Chapter 8: Lawmen, Criminals, and Victims of Crime)
Henry H. Sibley (this chapter)
Smith H. Simpson (this chapter)
Donaciano Vigil (Chapter 9: Political, Diplomatic, and Judicial Leaders)

Buffalo Soldiers (in alphabetical order)

Several thousand African American soldiers, respectfully known as Buffalo Soldiers, served bravely in the 9th and 10th Cavalry and the 24th and 25th Infantry Regiments throughout the West, including New Mexico, during the Indian wars of the late nineteenth century. Their gravesites in New Mexico are found in several locations, but especially at our national cemeteries in Santa Fe and at Fort Bayard. There are fifty-one Buffalo Soldiers buried at Fort Bayard alone. Others, including nine from the Old Military Cemetery at Fort Stanton, were reinterred in the 1890s when their former forts were closed. Statues in their honor stand on the old parade grounds at Fort Bayard, New Mexico, and at Fort Leavenworth, Kansas.[68]

James Betters
Buffalo Soldier; 9th Cavalry Corporal; eleven year Army veteran
Date of Birth: unknown
Place of Birth: unknown
Date of Death (age): October 3, 1877 (unknown)
Place of Death: in the Mogollon Mountains, New Mexico
Cause of Death: accidentally shot when his carbine discharged or, in another version, died of a pistol wound accidently discharged by Sergeant John Perry
Resting Place: National Cemetery, Fort Bayard, New Mexico

307.

Near death, Betters requested that he be buried at Fort Bayard. His request was honored, but his company commander, Captain Charles D. Beyer, and Betters's fellow Buffalo Soldiers were outraged when they later learned of the treatment Betters received when he was unceremoniously interred at the Fort Bayard cemetery. His unwashed remains had been transported by a convict using a cart normally used to collect trash. No service was held, no flag covered his coffin, no prayer was said, and not even the spelling of his name on his headstone was correct. To help rectify this injustice, the Fort Bayard Historic Preservation Society paid homage to Betters with a full military funeral on September 20, 2003. Colonel Edward Hatch (played by reenactor soldier William A. Aleshire) gave the eulogy, and the ceremony ended with a rifle salute and taps. The Preservation Society plans to correct the misspelling of Betters's name in the near future.[69] No. 307

Cathy "Miss Kate" Williams; alias Private William Cathy
Black woman, born a slave, who impersonated a male infantry soldier from November 15, 1866, when she enlisted in the U.S. Army at the age of twenty-two, until her true identity was revealed by a post physician and she was discharged from the Army at Fort Bayard, New Mexico, October 14, 1868; said to be the only female Buffalo Soldier
Date of Birth: September 1844
Place of Birth: near Independence, Missouri
Date of Death (age): probably between 1892 and 1900 (probably between 48 and 56)
Place of Death: probably Trinidad, Colorado
Cause of Death: probably diabetes
Resting Place: unknown, although some insist that it is in Raton, New Mexico, while other sources claim it is in the black cemetery on the north end of Trinidad, Colorado[70]

In July 1891 Cathy Williams applied for an Army pension, writing that during her nearly two years of military service her health had been impaired when she was "compelled to swim" the Rio Grande, suffered from smallpox, and experienced deafness. Despite these several illnesses, the nation's only female Buffalo Soldier's application was denied.[71]

Other Buffalo Soldiers and their Officers include:
Thomas Boyne (this chapter)
Matthias W. Day (this chapter)
John Denny (this chapter)
Clinton Greaves (this chapter)
George Jordon (this chapter)
John J. Pershing (Chapter 13: Wartime Leaders and Victims Since the Spanish-American War, 1898)
Thomas Shaw (this chapter)
Augustus Walley (this chapter)
Moses Williams (this chapter)
Brent Woods (this chapter)

Medal of Honor Recipients: Indian Wars *(in alphabetical order)*
A total of 424 Medals of Honor were awarded during the Indian wars in the United States. Twenty-six recipients, including eight Buffalo Soldiers and an Indian scout, served in New Mexico and/or were subsequently buried in the Territory.[72]

Alonzo Bowman
U.S. Army First Sergeant, 8th Cavalry; Medal of Honor recipient for his heroic action displayed at Cibicu Creek, Arizona, August 30, 1881; Medal of Honor issued, November 4, 1882
Date of Birth: June 15, 1848

Place of Birth: Washington Township, Maine
Date of Death (age): October 4, 1885 (37)
Place of Death: Fort Bayard, New Mexico
Cause of Death: shot in Silver City, New Mexico
Resting Place: National Cemetery, Fort Bayard, New Mexico[73] No. 308

Thomas Boyne; also known as Thomas Bowen
Union soldier in the Civil War; U.S. Army Buffalo Solider Sergeant, C Troop, 9th Cavalry; Medal of Honor recipient for his heroic action against Victorio in the Mimbres Mountains on May 29, 1879, and at Cuchillo Negro, New Mexico, September 27, 1879; Medal of Honor received, January 6, 1882; over twenty-three years of military service
Date of Birth: 1849
Place of Birth: Prince George's County, Maryland
Date of Death (age): April 21, 1896 (about 47)
Place of Death: Soldiers Home, Washington, D.C.
Cause of Death: consumption (tuberculosis)
Resting Place: Soldiers and Airmen Home National Cemetery, Washington, D.C.[74] No. 308

308.

Frank Bratling
U.S. Army Corporal, 8th Cavalry; Medal of Honor recipient for his heroic action displayed near Fort Selden, New Mexico, in the Indian wars, July 8-11, 1873; Medal of Honor issued August 12, 1875
Date of Birth: 1845
Place of Birth: Bavaria, Germany
Date of Death (age): July 13, 1873 (about 28)
Place of Death: near Cañada Alamosa, New Mexico
Cause of Death: gunshot wounds suffered in battle with hostile Indians[75]
Resting Place: originally at Fort McRae, New Mexico; removed to the Fort Leavenworth, Kansas, military cemetery in 1886; cenotaphs, or headstones in his memory, were dedicated at both the Fort Bliss National Cemetery, El Paso, Texas, and at the National Cemetery, Fort Leavenworth, Kansas

A monument was dedicated to Fort McRae and Bratling by the New Mexico Hometown Heroes Committee at Elephant Butte Lake State Park on April 5, 2003, near the now-submerged remains of Fort McRae where Bratling was stationed and originally buried.[76] No. 309

George Ritter Burnett
U.S. Army Second Lieutenant, 9th Cavalry; Medal of Honor recipient for his heroic action in rescuing a dismounted soldier under heavy enemy fire in the Cuchillo Negro Mountains, New Mexico, August 16, 1881; Medal of Honor received, July 23, 1897
Date of Birth: April 21, 1858

309.

310. Photo courtesy of David N. Lotz.

Place of Birth: Lower Providence Township, Pennsylvania
Date of Death (age): November 1, 1908 (50)
Place of Death: Lincoln, Nebraska
Cause of Death: unknown
Resting Place: National Cemetery, Arlington, Virginia[77]

Matthias W. Day
U.S. Army Second Lieutenant, 9th Cavalry; Medal of Honor recipient for his heroic action in rescuing a wounded soldier at the Battle of Las Animas, New Mexico, September 18, 1879; Medal of Honor received, May 7, 1890
Date of Birth: August 8, 1853
Place of Birth: Oberlin, Ohio
Date of Death (age): September 12, 1927 (74)
Place of Death: Los Angeles, California
Cause of Death: unknown
Resting Place: National Cemetery, San Francisco, California

A special ceremony honoring Day, two other recipients of the Medal of Honor (John Denny and Robert Emmet), and the eight or more soldiers who died and were hastily buried at the Battle of Las Animas, New Mexico, was held at the remote battlesite on June 14, 1997.[78] No. 310

John Denny
U.S. Army Buffalo Solider Sergeant, C Troop, 9th Cavalry; Medal of Honor recipient for his heroic action against Victorio, rescuing a wounded fellow private while under heavy enemy fire during the Battle of Las Animas, New Mexico, September 18, 1879; Medal of Honor received, November 27, 1895
Date of Birth: 1846
Place of Birth: Big Flats, New York
Date of Death (age): November 28, 1901 (about 55)
Place of Death: Soldiers Home, Washington, D.C.
Cause of Death: unstated natural causes
Resting Place: Soldiers and Airmen Home National Cemetery, Washington, D.C.

A special ceremony honoring Denny, two other recipients of the Medal of Honor (Matthias Day and Robert Emmet), and the eight or more soldiers who died and were hastily buried at the Battle of Las Animas, New Mexico, was held at the remote battlesite on June 14, 1997.[79]

At the time of his death, Denny's "estate" consisted of his Medal of Honor, a silver watch, and sixty-eight cents.[80]

Edwin L. Elwood
U.S. Army Private, 8th Cavalry; Medal of Honor recipient for his heroic action in the Chiricahua Mountains, Arizona, during the Indian wars, October 20, 1869; Medal of Honor issued February 14, 1870
Date of Birth: 1847
Place of Birth: St. Louis, Missouri

Date of Death (age): September 13, 1907 (about 60)
Place of Death: St. Louis, Missouri
Cause of Death: unknown
Resting Place: National Cemetery, Santa Fe, New Mexico[81] No. 311

Robert Temple Emmet
U.S. Army 9th Cavalry officer; Medal of Honor recipient for his heroic action against Apache warriors at Las Animas Canyon, New Mexico, on September 18, 1879
Date of Birth: December 13, 1854
Place of Birth: New York, New York
Date of Death (age): October 25, 1936 (81)
Place of Death: Ashfield, Massachusetts
Cause of Death: unstated natural causes
Resting Place: Beechwoods Cemetery, New Rochelle, New York

A special ceremony honoring Emmet, two other recipients of the Medal of Honor (Matthias Day and John Denny), and the eight or more soldiers who died and were hastily buried at the Battle of Las Animas, New Mexico, was held at the remote battlesite on June 14, 1997.[82]

311.

Clinton Greaves
U.S. Army Buffalo Soldier Corporal, C Troop, 9th Cavalry; Medal of Honor recipient for his heroic action in hand-to-hand combat with Apache warriors on January 24, 1877, in the Florida Mountains, New Mexico; Medal of Honor received, June 26, 1879
Date of Birth: August 12, 1855
Place of Birth: Madison County, Virginia
Date of Death (age): August 18, 1906 (51)
Place of Death: Columbus, Ohio
Cause of Death: heart disease
Resting Place: Greenlawn Cemetery, Columbus, Ohio

The Buffalo Soldiers' monument in the center of the old parade grounds at Fort Bayard is artist Greg Whipple's depiction of Corporal Greaves in combat.[83]

Jacob Guenther; also Gunther
U.S. Army Corporal, 8th Cavalry; Medal of Honor recipient for heroic action displayed in the Indian wars, August 1869; Medal of Honor issued September 6, 1869
Date of Birth: November 13, 1844
Place of Birth: Schuylkill, Pennsylvania
Date of Death (age): March 29, 1871 (26)
Place of Death: Fort Wingate, New Mexico
Cause of Death: unknown
Resting Place: National Cemetery, Santa Fe, New Mexico[84] No. 312

312. A military gravestone at last acknowledging Corporal Guenther's Medal of Honor was placed at his gravesite by the New Mexico Hometown Heroes Committee on Memorial Day, 1991.[85] The birth year on Guenther's headstone is incorrect.

George Jordon

U.S. Army Buffalo Soldier Sergeant, K Troop, 9th Cavalry; Medal of Honor recipient for his heroic action in organizing and directing the defense of a civilian settlement with nineteen men against approximately one hundred Apache warriors at old Fort Tularosa, New Mexico, May 14, 1880; also for combat at Carrizo Canyon, New Mexico, August 12, 1881; Medal of Honor received, May 7, 1890; enlisted six times, serving a total of thirty years
Date of Birth: 1847
Place of Birth: Williamson County, Kentucky
Date of Death (age): October 24, 1904 (about 57)
Place of Death: Crawford, Nebraska
Cause of Death: unstated natural causes
Resting Place: National Cemetery, Fort McPherson, Nebraska[86]

    Two years before his death, Jordon's assessed value of personal property equaled eleven dollars. According to the chaplain at Fort Robinson, Nebraska, Jordon "died for the want of proper attention. He lived alone and had no one to attend to his wants. The doctor made two applications for his admittance into Fort Robinson Hospital and was refused." Jordon was nevertheless buried with full military honors, attended by the entire command at Fort Robinson.[87]

313.

Leonidas Steward Lytle

U.S. Army First Sergeant, 8th Cavalry; Medal of Honor recipient for his heroic action displayed near Fort Selden, New Mexico, July 8-11, 1873; Medal of Honor issued, April 12, 1875
Date of Birth: September 4, 1846
Place of Birth: Warren County, Pennsylvania
Date of Death (age): January 23, 1924 (77)
Place of Death: Silver City, New Mexico
Cause of Death: unstated natural causes
Resting Place: Memory Lane Cemetery, Silver City, New Mexico[88]
No. 313

James McNally

Civil War Union soldier wounded at the Battle of Valverde, February 21, 1862; U.S. Army First Sergeant, 8th Cavalry; Medal of Honor recipient for his heroic action displayed in the Indian wars, 1868 and 1869; later a miner in New Mexico's Hatch, Hillsboro, and Kingston area
Date of Birth: 1839
Place of Birth: County Monaghan, Ireland
Date of Death (age): November 26, 1904 (about 65)
Place of Death: Kingston, New Mexico
Cause of Death: unknown
Resting Place: Kingston Cemetery, Kingston, New Mexico[89]
No. 314

314. Although the exact location of James McNally's grave in the Kingston Cemetery is unknown, the Hometown Heroes Committee dedicated this cenotaph, or monument, in his honor on October 16, 1999.[90]

James L. Morris

U.S. Army First Sergeant, 8th Cavalry; Medal of Honor recipient for his heroic action near Fort Selden, New Mexico, July 8-11, 1873; Medal of Honor issued August 12, 1875

Date of Birth: 1844

Place of Birth: Ireland

Date of Death: 1903 (about 59)

Place of Death: probably Albuquerque, New Mexico

Cause of Death: unknown

Resting Place: Fairview Cemetery, Albuquerque, New Mexico[91]

Originally buried in a pauper's grave, Sergeant Morris was reburied in 1989 when New Mexico historians rectified this tragic neglect of a Medal of Honor recipient. The National Congressional of Honor Society (and the New Mexico Hometown Heroes Committee) honored Morris at his new gravesite during the society's annual convention, held in Albuquerque that year.[92] As one organizer described the event, "We put together a display of men wearing uniforms from every American war, and, in addition to bugles and music, we fired three guns."[93] No. 315

315. The inscription on the plaque below James Morris's gravestone reads: "Sergeant Morris received the Medal of Honor on August 12, 1875, for 'services against hostile Indians' near Fort Selden, New Mexico. He led a small party of cavalrymen in pursuit of Apache Indians, showing outstanding bravery and courage."

Y.B. Rowdy

U.S. Army Indian Scout Sergeant; Medal of Honor recipient for his heroic action displayed in Arizona, March 7, 1890; one of only seventeen Medals of Honor awarded to Indian Scouts; Medal of Honor issued, May 15, 1890

Date of Birth: unknown

Place of Birth: Arizona Territory

Date of Death (age): March 29, 1893 (unknown)

Place of Death: unknown

Cause of Death: unknown

Resting Place: National Cemetery, Santa Fe, New Mexico[94]

Little is known about this courageous scout, including where he was originally buried. He is now buried in the southeastern quadrant of the National Cemetery, a section largely occupied by soldiers who were originally buried in fort cemeteries around New Mexico until most forts and their military cemeteries were closed in the late nineteenth century and most bodies were transferred to national cemeteries, especially the cemetery in Santa Fe. No. 316

Albert D. Sale

U.S. Army Private, 8th Cavalry; Medal of Honor recipient for his heroic action displayed at Santa Maria River, Arizona, June 29, 1869; Medal of Honor issued, March 3, 1870; he had risen to the rank of captain by the time of his death

Date of Birth: 1850

Place of Birth: Broome County, New York

Date of Death: November 29, 1874 (about 24)

Place of Death: Post Hospital, Fort Union, New Mexico

Cause of Death: typhoid fever

316. A military gravestone at last acknowledging Sergeant Rowdy's Medal of Honor was placed at his gravesite on Memorial Day, 1991.[95]

317. Photo courtesy of Kent Kool.

318. Although some sources give John Schnitzer's year of death as 1906, the date on his headstone is 1904.

Resting Place: originally at the Post Cemetery, Fort Union, New Mexico; reburied with some 286 others in May 1892 at what is now the National Cemetery, Fort Leavenworth, Kansas[96]

The Medal of Honor Historical Society placed a new Medal of Honor headstone at Sale's gravesite in a special ceremony held on May 24, 1992.[97]
No. 317

John P. Schnitzer

U.S. Army Wagoner, 4th Cavalry; Medal of Honor recipient for his heroic rescue of a wounded comrade while under heavy enemy fire at Horseshoe Canyon, New Mexico, April 23, 1882; Medal of Honor issued August 17, 1896
Date of Birth: 1854
Place of Birth: Kempten, Bavaria, Germany
Date of Death (age): October 26, 1906 (about 52)
Place of Death: unknown
Cause of Death: unknown
Resting Place: National Cemetery, Fort Bayard, New Mexico[98] No. 318

Edward Clay Sharpless

U.S. Army Corporal, 6th Cavalry; Medal of Honor recipient for his heroic action in fighting off Indian attacks for two days at Upper Washita, Texas, September 9-11, 1874; Medal of Honor issued April 23, 1875
Date of Birth: August 10, 1853
Place of Birth: Marion County, Ohio
Date of Death (age): January 12, 1934 (80)
Place of Death: Mountainair, New Mexico
Cause of Death: unstated natural causes
Resting Place: Mountainair Cemetery, Mountainair, New Mexico[99]

Sharpless's original headstone did not mention that he had received the Medal of Honor. The New Mexico Hometown Heroes Committee rectified this oversight by erecting a new stone at his gravesite on Labor Day, 1990.[100] No. 319

Thomas Shaw

Union soldier in the Civil War; U.S. Army Buffalo Soldier Sergeant, K Troop, 9th Cavalry; Medal of Honor recipient for his heroic action against Nana's Apache warriors on August 12, 1881, at Carrizo Canyon, New Mexico; Medal of Honor received on December 7, 1890
Date of Birth: 1846
Place of Birth: Covington, Kentucky
Date of Death (age): June 23, 1895 (about 49)
Place of Death: Rosslyn, Virginia
Cause of Death: unstated natural causes
Resting Place: National Cemetery, Arlington, Virginia

Sergeant Shaw is the main subject in D.J. Neary's stirring painting, "Edge of the Storm."[101]

John Sheerin

Blacksmith, 8th Cavalry; Medal of Honor recipient for his heroic action in fighting near Fort Seldon, New Mexico, July 8-11, 1873
Date of Birth: 1841
Place of Birth: Camden, New Jersey
Date of Death (age): unknown
Place of Death: unknown
Cause of Death: unknown
Resting Place: unknown[102]

Ebin (or Eben) Stanley

Rancher, miner, hotel operator, outlaw, and Indian scout; U.S. Army Private, 5th Cavalry; Medal of Honor recipient for his heroic action displayed in the Indian wars near Turret Mountain, Arizona, March 25-27, 1873: Medal of Honor issued April 12, 1875
Date of Birth: February 14, 1844
Place of Birth: Decauter County, Iowa
Date of Death (age): November 19, 1904 (60)
Place of Death: Cold Springs, New Mexico
Cause of Death: unstated natural causes
Resting Place: Hillsboro Community Cemetery, Hillsboro, New Mexico[103]
The engraving on the top of Stanley's monument reads:

> Near this spot lie the unidentified remains of a true American hero, Ebin Stanley. Born in Decauter County, Iowa, Ebin served with the 3rd and 5th U.S. Cavalry from 1861 to 1873. Variously described as a rancher, miner, hotel operator, Indian scout, and outlaw (the Clanton Gang), he died in Cold Springs, New Mexico. He was survived by his wife Mary Elsie (Clanton) and two stepsons, Burt and Joe Slinkard. Sergeant Ebin Stanley was presented the nation's highest award for valor, the Medal of Honor, for his gallantry in action at the Battle of Turret Mountain, Arizona, 25-27 March 1873.

Stanley's first name is spelled Ebin on the top of his stone and Eben on its front. No. 320

Augustus Walley

U.S. Army Buffalo Soldier Sergeant, E Troop, 10th Cavalry; Medal of Honor recipient for his heroic action against Nana and his Apache warriors on August 16, 1881, in the Cuchillo Negro Mountains, New Mexico; Medal of Honor received, October 1, 1890; also served with bravery at the Battle of Las Guasimas, Cuba, June 24, 1898, in the Spanish-American War; recommended for a second Medal of Honor, but instead received a Certificate of Merit; retired after twenty-nine years of service, 1907; volunteered to fight in World War I,

319. Although some sources give Edward Sharpless's date of birth as August 10, the date on his headstone is August 20.

320. Although the exact location of Stanley's grave in the Hillsboro cemetery is unknown, the New Mexico Hometown Heroes Committee dedicated this cenotaph, or monument, in his honor on October 16, 1999.[104]

but was rejected as too old for service
Date of Birth: March 10, 1856
Place of Birth: Reisterstown, Maryland
Date of Death (age): April 9, 1938 (82)
Place of Death: Baltimore, Maryland
Cause of Death: unstated natural causes
Resting Place: St. Luke's Methodist Church Cemetery, Reisterstown, Maryland

    A Medal of Honor headstone was finally placed at his gravesite on Memorial Day, 1995.[105]

Wilber Elliott Wilder
U.S. Army First Lieutenant, 4th Cavalry; Medal of Honor recipient for his heroic action in rescuing a wounded fellow soldier under heavy fire from Indian warriors at Horseshoe Canyon, New Mexico, 1882; a veteran of the Spanish-American War, the Punitive Expedition of 1916, and World War I, retiring with the rank of general in 1927
Date of Birth: August 16, 1857
Place of Birth: Atlas, Michigan
Date of Death (age): January 30, 1952 (94)
Place of Death: Ridgefield, Connecticut
Cause of Death: unstated natural causes
Resting Place: Fairlawn Cemetery, Ridgefield, Connecticut[106]

Moses Williams
U.S. Army Buffalo Soldier First Sergeant, I Troop, 9th Cavalry; Medal of Honor recipient for his heroic action against about fifty of Nana's Apache warriors in a running battle of three to four hours, saving at least three of his comrades in the foothills of the Cuchillo Negro Mountains, New Mexico, August 16, 1881; Medal of Honor received, November 12, 1896
Date of Birth: 1845
Place of Birth: Carrollton, Louisiana
Date of Death (age): August 23, 1899 (about 54)
Place of Death: Vancouver, Washington
Cause of Death: heart failure
Resting Place: Vancouver Barracks Cemetery, Vancouver, Washington[107]

    Sergeant Williams's estate at the time of his death consisted of nine books, a pipe, a cigar holder, some two cent stamps, a pen, a bed, four chairs, six neckties, and twenty-three dollars in cash.[108] According to the commanding officer at Vancouver Barracks, "the sergeant died alone and without friends."[109]

Henry Wills
U.S. Army Private, 8th Cavalry; Medal of Honor recipient for his heroic action displayed near Fort Selden, New Mexico, July 8-11, 1873; Medal of Honor issued, August 12, 1875.

Date of Birth: 1842
Place of Birth: Gracon, Pennsylvania
Date of Death (age): unknown
Place of Death: unknown
Cause of Death: unknown
Resting Place: unknown[110]

Brent Woods
U.S. Army Buffalo Soldier Sergeant, B Troop, 9th Cavalry; Medal of Honor recipient for heroically rescuing white cowboys ambushed by Nana's Apache warriors in Gavilan Canyon, New Mexico, August 19, 1881; Medal of Honor received, July 12, 1894
Date of Birth: 1855
Place of Birth: Pulaski County, Kentucky
Date of Death (age): March 31, 1906 (about 51)
Place of Death: probably Kentucky
Cause of Death: unstated natural causes
Resting Place: Mill Springs National Cemetery, Nancy, Kentucky[111]

Sergeant Woods's remains were moved from a community cemetery, where only a rock had marked his gravesite, to the Mill Springs National Cemetery, Nancy, Kentucky, with an official Medal of Honor headstone to mark their location, in 1984.[112]

Native American Military Leaders (in alphabetical order)

Alfred Chato; "Chatto" (Flat Nose)
One of the most daring Chiricahua Apache leaders; U.S. Army scout; imprisoned in Florida and at Fort Sill, Oklahoma; helped negotiate the return of many Apache to New Mexico
Date of Birth: about 1860
Place of Birth: Arizona
Date of Death (age): August 16, 1934 (about 74)
Place of Death: Mescalero Reservation, New Mexico
Cause of Death: Model T car accident off a cliff at night
Resting Place: Mescalero Reservation Cemetery, Mescalero, New Mexico; not accessible to the general public[113]

Cochise
Chiricahua Apache chief, 1856-74; a main leader of Apache resistance to non-Indian expansion in the Southwest
Date of Birth: about 1810
Place of Birth: northern Mexico or southeastern Arizona
Date of Death (age): June 8, 1874 (about 64)
Place of Death: southeastern Arizona

Cause of Death: probably a form of stomach cancer
Resting Place: buried somewhere in the Dragoon Mountains of Arizona[114]

Cochise's last directions to his tribe were "to forever live at peace" with the white man.[115] According to a witness at Cochise's burial:

> [Cochise's body] was dressed in his best war garments, decorated with war paint and head feathers, and wrapped in a splendid heavy, red, woolen blanket.... He was then placed on his favorite horse...[which] was guided to a rough and lonely place among the rocks and chasms in the stronghold, where there was a deep fissure in the cliff. The horse was killed and dropped into the depths; also, Cochise's favorite dog. His gun and other arms were then thrown in; and last, Cochise was lowered with lariats into the rocky sepulcher—deep in the gorge.[116]

Geronimo "Goyathlay" or "Goyahkla" (Sleepy or One Who Yawns)
Apache Shaman and warrior with special powers; famous for his breakouts from the San Carlos Reservation, 1878-79, 1882-83, and 1885-86, before becoming the last major warrior to surrender to the U.S. Army in New Mexico; eluded some five thousand U.S. troops, or one quarter of the U.S. Army, with his band of sixteen warriors, fourteen women, and six children from 1885 to September 4, 1886; Geronimo Springs and Geronimo Springs Museum on Main Street in Truth or Consequences, New Mexico, were named in his honor
Date of Birth: according to Geronimo, June 1829, but probably earlier
Place of Birth: No-doyohn Canyon, Arizona (then part of Mexico, prior to the Gadsden Purchase, 1853) near the confluence of the middle and west forks of the Gila River
Date of Death (age): 6:15 a.m., February 17, 1909 (about 79)
Place of Death: Indian hospital at Fort Sill, Oklahoma
Cause of Death: pneumonia, six days after falling from a horse and lying outside, partly submerged in a creek, on a winter night
Resting Place: Apache Cemetery, Fort Sill, Lawton, Oklahoma

Shortly before his death, Geronimo had asked his relatives "to tie his horse to a certain tree and to hang up his belongings on the east side of his grave [because] in three days he would come and get them." Despite this request, his widow "decided to bury his possessions with him."[117]

Rumors persist that Geronimo's remains were stolen by Army officers in 1918 and taken to New Haven, Connecticut, where they are still used in rituals performed by Yale University student members of the Skull and Bones Society. A lawyer representing the Skull and Bones Society denies the accusation, although accusations still circulate.[118]

According to another legend, Geronimo's remains were secretly removed shortly after his death "and taken somewhere to the Southwest—perhaps to the Mogollons, or the Chiricahua Mountains, or deep into the Sierra Madres of Mexico" that he knew so well in life.[119]

Today Geronimo's grave attracts many visitors, hundreds of whom leave tokens, including, on a typical day, gifts of geodes, quartz, leather strips, a quarter, a nickel, and nineteen pennies. Feathers and pouches are often tied to a nearby cedar tree. Some say that Geronimo's stone and cement grave imprisons him in Oklahoma, assuring that not even his remains are allowed to return home to the Southwest.[120]

A monument at the Gila Cliff Dwellings National Monument near Geronimo's birth place was dedicated to him on October 9, 2004. The four-foot high cairn faces east and includes a famous photograph of the proud warrior, with the quote, "I was born by the headwaters of the Gila." Over a hundred visitors watched Geronimo's great-grandson, Harlyn Geronimo, help dedicate the monument with Apache prayers and smudges of yellow cattail pollen.[121] No. 321

321. Geronimo's monument of stones was erected in 1931. Photo courtesy of David N. Lotz.

Lozen "The Woman Warrior"
Victorio's younger sister or cousin; Warm Springs Apache warrior said to have the power to find the enemy; fought alongside Victorio, Nana, and Geronimo; among Geronimo's band when he surrendered in 1886; held prisoner in Florida and at Mount Vernon Barracks, Mobile, Alabama
Date of Birth: late 1840s
Place of Birth: near U.S.-Mexico border at Apacheria
Date of Death (age): 1890s (about 50)
Place of Death: Mount Vernon Barracks, Mobile, Alabama
Cause of Death: tuberculosis; as much as twenty-five percent of the Apaches imprisoned at Mount Vernon Barracks died of disease, especially tuberculosis
Resting Place: Mount Vernon Barracks, Mobile, Alabama, although the exact location of her grave is unknown, in keeping with Apache custom

Victorio once declared that "Lozen is as my right hand. Strong as a man, braver than most, and cunning in strategy, Lozen is a shield to her people."[122]

Mangas Coloradas "Red Sleeves" "Roan Shirt"
Six-foot, six-inch Warm Springs Apache chief; led numerous raids against settlers in Arizona, Texas, New Mexico, and Chihuahua, Mexico
Date of Birth: about 1795
Place of Birth: probably in southern New Mexico
Date of Death (age): January 18, 1863 (about 68)
Place of Death: Fort McLane, New Mexico
Cause of Death: according to U.S. Army records, he was killed while trying to escape; probably killed when he objected to torture by soldiers who had burned his feet and legs with heated bayonets
Resting Place: unmarked grave on Bureau of Reclamation land, once the site of Fort McLane, New Mexico[123]

Manuelito
Mescalero Apache Chief
Date of Birth: about 1787
Place of Birth: probably in the mountain region of southeastern New Mexico
Date of Death (age): October 18, 1862 (about 75)
Place of Death: Gallinas Springs (or Cement Spring), New Mexico
Cause of Death: shot in head and killed along with eleven Apache followers by Captain James Graydon and his troops, although Manuelito had approached Graydon with his hand raised in a sign of peace
Resting Place: unknown, but probably at Cement Spring, New Mexico[124]

Manuelito; Hastiin Ch'ilhaajinii (Man of the Black Plants Place)
Powerful Navajo warrior and chief; a tribal leader, especially during the Bosque Redondo period, 1864-68; chief of the first Navajo police organization
Date of Birth: about 1818
Place of Birth: Navajo homeland
Date of Death (age): 1893 (75)
Place of Death: Navajo homeland
Cause of Death: pneumonia
Resting Place: Navajo homeland[125]

Nana; also known as Nanay "Kas-Tziden"
Famous Warm Springs Apache chief; broke out of the San Carlos Reservation at least three times, terrorizing settlers in Texas, New Mexico, and Chihuahua; most infamous for his raids of 1881 when he (at the age of about eighty) led fifteen to forty warriors on a campaign covering over a thousand miles, causing the deaths of thirty to fifty settlers; four Buffalo Soldiers (Thomas Shaw, Augustus Walley, Moses Williams, and Brent Woods) earned Medals of Honor in his pursuit; surrendered with Geronimo, 1886
Date of Birth: about 1800
Place of Birth: probably the mountain region of southwestern New Mexico
Date of Death (age): May 9, 1896 (about 96)
Place of Death: Fort Sill, Oklahoma
Cause of Death: unstated natural causes
Resting Place: Apache Cemetery, Fort Sill, Lawton, Oklahoma[126] No. 322

322. Photo courtesy of David N. Lotz.

Popé or Popay ("Squash Mountain" or "Red Moon" or "Ripe Cultigens")
San Juan shaman or spiritual leader; leader of the Pueblo Revolt, 1680
Date of Birth: about 1630
Place of Birth: San Juan Pueblo, New Mexico
Date of Death (age): probably 1688 (about 58)
Place of Death: probably San Juan Pueblo, New Mexico

Cause of Death: probably natural causes

Resting Place: probably San Juan Pueblo, New Mexico[127]

Each state has two statues in the National Statutory Hall of Congress. A bronze statue of Senator Dennis Chavez was erected in 1966 and remained New Mexico's sole statue until 2005 when it was joined by a seven-foot tall, three-and-a-half ton marble statue of Popé created by sculptor Cliff Fragua of Jemez Pueblo.[128]

Victorio; Beduiat

Famous Warm Springs Apache chief; fled from the San Carlos Reservation at least twice, terrorizing settlers in Texas, New Mexico, and Chihuahua; Victorio Park in Sierra County, Victorio Peak in Doña Ana County, and the Victorio Mountains in Luna County were named in his honor

Date of Birth: about 1825

Place of Birth: probably in the Black Range, New Mexico

Date of Death (age): October 16, 1880 (about 55)

Place of Death: in the Tres Castillos Mountains, Chihuahua, Mexico

Cause of Death: either killed by Mexican forces, by a Tarahumara scout working for the Mexican army, or with a knife by his own hand

Resting Place: in the Tres Castillos Mountains, Chihuahua, Mexico, although some claim that a Mexican soldier carried Victorio's head through the streets of the city of Chihuahua[129]

13
WARTIME LEADERS AND VICTIMS SINCE THE SPANISH-AMERICAN WAR, 1898

The giant-blooming cereus are out tonight
In rows of cross-shaped stars along an avenue
Of sentry palms beneath a phosphorescent sky,
A lovely sight to view, but oh! The roots, the roots...

We saw them planted day by day not far apart—
Dank roots of mandrake foully mocking human forms,
Their twisted limbs and bloated bellies mottled dark
With mud and mildew, and their clotted say like gore.

Forgive us, fellows, for forgetting what we know,
For letting earth's erasure banish what we saw.
But you we will remember blooming white, O souls
More glorious than the Pleiades or Southern Cross!
—"Pacific Island Cemetery"
Chaplain Fray Angélico Chávez, O.F.M.[1]

Spanish-American War, April-August 1898

Eager to prove their loyalty to the United States against Spain, New Mexico's former mother country, 351 New Mexicans volunteered to fight in the First U.S. Volunteer Cavalry Regiment, better known as the Rough Riders, during the Spanish-American War in 1898. Two hundred and seventy of these 351 brave men saw combat in Cuba, suffering forty-one casualties, including ten deaths. A small number of Rough Rider reinforcements and a volunteer infantry company also served from New Mexico. All fought ably in key battles, following the leadership and winning the admiration of Colonel Theodore Roosevelt, the Rough Riders' second in command and a future president of the United States (1901-09).[2]

Rough Riders *(in alphabetical order)*

Frank C. Brito

Last surviving Rough Rider in New Mexico; second to last surviving Rough Rider in the United States; served with the National Guard on the border following Pancho Villa's 1916 raid on Columbus, New Mexico; at various times a miner, bartender, deputy sheriff, town constable, city jailer, and game warden

Date of Birth: August 24, 1877
Place of Birth: Pinos Altos, New Mexico
Date of Death (age): April 22, 1973 (95)
Place of Death: at a nursing home in El Paso, Texas
Cause of Death: gangrene following amputation of his right leg above the knee
Resting Place: San José Catholic Cemetery, Las Cruces, New Mexico[3] No. 323

323.

William Henry Harrison Llewellyn

Arrived in New Mexico in 1885; helped capture the notorious horse thief David "Doc" Middleton (1851-1913); Indian agent, 1881-85; legislative leader; U.S. District Attorney; Rough Rider captain (Troop G); Troop G, as well as Troops E and F from New Mexico; had the honor of planting the first guidons on the summit following the famous American charge up Kettle Hill, Cuba, July 1898

Date of Birth: September 9, 1851
Place of Birth: Monroe, Wisconsin
Date of Death (age): afternoon, June 11, 1927 (75)
Place of Death: William Beaumont Hospital, El Paso, Texas
Cause of Death: poor health complicated by yellow fever first contracted in Cuba during the Spanish-American War
Resting Place: Masonic Cemetery, Las Cruces, New Mexico[4]

A few months before his death, Llewellyn visited Santa Fe and dropped by the offices of the city's major newspaper, the *New Mexican*. With typical good humor he announced:

> He [recently] had been so close to the hereafter that he could see the people in it. "What place was it?" the major was asked. "It was my favorite heaven," said the major, "the one of that denomination which interferes neither with your religion nor your politics."
> "How is your conduct?" he was asked.
> "Excellent," responded the major. "Not from choice, however, but from necessity."[5] No. 324

324.

Maximiliano Luna

Valencia County Sheriff, 1892-94; only Hispanic Rough Rider Captain (Troop F) in the Spanish-American War, 1898; Troop F, as well as Troops E and G from

New Mexico, had the honor of planting the first guidons on the summit following the famous American charge up Kettle Hill, Cuba; Speaker of the New Mexico Territorial Legislature (elected by unanimous vote), 1898-99; member of General Henry W. Lawton's U.S. Army staff in the Philippines; Los Lunas, New Mexico, was named in the Luna family's honor; the New Mexico National Guard's Camp Luna in Las Vegas, New Mexico, was renamed in his honor, 1929; Luna Technical College in Las Vegas was also named in his honor; a monument to him was erected on the college's campus; Luna's bust in the Roundhouse in Santa Fe is one of only two such statues in the state capitol building

Date of Birth: June 16, 1870
Place of Birth: Los Lunas, New Mexico
Date of Death (age): November 15, 1900 (30)
Place of Death: Rio Agno near San Nicolas, Luzon, Philippines
Cause of Death: drowned with his aide and two Filipino escorts while crossing the Rio Agno
Resting Place: body never recovered for burial[6]

The press reported Luna's death twice, including in June 1898, during the Spanish-American War, when he was confused with a Captain Luna of the Cuban army.[7]

In August 1929 the National Guard camp in Las Vegas was renamed in Luna's honor. Until that time, the camp had been named after each incumbent governor, creating a problem since governors served only two-year terms, requiring frequent name changes at the camp. Colonel Norman L. King declared that the permanent name change to Camp Luna was a "splendid action," adding "No man in New Mexico's history had a better claim to lasting distinction."[8]

A drive to raise funds to create a memorial in Luna's honor was begun as early as January 1901.[9]

Frederick "Fritz" Mueller
U.S. Cavalry, 1882-87; Santa Fe businessman; Santa Fe County treasurer; Rough Rider Captain (Troop E); Troop E, as well as Troops F and G from New Mexico, had the honor of planting the first guidons on the summit following the famous American charge up Kettle Hill, Cuba, July 1898; 33rd degree Scottish Rite Mason
Date of Birth: January 28, 1863
Place of Birth: Wurtenberg, Germany
Date of Death (age): 5:30 a.m., September 16, 1934 (71)
Place of Death: Albuquerque, New Mexico
Cause of Death: stomach cancer
Resting Place: National Cemetery, Santa Fe, New Mexico[10] No. 325

Theodore "T.R." "Teddy" "Teedie" Roosevelt
Rough Rider second in command (to Colonel Leonard Wood); Governor of New York, 1898-1901; Vice President of the United States, 1901; President

325.

326. A plaque near the president's grave quotes Teddy Roosevelt's words: "Keep your eyes on the stars and keep your feet on the ground." Photo courtesy of Jack Gundolfi.

of the United States, 1901-09; visited New Mexico several times before and during his terms as president; a U.S. postage stamp was issued in his honor; the now-abandoned Quay County community of Roosevelt was probably named in his honor; Roosevelt Middle School in Tijeras, New Mexico, and Roosevelt County, New Mexico, (created in 1903) were named in his honor[11]

Date of Birth: October 27, 1858

Place of Birth: New York City, New York

Date of Death (age): 4:00 a.m., January 6, 1919 (60)

Place of Death: at his Sagamore Hill estate in Oyster Bay, New York

Cause of Death: embolism

Resting Place: Young's Memorial Cemetery, Oyster Bay, New York

Devastated by the loss of his youngest son in World War I, Roosevelt became weaker and weaker. His last words were to his valet, James Amos. After taking medication to help him sleep, the former president said, "James, will you please put out the light?" Having survived heavy fire in battle, dangerous safaris, and an assassin's bullet on October 14, 1912, in Milwaukee (saved by a pair of glasses and his folded speech in his breast coat pocket), the indefatigable Teddy Roosevelt passed on at last.[12]

Roosevelt was buried on a cold, snowy day. A teary-eyed William Howard Taft, Roosevelt's vice president and successor in the White House, was one of the last to leave the cemetery that day.[13] No. 326

Other Rough Riders include:
Charles Littlepage Ballard (Chapter 8: Lawmen, Criminals, and Victims of Crime)
George Curry (Chapter 9: Political, Diplomatic, and Judicial Leaders)
Fred Fornoff (Chapter 8: Lawmen, Criminals, and Victims of Crime)
Wilber Elliott Wilder (this chapter)

Other Spanish-American War Veterans include:
Albert B. Fall (Chapter 9: Political, Diplomatic, and Judicial Leaders)
Augustus Walley (this chapter)

Inter-War Medal of Honor Recipient

Edward Alvin Clary
Watertender, U.S. Navy; Medal of Honor recipient for his heroic action following a boiler room accident aboard the *U.S.S. Hopkins*, February 14, 1910; served in the U.S. Navy for thirty years; prohibition agent

Date of Birth: May 6, 1883

Place of Birth: Foxport, Kentucky

Date of Death (age): 2:50 a.m., April 30, 1939 (55)

Place of Death: at his home in Santa Fe, New Mexico

Cause of Death: coronary thrombosis

Resting Place: National Cemetery, Santa Fe, New Mexico[14] No. 327

327.

The Mexican Revolution, 1910-20 *(in alphabetical order)*

The Mexican Revolution was a long, chaotic conflict involving not one, but many revolutionary armies and political contenders. Tragically, the conflict often spilled over the U.S.-Mexican border, drawing New Mexico and other border states into the violence with dire consequences for both the United States and Mexico.[15]

Cayetano Romero
Mexican Federalist Army Brigadier General captured with 3,333 of his men (and their families) by American troops following their defeat at the hands of Pancho Villa's Constitutionalist rebel forces in the Battle of Ojinaga, December 1913-January 1914; incarcerated with his men at Fort Wingate, New Mexico
Date of Birth: unknown
Place of Birth: unknown
Date of Death (age): July 22, 1914 (unknown)
Place of Death: Fort Wingate, New Mexico
Cause of Death: unstated natural causes
Resting Place: Fort Wingate Cemetery, Fort Wingate, New Mexico

328.

At General Romero's funeral, his ragged fellow Mexican soldiers were said to honor Romero by wearing whatever uniforms they still possessed. A Mexican soldier played taps and U.S. soldiers fired a twenty-one gun salute.[16] No. 328

Benjamin J. Viljoen
General in the Boer War; journalist; novelist; military advisor to Francisco Madero in the Mexican Revolution; Mexican diplomat; farmer
Date of Birth: 1868
Place of Birth: Wodehouse, South Africa
Date of Death (age): January 14, 1917 (about 49)
Place of Death: La Mesa, New Mexico
Cause of Death: pneumonia
Resting Place: Masonic Cemetery, Las Cruces, New Mexico

When told of her husband's death, Myrtle Viljoen was "so bitterly distressed that she picked up a bottle of his adrenaline [used to treat his asthma] and just smashed it against the wall. She didn't say a word. She just smashed that bottle against the wall."[17] No. 329

Pancho Villa's Raid on Columbus, March 9, 1916, and the Punitive Expedition, 1916-17 *(in alphabetical order)*

In the early morning hours of March 9, 1916, Pancho Villa and approximately 485 soldiers from his Mexican revolutionary army invaded Columbus, New Mexico. Eleven civilians, eight U.S. soldiers, and between eighty-seven and 190 of Villa's men were killed in an international incident that led to a frustrating, unsuccessful search for Villa by the American

329.

Punitive Expedition into Mexico from March 1916 to February 1917.[18]

In March 1991, Columbus celebrated the seventy-fifth anniversary of Villa's raid with several events, including a parade through town, the encampment of reenactment soldiers at Pancho Villa State Park, a dance at Columbus's Pancho Villa Lounge, and the dedication of a monument by two elderly women, Margaret Epps and Marylee Gaskill, who were small children in Columbus at the time of the infamous raid.[19]

James Todd Dean

Columbus grocer and homesteader; one of only two victims of Villa's raid to be buried in Columbus
Date of Birth: December 17, 1854
Place of Birth: Philadelphia, Pennsylvania
Date of Death (age): March 9, 1916 (61)
Place of Death: near Broadway and Main Street, Columbus, New Mexico
Cause of Death: killed by Villista raiders
Resting Place: Valley Heights Cemetery, Columbus, New Mexico

Dean was killed when he left his house to help fight the fires he saw in the business district of town. His twenty-three-year-old son, Edwin, later found his father's body on the street in a pile of dead Villista bodies.[20]

Dean is buried to the right of Bessy James's gravesite, No. 330.

Bessy James

Wife of railroad worker, Milton James; one of only two victims of Villa's raid to be buried in Columbus
Date of Birth: October 6, 1897
Place of Birth: unknown
Date of Death (age): March 9, 1916 (18)
Place of Death: outside the Hoover Hotel, Columbus, New Mexico
Cause of Death: shot in chest by Villista raiders
Resting Place: Valley Heights Cemetery, Columbus, New Mexico

Pregnant at the time of the raid, Bessy, her husband Milton, and her sister Alice ran from their wood-frame house toward the Hoover Hotel to seek protection from Villa's men. Holding Alice's hand as they ran, Bessy was shot just as they reached the hotel. Milton was shot in the leg, but Alice was unharmed. Although advanced in age, Alice survived to attend the seventy-fifth anniversary of the raid in 1991.[21] No. 330

330. Bessy's is the tall headstone to the left. Beneath Bessy's name and dates are the words: "A place is vacant in our hearts that never can be filled." James Dean's headstone is to the right, just outside the fence.

Susan "Susie" Parks Kendrick

Heroic Columbus telephone operator during Villa's raid on Columbus; wife of G.E. Parks, owner of the *Columbus Courier*; left New Mexico in 1919; the first woman

sheet metal worker in a Seattle shipyard during World War II; was among thousands of women nicknamed Rosie the Riveter during the war
Date of Birth: October 22, 1895
Place of Birth: Cinabar, Washington
Date of Death (age): April 19, 1981 (85)
Place of Death: Valley Terrace Rest Home, Puyallup, Washington
Cause of Death: unstated natural causes
Resting Place: cremated with ashes at the Rose Hill Cemetery, Kirkland, Washington

Despite bullets that flew through her house, threatening her and her infant Gwen's lives, Susie Parks bravely used the telephone exchange in her home to call for help from Fort Bliss, Texas, during Villa's raid on Columbus. Although injured in the raid, Gwen Parks Conyea lived to be ninety years old, dying in 2004. Susan had six other children after Gwen.

Susan's bullet-riddled switchboard is on display at the Columbus Historical Museum. A replica of the switchboard is on display at the Telephone Pioneers Museum in Albuquerque, New Mexico.[22]

Maud S. Hawk Wright Medders
Captured on March 1, 1916, with her two-year-old son Johnnie, by Villa's army on her family's ranch outside Pearson, Chihuahua, Mexico; finally released by Villa prior to his raid on Columbus, New Mexico, March 9, 1916; settled on a ranch west of Mountainair with her second husband, Will Medders (1895-1965), in 1917
Date of Birth: May 31, 1889
Place of Birth: Alabama
Date of Death (age): (Christmas) December 25, 1980 (91)
Place of Death: probably at her ranch in Abo, New Mexico
Cause of Death: unstated natural causes
Resting Place: Mountainair Cemetery, Mountainair, New Mexico[23]

331. Maud's grave lies beneath a juniper tree in the far southwest corner of the Mountainair Cemetery. Mexico, where she experienced her horrifying days as Villa's prisoner, lies hundreds of miles in the distance.

Apparently Villa was glad to release Maud. According to her descendents, Villa bid her farewell with the words, "Cursed is the man that is burdened with you." Maud's descendents also recall her disgust when she heard that a new state park in Columbus was going to be named for Pancho Villa. According to Maud, "it was like naming a park in a Jewish community after Adolf Hitler!"[24]

Active until late in life, Maud injured her back while bulldogging a calf and, later, broke her hip while roping a calf in her 80's![25] No. 331

John G. Nievergelt
Sergeant and member of the 13th Cavalry Band
Date of Birth: unknown
Place of Birth: unknown

332.

Date of Death (age): March 9, 1916 (unknown)
Place of Death: Columbus, New Mexico
Cause of Death: killed during Villa's raid on Columbus, New Mexico
Resting Place: Fort Bliss National Cemetery, El Paso, Texas[26] No. 332

John Joseph "Black Jack" Pershing
Commander of the Punitive Expedition, 1916-17, that fruitlessly pursued Pancho Villa after his raid on Columbus, New Mexico; Commander of the American Expeditionary Force (AEF) in World War I, 1917-18; Chief of Staff of the U.S. Army, 1921-24, with the title of "General of the Armies"; a U.S. postage stamp was issued in his honor
Date of Birth: September 13, 1860
Place of Birth: near Laclede, Missouri
Date of Death (age): July 15, 1948 (87)
Place of Death: Walter Reed Army Medical Center, Washington, D.C.
Cause of Death: "generalized arteriosclerosis, auricular fibrillation and, finally, the immediate cause—a blood clot in the lungs."[27]
Resting Place: as was his wish, under a simple white military gravestone in Section 34 of Arlington National Cemetery, now known as Pershing Hill, near the gravestones of his Doughboys of World War I and near his grandsons, Colonel John Warren Pershing (1941-99) and Lieutenant Richard Pershing (1942-68), the latter killed in action in Vietnam[28] No. 333

333. Photo courtesy of Sam Jackson.

Samuel "Sam" Ravel
Arrived in the United States from Lithuania, 1905, and in Columbus, New Mexico, 1910; co-owner (with brothers Luis and Arthur) of the general store and Commercial Hotel attacked by Villista soldiers some say because he reneged on a business deal with Villa; he was reportedly in El Paso at a dentist appointment (or, according to another account, recovering from an operation) on the day of the raid
Date of Birth: 1885
Place of Birth: Shakie, Lithuania
Date of Death (age): July 16, 1937 (about 52)
Place of Death: El Paso, Texas
Cause of Death: unstated natural causes
Resting Place: B'nai Zion Cemetery, El Paso, Texas[29]

Hearing of Villa's raid on Columbus, Ravel reportedly sent a telegram from El Paso to his brothers in Columbus, asking, "Are you dead or alive? Answer." Ravel gave no instructions as to how Luis and Arthur were to answer his question if they were both dead!

The Ravels filed claims for the value of the property they lost in the raid, but received no compensation from their insurance company because the company insisted that it was not responsible for losses caused by "raids, commotions, or civil disorders."[30] No. 334

Other Victims of the Villa Raid:

Soldiers of the 13th U.S. Cavalry:
Private Thomas F. Butler
Sergeant Mark A. Dobbs
Private Fred A. Griffin
Private Frank T. Kindval
Corporal Paul Simon
Private Jessie P. Taylor
Corporal Harry E. Wiswell

Civilians:
W.A. Davidson
Harry Davis
Dr. H.M. Hart: an El Paso veterinarian
C.C. Miller: local druggist
C.D. Miller: a civil engineer from Las Cruces, New Mexico
J.J. Moore: a local farmer
José Pereyra: a Mexican citizen visiting from Parral, Mexico
William T. Ritchie: manager of Columbus's Commercial Hotel
J. Waton Walker: a visitor from Playas, New Mexico[32]

Other Punitive Expedition Soldiers include:
Frank C. Brito (this chapter)
Wilber Elliott Wilder (this chapter)

334. Translated, the Hebrew words on Sam Ravel's gravestone mean: "Here Lies Samar-Hu, Son of the Worthy Son, Abraham David. 16 Tammuz 5697 (the date of death in the Hebrew calendar) May his soul be bound up in the bond of eternal life." 1 Samuel 25:29[31] Photo courtesy of Richard Dean.

Villistas

Pancho Villa raided Columbus with a force of about 485 men. At least eighty-seven (and as many as 190) Villistas were killed during the raid. Most of their remains were piled eight to ten feet high on rows of cordwood, covered with kerosene, and burned. Three captured Villistas died from their wounds. Seven captured soldiers were tried, found guilty of murder, and sentenced to be executed in Deming. José Rodriguez's sentence was commuted to life in the New Mexico State Penitentiary. The other six were hanged. It is believed that they were buried in unmarked graves on the east end of Mountain View Cemetery in Deming. The six were (in alphabetical order):

Francisco Alvarez (22-year-old laborer, hanged at 6:36 a.m., June 9, 1916)
Juan Castillo (26-year-old laborer, hanged at 7:17 a.m., June 30, 1916)
Taurino Garcia (21-year-old laborer, hanged at 6:00 a.m., June 30, 1916)
José Rangel (23-year-old laborer, hanged at 7:17 a.m., June 30, 1916)
Eusevio Renteria (24-year-old laborer, hanged at 6:00 a.m., June 30, 1916)
Juan Sanchez (16-year-old laborer, hanged at 7:13 a.m., June 9, 1916)[33]

Francisco "Pancho" Villa; originally Doroteo Arango
Mexican revolutionary general and bandit whose forces attacked Columbus, New Mexico, March 9, 1916; strangely, Pancho Villa State Park in Columbus was named

for the man who was responsible for causing so much death and destruction in that border town

Date of Birth: 1877

Place of Birth: San Juan del Rio, Durango, Mexico

Date of Death (age): early morning, July 20, 1923 (about 46)

Place of Death: Juárez Street, Parral, Mexico, not far from his 25,000-acre La Rancho de Cañutillo, the elaborate fifty-room *hacienda* where he had retired in 1920; a plaque marks the place where he was murdered

Cause of Death: assassinated in a well-planned ambush as he drove by a rented house in his black 1919 Dodge roadster with his three-man bodyguard (two of whom were also killed in the attack); dozens of rounds were fired in a two-minute span before Villa's car crashed into a tree

Resting Place: Cementerio Municipal, Parral, Mexico[34]

Villa had been the target of several assassination attempts, including an American attempt during John J. Pershing's Punitive Expedition of 1916-17. In the latter episode, two Japanese men, K. Fuzita and T. Suzuki, infiltrated Villa's camp with plans to kill Villa by adding poison to his coffee. Although Villa drank at least half the laced cup of coffee, the poison clearly failed. Fuzita and Suzuki fled the camp, unharmed as well.[35]

Only one man confessed to Villa's murder in 1923. Jesús Salas Barraza was sentenced to twenty years in prison, but was released from custody by the end of 1923.

Villa remained a legendary figure in death, just as he had been in life. There are at least three macabre legends regarding his remains and their whereabouts. First, it's said that grave robbers dug up his body in early 1926 to remove its head to sell it to a Chicago millionaire who collected the skulls from historic cadavers! Next, it is rumored that members of the highly secretive Skull and Bones Society at Yale University acquired Villa's head, much as they had supposedly acquired Geronimo's skull in 1918.

Finally, when President Luis Echeverria requested that Villa's body be entombed in Mexico City's Monument to the Mexican Revolution in 1976, it's said that the mayor of Parral sent another body rather than surrender Villa's, if only because Villa's gravesite is such a large tourist attraction in Parral. In fact, a commemorative event is held in Parral each July with reenactments of Villa's assassination and hundreds of horsemen in period costume riding into town from throughout northern Mexico. Meanwhile, Villa's grave in Parral is continuously guarded and is almost always covered with flowers and other tributes left by those who admire him still.[36]

Several *corridos* (ballads) have been written in Villa's memory, including:

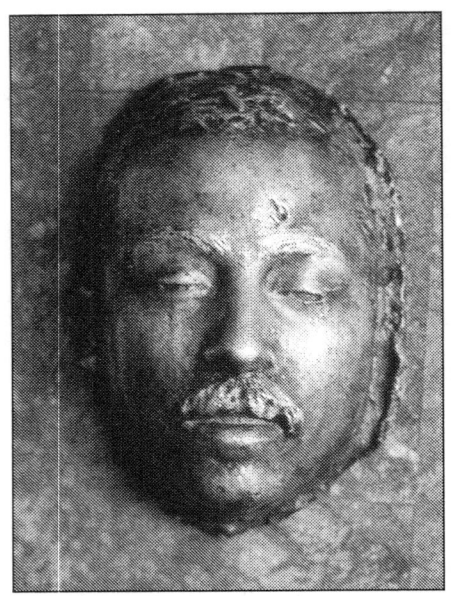

335. Pancho Villa's death mask.
Photo courtesy of Gary Chrisman.

Pobre Pancho Villa.	Poor Pancho Villa.
Fue muy triste su destino	How sad is his fate
Morir en una emboscada	To die in an ambush
Ya la mitad del camino.	In the middle of the road.

Ay, Mexico está de luto.
Tiene una gran pesadilla.
Pues mataron en Parral
al valiente Pancho Villa.

Poor Mexico is mourning.
It is afflicted by a nightmare.
They've killed brave Pancho Villa in Parral.[37]

It is perhaps fitting that one of only three copies of Villa's death mask is on display at the Columbus Historical Society Museum in Columbus, New Mexico. The other two masks are in the Museo de General Francisco Villa in Parral, Mexico, and at the Museo de Pancho Villa in Chihuahua City, Mexico. Villa's bullet-ridden Dodge is also on display in the Museo de Pancho Villa. No. 335, No. 336

World War I Soldiers and Officers, 1917-18

At least 17,251 New Mexicans served in the U.S. military during World War I. Five hundred and one of these men died, an above average number per capita among the states.[39] A monument for the 1,750 Bernalillo County men who served and the fifty who died in the war was erected at the New Mexico Veterans Memorial in southeast Albuquerque.

336. Translated, the words on Villa's gravestone read: "The insults and their instigators supplanted the soldier in historical importance and indeed show their baseness. General Juan N. Medina." General Medina was Villa's chief of staff during the Mexican Revolution.[38] Photo courtesy of Gary Chrisman.

Harry Perkins Stagg

Recipient of the Silver Star, a Purple Heart, and the French Legion of Honor; healthseeker who came to New Mexico in 1925; Baptist minister and executive director of the Southern Baptist Convention of New Mexico, 1938-68
Date of Birth: October 1, 1898
Place of Birth: Hamburg, Louisiana
Date of Death (age): February 6, 2000 (101)
Place of Death: at his home in Albuquerque, New Mexico
Cause of Death: unstated natural causes
Resting Place: Sunset Memorial Cemetery, Albuquerque, New Mexico

Stagg's regiment made the first all-American charge on the enemy in World War I. Despite sweeping artillery fire, Stagg survived the charge of approximately nine hundred yards. In his words, as he began the charge, "There came a bright light, brighter than any ordinary sunlight that came down in a funnel shape, very small, just around my feet and then slanting outward and upward. It seemed that no bullet could penetrate this white light. I was not touched." Although most of his fellow soldiers were killed in the action, Stagg made it safely, falling into a deep shell hole at the end of the charge. Years later, Stagg still asserted, "I knew that there had been a great miracle from heaven."[40]

337.

After turning one hundred years of age, Stagg said, "[T]o think I'm still living at over one hundred now, after [so many] things happened. I should have been killed or just died. I can't imagine still being alive. It's of the Lord. It makes me wonder what's coming next."[41] No. 337

Other World War I Soldiers, Chaplains, and Officers include:
Father Albert Braun (Chapter 10: Religious Leaders)
Bronson Cutting (Chapter 9: Political, Diplomatic, and Judicial Leaders)
Conrad Hilton (Chapter 5: Business Leaders)
Roy Johnson (Chapter 6: Educational Leaders)
Harry P. Mera (Chapter 4: Cultural Preservationists)
John J. Pershing (this chapter)
Frances V. Scholes (Chapter 4: Cultural Preservationists)
Will Shuster (Chapter 2: Artists, Performers, and Directors)
Kenneth N. Walker (this chapter)
Wilber Elliott Wilder (this chapter)

World War II Soldiers, Chaplains, and Officers, 1941-45

New Mexico suffered 2,263 fatalities, including 1,242 combat deaths, during World War II.[42] New Mexico made many other significant contributions to the war. Indeed, the state and its people did as much, in proportion to its size and resources, as any state in the Union to finally end the deadliest conflict in world history.[43]

Bataan Death Marchers (in alphabetical order)

New Mexico National Guardsmen, mobilized on January 6, 1941, were deployed to the Philippines as the 200th Coast Guard Artillery Regiment, unfortunately in time for the Japanese attack on the Philippines immediately following the Japanese surprise attack on Pearl Harbor on December 7, 1941. With no reinforcements and dwindling supplies, the 200th, along with the 515th Coast Guard Artillary and approximately seventy thousand other U.S. and Filipino soldiers, held out against the enemy as long as they could before finally surrendering on April 9, 1942. Already weakened and often injured, those who surrendered were forced on a terrible Bataan Death March over as many as sixty-five miles with little food, water, or medical supplies. Those who survived faced months of agony in Japanese prison camps. Others perished on the infamous Japanese Death Ships, often bombed by U.S. planes that had no idea they were attacking ships with fellow Americans aboard. In all, 687 New Mexicans died before, during, or after the Death March.[44]

New Mexicans have honored the memory of the Bataan Death March in many ways, including with an annual memorial march on White Sands Missile Range since 1990, the creation of a museum, a monument, and the renaming of New Mexico's state capitol building (until 1966) in Santa Fe, the naming of a memorial park and Methodist hospital (from 1952-65) in Albuquerque, and the April 19, 1991, dedication of an impressive monument outside the Deming Luna Mimbres Museum in Deming, New Mexico.[45]

338.

Calvin Robert Graef
Sergeant, Battery H, 200th Coast Guard Artillery Regiment; miraculous survivor of

the Bataan Death March, Prisoner of War camps, and the Japanese Death Ship, *Arisan*
Date of Birth: July 24, 1915
Place of Birth: Brooklyn, New York
Date of Death (age): March 6, 1997 (81)
Place of Death: Columbia Medical Center, Carlsbad, New Mexico
Cause of Death: unstated natural causes "after a lengthy illness"
Resting Place: National Cemetery, Santa Fe, New Mexico[46] No. 338

Charles Gurdon "The Kipper" Sage
Highly decorated commander of the 200th Coastal Artillery Regiment; survivor of the Bataan Death March; Prisoner of War in the Philippines, Formosa, Japan, and Manchuria, April 1942-August 1945; General of the New Mexico National Guard, 1946-57; forty-year military veteran; newspaper owner; a street in Santa Fe was named in his honor; a memorial bench at the New Mexico Veterans Memorial in southeast Albuquerque was dedicated in his honor
Date of Birth: April 10, 1895
Place of Birth: Sparks, Kansas
Date of Death (age): February 4, 1967 (71)
Place of Death: St. Vincent Hospital, Santa Fe, New Mexico
Cause of Death: unstated natural causes
Resting Place: National Cemetery, Santa Fe, New Mexico

At Sage's funeral, the First Presbyterian Church in Santa Fe was filled to capacity with a crowd that included many of the general's fellow survivors of the Bataan Death March and POW camps of World War II. Bataan veterans formed the honor guard when Sage's casket was taken to the National Cemetery for burial.[47] No. 339

339.

John Jerome Wilcoxson; POW No. 1363
Sergeant, Battery A, 200th Coast Guard Artillery Regiment; Bataan Death March survivor; Japanese Prisoner of War, April-December 1942
Date of Birth: November 20, 1918
Place of Birth: unknown
Date of Death (age): December 4, 1942 (24)
Place of Death: Camp Hoten, Mukden, Manchuria
Cause of Death: horrible POW camp conditions; among the 250 Allied POWs to die at Camp Hoten during the first year of its operation
Resting Place: Fairview Cemetery, Albuquerque, New Mexico[48] No. 340

Navajo Code Talkers (in alphabetical order)
The U.S. Marine Corps recruited twenty-nine young Navajo men to help develop a military code in the Navajo language. The "Original 29" Navajo Code Talkers arrived at Camp Pendleton, California, in May 1942. Soon joined by

340.

over three hundred fellow Navajos in the 382nd Platoon, these brave radio operators used their secret code to help win several major battles in the Pacific, including the battles of Guadalcanal, Tarawa, Saipan, Iwo Jima, and Okinawa. At the Battle of Iwo Jima alone, the Code Talkers sent more than eight hundred error-free messages in a forty-eight-hour period. The Japanese never broke the code, and the Code Talkers maintained their secrecy until their code was officially declassified in 1968.

Since then, the group has been deservedly honored with special events and medals on both the state and national levels. The Code Talkers were formally recognized for the first time on June 28, 1969. President Ronald Reagan proclaimed August 14, 1982, "National Navajo Code Talkers Day," creating a holiday that's been celebrated ever since. Surviving members of the "Original 29" Code Talkers received Congressional Gold Medals of Honor, the highest honor an American civilian can achieve, on December 21, 2000. A movie about the Code Talkers, entitled *Windtalkers*, opened to mixed reviews in June 2002. Beautiful sculptures of a Code Talker, by Kirtland, New Mexico, artist Oreland Joe, stand in the Gallup Cultural Center and near the Navajo tribal offices in Window Rock, Arizona. The Code Talkers are also honored at the New Mexico Veterans Memorial in southeast Albuquerque.[49]

The "Original 29" Code Talkers were (in alphabetical order):

Charley Tsosie Begay (May 12, 1912-July 15, 1998)
Roy L. Begay (unknown-1944, dying on Palau Island)
Samuel Hosteen Nez Begay (July 15, 1914-July 1984)
John Ashi Benally (August 29, 1917-December 4, 1980)
Wilsie H. Bitsie (deceased, dates unknown)
Cosey Stanley Brown (December 5, 1925-January 26, 1974)
John Brown, Jr. (unknown-   )
John Chee (deceased, dates unknown)
Benjamin Cleveland (deceased, dates unknown)
Eugene Roanhorse Crawford (deceased, dates unknown)
David Curley (deceased, dates unknown)
Lowell Smith Damon (deceased, dates unknown)
George H. Dennison (July 15, 1918-May 1973)
James Dixon (September 10, 1924-June 21, 1997)
Carl Nelson Gorman (October 5, 1907-January 29, 1998)
Oscar B. Ilthma (deceased, dates unknown)
Alan Dale June (unknown-   )
Alfred Leonard (deceased, dates unknown)
James C. Manuelito, Sr. (October 9, 1909-June 1985)
William McCabe (February 3, 1913-October 1969)
Chester Nez (about 1921-   )
Jack Nez (January 15, 1914-June 1976)
Lloyd Oliver (unknown-   )

Joe Palmer (also known as Balmer Slowtalker) (unknown-)
Frank Denny Pete (July 4, 1920-May 1974)
Nelson S. Thompson (December 15, 1910-February 1983)
Harry Tsosie (about 1920-1944, dying at Bougainville, Solomon Islands)
John W. Willie, Jr. (deceased, dates unknown)
William Dean Wilson (deceased, dates unknown)

James Dixon
One of the "Original 29" Navajo Code Talkers in the 382nd Platoon, U.S. Marine Corps
Date of Birth: September 10, 1924
Place of Birth: Shiprock, New Mexico
Date of Death (age): June 21, 1997 (72)
Place of Death: at his home in Kirtland, New Mexico
Cause of Death: unstated natural causes
Resting Place: Greenlawn Cemetery, Farmington, New Mexico[50] No. 341

341.

Jerome Cody Dodge
U.S. Marine Corps Navajo Code Talker
Date of Birth: June 25, 1917
Place of Birth: unknown
Date of Death (age): January 6, 1996 (78)
Place of Death: St. Joseph Hospital, Albuquerque, New Mexico
Cause of Death: unstated natural causes
Resting Place: Kirtland Community Cemetery, Kirtland, New Mexico[51] No. 342

Carl Nelson Gorman
Albuquerque Indian School graduate; one of the "Original 29" Navajo Code Talkers in the 382nd Platoon, U.S. Marine Corps; past President of the Navajo Code Talkers Association; artist; father of artist R.C. Gorman; staunch supporter of the Navajo tradition, teaching it and his art at several schools, including the University of California-Davis and the University of New Mexico-Gallup Campus; University of New Mexico honorary degree recipient, 1990
Date of Birth: October 5, 1907
Place of Birth: ranch near Chinle, Arizona
Date of Death (age): shortly after midnight, January 29, 1998 (90)
Place of Death: Rehoboth-McKinley Christian Hospital, Gallup, New Mexico
Cause of Death: congestive heart failure
Resting Place: cremated

342.

   Gorman's funeral was in Gallup's Sacred Heart Catholic Cathedral, although his son, R.C. Gorman, said, "My father was baptized four times, so he had a choice. He was respectful of all religions. I never heard him putting down anything or anyone. That's what made him a great man."[52]

343.

Harrison Lapahie; Diné name: Yieh Kinne yah (He Finds Things)
U.S. Marine Navajo Code Talker, 1943-November 1945; worked as a mechanic for Rockwell International in Los Angeles, California, for thirty-three years, 1952-85
Date of Birth: January 18, between 1923 and 1928 (his gravestone reads 1924)
Place of Birth: near Shiprock, New Mexico
Date of Death (age): about 6:00 a.m., November 26, 1985 (between 57 and 62)
Place of Death: at his apartment in Los Angeles, California
Cause of Death: heart attack
Resting Place: Memory Garden, Farmington, New Mexico[53] No. 343

A U.S. Army Commander

344.

Patrick Jay Hurley
U.S. Secretary of War, 1929-33; U.S. Minister to New Zealand, 1942-43; Major General, 1943; U.S. Ambassador to China, 1944-45; unsuccessful Republican candidate of the U.S. Senate in the controversial election of 1952
Date of Birth: January 8, 1883
Place of Birth: Indian Territory
Date of Death (age): July 30, 1963 (80)
Place of Death: at his home in Santa Fe, New Mexico
Cause of Death: heart attack
Resting Place: National Cemetery, Santa Fe, New Mexico[54] No. 344

Medal of Honor Recipients: World War II (in alphabetical order)

Eight of the 433 recipients of the Medal of Honor during World War II were either native New Mexicans (in the case of four men) or soldiers who had spent part of their lives in the state (in the case of four others).[55]

345.

Alexander "Sandy" Bonnyman, Jr.
U.S. Marine First Lieutenant; entered the military in New Mexico; Medal of Honor recipient for his heroic action in the Gilbert Islands of the South Pacific, November 20-22, 1943
Date of Birth: May 2, 1910
Place of Birth: Atlanta, Georgia
Date of Death (age): November 22, 1943 (33)
Place of Death: Tarawa in the Gilbert Islands
Cause of Death: killed in action
Resting Place: body never recovered; a cenotaph, or memorial headstone, has been placed in his honor at the National Cemetery, Santa Fe, New Mexico[56] No. 345

Joseph Pantillion Martinez

U.S. Army Private; only American to receive the Medal of Honor on U.S. soil during World War II; the first Hispanic and the first drafted soldier of World War II to receive the Medal of Honor, earned for his heroic action on Attu in the Aleutian Islands, Alaska, May 26, 1943; Medal of Honor issued posthumously on October 27, 1943
Date of Birth: July 27, 1920
Place of Birth: Taos, New Mexico
Date of Death (age): May 26, 1943 (22)
Place of Death: Attu in the Aleutian Islands, Alaska
Cause of Death: killed in action
Resting Place: Ault Cemetery, Ault, Colorado

    Urging his fellow soldiers to advance against heavy enemy fire, Martinez yelled, "Come on! Let's go!" as he charged forward. These words were used to help promote war bond sales in the United States thereafter.[57]

Harold Herman Moon, Jr.

Medal of Honor recipient for his heroic action holding off an enemy attack; almost two hundred dead Japanese soldiers were found within a hundred yards of his foxhole, October 21, 1944, at Pawig, Leyte, Philippine Islands; first Albuquerque native to receive the Medal of Honor
Date of Birth: March 15, 1921
Place of Birth: Albuquerque, New Mexico
Date of Death (age): October 21, 1944 (23)
Place of Death: Pawig, Leyte, Philippine Islands
Cause of Death: killed by enemy fire

346.

Resting Place: originally buried in the Philippines; reburied at Fairview Cemetery, Albuquerque, New Mexico, in 1948[58]

    Moon's original gravestone at Fairview Cemetery gave no indication that he had received the Medal of Honor. The New Mexico Hometown Heroes Committee rectified this oversight on Memorial Day, 1990, with a formal military ceremony that included a symbolic riderless horse and canon fire.[59] No. 346

John Cary "Red" Morgan

New Mexico Military Institute student, 1934; Second Lieutenant, U.S. Army Air Corps; Medal of Honor recipient for his heroic action flying a badly damaged B-17 during a bombing mission over Germany, July 28, 1943; his heroism inspired the popular 1949 movie, *Twelve O'Clock High*; the only New Mexico Military Institute alum to ever receive the Medal of Honor
Date of Birth: August 24, 1914
Place of Birth: Vernon, Texas
Date of Death (age): January 17, 1991 (76)
Place of Death: Papillton, Nebraska

347. Photo courtesy of J. Donald Morfe.

Cause of Death: unstated natural causes
Resting Place: National Cemetery, Arlington, Virginia[60] No. 347

Robert Sheldon Scott
University of New Mexico athlete and graduate, 1937; Medal of Honor recipient for his heroic action holding off an enemy attack on the Solomon Islands after the remainder of his company had retreated, July 29, 1943; reenlisted after World War II and also served in Korea and in Vietnam, retiring after twenty-five years of service with the rank of colonel
Date of Birth: November 30, 1913
Place of Birth: Washington, D.C.
Date of Death (age): February 5, 1999 (85)
Place of Death: at his home in Santa Fe, New Mexico
Cause of Death: unknown natural causes following a case of the flu
Resting Place: National Cemetery, Santa Fe, New Mexico[61]

After retiring, Scott told a reporter, "I spent my life taking orders. Now I'm my own man. I'm in a position to tell anybody to go to hell, even though it might cost me. But that's the nice thing about being old—you can say what you really think."[62]

Two years prior to his death, the New Mexico State Legislature declared his birthday "Colonel Robert Scott Day." Interviewed on the occasion, Scott asked, "A day named after me? I'm glad I know now. That way I can call up my friends and brag." Normally humble, he referred to his heroic action during World War II as "a critical little deal."[63] No. 348

349.

José F. Valdez
U.S. Army Private; Medal of Honor recipient for his heroic action holding off the German enemy near Rosenkrantz, France, calling in artillery fire within fifty yards of his position, January 25, 1945; Medal of Honor posthumously issued, February 8, 1946; a monument in Valdez's hometown of Gobernador, New Mexico, a naval vessel, a New Mexico highway (from Tierra Amarilla to Bloomfield, New Mexico, dedicated on August 27, 2004), as well as several schools, streets, training centers, and armories in Utah, Colorado, and Georgia have been named in his honor
Date of Birth: January 3, 1925
Place of Birth: Gobernador, New Mexico
Date of Death (age): February 17, 1945 (20)
Place of Death: near Rosenkrantz, France
Cause of Death: wounds suffered in battle
Resting Place: National Cemetery, Santa Fe, New Mexico[64] No. 349

Kenneth Newton Walker
U.S. Army Brigadier General and pilot; in 1934, with three other officers, he created AWDP-Plan 1, a blueprint for a possible future war with Germany; commander of the 5th Bomber Command in the Pacific theater, 1942-43; Medal of Honor recipient for his heroic action leading twelve B-17's on a daring daylight bombing raid on Japanese ships in the harbor at Rabaul, New Britain, resulting in nine direct hits on enemy vessels, January 5, 1943; Medal of Honor posthumously issued, March 11, 1943; medal presented to his son by President Franklin D. Roosevelt at the White House, March 25, 1943; Walker Air Force Base in Roswell, New Mexico, was named in his honor in 1948 until it was decommissioned in 1967
Date of Birth: July 17, 1898
Place of Birth: Cerrillos, New Mexico
Date of Death (age): January 5, 1943 (44)
Place of Death: near Rabaul, New Britain
Cause of Death: killed when his plane, a B-17 Flying Fortress nicknamed the "San Antonio Rose," was shot down
Resting Place: remains never recovered; a memorial headstone was erected in his honor at the National Cemetery, Arlington, Virginia

      A public memorial service for General Walker did not take place until years after his death. Such an event was finally held at Arlington National Cemetery on Pearl Harbor Day, December 7, 2001, when a memorial headstone was erected while a World War II-era B-29 Superfortress flew overhead.[65]

Other World War II Soldiers, Chaplains, and Officers include:
Frank Angel, Jr. (Chapter 6: Educational Leaders)
Father Albert Braun (Chapter 10: Religious Leaders)
Jack Campbell (Chapter 9: Political, Diplomatic, and Judicial Leaders)
Fray Angélico Chávez (Chapter 4: Cultural Preservationists)
John O. Crosby (Chapter 2: Artists, Performers, and Directors)
Walter G. Haut (Chapter 7: Sung and Unsung Heroes)
Paul Horgan (Chapter 3: Authors and Composers)
Clinton Jencks (Chapter 7: Sung and Unsung Heroes)
Roy Johnson (Chapter 6: Educational Leaders)
Oliver LaFarge (Chapter 3: Authors and Composers)
Roy Nakayama (Chapter 11: Scientists and Medical Personnel)
Frank V. Ortiz (Chapter 9: Political, Diplomatic, and Judicial Leaders)
Rabbi David Shor (Chapter 10: Religious Leaders)
John Paul Stapp (Chapter 11: Scientists and Medical Personnel)
Quincy Tahoma (Chapter 2: Artists, Performers, and Directors)
Miguel H. Trujillo (Chapter 7: Sung and Unsung Heroes)
Sabine Reyes Ulibarri (Chapter 3: Authors and Composers)
Johnny Walker (Chapter 9: Political, Diplomatic, and Judicial Leaders)
Victor Westphall (Chapter 7: Sung and Unsung Heroes)

Manhattan Project Scientists and Leaders, 1943-45 (in alphabetical order)

The Manhattan Engineer District (MED), more commonly known as the Manhattan Project, was the code name given to the enormous American and British effort to develop an atomic weapon that could be used to help end World War II. The project included thirty-seven sites across the United States, including Site Y in Los Alamos, New Mexico, where top scientists and engineers worked to create an atomic weapon between March 1943 and July 16, 1945, when they successfully tested the world's first atomic bomb at Trinity Site in southern New Mexico. Atomic bombs developed at Los Alamos were dropped on Hiroshima (August 6, 1945) and on Nagasaki (August 9, 1945), Japan, leading to Japan's unconditional surrender on V-J Day, August 15, 1945.[66]

Frederick L. "Dick" Ashworth

After three months at Los Alamos, designated the Director of Operations of Project A (Alberta) on Tinian Island where the atomic bombs were prepared for delivery and use over Japan; weaponeer on Bock's Car, the B-29 that dropped the atomic bomb (nicknamed Fat Man) on Nagasaki, Japan, August 9, 1945, leading to Japan's unconditional surrender on August 15, 1945, ending World War II; later the commander of the 6th Fleet in the Mediterranean and Deputy Commander in Chief of the Atlantic Fleet; retired as a three-star Vice Admiral, 1968, living most of his retirement in Santa Fe

Date of Birth: January 24, 1912

Place of Birth: Beverly, Massachusetts

Date of Death (age): December 3, 2005 (93)

Place of Death: Arizona Heart Institute, Scottsdale, Arizona

Cause of Death: heart failure during surgery

Resting Place: National Cemetery, Santa Fe, New Mexico

While planning his will and last wishes, Admiral Ashworth wrote his own obituary, including a short paragraph about his mission to Nagasaki, about a year before his death.[67]

350. Photo courtesy of Sam Jackson.

Leslie Richard Groves, Jr.

U.S. Army General; military leader of the entire Manhattan Engineer District, including Site Y at Los Alamos, New Mexico

Date of Birth: August 17, 1896

Place of Birth: Albany, New York

Date of Death (age): 11:15 p.m., July 13, 1970 (73)

Place of Death: Walter Reed Hospital, Washington, D.C.

Cause of Death: pulmonary edema of congestive heart failure caused by aortic stenosis[68]

Resting Place: National Cemetery, Arlington, Virginia

Reflecting the clear clash of cultures between the military and scientific communities in Los Alamos, General Groves reportedly said, "If this were a country like Germany,...there were a dozen [scientists at Los Alamos] we should have shot right off [for lapses in security and] another dozen we could have shot for suspicion and carelessness."[69] No. 350

Dorothy Scarritt "D" McKibbin
Arrived as a TB patient in Santa Fe, 1925; famed "gatekeeper" at 109 East Palace Avenue, Santa Fe, where she greeted hundreds of scientists and their families assigned to the Manhattan Project at Site Y, Los Alamos, during World War II; retired on June 28, 1963, when her office at 109 East Palace Avenue was finally closed after twenty years of service
Date of Birth: December 12, 1897
Place of Birth: Kansas City, Missouri
Date of Death (age): December 17, 1985 (88)
Place of Death: at her home in Santa Fe, New Mexico
Cause of Death: unknown natural causes
Resting Place: Memorial Cemetery, Santa Fe, New Mexico

351.

At Dorothy's memorial service, Peggy Pond Church read a poem she had written for her old friend. It read, in part:

> She yields her hair to the wind;
> she yields her face to the sun;
> her love, like the evening star,
> shines clear for everyone.[70]

No. 351

Julius Robert "Oppie" or "Opje" Oppenheimer; Manhattan Project Code Name: James Oberhelm
Theoretical nuclear physicist and scientific director of the Manhattan Project at Site Y in Los Alamos during World War II, 1942-October 1945; University of New Mexico honorary degree recipient, 1947; lost his top security clearance after controversial hearings before the Atomic Energy Commission, 1954; largely vindicated when he received the Atomic Energy Commission's Enrico Fermi Award, April 5, 1963; the J. Robert Oppenheimer Study Center at the Los Alamos National Labs and a street in Los Alamos were named in his honor
Date of Birth: April 22, 1904
Place of Birth: New York City, New York
Date of Death (age): 8:00 p.m., February 18, 1967 (62)
Place of Death: Princeton, New Jersey
Cause of Death: throat cancer after years of smoking cigarettes and pipes
Resting Place: In keeping with his Hindu beliefs, Oppenheimer's remains were cremated with his ashes scattered off the Virgin Islands, near his home on St. John, by his wife, Kitty. The Oppenheimers' daughter scattered her mother's ashes at the same place when Kitty died and was cremated in October 1972.[71]

352. Photo courtesy of Clara Parsons.

William Sterling "Deak" or "Deke" Parsons; Code Name on the *Enola Gay*: Judge

Navy Captain; ordnance chief and Associate Director at Site Y of the Manhattan Project; completed the assembly of the "Little Boy" atomic bomb en route to Hiroshima, Japan, aboard the B-29 named the *Enola Gay*, August 6, 1945

Date of Birth: November 26, 1901

Place of Birth: Chicago, Illinois (raised in Fort Sumner, New Mexico, where highway signs into town proudly announce that this was once his home)

Date of Death (age): December 5, 1953 (52)

Place of Death: Bethesda Naval Hospital, Bethesda, Maryland

Cause of Death: heart attack

Resting Place: National Cemetery, Arlington, Virginia

Upset by news that his Manhattan Project colleague J. Robert Oppenheimer would have to face hearings regarding his loyalty to the United States, Parsons complained of chest pains on Friday night, December 4, 1953. His wife Martha persuaded him to go to Bethesda Naval Hospital to be checked the next morning. Although he usually worked on Saturday mornings, he told Martha, "And I won't work today; we'll just play golf." Within moments after arriving at the hospital and before doctors could complete their examination, Deak Parsons suffered a massive heart attack and died.[72] No. 352

Others Associated with the Manhattan Project include:

Enrico Fermi (Chapter 11: Scientists and Medical Personnel)
Klaus Fuchs (Chapter 11: Scientists and Medical Personnel)
Theodore Hall (Chapter 11: Scientists and Medical Personnel)
Eric Jette (Chapter 11: Scientists and Medical Personnel)
Edward Teller (Chapter 11: Scientists and Medical Personnel)
Edith Warner (Chapter 3: Authors and Composers)
Charles B. Winstead (Chapter 8: Lawmen, Criminals, and Victims of Crime)
E.J. Workman (Chapter 6: Educational Leaders)

World War II Journalists *(in alphabetical order)*

William "Bill" Mauldin

Political cartoonist; most famous for his "Willie and Joe" satirical military cartoons during World War II; winner of two Pulitzer Prizes, 1945 and 1959; after 1989, a sculptor of bronze statues depicting some of his most famous cartoons; resident of Santa Fe, 1970-97

Date of Birth: October 29, 1921

Place of Birth: Mountain Park, New Mexico

Date of Death (age): January 22, 2003 (81)

Place of Death: in a nursing home in Newport Beach, California

353. Photo courtesy of Sam Jackson.

Cause of Death: pneumonia and complications from Alzheimer's disease
Resting Place: National Cemetery, Arlington, Virginia

Mauldin's favorite cartoon of World War II (and his first cartoon-to-sculpture created in the late 1980s) shows a cavalry sergeant looking away as he shoots his beloved disabled jeep, much as a sad cowboy might have shot his beloved ailing horse.

In a fitting farewell, the *Santa Fe New Mexican* concluded that "Bill Mauldin leaves big combat boots to fill."[73]
No. 353

Ernest Taylor "Ernie" Pyle
Most famous American war correspondent of World War II; the Albuquerque Public Library's first branch was named in his honor and created in his former house at 900 Girard Boulevard in Albuquerque, 1948; a beach, a movie theatre, and a middle school in Southwest Albuquerque were also named in his honor; until recently the Ernie Pyle Middle School was the only middle school in the city not named after a president of the United States; University of New Mexico honorary degree recipient, 1944; a U.S. postage stamp was issued in his honor
Date of Birth: August 3, 1900
Place of Birth: Dana, Indiana
Date of Death (age): about 10:15 a.m., April 18, 1945 (44)
Place of Death: Ie Shima
Cause of Death: shot by a Japanese sniper

354. Photo courtesy of Chris Kent.

Resting Place: originally buried on Ie Shima, but later reinterred at the National Memorial Cemetery of the Pacific, Honolulu, Hawaii; one of the first five men interred at the National Memorial Cemetery of the Pacific when it opened on July 19, 1949; besides New Mexico, Hawaii was one of Pyle's five favorite states or territories of the United States

Having jumped into a ditch when under fire from a Japanese sniper, Pyle looked up to check on a companion and asked, "Are you all right?" The sniper opened fire, hitting Pyle in the left temple and killing him instantly. Pyle was originally buried near where he died, with a marker that read, "At This Spot the 77th Infantry Division Lost a Buddy, Ernie Pyle, 18 April 1945."[74]

The marker still stands, along with a plaque, a photo of Pyle, a brief outline of his life, and a statement (in Japanese and in English) composed by the residents of Ie Shima, which reads: "We, the people of Ie [sic] village, vow that we will never have such a horrible war again, and will try to make the world a peaceful place." The plaque also notes that the Okinawa chapter of the American Legion holds memorial services for Pyle each year on the Sunday closest to the date of his death.
No. 354

World War II Prisoners Held in New Mexico

Japanese-American Internment (in alphabetical order)

Shocked by the Japanese surprise attack on Pearl Harbor in late 1941, many Americans feared additional attacks on U.S. soil with the assistance of Japanese men and women already in this country. As a result, President Franklin D. Roosevelt issued Executive Order 9066 of February 19, 1942, which led to the rounding up and detainment of over 112,000 men, women, and children of Japanese descent into isolated relocation camps throughout the West, including at Fort Stanton from January to December 1942.

Over five thousand Japanese-American males classified as potentially most dangerous to American interests were separated from their families and imprisoned in internment camps in Santa Fe and Lordsburg. Many of these men were American citizens. Most were unfairly identified as threats to the United States. A good many had sons and other relatives who fought bravely as part of the U.S. Army's highly-decorated 100th Infantry Battalion/442nd Regimental Combat Team in Europe.

Despite the unfairness of their imprisonment, few internees attempted to escape from their camps in New Mexico. Two were killed in their attempts in Lordsburg, although their intentions were highly questionable.

A monument at Ortiz Park near the site of the Santa Fe internment camp was dedicated in 2000.[75]

Hirota Isomura

California fisherman; thirty-seven year resident of the United States; Japanese-American internee transported to the Lordsburg, New Mexico, internment camp during World War II
Date of Birth: November 11, 1883
Place of Birth: Japan
Date of Death (age): about 3:30 a.m., July 27, 1942 (58)
Place of Death: near a path outside the Japanese-American Internment Camp, Lordsburg, New Mexico
Cause of Death: although lame from a job-related injury, Isomura was shot in the neck and left shoulder by Sergeant. John A. Beckham who suspected that Isomura and a fellow internee, Toshiro Kobata, were attempting to escape
Resting Place: Fort Bliss National Cemetery, El Paso, Texas[76] No. 355

355. There is no explanation why Hirota Isomura's surname is given first on his gravestone.

Toshiro Kobata

California laborer; eleven-year resident of the United States; Japanese-American internee transported to the Lordsburg, New Mexico, internment camp during World War II
Date of Birth: June 2, 1884
Place of Birth: Japan
Date of Death (age): about 3:30 a.m., July 27, 1942 (58)
Place of Death: near a path outside the Japanese-American Internment Camp, Lordsburg, New Mexico

Cause of Death: shot in the center and upper left back by Sergeant John A. Beckham who suspected that Kobata and a fellow internee, Hirota Isomura, were attempting to escape
Resting Place: unknown[77]

N. Sudo
Japanese-American Issei internee held at the Santa Fe internment camp during World War II
Date of Birth: January 23, 1894
Place of Birth: Japan
Date of Death (age): January 3, 1945 (50)
Place of Death: Santa Fe, New Mexico
Cause of Death: unstated natural causes
Resting Place: Rosario Cemetery, Santa Fe, New Mexico[78] No. 356

D. Yoshikawa
Japanese-American Issei internee held at the Santa Fe internment camp during World War II
Date of Birth: December 27, 1891
Place of Birth: Japan
Date of Death (age): June 6, 1945 (53)
Place of Death: Santa Fe, New Mexico
Cause of Death: unstated natural causes
Resting Place: Rosario Cemetery, Santa Fe, New Mexico[79] No. 357

356. N. Sudo and fellow internee D. Yoshikawa were buried at the extreme western edge of Rosario Cemetery, just south of the Santa Fe National Cemetery.

Prisoners of War (POWs) (in alphabetical order)
    Roswell and Lordsburg hosted large POW camps through most of World War II. In all, approximately twelve thousand POWs, mostly Germans, were detained in the camps. Other POWs were detained in smaller camps in Las Cruces and Albuquerque. Treated well by their American captors, many POWs worked as farm laborers and in other useful capacities in accordance with Article 27 of the Geneva Convention of 1929. Few prisoners attempted to escape. Tragically, two who did escape were shot and killed.[80]

Walter Jaeger
German *obergefreiter* (leading seaman); prisoner of war held at the POW camp, Roswell, New Mexico
Date of Birth: probably 1923
Place of Birth: probably Germany
Date of Death (age): about 10:00 p.m., January 13, 1943 (about 20)
Place of Death: at a farm outside Artesia, New Mexico
Cause of Death: shot by farmer Mart (sometimes misspelled Mark) Fanning after escaping from the Roswell POW camp and trying to steal Fanning's car with two other escaped POWs

357. D. Yoshikawa and fellow internee N. Sudo were buried at the extreme western edge of Rosario Cemetery, just south of the Santa Fe National Cemetery.

358.

359.

Resting Place: originally buried in a grave across from the main entrance to the Roswell POW camp; later removed to Fort Bliss National Cemetery, El Paso, Texas[81]

American authorities at the Roswell POW camp allowed his fellow POWs to view Jaeger's body before a detail of twenty-five men (selected from among the prisoners) conducted the interment service. A squad of American riflemen shot three volleys over the open grave and taps were sounded. The German prisoners sought permission to erect a grave marker with a swastika on it, but, while the marker was approved, the swastika was not.[82]

About ten days after the fatal shooting P.E. Ford of Roswell mailed a dollar to Mart Fanning "in appreciation of his fine work in cutting off the escape of three German prisoners of war…. Mr. Ford said he had three brothers in [the] service, one of whom was killed at Pearl Harbor."[83]

Learning of Jaeger's death, the *Kansas City Times* editorialized that "We suspect that if any Nazi prisoners ever are fortunate enough to escape and reach Germany they'll report that the southwest is not a favorable point for any invasion plans. Folks down there are too nervous with their shooting irons."[84] No. 358

Wolfgang Schlegel
German *obergefreiter* (leading seaman); prisoner of war held at the POW camp, Roswell, New Mexico
Date of Birth: probably 1919
Place of Birth: probably Germany
Date of Death (age): February 5, 1945 (probably 26)
Place of Death: William Beaumont General Hospital, Fort Bliss, El Paso, Texas
Cause of Death: shot in right leg by a guard while attempting to escape from the Las Cruces POW camp
Resting Place: originally buried in Roswell; later removed to Fort Bliss National Cemetery, El Paso, Texas[85] No. 359

SS Columbus German Prisoners

Four hundred and ten German seamen from a luxury liner, the *SS Columbus*, were interred at Fort Stanton, New Mexico, from early 1941 to August 1945, during World War II. Four seamen died at the fort and were buried in the far northwestern corner of the large cemetery west of the fort. According to historian James McBride, there has never been a good explanation for why the four were buried about fifty yards from hundreds of the interred who had died of tuberculosis when the fort served as a merchant marine hospital to treat TB patients after 1899. Most likely it was because the United States was at war with Nazi Germany, although these Germans were not sailors in their nation's armed forces. Castaways in the war, they remained castaways in death.

The Germans were buried in compliance with the Geneva Convention, with caskets provided and honorable burials, as witnessed by about fifty of their fellow crewmembers.[86]

The four Germans buried at Fort Stanton (in alphabetical order) are:

Hermann Neuhoff
German merchant marine seaman
Date of Birth: February 22, 1910
Place of Birth: Germany
Date of Death (age): March 18, 1944 (34)
Place of Death: Fort Stanton immigration camp
Cause of Death: "asphyxia due to hanging….suicide"
Resting Place: Merchant Marine Cemetery, Fort Stanton, New Mexico[87] No. 360

360.

Heinrich Renken
German merchant marine cook
Date of Birth: September 29, 1911
Place of Birth: Germany
Date of Death (age): 8:43 p.m., February 20, 1942 (30)
Place of Death: Fort Stanton immigration camp
Cause of Death: trichinosis; the entire crew had come down with trichinosis after eating bad pork
Resting Place: Merchant Marine Cemetery, Fort Stanton, New Mexico[88] No. 360

Friedrich Heinrich Steffens
German merchant marine steward
Date of Birth: January 17, 1894
Place of Birth: Hanover, Germany
Date of Death (age): February 11, 1942 (48)
Place of Death: Fort Stanton immigration camp
Cause of Death: heart attack while being treated for trichinosis
Resting Place: Merchant Marine Cemetery, Fort Stanton, New Mexico[89] No. 360

Otto Erich Theodor Zeitsch
German merchant marine cook
Date of Birth: April 1, 1910
Place of Birth: Hamburg, Germany
Date of Death (age): 9:20 p.m., May 13, 1944 (34)
Place of Death: Fort Stanton immigration camp
Cause of Death: "several blows about head with unknown blunt instrument" suffered during a fight with three of his fellow cooks
Resting Place: Merchant Marine Cemetery, Fort Stanton, New Mexico[90]
No. 360 The Germans' original headstones were made by fellow internees. They were removed for safekeeping and replaced by new headstones in 1995, thanks to the efforts of the Lincoln County Historical Society.[91] No. 360

Korean War Soldiers, Officers, and MIA's, 1950-52
Over 25,000 New Mexicans served in the U.S. Armed Forces during the Korean War, sometimes known as the "forgotten war" in American history because it was overshadowed by World War II before it and the Vietnam War after it. Sergeant Hiroshi "Hershey" Miyamura (1925-) of Gallup earned the Medal of Honor for his heroic action near Taejon, South Korea, on April 24, 1951. Raymond G. "Jerry" Murphy (1930-), now of Albuquerque, earned his Medal of Honor for heroic action displayed on February 3, 1953.

One hundred and eighty-four New Mexicans lost their lives in the conflict. Forty-six New Mexicans are still listed as Missing in Action (MIA) from this conflict.

The Korean War Veterans Memorial in Washington, D.C., honors all Americans killed in the two-year war. New Mexico's Korean War veterans are honored at the New Mexico Veterans Memorial in southeast Albuquerque.[92]

See (in alphabetical order):
Fray Angélico Chávez (Chapter 4: Cultural Preservationists)
Robert Sheldon Scott (this chapter)
John Paul Stapp (Chapter 11: Scientists and Medical Personnel)
Jerry Unser (Chapter 7: Sung and Unsung Heroes)

Vietnam War Soldiers, Officers, and MIA's, 1954-75
New Mexico suffered 399 deaths during the Vietnam War. These men and women are honored at the Vietnam Veterans National Monument in Angel Fire, New Mexico, at the New Mexico Veterans Memorial in southeast Albuquerque, at the Vietnam Memorial in Washington, D.C., and at a replica of the Washington memorial in Truth or Consequences. As of mid 2005, thirteen New Mexican servicemen are still listed as Missing In Action (MIA).

A renowned Santa Fe sculptor, Glenna Goodacre (1939-), designed the Vietnam Women's Memorial that stands about a hundred yards from the Vietnam Memorial in Washington. Honoring the 11,500 American women who served in Vietnam and the estimated twenty women who died there, the memorial was dedicated in Washington, D.C., on Veterans Day, November 11, 1993.[93]

Medal of Honor Recipients: Vietnam War (in alphabetical order)
Five of the 239 recipients of the Medal of Honor during the Vietnam War were from New Mexico.[94]

Daniel D. "Uncle Dan" Fernández
U.S. Army Specialist Fourth Class; Purple Heart, March 1965; Air Medal, May 1965; Medal of Honor recipient for his heroic action in saving the lives of his fellow U.S. soldiers, February 18, 1966; recipient of the Republic of Vietnam's Military Merit Medal and Gallantry Cross; VFW Post 9676, a Los Lunas, New Mexico, school, and the largest park in Los Lunas were named in his honor

Date of Birth: June 30, 1944
Place of Birth: Albuquerque, New Mexico
Date of Death (age): about 7:00 a.m., February 18, 1966 (21)
Place of Death: near Cu Chi Hau, about twenty-five miles west of Saigon, Vietnam
Cause of Death: battle wounds, after throwing himself on a live grenade in order to save the lives of four fellow U.S. soldiers
Resting Place: National Cemetery, Santa Fe, New Mexico[95]

361.

Carried to an open area where a helicopter could land to evacuate him, Fernández was badly hurt, but still conscious. A fellow Catholic soldier urged Fernández to "make a good act of contrition," to which the injured man replied, "I will." He died moments later.

Hearing of Daniel's death, his father said, "Daniel was a man who didn't have any hatred. He had lots of friends among the South Vietnamese [and even] considered [the Viet Cong to be] very brave people.... When I heard [that Daniel had sacrificed himself for others], I just couldn't believe it.... I can say that I feel humble...to know that my son did such a thing."[96]

Many honored Fernández at every train stop when his remains were returned to New Mexico in late February 1966. About seven hundred "braved a light snow and chilly winds" when his body arrived in Belen. Hundreds passed at his viewing in a local mortuary. An estimated fifteen hundred attended his funeral mass at the Los Lunas High School gym, the only local facility large enough to accommodate the crowd. Two thousand accompanied the remains to the gravesite where Fernández was buried on a hillside at the National Cemetery in Santa Fe. His family received hundreds of letters and telegrams offering condolences from across the United States.[97]

The Fernández family received Daniel's Medal of Honor from President Lyndon B. Johnson in a special ceremony held at the White House on April 6, 1967, the Fernández's twenty-sixth wedding anniversary. Flown to and from Washington, D.C., in a U.S. Air Force jet, the family was received back in Los Lunas in a large reception that featured the singing of "The Ballad of Daniel D. Fernández" by a mariachi band, Los Reyes de Albuquerque.[98] No. 361

Delbert Owen Jennings
U.S. Army Sergeant Major; Medal of Honor recipient for his heroic action in the Kim Song Valley, Vietnam, December 27, 1966; medal awarded by President Lyndon B. Johnson at a White House ceremony held on September 19, 1968
Date of Birth: July 23, 1936
Place of Birth: Silver City, New Mexico
Date of Death (age): March 16, 2003 (66)
Place of Death: Honolulu, Hawaii
Cause of Death: unstated natural causes
Resting Place: National Memorial Cemetery of the Pacific, Honolulu, Hawaii[99]

Franklin Douglas Miller

Entered the U.S. Army in Albuquerque, New Mexico; Staff Sergeant; Medal of Honor recipient for his heroic action in saving the lives of his fellow soldiers on January 5, 1970, Kontum Province, Vietnam; medal awarded by President Richard Nixon at a White House ceremony held on June 15, 1971

Date of Birth: January 27, 1945
Place of Birth: Elizabeth City, North Carolina
Date of Death (age): June 30, 2000 (55)
Place of Death: Tampa, Florida
Cause of Death: unstated natural causes
Resting Place: cremated[100]

Louis Richard Rocco

U.S. Army Warrant Officer; Medal of Honor recipient for heroic action in rescuing fellow soldiers from a crashed helicopter northeast of Katum, Vietnam, May 24, 1970; medal awarded by President Gerald Ford at a White House ceremony held on December 15, 1974; veterans' rights activist; a park next to the Westside Community Center in southwest Albuquerque was named in his honor; he is also honored at the New Mexico Veterans Memorial in southeast Albuquerque

Date of Birth: November 19, 1938
Place of Birth: Albuquerque, New Mexico
Date of Death (age): October 31, 2002 (63)
Place of Death: at his home in San Antonio, Texas
Cause of Death: cancer
Resting Place: National Cemetery, San Antonio, Texas

In 1983 Rocco told a newspaper reporter, "I didn't join the Army out of any sense of patriotism. It was either the Army or reform school.... It was the best move I ever made." He later became active in a juvenile gang intervention program.[101] No. 362

362. Photo courtesy of Elaine Lucarini.

Kenneth Lee Worley

U.S. Marine Corps Lance Corporal; Medal of Honor recipient for his heroic action in throwing himself on a live grenade to save several of his fellow Marines; medal awarded posthumously by Vice President Spiro T. Agnew at a White House ceremony held on April 20, 1970

Date of Birth: March 27, 1948
Place of Birth: Farmington, New Mexico
Date of Death (age): August 12, 1968 (20)
Place of Death: Bo Ban, Hamlet of Quang Nam Province, Vietnam
Cause of Death: grenade explosion
Resting Place: Westminster Memorial Park, Westminster, California[102]

Vietnam War Missing in Action/Prisoners of War (MIA/POWs) *(in alphabetical order)*

Robert Charles Lopez
Raised and schooled in Albuquerque, New Mexico; Private First Class, U.S. Marine
Missing in Action for thirty-seven years, 1968-2005; remains identified with the help of DNA testing, July 2005
Date of Birth: September 30, 1948
Place of Birth: California
Date of Death (age): May 10, 1968 (19)
Place of Death: a hill near the North Vietnam border
Cause of Death: killed in battle, along with eleven others, as searched for two lost Marines, including a medic
Resting Place: National Cemetery, Arlington, Virginia, with seven of the eleven Marines he died with, as a group in a single coffin, on October 7, 2005[103]

John Wesley Frink
U.S. Warrant Officer and co-pilot shot down with three fellow crewmembers on an Army assault helicopter during a search and rescue mission, April 2, 1972
Date of Birth: November 7, 1945
Place of Birth: Albuquerque, New Mexico
Date of Death (age): April 2, 1972 (26)
Place of Death: South Vietnam
Cause of Death: killed by enemy fire following his helicopter's crash
Resting Place: long Missing In Action, but his body was finally recovered, identified, and returned from Vietnam and buried beside his father's at the National Cemetery, Santa Fe, New Mexico[104]

Roy Francis Townley
Civilian co-pilot for Air America (the CIA's covert airlines) active in supplying American allied forces in Laos
Date of Birth: November 3, 1919
Place of Birth: unknown
Date Lost (age): December 27, 1971 (52)
Place Lost: somewhere between Ban Xieng and Ban Hong Sa, Laos
Memorial Stone: National Cemetery, Santa Fe, New Mexico[105] No. 363

363.

New Mexico's other MIA/POWs (in alphabetical order):
Stan Leroy Corfield of Gallup; born August 25, 1940, lost May 1, 1967
Ricardo Gonzales Davis of Carlsbad; born March 17, 1941, lost March 20, 1969
Frederick D. Herrera of Albuquerque; born August 7, 1949, lost March 25, 1969
Mitchell S. Lane of Albuquerque; born October 4, 1940, lost January 4, 1969
Calvin Walter Maxwell of Eddy; born November 6, 1943, lost October 10, 1969

Scott Winston McIntire of Albuquerque; born July 7, 1924, lost December 10, 1971
Robert D. Morrissey of Albuquerque; born April 24, 1930, lost November 7, 1972
Bobby G. Neeld of Albuquerque; born October 8, 1928, lost January 4, 1969
John Sanders Oldham of Tinnie; born July 3, 1933, lost June 11, 1967
Max Coleman Simpson of Carlsbad; born March 28, 1944, lost January 24, 1967
Robert S. Trujillo of Santa Fe; born August 3, 1946, lost January 7, 1968
Bain Wendell Wiseman, Jr., of Truth or Consequences; born November 8, 1947, lost December 23, 1970[106]

Other Vietnam War Soldiers and Officers include:
Robert Sheldon Scott (this chapter)
John Paul Stapp (Chapter 11: Scientists and Medical Personnel)
Jacob Viarrial (Chapter 9: Political, Diplomatic, and Judicial Leaders)

War on Terrorism and in Iraq, 2001-present

As of mid 2006 twenty-seven New Mexicans had been killed in Afghanistan and Iraq. Honored at the New Mexico Veterans Memorial in southeast Albuquerque, they are *(in alphabetical order)*:

Christopher S. Adlesperger, died December 9, 2004
Tamara Long Archuleta, died March 23, 2003
Aaron Austin, died April 26, 2004
Lyle J. Cambridge, died July 5, 2005
Jeremy E. Christensen, died November 27, 2004
Jason Cunningham, died March 4, 2002
Jeremy Fresques, died May 30, 2005
Damian J. Garza, died August 4, 2005
Jonathan Grant, died May 11, 2005
Tommy L. Gray, died August 3, 2004
Chad R. Hildebrandt, died October 17, 2005
Christopher A. Merville, died October 12, 2004
Lori Plestewa, died March 23, 2003
James "Heath" Pirtle, died October 4, 2003
Steven Plumhoff, died November 23, 2003
Christopher Ramos, died April 5, 2004
Mario A. Reyes, died November 7, 2005
Demetrius L. Rice, died July 14, 2005
Moses Daniel Rocha, died August 5, 2004
Joseph E. Rodriguez, died January 28, 2005
Rick Salas, Jr., died March 7, 2006
Christopher James Speer, died August 6, 2002
Lee Todacheene, died April 6, 2004
Marshall A. Westbrook, died October 1, 2005
Vernon R. Widner, died November 17, 2005

Clifton J. Yazzie, died January 20, 2006
Jesse Maria Zamora, died February 3, 2006[107]

Tamara Lee "Tammy" "Skyfab" Long Archuleta
Girl Scout; Third degree black belt; undefeated world karate champion; University of New Mexico honor graduate; first female UNM Air Force ROTC student to earn her wings; U.S. Air Force Captain; HH-60 G Pavehawk helicopter co-pilot in Operation Enduring Freedom; a memorial was created in her honor at Rescue Rock at the Girl Scout camp she attended near Cuba, New Mexico; a scholarship and the nation's first women's veterans organization was created and named in her honor, 2004
Date of Birth: May 12, 1979
Place of Birth: Belen, New Mexico
Date of Death (age): March 23, 2003 (23)
Place of Death: eighteen miles north of Ghazni, Afghanistan
Cause of Death: with five fellow airmen, killed in a HH-60 G Pavehawk helicopter crash on a rescue mission to assist two Afghan children who had suffered severe head wounds; one of three female service members killed in Afghanistan and one of forty-four female service members killed in Afghanistan and Iraq since 2001
Resting Place: Terrace Grove Cemetery, Belen, New Mexico[108]

364. An image of the HH-60 G Pavehawk helicopter Captain Long Archuleta co-piloted appears in the upper right hand corner of her gravestone.

Shortly before her death, Long Archuleta wrote letters from Afghanistan to students in elementary schools in Colorado and in Valdosta, Georgia, her home base. To one third grade student, she explained that her helicopter squadron had a "very special job":

> In peacetime, we do civilian rescues for people that are lost and hurt at sea or in the mountains and need to get to a hospital. That is a lot of what we have been doing here to help show the people of Afghanistan that we are here to help them.

In closing, the young pilot encouraged the third grader to "Keep working hard in school and you can be anything you want to be when you grow up!"[109]

To help maintain high troop morale, Long Archuleta decorated the walls of her crew's break room in Afghanistan with letters she received from children in the United States.[110] No. 364

14
UNUSUAL GRAVES

Unusual Materials

365. San José Cemetery, Albuquerque, New Mexico

366. Cuba Catholic Cemetery, Cuba, New Mexico

367. Monticello Cemetery, Monticello, New Mexico

368. Capitan Cemetery, Capitan, New Mexico

369. Grave with putting green surface and hole. Bernalillo Catholic Cemetery, Bernalillo, New Mexico

370. Sierra Vista Cemetery, Taos, New Mexico

371. The words on this gas container grave marker read: "Going for Gas." Photo courtesy of Thomas Broderick. Madrid Cemetery, Madrid, New Mexico

372. Martin Brito loved his motorcycle, but did not die in a motorcycle accident. "According to the locals (in Truchas, New Mexico), Martin often led children and groups of his peers on hikes in the nearby mountains. He was a bit of a clown, and on one trek he went to the edge of a high overlook and pretended to lose his balance for the entertainment of the rest of the hikers. His loss of balance became genuine and he fell to his death at the age of twenty-six."[1] Truchas Catholic Cemetery, Truchas, New Mexico

373. Hillcrest Cemetery, Gallup, New Mexico

374. Reserve Cemetery, Reserve, New Mexico

375. Hillsboro Cemetery, Hillsboro, New Mexico

Famous and Unusual Gravesites in New Mexico History

376. The epitaph on the accompanying headstone reads: "Riding My Horse Through Eternity." Edgewood Cemetery, Edgewood, New Mexico

377. Cemetery near Route 180 in western New Mexico

378. Dusty Cemetery, Dusty, New Mexico

Also see:

Geronimo (Chapter 12: Wartime Leaders and Victims to the End of the Indian Wars in New Mexico, 1886)

Zebulon M. Pike (Chapter 12: Wartime Leaders and Victims to the End of the Indian Wars in New Mexico, 1886)

Unusual Shapes and Designs

380. Abo Catholic Cemetery, Abo, New Mexico

379. Horace McAfee returned from World War II to find his father's gravesite in Chilili, New Mexico, in terrible disrepair. Remembering a handmade metal monument he had seen in an Australian cemetery during the war, McAfee vowed to make a similar monument for his father. The unique product of his labor was so admired by cemetery visitors that family members and local residents asked McAfee to create ssimilar monuments for their deceased loved ones buried in Chilili. Over the years, McAfee created about a dozen monuments in the cemetery, using a wide assortment of collected materials, including (but hardly limited to) scrap metal, car parts, cable, an army helmet, a bowling ball, and doorknobs. After welding these various parts together, McAfee sprayed each monument with aluminum paint and attached sheet-metal plaques inscribed with names, dates, and relevant scripture punched with an ice pick and hammer. These unique memorials have attracted visitors from across the country, although all newcomers are warned (in a typical McAfee metal sign) that "vandals will face court action."[2] Chilili Cemetery, Chilili, New Mexico

381. Floyd Cemetery, Floyd, New Mexico

382. Bernalillo Catholic Cemetery, Bernalillo, New Mexico

383. A post laundress's headstone is the last standing gravesite left at the Old Post Cemetery, Fort Union, New Mexico; not accessible to the general public.

384. Mary D. Merriott Kilgore (September 18, 1937-January 12, 1996), Sierra Vista Cemetery, Taos, New Mexico. Artist John Suazo, a Taos Indian friend, carved Mary Kilgore's gravestone from Indiana limestone. Her family reports that Mary was an avid reader.[3]
Photo courtesy of Gina Marie Torres.

385. Veguita Catholic Cemetery, Veguita, New Mexico. Sarah Carrillo's family says that she loved hummingbirds.

386. Madrid Cemetery, Madrid, New Mexico

Famous and Unusual Gravesites in New Mexico History

387. Nuestra Señora de los Remedios Catholic Cemetery, Galisteo, New Mexico[4]

388. Nuestra Señora de los Remedios Catholic Cemetery, Galisteo, New Mexico

389. Nuestra Señora de los Remedios Catholic Cemetery, Galisteo, New Mexico. Gravestones with six-pointed Stars of David are found in scattered cemeteries across New Mexico, with as many as three found in a single cemetery, according to photographer Cary Herz.[5] A gravestone in central New Mexico also features parts of the Ten Commandments written in Hebrew. These gravestones are considered among the best historical indicators of crypto-Judaism in New Mexico's material culture, although historian Stanley Hordes cautions that "Symbols that may seem to impart a Jewish connection may well derive from other, unrelated cultural contexts."[6]

Also see:

Ben Abruzzo (Chapter 7: Sung and Unsung Heroes)
Brother Mathias Barrett (Chapter 10: Religious Leaders)
Witter Bynner (Chapter 3: Authors and Composers)
José Felipe Chávez (Chapter 5: Business Leaders)
E. Irving Couse (Chapter 2: Artists, Performers, and Directors)
Dena Lynn Gore (Chapter 8: Lawmen, Criminal, and Victims of Crime)
Victor Higgins (Chapter 2: Artists, Performers, and Directors)
William J. Mills (Chapter 9: Political, Diplomatic, and Judicial Leaders)
Dennis O'Leary (this chapter)
Cayetano Romero (Chapter 13: Wartime Leaders and Victims Since the Spanish-American War, 1898)
Benjamin J. Viljoen (Chapter 13: Wartime Leaders and Victims Since the Spanish-American War, 1898)

Occupations

390. Santa Fe Trail freighter buried in Wagon Mound near the old Santa Fe Trail. Wagon Mound Cemetery, Wagon Mound, New Mexico

391.

No. 391 Dawson, New Mexico, a large coal camp owned and operated by the Phelps Dodge Corporation from 1905 to its closing in 1950, suffered two major mining disasters. On October 23, 1913, 265 men lost their lives, and on February 8, 1923, another 120 miners perished in some of the worst coal mining tragedies in American history. A white metal miner's cross marks the grave of each lost miner, many of whom were of Croatian, Greek, Italian, German, Serbian, Slovenian, and Hispanic descent. About seventy markers have neither names nor dates, designating the graves of unidentified or unidentifiable bodies. Greek descendents of those killed still gather at the cemetery each year on the weekend after Thanksgiving to honor their family members and all those who perished in the mines.[7] Here an Italian miner's gravestone stands beside one of the 385 white metal miners' crosses. Dawson Cemetery, Dawson, New Mexico

No. 392 White Oaks's Old Abe gold mine was one of the largest, richest gold mines in New Mexico during the late nineteenth century. Sadly, Old Abe was also the site of White Oaks's greatest tragedy. Twenty men were working in the mine on March 9, 1895, when a kerosene lamp hanging on the wooden frame of the hoist house exploded. Somehow, eleven miners escaped with their lives. Despite two days and three nights of fighting the fire, townspeople were unable to rescue nine other men who had apparently died of monoxide gas poisoning in the mine.

Practically the entire population of White Oaks attended the dead miners' funeral. With not enough factory-made coffins in stock, local carpenters hastily constructed pine boxes. The nine coffins, laid side-by-side, "filled the width of the church," according to an eyewitness. "[T]he funeral cortege, including every passenger vehicle in town—buggies, hacks, light spring wagons—strung out along the dry, dusty road leading to the cemetery west of town."[8]

The miners' original wooden markers were later replaced by this headstone, although the ninth miner's name is missing. Cedarvale Cemetery, White Oaks, New Mexico

392.

393. Socorro Cemetery, Socorro, New Mexico

James C. Cooney

U.S. Army Cavalry Sergeant, Fort Bayard, New Mexico; miner along Cooper and Mineral creeks, New Mexico; the now-abandoned settlement of Cooney and Cooney Peak in Catron County were named in his honor
Date of Birth: 1840
Place of Birth: Canada
Date of Death (age): April 30, 1880 (about 40)
Place of Death: near Alma, New Mexico
Cause of Death: killed by Apaches while attempting to warn settlers of an impending Indian raid
Resting Place: originally buried where he and his friend, Jack Chick, were killed; later, to protect his remains, reburied by his brother Michael (1838-1914), in a vault carved into a large boulder by Mineral Creek in Catron County, New Mexico[9] No. 394

394. The stone slab at the sealed door reads, "J.C. Cooney, Killed by Victorio's Apaches, April 29, 1880. Aged 40 years." Cooney actually died on April 30.

395. "Jack of all Trades." Terrace Grove Cemetery, Belen, New Mexico

396. Portales Cemetery, Portales, New Mexico

Dennis O'Leary

U.S. Army Private
Date of Birth: July 1877
Place of Birth: unknown
Date of Death (age): April 1, 1901 (23)
Place of Death: Fort Wingate, New Mexico
Cause of Death: suicide
Resting Place: originally in the Fort Wingate Post Cemetery; later interred in the National Cemetery, Santa Fe, New Mexico, 1912

According to legend, Private O'Leary suffered from severe despondency while serving at Fort Wingate in the first years of the twentieth century. In fact, O'Leary went AWOL for several weeks in early 1901, eventually returning to duty, but hardly improved in spirit. On April 1, 1901, the twenty-three-year-old shot himself.

397. Fruitland Cemetery, Fruitland, New Mexico

398. Private Dennis O' Leary. National Cemetery, Santa Fe, New Mexico.

Soldiers who discovered O'Leary's body also discovered a strange suicide note. The note instructed the soldiers to go to a specific location where they found a life-size carved image of the deceased with the exact date of his suicide. According to one story, the private had carved the image with his own bayonet blade. It was now clear what O'Leary had done during the time he had gone AWOL.[10]

Using his carved image as a rather macabre headstone, O'Leary's fellow soldiers buried him at the Fort Wingate post cemetery. When the post cemetery was closed and most of those buried in the graveyard were moved to the National Cemetery in Santa Fe, O'Leary and his unique gravestone were moved as well. His stone remains the most unusual headstone at the National Cemetery, conspicuous by its design among rows of far more traditional military headstones. Unable—or unwilling—to adjust to military requirements in life, O'Leary remains a non-conformist in death.[11]

Many have been left spellbound by this sad story of a lonely soldier on the Western frontier. However, after considerable research, historian Robert R. White has been unable to prove any part of the O'Leary legend with sound evidence from military records. Despite its appeal, the legend is probably false, although no other explanation has been offered for this unique gravestone.[12] No. 398

399. " A rancher, a cattleman, and a friend to all." Claunch Cemetery, Claunch, New Mexico

400. "Lonesome Dove." Chloride Cemetery, Chloride, New Mexico

401. "The last goodbye, the hardest one to say. This is where the cowboy rides away." Terrace Grove Cemetery, Belen, New Mexico

Famous and Unusual Gravesites in New Mexico History

402. The words at the base of this military headstone read: "This Ole Cowboy blessed every life he touched." Ramah Cemetery, Ramah, New Mexico

403. Ranchers often mark their headstones with their cattle brand. Portales Cemetery, Portales, New Mexico

Also see:

Tamara Long Archuleta (Chapter 13: Wartime Leaders and Victims Since the Spanish-American War, 1898)
Dionisio "Dennis" Chavez (Chapter 9: Political, Diplomatic, and Judicial Leaders)
Tibo J. Chavez, Sr. (Chapter 9: Political, Diplomatic, and Judicial Leaders)
Buddy Holly (Chapter 2: Artists, Performers, and Directors)
Kathryn O'Connor (Chapter 2: Artists, Performers, and Directors)
Wernher Von Braun (Chapter 11: Scientists and Medical Personnel)

Unusual Icons[12]

404. Portales Cemetery, Portales, New Mexico

405. Mountain View Cemetery, Deming, New Mexico

406. "We liked his style." Cedarvale Cemetery, White Oaks, New Mexico

407. Edgewood Cemetery, Edgewood, New Mexico

408. "Wabash Cannonball." Sunset Cemetery, Albuquerque, New Mexico

409. "Rock 'n' Roll Forever." Portales Cemetery, Portales, New Mexico

410. Fruitland Cemetery, Fruitland, New Mexico

411. Capitan Cemetery, Capitan, New Mexico

412. "He played the main room." Congregation Albert Section, Fairview Cemetery, Albuquerque, New Mexico[14]

No. 413 Each line of music on Martha R. Maschhoff's gravestone represents another song. The first is from "Jesus, Joy of Man's Desiring," a Lutheran hymn by Johann Sebastian Bach. The second song is "Duke Street," a hymn by John Hatton (1793), with words by Isaac Watts (1719). The third song is "Silent Night," composed by Franz Grueber (1818), with words by Joseph Mohr. Sunset Cemetery, Albuquerque, New Mexico[15]

413.

Also see:
Maxie Anderson (Chapter 7: Sung and Unsung Heroes)
Gerald Cassidy (Chapter 2: Artists, Performers, and Directors)
Lucien Maxwell (Chapter 5: Business Leaders)
John B. Newbrough (Chapter 10: Religious Leaders)

Unique Epitaphs

414. "Good Night Sweet Prince." Memorial Gardens, Santa Fe, New Mexico

415. "The One and Only." Portales Cemetery, Portales, New Mexico

No. 416 Like many new communities in the United States, Rio Rancho is populated by people from across the country. Reflecting this modern mobility, and in an admirable effort to assist family genealogists, Robert Lenberg and his brother have created a marker listing the locations of their relatives' gravesites from Rhode Island in the East to California in the West. Having run out of space on their small bronze marker, the Lenbergs added a note at the end of their litany, urging interested persons to check the Vista Verde Cemetery office for additional family information! The brothers plan to place similarly informative markers in other cemeteries where family members are buried in states like Minnesota and Washington. With fourteen children and dozens of grandchildren between them, the Lenbergs want future generations of family members buried in a single place, rather than spread across the country. Each brother has purchased thirty-six plots at the Vista Verde Cemetery; only two of the seventy-two plots have been used thus far.[16] Vista Verde Cemetery, Rio Rancho, New Mexico

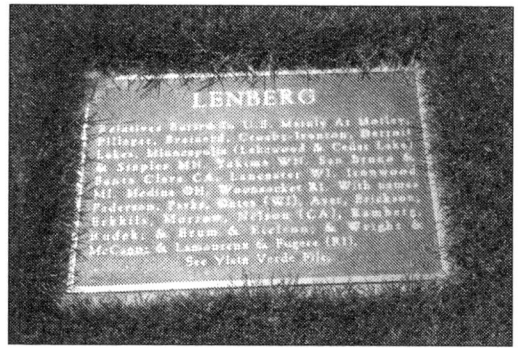

416.

417. "And dance beneath the diamond sky with one hand waving free." Guaje Pines Cemetery, Los Alamos, New Mexico

418. "Free bird." Elizabethtown Cemetery, Elizabethtown, New Mexico

419. The epitaph on Charles A. Byrd's gravestone reads: "Here lies the remains of a class conscious socialist." Fairview Cemetery, Albuquerque, New Mexico

420. Kay Bonneau's epitaph reads: "Povee: '…Thou shalt die in a polluted land.' Amos 7:17 Martyred by our nation's polluted air, water, and food. Hodgkin's disease is caused by the upper." Mountainair Cemetery, Mountainair, New Mexico

Also see:

Thomas J. Maeston (Chapter 12: Wartime Leaders and Victims to the End of the Indian Wars in New Mexico, 1886)

Famous and Unusual Gravesites in New Mexico History

Humorous Epitaphs[17]

421. The last line on Narsise Reams's gravestone reads: "Rest in Peas." Our Lady de La Luz Cemetery, La Luz, New Mexico

424. "I hope God has a sense of humor." Mount Calvary Cemetery, Albuquerque, New Mexico

426. "Gone Fishin'." Fruitland Cemetery, Fruitland, New Mexico

422. "I told you I was sick." Farmington Cemetery, Farmington, New Mexico

423. "Shit happens." Memorial Gardens Cemetery, Santa Fe, New Mexico

425. "Entered life via Baltimore. Exit via Albuquerque." Santa Barbara Cemetery, Albuquerque, New Mexico

427. Mountain View Cemetery, Deming, New Mexico

Animals

Many Southwestern pet owners have wanted to be buried with or near their beloved animals. In fact, Dody Fugate at the Museum of Indian Arts and Culture's Laboratory of Anthropology in Santa Fe has compiled a database of every dog burial she has identified in the region. As of March 2003, her database included some eight hundred burials, with many dating back to the late Archaic through Pueblo II periods.[18]

More recently, the owners of a mortuary in Taos reported that a woman who had just lost her husband "wanted us to kill his dog and bury him in the same grave [with the deceased] as she insisted that the dog would simply die from grief at losing his master!" The owners of the mortuary had "always tried to comply with the wishes of [grieving] families," but in this case decided that the request was impossible—and inhumane by modern standards!"[19]

At least one rancher was reportedly buried on his horse at his ranch near Tucumcari, New Mexico.[20] A rancher in the mid Rio Grande Valley has placed gravestones near the gate to his property in memory of his favorite horses.

Pet cemeteries, like Rainbow's End in Williamsburg, New Mexico, are increasingly popular. So are specially designed pet gravestones. Granite stones featuring laser etched images of one's pet are available for costs ranging from $120 to $329 at an Albuquerque monument company.[21]

428.

No. 428 Sheriffs and National Guardsmen from three New Mexico counties searched the Upper Pecos region when sixteen-year-old Alfonso Sedillo (November 13, 1913, to November 7, 1929) of Albuquerque went missing while picking piñon with two of his friends and his little brown dog, Fido, in 1929. Alfonso was eventually found when Fido was seen huddled in the snow, loyally stationed by the boy's dead body.[22] Although a bronze statue of the dog was originally proposed, a concrete carving of the faithful companion was placed atop Alfonso's headstone at Santa Barbara Cemetery in Albuquerque. The carving has since been destroyed by either age or vandalism or both.[23] A plaque on Alfonso's gravestone reads: "Fido. For seven days and nights he guarded the frozen body of his little master in a mountain wilderness." Santa Barbara Cemetery, Albuquerque, New Mexico

429.

No. 429 "Herbie, Daddy's Dog, c. 1979- August 8, 1995," rests at his master's feet in death as he had often rested there in life. Socorro Protestant Cemetery, Socorro, New Mexico

No. 431 Rocky I, a beloved miniature Dobermanpinscher, was buried in a corner of his mourning owners' backyard in Los Lunas, New Mexico. Rocky II, of the same breed, plays in the same yard where his namesake now rests.

No. 432 Ernie Pyle's beloved shelty was named Cheetah because Ernie's wife, Jerry, had always wanted a Cheetah as a pet. While Ernie was buried in Hawaii (Chapter 13, No. 354) and Jerry was buried in her homestate of Minnesota, only their beloved Cheetah was buried in Albuquerque, in the backyard of the family's former home, now the Ernie Pyle Public Library.[24]

No. 433 Amelia Elizabeth and Martha White (daughters of Horace White, editor of the *New York Evening Post*) moved to Santa Fe in 1922, establishing their home, known as El Delirio, designed by William P. Henderson. The sisters were involved in countless community projects, ranging from the Indian Arts Fund to archeology. They donated property for the creation of the Laboratory of Anthropology and the International Folk Art Museum.

    The White sisters also donated their property at 630 Garcia to the School of American Research with the understanding that the cemetery that held dozens of their prized Afghan hounds and wolfhounds would be cared for and would never be disturbed. This promise has been kept. Martha White died in 1947. Amelia, who founded the Santa Fe Animal Shelter, lived to be ninety-four, dying on her birthday in 1972.[25]

431.

432.

433.

430. Our Lady de La Luz Cemetery, La Luz, New Mexico

434. Hillsboro Cemetery, Hillsboro, New Mexico

HAM (Holloman Aero Med); HAM the Chimp, HAM the Astrochimp

One of sixty-five chimps originally tested for flight in the Mercury space program at the Holloman Aeromedical Lab, New Mexico; first higher primate animal launched into space, January, 31, 1961

Date of Birth: 1955

Place of Birth: Caneroons, Equatorial Africa

Date of Death (age): January 18, 1983 (about 27)

Place of Death: North Carolina Zoological Park where he had "retired" from space travel and had lived the last twenty years of his life

Cause of Death: enlarged heart and liver ailments

Resting Place: HAM Memorial Garden, located below the sign welcoming visitors to the International Space Museum, Alamogordo, New Mexico[26]

A plaque was dedicated to HAM at the HAM Memorial Garden on March 28, 1983. Speaking at the ceremony, Colonel John Paul Stapp, who had organized the Holloman Aeromedical Field Laboratory where HAM was trained, remembered HAM's historic 1961 flight and the many problems it encountered. The flight was delayed for four hours and HAM's space capsule almost sank before it could be recovered. Despite these flaws, HAM performed well and eagerly accepted an apple as his much-deserved reward once he was recovered. Stapp concluded, "We are indebted to the experiments [conducted on animals like HAM]. We owe a debt…and should be thankful."[27]

435. The inscription on HAM's plaque reads in part: "HAM was trained at Holloman Air Force Base Medical Research Laboratory. His name is an acronym for Holloman Aero Med. HAM's training culminated on January 31, 1961, by riding in a capsule perched atop an eighty-three-foot Redstone rocket launched from Cape Canaveral, Florida. Reaching a top speed of 5,800 MPH and an altitude of 155 miles, he was recovered at sea 420 miles down range from the launch site. HAM proved that mankind could live and work in space."

Smokey Bear; originally Hot Foot Teddy

Rescued as a four-pound cub from a 17,000-acre forest fire in the Capitan Mountains, May 9, 1950; became the nation's symbol for forest fire protection; long-time attraction at the National Zoo in Washington, D.C.; received so much fan mail at the zoo that the U.S. Postal Service assigned him his own zip code: 20252; a special shapes Smokey Bear hot air balloon was named in his honor

Date of Birth: 1950

Place of Birth: Capitan Mountains, New Mexico

Date of Death (age): November 9, 1976 (about 26)

Place of Death: National Zoo, Washington, D.C.

Cause of Death: unstated natural causes

Resting Place: Smokey Bear Capitan Historical State Park, Capitan, New Mexico[28]

In 2000, on what would have been Smokey's fiftieth birthday, Capitan celebrated with a Smokey Bear parade and a number of other festivities. A community of about a thousand residents, Capitan is so proud of its fame as Smokey's hometown that it has a Smokey Bear Boulevard, a Smokey Bear State Park, a Smokey Bear Museum, and a Smokey Bear Visitor Center. Capitan has been good to Smokey and Smokey has been good to Capitan, bringing much-appreciated tourist dollars to the local economy.[29] No. 439

Unusual Cemetery Signs

436. Capitan Cemetery, Capitan, New Mexico

437. Veguita Catholic Cemetery, Veguita, New Mexico

438. Sacred Heart Cemetery, Española, New Mexico

439. Smokey Bear, Capitan, New Mexico

440. Memory Lane Cemetery, Silver City, New Mexico

441. Lomas Boulevard Cemetery, Albuquerque, New Mexico

442. Rainbow Pet Cemetery, Williamsburg, New Mexico

Also see:

"No Hunting" (Chapter 1: Not Forgotten)
"24 Hour Surveillance with Hidden Camera" (Chapter 1: Not Forgotten)
"Respect Our Beloved Dead or May God Bless You" (Chapter 1: Not Forgotten)

443. Arroyo Hondo Cemetery, Arroyo Hondo, New Mexico

APPENDIX A

FAMOUS NEW MEXICANS INTERRED IN PUBLIC CEMETERIES IN NEW MEXICO

The author has visited over 150 cemeteries across New Mexico. Some cemeteries have no notable New Mexicans buried among their dead, while others have dozens. Indeed, the history of New Mexico unfolds as one walks down rows of graves in cemeteries like Fairview Cemetery in Albuquerque, Fairview Cemetery in Santa Fe, Kit Carson Cemetery in Taos, the Masonic Cemetery in Las Cruces, and the national cemeteries in Santa Fe and Fort Bayard.

Cemeteries listed here can boast the inclusion of one or more famous New Mexicans.

Each famous New Mexican's chapter is listed in parentheses. Names marked with asterisks (*) include gravestone photographs in the text.

Famous New Mexicans buried in non-public cemeteries or on private, usually inaccessible land are not listed in Appendix A.

Alamogordo

Monte Vista Cemetery
  Howard Beacham (Chapter 8: Lawmen, Criminals, and Victims of Crime)*
  Oliver Lee (Chapter 8: Lawmen, Criminals, and Victims of Crime)*

Albuquerque (in alphabetical order by cemetery names)

Fairview Cemetery
  Clinton P. Anderson (Chapter 9: Political, Diplomatic, and Judicial Leaders)*
  Frank Bond (Chapter 5: Business Leaders)*
  John Braden (Chapter 7: Sung and Unsung Heroes)
  Sam G. Bratton (Chapter 9: Political, Diplomatic, and Judicial Leaders)*
  Ross Calvin (Chapter 10: Religious Leaders)*
  Richard Dillon (Chapter 9: Political, Diplomatic, and Judicial Leaders)*
  Arthur T. Hannett (Chapter 9: Political, Diplomatic, and Judicial Leaders)*
  Emily Harwood (Chapter 10: Religious Leaders)*
  Thomas Harwood (Chapter 10: Religious Leaders)*
  Carl Hatch (Chapter 9: Political, Diplomatic, and Judicial Leaders)*
  Opal Hill (Chapter 5: Business Leaders)*
  Santiago Hubbell (Chapter 5: Business Leaders)*

Franz Huning (Chapter 5: Business Leaders)*
William Randolph Lovelace I (Chapter 11: Scientists and Medical Personnel)*
William Randolph "Randy" Lovelace II (Chapter 11: Scientists and Medical Personnel)*
Thomas J. Mabry (Chapter 9: Political, Diplomatic, and Judicial Leaders)*
Edwin L. "Ed" Mechem (Chapter 9: Political, Diplomatic, and Judicial Leaders)*
James Menaul (Chapter 10: Religious Leaders)*
Harold Moon (Chapter 13: Wartime Leaders and Victims Since the Spanish-American War, 1898)*
James L. Morris (Chapter 12: Wartime Leaders and Victims to the End of the Indian Wars in New Mexico, 1886)*
Francisco Perea (Chapter 9: Political, Diplomatic, and Judicial Leaders)
Bernard S. Rodey (Chapter 9: Political, Diplomatic, and Judicial Leaders)*
Edmund G. Ross (Chapter 9: Political, Diplomatic, and Judicial Leaders)*
Steven "Steve" Schiff (Chapter 9: Political, Diplomatic, and Judicial Leaders)*
David Shor (Chapter 10: Religious Leaders)*
A.G. Shortle (Chapter 11: Scientists and Medical Personnel)*
Albert G. Simms (Chapter 9: Political, Diplomatic, and Judicial Leaders)*
John F. Simms, Jr. (Chapter 9: Political, Diplomatic, and Judicial Leaders)*
Ruth Hanna McCormick Simms (Chapter 6: Educational Leaders)*
Montague Stevens (Chapter 7: Sung and Unsung Heroes)*
Carrie Tingley (Chapter 7: Sung and Unsung Heroes)*
Clyde Tingley (Chapter 9: Political, Diplomatic, and Judicial Leaders)*
John J. Wilcoxson (Chapter 13: Wartime Leaders and Victims Since the Spanish-American War, 1898)*
James Zimmerman (Chapter 6: Educational Leaders)*

Gate of Heaven Cemetery
Ben Abruzzo (Chapter 7: Sung and Unsung Heroes)*
John Baker (Chapter 7: Sung and Unsung Heroes)*

Mount Calvary Cemetery
Phil Chacon (Chapter 8: Lawmen, Criminals, and Victims of Crime)*
Dionisio "Dennis" Chavez (Chapter 9: Political, Diplomatic, and Judicial Leaders)*
Soledad Chávez de Chacón (Chapter 9: Political, Diplomatic, and Judicial Leaders)*
A.J. Connell (Chapter 6: Educational Leaders)*
Antonio Gilberto Espinosa (Chapter 4: Cultural Preservationists)*
Merritt Mechem (Chapter 9: Political, Diplomatic, and Judicial Leaders)*
Kathryn O'Connor (Chapter 2: Artists, Performers, and Directors)*
Sabine R. Ulibarri (Chapter 3: Authors and Composers)*

Santa Barbara Cemetery
William "Will" Keleher (Chapter 4: Cultural Preservationists)*
Octaviano Larrazolo (Chapter 9: Political, Diplomatic, and Judicial Leaders)*
Solomon Luna (Chapter 9: Political, Diplomatic, and Judicial Leaders)*
Nestor Montoya (Chapter 9: Political, Diplomatic, and Judicial Leaders)
Mariano Otero (Chapter 9: Political, Diplomatic, and Judicial Leaders)
Milton Yarberry (Chapter 8: Lawmen, Criminals, and Victims of Crime)*

Sunset Memorial Cemetery
"Maxie" Anderson (Chapter 7: Sung and Unsung Heroes)*

Kaitlyn Arquette (Chapter 8: Lawmen, Criminals, and Victims of Crime)*
Elfego Baca (Chapter 8: Lawmen, Criminals, and Victims of Crime)*
Melanie Cravens (Chapter 8: Lawmen, Criminals, and Victims of Crime)*
Evelyn Frey (Chapter 5: Business Leaders)*
Alice Hoppes (Chapter 7: Sung and Unsung Heroes)*
Harry P. Stagg (Chapter 13: Wartime Leaders and Victims Since the Spanish-American War, 1898)*
Jerry Unser (Chapter 7: Sung and Unsung Heroes)*

Belen (in alphabetical order by cemetery names)

Our Lady of Belen Catholic Cemetery
José Felipe Chávez (Chapter 5: Business Leaders)*
Tibo J. Chavez, Sr. (Chapter 9: Political, Diplomatic, and Judicial Leaders)*

Terrace Grove Cemetery
Tamara Long Archuleta (Chapter 13: Wartime Leaders and Victims Since the Spanish-American War, 1898)*

Bernalillo

Our Lady of Sorrows Catholic Cemetery
Francisco "Pedro" Perea (Chapter 9: Political, Diplomatic, and Judicial Leaders)*

Cañon

Nuestra Señora de Dolores Cemetery
Patrocinio Barela (Chapter 2: Artists, Performers, and Directors)*
Leo Salazar (Chapter 2: Artists, Performers, and Directors)*

Carlsbad (in alphabetical order by cemetery names)

Carlsbad Municipal Cemetery
Bruce Cabot (Chapter 2: Artists, Performers, and Directors)*
James "Jim" White (Chapter 7: Sung and Unsung Heroes)*

Sunset Gardens Memorial Park
Georgia Lusk (Chapter 9: Political, Diplomatic, and Judicial Leaders)*

Cimarron

Mountain View Cemetery
Charles Fred Lambert (Chapter 8: Lawmen, Criminals, and Victims of Crime)*
Henry Lambert (Chapter 5: Business Leaders)*
Franklin Tolby (Chapter 8: Lawmen, Criminals, and Victims of Crime)*

Clayton

Clayton Cemetery
Thomas E. "Black Jack" Ketchum (Chapter 8: Lawmen, Criminals, and Victims of Crime)*
Bernice McLaughlin (Chapter 7: Sung and Unsung Heroes)*
Raymond "Ray" Sutton, Sr. (cenotaph) (Chapter 8: Lawmen, Criminals, and Victims of Crime)*

Clovis

Mission Garden of Memories Cemetery
Andrew Hockenhull (Chapter 9: Political, Diplomatic, and Judicial Leaders)*
Norman Petty (Chapter 2: Artists and Composers)*

Columbus

Valley Heights Cemetery
James Todd Dean (Chapter 13: Wartime Leaders and Victims Since the Spanish-American War, 1898)*
Bessy James (Chapter 13: Wartime Leaders and Victims Since the Spanish-American War, 1898)*

Córdova

San Antonio Church Cemetery
José D. López (Chapter 2: Artists and Composers)*

Deming

Mountain View Cemetery
Francisco Alvarez (Chapter 13: Wartime Leaders and Victims Since the Spanish-American War, 1898)
Juan Castillo (Chapter 13: Wartime Leaders and Victims Since the Spanish-American War, 1898)
Taurino Garcia (Chapter 13: Wartime Leaders and Victims Since the Spanish-American War, 1898)
José Rangel (Chapter 13: Wartime Leaders and Victims Since the Spanish-American War, 1898)
Eusevio Renteria (Chapter 13: Wartime Leaders and Victims Since the Spanish-American War, 1898)
Juan Sanchez (Chapter 13: Wartime Leaders and Victims Since the Spanish-American War, 1898)
George Scarborough (Chapter 8: Lawmen, Criminals, and Victims of Crime)*
Charlotte "Lottie Deno" Thurmond (Chapter 8: Lawmen, Criminals, and Victims of Crime)*

Dixon

Father Cooper's Cemetery
Horacio E. Valdez (Chapter 2: Artists, Performers, and Directors)*

Dwyer

San José Catholic Cemetery
Juan Chacón (Chapter 7: Sung and Unsung Heroes)*

Edgewood

Mountain Valley Cemetery
Richard B. Williams (Chapter 8: Lawmen, Criminals, and Victims of Crime)*

Farmington (in alphabetical order by cemetery names)

Greenlawn Cemetery
    James Dixon (Chapter 13: Wartime Leaders and Victims Since the Spanish-American War, 1898)*

Memory Garden
    Harrison Lapahie (Chapter 13: Wartime Leaders and Victims Since the Spanish-American War, 1898)*

Folsom

Folsom Cemetery
    George McJunkin (Chapter 7: Sung and Unsung Heroes)*
    Sarah "Sallie" Rooke (Chapter 7: Sung and Unsung Heroes)*

Fort Bayard

National Cemetery
    James Betters (Chapter 12: Wartime Leaders and Victims to the End of the Indian Wars in New Mexico, 1886)*
    Alonzo Bowman (Chapter 12: Wartime Leaders and Victims to the End of the Indian Wars in New Mexico, 1886)*
    Mildred C. "Madame Millie" Cusey (Chapter 8: Lawmen, Criminals, and Victims of Crime)*
    John P. Schnitzer (Chapter 12: Wartime Leaders and Victims to the End of the Indian Wars in New Mexico, 1886)*

Fort Stanton

Merchant Marine Cemetery
    Hermann Neuhoff (Chapter 13: Wartime Leaders and Victims Since the Spanish-American War, 1898)*
    Heinrich Renken (Chapter 13: Wartime Leaders and Victims Since the Spanish-American War, 1898)*
    Friedrich Steffens (Chapter 13: Wartime Leaders and Victims Since the Spanish-American War, 1898)*
    Otto Zeitsch (Chapter 13: Wartime Leaders and Victims Since the Spanish-American War, 1898)*

Fort Sumner

Old Military Cemetery
    William H. "Billy the Kid" Bonney (Chapter 8: Lawmen, Criminals, and Victims of Crime)*
    Lucien Maxwell (Chapter 5: Business Leaders)*
    Peter "Pete" Maxwell (Chapter 8: Lawmen, Criminals, and Victims of Crime)*

Fort Wingate

Fort Wingate Cemetery
    Cayetano Romero (Chapter 13: Wartime Leaders and Victims Since the Spanish-American War, 1898)*

Fruitland

Fruitland Cemetery
Joseph Edward Wheeler (Chapter 10: Religious Leaders)*

Gallup

Hillcrest Cemetery
Lucy Whiteside (Chapter 11: Scientists and Medical Personnel)*
"Bobcat" Wilson (Chapter 8: Lawmen, Criminals, and Victims of Crime)*

Grants

Grants Memorial Park
Patricio "Paddy" Martinez (Chapter 5: Business Leaders)*

Hachita

Hachita Cemetery
William H. "Bronco Bill" Walters (Chapter 8: Lawmen, Criminals, and Victims of Crime)*

Hillsboro

Hillsboro Community Cemetery
Ebin Stanley (Chapter 12: Wartime Leaders and Victims to the End of the Indian Wars in New Mexico, 1886)*

Kingston

Kingston Cemetery
James McNally (Chapter 12: Wartime Leaders and Victims to the End of the Indian Wars in New Mexico, 1886)*

Kirtland

Kirtland Community Cemetery
Jerome C. Dodge (Chapter 13: Wartime Leaders and Victims Since the Spanish-American War, 1898)*

La Luz

Our Lady de la Luz Cemetery
François-Jean "Frenchy" Rochas (Chapter 2: Artists, Performers, and Directors)*

Las Cruces (in alphabetical order by cemetery names)

IOOF Cemetery
Samuel "Sam" Steel (Chapter 8: Lawmen, Criminals, and Victims of Crime)*

Masonic Cemetery
Ovida "Cricket" Coogler (Chapter 8: Lawmen, Criminals, and Victims of Crime)*
Albert and Henry Fountain (cenotaph) (Chapter 8: Lawmen, Criminals, and Victims of Crime)*
Fabian Garcia (Chapter 11: Scientists and Medical Personnel)

Patrick "Pat" Garrett (Chapter 8: Lawmen, Criminals, and Victims of Crime)*
Ralph W. Goddard (Chapter 6: Educational Leaders)*
Hiram Hadley (Chapter 6: Educational Leaders)*
William H.H. Llewellyn (Chapter 13: Wartime Leaders and Victims Since the Spanish-American War, 1898)*
John Ballou Newbrough (Chapter 10: Religious Leaders)*
Milton E. "Doc" Noss (Chapter 7: Sung and Unsung Heroes)
William Rynerson (Chapter 12: Wartime Leaders and Victims to the End of the Indian Wars in New Mexico, 1886)
Benjamin Viljoen (Chapter 13: Wartime Leaders and Victims Since the Spanish-American War, 1898)*

San José Catholic Cemetery
Frank C. Brito (Chapter 13: Wartime Leaders and Victims Since the Spanish-American War, 1898)*

Las Vegas (in alphabetical order by cemetery names)

Masonic Cemetery
Charles Ilfeld (Chapter 5: Business Leaders)*
Andrieus A. Jones (Chapter 9: Political, Diplomatic, and Judicial Leaders)*
William J. Mills (Chapter 9: Political, Diplomatic, and Judicial Leaders)*
Frank Springer (Chapter 6: Educational Leaders)*

Mount Calvary Catholic Cemetery
Ezequiel C de Baca (Chapter 9: Political, Diplomatic, and Judicial Leaders)*
Francisco A. Manzanares (Chapter 9: Political, Diplomatic, and Judicial Leaders)
Trinidad Romero (Chapter 9: Political, Diplomatic, and Judicial Leaders)*

Lincoln
Lincoln Cemetery
George "Dad" Peppin (Chapter 8: Lawmen, Criminals, and Victims of Crime)*

Los Alamos

Guaje Pines Cemetery
Norris Bradbury (Chapter 11: Scientists and Medical Personnel)*
Eric Jette (Chapter 11: Scientists and Medical Personnel)*

Los Lunas

San Clemente Catholic Cemetery
Tranquilino Luna (Chapter 9: Political, Diplomatic, and Judicial Leaders)*

Lovington

Resthaven Memorial Gardens
Harold Runnels (Chapter 9: Political, Diplomatic, and Judicial Leaders)*

Mescalero
Blazer Cemetery
Richard M. "Dick" Brewer (Chapter 8: Lawmen, Criminals, and Victims of Crime)
Andrew L. "Buckshot" Roberts (Chapter 8: Lawmen, Criminals, and Victims of Crime)

Mesilla

San Albino Cemetery
Giovanni María Augustini (Chapter 10: Religious Leaders)*

Mountainair

Mountainair Cemetery
Maud Medders (Chapter 13: Wartime Leaders and Victims Since the Spanish-American War, 1898)*
Edward Clay Sharpless (Chapter 12: Wartime Leaders and Victims to the End of the Indian Wars in New Mexico, 1886)*

Newkirk

Newkirk Cemetery
Fabiola C de Baca Gilbert (Chapter 4: Cultural Preservationist)*

Pinos Altos

Pinos Altos Cemetery
Thomas J. Maeston (Chapter 12: Wartime Leaders and Victims to the End of the Indian Wars in New Mexico, 1886)*

Portales

Portales Cemetery
John Burroughs (Chapter 9: Political, Diplomatic, and Judicial Leaders)*
Washington E. Lindsey (Chapter 9: Political, Diplomatic, and Judicial Leaders)*

Puerto de Luna

Nuestra Señora de El Refugio Cemetery
Alexander Grzelachowski (Chapter 12: Wartime Leaders and Victims to the End of the Indian Wars in New Mexico, 1886)*

Ranchos de Taos

Descanso Cemetery
John Collier (Chapter 7: Sung and Unsung Heroes)*

Raton

Fairmont Cemetery
John Morrow (Chapter 9: Political, Diplomatic, and Judicial Leaders)*

Roswell

South Park Cemetery
Robert Crosby (Chapter 7: Sung and Unsung Heroes)*
Elizabeth Garrett (Chapter 3: Authors and Composers)*
Walter G. Haut (Chapter 7: Sung and Unsung Heroes)
James Hinkle (Chapter 9: Political, Diplomatic, and Judicial Leaders)*
Addison Jones (Chapter 7: Sung and Unsung Heroes)*

Joseph C. Lea (Chapter 5: Business Leaders)*
Jacob B. "Billy" Mathews (Chapter 8: Lawmen, Criminals, and Victims of Crime)*

Santa Fe (in alphabetical order by cemetery names)

Fairview Cemetery
Ruth Laughlin Alexander (Chapter 3: Authors and Composers)*
Frank Applegate (Chapter 4: Cultural Preservationists)
Julia Asplund (Chapter 6: Educational Leaders)*
Gerald Cassidy (Chapter 2: Artists, Performers, and Directors)*
Ina Cassidy (Chapter 3: Authors and Composers)*
Thomas Catron (Chapter 9: Political, Diplomatic, and Judicial Leaders)*
Amado Chaves (Chapter 6: Educational Leaders)*
Max Frost (Chapter 5: Business Leaders)*
Alice Corbin Henderson (Chapter 3: Authors and Composers)*
William Henderson (Chapter 2: Artists, Performers, and Directors)*
E. Dana Johnson (Chapter 5: Business Leaders)*
Antonio Joseph (Chapter 9: Political, Diplomatic, and Judicial Leaders)
Frank E. Mera (Chapter 11: Scientists and Medical Personnel)*
Harry P. Mera, Jr. (Chapter 4: Cultural Preservationists)*
Miguel Otero, Jr. (Chapter 9: Political, Diplomatic, and Judicial Leaders)*
William Hayes Pope (Chapter 9: Political, Diplomatic, and Judicial Leaders)*
Arthur Seligman (Chapter 9: Political, Diplomatic, and Judicial Leaders)*
Abraham Staab (Chapter 5: Business Leaders)*
William T. Thornton (Chapter 9: Political, Diplomatic, and Judicial Leaders)*
N. Howard Thorp (Chapter 4: Cultural Preservationists)*
Ralph Twitchell (Chapter 4: Cultural Preservationists)*
Carlos Vierra (Chapter 2: Artists, Performers, and Directors)*

IOOF Cemetery
Sam Ketchum (cenotaph) (Chapter 8: Lawmen, Criminals, and Victims of Crime)*

Memorial Gardens
Elliott Speer Barker (Chapter 7: Sung and Unsung Heroes)*
George Fitzpatrick (Chapter 5: Business Leaders)*
Allan Houser (Chapter 2: Artists, Performers, and Directors)*
Dorothy McKibbin (Chapter 13: Wartime Leaders and Victims Since the Spanish-American War, 1898)*
John E. Miles (Chapter 9: Political, Diplomatic, and Judicial Leaders)*

National Cemetery
Joseph G.H. Able (Chapter 12: Wartime Leaders and Victims to the End of the Indian Wars in New Mexico, 1886)*
Richard Alday (Chapter 12: Wartime Leaders and Victims to the End of the Indian Wars in New Mexico, 1886)*
William F.M. Arny (Chapter 9: Political, Diplomatic, and Judicial Leaders)*
Frederick L. Ashworth (Chapter 13: Wartime Leaders and Victims Since the Spanish-American War, 1898)
S. Omar Barker (Chapter 3: Authors and Composers)*
Charles Bent (Chapter 9: Political, Diplomatic, and Judicial Leaders)*
Reuben P. Bentley (Chapter 12: Wartime Leaders and Victims to the End of the Indian Wars in New Mexico, 1886)*
Alexander Bonnyman, Jr. (cenotaph) (Chapter 13: Wartime Leaders and Victims Since the Spanish-American War, 1888)*

William Booker (Chapter 12: Wartime Leaders and Victims to the End of the Indian Wars in New Mexico, 1886)*

Edward T. Burrowes (Chapter 12: Wartime Leaders and Victims to the End of the Indian Wars in New Mexico, 1886)*

J. Francisco Chaves (Chapter 9: Political, Diplomatic, and Judicial Leaders)*

Edward Clary (Chapter 13: Wartime Leaders and Victims Since the Spanish-American War, 1898)*

Charles P. Clever (Chapter 9: Political, Diplomatic, and Judicial Leaders)

J.S.L. Cotton (Chapter 12: Wartime Leaders and Victims to the End of the Indian Wars in New Mexico, 1886)*

John O. Crosby (Chapter 2: Artists, Performers, and Directors)

George Curry (Chapter 9: Political, Diplomatic, and Judicial Leaders)*

Edwin L. Elwood (Chapter 12: Wartime Leaders and Victims to the End of the Indian Wars in New Mexico, 1886)*

Daniel Fernandez (Chapter 13: Wartime Leaders and Victims Since the Spanish-American War, 1898)*

Everett C. Foley (Chapter 12: Wartime Leaders and Victims to the End of the Indian Wars in New Mexico, 1886)*

Frederick "Fred" Fornoff (Chapter 8: Lawmen, Criminals, and Victims of Crime)*

John W. Frink (Chapter 13: Wartime Leaders and Victims Since the Spanish-American War, 1898)

Christopher Gollmer (Chapter 12: Wartime Leaders and Victims to the End of the Indian Wars in New Mexico, 1886)*

Calvin R. Graef (Chapter 13: Wartime Leaders and Victims Since the Spanish-American War, 1898)*

James "Paddy" Graydon (Chapter 12: Wartime Leaders and Victims to the End of the Indian Wars in New Mexico, 1886)*

Benjamin G. Greely (Chapter 12: Wartime Leaders and Victims to the End of the Indian Wars in New Mexico, 1886)*

Jacob Guenther (Chapter 12: Wartime Leaders and Victims to the End of the Indian Wars in New Mexico, 1886)*

August Habermann (Chapter 12: Wartime Leaders and Victims to the End of the Indian Wars in New Mexico, 1886)*

Peter Hail (Chapter 12: Wartime Leaders and Victims to the End of the Indian Wars in New Mexico, 1886)*

Ebineezer Hanna (Chapter 12: Wartime Leaders and Victims to the End of the Indian Wars in New Mexico, 1886)*

Jacob Henson (Chapter 12: Wartime Leaders and Victims to the End of the Indian Wars in New Mexico, 1886)*

F.J. Hopkins (Chapter 12: Wartime Leaders and Victims to the End of the Indian Wars in New Mexico, 1886)*

Patrick J. Hurley (Chapter 13: Wartime Leaders and Victims Since the Spanish-American War, 1898)*

Roy W. Johnson (Chapter 6: Educational Leaders)*

August Juhl (Chapter 12: Wartime Leaders and Victims to the End of the Indian Wars in New Mexico, 1886)*

Robert Lee "Bob" King (Chapter 6: Educational Leaders)*

Oliver LaFarge (Chapter 3: Authors and Composers)*

William Langston (Chapter 12: Wartime Leaders and Victims to the End of the Indian Wars in New Mexico, 1886)*

James Manus (Chapter 12: Wartime Leaders and Victims to the End of the Indian Wars in New Mexico, 1886)*

Stephen Marbach (Chapter 12: Wartime Leaders and Victims to the End of the Indian Wars in New Mexico, 1886)*

John R. Martin (Chapter 12: Wartime Leaders and Victims to the End of the Indian Wars in New Mexico, 1886)*
James McCord (Chapter 12: Wartime Leaders and Victims to the End of the Indian Wars in New Mexico, 1886)*
William McCormick (Chapter 12: Wartime Leaders and Victims to the End of the Indian Wars in New Mexico, 1886)*
John R. McFie (Chapter 9: Political, Diplomatic, and Judicial Leaders)*
John N. McKnight (Chapter 12: Wartime Leaders and Victims to the End of the Indian Wars in New Mexico, 1886)*
Alexander Montgomery (Chapter 12: Wartime Leaders and Victims to the End of the Indian Wars in New Mexico, 1886)*
Frederick "Fritz" Mueller (Chapter 13: Wartime Leaders and Victims Since the Spanish-American War, 1898)*
Lawrence G. Murphy (Chapter 8: Lawmen, Criminals, and Victims of Crime)*
Dennis O'Leary (Chapter 14: Unusual Graves)*
William T. Parsons (Chapter 12: Wartime Leaders and Victims to the End of the Indian Wars in New Mexico, 1886)*
William Ritch (Chapter 9: Political, Diplomatic, and Judicial Leaders)*
Y.B. Rowdy (Chapter 12: Wartime Leaders and Victims to the End of the Indian Wars in New Mexico, 1886)*
Charles G. Sage (Chapter 13: Wartime Leaders and Victims Since the Spanish-American War, 1898)*
Fritz Schaefer (Chapter 12: Wartime Leaders and Victims to the End of the Indian Wars in New Mexico, 1886)*
Frances Scholes (Chapter 4: Cultural Preservationists)*
Otto Schroeder (Chapter 12: Wartime Leaders and Victims to the End of the Indian Wars in New Mexico, 1886)*
Robert S. Scott (Chapter 13: Wartime Leaders and Victims Since the Spanish-American War, 1898)*
William H. "Will" Shuster, Jr. (Chapter 2: Artists, Performers, and Directors)*
E.R. Slaughter (chapter 12: Wartime Leaders and Victims to the End of the Indian Wars in New Mexico, 1886)*
James R. Stevens (Chapter 12: Wartime Leaders and Victims to the End of the Indian Wars in New Mexico, 1886)*
Katherine Stinson-Otero (Chapter 2: Artists, Performers, and Directors)*
Burton R. Stone (Chapter 12: Wartime Leaders and Victims to the End of the Indian Wars in New Mexico, 1886)*
William Straughn (Chapter 12: Wartime Leaders and Victims to the End of the Indian Wars in New Mexico, 1886)*
G.N. Taylor (Chapter 12: Wartime Leaders and Victims to the End of the Indian Wars in New Mexico, 1886)*
Roy Townley (cenotaph) (Chapter 13: Wartime Leaders and Victims Since the Spanish-American War, 1898)*
Miguel Trujillo (Chapter 7: Sung and Unsung Heroes)*
José F. Valdez (Chapter 13: Wartime Leaders and Victims Since the Spanish-American War, 1898)*
Elver S. "Johnny" Walker (Chapter 9: Political, Diplomatic, and Judicial Leaders)
Robert P. Walker (Chapter 12: Wartime Leaders and Victims to the End of the Indian Wars in New Mexico, 1886)*
Thomas D. Wilson (Chapter 12: Wartime Leaders and Victims to the End of the Indian Wars in New Mexico, 1886)*

Rosario Cemetery
Jozef Bakos (Chapter 2: Artists, Performers, and Directors)*

Fray Angélico Chávez (Chapter 4: Cultural Preservationist)*
Francisco "Frank" Chávez (Chapter 8: Lawmen, Criminals, and Victims of Crime)
Henry Connelly (Rosario Chapel) (Chapter 9: Political, Diplomatic, and Judicial Leaders)*
John Dempsey (Chapter 9: Political, Diplomatic, and Judicial Leaders)*
Brian Boru Dunne (Chapter 3: Authors and Composers)*
Fremont Ellis (Chapter 2: Artists, Performers, and Directors)*
Antonio Fernandez (Chapter 9: Political, Diplomatic, and Judicial Leaders)*
José Manual Gallegos (Chapter 9: Political, Diplomatic, and Judicial Leaders)*
Juan F. "Pancho" Griego (Chapter 8: Lawmen, Criminals, and Victims of Crime)*
Angelina Jaramillo (Chapter 8: Lawmen, Criminals, and Victims of Crime)*
Cleofas Martinez Jaramillo (Chapter 4: Cultural Preservationist)*
Sister Catherine Mallon (Chapter 10: Religious Leaders)*
William Manderfield (Chapter 5: Business Leaders)*
Joseph Montoya (Chapter 9: Political, Diplomatic, and Judicial Leaders)*
Francis "Frank" Ortiz, Jr. (Chapter 9: Political, Diplomatic, and Judicial Leaders)
Maria Adelina "Nina" Otero-Warren (Chapter 7: Sung and Unsung Heroes)*
Benjamin Read (Chapter 4: Cultural Preservationists)*
N. Sudo (Chapter 13: Wartime Leaders and Victims Since the Spanish-American War, 1898)*
Donaciano Vigil (Chapter 9: Political, Diplomatic, and Judicial Leaders)
D. Yoshikawa (Chapter 13: Wartime Leaders and Victims Since the Spanish-American War, 1898)*

Shakespeare

Shakespeare Cemetery
William "Russian Bill" Tettenborn (Chapter 8: Lawmen, Criminals, and Victims of Crime)*

Silver City (in alphabetical order by cemetery names)

Masonic Cemetery
William "Billy" Walton (Chapter 9: Political, Diplomatic, and Judicial Leaders)*
Harvey Whitehill (Chapter 8: Lawmen, Criminals, and Victims of Crime)

Memory Lane Cemetery
Catherine Antrim (Chapter 8: Lawmen, Criminals, and Victims of Crime)*
John M. Bullard (Chapter 12: Wartime Leaders and Victims to the End of the Indian Wars in New Mexico, 1886)*
Benjamin "Ben" Lilly (Chapter 7: Sung and Unsung Heroes)*
Leonidas S. Lytle (Chapter 12: Wartime Leaders and Victims to the End of the Indian Wars in New Mexico, 1886)*

Socorro

Socorro Cemetery
Holm O. Bursum, Sr. (Chapter 9: Political, Diplomatic, and Judicial Leaders)*

Taos (in alphabetical order by cemetery names)

Kit Carson Cemetery
Christopher "Kit" Carson (Chapter 12: Wartime Leaders and Victims to the End of the Indian Wars in New Mexico, 1886)*

John "Long John" Dunn (Chapter 5: Business Leaders)*
Mabel Dodge Luhan (Chapter 4: Cultural Preservationists)*
Arthur Manby (Chapter 8: Lawmen, Criminals, and Victims of Crime)*
Antonio José Martínez (Chapter 10: Religious Leaders)*
Smith Henry Simpson (Chapter 12: Wartime Leaders and Victims to the End of the Indian Wars in New Mexico, 1886)*

Sierra Vista Cemetery
Oscar Berninghaus (Chapter 2: Artists, Performers, and Directors)*
E. Irving Couse (Chapter 2: Artists, Performers, and Directors)*
William Herbert "Buck" Dunton (Chapter 2: Artists, Performers, and Directors)*
William Victor Higgins (Chapter 2: Artists, Performers, and Directors)*
Bert Geer Phillips (Chapter 2: Artists, Performers, and Directors)*
Mary Millicent Rogers (Chapter 4: Cultural Preservationists)*

Truth or Consequences (formerly Hot Springs)

Hot Springs Cemetery
Sarah "Sadie" Orchard (Chapter 8: Lawmen, Criminals, and Victims of Crime)*

Tularosa

Tularosa Cemetery
William "Mack" Brazel (Chapter 7: Sung and Unsung Heroes)*
James R. Gililland (Chapter 8: Lawmen, Criminals, and Victims of Crime)*

Vado

Vado Cemetery
Francis "Frank" Boyer (Chapter 7: Sung and Unsung Heroes)*

White Oaks

Cedarvale Cemetery
James Bell (Chapter 8: Lawmen, Criminals, and Victims of Crime)*
Dena Lynn Gore (Chapter 8: Lawmen, Criminals, and Victims of Crime)*
William McDonald (Chapter 9: Political, Diplomatic, and Judicial Leaders)*
Susan McSween Barber (Chapter 8: Lawmen, Criminals, and Victims of Crime)*

Additional public cemeteries visited in New Mexico towns (in alphabetical order by town names):

Abbott, Abo, Alamogordo, Albuquerque, Algodones, Arroyo Hondo, Arroyo Seco, Aztec, Bayard, Bloomfield, Bueyeros, Cabezon, Capitan, Carrizozo, Casa Colorada, Cerrillos, Chama, Chilili, Chimayo, Chloride, Claunch, Cordova, Corona, Corrales, Cuba, Datil, Dawson, Dexter, Dixon, Dusty, Elizabethtown (E-Town), Escondida, Española, Estancia, Floyd, Fort Stanton, Fort Sumner, Golden, Hagerman, Hatch, Hernandez, Kelly, La Cienega, La Joya, La Luz, Lemitar, Los Lunas, Madrid, Magdalena, Manzano, Mayhill, Monticello, Mora, Moriarty, Peralta, Placitas, Ramah, Raton, Reserve, Riley, Rio Rancho, Ruidoso, San Acacia, San Antonio, San Marcial, Santa Cruz, Santa Rosa, Springer, Stanley, Tajique, Tomé, Torreon, Truchas, Truth or Consequences, Tucumcari, Veguita, Villanueva, Wagon Mound, Watrous, Willard, Williamsburg

APPENDIX B

FAMOUS NEW MEXICANS INTERRED IN PUBLIC CEMETERIES IN OTHER STATES AND COUNTRIES

Famous New Mexicans have been buried in at least thirty states and three foreign countries, although few of their gravestones mention the important roles they played in New Mexico history.

The following is a list of famous New Mexicans and the cities, states, and cemeteries where they have been buried. As in Appendix A, each famous New Mexican's chapter is listed in parentheses. Names marked with asterisks (*) include gravestone photographs in the text.

Famous New Mexicans buried in non-public cemeteries or on private, usually inaccessible land are not listed in Appendix B.

STATES AND THE DISTRICT OF COLUMBIA *(public cemeteries in alphabetical order)*

ALABAMA

    Mount Vernon Barracks Cemetery, Mobile, Alabama
      Lozen (Chapter 12: Wartime Leaders and Victims to the End of the Indian Wars in New Mexico, 1886)

ARIZONA (in alphabetical order by cemetery names)

    Arizona Pioneers' Home Cemetery, Prescott, Arizona
      John Miller (Chapter 8: Lawmen, Criminals, and Victims of Crime)

    Fort Defiance Cemetery, Fort Defiance, Arizona
      Henry Chee Dodge (Chapter 9: Political, Diplomatic, and Judicial Leaders)

    Holy Hope Catholic Cemetery, Tucson, Arizona
      Jean B. Salpointe (Chapter 10: Religious Leaders)*

    IOOF Cemetery, Prescott, Arizona
      John Kinney (Chapter 8: Lawmen, Criminals, and Victims of Crime)

    Safford Union Cemetery, Safford, Arizona
      Everett Bowman (Chapter 7: Sung and Unsung Heroes)

CALIFORNIA (in alphabetical order by cemetery names)

Ascension Cemetery, Lake Forest, California
    William Hanna (Chapter 2: Artists, Performers, and Directors)

Calvary Memorial Pioneer Cemetery, San Diego, California
    Charles F. Walsh (Chapter 7: Sung and Unsung Heroes)

Forest Lawn Memorial Park, Glendale, California
    Edward Sheriff Curtis (Chapter 2: Artists, Performers, and Directors)
    Ralph Edwards (Chapter 2: Artists, Performers, and Directors)
    Arthur "Art" Goebel (Chapter 7: Sung and Unsung Heroes)
    Louis L'Amour (Chapter 3: Authors and Composers)
    Tom Mix (Chapter 2: Artists, Performers, and Directors)

Inglewood Park Cemetery, Inglewood, California
    Benigno C. Hernández (Chapter 9: Political, Diplomatic, and Judicial Leaders)
    Charles A. Siringo (Chapter 8: Lawmen, Criminals, and Victims of Crime)*

Live Oak Memorial Park, Monrovia, California
    William A. Pile (Chapter 9: Political, Diplomatic, and Judicial Leaders)*

Mountain View Cemetery, Altadena, California
    Richard Feynman (Chapter 11: Scientists and Medical Personnel)
    Joseph Henry Sharp (Chapter 2: Artists, Performers, and Directors)*

National Cemetery, Los Angeles, California
    Louis Felsenthal (Chapter 12: Wartime Leaders and Victims to the End of the Indian Wars in New Mexico, 1886)

National Cemetery, San Francisco, California
    Matthias W. Day (Chapter 12: Wartime Leaders and Victims to the End of the Indian Wars in New Mexico, 1886)*

San Gorgonio Memorial Park, Banning, California
    Dorothy Dunn Kramer (Chapter 6: Educational Leaders)

Westminster Memorial Park, Westminster, California
    Kenneth Lee Worley (Chapter 13: Wartime Leaders and Victims Since the Spanish-American War, 1898)

COLORADO (in alphabetical order by cemetery names)

Ault Cemetery, Ault, Colorado
    Joseph P. Martinez (Chapter 13: Wartime Leaders and Victims Since the Spanish-American War, 1898)

Evergreen Cemetery, Colorado Springs, Colorado
    Laura Gilpin (Chapter 2: Artists, Performers, and Directors)*

Fairmont Cemetery, Denver, Colorado
    John Chivington (Chapter 12: Wartime Leaders and Victims to the End of the Indian Wars in New Mexico, 1886)*

Stephen Dorsey (Chapter 5: Business Leaders)*
Myra Ellen Jenkins (Chapter 4: Cultural Preservationists)*

Green Mountain Cemetery, Boulder, Colorado
Robert S. Goss (Chapter 6: Educational Leaders)

Las Animas Cemetery, Las Animas, Colorado
William Bent (Chapter 5: Business Leaders)*

Linwood Cemetery, Glenwood Springs, Colorado
John Henry "Doc" Holiday (Chapter 8: Lawmen, Criminals, and Victims of Crime)*

Mount Olive Cemetery, Denver, Colorado
Joseph P. Machebeuf (Chapter 10: Religious Leaders)*
Jean B. Pitaval (Chapter 10: Religious Leaders)*

Riverside Cemetery, Denver, Colorado
Miguel Otero, Sr. (Chapter 9: Political, Diplomatic, and Judicial Leaders)

Stonewall Cemetery, Stonewall, Colorado
Oscar P. McMains (Chapter 8: Lawmen, Criminals, and Victims of Crime)
Marion Russell (Chapter 5: Business Leaders)*

Trinidad Catholic Cemetery, Trinidad, Colorado
Rafael Chacon (Chapter 12: Wartime Leaders and Victims to the End of the Indian Wars in New Mexico, 1886)*
Richens "Uncle Dick" Wootton (Chapter 5: Business Leaders)*

Trinidad Masonic Cemetery, Trinidad, Colorado
Isaac Hamilton Rapp (Chapter 2: Artists, Performers, and Directors)

CONNECTICUT

Fairlawn Cemetery, Ridgefield, Connecticut
Wilber E. Wilder (Chapter 12: Wartime Leaders and Victims to the End of the Indian Wars in New Mexico, 1886)

HAWAII

National Memorial Cemetery of the Pacific (AKA The Punch Bowl), Honolulu, Hawaii
Delbert O. Jennings (Chapter 13: Wartime Leaders and Victims Since the Spanish-American War, 1898)
Ernie Pyle (Chapter 13: Wartime Leaders and Victims Since the Spanish-American War, 1898)*

ILLINOIS (in alphabetical order by cemetery names)

Graceland *Cemetery, Chicago, Illinois*
John A. "Jack" Johnson (Chapter 7: Sung and Unsung Heroes)*

Memorial Park Cemetery, Evanston, Illinois
Ernest Martin Hennings (Chapter 2: Artists, Performers, and Directors)

Oak Woods Cemetery, Chicago, Illinois
Enrico Fermi (Chapter 11: Scientists and Medical Personnel)*

Queen of Heaven Cemetery, Hillside, Illinois
    Lawrence Martin Jenco (Chapter 10: Religious Leaders)

INDIANA (in alphabetical order by cemetery names)

Crown Hill Cemetery, Indianapolis, Indiana
    Edward R.S. Canby (Chapter 12: Wartime Leaders and Victims to the End of the Indian Wars in New Mexico, 1886)*

Oak Hill Cemetery, Crawfordsville, Indiana
    Lewis "Lew" Wallace (Chapter 9: Political, Diplomatic, and Judicial Leaders)*
    Susan Wallace (Chapter 3: Authors and Composers)

Park Cemetery, Fairmont, Indiana
    Olive Rush (Chapter 2: Artists, Performers, and Directors)

Rose Hill Cemetery, Bloomington, Indiana
    John S. Watts (Chapter 9: Political, Diplomatic, and Judicial Leaders)

IOWA

Aspen Grove Cemetery, Burlington, Iowa
    Aldo Leopold (Chapter 7: Sung and Unsung Heroes)*

KANSAS (in alphabetical order by cemetery names)

Evergreen Cemetery, Fort Scott, Kansas
    H.C. McComas (Chapter 12: Wartime Leaders and Victims to the End of the Indian Wars in New Mexico, 1886)*
    Juanita McComas (Chapter 12: Wartime Leaders and Victims to the End of the Indian Wars in New Mexico, 1886)*

Maple Grove Cemetery, Wichita, Kansas
    Jeremiah "Shoeless Jerry" Simpson (Chapter 9: Political, Diplomatic, and Judicial Leaders)

Mount Muncie Cemetery, Lansing, Kansas
    Frederick Henry "Fred" Harvey (Chapter 5: Business Leaders)*

National Cemetery, Fort Leavenworth, Kansas
    Frank Bratling (cenotaph) (Chapter 12: Wartime Leaders and Victims to the End of the Indian Wars in New Mexico, 1886)
    Albert D. Sale (Chapter 12: Wartime Leaders and Victims to the End of the Indian Wars in New Mexico, 1886)*

KENTUCKY (in alphabetical order by cemetery names)

Cave Hill Cemetery, Louisville, Kentucky
    David Meriwether (Chapter 9: Political, Diplomatic, and Judicial Leaders)

Mill Springs National Cemetery, Nancy, Kentucky
    Brent Woods (Chapter 12: Wartime Leaders and Victims to the End of the Indian Wars in New Mexico, 1886)

MARYLAND

St. Luke's Methodist Church Cemetery, Reisterstown, Maryland
Augustus Walley (Chapter 12: Wartime Leaders and Victims to the End of the Indian Wars in New Mexico, 1886)

MASSACHUSETTS (in alphabetical order by cemetery names)

Hope Cemetery, Worchester, Massachusetts
Robert Goddard (Chapter 11: Scientists and Medical Personnel)*

Mount Auburn Cemetery, Cambridge, Massachusetts
James Carleton (Chapter 12: Wartime Leaders and Victims to the End of the Indian Wars in New Mexico, 1886)*

MICHIGAN (in alphabetical order by cemetery names)

Elmwood Cemetery, Detroit, Michigan
Philip St. George Cooke (Chapter 12: Wartime Leaders and Victims to the End of the Indian Wars in New Mexico, 1886)

Mountain Home Cemetery, Kalamazoo, Michigan
Marsh Giddings (Chapter 9: Political, Diplomatic, and Judicial Leaders)

MINNESOTA

Oakland Cemetery, St. Paul, Minnesota
Mary Elizabeth Colter (Chapter 2: Artists, Performers, and Directors)*

MISSOURI (in alphabetical order by cemetery names)

Bellefontaine Cemetery, St. Louis, Missouri
George Bent (Chapter 5: Business Leaders)
Stephen Watts Kearny (Chapter 12: Wartime Leaders and Victims to the End of the Indian Wars in New Mexico, 1886)*
William Carr Lane (Chapter 9: Political, Diplomatic, and Judicial Leaders)
Susan Magoffin (Chapter 5: Business Leaders)*
Sterling Price (Chapter 12: Wartime Leaders and Victims to the End of the Indian Wars in New Mexico, 1886)*

Liberty Cemetery, Richmond, Missouri
Alexander Doniphan (Chapter 12: Wartime Leaders and Victims to the End of the Indian Wars in New Mexico, 1886)

National Cemetery, Springfield, Missouri
Richard H. Weightman (Chapter 9: Political, Diplomatic, and Judicial Leaders)

Richmond City Cemetery, Richmond, Missouri
Robert Newton "Bob" Ford (Chapter 8: Lawmen, Criminals, and Victims of Crime)*

Union Cemetery, Kansas City, Missouri
James S. Calhoun (Chapter 9: Political, Diplomatic, and Judicial Leaders)*

NEBRASKA

National Cemetery, Fort McPherson, Nebraska
George Jordon (Chapter 12: Wartime Leaders and Victims to the End of the Indian Wars in New Mexico, 1886)

NEW HAMPSHIRE

Old Burying Ground, Jaffery, New Hampshire
Willa Cather (Chapter 3: Authors and Composers)*

NEW JERSEY

First Presbyterian Church Cemetery, Morristown, New Jersey
Samuel B. Axtell (Chapter 9: Political, Diplomatic, and Judicial Leaders)

NEW YORK (in alphabetical order by cemetery names)

Beechwoods Cemetery, New Rochelle, New York
Robert T. Emmet (Chapter 12: Wartime Leaders and Victims to the End of the Indian Wars in New Mexico, 1886)

Greenwood Cemetery, Brooklyn, New York
Bronson Cutting (Chapter 9: Political, Diplomatic, and Judicial Leaders)*

Milford Cemetery, Milford, New York
Charles Eddy (Chapter 5: Business Leaders)

Military Cemetery, Sacketts Harbor, New York
Zebulon Pike (Chapter 12: Wartime Leaders and Victims to the End of the Indian Wars in New Mexico, 1886)*

National Cemetery, Brooklyn, New York
John W. "Captain Jack" Crawford (Chapter 2: Artists, Performers, and Directors)*

St. George's Cemetery, Flushing, New York
L. Bradford Prince (Chapter 9: Political, Diplomatic, and Judicial Leaders)

St. Stanislaus Cemetery, Cheektowaga, New York
Walter Mruk (Chapter 2: Artists, Performers, and Directors)

United German and French Grounds, Mount Calvary Cemetery, Cheektowaga, New York
Paul Horgan (Chapter 3: Authors and Composers)*

West Point Cemetery, West Point, New York
Alexander McRae (Chapter 12: Wartime Leaders and Victims to the End of the Indian Wars in New Mexico, 1886)*

Woodlawn Cemetery, Bronx, New York
Ralph Bunche (Chapter 7: Sung and Unsung Heroes)

Young's Memorial Cemetery, Oyster Bay, New York

Theodore Roosevelt (Chapter 13: Wartime Leaders and Victims Since the Spanish-American War, 1898)*

NORTH CAROLINA

St. Bartholomew's Episcopal Churchyard, Pittsboro, North Carolina
Abraham Rencher (Chapter 9: Political, Diplomatic, and Judicial Leaders)

OHIO (in alphabetical order by cemetery names)

Greenlawn Cemetery, Columbus, Ohio
Clinton Greaves (Chapter 12: Wartime Leaders and Victims to the End of the Indian Wars in New Mexico, 1886)

Sisters of Charity Cemetery, Cincinnati, Ohio
Rosaister Maria Segale (Chapter 10: Religious Leaders)

Spring Grove Cemetery, Cincinnati, Ohio
John P. Slough (Chapter 12: Wartime Leaders and Victims to the End of the Indian Wars in New Mexico, 1886)

OKLAHOMA (in alphabetical order by cemetery names)

Apache Cemetery, Fort Sill, Lawton, Oklahoma
Geronimo (Chapter 12: Wartime Leaders and Victims to the End of the Indian Wars in New Mexico, 1886)*
Nana (Chapter 12: Wartime Leaders and Victims to the End of the Indian Wars in New Mexico, 1886)*

Rose Hill Memorial Park, Tulsa, Oklahoma
Carlton "Carl" Magee (Chapter 5: Business Leaders)

PENNSYLVANIA (in alphabetical order by cemetery names)

Doylestown Cemetery, Doylestown, Pennsylvania
W.W.H. Davis (Chapter 9: Political, Diplomatic, and Judicial Leaders)*

Woodlawn Cemetery, Titusville, Pennsylvania
William "Bull" Andrews (Chapter 9: Political, Diplomatic, and Judicial Leaders)

TEXAS (in alphabetical order by cemetery names)

Ascension Montell Church Cemetery, Montell, Texas
John R. Baylor (Chapter 12: Wartime Leaders and Victims to the End of the Indian Wars in New Mexico, 1886)*

B'nai Zion Cemetery, El Paso, Texas
Samuel "Sam" Ravel (Chapter 13: Wartime Leaders and Victims Since the Spanish-American War, 1898)*

Boerne City Cemetery, Boerne, Texas
George Kendall (Chapter 12: Wartime Leaders and Victims to the End of the Indian Wars in New Mexico, 1886)

Bovina Cemetery, Bovina, Texas
    Pedro "Pete" Cervántez (Chapter 2: Artists, Performers, and Directors)

Calvary Hills Cemetery, Dallas, Texas
    Conrad Hilton (Chapter 5: Business Leaders)*

Clarksville Cemetery, Clarksville, Texas
    Mary Donoho (Chapter 5: Business Leaders)*

Evergreen Cemetery, El Paso, Texas
    Charles Ballard (Chapter 8: Lawmen, Criminals, and Victims of Crime)*
    Albert B. Fall (Chapter 9: Political, Diplomatic, and Judicial Leaders)*

Forest Oaks Cemetery, Austin, Texas
    George I. Sánchez (Chapter 6: Educational Leaders)

Fort Bliss National Cemetery, El Paso, Texas
    Frank Bratling (cenotaph) (Chapter 12: Wartime Leaders and Victims to the End of the Indian Wars in New Mexico, 1886)*
    Hirota Isomura (Chapter 13: Wartime Leaders and Victims Since the Spanish-American War, 1898)*
    Walter Jaeger (Chapter 13: Wartime Leaders and Victims Since the Spanish-American War, 1898)*
    John G. Nievergelt (Chapter 13: Wartime Leaders and Victims Since the Spanish-American War, 1898)*
    Wolfgang Schlegel (Chapter 13: Wartime Leaders and Victims Since the Spanish-American War, 1898)*
    John Paul Stapp (Chapter 11: Scientists and Medical Personnel Since the Spanish-American War, 1898)*

Goodnight Cemetery, Goodnight, Texas
    Charles Goodnight (Chapter 5: Business Leaders)*

Greenwood Cemetery, Weatherford, Texas
    Oliver Loving (Chapter 5: Business Leaders)*

Higgins Cemetery, Higgins, Texas
    Mack Carmichael (Chapter 8: Lawmen, Criminals, and Victims of Crime)*

Hillcrest Memorial Park, Dallas, Texas
    Greer Garson (Chapter 2: Artists, Performers, and Directors)*

Lubbock City Cemetery, Lubbock, Texas
    Charles "Buddy" Holly (Chapter 2: Artists, Performers, and Directors)*

National Cemetery, San Antonio, Texas
    Louis R. Rocco (Chapter 13: Wartime Leaders and Victims Since the Spanish-American War, 1898)*

Oakwood Cemetery, Hamilton, Texas
    Ollie P. "Brushy Bill" Roberts (Chapter 8: Lawmen, Criminals, and Victims of Crime)*

Oakwood Cemetery, Austin, Texas
    Thomas "Tom" Green (Chapter 12: Wartime Leaders and Victims to the End of the Indian Wars in New Mexico, 1886)*

Restland Memorial Park Cemetery, Dallas, Texas
    B.J.O. Nordfeldt (Chapter 2: Artists, Performers, and Directors)

Texas State Cemetery, Austin, Texas
    Hugh McLeod (Chapter 12: Wartime Leaders and Victims to the End of the Indian Wars in New Mexico, 1886)*

West of the Pecos Museum, Pecos, Texas
    Robert Clay Allison (Chapter 8: Lawmen, Criminals, and Victims of Crimes)*

VIRGINIA (in alphabetical order by cemetery names)

Fredericksburg City Cemetery, Fredericksburg, Virginia
    Henry H. Sibley (Chapter 12: Wartime Leaders and Victims to the End of the Indian Wars in New Mexico, 1886)*

Ivy Hill Cemetery, Alexandria, Virginia
    Catharine Carter Critcher (Chapter 2: Artists, Performers, and Directors)
    Werner Von Braun (Chapter 11: Scientists and Medical Personnel)*

National Cemetery, Arlington, Virginia
    George Burnett (Chapter 12: Wartime Leaders and Victims to the End of the Indian Wars in New Mexico, 1886)*
    Nathan A.M. Dudley (Chapter 8: Lawmen, Criminals, and Victims of Crime)*
    Leslie Groves (Chapter 13: Wartime Leaders and Victims Since the Spanish-American War, 1898)*
    Robert C. Lopez (Chapter 13: Wartime Leaders and Victims Since the Spanish-American War, 1898)
    William "Bill" Mauldin (Chapter 13: Wartime Leaders and Victims Since the Spanish-American War, 1898)*
    Robert B. Mitchell (Chapter 9: Political, Diplomatic, and Judicial Leaders)
    John Cary "Red" Morgan (Chapter 13: Wartime Leaders and Victims Since the Spanish-American War, 1898)*
    William Sterling "Deak" Parsons (Chapter 13: Wartime Leaders and Victims Since the Spanish-American War, 1898)*
    John J. "Black Jack" Pershing (Chapter 13: Wartime Leaders and Victims Since the Spanish-American War, 1898)*
    Thomas Shaw (Chapter 12: Wartime Leaders and Victims to the End of the Indian Wars in New Mexico, 1886)
    William Howard Taft (Chapter 9: Political, Diplomatic, and Judicial Leaders)*
    Kenneth Walker (Chapter 13: Wartime Leaders and Victims Since the Spanish-American War, 1898)

WASHINGTON

Rose Hill Cemetery, Kirkland, Washington
    Susan "Susie" Parks Kendrick (Chapter 13: Wartime Leaders and Victims Since the Spanish-American War, 1898)

Vancouver Barracks Cemetery, Vancouver, Washington
    Moses Williams (Chapter 12: Wartime Leaders and Victims to the End of the Indian Wars in New Mexico, 1886)

WASHINGTON, D.C.

Soldiers and Airmen Home National Cemetery, Washington, D.C.
    Thomas Boyne (Chapter 12: Wartime Leaders and Victims to the End of the Indian Wars in New Mexico, 1886)
    John Denny (Chapter 12: Wartime Leaders and Victims to the End of the Indian Wars in New Mexico, 1886)

WEST VIRGINIA

Maplewood Cemetery, Elkins, West Virginia
    Stephen B. Elkins (Chapter 9: Political, Diplomatic, and Judicial Leaders)*

FOREIGN COUNTRIES *(public cemeteries in alphabetical order)*

DENMARK

Assistens Cemetery, Copenhagen, Denmark
    Niels Bohr (Chapter 11: Scientists and Medical Personnel)

FRANCE

Cimetière du Pére Lachaise, Paris, France
    James D. "Jim" Morrison (Chapter 2: Artists, Performers, and Directors)*

MEXICO

Cementario Municipal, Parral, Mexico
    Francisco "Pancho" Villa (Chapter 13: Wartime Leaders and Victims Since the Spanish-American War, 1898)*

Appendix C

Famous New Mexicans Who Have Been Cremated

"*Cuando Muera*"	"When I Die"
Cuando muera	When I die
no me entierren	don't bury me
debajo de la tierra	beneath the earth
de un camposanto.	of a cemetery.
Que desparramen	Have my ashes
mis cenizas	scattered
alrededor de mi	around my little
casita en la lomita	house atop the tiny hill
donde yo me crié.	where I was raised.
Que se las lleve	Let the wind carry
el viento a las milpas	them to the cornfields
donde yo escardé.	where I once hoed.
Que den sus	Let them skip
golpes y saltos	and jump freely
igual	just like the
que las libertad	freedom
de la cual yo gocé.	I once enjoyed.
Que lleguen	Let them
a parar	rest
en sus propio destino	in their just destiny
sin estar enterradas	without being buried
y amarradas	and tied
debajo de la tierra	below the earth
sin poder volar.	without being able to fly.
	—Nasario García[1]

Chapter 2: Artists, Performers, and Directors
Ansel Adams: ashes scattered off a cliff in Yosemite National Park, California
Kenneth Adams
Gustave Baumann: ashes buried beside an Aspen tree along the road to the Santa Fe ski basin
Ernest Blumenschein
Dorothy Brett: ashes scattered on rocks below Lobo Peak near D.H. Lawrence's ranch
Andrew Dasburg
John Denver
Laura Gilpin: ashes buried at Evergreen Cemetery, Colorado Springs, Colorado
Peter Hurd: ashes buried at his Sentinel Ranch, San Patricio, New Mexico
Carl Raymond Jonson: ashes kept in a vault at the Jonson Gallery on the University of New Mexico campus, Albuquerque, New Mexico
Dorothea Lange: ashes scattered in the Pacific Ocean
Herbert "Herbie" Mann
John Gaw Meem: ashes kept in a wall niche at the Church of the Holy Faith, Santa Fe, New Mexico
Roger Miller
Willard Nash
Georgia O'Keeffe: ashes scattered over Ghost Ranch, New Mexico
Orrin Sheldon Parsons
Esquípula Romero de Romero: ashes scattered over the Sandia Mountains east of Albuquerque, New Mexico
Olive Rush: ashes buried in family plot in Park Cemetery, Fairmont, Indiana
John Henry Sharp: ashes buried at the Mountain View Mausoleum, Mountain View, Altadena, California
John Sloan: ashes scattered near his birthplace in Lock Haven, Pennsylvania
Katherine Stinson-Otero: ashes buried at the National Cemetery, Santa Fe, New Mexico
Walter Ufer: ashes scattered over Taos Valley
Vivian Vance

Chapter 3: Authors and Composers
Mary Austin: ashes buried in concrete vault on Mount Picacho, New Mexico
Harold Witter Bynner: ashes buried below stone sculpture in house yard on Atalaya Hill, Santa Fe, New Mexico
Ina Sizer Cassidy: ashes buried at Fairview Cemetery, Santa Fe, New Mexico
Margaret "Peggy" Pond Church: ashes scattered near Garcia Canyon, east of Los Alamos, New Mexico
Agnes Morley Cleaveland: ashes scattered at her Cleaveland Ranch, Datil, New Mexico
Erna Fergusson: ashes scattered over the West Mesa, Albuquerque, New Mexico
Harvey Fergusson
D.H. Lawrence: ashes mixed in concrete at his monument at Kiowa Ranch, San Cristobal, New Mexico
John Sinclair: ashes scattered over "my beloved New Mexico," in his words
Frank Waters: ashes buried or scattered at various places in his house yard, Arroyo Seco, New Mexico

Chapter 4: Cultural Preservationists
Adolph Bandelier: ashes scattered in Frijoles Canyon, Bandelier National Park, New Mexico

E. Boyd: ashes scattered in hills surrounding the Cerro Gordo Park, Santa Fe, New Mexico

Kenneth M. Chapman: ashes scattered on foothills near the School of American Research, Santa Fe, New Mexico

Florence Hawley Ellis: ashes scattered at Ghost Ranch, New Mexico

Antonio Gilberto Espinosa: ashes buried at Mount Calvary Cemetery, Albuquerque, New Mexico

Edgar Hewett: ashes in a wall niche in the south wall of the interior courtyard at the Museum of Fine Arts, Santa Fe, New Mexico

Janaloo Hill Hough: ashes buried on a hill overlooking Shakespeare, New Mexico

Clyde Kluckhohn: ashes scattered over Ramah, New Mexico

Charles Lummis: ashes in a wall niche in the courtyard of his home, El Alisal, Los Angeles, California

Alfonso Ortiz: ashes scattered over a sacred mountain near his native San Juan Pueblo, New Mexico

Elsie Clews Parsons: ashes left at the crematoria

John D. Robb

Chapter 5: Business Leaders
Franz Huning: ashes buried at Fairview Cemetery, Albuquerque, New Mexico

Chapter 6: Educational Leaders
Francisco "Frank" Angel, Jr.: half his ashes scattered in Brazil and half near the Gallinas River in New Mexico

Thomas C. Donnelly

Dorothy Dunn Kramer: ashes buried at the San Gorgonio Memorial Park, Banning, California

Ashley Pond, Jr.: ashes sent to Detroit, Michigan, for burial at an unspecified cemetery

Thomas "Tom" Popejoy

George I. Sánchez: ashes buried at the Forest Oaks Cemetery, Austin, Texas

Frank Springer: ashes buried at the Masonic Cemetery, Las Vegas, New Mexico

William Tight: ashes sent from California to an unspecified destination in Ohio via Albuquerque

E.J. "Jack" Workman: ashes scattered over the New Mexico Tech golf course

Chapter 7: Sung and Unsung Heroes
Irma Flores Gonzales

Clinton Jencks

Ernest T. "Ernie" Mills

Ernest Thompson Seton: ashes scattered over High Cone, northeast of his Seton Castle near Santa Fe, New Mexico

Chapter 8: Lawmen, Criminals, and Victims of Crime
John Ehrlichman

Edward Lee Howard

Charles Winstead

Chapter 9: Political, Diplomatic, and Judicial Leaders
Thomas F. "Tom" Bolack: most of his ashes scattered over his B-Square Ranch near Farmington, New Mexico
John Campbell: ashes scattered in the Pecos Wilderness, New Mexico
Louise Holland Coe: ashes buried at the private Coe family cemetery, Glencoe, New Mexico
H.B. Fergusson
Herbert James Hagerman: ashes buried at the family plot in an unspecified cemetery in Milwaukee, Wisconsin
Lionel Allen Sheldon
Elver S. "Johnny" Walker: ashes buried at the National Cemetery, Santa Fe, New Mexico

Chapter 10: Religious Leaders
Yogi Bhajan

Chapter 11: Scientists and Medical Personnel
Carl H. Gellenthien: ashes scattered near Valmora, New Mexico
Eric Jette: ashes buried at Guaje Pines Cemetery, Los Alamos, New Mexico
Roy Nakayama: ashes scattered in his favorite places
John P. Stapp: ashes buried at the Fort Bliss National Cemetery, El Paso, Texas
Clyde Tombaugh: ashes scattered over Tortugas Mountain east of Las Cruces, New Mexico
Stanislaw "Stan" Ulam

Chapter 13: Wartime Leaders and Victims Since the Spanish-American War, 1898
Carl Gorman
Susan "Susie" Parks Kendrick: ashes buried at the Rose Hill Cemetery, Kirkland, Washington
Franklin D. Miller
J. Robert Oppenheimer: ashes scattered off the Virgin Islands in the Atlantic Ocean

APPENDIX D

FAMOUS NEW MEXICANS WHO ORIGINALLY CAME TO NEW MEXICO TO RECOVER THEIR HEALTH OR TO ACCOMPANY SOMEONE ELSE WHO WAS ILL

After learning that he had tuberculosis, Kenneth Chapman "had an unexpected opportunity to talk with an acquaintance...who had just returned [to Wisconsin] from New Mexico, fit as a fiddle, after a year out of doors, part of it traveling by wagon with another health seeker, from end to end of the [New Mexico] Territory." Impressed by what he heard about the healing qualities of New Mexico, Chapman declared, "for [me] the Southwest and sunshine!"[1]

Thousands have come to New Mexico to attempt to recover their health. The territory, and later the state, was so well known for its salubrious conditions that it billed itself the "Wellness Country." Most healthseekers of the period from the late nineteenth century to the 1920s came to New Mexico to recover from tuberculosis (also known as the White Plague, TB, or, most commonly, consumption).[2] While many came alone, others came with friends or family members. According to one estimate, by 1920 ten percent of all New Mexicans were either healthseekers or their relatives. An estimated third of Santa Fe's artists and intellectuals of the 1920s originally came to recover from TB or from other respiratory ailments. In towns like Silver City as high as sixty percent of all households had at least one so-called "lunger" or patient with TB.[3]

For one reason or another, a large percentage of healthseekers were unsuccessful in their quest. Others enjoyed greater success, either returning to their home states or deciding to live out their years in New Mexico. Several of the latter remained to make major contributions in New Mexico history. In fact, only two of the thirty-one healthseekers listed below died of tuberculosis or whatever ailment that had first brought them to New Mexico.[4] Most lived to an old age, with an average life span of seventy-one highly productive years.

Individuals listed with an asterisk (*) suffered from tuberculosis when they first arrived in New Mexico. Ages at death are noted in parentheses.

Chapter 2: Artists, Performers, and Directors
Gerald Cassidy: 1869-1934 (64): arrived in Santa Fe, 1912
John O. Crosby: 1926-2002 (76): arrived in Los Alamos, 1940
William Henderson (arrived with his ill wife, Alice Corbin Henderson, 1916): 1877-1943 (66)
Oliver LaGrone (arrived with his ill sister who had TB, 1931): 1906-95 (88)
John Gaw Meem: 1894-1983 (88); arrived in Santa Fe, 1920*
Kathryn Kennedy O'Connor: 1894-1965 (71); arrived in Albuquerque, 1927*
Orrin Sheldon Parsons: 1866-1943 (77)
William "Will" Shuster: 1893-1969 (75); arrived in Santa Fe, 1920*
Katherine Stinson-Otero: 1896-1977 (81)*
Carlos Vierra: 1876-1937 (61); arrived in Santa Fe, 1904

Chapter 3: Authors and Composers
S. Omar Barker (arrived with his asthmatic mother): 1894-1985 (90)
Witter Bynner: 1881-1968 (86): arrived in Santa Fe, 1922
Alice Corbin Henderson: 1881-1949 (68): arrived in Santa Fe, 1916*
Paul Horgan (arrived with his ill father who had TB, 1915): 1903-1995 (91)
D.H. Lawrence: 1885-1930 (44); arrived in Taos, 1922*
Frieda Lawrence (arrived with her husband, D.H.): 1879-1956 (77)

Chapter 4: Cultural Preservationists
Kenneth Chapman: 1875-1968 (92)*
Charles Lummis: 1859-1928 (69); arrived in New Mexico, 1884; returned as a healthseeker, 1888
Frances V. Scholes: 1897-1979 (82); arrived in Albuquerque, 1924*

Chapter 5: Business Leaders
Josiah Gregg: 1806-50 (43); arrived in Santa Fe, 1831*

Chapter 7: Sung and Unsung Heroes
Elliott S. Barker (arrived with his asthmatic mother): 1886-1988 (101)
Ralph Bunche (arrived with his ill mother, father, and uncle, 1915): 1904-1971 (67)
Carrie Tingley: 1877-1961 (84); arrived in Albuquerque, 1911*

Chapter 8: Lawmen, Criminals, and Victims of Crime
Catherine Antrim: 1829-74 (45); arrived in Santa Fe, 1873*

Chapter 9: Political, Diplomatic, and Judicial Leaders
Clinton P. Anderson: 1895-1975 (80); arrived in Albuquerque, 1917*
Holm O. Bursum, Sr.: 1867-1953 (86); arrived in New Mexico, 1881
Bronson M. Cutting: 1888-1935 (46); arrived in Santa Fe, 1910*
Merritt C. Mechem: 1870-1946 (75)
William G. Ritch: 1830-1904 (74)
Albert G. Simms: 1882-1964 (82); arrived in Albuquerque, 1906*
Clyde Tingley (arrived with his ill fiancée, Carrie): 1881-1960 (79)

Chapter 10: Religious Leaders
Ross Calvin: 1889-1970 (80)

Chapter 11: Scientists and Medical Personnel
Carl Gellenthien: 1900-89 (89); arrived at Valmora, 1924*
Robert H. Goddard: 1882-1945 (62); arrived in Roswell, 1930*
William Randolph Lovelace I: 1883-1968 (85); arrived in Fort Sumner, 1906*
Lucy Whiteside: 1871-1958 (87)

Chapters 12 and 13: Wartime Leaders and Victims
Christopher "Kit" Carson: 1809-68 (58); arrived in Santa Fe, 1826
Dorothy McKibbin: 1897-1985 (88); arrived in Santa Fe, 1925*
Harry P. Stagg, 1898-2000 (101); arrived in New Mexico, 1925

ACKNOWLEDGEMENTS

1. Quoted in Dayton Duncan, *Horatio's Drive: America's First Road Trip* (New York: Alfred A. Knopf, 2003): xiv.

2. Quentin, *Eternal New Mexicans: A Guide to the Final Resting Places of 350 Noteworthy Persons of the Land of Enchantment* (Oakland: Lawrence W. Rand, 1994).

1
NOT FORGOTTEN?

1. Carlos Ruiz Zafón, *The Shadow of the Wind* (New York: Penguin Books, 2005): 172.

2. Ansel Adams's *Moonrise, Hernandez, New Mexico* (October 31, 1941) is the most famous example of cemeteries depicted in New Mexico art. Adams recalled the moment he took this extraordinary photograph with the afternoon sun "blaz[ing] a brilliant white upon the crosses in the [San Juan del Chama] church cemetery." Ansel Adams, *Ansel Adams: An Autobiography* (Boston: Little, Brown and Company, 1996): 231; Ansel Adams, *Examples: The Making of Forty Photographs* (Boston: Little, Brown, and Company, 1983): 40-3. The cost of a silver print of *Moonrise, Hernandez, New Mexico* was listed at $165,000 at the Andrew Smith Gallery in Santa Fe, New Mexico, in April 2005. Also see Isabel Foreman, "Hernandez and the Photo," *Impact Magazine*, May 27, 1986. Other examples of famous photographs featuring New Mexico cemeteries include Russell Lee's *Monument in a Catholic Cemetery* and *Entrance to the Cemetery*, both taken in Peñasco, New Mexico, and included in William Wroth, ed., *Russell Lee's FSA Photographs of Chamiscal and Peñasco, New Mexico* (Santa Fe: Ancient City Press, 1985): 118-19. John Young-Hunter's *Campo Santo* (n.d.) is part of the Museum of Albuquerque's permanent collection, and Stuart Davis's painting of the entrance to Santa Fe's Rosario Cemetery, entitled *New Mexican Gate* (1923), is included in Sharyn Rohlfsen Udall, *Modernist Painting in New Mexico, 1913-1935* (Albuquerque: University of New Mexico Press, 1988): 156. For examples of cemeteries in New Mexico literature see Mari Ulmer, *Midnight at the Camposanto: A Taos Festival Mystery* (Scottsdale, Arizona: Poisoned Pen Press, 2000) and Armand Garnet Ruffo, *At Geronimo's Grave* (Regina, Saskatchewan: Coteau Books, 2001). For guides to important cemeteries see Margaret Nava, *Remembering: A Guide to New Mexico Cemeteries, Monuments, and Memorials* (Santa Fe: Sunstone Press, 2006); Bryan Wooley *et. al.*, *Final Destinations: A Travel Guide for Remarkable Cemeteries* (Denton: University of North Texas Press, 2000); Jean Arbeiter and Linda D. Cirino, *Permanent Addresses: A Guide to the Resting Places of Famous Americans* (New York: M. Evans, 1983), and Sarach Vowell's off-beat, but politically savvy, *Assassination Vacation* (New York: Simon and Shuster, 2005): 88-92, 106-09, 189-93. Also see Marc Simmons, "Grave Matters," *Santa Fe Reporter*, July 4, 1984.

3. The best example of generational exploitation is described in Stephen Tatum, *Inventing Billy the Kid: Visions of the Outlaw in America* (Albuquerque: University of New Mexico Press, 1982).

4. New Mexico cemetery folk art represents a field of study worthy of much additional attention. Previous studies have focused on *camposantos*, or traditional Hispanic Catholic cemeteries. These works include Nancy Hunter Warren, "New Mexico Village *Camposantos*," *Markers*, vol. 4 (1987): 115-29; Laura Sue Sanborn, "*Camposantos*: Sacred Places of the Southwest," *Markers*, vol. 6 (1989): 158-79; Susan Hazen-Hammond, "*Camposantos*: Dios Da y Dios Quita," *New Mexico Magazine*, vol. 64 (July 1986): 30-6; Dorothy Benrimo, *Camposantos: A Photographic Essay* (Fort Worth: Amon Carter Museum of Western Art, 1966).

5. On cemeteries as tourist attractions, see Kevin Britz, "'Boot Hill Burlesque': The Frontier Cemetery as Tourist Attraction in Tombstone, Arizona, and Dodge City, Kansas," *Journal of Arizona History*, vol. 44 (Autumn 2003): 211-42; Ben T. Traywick, *Tombstone's Boothill* (Tombstone: Red Marie's Bookstore, 1994). Western towns have no monopoly on the commercial use of cemeteries. Tourist literature advertises a tour of "Boston's oldest burying grounds" led by "your personal gravedigger guide" who gladly "shares an in depth knowledge of all things shadowy and sinister." On cemeteries as intentionally well-manicured parks, see David Charles Sloane, *The Last Great Necessity: Cemeteries in American History* (Baltimore: Johns Hopkins University Press, 1991): 159-90.

6. For details about New Mexicans who have received the Medal of Honor, see Chapters 12 and 13 and Mike Cody and Ken Dusenberry, "The Medal of Honor in New Mexico" enclosed in correspondence from Ken Dusenberry to the author, November 18, 2004.

7. For early Native American burial rites, see Douglas R. Mitchell and Judy L. Brunson-Hadley, eds., *Ancient Burial Practices in the American Southwest* (Albuquerque: University of New Mexico, 2004). For early Hispanic traditions, see Martina E. Will de Chaparro, "God Gives and God Takes Away: Death and Dying in New Mexico, 1760-1850" (Unpublished Ph.D. dissertation, University of New Mexico, 2000) and Martina E. Will de Chaparro, "From Body to Corpse: The Treatment of the Dead in Eighteenth- and Nineteenth-Century New Mexico," *New Mexico Historical Review*, vol. 79 (Winter 2004): 1-29 and Martina E. Will de Chaparro, *Death and Dying in New Mexcio* (Albuquerque: University of New Mexico Press, 2007).

8. Will de Chaparro, "God Gives," 189, 225. On burials beneath the floor of the Parroquia, the old Catholic church in Santa Fe before its replacement by St. Francis Cathedral, see Bruce Ellis, *Bishop Lamy's Santa Fe Cathedral* (Albuquerque: University of New Mexico Press, 1985): 161, 166, 191n. The high cost of mid-nineteenth century church funerals in New Mexico was described and criticized in W.W. Davis, *El Gringo: New Mexico and Her People* (Lincoln: University of Nebraska Press, 1982; originally published in 1857): 185-87. The practice of burying the dead beneath church floors was not unique to New Mexico. See, for example, Sharon Debartolo Carmack, *Your Guide to Cemetery Research* (Cincinnati: Betterway Publications, 2002): 176.

9. James Henry Carleton, *Diary of An Excursion to the Ruins of Abó, Quarai, and Gran Quivira in New Mexico in 1853* (Santa Fe: Stagecoach Press, 1965): 50; Richard Melzer, *Coming of Age in the Great Depression: The Civilian Conservation Corps Experience in New Mexico, 1933-42* (Las Cruces: Yucca Tree Press, 2000): 76.

10. Douglas R. Givens, *Alfred Vincent Kidder and the Development of Americanist Archaeology* (Albuquerque: University of New Mexico Press, 1992): Figure 12, following page 76. This photo is also included in John L. Kessell, *Kiva, Cross, and Crown, The Pecos Indians and New Mexico, 1540-1840* (Washington, D.C.: National Park Service,

1979): 485. An equally gruesome photo of Native American "mummies" collected by archeologist Richard Wetherill in Grand Gulch is included in Kathryn Gabriel, *Marietta Wetherill: Life With the Navajos in Chaco Canyon* (Albuquerque: University of New Mexico Press, 1997): 129. Wetherill's widow described her husband's excavations of Indian remains in Ibid., 64-76.

11. E. Boyd, Historical Notes, in Benrimo, *Camposantos*, 2.

12. Interview with John L. Kessell (Vargas biographer), February 21, 2004; John L. Kessell, ed., *Remote Beyond Compare: Letters of Don Diego de Vargas to His Family from New Spain and New Mexico, 1675-1706* (Albuquerque: University of New Mexico Press, 1989): 82-90. Also see Marc Simmons, "The Death of New Mexico Governor Diego de Vargas," *Santa Fe New Mexican*, April 5, 2003.

13. E. Boyd, Historical Notes, in Benrimo, *Camposantos*, 2. The colonial exceptions are two Franciscans, Father Asencio de Zárate and Father Gerónimo de la Llana, whose remains were discovered in the Conquistadora chapel of what is now St. Francis Cathedral in Santa Fe. Fray Angélico Chávez, "The Unique Tomb of Fathers Zárate and de la Llana in Santa Fe," *New Mexico Historical Review*, vol. 40 (April 1965): 101-15.

14. Father Padilla's remains have been the subject of much mystery, having risen from the ground (or been dug up) on at least six occasions, in 1775, 1819, 1889, 1895, 1914, and 1948. See Fray Angélico Chávez, "The Mystery of Father Padilla," *El Palacio*, vol. 54 (November 1947): 251-68, and Fray Angélico Chávez, "A Sequel to 'The Mystery of Father Padilla,'" *El Palacio*, vol. 59 (December 1952): 386-89; Richard Melzer, "Mystery of the Priest's Coffin," *Valencia County News-Bulletin*, January 19, 2002.

15. Martina E. Will de Chaparro, "The 'Abominable Stench' of Rotting Corpses: Protecting Public Health by Exiling New Mexico's Dead, 1804-50," *La Crónica de Nuevo México*, no. 53 (August 2000): 2-5; Will de Chaparro, "God Gives," 217n, 239, 267. Hispanic artisans employed their skills to design grave markers in several villages. Some of the best examples of this folk art can be found in the Galisteo Catholic cemetery. Simmons, "Grave Lessons," 20; Stanley M. Hordes, *To the End of the Earth: A History of the Crypto-Jews of New Mexico* (New York: Columbia University Press, 2005): 252-53. In an effort to protect their dead, Hispanics often built highly decorative small iron or wooden picket fences, known as *cerquitas*, around gravesites.

16. David L. Cohn, *The Good Old Days: A History of American Morals and Manners as Seen Through the Sears, Roebuck Catalog* (New York: Simon and Shuster, 1940): 233-34. For an example of a "Memorial Department" in a Sears, Roebuck Catalog, see *The Sears, Roebuck and Company Consumers Guide, Fall 1900, Catalog 110* (reprinted by Northfield, Illinois: DBI Books, 1970): 739. Unfortunately, there is no way to determine how many Sears, Roebuck tombstones were ordered in New Mexico, no less how many still exist in cemeteries across the state today.

17. Other contenders for this distinction include Slap Jack Bill, Handsome Harry, Scarface Charlie, Rattlesnake Sam, Dirty-face Mike, Cockeyed Frank, Mysterious Dave, and Coal Oil Johnnie. Marc Simmons, "Trail Robbers," *Santa Fe Reporter*, July 15, 1987.

18. Carmack, *Cemetery Research*, 20; *Laws of the State of New Mexico Passed by the Fourth Regular Session of the Legislature of the State of New Mexico, 1919* (Albuquerque: Albright and Anderson, 1919): Chapter 85, 161-71. On the creation of New Mexico's Department of Public Health see Richard Melzer, "A Dark and Terrible Moment: The Spanish Flu Epidemic of 1918 in New Mexico," *New Mexico Historical Review*, vol. 57 (July 1982): 229-32.

19. Carmack, *Cemetery Research*, 23. Starting in 1995, the University of Maryland's School

of Medicine has held an annual clinicopathological conference to consider the cause of death of such famous individuals as Alexander the Great, Ludwig van Beethoven, Christopher Columbus, King George III, Napoleon Bonaparte, Edgar Allan Poe, and Florence Nightingale. Despite using the most modern medical diagnoses, conference findings for even these historical figures remain quite speculative. *Newsweek*, August 8, 2005

20. A good medical glossary explaining main causes of death is found in Carmack, *Cemetery Research*, Appendix C, 234-43.

21. Edwin Murphy, *After the Funeral: The Posthumous Adventures of Famous Corpses* (New York: Barnes and Noble Books, 1995): ix.

22. Frederick Nolan, *The West of Billy the Kid* (Norman: University of Oklahoma Press, 1998): 28, with a photo of Catherine's headboard while it still marked her grave in Silver City. Silver City has recently attempted to have this wooden marker returned from Lincoln, but without success. *Albuquerque Journal*, January 18, 2004

23. According to the New Mexico Office of Vital Records and Health Services, the percentage of cremations in New Mexico increased from twenty-five percent of all final dispositions to forty percent in just ten years, 1991 to 2001. *Albuquerque Journal*, March 28, 2004

24. Agnes Morley Cleaveland, *No Life for a Lady* (Lincoln: University of Nebraska Press, 1977): 39.

25. *Silver City Enterprise*, September 15, 1933

26. *Lincoln County News*, October 27, 1939. Cree had died in February 1929. *Alamogordo News*, April 4, 1929

27. Robert Julyan, *The Place Names of New Mexico* (Albuquerque: University of New Mexico, 1998): xxiii, 107; interview with Robert Julyan, November 6, 2004.

28. Robert Julyan to the author, February 5, 2005.

29. John A. Lomax and Alan Lomax, *Cowboy Songs and Other Frontier Ballads* (New York: Macmillan, 1945): 300-02; interview with Mark L. Gardner (Western music historian), July 7, 2005. Death and burial are common themes in many Western songs, including "The Dying Cowboy," "I Wanted to Die in the Desert," and "The Cowboy's Lament." Lomax and Lomax, *Cowboy Songs*, 48-51, 323-24, 417-22.

30. Sister Blandina Segale, *At the End of the Santa Fe Trail* (Cincinnati: Sisters of Charity, 1996): 91, 289n. A photo depicting Sister Alphonsa Thompson's burial on the Santa Fe Trail was taken at a reenactment outside Santa Fe in 1902 as part of the fiftieth anniversary of the Sisters of Loretto's arrival in New Mexico. Marc Simmons, "Lamy's 1867 Caravan Faced Hardships on the Santa Fe Trail," *Santa Fe New Mexican*, September 29, 2001. The photo, frequently claimed to have been taken at the actual funeral in 1867, appeared in Clark Kimball and Marcus J. Smith, *The Hospital at the End of the Santa Fe Trail: A Photographic History of St. Vincent Hospital* (Santa Fe: Rydal Press, 1995): 36.

31. Quoted in Richard Melzer, *When We Were Young in the West* (Santa Fe: Sunstone Press, 2003): 26.

32. Marc Simmons, *Murder on the Santa Fe Trail* (El Paso: Texas Western Press, 1987): 33, 70-1.

33. Julyan, *Place Names*, 94; George Hackler, *The Butterfield Trail in New Mexico* (Las Cruces: Yucca Enterprises, 2005): 123; Richard C. Hindley, "On the Trail of Butterfield," *New Mexico Magazine*, vol. 48 (May-June 1970): 34. For photos of isolated gravesites along the Butterfield Trail, see Hackler, *Butterfield Trail*, 114, 121, 187.

34. Julyan, *Place Names*, 12, 180, 198. For a similarly grisly tale of isolated gravesites near Las Cruces see the *New Mexico Sentinel*, June 5, 1938. Julyan counted as many as twenty-nine places in New Mexico named Dead Man or Deadman. Julyan also lists places like Dead Horse, Dead Cow, and Dead Dog in Ibid., 106-07. Some say that Ghost Ranch was named, in part, because "cottonwoods on the property were reputed to have served as gallows for local cattle thieves." Ibid., 146. Others say that the ranch is named after Ghost House, the oldest structure on the property, where "a family had been murdered...and now a ghostly woman haunted the building by night, clutching a spectral infant in her arms." Michael Berry, *Georgia O'Keeffe* (New York: Chelsea House, 1988): 78. Still others refer to *el Rancho de los Brujos*, or the Ranch of the Witches, "associated with legendary evildoers." Lesley Poling-Kempes, *Ghost Ranch* (Tucson: University of Arizona Press, 2005): 3. Roadside gravesites should not be confused with roadside crosses, known as *descansos*, that mark the locations of accidental or unattended deaths, with the victims of these tragedies buried elsewhere. See Anita Torres Smith, "*Descansos*: Markers to Heaven," *Journal of Big Bend Studies*, vol. 12 (2000): 259-69. According to research conducted by Kathleen McRee and Troy Fernandez, the earliest reference to a *descanso* in New Mexico dates back to 1744. An 1826 map shows the locations of numerous *descansos* along the pathways and roads of northern New Mexico. *Albuquerque Journal*, June 12, 2005

35. Clifford E. Trafzer, *The Kit Carson Campaign: The Last Great Navajo War* (Norman: University of Oklahoma Press, 1982): 190-93.

36. *Albuquerque Journal*, May 8 and June 3, 2005

37. *Albuquerque Journal*, June 5, 2005

38. Quoted in Mark L. Gardner and Marc Simmons, *The Mexican War Correspondence of Richard Smith Elliott* (Norman: University of Oklahoma Press, 1997): 224. Emphasis in the original.

39. Ann and Albert Manchester, "Return to Massacre Canyon," *Persimmon Hill*, vol. 28 (Autumn 2000): 66-7; New Mexico Hometown Heroes Committee flyer, June 1997; Ken Dusenberry, "The Medal of Honor Society and the New Mexico Hometown Heroes Committee: A Brief History," 5, enclosed in correspondence from Ken Dusenberry to the author, November 18, 2004.

40. Dean W. Holt, *American Military Cemeteries* (Jefferson, North Carolina: McFarland and Company, 1992): 337; *Carlsbad Current-Argus*, March 13, 1949; *Albuquerque Journal North*, June 8, 1985. Remains were transferred to the Santa Fe National Cemetery from Fort Stanton in 1896, Forts Sumner and Marcy in 1906, Forts Wingate and Craig in 1912, and Fort Hatch in 1933. Holt, *Military Cemeteries*, 337.

41. Leo E. Oliva, *Fort Union and the Frontier Army in the Southwest* (Santa Fe: National Park Service Professional Paper, 1993): 577. On an unmarked cemetery discovered at Fort Fillmore, see Richard Wadsworth, "The Fort Fillmore Cemetery," *Southern New Mexico Historical Review*, vol. 8 (January 2001): 1-6. The post cemetery at Fort McRae was submerged with the construction of the Elephant Butte dam and reservoir in 1916.

42. See Chapter 14, No. 383. Jim Harris found a rather mysterious non-military gravestone with the words "unknown soldier" in the Antioch Cemetery in Lea County, New Mexico. Reportedly, an ill soldier came to the door of a local family near the end of World War

I, but died in the Spanish flu epidemic before anyone had a chance to learn his name, no less anything else about him. See Harris, "The Lea County Museum History Notebook," *Lovington Daily Leader*, February 11, 2005.

43. On the Alameda cemetery and its excavation, see the *Albuquerque Journal*, December 12, 2003. On the discovery of other, long-forgotten Albuquerque cemeteries, see the *Albuquerque Journal*, January 15, 1955, and the *Albuquerque Tribune*, September 4, 1969. In the most recent discovery of human remains below a New Mexico construction site, an estimated twenty-five bodies have been discovered, buried beneath the parking lot of the Sweeney Convention Center in Santa Fe. The remains were found in what is believed to be an ancient Tewa Indian village dating back to about 1200 A.D. Work at the site was interrupted until issues regarding the bodies were resolved to the satisfaction of both pueblo tribal leaders and city officials. *Albuquerque Journal*, November 6 and December 16, 2005; *Santa Fe New Mexican*, December 16, 2005

44. *Santa Fe New Mexican*, November 13, 1997; Antonio R. Garcez, *Adobe Angels: The Ghosts of Las Cruces and Southern New Mexico* (Santa Fe: Red Rabbit Press, 1996): 76-8; Glenna Dean, "Endangered Cemeteries and Burial Grounds," Paper presented at the Historical Society of New Mexico's Annual Conference, Clayton, New Mexico, April 22, 2005; interview with Robert L. Hart (President, Socorro Historical Society), October 22, 2005.

45. Jenkins quoted in John Pen LaFarge, *Turn Left at the Sleeping Dog: Scripting the Santa Fe Legend, 1920-1955* (Albuquerque: University of New Mexico Press, 2001): 222. Also see the *Albuquerque Journal North*, June 8, 1985. At least one ghost from the former graveyard is rumored to haunt the PERA building.

46. Will de Chaparro, "God Gives," 193; Enrique R. Lamadrid, *Hermanitos Comanchitos* (Albuquerque: University of New Mexico Press, 2003): 184.

47. *Socorro Defensor Chieftain*, March 6, 2004; *Albuquerque Journal*, March 31, 2002

48. *Albuquerque Tribune*, November 7, 1988. Also see the *Albuquerque Journal*, May 30, 1956, and Chapter 12, No. 301.

49. Thomas J. Steele, *Works and Days: A History of San Felipe Neri Church, 1867-95* (Albuquerque: Albuquerque Museum, 1983): 75; Ezekiel Gutiérrez, "Forgotten Cemeteries in Albuquerque," *La Herencia*, vol. 48 (Winter 2005: 33.

50. *Sierra County Advocate*, January 14, 1927; H.E. Blake, "How the Law Came to White Oaks, New Mexico," *Farmington Times Hustler*, June 23, 1933. Mortician Harry Strong said that in the 1880s, "Gamblers and transients who died with their boots on were often buried in unmarked graves in the sandhills east of the railroad tracks" in New Town Albuquerque. Bryan, *Albuquerque Remembered*, 189.

51. See, for example, Ellen S. Mills, "Graves in the Gravel: The Unmarked Cemetery of Las Vegas, New Mexico" (Unpublished M.A. thesis, New Mexico Highlands University, 1979).

52. Bainbridge Bunting, Thomas R. Lyons, and Margil Lyons, "Penitente Brotherhood *Moradas* and Their Architecture" in Marta Weigle, ed., *Hispanic Arts and Ethnohistory* (Santa Fe: Ancient City Press, 1983): 37.

53. Howard Bryan, *True Tales of the American Southwest* (Santa Fe: Clear Light Publishers, 1998): 136-37. Native American gravesites are not the only sites raided by greedy grave robbers. The digging of treasure hunters among interred bodies at Gran Quivira has already been noted. In early 2005 a Buffalo Soldier's skull, taken from the abandoned

post cemetery at Fort Craig, was discovered among the pilfered belongings of a recently deceased resident of Bosque Farms, New Mexico. Don E. Alberts interview, May 7, 2005.

54. Dean, "Endangered Cemeteries"; Tony Hillerman, *A Thief of Time* (New York: Harper Collins, 1988).

55. *Albuquerque Journal*, May 11 and 23, 1999; Nicky Leach, "Pecos National Historical Park," *New Mexico Magazine*, vol. 81 (June 2003): 75. The remains of another 224 Native Americans were reburied at the Gila Cliff Dwellings National Monument in August 2005. *Albuquerque Journal*, August 28, 2005

56. *Albuquerque Journal*, August 27, 2000

57. Ollie Reed, Jr., "Village Vestiges," *Albuquerque Tribune*, January 6, 2005.

58. Wooley *et. al.*, *Final Destinations*, 190-91.

59. *Valencia County News-Bulletin*, March 22, 1982; interview with Henry Perea (President, San Clemente Church Cemetery Association), January 6, 2004.

60. Quoted in the *Taos News*, November 7, 1968.

61. *Taos News*, September 26, 1968. The vast majority of Taos residents displayed far greater respect for their local cemeteries. See Spud Johnson's comments in the *Taos News*, November 30, 1967, and John B. Sanchez's moving letter to the editor, *Taos News*, June 5, 1969. Nearly every "resting place" in New Mexico has suffered senseless vandalism to one degree or another. See, for example, Stanley M. Hordes's introduction to n.a., *Stones of Remembrance: The Historic Jewish Cemetery in Las Vegas, New Mexico* (n.p.: New Mexico Jewish Historical Society, 1990): 4. Vandals come in various forms. According to a recent newspaper report, prairie dogs are digging up human remains at Fairview Cemetery in Santa Fe. "Bones and hardware from coffins are visible around prairie dog burrows in the southernmost end of the four-acre cemetery where indigents were buried." A city ordinance requiring "humane relocation" of the rodents has thus far frustrated efforts to solve this "catastrophic" problem. *Santa Fe New Mexican*, October 10, 2004

62. The Association of Gravestone Studies' web-site is www.gravestonestudies.org. The latter also provides helpful tips on the best ways to photograph gravestones. Other practical suggestions are offered in Carmack, *Cemetery Research*: 113-18; Mary-Ellen Jones, *Photographing Tombstones: Equipment and Techniques,* Technical Leaflet 92 (Nashville: American Association for State and Local History, 1977).

63. Ray Robinson, *Famous Last Words* (New York: Workman, 2003): ix.

64. For John Kinney's obituary in the *Prescott (Arizona) Journal Miner*, see Robert N. Mullin, "Here Lies John Kinney," *Journal of Arizona History*, vol. 14 (Autumn 1973): 224. For Lottie Deno's obituary, see the *Deming Graphic*, February 15, 1934. Also see Janice Hume, *Obituaries in American Culture* (Jackson: University of Mississippi Press, 2000).

2
ARTISTS, PERFORMERS, AND DIRECTORS

1. Quoted in the *Santa Fe New Mexican*, February 10, 1969.

2. Edgar L. Hewett, "Address by Edgar L. Hewett at the Opening of the New Museum at Santa Fe," *El Palacio*, vol. 4 (November 1917): 74-5.

3. The TSA's constitution and by-laws appear in Robert R. White, ed., *The Taos Society of Artists* (Albuquerque: University of New Mexico Press, 1983); 17-21. Minutes of the group's annual meetings appear in Ibid., 23-102. Also see a special edition of the *Taos News*, September 12, 1968.

4. New Deal artists included painters, muralists, potters, and sculptors who participated in New Deal programs such as the Federal Art Project (FAP) during the Great Depression. See Kathryn A. Flynn, ed., *Treasures on New Mexico Trails: Discover New Deal Art and Architecture* (Santa Fe: Sunstone Press, 1995).

5. *Albuquerque Journal*, April 28, 1952; Flynn, *Treasures*, 204-5; David L. Witt, *The Taos Artists: A Historical Narrative and Biographical Dictionary* (Colorado Springs: Ewell Fine Art Publications, 1984): 25; Quentin, *Eternal New Mexicans*, 71-2; Edmund H. Wuerpel, "Oscar E. Berninghaus," *New Mexico Quarterly*, vol. 21 (Summer 1951): 212-19; Tomas Jaehn, *Germans in the Southwest, 1850-1920* (Albuquerque: University of New Mexico, 2005): 125-27.

6. Quoted in Gordon E. Sanders, *Oscar E. Berninghaus, Taos, New Mexico: Master Painter of American Indians and the Frontier West* (Taos: Taos Frontier Publishing Company, 1985): 110.

7. Patricia Janis Broder, *Taos: A Painter's Dream* (Boston: New York Graphic Society, 1980): 115, 128.

8. *Albuquerque Journal*, June 7, 1960; Helen Greene Blumenschein, *Recuerdos: Early Days of the Blumenschein Family* (Silver City: Tecolote Press, 1979): 4; Flynn, *Treasures*, 207; Jaehn, *Germans in the Southwest*, 124-27.

9. Couse was affectionately known as Green Mountain among the Indians of Taos because he always wore a green sweater.

10. *Santa Fe New Mexican*, April 26 and June 23, 1936; Witt, *Taos Artists*, 29; Broder, *A Painter's Dream*, 144, 154; Victoria E. Dye, *All Aboard for Santa Fe: Railway Promotion of the Southwest, 1890s to 1930s* (Albuquerque: University of New Mexico Press, 2005): 41.

11. Loraine Carr quoted in Virginia Couse Leavitt, *Eanger Irving Couse: Image Maker for America* (Albuquerque: Albuquerque Museum, 1991): 42-3. For a "tour" of Couse's studio in Taos, see the *Taos Valley News*, July 28, 1923.

12. Certificate of Death, New Mexico State Department of Public Health, Taos County, March 18,1936; Julie Schimmel, *The Art and Life of W. Herbert Dunton, 1878-1936* (Austin: University of Texas Press, 1984): 18, 42; Flynn, *Treasures*, 217; Mary Carroll Nelson, *Legendary Artists of Taos* (New York: Watson-Guptill, 1980): 65, 69; Broder, *A Painter's Dream*, 163.

13. *Albuquerque Tribune*, June 16, 1956; Flynn, *Treasures*, 257-58; Quentin, *Eternal New Mexicans*, 72; Julie Schimmel and Robert R. White, *Bert Geer Phillips and the Taos Art Colony* (Albuquerque: University of New Mexico Press, 1994): 1-2, 184.

14. *Santa Fe New Mexican*, September 27, 1951; *El Crepusculo*, September 3, 1953; Forrest Fenn, *The Beat of the Drum and the Whoop of the Dance: A Study of the Life and Work of Joseph Henry Sharp* (Santa Fe: Fenning Publishing Co., 1983): 12, 29, 296, 299; Edan M. Hughes, *Artists in California, 1786-1940* (San Francisco: Hughes Publishing Company, 1989): 507. All references to streets named in a person's honor are from Donald A. Gill, *Stories Behind the Street Names of Albuquerque, Santa Fe, and Taos* (Chicago: Bonus Books, 1994).

15. *The (University of New Mexico) Lobo*, February 8, 1939

16. *Albuquerque Review*, March 15, 1962; *Albuquerque Journal*, June 28, 1966; *Albuquerque Tribune*, June 28, 1966; *Taos News*, June 30, 1966; Witt, *Taos Artists*, 23; Marta Weigle, *New Mexicans in Cameo and Camera* (Albuquerque: University of New Mexico Press, 1985): 184-85; Flynn, *Treasures*, 197-98.

17. *Alexandria (Virginia) Gazette*, June 13, 1964; Patricia Janis Broder, "Catharine C. Critcher: Portraits of the Pueblo People," *Southwest Art*, vol. 10 (April 1981): 110-15; Phil Kovinick and Marian Yoshiki-Kovinick, *An Encyclopedia of Women Artists of the American West* (Austin: University of Texas Press, 1998): 59-60; Witt, *Taos Artists*, 30; Broder, *A Painter's Dream*, 241, 248; Nelson, *Legendary Artists of Taos*, 96-8.

18. *Albuquerque Journal*, May 20, 1956; Witt, *Taos Artists*, 38; Broder, *A Painter's Dream*, 256, 264; Flynn, *Treasures*, 225; Nelson, *Legendary Artists of Taos*, 100-07.

19. *Taos Star*, September 1, 1949; Flynn, *Treasures*, 226-27; Udall, *Modernist Painting in New Mexico*, 189-91; Nelson, *Legendary Artists of Taos*, 70, 75; Dean A. Porter, *Victor Higgins: An American Master* (Salt Lake City: Peregrine Smith Books, 1991): 19, 243.

20. Certificate of Death, New Mexico State Department of Public Health, Santa Fe County, August 2, 1936; *New York Times*, August 3, 1936; Broder, *A Painter's Dream*, 211, 229; Nelson, *Legendary Artists of Taos*, 76-80; Witt, *Taos Artists*, 55; Flynn, *Treasures*, 272-73; Jaehn, *Germans in the Southwest*, 125-28.

21. Edna Robertson, *Los Cinco Pintores* (Santa Fe: Museum of New Mexico Press, 1975); Edna Robertson and Sarah Nestor, *Artists of the Canyons and Caminos: Santa Fe, The Early Years* (Salt Lake City: Gibbs M. Smith, 1982): 82-6; *Santa Fe New Mexican*, October 29, 1921. Their houses on Camino del Monte Sol were numbered between 538 and 586.

22. Quoted in the *Santa Fe New Mexican*, May 23, 1968. Eliseo Rodriguez (1915-), one of New Mexico's foremost Hispanic artists, is sometimes referred to as El Sexto Pintor (The Sixth Painter) because he lived near the five, did odd jobs for them as a boy, and received strong encouragement from them in his youth.

23. *Santa Fe New Mexican*, May 19, 1968, and April 26, 1977; Flynn, *Treasures*, 198-99; interview with Norman Bakos (nephew), September 15, 2003.

24. Quoted in the *Santa Fe New Mexican*, March 21, 1976.

25. *Santa Fe New Mexican*, January 14, 1985; *Albuquerque Tribune*, January 14, 1985; Jill Warner, "Fremont Ellis: Always a Ray of Sunlight," *New Mexico Magazine*, vol. 62 (July 1984): 28-32; Flynn, *Treasures*, 218.

26. Stanley L. Cuba, "Walter Mruk: The Elusive Cinco," *El Palacio*, vol. 105 (Winter-Spring 2000-2001): 40-8.

27. Certificate of Death, New Mexico State Department of Public Health, Bernalillo County,

September 2, 1942; *Albuquerque Journal*, September 3 and 4, 1942; Flynn, *Treasures*, 252-53.

28. Walter E. Mruk had died in 1941, nine months before this editorial in Nash's honor was written.

29. Quoted in the *Albuquerque Tribune*, February 11, 1969.

30. *Santa Fe New Mexican*, February 10-12, 1969, with a commemorative editorial on February 11, 1969; *Albuquerque Journal*, February 11, 1969; *Albuquerque Tribune*, February 11, 1969; *Taos News*, February 13, 1969; Joseph Despenza and Louise Turner, *Will Shuster: A Santa Fe Legend* (Santa Fe: Museum of New Mexico Press, 1989): 3, 102; Flynn, *Treasures*, 266-67.

31. Robert R. White, "The New Mexico Painters, 1923-1926," *Southwest Art*, vol. 15 (May 1986): 76-81.

32. *Santa Fe New Mexican*, October 8, 1971; Martin F. Krause *et. al.*, *Gustave Baumann: Nearer to Art* (Santa Fe: Museum of New Mexico Press, 1993): 12, 76; Ellen Zieselman, *The Hand-Carved Marionettes of Gustave Baumann* (Santa Fe: Museum of Fine Arts, 1999: 12, 16; Jaehn, *Germans in the Southwest*, 124-25; Flynn, *Treasures*, 202-3; interview with Robert R. White (art historian), December 4, 2003.

33. *Albuquerque Journal*, November 8, 1964; *New York Times*, November 10, 1964; *Santa Fe New Mexican*, November 8, 9, and 10, 1964; Donelson F. Hoopes, "Randall Vernon Davey (1887-1964)" in *Randall Davey: Artist/Bon Vivant, A Retrospective Exhibition, 1910-1963* (Santa Fe: Museum of Fine Arts, 1984); Flynn, *Treasures*, 214-15; literature distributed at the Randall Davey Audubon Center, Santa Fe, New Mexico; Deanna Einspahr (Operations Manager, Randall Davey Audubon Center, Santa Fe) to the author, September 10, 2003. Davey liked to drive at high speeds, once boasting that he could drive from Santa Fe to Albuquerque in forty-five minutes in an era when most drivers took up to two hours to cover the distance. Davey's former home is a New Mexico Registered Cultural Property.

34. Quoted in John Sloan, "Randall Davey," *New Mexico Quarterly*, vol. 21 (Spring 1951): 25.

35. Certificate of Death, New Mexico State Department of Public Health, Santa Fe County, October 15, 1943; *Santa Fe New Mexican*, April 1, 1916, and October 15, 1943; Special edition on William Penhallow Henderson, *El Palacio*, vol. 93 (Winter 1987): 45; Flynn, *Treasures*, 224-25.

36. Van Deren Coke, *Nordfeldt the Painter* (Albuquerque: University of New Mexico Press, 1972): 135-36; Flynn, *Treasures*, 254-55.

37. Fourteenth U.S. Census, 1920, included in Louise Moye (Rusk County Public Library, Henderson, Texas) to the author, August 24, 2004.

38. Quoted in Mary Cable, "John Sloan in New Mexico," *American Heritage*, vol. 33 (April/May 1982): 100.

39. John Loughery, *John Sloan: Painter and Rebel* (New York: Henry Holt and Company, 1995): 2, 370-71; James Kraft and Helen Farr Sloan, *John Sloan in Santa Fe* (Washington, D.C.: Smithsonian Institution, 1981): 21-35..

40. Quoted in the *Santa Fe New Mexican*, September 9, 1951.

41. Certificate of Death, New Mexico State Department of Public Health, Santa Fe County, February 12, 1934; *Albuquerque Journal*, February 13, 1934; Quentin, *Eternal New Mexicans*, 51; Flynn, *Treasures*, 208-09.

42. Certificate of Death, New Mexico State Department of Public Health, Bernalillo County, September 24, 1943.

43. *Santa Fe New Mexican*, September 25, 1943, with a commemorative editorial on September 27, 1943; *Albuquerque Journal*, September 25, 1943; Flynn, *Treasures*, 255.

44. Quoted in the *Santa Fe New Mexican*, September 25, 1966.

45. *Santa Fe New Mexican*, September 18, 1963, August 22, 1966; Robertson and Nestor, *Artists of the Canyons and Caminos,* 111; Catherine Coggan, "Olive Rush: A Forgotten Artist Who Left Her Mark," *New Mexico Magazine*, vol. 81 (June 2003): 84-7; Grace Dunham Guest, "Olive Rush, Painter," *New Mexico Quarterly*, vol. 21 (Winter 1951): 406-12; Flynn, *Treasures*, 263. Rush's former house is now a New Mexico Registered Cultural Property.

46. Certificate of Death, New Mexico State Department of Public Health, Santa Fe County, December 19, 1937; Ralph Emerson Twitchell, *The Leading Facts of New Mexican History* (Cedar Rapids, Iowa: Torch Press, 1912): V:343n; *Santa Fe New Mexican*, April 27, 1918, July 30, 1919, December 20, 1937, and October 8, 1972.

47. *New Mexico Sentinel*, December 29, 1937. Vierra's former home at 1002 Las Vegas Road, Santa Fe, New Mexico, is now a New Mexico Registered Cultural Property.

48. *Albuquerque Journal*, August 14, 1977; Sean Hignett, *Brett: From Bloomsbury to New Mexico* (New York: Franklin Watts, 1983): 12, 262-63, 270; *Albuquerque Tribune*, September 26, 1968; *Albuquerque Journal*, August 29, 1977; *Taos News*, October 1, 1970, and September 1, 1977; Frank Waters, *Of Time and Change* (Denver: MacMurray and Beck, 1998): 132.

49. Quoted in the *Taos News*, September 8, 1971.

50. *Albuquerque Tribune*, May 2, 1975; *Santa Fe New Mexican*, May 15, 1977; *Taos News*, August 16, 1979; Waters, *Of Time and Change*, 219; Van Deren Coke, *Andrew Dasburg* (Albuquerque: University of New Mexico Press, 1979): v, 1; Nelson, *Legendary Artists of Taos*, 128-29; Udall, *Modernist Painting in New Mexico,* 69; interview with Robert R. White (art historian), December 4, 2003.

51. *Albuquerque Tribune*, February 4, 1971; *Albuquerque Journal*, April 4, 1997; *New York Times*, April 6, 1997; Paul Horgan, essayist, *Henriette Wyeth: The Artifice of Blue* (Santa Fe: Museum of New Mexico Press, 1994); Dorothy Cave Aldrich (historian and Hurd family friend) to the author, December 30, 2004.

52. *New York Times*, July 10, 1984; *Taos News*, December 14, 1970; Robert Metzger, ed., *My Land Is the Southwest: Peter Hurd's Letters and Journals* (College Station: Texas A&M Press, 1983): xxvii-xxviii; Paul Horgan, *Peter Hurd: A Portrait Sketch From Life* (Austin: University of Texas Press, 1965): Flynn, *Treasures*, 232.

53. Quoted in Elvis E. Fleming, "Peter Hurd Paints LBJ" in Elvis E. Fleming and Ernestine Chesser Williams, *Treasures of History* (Roswell: Chaves County Historical Society, 1991): II: 97-8. Also see Dorothy Cave Aldrich (historian and Hurd family friend) to the author, December 30, 2004. Apparently, LBJ was not opposed to all art created by the Hurd family of New Mexico. In November 1967, the president gave a painting by

Henriette Wyeth Hurd to his wife, Lady Bird, on their thirty-third wedding anniversary. The gift giving made front-page headlines in the *Albuquerque Tribune*, November 22, 1967.

54. Jonson's father, on arriving in the United States from Sweden, had changed his surname Jonsson to the more American Johnson. Jonson changed his name back to the original Jonson (with only one "s") and insisted that his name be pronounced "Joanson."

55. Ed Garman, *The Art of Raymond Jonson, Painter* (Albuquerque: University of New Mexico Press, 1976): 7, 173-83; Skip Ware (Curator, Jonson Gallery, University of New Mexico) to the author, December 19, 2003, and interview, January 30, 2004; *Albuquerque Journal*, May 28, 1954; Flynn, *Treasures,* 234-35.

56. Gail T. South, "Oliver LaGrone: Time Walker" (Unpublished Masters thesis, Pennsylvania State University, 1976): 7; Flynn, *Treasures,* 25, 237-38; n.a., *History of Hope: The African American Experience in New Mexico* (Albuquerque: Albuquerque Museum, 1996), 57.

57. *Albuquerque Journal*, March 7, 1986, with a commemorative editorial on that same date; Hunter Drohojowska-Philp, *Full Bloom: The Art and Life of Georgia O'Keeffe* (New York: W.W. Norton, 2004): 13, 545.

58. O'Keeffe's husband, Alfred Stieglitz, was also cremated, although his ashes were placed under a tall pine tree at his favorite rural haven, Lake George, New York.

59. Quoted in Michael Berry, *Georgia O'Keeffe* (New York: Chelsea House, 1988): 105.

60. Drohojowska-Philp, *Full Bloom*, 545.

61. Quoted in the *Santa Fe New Mexican*, July 26, 1994. Also see Barbara A. Babcock, "Pueblo Storytellers," *Impact Magazine*, May 27, 1986; *Albuquerque Journal*, July 26, 1994.

62. *Santa Fe New Mexican*, November 4, 2005; *Albuquerque Journal*, November 4, 6, and 8, 2005; *New York Times*, November 5, 2005; S. Derrickson Moore, "Remembering R.C.," *New Mexico Magazine*, vol. 84 (June 2006): 64-8; rcgormangallery.com

63. Quoted in the *Albuquerque Journal*, August 23, 1994. Also see the *Albuquerque Journal*, August 20, 1998, and W. Jackson Rushing, *Allan Houser: An American Master* (New York: Harry N. Abrams, 2004).

64. Flynn, *Treasures*, 229.

65. Susan Peterson, *Lucy M. Lewis: American Indian Potter* (Tokyo: Kodansha International, 1984): 35. Prior to 1950, Lewis printed "Acoma, N.M." on the bottom of her pots. After 1950, she printed "Lucy M. Lewis, Acoma, N.M."

66. *Albuquerque Journal*, March 8, 1943; Flynn, *Treasures*, 244-45.

67. Maria often signed her pots as "Marie" because this name was more familiar to the non-Indians who bought most of her pottery. *Albuquerque Journal*, August 10, 2003

68. *Santa Fe New Mexican*, July 21, 1980, with a commemorative editorial on July 22, 1980; *Albuquerque Journal*, July 22, 1980, with a commemorative editorial on that same date; *Rocky Mountain News*, July 22, 1980; Richard L. Spivey, *The Legacy of Maria Poveka Martinez* (Santa Fe: Museum of New Mexico Press, 2003); Flynn, *Treasures*, 244-45.

69. *Santa Fe New Mexican*, February 27, 2001; *Albuquerque Journal*, February 28, 2001; *New York Times*, March 5, 2001.

70. Bruce Bernstein, *Modern by Tradition: Dorothy Dunn and the Studio Style* (Santa Fe: Museum of New Mexico Press, 1995): 24, 25; www.lapahie.com/Quincy_Tahoma.cfm

71. Quoted in Marcella J. Ruch, *Pablita Velarde: Painting Her People* (Santa Fe: New Mexico Magazine, 2001): 68. Also see Ibid., 32 and 66; *Santa Fe New Mexican*, January 12, 2006; *Albuquerque Journal*, January 12, 2006; Joe S. Sando, *Pueblo Profiles: Cultural Identity through Centuries of Change* (Santa Fe: Clear Light Publishers, 1998): 200-15.

72. Barbe Awalt and Paul Rhetts, *Our Saints Among Us: 400 Years of New Mexican Devotional Art* (Albuquerque: LPD Press, 1998): 130; Donna Pierce and Marta Weigle, eds., *Spanish New Mexico* (Santa Fe: Museum of New Mexico Press, 1996): 40, 42; interview with Félix López (*santero*), January 7, 2004.

73. Some have spelled Barela's first name Patrociño, but his family continues to spell it as Patrocinio. Tey Marianna Nunn, *Sin Nombre: Hispana and Hispano Artists of the New Deal Era* (Albuquerque: University of New Mexico Press, 2001): 144-49, 166n; Flynn, *Treasures*, 200-01.

74. *Rocky Mountain News*, June 24, 2006; *Albuquerque Journal*, June 14, 2006; *Santa Fe New Mexican*, June 14, 2006; *Roswell Daily Record*, June 15, 2006; *New York Times*, June 15, 2006; *Los Angeles Times*, June 15, 2006; *Washington Post*, June 16, 2006; Rudolfo Anaya et al., *Man on Fire: Luis Jimémez* (Albuquerque: Albuquerque Museum, 1994); Camille Flores-Turney, *Howl: The Artwork of Luis Jimémez* (Santa Fe: New Mexico Magazine, 1997): 11, 72-4.

75. *Albuquerque Journal*, October 2, 2005; Pierce and Weigle, *Spanish New Mexico*, 38-40; Marta Weigle and Peter White, *The Lore of New Mexico* (Albuquerque: University of New Mexico Press, 1988): 139; Charlie Sanchez (*santero*) to the author, January 5, 2004.

76. Nunn, *Sin Nombre*, 47-56; Flynn, *Treasures*, 209-10.

77. *Albuquerque Journal*, April 23, 1975; *Albuquerque Tribune*, April 23, 1975; Nunn, *Sin Nombre*, 66-70; Flynn, *Treasures*, 262.

78. Awalt and Rhetts, *Our Saints*, 152; Pierce and Weigle, *Spanish New Mexico*, 53-4.

79. Awalt and Rhetts, *Our Saints*, 157; "Obituaries," *Folk Art Messenger*, vol. 6 (Fall 1992): 10.

80. Quoted in Pierce and Weigle, *Spanish New Mexico*, 81.

81. *Santa Fe New Mexican*, January 8, 1958

82. Quoted in Virginia L. Grattan, *Mary Colter: Builder Upon the Red Earth* (Grand Canyon: Grand Canyon Natural History Association, 1992): 2, 111, 125-26; Arnold Blake, *Mary Colter: Architect of the Southwest* (New York: Princeton Architectural Press, 2002): 23, 271-72.

83. *New York Times*, August 7, 1983; Quentin, *Eternal New Mexicans*, 36; Chris Wilson, *Facing Southwest: The Life and Houses of John Gaw Meem* (New York: W.W. Norton, 2001): 5, 58. Meem designed several buildings on the Holy Faith of Santa Fe grounds. Stanford Lehmberg, *Holy Faith of Santa Fe, 1863-2000* (Albuquerque: LPD Press, 2004): 57-9, 79-91, 155.

84. Quoted in Van Dorn Hooker, *Only In New Mexico: An Architectural History of the University of New Mexico* (Albuquerque: University of New Mexico Press, 2000): 272.

85. *Santa Fe New Mexican*, March 28, 1933; Carl D. Sheppard, *Creator of the Santa Fe Style: Isaac Hamilton Rapp, Architect* (Albuquerque: University of New Mexico Press, 1988): 11, 102, 129n.

86. A.M. Gibson, *The Life and Death of Colonel Albert Jennings Fountain* (Norman: University of Oklahoma Press, 1965): 259.

87. Mary J. Straw Cook, *Loretto: The Sisters and Their Chapel* (Santa Fe: Museum of New Mexico Press, 2002): 60-70; Peter Eidenbach, "The Stockman and the Carpenter" in Linnie L. Townsend, ed., *Things Remembered: Otero County, New Mexico, 1899-1999* (Alamogordo: Alamogordo/Otero County Centennial Celebration, 1998): 43-61; *Santa Fe New Mexican*, September 10, 1995; *Albuquerque Journal*, June 7, 2002.

88. Quoted in C.L. Sonnichsen, *Tularosa* (Albuquerque: University of New Mexico Press, 1980): 98. Sonnichsen admired Rochas so much that he called his chapter on the Frenchman, "The Bravest Man in New Mexico."

89. Frank Rochas to Q. Monier, December 23, 1894, translated and quoted in Sonnichsen, *Tularosa*, 104; Cook, *Loretto*, 64.

90. Sonnichsen, *Tularosa*, 105.

91. *New York Times*, November 4, 1936, and July 11, 1977; Sheppard, *Santa Fe Style*, 92.

92. *Albuquerque Journal*, April 24, 1984, and June 7, 1989. Adams described the moment on October 31, 1941, when he took his most famous photograph with the afternoon (4:05 p.m.) sun "blaz[ing] a brilliant white upon the crosses in the [San José] church cemetery" at Hernandez, New Mexico, in Adams, *Autobiography*, 231, and in Adams, *Examples*, 40-3. Also see Foreman, "Hernandez and the Photo."

93. Adams, *Autobiography,* ix, 1, 4; *New York Times*, April 24, 1984.

94. Quoted in transcript, *Ansel Adams: A Documentary Film*, www.pbs.org/wgbh/amex/ansel/filmmore/pt.

95. World Heritage Site and Mount Ansel Adams Dedication Program, August 24, 1985, and newspaper clippings from the *Fresno (California) Bee*, August 24, 1985, and the *Merced (California) Sun-Star*, August 26, 1985, included in correspondence from Jim Snyder (Historian, Yosemite Research Library) to the author, January 17, 2001.

96. Laurie Lawlor, *Shadow Catcher: The Life and Work of Edward S. Curtis* (New York: Walker and Company, 1994): 9, 122; James Abarr, "Curtis in New Mexico," *Impact Magazine*, November 29, 1983; Jon Bowman, "Edward S. Curtis," *New Mexico Magazine*, vol. 72 (August 1994): 64-73.

97. *Santa Fe New Mexican*, December 1, 1979; *Albuquerque Journal*, December 1, 1979

98. Margaret Lafranc quoted in the *Santa Fe New Mexican*, December 1, 1979.

99. Quoted in Martha A. Sandweiss, *Laura Gilpin: An Enduring Grace* (Fort Worth: Amon Carter Museum, 1986): 98, 113. Also see Martha A. Sandweiss, "Laura Gilpin: Photographer Brought Timeless Southwest to Life," *New Mexico Magazine*, vol. 65 (July 1987): 48-53; *Christian Science Monitor*, September 13, 1971; *Santa Fe New*

Mexican, November 30, 1979, and December 1, 1979; Barbara McCandless (Curator of Photographs, Amon Carter Museum, Fort Worth, Texas) to the author, July 11, 2003.

100. Dorothea changed her name to her mother's maiden name in 1918 because her father had abandoned his family when she was twelve and because she intended to start a new life in San Francisco, California. Julie Danneberg, *Women Artists of the West* (Golden, Colorado: Fulcrum, 2002): 52.

101. *New York Times*, October 14, 1965; Elizabeth Partridge, *Restless Spirit: The Life and Work of Dorothea Lange* (New York: Viking, 1998): 111; Milton Meltzer, *Dorothea Lange: A Photographer's Life* (Syracuse: Syracuse University Press, 2000): 3, 359.

102. Weigle, *New Mexicans in Cameo and Camera*, 191. Lee's work in New Mexico is featured in William Wroth, ed., *Russell Lee's FSA Photographs of Chamisal and Peñasco, New Mexico* (Santa Fe: Ancient City Press, 1985); Russell Lee, "Pie Town, New Mexico," *U.S. Camera*, vol. 4 (October 1941): 39-54, 88-9, 106-07; Joan Meyers, *Pie Town Woman* (Albuquerque: University of New Mexico Press, 2001).

103. *Santa Fe New Mexican*, November 3, 1990; Joy Waldron, "Eliot Porter: Images of a Master," *New Mexico Magazine*, vol. 69 (June 1991): 41.

104. *Carlsbad Current Argus*, May 4, 1972; Quentin, *Eternal New Mexicans*, 186.

105. Quoted in Darlis Miller, *Captain Jack Crawford: Buckskin Poet, Scout, and Showman* (Albuquerque: University of New Mexico Press, 1993): 271.

106. Quoted in Ibid, 269. Also see Marc Simmons, *Ranchers, Ramblers, and Renegades* (Santa Fe: Ancient City Press, 1984): 17.

107. Miller, *Captain Jack*, 270.

108. Quoted in Eleanor Scott, *The First Years of the Santa Fe Opera* (Santa Fe: Sunstone Press, 1976): 4. Also see Ibid., 5; *New York Times*, September 6, 2000; *Santa Fe New Mexican*, December 16, 2002; *Albuquerque Journal*, December 17, 2002; Winfield Townley Scott, "Guaranteed Performance," *New Mexico Magazine*, vol. 43 (April 1965): 14-17; LaFarge, *Turn Left*, 317-19, 331-32.

109. *Albuquerque Journal*, October 14, 1997

110. *Las Cruces Sun-News*, November 17 and December 2, 2005; *Albuquerque Journal*, November 17, 2005; *Truth or Consequences Herald*, November 23, 2005; *Sierra County Sentinel*, November 23, 2006. An effort to return the town's name to Hot Springs failed in a local election held in 1964.

111. *Albuquerque Journal*, April 7, 1996, with a commemorative editorial on April 9, 1996.

112. Quoted in Michael Truyan, *A Rose for Mrs. Miniver: The Life of Greer Garson* (Lexington: University Press of Kentucky, 1999): 7-8, 365.

113. *Albuquerque Journal*, March 26, 2001; William Harmann, *A Cast of Friends* (Cambridge, Massachusetts: Da Carpo Press, 1999): 5.

114. Holley changed his name to Holly after a February 1956 record company contract had misspelled his original name.

115. Philip Norman, *Rave On: The Biography of Buddy Holly* (New York: Simon and Shuster, 1996): 13-14, 18-9, 32-3, 283-86, 93-4; www.buddyhollyonline.com

116. *Albuquerque Journal*, July 3, 2003

117. www.countrymusichalloffame.com/inductees/roger_miller

118. Paul E. Mix, *The Life and Legend of Tom Mix* (New York: A.S. Barnes, 1972): 16, 151-54.

119. Quoted in Joseph Dispenza, "The Romance of New Mexico" in Mikelle Cosandaey et. al., *One Hundred Years of Filmmaking in New Mexico* (Santa Fe: New Mexico Magazine, 1998): 14.

120. Mix, *Tom Mix*, 14.

121. *Albuquerque Journal*, October 9, 2000; James Riordan and Jerry Prochnicky, *Break On Through: The Life and Death of Jim Morrison* (New York: William Morrow, 1991): 26-8, 450-51.

122. *Albuquerque Journal*, November 17, 18, and 19, 1965; *Albuquerque Tribune*, November 16 and 17, 1965; Kathryn K. O'Connor, *Theatre in the Cow Country* (Albuquerque: Albuquerque Little Theater, 1966): 17-20; Quentin, *Eternal New Mexicans*, 21.

123. Frank Castelluccio and Alvin Walker, *The Other Side of Ethel Mertz: The Life Story of Vivian Vance* (New York: Berkley Boulevard Books, 1998): 1-6, 31-59, 115-18, 284-91; O'Connor, *Theatre in the Cow Country*, 66-8.

3
AUTHORS AND COMPOSERS

1. From William Faulkner's speech when receiving the Nobel Prize for Literature, 1950.

2. James M. Cahalan, *Edward Abbey: A Life* (Tucson: University of Arizona Press, 2001): 3, 260-69; Edward Abbey, *One Life at a Time, Please* (New York: Henry Holt, 1988); Marc Simmons, "A Tribute to Edward Abbey," *Socorro Defensor Chieftain*, May 8, 1989.

3. Edward Abbey, *A Fool's Progress: An Honest Novel* (New York: Henry Holt, 1988).

4. Cahalan, *Abbey*, 261.

5. Ibid., 264; interview with Jack Loeffler, June 7, 2006.

6. *Santa Fe New Mexican*, July 31, 1962; *Albuquerque Journal*, July 31, 1962

7. Certificate of Death, New Mexico State Department of Public Health, Santa Fe County, August 13, 1934; Mary Austin, *Earth Horizon: An Autobiography* (Albuquerque: University of New Mexico Press, 1991): 38-9; Augusta Fink, *I-Mary: A Biography of Mary Austin* (Tucson: University of Arizona Press, 1983): 9, 257-59; Marc Simmons, "Remembering Mary Austin," *Santa Fe New Mexican*, March 13, 2004.

8. *Santa Fe New Mexican*, August 14, 1934; *Albuquerque Journal*, August 14 and 17, 1934; Quentin, *Eternal New Mexicans*, 32-3. Austin wrote the introduction to Frank G. Applegate's *Native Tales of New Mexico* (Philadelphia: J.B. Lippincott, 1932).

9. Quoted in www.cowboydirectory.com/B/omar/omar-bio.html. Also see the *Las Vegas Optic*, April 3, 1985.

10. Corinne P. Sze, "The Witter Bynner House," *Bulletin of the Historic Santa Fe Foundation*, vol. 20 (September 1992): 1-16.

11. Quoted in Sharyn Rohlfsen Udall, *Spud Johnson and Laughing Horse* (Albuquerque: University of New Mexico Press, 1994): 273; *Santa Fe New Mexican*, June 2, 1968; James Kraft, *Who Is Witter Bynner?: A Biography* (Albuquerque: University of New Mexico, 1995): 1, 111. Robert Hunt died of a heart attack on January 18, 1964. A tribute to Bynner, written by many artists and authors, appeared in the *Santa Fe New Mexican*, August 12, 1956.

12. *Santa Fe New Mexican*, November 20, 1952; *Albuquerque Journal*, August 3, 1956, and September 10, 1965; *Albuquerque Tribune*, September 9, 1965; Andre Dumont, "Ina Sizer Cassidy and the Writers Project," *Impact Magazine*, January 19, 1982

13. *Santa Fe New Mexican*, September 9 and 12, 1965

14. *Albuquerque Journal*, April 25, 1947; Phyllis C. Robinson, *Willa: The Life of Willa Cather* (Garden City: Doubleday and Company, 1983): 280; Robert F. Gish, "Willa Cather in New Mexico: A Review Essay," *New Mexico Historical Review*, vol. 64 (April 1989): 221-29. Cather first went to Jaffery, New Hampshire, in 1917 and called it the best place for her to work. She requested that she be buried in the town's Old Burying Ground, with her long-time companion Edith Lewis making the final arrangements.

15. Edith Lewis, *Willa Cather Living: A Personal Record* (New York: Alfred A. Knopf, 1953): 197.

16. *Santa Fe New Mexican*, October 26, 1986; Sharon Snyder (Peggy Pond Church's biographer) to the author, September 12, 2003.

17. Peggy Pond Church, *Accidental Magic* (Albuquerque: Wildflower Press, 2004): 143-44. Used by permission of Kathleen D. Church.

18. Quoted in Sharon Snyder, "Peggy Pond Church: She Existed in a Landscape," Paper read at the Historical Society of New Mexico Conference, Los Alamos, New Mexico, April 23, 2004.

19. *Santa Fe New Mexican*, December 13, 1995, and November 24, 1996; *Albuquerque Journal*, December 13, 1995; Jeanne Whitehouse Peterson, "The Early Life of Ann Nolan Clark: A Contextual Biography" (Unpublished Ph.D. dissertation, University of New Mexico, 1987); Jeanne Whitehouse Peterson to the author, July 3, 2004.

20. *Albuquerque Tribune*, March 8, 1958; *Albuquerque Journal*, March 9, 1958; *Santa Fe New Mexican*, March 9, 1958; Quentin, *Eternal New Mexicans*, 135.

21. Cleaveland, *No Life For a Lady*, 41-2.

22. Quoted in Bryan, *True Tales*, 53.

23. *Santa Fe New Mexican*, December 31, 1962, and January 6, 1963; *Albuquerque Journal*, January 1, 1963

24. John L. Sinclair, *A Cowboy Writer in New Mexico* (Albuquerque: University of New Mexico Press, 1996): 93.

25. LaFarge, *Turn Left*, 290.

26. William A. Keleher, "Erna Mary Fergusson," *New Mexico Historical Review*, vol. 39

(October 1964): 345-50; Robert F. Gish, *Beautiful Swift Fox: Erna Fergusson and the Modern Southwest* (College Station: Texas A&M Press, 1996): ix, 17-19; Quentin, *Eternal New Mexicans*, 28.

27. *Albuquerque Tribune*, July 30, 1964, and August 1, 1964; *Albuquerque Journal*, July 31, 1964; D.H. Thomas, *The Southwestern Indian Detours* (Phoenix: Hunter Publishing Company, 1978): 75-9; Dorothy Woodward, "Erna Fergusson," *New Mexico Quarterly*, vol. 22 (Spring 1952): 75-89.

28. Lawrence Clark Powell, "Southwest Classics Reread: Erna Fergusson and *Dancing Gods*," *Westways,* vol. 63 (March 1971): 62.

29. *Albuquerque Tribune*, August 28, 1971; *Albuquerque Journal*, August 29, 1971; *Santa Fe New Mexican,* August 29, 1971; *New York Times*, August 29, 1971; Harvey Fergusson, *Home in the West: An Inquiry Into My Origins* (New York: Duell, Sloan and Pearce, 1944); Robert F. Gish, *Frontier's End: The Life and Literature of Harvey Fergusson* (Lincoln: University of Nebraska Press, 1988): 3, 5, 316.

30. Ibid., 309.

31. Quoted in Powell, "Southwest Classics Reread," 62.

32. *Albuquerque Journal*, July 19, 1949

33. *Santa Fe New Mexican*, July 19, 1949. Also see the *New Mexico Quarterly Review*, vol. 19 (Spring 1949): 5-79. Authors who wrote tributes included not only LaFarge and Bynner, but also Carl Sandburg, Ruth Laughlin, and Spud Johnson.

34. Quoted in the *New York Times*, March 9, 1995. Also see the *Albuquerque Journal*, March 12, 1995, with a commemorative editorial on that same date; Robert F. Gish, *Nueva Granada: Paul Horgan and the Southwest* (College Station: Texas A&M Press, 1995): 61; William E. Gibbs and Eugene T. Jackman, *New Mexico Military Institute: A Centennial History* (Roswell: New Mexico Military Institute Centennial Commission, 1991): 271; Marc Simmons, "Deaths of Horgan, Waters Major State Loss," *Socorro Defensor Chieftain*, August 5-6, 1995; Dorothy Cave Aldrich (historian and Horgan friend) to the author, December 30, 2004.

35. River Madison (St. James Episcopal Church, Taos, New Mexico) to the author, May 27, 2004. Also see Udall, *Spud Johnson and Laughing Horse,* 98; *Taos News,* November 7, 1968, with a commemorative editorial on that same date; *Santa Fe New Mexican*, November 7, 1968.

36. Quoted in the *Taos News*, November 7, 1968.

37. *Albuquerque Journal*, August 3, 4, and 6, 1963; *Santa Fe New Mexican*, August 4, 5, and 11, 1963; *Las Vegas Optic*, August 5, 1963; Marc Simmons, "Indian Man," *Santa Fe Reporter*, February 1, 1979; Oliver LaFarge, *Raw Material* (Boston: Houghton Mufflin, 1945); Quentin, *Eternal New Mexicans*, 48.

38. Louis L'Amour, *Education of a Wandering Man* (New York: Bantam Books, 1990); Bertram H. Murphy, *Trailing Louis L'Amour in New Mexico* (Roswell: MBAR, 1995).

39. Keith Sagar, ed., *D.H. Lawrence and New Mexico* (Salt Lake City: Gibbs M. Smith, 1982): vii, 102; Arthur J. Bachrach, *D.H. Lawrence in New Mexico* (Albuquerque: University of New Mexico Press, 2006).

40. Frieda Lawrence quoted from her memoirs, "Not I, But the Wind," included in Rosie

Jackson, *Frieda Lawrence* (San Francisco: Pandora, 1994): 195.

41. Also see Woolley *et. al.*, *Final Destinations*, 122-23; Murphy, *After the Funeral*, 219-20. For the several mishaps in transporting Lawrence's ashes from France to New Mexico, see Ibid., 216-18.

42. John Sherman, *Taos* (Santa Fe: William Gannon, 1990): 95.

43. See, for example, John R. Milton's poem, "Lawrence, Resting Near Taos," in the *Taos News*, May 21, 1970.

44. *Santa Fe New Mexican*, August 12, 1956; Jackson, *Frieda Lawrence,* 91, 95-6.

45. Ibid., 96.

46. William A. Keleher, *New Mexicans I Knew* (Albuquerque: University of New Mexico Press, 1983): 234-38; William A. Keleher, *The Fabulous Frontier* (Albuquerque: University of New Mexico Press, 1982): 172-73; Sonnichsen, *Tularosa*, 202-27; Mrs. Tom Charles's introduction to a special edition of Eugene Manlove Rhodes, *Pasó Por Aquí* (Alamogordo: Friends of the Alamogordo Public Library, 1963): ii; "Rhodes Memorial," *New Mexico Magazine,* vol. 19 (June 1941): 45; David Townsend, *You Take the Sundials and Give Me the Sun* (Alamogordo: Alamogordo Daily News, 1984): 82-9; Julyan, *Place Names*, 290.

47. May Davison Rhodes, *The Hired Man on Horseback: My Story of Eugene Manlove Rhodes* (Boston: Houghton Mifflin, 1938): 15, 238, 254-56.

48. John L. Sinclair, *A Cowboy Writer in New Mexico: The Memoirs of John L. Sinclair* (Albuquerque: University of New Mexico Press, 1996): viii, 1; *Albuquerque Journal*, December 18, 1993; Marc Simmons, "Remembering John Sinclair," *Santa Fe Reporter*, February 2-8, 1994; Ollie Reed, Jr., "Trail Tales," *Albuquerque Tribune*, December 16, 2000.

49. *New York Times*, October 11, 1965; James L. Thorson, "Gomorrah on the Puerco: A Critical Study of Philip Stevenson's Proletarian Epic" in Robert Kern, ed., *Labor in New Mexico* (Albuquerque: University of New Mexico Press, 1983): 149, 152

50. *Albuquerque Journal*, April 10, 1972

51. Quoted in Robert E. and Katherine M. Morsberger, *Lew Wallace: Militant Romantic* (New York: McGraw-Hill, 1980): 444; *Denver Post*, October 11, 1959. Also see Marc Simmons, "New Mexico Supplied Lew and Susan Wallace with Plenty of Stories to Record," *Santa Fe New Mexican*, May 25, 2002.

52. *Santa Fe New Mexican*, June 5, 1995; interview with Barbara Waters (widow), October 12, 2001.

53. *Albuquerque Tribune*, May 10, 1975. Also see the *Taos News*, September 13, 1990, and Marc Simmons, "Deaths of Horgan, Waters Major State Loss," *Socorro Defensor Chieftain*, August 5-6, 1995.

54. Certificate of Death, New Mexico State Department of Public Health, Chaves County, October 16, 1947.

55. Quoted in the *Albuquerque Journal*, October 18, 1947. Also see the *Alamogordo News*, December 9, 1926; Linda G. Harris, *Las Cruces* (Las Cruces: Arroyo Press, 1993): 87-8; David Townsend and Cliff McDonald, *Centennial: Where the Old West Meets*

the New Frontier (Alamogordo: Alamogordo/Otero County Centennial Celebration, 1999): 31, 44; Quentin, *Eternal New Mexicans*, 176. Garrett's talent and character were praised in newspapers as far east as New York. See a *New York Sun* article quoted in the *Alamogordo News*, December 13, 1928.

56. Norman, *Rave On*, 89, 305-07; Emily Drabanski and Tom Gasparoli, "The Norman Petty Story," *New Mexico Magazine*, vol. 64 (September 1986): 41-5.

4
CULTURAL PRESERVATIONISTS

1. Quoted in Beatrice Chauvenet, *Hewett and Friends: A Biography of Santa Fe's Vibrant Era* (Santa Fe: Museum of New Mexico Press, 1983): 213.

2. *Santa Fe New Mexican*, February 13, 14, 16, and 18, 1931; Daria Labinsky and Stan Hieronymus, *Frank Applegate of Santa Fe: Artist and Preservationist* (Albuquerque: LPD Press, 2001): 12, 268-71; Wilson, *Myth of Santa Fe*, 245-46.

3. Charles H. Lange and Carroll L. Riley, *Bandelier: The Life and Adventures of Adolph Bandelier* (Salt Lake City: University of Utah Press, 1996): 1, 3, 42, 208, 210, 236-37; Jaehn, *Germans in the Southwest*, 22-6; Julyan, *Place Names*, 29; Chris Judson (Park Ranger, Bandelier National Monument) to the author, August 26, 2003.

4. *Santa Fe New Mexican*, October 1 and 6, 1974, with a commemorative editorial on October 2, 1974; *Albuquerque Journal*, October 1, 1974; *Albuquerque Tribune*, April 4, 1974, and October 2, 1974; Quentin, *Eternal New Mexicans*, 35; Marta Weigle (anthropologist and Boyd's friend) to the author, December 9 and 12, 2003. Boyd was never known to use her first name.

5. *Albuquerque Journal*, February 15, 1981

6. Tey Diana Rebolledo, ed., *Nuestras Mujeres: Hispanas of New Mexico, Their Images and Their Lives, 1582-1992* (Albuquerque: El Norte Publications, 1992): 44-6; A. Gabriel Meléndez, *Spanish-Language Newspapers in New Mexico, 1834-1958* (Tucson: University of Arizona Press, 2005): 185; Maureen Reed, *A Woman's Place: Women Writing New Mexico* (Albuquerque: University of New Mexico, 2005): 121-69.

7. *Santa Fe New Mexican*, February 25, 1968, with commemorative articles by John Gaw Meem and Alice Bullock on February 25, 1968, and a commemorative editorial, February 26, 1968; *Kansas City Star*, April 4, 1968; Wilson, *Myth of Santa Fe*, 94, 120, 125, 129, 134-35, 250, 349n; "Biographical Information," Box 1, Folder AC2:83, Kenneth M. Chapman Collection, Catherine McElvain Library, School of American Research, Santa Fe, New Mexico; Len Leschander (Catherine McElvain Library, School of American Research) to the author, June 8, 2004.

8. Quentin, *Eternal New Mexicans*, 63-4.

9. Chauvenet, *Hewett and Friends*, 3, 213, 218-21; *Santa Fe New Mexican*, December 31, 1946; Edgar Lee Hewett, *Campfire and Trail* (Albuquerque: University of New Mexico Press, 1944); Paul A.F. Walter, "Edgar Lee Hewett," *New Mexico Historical Review*, vol. 22 (April 1947): 190-96; Don D. Fowler, *A Laboratory for Anthropology: Science and Romanticism in the American Southwest, 1846-1930* (Albuquerque: University of New Mexico Press, 2000): 261-74; Malinda Elliott, *The School of American Research: A History* (Santa Fe: School of American Research, 1987): 1-35; Maurilio E. Vigil, *Defining Our Destiny: The History of New Mexico Highlands University* (Las Vegas: New Mexico Highlands University, 1993): 27-34; Marc Simmons, "Unearthing Edgar Hewett's Contributions to Archaeology," *Santa Fe New Mexican*, February 22, 2003.

10. Edgar L. Hewett, *Man in the Pageant of the Ages* (Albuquerque: University of New Mexico Press, 1943): 3-4.

11. *Santa Fe New Mexican*, December 3, 1956; Rebolledo, *Nuestras Mujeres*, 42-3; Reed, *A Woman's Place*, 69-119; Wilson, *Myth of Santa Fe*, 152-54.

12. *New York Times*, June 15, 1963; Richard B. Woodbury, *Alfred V. Kidder* (New York: Columbia University Press, 1973); Marjorie Lambert, "Alfred V. Kidder, Sr., 1885-1963," *El Palacio*, vol. 70 (Autumn 1963); Givens, *Kidder*; Kessell, *Kiva, Cross, and Crown*, 480-88, 516n; Fowler, *Laboratory*, 265, 284-88, 315.

13. *Santa Fe New Mexican*, July 31, 1960

14. Mark Thompson, *American Character: The Curious Life of Charles Fletcher Lummis and the Rediscovery of the Southwest* (New York: Arcade Publishing, 2001): 331; Dudley Gordon, *Charles F. Lummis: Crusader in Corduroy* (n.c.: Cultural Assets Press, 1972): 24, 320-25; Edwin R. Bingham, *Charles F. Lummis: Editor of the Southwest* (San Marino, California: Huntington Library, 1955): 4, 28-9; Turbesé Lummis Fiske and Keith Lummis, *Charles F. Lummis: The Man and His West* (Norman: University of Oklahoma Press, 1975); Ramón A. Gutiérrez, "Charles Fletcher Lummis and Orientalization of New Mexico" in Francisco a. Lomelf, Victor A. Sorell, and Genaro M. Padilla, eds., *Nuevomexicano Cultural Legacy* (Albuquerque: University of New Mexico Press, 2002): 11-27; Wilson, *Myth of Santa Fe*, 87-9; Julyan, *Place Names*, 215.

15. *Los Angeles Times*, November 25, 1928

16. *Santa Fe New Mexican*, April 16, 1951, and January 7, 1968; H.P. Mera, *Style Trends of Pueblo Pottery, 1500-1840* (Albuquerque: Avanyu Publishing Company, 1991; reprint of 1939 edition): v, vi; Richard Polese, "The Zia Sun Symbol," *El Palacio*, vol. 74 (Summer 1968); interview with Dody Fugate (Curator, Laboratory of Anthropology, Santa Fe), April 8, 2005.

17. *Albuquerque Tribune*, January 29, 1997; *Albuquerque Journal*, January 30, 1997; *Santa Fe New Mexican*, January 30, 1997; Marc Simmons, "Remembering Alfonso Ortiz," *Santa Fe Reporter*, April 2-8, 1997; Sando, *Pueblo Profiles*, 271-79.

18. *New York Times*, December 20, 1941; Desley Deacon, *Elsie Clews Parsons: Inventing a Modern Life* (Chicago: University of Chicago Press, 1997): 1, 378-80; Fowler, *Laboratory*, 325-32.

19. Elsie Clews Parsons to Lisa Parsons, February 11, 1940, Elsie Clews Parsons Papers, American Philosophical Society, Philadelphia, Pennsylvania, citation enclosed in correspondence from Catherine Lavender (archivist, American Philosophical Society) to the author, May 29, 2004.

20. *Albuquerque Tribune*, December 19, 1972; *Albuquerque Journal*, April 7, 1975, and January 19, 1989; Scott Meredith, "Many-Sided Man: John Donald Robb and Music in New Mexico," *La Crónica de Nuevo México*, no. 60 (October 2003): 2-5.

21. Certificate of Death, New Mexico State Department of Public Health, Bernalillo County, June 4, 1940; *Santa Fe New Mexican*, June 5, 1940; Mark L. Gardner, ed., *Jack Thorp's Songs of the Cowboys* (Santa Fe: Museum of New Mexico Press, 2005): 12, 17.

22. Lomax and Lomax, *Cowboy Songs*, 91-3; Gardner, *Jack Thorp's Songs of the Cowboys*, 40-41.

23. Mark L. Gardner, "Hunting Ballads: Cowboy Jack Thorp Hits Trail in Search of Tunes," *New Mexico Magazine*, vol. 82 (March 2004): 76-7; Marc Simmons, "Cowboy Songs," *Santa Fe Reporter*, October 12-18, 1989. Also see Peter White and Mary Ann White, eds., *Along the Rio Grande: Cowboy Jack Thorp's New Mexico* (Santa Fe: Ancient City Press, 1988).

24. Fray Angélico Chávez received his religious name after the saintly medieval Italian painter, Frá Angélico da Fiesole. Phyllis S. Morales, *Fray Angélico Chávez: A Bibliography of His Published Writings, 1925-1978* (Santa Fe: Lightning Tree Press, 1980): 9; *Santa Fe New Mexican*, March 20, 1996; *Albuquerque Journal*, March 22, 1996; *New York Times*, March 22, 1996; Nasario Garcia, "In Passing: Fray Angélico Chávez," *New Mexico Historical Review*, vol. 71 (July 1996): 269; Marc Simmons, "Fray Angélico Was a New Mexico Original," *Santa Fe New Mexican*, April 7, 2001; Robert Huber, "Fray Angélico Chávez, Twentieth Century Renaissance Man," *New Mexico Magazine*, vol. 48 (March-April 1970): 18-23; Ellen McCracken, ed., *Fray Angélico Chávez: Poet, Priest, and Artist* (Albuquerque: University of New Mexico Press, 2000): 111, 135, 139-41; Wilson, *Myth of Santa Fe*, 154-55.

25. *Santa Fe New Mexican*, March 20, 1996

26. *Albuquerque Journal*, August 5, 1983; Narsario García and Richard McCord, *Albuquerque: Three Centuries to Remember* (Santa Fe: La Herencia, 2005): 168-69; interview with Margaret Espinosa McDonald (daughter and New Mexico historian), July 11, 2005.

27. *Albuquerque Tribune*, May 30, 2005; Janaloo Hill, *The Hill Family of Shakespeare* (n.c.: n.p., 2001): 126, 301; Carleen Lazzell, "Tribute to Janaloo Hill," *La Crónica de Nuevo México*, no. 65 (July 2005): 2 and 8.

28. Quoted in the *Albuquerque Tribune*, May 30, 2005. Also see www.shakespeareghostown.com/passing.html.

29. Hill, *Hill Family*, 277.

30. Quoted in *Santa Fe New Mexican*, June 24, 1993, with a commemorative editorial on June 25, 1993. Also see the *Santa Fe New Mexican*, July 8, 1992; Marc Simmons, "State's Own 'Dr. J' Knew It All," *Socorro Defensor Chieftain*, August 14-15, 1993; and John W. Grassham, "In Passing: Myra Ellen Jenkins," *New Mexico Historical Review*, vol. 68 (October 1993): 407.

31. *Albuquerque Tribune*, December 19, 1972

32. Gaspar Pérez de Villagrá, *Historia de la Nueva México, 1610*, Miguel Encinias, Alfred Rodríguez, and Joseph P. Sánchez, trans. (Albuquerque: University of New Mexico Press, 1992): xvii-xviii; Thomas E. Chávez, "La Historia de la Nueva México," *El Palacio*, vol. 102 (Winter/Spring 1997-98): 37-43.

33. *Santa Fe New Mexican*, September 15 and 16, 1927, with a commemorative editorial on September 15, 1927; Necrology, *New Mexico Historical Review*, vol. 2 (October 1927): 394-97; Meléndez, *Spanish-Language Newspapers*, 123-32.

34. *Albuquerque Journal*, February 13, 1979; *Albuquerque Tribune*, February 21, 1979; Marc Simmons, "A Fond Farewell to 'Papa Scholes,'" *Santa Fe Reporter*, March 15, 1979; "Memorial to Frances V. Scholes," *New Mexico Historical Review*, vol. 54. (April 1979): 88; Richard E. Greenleaf, "Frances V. Scholes: Historian's Historian, 1897-1979," *New Mexico Historical Review*, vol. 75 (July 2000): 320-38; Hooker, *Only In New Mexico*, 198; Dr. Fred H. Hanold, Scholes's physician, as reported in Jake Spidle (historian and Scholes's colleague) to the author, September 21, 2004.

35. *Albuquerque Journal*, February 14, 1979

36. Quentin, *Eternal New Mexicans*, 57.

37. *Santa Fe New Mexican*, August 26-29 and 31, 1925, with a commemorative editorial on August 26, 1925; Obituary, *New Mexico Historical Review*, vol. 1 (January 1926): 78-85; Myra Ellen Jenkins, "Ralph Emerson Twitchell," *Arizona and the West*, vol. 8 (Summer 1966): 102-06.

38. *New York Times*, August 14, 1962; *Taos News*, August 16 and 18, 1962

39. Lois Palken Rudnick, *Mabel Dodge Luhan: New Woman, New Worlds* (Albuquerque: University of New Mexico Press, 1984): 329-30, 361n; Waters, *Of Time and Change*, 98-9. Mabel changed the spelling of her last husband's name from Lujan to Luhan because so many people mispronounced the "j".

40. Emily Hahn, *Mabel* (Boston: Houghton Mifflin, 1977): 217, with a copy of Brett's painting included among the illustrations printed after 116.

41. Quoted in Ibid., 217.

42. Antonio R. Garcez, *Adobe Angels: The Ghosts of Santa Fe and Taos* (Santa Fe: Red Rabbit Press, 1995): 126-29.

43. *Santa Fe New Mexican*, January 2 and 5, 1953; *Albuquerque Journal*, January 2, 1953; *Albuquerque Tribune*, January 2, 1953; *New York Times*, January 2, 1953; Anna Dooling, "The Lady and the Legend," *Impact Magazine*, July 15, 1986; Tricia Hurst, "Heiress Brings Lavish Lifestyle to Taos," *New Mexico Magazine*, vol. 67 (November 1989): 28-33; Dean A. Porter *et. al.*, *Taos Artists and Their Patrons, 1898-1950* (South Bend, Indiana: University of Notre Dame Press, 1999): 293-98.

44. *Albuquerque Journal*, January 1, 1953

5
BUSINESS LEADERS

1. Quoted in Susan Calafate Boyle, *Los Capitalistas: Hispanic Merchants and the Santa Fe Trail* (Albuquerque: University of New Mexico Press, 1997): 57. Robledo was referring to the development of New Mexico's mercantile system, but his words certainly apply to business transactions in general.

2. Quoted in Thomas E. Chávez, *Manuel Alvarez, 1794-1856: A Southwestern Biography* (Niwot: University Press of Colorado, 1990): 9, 190, 225n.

3. Thomas E. Chávez, "Don Manuel Alvarez (de las Abelgas): Multi-Talented Merchant of New Mexico," *Journal of the West*, vol. 18 (1979): 22-31.

4. Larry M. Beachum, *William Becknell: Father of the Santa Fe Trail* (El Paso: Texas Western Press, 1982): 1, 29, 69-70, 89n; Lawrence O. Christensen, William E. Foley, Gary R. Kremer, and Kenneth H. Winn, eds., *Dictionary of Missouri Biography* (Columbia: University of Missouri Press, 1999): 48.

5. Howard R. Lamar, *Reader's Encyclopedia of the West* (New York: Harper and Row, 1977): 87; Ruth Ellenwood McGuyre, "Bent Family," unpublished genealogy, Charles Bent Family File, Harwood Museum, Taos, New Mexico; Twitchell, *Leading Facts*, II:256; James A. Browning, *Violence Was No Stranger: A Guide to the Grave Sites*

of Famous Westerners (Stillwater, Oklahoma: Barbed Wire Press, 1993): 19; David Lavender, *Bent's Fort* (Garden City, New York: Doubleday, 1954): 303-04.

6. Ibid., 21, 366; Ellenwood, "Bent Family"; Linda Wommack, *From the Grave: A Roadside Guide to Colorado's Pioneer Cemeteries* (Caldwell, Idaho: Caxton Press, 1998): 285-86.

7. Simmons, *Murder on the Santa Fe Trail*, 1, 29-32.

8. Ibid., 33, 70-1.

9. *Albuquerque Morning Journal*, April 12, 1905

10. *Albuquerque Morning Journal*, April 12 and 13, 1905; *Valencia County News-Bulletin*, June 11, 1981; Boyle, *Las Capitalistas*, 73-88; R.M. Biggs, "Monument for Don Felipe," *New Mexico Magazine*, vol. 30 (June 1952): 10, 51; Tibo J. Chavez, "El Millonario," *New Mexico Magazine*, vol. 67 (June 1989): 73-9; Gilberto Espinosa and Tibo J. Chavez, *El Rio Abajo* (Portales: Bishop, n.d.): 157-71.

11. Max L. Moorhead's introduction to Josiah Gregg, *Commerce of the Prairies* (Norman: University of Oklahoma Press, 1954): xviii, xxix. Also see Paul Horgan, *Josiah Gregg and His Vision of the Early West* (New York: Farrar Straus Giroux, 1979).

12. Fergusson, *Home in the West*, 44, 46-7.

13. *Santa Fe New Mexican*, November 7, 1905; Franz Huning, *Trader on the Santa Fe Trail: The Memoirs of Franz Huning* (Albuquerque: University of Albuquerque, 1973): x, 148; Howard Bryan, *Albuquerque Remembered* (Albuquerque: University of New Mexico Press, 2006): 107-09.

14. Quoted in Jaehn, *Germans in the Southwest*, 55. Also see Bryan, *Albuquerque Remembered*, 64-6.

15. W.H. Timmons, *James Wiley Magoffin: Don Santiago—El Paso Pioneer* (El Paso: West Texas Press, 1999): 6, 88; Marc Simmons, "Magoffin Responsible for Bloodless Conquest of New Mexico," *Santa Fe New Mexican*, October 18, 2003.

16. Howard R. Lamar's foreword in Stella M. Drumm, *Down the Santa Fe Trail and into Mexico: the Diary of Susan Shelby Magoffin, 1846-47* (Lincoln: University of Nebraska, 1982): xiv, xxxii-xxxiii; Christensen *et. al.*, *Missouri Biography*, 512; Marc Simmons, "Frontier Heroine," *Santa Fe Reporter*, August 17, 1983; Sharman Apt Russell, "The Life of a Wandering Princess," *New Mexico Magazine*, vol. 64 (June 1986): 49-51.

17. Don Bullis, *Ellos Pasaron por Aqui* (Chesterfield, Missouri: Science and Humanities Press, 2005): 240-42; Hordes, *To the End of the Earth*, 197-98; Quentin, *Eternal New Mexicans*, 91.

18. Marian Russell, *Land of Enchantment: Memoirs of Marian Russell Along the Santa Fe Trail* (Albuquerque: University of New Mexico, 1981): xiv, 1-2.

19. Ibid., 113-14.

20. Ibid., 139.

21. Marc Simmons, "Trail Lady," *Santa Fe Reporter*, March 14, 1990.

22. *Santa Fe Daily New Mexican*, October 29, 1870; Quentin, *Eternal New Mexicans*,

101; Browning, *Violence Was No Stranger*, 216-17; Harold H. Dunham, "Cerán St. Vrain" in LeRoy R. Hafen, ed., *The Mountain Men and the Fur Trade of the Far West: Biographical Sketches of the Participants by Scholars of the Subjects* (Glendale, California: A.H. Clark Company, 1968): V:297-316; David J. Weber, *The Taos Trappers* (Norman: University of Oklahoma Press, 1971): 89, 169-75, 211-13, 228; Lavender, *Bent's Fort*, 51, 420n; Julyan, *Place Names*, 307.

23. *Santa Fe New Mexican*, April 8, 1930, and July 17, 1988; Henry J. Tobias, *A History of the Jews in New Mexico* (Albuquerque: University of New Mexico Press, 1990): 43; Floyd S. Fierman, *The Spiegelbergs of New Mexico: Merchants and Bankers, 1844-98* (El Paso: Southwestern Studies, 1964): 11-15; Wilson, *Myth of Santa Fe*, 65, 67-9. According to Spiegelberg family legend, the family name was given in 1812 by Baron Von Spiegelberg as a reward to a Spiegelberg ancestor, the baron's estate manager. Tomás Jaehn, *Jewish Pioneers of New Mexico* (Santa Fe: Museum of New Mexico Press, 2003): 7.

24. H.L. Conard, ed., *Uncle Dick Wootton* (Santa Barbara, California: Narrative Press, 2001); Agnes Morley Cleaveland, *Satan's Paradise* (Boston: Houghton Mifflin Company, 1952): 22-6; Bullis, *Pasaron por Aquí*, 313-15; Wommack, *From the Grave*, 322.

25. *Albuquerque Journal*, June 22, 1945; Frank Bond, "Memoirs of Forty Years in New Mexico," *New Mexico Historical Review*, vol. 21 (October 1946): 340-49; Necrology, *New Mexico Historical Review*, vol. 20 (July 1945); Frank H. Grubbs, "Frank Bond: Gentleman Sheepherder of Northern New Mexico," *New Mexico Historical Review*, vol. 35 (July 1960): 169-99; vol. 35 (October 1960): 293-308; vol. 36 (April 1961): 138-58; vol. 36 (July 1961): 230-43; vol. 36 (October 1961): 274-345; Quentin, *Eternal New Mexicans*, 6-7.

26. Carole Larson, *Forgotten Frontier: The Story of Southeastern New Mexico* (Albuquerque: University of New Mexico Press, 1993): 105-22; Marc Simmons, "Chisum's Legend as Pioneer Cattleman Lives On," *Santa Fe New Mexican*, March 17, 2001.

27. Quoted in Harwood P. Hinton, Jr., "John Simpson Chisum," *New Mexico Historical Review*, vol. 32 (January 1957): 61-5. Also see Twitchell, *Leading Facts*, V:282n-83n; Julyan, *Place Names*, 82.

28. Morris F. Taylor, "Stephen W. Dorsey: Speculator-Cattleman," *New Mexico Historical Review*, vol. 49 (January 1974): 27-48; Thomas J. Caperton, *Rogue!: Being an Account of the Life and High Times of Stephen W. Dorsey* (Santa Fe: Museum of New Mexico Press, 1978): 7, 38; Robert Beauvais with George Pearl, "The Residence of Stephan W. Dorsey," *New Mexico Architecture*, vol. 14 (November-December 1972): 12-23; Phil T. Archuletta and Sharyl S. Holden, *Traveling New Mexico: A Guide to the Historical and State Park Markers* (Santa Fe: Sunstone Press, 2004): 54.

29. Quoted in Ibid., 36. W. Hagan, *Charles Goodnight* (Norman: University of Oklahoma Press, 2007).

30. *Albuquerque Evening Democrat*, February 5, 1885; Marc Simmons, *Albuquerque* (Albuquerque: University of New Mexico Press, 1982): 161.

31. Browning, *Violence Was No Stranger*, 148-49; Julyan, *Place Names,* 212-13.

32. Ralph Emerson Twitchell, *The History of the Military Occupation of the Territory of New Mexico, 1846-51* (Chicago: Rio Grande Press, 1963): 267-8; Quentin, *Eternal New Mexicans*, 66-7.

33. *Alamogordo News*, April 16, 1931; Keleher, *Fabulous Frontier*, 278n-279n, 298; David F. Myrick, *New Mexico's Railroads* (Albuquerque: University of New Mexico Press, 1999): 73-87; Julyan, *Place Names*, 117.

34. Quoted in the *Alamogordo News*, April 16, 1931.

35. Keleher, *Fabulous Frontier*, 191n, 206; Larson, *Forgotten Frontier*, 250-77; Julyan, *Place Names*, 160; Gibbs and Jackman, *New Mexico Military Institute*, 83.

36. Quoted in Elvis E. Fleming, "J.J. Hagerman: Building the Pecos River Railroad," *Greater Llano Estacado Southwest Heritage*, vol. 7 (Spring 1977): 12.

37. Elvis E. Fleming, *Captain Joseph C. Lea* (Las Cruces: Yucca Tree Press, 2002): 3-4, 216; Larson, *Forgotten Frontier*, 197-211; Nolan, *West*, 228; Gibbs and Jackman, *New Mexico Military Institute*, 142; Julyan, *Place Names*, 201.

38. Lawrence R. Murphy, *Lucien Bonaparte Maxwell: The Napoleon of the Southwest* (Norman: University of Oklahoma Press, 1983): 3; María E. Montoya, *Translating Property: The Maxwell Land Grant and the Conflict Over Land in the American West, 1840-1900* (Berkeley: University of California Press, 2002): 48-54, 63, 230n; Cleaveland, *Satan's Paradise*, 7-21; Julyan, *Place Names*, 222.

39. *El Paso Times*, May 29, 1949; Murphy, *Maxwell*, 216-19.

40. Quoted in Marian Meyer, *Mary Donoho: New First Lady of the Santa Fe Trail* (Santa Fe: Ancient City Press, 1991): 20, 99-100, with a copy of Mary's funeral notice on 98.

41. Carmack, *Cemetery Research*, 215.

42. Mary D. Burchill, *Lady of the Canyon: Evelyn Cecil Frey* (Los Alamos: Otowi Crossing, 2001): 6, 69, 70.

43. Quoted in Robinson, *Famous Last Words*, 41.

44. Quoted in William Patrick Armstrong, *Fred Harvey: Creator of Western Hospitality* (Bellemont, Arizona: Canyonlands, 2000): 24.

45. Ibid.

46. *Albuquerque Journal*, May 20, 1987; *Albuquerque Tribune*, May 20, 1987; Lenore Dils, *Horny Toad Man* (El Paso: Boots and Saddle Press, 1966): 67; Lesley Poling Kempes, *The Harvey Girls: Women Who Opened the West* (New York: Paragon House, 1989): 57, 76, 97-8, 141; interview with Shirley Boles (step-daughter), January 13, 2004.

47. Quoted in Kempes, *Harvey Girls*, 208.

48. Quoted in Robinson, *Famous Last Words*, 170.

49. *Albuquerque Journal*, January 5, 1979; Conrad Hilton, *Be My Guest* (Englewood Cliffs, New Jersey: Prentice-Hall, 1957): 31; Bullis, *Pasaron por Aquí*, 135-37.

50. *Raton Range*, January 28, 1913; Cleaveland, *Satan's Paradise*, 48-60; Browning, *Violence Was No Stranger*, 135.

51. Quentin, *Eternal New Mexicans*, 34.

52. Ibid., 50; Twitchell, *Leading Facts*, II:499n; Porter A. Stratton, *The Territorial Press of New Mexico, 1834-1912* (Albuquerque: University of New Mexico Press, 1969): 27, 86-7, 202-3, 212n, 226n.

53. Quoted in "Obituary As Written by Mr. Johnson," *New Mexico Historical Review*, vol.

13 (January 1938): 127. Also see the *Santa Fe New Mexican*, December 10, 1937, with a commemorative editorial on December 11, 1937; Cyrus McCormick, "In Memoriam: E. Dana Johnson, 1879-1937," *New Mexico Sentinel*, December 15, 1937.

54. Susan A. Roberts, "The Political Trials of Carl C. Magee," *New Mexico Historical Review*, vol. 50 (October 1975): 291-311; Bryan, *Albuquerque Remembered*, 222-27.

55. Quoted in the *New York Times*, February 2, 1946.

56. Stratton, *Territorial Press*, 3, 180, 207; Twitchell, *Old Santa Fe*, 471-72.

57. *New Mexico Sentinel*, July 10, 1938; Max Evans, *Long John Dunn of Taos: From Texas Outlaw to New Mexico Hero* (Santa Fe: Clear Light, 1993): 151-52.

58. Certificate of Death, New Mexico State Department of Public Health, San Miguel County, January 3, 1929; William J. Parish, *The Charles Ilfeld Company: A Study of the Rise and Decline of Mercantile Capitalism in New Mexico* (Cambridge: Harvard University Press, 1961): 359n, 409n; Jaehn, *Jewish Pioneers*, 13, 32; Sophia Truneh, "The Ilfelds: A Family Story of Jewish Pioneers in New Mexico," *Southwest Jewish History*, vol. 3 (Winter 1995); Julyan, *Place Names*, 173.

59. Abe Peña, *Memories of Cibola* (Albuquerque: University of New Mexico Press, 1997): 155-58; Quentin, *Eternal New Mexicans*, 76; Peter H. Eichstaedt, *If You Poison Us: Uranium and Native Americans* (Santa Fe: Red Crane Books, 1994): 39; *Santa Fe New Mexican*, August 27, 1969.

60. Quoted in the *Albuquerque Tribune*, August 27, 1969.

61. *Grants Beacon*, August 26, 1969

62. Several scholars agree that Staab and other Jewish merchants in Santa Fe helped finance the cathedral, but disagree about the "deal" Staab supposedly made with Lamy regarding the Tetragrammaton. Floyd S. Fierman argues that the Hebrew words above the cathedral's main entrance are enclosed in a triangle, making it a Catholic symbol rather than a Jewish one. Floyd S. Fierman, *The Triangle and the Tetragrammaton* (El Paso: Texas Western College Press, 1961): 1-7.

63. Floyd S. Fierman, "The Staabs of Santa Fe: Pioneer Merchants in New Mexico Territory," *Rio Grande History*, vol. 13 (1983): 6n-7n, 22; Tobias, *History of the Jews of New Mexico*, 58, 66, 79-81, 113, 117; Twitchell, *Old Santa Fe*, 479-80; *Santa Fe New Mexican*, January 6 and 23, 1913.

64. Quoted in Quentin, *Eternal New Mexicans*, 54.

6
EDUCATIONAL LEADERS

1. Don Pedro Baptista Pino, *The Exposition on the Province of New Mexico, 1812*, trans. by Adrian Bustamante and Marc Simmons (Albuquerque: El Rancho de las Golondrinas and the University of New Mexico Press, 1995): 22.

2. Certificate of Death, New Mexico State Department of Public Health, Santa Fe County, December 30, 1930; Marc Simmons, *Little Lion of the Southwest: A Life of Manuel Antonio Chaves* (Chicago: Swallow Press, 1973): 112, 247n; Lynn I. Perrigo, *Hispanos: Historic Leaders in New Mexico* (Santa Fe: Sunstone Press, 1985): 62-4; John D. Mondragón and Ernest S. Stapleton, *Public Education in New Mexico* (Albuquerque:

University of New Mexico Press, 2005): 20, 32, 87, 223; Tom Wiley, *Public School Education in New Mexico* (Albuquerque: Division of Government Research, University of New Mexico, 1965): 24-5; A. Kenneth Stern and Dan D. Chávez, "From Clerk to Professional: New Mexico's Superintendency and the Superintendents of Public Instruction, 1891-1916," *New Mexico Historical Review*, vol. 80 (Spring 2005): 199-202; Twitchell, *Old Santa Fe*, 467-68; Quentin, *Eternal New Mexicans*, 53; Julyan, *Place Names*, 14.

3. For a complete list of New Mexico Superintendents of Public Instruction, 1891-2004, see Mondragón and Stapleton, *Public Education in New Mexico*, 223-24.

4. John D. Wirth and Linda Harvey Aldrich, *Los Alamos: The Ranch School Years, 1917-1943* (Albuquerque: University of New Mexico Press, 2003): 11; Ashley D. Pond IV (grandson) to the author, August 25, 2003.

5. *Santa Fe New Mexican*, February 11, 1944; Wirth and Aldrich, *Ranch School*, 19, 193.

6. Ann M. Velia, *KOB: Goddard's Magic Mast* (Las Cruces: New Mexico State University, 1972): 9, 70, 56, 131-39.

7. Quoted in Ibid., 131.

8. *Alamogordo News*, January 2, 1930, with a commemorative editorial on that same date; Simon F. Kropp, *That All May Learn: New Mexico State University, 1888-1964* (Las Cruces: New Mexico State University, 1972): 161, 173, 196, 205, 217, 220, 226. Facing various troubles following Goddard's death, KOB was closed down at New Mexico A&M in March 1932 and transferred to Albuquerque, to be run by the *Albuquerque Journal*. Velia, *KOB*, 148, 154.

9. Kropp, *That All May Learn*, 3, 165, 176; Paxton P. Price, *Mesilla Valley Pioneers, 1823-1912* (Las Cruces: Yucca Tree Press, 1995): 247, 249; Anna R. Hadley, Caroline H. Allen, and C. Frank Allen, *Hiram Hadley* (Boston: n.p., 1924): 10, 74-5; Mondragón and Stapleton, *Public Education in New Mexico*, 19, 97; Stern and Chávez, "From Clerk to Professional," 207-10; *The Round-Up*, December 12, 1922. Tributes at Hadley's funeral and at a memorial service appeared in Hadley *et. al.*, *Hadley*, 79-111. Also see Lee Priestley, *Journeys of Faith: the Story of Preacher and Edith Lewis* (Las Cruces: Arroyo Press, 1992): 177.

10. *Santa Fe New Mexican*, September 23, 1927. Springer's last work was *American Silurian Crinoids* (Washington, D.C.: Smithsonian Institution, 1926). Also see "Dr. Frank Springer," *El Palacio*, vol. 23 (September 17, 1927): 315-22, 363-411; Necrology, *New Mexico Historical Review*, vol. 2 (October 1927): 387-93; Vigil, *Defining Our Destiny*, 27-33; David L. Caffey, *A Renaissance Man in New Mexico: The Life and Work of Frank Springer in Law, Business, Cultural Affairs, and Science* (College Station: Texas A&M Press, 2006); Julyan, *Place Names*, 340. According to David Caffey, Springer had no middle name, although authors have erroneously inserted "E", "L", and "W" as his middle initial. David L. Caffey to the author, September 10 and 13, 2004, January 26, 2005, June 28, 2006.

11. *Albuquerque Tribune*, November 3, 1969; *Albuquerque Journal*, May 3, 1970; *Las Vegas Optic*, May 18, 1970, and April 14, 1980; Thomas C. Donnelly, *I Came Down From the Hills: An Autobiography* (Portales: Bishop Publishing Company, 1979): 3, 326; Cecilia Jensen Bell et. al., *A Centennial History: Western New Mexico University, 1893-1993* (Silver City: Western New Mexico University, 1993): 53; Vigil, *Defining Our Destiny*, 65-84; John M. Moore, ed., *Who Is Who in New Mexico* (Albuquerque: n.p., 1957): 89.

12. *Santa Fe New Mexican*, June 5, 2005; *Albuquerque Journal*, June 5, 2005; Vigil, *Defining Our Destiny*, 97-107; interview with Wendy Quintana (archivist, Thomas C. Donnelly Library, New Mexico Highlands University), July 27, 2005.

13. *Socorro Defensor Chieftain*, January 3, 1983; Paige W. Christiansen, *Of Earth and Sky: A History of New Mexico Institute of Mining and Technology, 1889-1964* (Socorro: New Mexico Institute of Mining and Technology, 1964), 72-4; Joe Chew, *Storms Above the Desert: Atmospheric Research in New Mexico, 1935-85* (Albuquerque: University of New Mexico Press, 1987): 6-16, 143. For a description of New Mexico Tech's earliest leaders and presidents see Christiansen, *Of Earth and Sky*, 59-74.

14. Gibbs and Jackman, *New Mexico Military Institute*; J.R. Kelly, *A History of the New Mexico Military Institute, 1891-1941* (Albuquerque: University of New Mexico Press, 1953): 9-20, 20n.

15. Quoted in Kristie Miller, *Ruth Hanna McCormick: A Life in Politics, 1880-1944* (Albuquerque: University of New Mexico Press, 1992): 288. Also see the *Albuquerque Tribune*, February 18, 1933, and August 18, 1933; *New Mexico Sentinel*, July 3, 1933; Lou Liberty, *Constant Possum: The History of Sandia Preparatory School* (Albuquerque: Sandia Preparatory School, 2001): 12; Miller, *Ruth Hanna McCormick*, 9-10, 288; Christiansen, *Of Earth and Sky*, 103.

16. On John Medill McCormick's tragic death, see the *Albuquerque Journal*, July 3, 1938.

17. C.E. Hodgin, "Dr. Tight: The President and the Man," *New Mexico Quarterly*, vol. 1 (May 1931): 115-24; *Albuquerque Morning Journal*, January 17, 1910, with a commemorative editorial on that same date; Hooker, *Only in New Mexico*, 18-24; García and McCord, *Albuquerque*, 187. On the early history of UNM, see Dorothy Hughes, *Pueblo on the Mesa* (Albuquerque: University of New Mexico Press, 1939); William E. Davis, *Miracle on the Mesa: A History of the University of New Mexico, 1889-2003* (Albuquerque: University of New Mexico Press, 2006): 53-79.

18. Necrology, *New Mexico Historical Review*, vol. 20 (January 1945): 83.

19. Edgar L. Hewett, "James Fulton Zimmerman," *El Palacio*, vol. 51 (November 1944): 205; *Albuquerque Journal*, October 21, and a commemorative editorial on October 22, 1944; *Albuquerque Tribune*, October 21 and 23, 1944; *New York Times*, October 22, 1944; Hooker, *Only In New Mexico*, 60-87; Davis, *Miracle on the Mesa*, 137-79.

20. *Albuquerque Journal*, October 24 and 25, 1975; *Albuquerque Tribune*, October 24, 1975, with a commemorative editorial on October 28, 1975; *New Mexico Daily Lobo*, October 28, 1975; James Defibaugh, "The Popejoy Years," *New Mexico Alumnus*, vol. 48 (December 1975); William E. Davis, "The Man Who Made UNM," *Mirage*, vol. 23 (Winter 2005): 22-6; Davis, *Miracle on the Mesa*, 171-72, 191-225.

21. Quoted in the *Santa Fe New Mexican*, April 28, 1968.

22. Hooker, *Only In New Mexico*, 166-67, 181-82.

23. *Santa Fe New Mexican*, July 28, 1958; Ann Burleson Honea, "Julia Brown Asplund: New Mexico Librarian, 1875-1958" (Unpublished Master of Library Science thesis, University of Texas Press, 1967): 4, 5, 45; Terry Gugliotta (University of New Mexico Archivist) to the author, January 11, 2005.

24. *Albuquerque Tribune*, September 21, 1989; Robert K. Barney, *Roy William Johnson: A Short Biography* (n.c.: n.p., 1963): 5; Hooker, *Only In New Mexico*, 126-27; Davis, *Miracle on the Mesa*, 130-33, 176.

25. *Albuquerque Journal*, December 11 and 16, 2004; Davis, *Miracle on the Mesa*, 222-23, 323-24; García and McCord, *Albuquerque*, 61-2.

26. Quoted in www.collectorsguide.com/fa/fa044.shtml; Bernstein, *Dorothy Dunn and the Studio Style*, vii, 3-25; 153n; Dorothy Dunn Kramer, "The Studio, 1932-37: Fostering Indian Art as Art," *El Palacio*, vol. 83 (Winter 1977): 2-17.

27. L. Glenn Smith et. al., *Lives in Education: A Narrative of People and Ideas* (Mahwah, New Jersey: Lawrence Erlbaum Associates, 1994): 345-54; Michael Welsh, "A Prophet Without Honor: George I. Sánchez and Bilingualism in New Mexico," *New Mexico Historical Review*, vol. 69 (January 1994): 19-34; Davis, *Miracle on the Mesa*, 173-74; Margo Gutierrez (archivist, University of Texas Library) to the author, June 1, 2004.

7
SUNG AND UNSUNG HEROES

1. Arthur Kopecky, *New Buffalo* (Albuquerque: University of New Mexico Press, 2004): xvii.

2. *Albuquerque Daily Citizen*, October 20 and 26, 1896; Bryan, *Albuquerque Remembered*, 160-63; Simmons, *Albuquerque*, 296-97; Marc Simmons, "There Was a Time When Heroism Was Respected," *Socorro Defensor Chieftain*, February 9, 2002. Years later, in a similar act of self-sacrifice, twenty-three-year-old H.W. "Buddy" Hendricks, Jr. (April 22, 1941-June 9, 1964), saved the lives of thirty-five high school girls and seven adults traveling in a passenger bus from Albuquerque to Farmington when he skidded his construction truck more than sixty feet in an attempt to avoid crashing into the larger vehicle, which had swerved to the wrong side of the road. Hendricks was crushed to death in the accident. He was buried at Sunset Cemetery, Albuquerque, New Mexico. *Albuquerque Journal*, June 10, 1964

3. *Albuquerque Journal*, February 1, 2003

4. *Albuquerque Journal*, February 1, 2004

5. *Albuquerque Journal*, February 27, 2003; Roger Morris, *The Devil's Butcher Shop: The New Mexico Prison Uprising* (Albuquerque: University of New Mexico Press, 1983): 135-36, 167-75; interview with Kenneth Mills (son), December 29, 2003.

6. Jacqueline Meketa, *From Martyrs to Murderers* (Las Cruces: Yucca Tree Press, 1993): 196-202; Bullis, *Pasaron por Aqui*, 267-69; Quentin, *Eternal New Mexicans*, 113.

7. Stan Steiner, "Living Pioneer Still Has Fire Burning in His Eyes," *New Mexico Magazine*, vol. 64 (December 1986): 82-3.

8. *Santa Fe New Mexican*, April 4 and 5, 1988. Also see Elliott S. Barker, *Western Life and Adventures, 1889-1970* (Albuquerque: Calvin Horn, 1970); Elliott S. Barker, *When the Dogs Bark "Treed": A Year on the Trail of the Longtails* (Albuquerque: University of New Mexico Press, 1946); Elliott S. Barker, *Ramblings in the Field of Conservation* (Santa Fe: Sunstone Press, 1976); Julyan, *Place Names*, 31.

9. Thomas J. Carey and Donald R. Schmitt, "Mack Brazel Reconsidered," www.nicap.dabsol.co.uk/rosbraz.htm. Ten newspapers across New Mexico and papers from Seattle, Washington, to Chicago, Illinois, carried the news of Brazel's controversial discovery.

10. *New York Times*, December 10, 1971; *Albuquerque Journal*, February 29, 2004; Ben Keppel, "Thinking Through a Life: Reconsidering the Origins of Ralph Bunche,"

Journal of Negro Education, vol. 73 (Spring 2004): 116-24. Although some publications list Bunche's year of birth as 1903, his school and college records indicate that he was born in 1904. His family name was originally Bunch; the "e" was added in 1917 when his mother died and his grandmother hoped to give him and his sister a new start after moving them from Albuquerque to Los Angeles. Charles P. Henry, ed., *Ralph J. Bunche: Selected Speeches and Writings* (Ann Arbor: University of Michigan Press, 1995): 2, 317n; Brian Urquhart, *Ralph Bunche: An American Life* (New York: W.W. Norton, 1998): 25, 454-58.

11. Quoted in Ibid., 454.

12. *Silver City Daily Press*, February 18, 1985; *Albuquerque Tribune*, February 18, 1985; interview with Virginia Chacón (widow), April 14, 2002. Rosaura Revueltas, Juan Chacón's co-star in *Salt of the Earth*, was born in Ciudad Lerdo, Mexico, about 1909, and died on April 30, 1996, at her home in Cuernavaca, Mexico, after a long illness. In addition to her role as Esperanza in *Salt of the Earth*, Revueltas starred in thirteen other movies during her long acting career from 1946 to 1976 in Mexico. A two-act opera, entitled *Esperanza*, was written and produced at the University of Wisconsin-Madison. It premiered in Madison on August 25, 2000. *Hidalgo County Herald*, May 6, 2005. For a history of the Hanover strike and the making of *Salt of the Earth*, see Jack Cargill, "Empire and Opposition: 'The Salt of the Earth' Strike" in Kern, *Labor in New Mexico*, 183-267; James J. Lorence, *The Suppression of Salt of the Earth* (Albuquerque: University of New Mexico Press, 1999): 19-90. For the screenplay of *Salt of the Earth*, see Michael Wilson, *Salt of the Earth* (New York: Feminist Press, 1978).

13. *Santa Fe New Mexican*, May 8, 1968; *Albuquerque Journal*, May 9, 1968; *Taos News*, May 16, 1968; John Collier, *From Every Zenith: A Memoir* (Denver: Sage Books, 1963): 20.

14. *Albuquerque Journal*, December 31, 2004

15. *Roswell Daily Record*, December 16, 2005; *Albuquerque Journal*, December 19, 2005

16. *Albuquerque Journal*, October 22, 2003. For the Kent family's experience in segregated Tucumcari see Melzer, *When We Were Young in the West*, 227-43.

17. Hispanics called Jencks "El Palomino" because he was so blond and light complected.

18. *Albuquerque Journal*, December 24, 2005. For a history of the Hanover strike and the making of *Salt of the Earth*, see Cargill, "Empire and Opposition," 183-267; Lorence, *Suppression of Salt of the Earth*, 19-90; Ellen R. Baker, *On Strike and On Film* (Chapel Hill: University of North Carolina Press, 2007).

19. *New York Times*, April 22, 1948; Marybeth Lorbiecki, *Aldo Leopold: A Fierce Green Fire* (Helena, Montana: Falson, 1996): 5, 178-79, 201n; Curt Meine, *Aldo Leopold: His Life and Work* (Madison: University of Wisconsin Press, 1988): 521; John R. Sweet, "Men and Varmints in the Gila Wilderness, 1909-1936," *New Mexico Historical Review*, vol. 77 (Fall 2002): 376-87; Julyan, *Place Names*, 12.

20. For a typical article that neglected to mention McJunkin's role in the discovery of Folsom Man, see the *Alamogordo News*, August 9, 1928.

21. Franklin Folsom, *Black Cowboy: The Life and Legend of George McJunkin* (Niwot, Colorado: Roberts Rinehart, 1992): 139-40; Bullis, *Pasaron por Aquí*, 216-18.

22. Certificate of Death, New Mexico State Department of Public Health, Doña Ana County, March 5, 1949. Noss was called "Doc" because he often falsely claimed that he was a

medical doctor. His death certificate listed his occupation as mining engineer.

23. David Leon Chandler, *One Hundred Tons of Gold* (Garden City, New York: Doubleday, 1978): 11-12, 103-7, Chapter 11.

24. Interview with Greg Angstrom (member, Victorio Peak Project), April 27, 2004.

25. *Albuquerque Journal*, October 1, 1922, and January 4 and 6, 1965; Perrigo, *Hispanos*, 75-7.

26. Quoted in Charlotte Whaley, *Nina Otero-Warren of Santa Fe* (Albuquerque: University of New Mexico Press, 1994): 203. Also see the *Albuquerque Journal*, January 4 and 6, 1965; Ann M. Massmann, "Adelina 'Nina' Otero-Warren: A Spanish-American Cultural Broker," *Journal of the Southwest*, vol. 42 (Winter 2000): 877-96; Elizabeth Salas, "Soledad Chávez de Chacón, Adelina Otero-Warren, and Concha Ortiz y Pino: Three Hispana Politicians in New Mexico Politics" in Melanie Gustafson, Kristie Miller, and Elisabeth I. Perry, eds., *We Have Come To Stay: American Women and Political Parties, 1880-1960* (Albuquerque: University of New Mexico Press, 1999): 164-69; Rebolledo, *Nuestras Mujeres*, 43-4.

27. *Fire on the Mountain* was made into a made-for-television movie with Buddy Ebsen playing John Vogelin (the John Prather character) and Ron Howard as his young co-star. At least one critic has concluded that the movie suffered "from too much Ron Howard and a poorly developed romantic angle conjured up for the television audience." Caffey, *Land of Enchantment, Land of Conflict*, 179.

28. Sara J. Chambers, "John Prather: Pioneer Versus the U.S. Army" in Townsend., *Things Remembered*, 133.

29. *Alamogordo Daily News*, February 12, 1965

30. *Alamogordo Daily News*, February 12, and 14, 1965; *Las Cruces Sun-News*, February 12, 1965; Sonnichsen, *Tularosa*, 291; Townsend, *You Take the Sundials*, 136-42; Robert K. Mortensen, "John Prather's War," *New Mexico Stockman*, vol. 49 (March 1983): 76-80.

31. *Albuquerque Journal*, August 29 and 30, 1989; Sando, *Pueblo Profiles*, 57-62. Miguel Trujillo had a middle initial, but no middle name. Interview with Josephine Waconda (daughter), July 7, 2003.

32. Albuquerque Journal, October 28, 2004

33. *Albuquerque Journal*, February 3, 2005; interview with James Williams II (grandson), February 16, 2005.

34. Gordon Owen, *Las Cruces, New Mexico, 1849-1999* (Las Cruces: Red Sky, 1999): 150-1; n.a., *History of Hope*, 49; Daniel Gibson, "Blackdom," *New Mexico Magazine*, vol. 64 (February 1986): 46-7, 50-1; Jeff Berg, "Quest for Freedom: Early Black Settlements Made a Dream Come True," *New Mexico Magazine*, vol. 83 (March 2005): 54-7; M.A. Walton, "Vado, New Mexico: A Dream in the Desert," *Southern New Mexico Historical Review*, vol. 2 (1995): 17, 20, 22.

35. Certificate of Death, New Mexico State Department of Public Health, Chaves County, March 24, 1926.

36. J. Evetts Haley quoted in Elvis E. Fleming and Ernestine Chesser Williams, *Treasures of History* (Roswell: Historical Society for Southeast New Mexico, 1995): III:44.

37. Certificate of Death, New Mexico State Department of Public Health, Santa Fe County, October 23, 1946. The Seton Castle was sold to the Academy for the Love of Learning in 2003. While undergoing major reconstruction, it burned on November 15, 2005. Fortunately, most of Seton's art collection and library had been stored in an off-site location. *Santa Fe New Mexican*, November 15, 2005; *Albuquerque Journal*, November 16, 2005.

38. *Santa Fe New Mexican*, October 23 and 24, 1946, with a commemorative editorial on October 24, 1946; Quentin, *Eternal New Mexicans*, 32; Necrology, *New Mexico Historical Review*, vol. 22 (January 1947): 107; H. Allen Anderson, "Ernest Thompson Seton's First Visit to New Mexico," *New Mexico Historical Review*, vol. 56 (October 1981): 369; Ernest Thompson Seton, *Trail of an Artist-Naturalist* (New York: Scribner's Sons, 1941); Julyan, *Place Names*,. 331-32. Seton Castle is a New Mexico Registered Cultural Property.

39. *Albuquerque Journal*, March 14, 1988; Bert Herrman, *Mountainair, New Mexico: Centennial History, 1903-2003* (Mountainair: Mountainair Public Schools, 2003): 61-2; interview with Martín Sisneros (grandson), October 27, 2004; interview with Benny Sisneros (son), August 8, 2005.

40. *Albuquerque Journal*, February 11, 1952, November 8, 10, 11, and 15, 1961, with a commemorative editorial on November 8, 1961; *Albuquerque Tribune*, November 11 and 14, 1961; Ruth K. Hall, *First Ladies of New Mexico* (Santa Fe: Lightning Tree Press, 1982): 85, 88.

41. Victor David Westphall III (January 30, 1940-May 22, 1968) is buried at the National Cemetery, Santa Fe, New Mexico. See Victor Westphall, *David's Story: A Casualty of Vietnam* (Springer, New Mexico: Center for the Advancement of Human Dignity, 1981).

42. *Denver Post*, August 16, 1970; *Albuquerque Tribune*, April 29, 1971, and May 19, 1971; *Albuquerque Journal*, May 23, 1971, and July 25, 2003; *Taos News*, May 26, 1971, and November 17-23, 2005; Marc Simmons, "Honoring the Life of Victor Westphall," *Santa Fe New Mexican*, November 1, 2003; Press Release, Vietnam Veterans National Memorial, July 24, 2003.

43. Walter D. Westphall correspondence to members of the David Westphall Veterans Foundation, Inc., n.d.

44. James Larkin White, *The Discovery and History of Carlsbad Caverns: Jim White's Own Story* (Carlsbad: Carlsbad Caverns Guadalupe Mountains Association, 1998): 1; *Carlsbad Current-Argus*, April 29 and 30, 1946; Marc Simmons, "Discoverer of Caverns Died a Poor Man," *Santa Fe Reporter*, September 12, 1982. Whites City near Carlsbad Caverns was not named for Jim White. Julyan, *Place Names*, 379.

45. *Albuquerque Journal*, February 12, 13, and 16, 1985, and October 1, 2005; Pamela Salmon, *Sandia Peak: A History of the Sandia Peak Tramway and Ski Area* (Albuquerque: Sandia Peak Ski and Tramway, 1998): 74, 98, 155; Quentin, *Eternal New Mexicans*, 26; historical literature distributed at the Anderson Abruzzo Albuquerque International Balloon Museum.

46. *Albuquerque Journal*, June 28 and 30, 1983, and October 1, 2005; historical literature distributed at the Anderson Abruzzo Albuquerque International Balloon Museum.

47. Marc Simmons, *Yesterday in Santa Fe* (Santa Fe: Sunstone Press, 1989): 50; Donald Chaput, *Francis X. Aubry: Trader, Trailmaker, and Voyageur in the Southwest* (Glendale, California: Arthur H. Clark Company, 1975): 1, 158-60; Twitchell, *Leading Facts*,

II:306n-8n; Arie W. Poldervaart, *Black-Robed Justice* (Santa Fe: Historical Society of New Mexico, 1948): 43-6.

48. *Honolulu (Hawaii) Advertiser*, August 17, 1927; *Washington Post*, December 8, 1973; Thomas L. Hedglen, "A Life in Flight," *Valencia County News-Bulletin*, November 16, 2002, December 24, 2002, and January 18, 2003; Thomas L. Hedglen (Goebel biographer) to the author, May 28, 2003.

49. *New York Times*, October 4, 1912; *San Diego Union*, October 4, 1912; Don E. Alberts, *Balloons to Bombers: Aviation in Albuquerque, 1882-1945* (Albuquerque: Museum of Albuquerque, 1987): 11-13; Marc Simmons, "Early Aviation Fascinated New Mexicans," *Santa Fe New Mexican*, November 24, 2001; Bryan, *Albuquerque Remembered*, 184-87; interview with Ernest Sansome (grandson), August 8, 2005; interview with Gene Walsh (grandson), August 12, 2005; Sue Walsh Campbell (great-granddaughter) to the author, August 14, 2005. Roy A. Stamm had recruited Walsh to perform at the 1911 fair. James S. and Ann L. Carson, eds., *For Me, The Sun: The Autobiography of Roy A. Stamm* (Albuquerque: Museum of Albuquerque, n.d.): 189-91.

50. *Albuquerque Journal*, November 27 and 28, 1970; William Buchanan, *A Shining Season* (New York: Bantam Books, 1979): 204-05.

51. *Wickkenburg (Arizona) Sun*, November 4, 1971

52. *Roswell Daily Record*, October 20 and 21, 1947; *Roswell Dispatch*, October 21, 1947; *Albuquerque Journal*, October 21, 1947; Thelma Crosby and Eve Ball, *Bob Crosby: World Champion Cowboy* (Clarendon, Texas: Clarendon Press, 1966): 22, 243-44.

53. Quoted in Randy Roberts, *Papa Jack: Jack Johnson and the Era of White Hopes* (New York: Free Press, 1983): 3, 226. Also see the *New York Times*, June 11, 1946; Geoffrey C. Ward, *Unforgivable Blackness: The Rise and Fall of Jack Johnson* (New York: Knopf, 2004).

54. Certificate of Death, New Mexico State Department of Public Health, Grant County, December 17, 1936. Lilly's death certificate incorrectly lists his year of birth as 1844.

55. Schimmel, *Dunton*, 78-9.

56. J. Frank Dobie, *The Ben Lilly Legend* (Austin: University of Texas Press, 1990): 16, 218; Quentin, *Eternal New Mexicans*, 130; Sweet, "Men and Varmints in the Gila Wilderness," 374-76; Reverend Clifton H. Henderson, Jr., and Jean Woodburn Henderson, "Directory of the Silver City Memory Lane Cemetery, 1871-1978," Unpublished manuscript, Silver City Museum, Silver City, New Mexico; roadside memorial outside Pino Altos.

57. Rhonda Coy Sedgwick, *Prairie Trails of Miz Mac: From Canada to the Cowgirl Hall of Fame* (Newcastle, Wyoming: Quarter Circle A Enterprises, 1990): 3, 15-20, 111; Quentin, *Eternal New Mexicans*, 114.

58. Interview with Wanda McLaughlin Hughes (daughter), August 25, 2004.

59. *Albuquerque Tribune*, February 16, 1950, December 7, 1951, and September 5, 1965; *Albuquerque Journal*, December 17, 1953

60. *Albuquerque Journal*, May 3, 1959, May 19, 1959, and May 29, 2005; *Albuquerque Tribune*, May 18, 1959, and December 20, 1975; Parnelli Jones, *The Unser Legacy* (Osceola, Wisconsin: Motorbooks International, 2005): 32-55; John Richard Arnold, "Unser Museum Revs Up," *New Mexico Magazine*, vol. 84 (January 2006): 58-63; interpretative historical display at the Unser Racing Museum, Albuquerque, New Mexico.

61. *Albuquerque Journal*, May 26, 1970

8
LAWMEN, CRIMINALS, AND VICTIMS OF CRIME

1. Certificate of Death, New Mexico State Department of Public Health, Bernalillo County, August 28, 1945. *Albuquerque Tribune*, August 28, 1945; *Las Cruces Sun-News*, August 28, 1945; *New York Times*, August 29, 1945; *Albuquerque Journal*, October 8, 2000; Larry D. Ball, *Elfego Baca in Life and Legend* (El Paso: Texas Western Press, 1992): 1, 101; Howard Bryan, *Incredible Elfego Baca* (Santa Fe: Clear Light Publishers, 1993): 7, 101-2; Bryan, *Albuquerque Remembered*, 201-7. Baca's death certificate, completed by his wife, claimed that February 7, 1865, was his birthday.

2. Browning, *Violence Was No Stranger*, 11.

3. David Townsend and Cliff McDonald, "Howard S. Beacham: Otero County's Eliot Ness," *Southern New Mexico Historical Review*, vol. 7 (January 2000): 49-52.

4. Chuck Hornung, *The Thin Gray Line: The New Mexico Mounted Police* (Fort Worth: Western Heritage Press, 1971): 31-2; *New Mexico Sentinel*, October 5, 1937; *Albuquerque Journal*, February 2, 1981; Browning, *Violence Was No Stranger*, 87-8; Frederick H. Fornoff (grandson) to the author, March 4, 1997.

5. Leon C. Metz, *Pat Garrett: The Story of a Western Lawman* (Norman: University of Oklahoma Press, 1974): 306; Nolan, *West*, 230; Keleher, *Fabulous Frontier*, 91n-92n.

6. Quoted in the *Alamogordo News*, October 22, 1931. Of Garrett's family only Elizabeth is not buried in the family plot in Las Cruces. See the photo of her gravesite at South Park Cemetery, Roswell, New Mexico, in Chapter 3, No. 53.

7. *Santa Fe New Mexican*, February 29, 1908; Sonnichsen, *Tularosa*, 228-44; Metz, *Garrett*, 290-306; Quentin, *Eternal New Mexicans*, 150-51.

8. *Albuquerque Tribune*, February 4, 1971; Cleaveland, *Satan's Paradise*, 99-274; Simmons, *When Six-Guns Ruled: Outlaw Tales of the Southwest* (Santa Fe: Ancient City Press, 1990): 116; Browning, *Violence Was No Stranger*, 135.

9. Robert K. DeArment, *George Scarborough: The Life and Death of a Lawman on the Closing Frontier* (Norman: University of Oklahoma Press, 1992): 6, 224-29.

10. Quoted in Howard R. Lamar, *Charlie Siringo's West* (Albuquerque: University of New Mexico Press, 2005): 301. Also see Clarence Siringo Adams, "Charlie Siringo: The Cowboy Detective," *New Mexico Magazine*, vol. 45 (October 1967): 18-19, 36, 40; Simmons, *When Six-Guns Ruled*, 76-9; Marc Simmons, "Siringo Road's Namesake Was a 'Cowboy Detective,'" *Santa Fe New Mexican*, February 14, 2004.

11. Bob Alexander, *Sheriff Harvey Whitehill: Silver City Stalwart* (Silver City: High-Lonesome Press, 2005): 9, 60-2, 283-84. A photo of Whitehill's gravesite is included in Ibid., 284.

12. *Gallup Daily Independent*, April 4, 1935; Gary L. Stuart, *The Gallup 14: A Novel* (Albuquerque: University of New Mexico Press, 2000).

13. *Albuquerque Tribune*, August 6, 1973

14. Lomax and Lomax, *Cowboy Songs*, 300-02; Gardner, *Jack Thorp's Songs of the Cowboys*, 71.

15. Simmons, *When Six-Guns Ruled*, 34.

16. Chuck Parsons, *Robert Clay Allison: Gentleman Gun Fighter* (Pecos, Texas: West of the Pecos Museum Press, 1977): 22. Also see Chuck Parsons, *Clay Allison: Portrait of a Shootist* (Seagraves, Texas: Pioneer Book Publishers, 1983): 1-2, 54; Cleaveland, *Satan's Paradise*, 36-41; Bullis, *Pasaron por Aquí*, 17-19.

17. Quoted in Parsons, *Robert Clay Allison*, 23.

18. *Silver City Enterprise*, May 20, 1892; Jess G. Hayes, *Apache Vengeance: The True Story of Apache Kid* (Albuquerque: University of New Mexico Press, 1954): 4; Simmons, *When Six-Guns Ruled*, 106-10; Stephen J. Andrews (historian and former San Mateo Mountains area resident) to the author, November 20, 2000; Julyan, *Place Names*, 20. One of the last accounts of his raids, the theft of "a large number of sheep," was reported in the *Santa Fe New Mexican*, August 21, 1905.

19. Sonnichsen, *Tularosa*, 229-30, 238-44; Robert N. Mullin, *The Strange Career of Wayne Brazel* (Canyon, Texas: Palo Duro Press, n.d.): 1-35.

20. Simmons, *Ranchers, Ramblers, and Renegades*, 97-9; Bullis, *Pasaron por Aquí*, 60-2; Browning, *Violence Was No Stranger*, 48. For another explanation of Black Jack's death (at the hands of one of his gang members), see Marc Simmons, "Murderous Desperadoes," *Santa Fe Reporter*, January 1, 1982.

21. *Santa Fe New Mexican*, February 16, 1999; *Albuquerque Journal*, February 16, 1999

22. Quoted in the *Santa Fe New Mexican*, February 16, 1999.

23. Howard Bryan, *Wildest of the Wild West* (Santa Fe: Clear Light, 1988): 200-07; Wommack, *From the Grave*, 416.

24. Lomax and Lomax, *Cowboy Songs*, 152-57. Originally buried on private land, Jesse James's body had to be reinterred to a Protestant cemetery in Kearney, Nebraska, when the man who leased the farm property exploited the gravesite by selling flowers grown on it for twenty-five cents each. T.J. Stiles, *Jesse James: Last Rebel of the Civil War* (New York: Vintage Books, 2002): 472n.

25. Bruce Ashcroft, *The Territorial History of Socorro* (El Paso: Western Texas Press, 1988): 25-6; Bullis, *Pasaron por Aquí*, 99-102.

26. Quoted in Howard Bryan, *Robbers, Rogues, and Ruffians: True Tales of the Wild West in New Mexico* (Santa Fe: Clear Light, 1991): 88, 106-08.

27. Quoted in Simmons, *When Six-Guns Ruled*, 92.

28. Certificate of Death, New Mexico State Department of Public Health, Sierra County, August 8, 1946.

29. Quoted in Keleher, *Fabulous Frontier*, 276n. Also see Gibson, *Fountain*, 271-81.

30. Wommack, *From the Grave*, 202-03.

31. *New York Times*, July 25, 2002; Edward Lee Howard, *Safe House: The Compelling Memoirs of the Only CIA Spy to Seek Asylum in Russia* (Bethesda, Maryland: National Press Books, 1995): 16. Also see David Wise, *The Spy Who Got Away: The Inside Story of Edward Lee Howard* (New York: Random House, 1988).

32. Bryan, *Robbers, Rogues, and Ruffians*, 7; Parsons, *Portrait*, 9-11; Cleaveland, *Satan's Paradise*, 42-7; Tom Hilton, "Charles Kennedy," in Stephen Zimmer, ed., *For Good or Bad: People of the Cimarron Country* (Santa Fe: Sunstone Press, 1999): 44-9. Marc Simmons writes of a similarly brutal thief named Moody in southern New Mexico. Before he was finally apprehended, Moody "had been killing every stranger who dropped by." Lawmen uncovered twenty skeletons near the killer's cabin. Simmons does not mention Moody's first name, nor his fate. Simmons, *Ranchers, Ramblers, and Renegades*, 77-8.

33. F. Stanley, *No Tears for Black Jack Ketchum* (Denver: World Press, 1958): 1-7, 132-46; Bryan, *True Tales*, 70; Bryan, *Robbers, Rogues, and Ruffians*, 251, 283-84; Bullis, *Pasaron por Aquí*, 193-94.

34. *Santa Fe New Mexican*, July 27, 1899

35. Berry Spradley (descendent) to the author, December 3, 2004.

36. On the origin of Ketchum's nickname, see Larry D. Ball, "Black Jack Ketchum in Life and Legend," *Panhandle Plains Historical Review*, vol. 64 (1991): 74-7. Black Jack gave his name as George Stevens when he was admitted to a Trinidad, Colorado, hospital following his capture in August 1899. Bryan, *Robbers, Rogues, and Ruffians*, 292.

37. Ball, "Black Jack Ketchum in Life and Legend," 66-85.

38. *Santa Fe New Mexican*, April 26 and 27, 1901. Also see Cleaveland, *Satan's Paradise*, 93-106.

39. Ball, "Black Jack Ketchum in Life and Legend," 80.

40. Stanley, *No Tears*, 7, 144-46.

41. Berry Spradley (descendent) to the author, December 3, 2004; D. Ray Blakeley (Director, Herzstein Memorial Museum, Clayton, New Mexico) to the author, December 1, 2004.

42. *Albuquerque Journal*, February 25, 2001; Black Jack Ketchum Centennial Festival Program, June 1-2, 2001, Clayton, New Mexico.

43. Berry Spradley (descendent) to the author, December 3, 2004.

44. Certificate of Death, New Mexico State Department of Public Health, Otero County, December 15, 1941; *Alamogordo News*, December 18, 1941; David H. Townsend, "Oliver Lee," *Rio Grande History*, vol. 1 (December 1973): 4-7; Eidenbach, "Stockman," 43-61; Gibson, *Fountain*, 271-81; Townsend and McDonald, *Centennial*, 127-29; Keleher, *Fabulous Frontier*, 244; Sonnichsen, *Tularosa*, 107-201; Bullis, *Pasaron por Aquí*, 183-90; Charles F. Coan, *A History of New Mexico* (Chicago: American Historical Society, 1925): III:134-35; Julyan, *Place Names*, 249-50.

45. A photo of the roadside cross appeared in a Howard Bryan article about Leyba in the *Albuquerque Tribune*, January 12, 1956.

46. Robert R. White, "The Murder of Colonel Charles Potter," *New Mexico Historical Review*, vol. 62 (July 1987): 249-62; Bullis, *Pasaron por Aquí*, 198-99.

47. Bryan, *Wildest of the Wild West*, 171-93; Bullis, *Pasaron por Aquí*, 273-76.

48. Alice Bullock, "Vicente Silva and the Bandidos," *New Mexico Magazine*, vol. 62

(August 1984): 37-9; Mills, "Unmarked Cemetery of Las Vegas," 20n; Simmons, *When Six-Guns Ruled*, 42.

49. Rita and Janaloo Hill, "Shakespeare Cemetery: Resting Place of Our Pioneers" (unpublished booklet): 10; Simmons, *When Six-Guns Ruled*, 87-8; Bullis, *Pasaron por Aquí*, 277-79; Browning, *Violence Was No Stranger*, 251.

50. Certificate of Death, New Mexico State Department of Public Health, Grant County, June 18, 1921. Walter's death certificate lists his name as J.C. Brown, his occupation as rancher, and his date of death as June 17, 1921.

51. Bryan, *Robbers, Rogues, and Ruffians*, 168, 197, 206; Philip J. Rasch, "An Incomplete Account of 'Bronco Bill' Walters," *The Brand Book*, vol. 19 (January 1977): 1, 8.

52. Bryan, *Wildest of the Wild West*, 192.

53. Yarberry was probably an assumed name, perhaps taken from a respected Colorado lawman. Bullis, *Pasaron por Aquí*, 316.

54. Quoted in Bryan, *Robbers, Rogues, and Ruffians*, 120-21.

55. Simmons, *When Six-Guns Ruled*, 60; Bullis, *Pasaron por Aquí*, 25, 316-19; Bryan, *Albuquerque Remembered*, 113-18. The case against Yarberry was summarized in the *Albuquerque Journal*, August 13, 1933. Marc Simmons notes an interesting early city ordinance in Santa Fe regarding legally executed bodies. According to this ordinance, dead bodies had to be buried within twenty-four hours, although an "exception will be made with bodies delivered over from hanging which can be buried later, so that officials can make certain that they are really dead." Ordinance quoted in Simmons, *Yesterday in Santa Fe*, 36.

56. Interview with Andy Gregg (photo journalist), June 8, 2001.

57. Robert J. Tórrez, *UFOs Over Galisteo and Other Stories of New Mexico's History* (Albuquerque: University of New Mexico Press, 2004): 75-8; Maurice Kildare, "They Hanged Her Twice," *New Mexico Lawman*, vol. 32 (June 1966): 3-9; Alice Bullock, "The Hanging Tree Didn't Forget," *Santa Fe New Mexican*, September 15, 1974; Quentin, *Eternal New Mexicans*, 96; Bryan, *Wild West*, 56-8; *Santa Fe New Mexican*, April 26, 1986. A photo (circa 1905) of Paula's grave was included in Kildare, "Hanged Her Twice," 7, although the site's location is currently unknown. In 1979 Myra Ellen Jenkins, then the New Mexico State Historian, believed that the grave was in Las Vegas's potter's field. Mills, "Graves in the Gravel," 20n.

58. The entire *corrido* appeared in Bob L'Aloge, *Knights of the Six-Gun* (Las Cruces: Yucca Tree Press, 1991): 158-60.

59. Fray Angélico Chávez, "Doña Tules: Her Fame and Her Funeral," *El Palacio*, vol. 62 (August 1950): 227-34; Janet Lecompte, "La Tules and the Americans," *Arizona and the West*, vol. 20 (Autumn 1978): 220; Walter Briggs, "The Lady They Called Tules," *New Mexico Magazine*, vol. 49 (March/April 1971): 9-16; Perrigo, *Hispanos*, 33-5; Deena J. González, "La Tules of Image and Reality" in Adela de la Torre and Beatríz M. Pesquera, *Building with Our Hands: New Directions in Chicana Studies* (Berkeley: University of California Press, 2004): 75-90.

60. Janet Lecompte, "La Tules: The Ultimate New Mexican Woman" in Glenda Riley and Richard W. Etulain, eds., *By Grit and Grace: Eleven Women Who Shaped the American West* (Golden, Colorado: Fulcrum, 1997): 17-18. Mary J. Straw Cook, *Doña Tules: Santa Fe's Courtesan and Gambler* (Albuquerque: University of New Mexico, Press, 2007): 3, 94-107.

61. Max Evans, *Madam Millie: Bordellos from Silver City to Ketchikan* (Albuquerque: University of New Mexico Press, 2002): 4, 308.

62. Interview with Peggy Wright (Millie's last caregiver), October 7, 2003.

63. *Sierra County News*, April 9, 1943

64. Certificate of Death, New Mexico State Department of Public Health, Sierra County, April 3, 1943; Meketa, *Martyrs to Murderers*, 147-60; Quentin, *Eternal New Mexicans*, 141-42. Sadie's death certificate incorrectly identifies Kansas as her place of birth.

65. WPA interview conducted by Clay W. Vaden, Quemado, New Mexico, August 10, 1936, History Files, New Mexico State Records Center and Archives, Santa Fe, New Mexico.

66. *Sierra County News*, April 9, 1943

67. Mary Frances Beverley, "Sadie Orchard Was a Good Ol' Girl," *New Mexico Magazine*, vol.61 (July 1983): 42; Marc Simmons, "The Remarkable Sadie," *Santa Fe Reporter*, August 19-25, 1998.

68. Certificate of Death, New Mexico State Department of Public Health, Luna County, February 9, 1934.

69. *Las Cruces Sun-News*, November 3, 1994; Browning, *Violence Was No Stranger*, 255.

70. Quoted in Cynthia Rose, *Lottie Deno: Gambling Queen of Hearts* (Santa Fe: Clear Light Publishers, 1994): 43.

71. Quoted in the *Deming Graphic*, February 15, 1934. Also see the *Deming Headlight*, February 16, 1934.

72. Rose, *Lottie Deno*, 113.

73. Certificate of Death, New Mexico State Department of Public Health, McKinley County, April 4, 1935.

74. *Gallup Independent*, April 4 and 5, 1935; Bullis, *New Mexico's Finest*, 41-43; Bullis, *Pasaron por Aquí*, 49-51. On the Gallup riot and its aftermath, see Harry R. Rubenstein, "Political Repression in New Mexico: The Destruction of the National Miners Union in Gallup" in Kern, *Labor in New Mexico*, 91-140. On the subsequent trial in Aztec, New Mexico, see the *Farmington Times Hustler*, October 11 and 18, 1935, and Gary L. Stuart's historical novel, *Gallup 14*.

75. *Albuquerque Journal*, September 11, 12, 13, 16, 25, 1980; Bullis, *New Mexico's Finest*, 51-52; interviews with Ed and Ted Chacon (brothers), September 13, 2005. Ed Chacon is finishing a biography of his brother entitled, *Only Butterflies Are Free*, the song sang at Phil's funeral in 1980.

76. Quoted in the *Santa Fe New Mexican*, May 31, 1892.

77. *Santa Fe New Mexican*, June 1, 1892

78. *Santa Fe New Mexican*, June 6, 1892

79. *Santa Fe New Mexican*, May 31, June 1, 2, 3, 4, 6, 27, 1892, and April 3, 1897; Tobias Duran, "Francisco Chávez, Thomas B. Catron, and Organized Political Violence in Santa

Fe in the 1890s," *New Mexico Historical Review*, vol. 59 (July 1984): 291-310; Marc Simmons, "One Murder Leads to Four Hangings," *Santa Fe New Mexican*, January 24, 2004. The four men executed for this murder were buried at Rosario Cemetery in Santa Fe.

80. *Albuquerque Journal*, December 26, 27, 29, 30, 1992, with an editorial on December 30, 1992; interview with Nadine Milford (mother), May 18, 2005. Sadly, this crash occurred in the same area of I-40 where three people had been killed in another head-on DWI crash just seven weeks earlier. *Albuquerque Journal*, December 27, 1992

81. *Albuquerque Journal*, December 30, 1992

82. Quoted in the *Albuquerque Journal*, December 30, 1992.

83. Quoted in the *Albuquerque Journal*, December 29, 1992.

84. *Santa Fe New Mexican*, February 4, 1896; Gibson, *Fountain*, 3-5, 228-29; Gordon R. Owen, *The Two Alberts: Fountain and Fall* (Las Cruces: Yucca Tree Press, 1996): 9, 291; Corey Recko, *Murder on the White Sands: The Disappearance of Albert and Henry Fountain* (Denton: University of North Texas Press, 2007):3-9; Like Fountain, twenty-five percent of the California Column settled in New Mexico.

85. *Silver City Enterprise*, April 22, 1892

86. *Las Cruces Sun-News*, May 25, 1948; Bryan, *True Tales*, 39-40.

87. Archuletta and Holden, *Traveling New Mexico*, 101. Colonel Fountain had five other children. Three (Albert, Jr., Margaret, and Jack) lived into their seventies, dying from natural causes, but two shared their father and Henry's violent fates. Edward Fountain was shot by his landlady in Pinos Altos, while Tom Fountain was either accidentally killed or assassinated during the Mexican Revolution. Lenore Harris Huges, *Adobe Abodes* (El Paso: Hughes Publishing Company, 1985): 179.

88. Two Certificates of Death, New Mexico State Department of Public Health, Taos County, July 3, 1929. One death certificate (claiming natural causes as the cause of death) was signed by Milton A. Spatts. The second death certificate (claiming homicide) was signed by Dr. T. P. Martin.

89. *Santa Fe New Mexican*, July 5, 1929; Quentin, *Eternal New Mexicans*, 67; Erna Ferguson, *Murder and Mystery in New Mexico* (Santa Fe: Lightning Tree Press, 1991): 133-52; Julyan, *Place Names*, 218.

90. *Albuquerque Journal*, September 12, 1929

91. Quoted in the *Albuquerque Journal*, September 18, 1929.

92. See, for example, the *New Mexico Sentinel*, March 27, 1938.

93. *Taos News*, September 29, 1977

94. Chuck Hornung, "The Mysterious Death of Prohibition Agent Ray Sutton," Paper presented at the Historical Society of New Mexico's Annual Conference, Clayton, New Mexico, April 22, 2005; Bullis, *Pasaron por Aquí*, 298-99; Don Bullis, *New Mexico's Finest: Peace Officers Killed in the Line of Duty, 1847-1999* (Santa Fe: New Mexico Department of Public Safety, 2000): 281-83.

95. Frank McNitt, *Richard Wetherill: Anasazi* (Albuquerque: University of New Mexico Press, 1957): 5-7, 9, 269-312; Gabriel, *Marietta Wetherill*, 237; Fowler, *Laboratory*,

187-200; Marc Simmons, "The Killing of Richard Wetherill," *Santa Fe Reporter*, October 28-November 3, 1992.

96. Edith Colgate Salsbury, *Susy and Mark Twain* (New York: Harper and Row, 1965): 385-93. For a summary of the Arquette case see the *Albuquerque Tribune*, July 16, 2004.

97. Certificate of Death, New Mexico State Department of Public Health, Doña Ana County, April 6, 1949; *Las Cruces Sun-News*, April 10 to May 17, 1949

98. Quoted in the *Las Cruces Sun-News*, December 3, 2000. Also see the *Santa Fe New Mexican*, February 17, 1999; *The Silence of Cricket Coogler*, a documentary film produced by Charles Cullin, Jack Flynn, and George Glass, Trespartes Films Venture Associates, 2000. Coogler was nicknamed Cricket because her high-heel shoes made a clicking sound when she walked.

99. *Roswell Daily Record*, July 20 to 28, 1986

100. www.clarkprosecutor.org

101. Certificate of Death, New Mexico State Department of Public Health, Santa Fe County, November 15, 1931; Reed, *A Woman's Place*, 91-104.

102. *Santa Fe New Mexican*, November 18, 1931; Ralph Melnick, *Justice Betrayed: A Double Killing in Old Santa Fe* (Albuquerque: University of New Mexico Press, 2002): 15, 31, 34; Cleofas M. Jaramillo, *Romance of a Little Village Girl* (Albuquerque: University of New Mexico Press, 2000): 115, 155-66.

103. *Silver City Enterprise*, March 17 and 24, 1893; Kropp, *That All May Learn*, 36. Known as a "cowardly...bad man," Roper was implicated in at least six other merciless murders in the Southwest. *Silver City Enterprise*, March 17, 1893

104. *Rio Grande Republican* quoted in the *Silver City Enterprise*, March 17, 1893.

105. Quoted in Jean Fulton, "Survey and Inventory of the IOOF Cemetery, Las Cruces, New Mexico," Unpublished manuscript, 1999.

106. *Rio Grande Republican*, March 10, 17, and 24, 1893; "The Sam Steel Story," New Mexico State University Sam Steel Society Online: www.samstelonloine.org. When Sam began his senior year at New Mexico A&M, he was the lone senior, with six juniors, seven sophomores, and twenty-three freshmen.

107. Bill Armstrong, "The Sam Steel Way," *Resources Magazine* (Summer 1996).

108. Montoya, *Translating Property*.

109. Quoted in Parsons, *Robert Clay Allison*, 20. Also see the *Santa Fe New Mexican*, June 7, 1875; Browning, *Violence Was No Stranger*, 100.

110. Quoted in Morris F. Taylor, *O.P. McMains and the Maxwell Land Grant Conflict* (Tucson: University of Arizona Press, 1979): 275.

111. Cleaveland, *No Life for a Lady*, 11-17.

112. Quoted in Norman Cleaveland, *The Morleys* (Albuquerque: Calvin Horn, 1971): 212-17. Also see Quentin, *Eternal New Mexicans*, 134.

113. Quoted in Fern Lyon, "Cracking the Ring," *New Mexico Magazine*, vol. 69 (March 1991): 65. Also see Cleaveland, *Satan's Paradise*, 61-79.

114. Norman Cleaveland, *Colfax County's Chronic Murder Mystery* (Santa Fe: Rydal Press, 1977): 11.

115. Montoya, *Translating Property*, 110-13; Cleaveland, *Chronic Murder Mystery*, 1-4; Marc Simmons, "The Murder of Parson Tolby," *Santa Fe Reporter*, August 10-16, 1994; Julyan, *Place Names*, 356; interview with Stephen Zimmer (Colfax County historian), October 27, 2005.

116. Kathleen P. Chamberlain, "In the Shadow of Billy the Kid," *Montana*, vol. 55 (Winter 2005): 53. The best books on the Lincoln County War include Maurice Garland Fulton with Robert N. Mullin, ed., *History of the Lincoln County War* (Tucson: University of Arizona Press, 1968); William Keleher, *Violence in Lincoln County* (Albuquerque: University of New Mexico Press, 1957); Frederick Nolan, *The Lincoln County War* (Norman: University of Oklahoma Press, 1992); Nolan, *West*; Robert M. Utley, *High Noon in Lincoln* (Albuquerque: University of New Mexico Press, 1987).

117. Marc Simmons, "Silver City Remembers Billy the Kid's Mom," *Santa Fe New Mexican*, October 27, 2001; Robert N. Mullin, *The Boyhood of Billy the Kid* (El Paso: Texas Western Press, 1967): 12.

118. Gordon Fikes, "Catherine McCarty: The Mother of Billy the Kid and a Jolly Irish Lady," www.zianet.com/snm/kidsmom; Jerry Weddle, *Antrim Is My Stepfather's Name* (n.p.: Arizona Historical Society, 1993): 14-15, 17-18.

119. Quoted in Nolan, *West*, 27.

120. Henderson and Henderson, "Directory of the Silver City Memory Lane Cemetery"; Robert N. Mullin, "A Grave Question," *Password*, vol. 17 (Winter 1972): 173-74; *(Silver City) Mining Life*, September 19, 1874. Catherine's other son, Joseph "Joe" "Josie" (August 25, 1854 or 1863-November 25, 1930), a professional gambler, died of apoplexy in Denver, Colorado, where his body was given to the Colorado Medical School. Browning, *Violence Was No Stranger*, 152; Nolan, *West*, 29.

121. Simmons, "Grave Matters," 20.

122. Utley, *Billy the Kid*, 2; Julyan, *Place Names*, 20. Robert Utley notes that, depending on one's source, Billy the Kid had several possible birth dates and places, including September 17, 1859, at 210 Greene Street, New York City, New York. Utley suggests that November 23, 1859, the date that is usually cited, is probably wrong. Utley, *Billy the Kid*, 210n. On Frederick Nolan's fruitless four-year search for documentation on the Kid's birth date, see Nolan, *West*, 3-6.

123. Quoted in the *Albuquerque Journal*, October 19, 1955.

124. Quoted in Robert M. Utley, "The Final Days of Billy the Kid," *New Mexico Historical Review*, vol. 64 (October 1989): 401-26.

125. Nolan, *West*, 289, 325n. Also see Paco Anaya, *I Buried Billy the Kid* (College Station, Texas: Early West Press, 1991).

126. For examples of these obituaries, see Harold L. Edwards, *Goodbye Billy the Kid* (College Station, Texas, 1995): 64-154.

127. John W. Poe, *The Death of Billy the Kid* (Boston: Houghton Mifflin Company, 1933): 45-7.

128. *Las Vegas Daily Optic*, September 10, 1881

129. *Las Vegas Daily Optic*, September 19, 1881

130. Tatum, *Inventing Billy the Kid*, 12.

131. Ibid.

132. Quoted in Bryan, *True Tales*, 193.

133. Nolan, *West*, 288.

134. *Alamogordo News*, July 5, 1928

135. *Fort Sumner Leader*, April 11 and October 31, 1930; editorial, *Alamogordo News*, May 15, 1930; Frederick Nolan to the author, November 1, 2005; Johnny D. Boggs, "Final Resting Places of the Famous and Infamous," *New Mexico Magazine*, vol. 84 (February 2006): 65. Thomas "Tom" O'Folliard (1858-December 19, 1880) was killed by lawmen led by Pat Garrett, while Charles "Charlie" Bowdre (about 1848-December 23, 1880) was killed by Garrett's posse in the famous shootout at Stinking Springs. Utley, *Billy the Kid*, 155-59; Nolan, *West*, 164; Browning, *Violence Was No Stranger*, 30, 179.

136. *New Mexican Sentinel*, August 14, 1938

137. *De Baca County News*, June 4, 1981

138. Marc Simmons, "Grave in Shackles," *Santa Fe Reporter*, October 3, 1982

139. Keleher, *Fabulous Frontier*, 73n-74n.

140. *Albuquerque Journal*, March 5, 2004

141. Efforts have also been made to exhume Billy's mother so that her DNA can be tested and eventually compared to her son's. However, many of the same problems about the correct location of Billy's remains in Fort Sumner also exist for his mother's remains in Silver City. Meanwhile, a state district court judge has declined to rule on a request to exhume Catherine Antrim's remains before Billy's remains are exhumed first. *Albuquerque Journal*, April 3, 2004

142. *Dallas Morning News*, October 11, 2003; *Albuquerque Journal*, December 7, 2003

143. *Portales News-Tribune*, June 21, 2005

144. *Albuquerque Journal*, September 25, 2004; Jay Miller, *Billy the Kid Rids Again: Digging for the Truth* (Santa Fe: Sunstone Press, 2005).

145. Quoted in the *Albuquerque Journal*, September 28, 2004.

146. Famous visitors have included Wild West showman Major Gordon W. "Pawnee Bill" Lillie in 1938. *Albuquerque Journal*, June 23, 1938; *New Mexico Sentinel*, July 3, 1938. The second and third most often visited graves among famous New Mexicans probably belong to Kit Carson, buried in Taos, and Geronimo, buried at Fort Sill, Oklahoma.

147. *De Baca County News*, June 25, 1981; *Albuquerque Journal*, September 23, 1998. Most recently, promoters have organized a "Billy the Kid ride, open to twenty rugged-rumped riders willing to fork over $1,250, cover 125 miles in eight days, tracing the outlaw's travels after his escape from the Lincoln County jail in 1881." *Albuquerque Journal*, February 19, 2005. For other activities organized "to preserve, promote, and protect Billy the Kid/Pat Garrett history in New Mexico," see the Billy the Kid Outlaw Gang, Inc., web-site: frontpage.nmia.com/btkog.

148. Frederick Nolan, "Dick Brewer, The Unlikely Gunfighter," *NOLA Quarterly*, vol. 15 (July-September 1991); Nolan, *West*, 68; Browning, *Violence Was No Stranger*, 33.

149. Frederick W. Nolan, "The Search for Alexander McSween," *New Mexico Historical Review*, vol. 62 (July 1987): 289; Chamberlain, "In the Shadow of Billy the Kid," 52; Nolan, *West*, 38; Larson, *Forgotten Frontier*, 133, 146-48; Quentin, *Eternal New Mexicans*, 163.

150. Robert M. Utley, *Billy the Kid: A Short and Violent Life* (Lincoln: University of Nebraska Press, 1989): 97-8.

151. Certificate of Death, New Mexico State Department of Public Health, Lincoln County, January 3, 1931; Richard W. Etulain, ed., *New Mexican Lives* (Albuquerque: University of New Mexico Press, 2002): 202, 217; Chamberlain, "In the Shadow of Billy the Kid," 36-53; Marc Simmons, "Susan McSween," *Santa Fe Reporter*, May 17-23, 2000; Nolan, *West*, 46; Bullis, *Pasaron por Aqui*, 219-21.

152. Quoted in Fulton, *History of the Lincoln County War*, 420.

153. *Alamogordo News*, January 8, 1931

154. *Prescott (Arizona) Evening Courier*, November 9, 1937. John Miller's private contention that he was Billy the Kid is the focus of Helen L. Airy, *Whatever Happened to Billy the Kid?* (Santa Fe: Sunstone Press, 1993): 146-49. Also see the *Prescott Daily Courier*, October 31, 2003.

155. C.L. Sonnichsen and William V. Morrison, *Alias Billy the Kid* (Albuquerque: University of New Mexico Press, 1955): 10-11, 14-15. The latest case for Brushy Bill as Billy the Kid is made in W.C. Jameson, *Billy the Kid: Beyond the Grave* (Dallas: Taylor, 2005).

156. *De Baca County News*, March 9, 1989

157. *Albuquerque Journal*, April 9, 1989

158. Tourist literature enclosed in Barbara Thomas (Hico, Texas, Chamber of Commerce) to the author, August 22, 2003.

159. Julyan, *Place Names*, 363.

160. Frederick W. Nolan, *The Life and Death of John H. Tunstall* (Albuquerque: University of New Mexico Press, 1965): 272-73, 448, 454; Nolan, *West*, 39; Larson, *Forgotten Frontier*, 139.

161. Frederick W. Nolan, "A Sidelight on the Tunstall Murder," *New Mexico Historical Review*, vol. 31 (July 1956): 206-22. On Susan McSween's refusal to later spend any Tunstall family money on a gravestone for their relative, see Chamberlain, "In the Shadow of Billy the Kid," 52n.

162. Jerry Ueckert, "Just Another Billy the Kid Tale?" *1992 Regional Guide Book and Business Directory* (Edgewood: East Mountain Telegraph, 1992).

163. *Albuquerque Journal*, December 7, 2003

164. Donald R. Lavash, *Sheriff William Brady: Tragic Hero of the Lincoln County War* (Santa Fe: Sunstone Press, 1986): 15, 96, 105-6, 109; Nolan, *West*, 118. Brady's granddaughter, Nadine Brady, recounted her ancestor's murder in the *Valencia County News-Bulletin*, October 8, 1973.

165. Nolan, *Lincoln County War*, 455-56; Nolan, *West*, 154; Fulton, *Lincoln County War*, 414; Larson, *Forgotten Frontier*, 149.

166. Frederick Nolan, "Boss Rustler: The Life and Crimes of John Kinney," *True West*, vol. 43 (September 1996): 14-21, and (October 1996): 12-19; Nolan, *West*, 65; Mullin, "Here Lies," 223-24, 226; Price, *Pioneers of the Mesilla Valley*, 212; Bullis, *Pasaron por Aqui*, 180-82.

167. Quoted in Price, "Here Lies," 224.

168. Nolan, *West*, 102.

169. Quoted in Elvis Fleming, *J.B. "Billy" Mathews: Biography of a Lincoln County Deputy* (Las Cruces: Yucca Tree Press, 1999): 2, 88-9.

170. Nolan, *West*, 41, 318n; Larson, *Forgotten Frontier*, 124, 149.

171. Nolan, *West*, 122; Browning, *Violence Was No Stranger*, 191.

172. Browning, *Violence Was No Stranger*, 212.

173. Grady E. McCright and James H. Powell, "Disorder in Lincoln County: Frank Warner Angel's Reports," *Rio Grande History*, vol. 12 (1981): 3-25; Nolan, *West*, 144. Frederick Nolan notes that Angel's obituary in the *New Jersey Evening Journal*, March 17, 1906, makes no mention of a burial place. Frederick Nolan to the author, October 24 and 27, 2004.

174. Nolan, *West*, 146, 269-75.

175. Nolan, *West*, 125; E. Donald Kaye, *Nathan Augustus Monroe Dudley* (n.c.: Outskirts Press, 2007): 3, 64.

176. Utley, "Final Days," 419-20; Browning, *Violence Was No Stranger*, 164.

177. Nolan, *West*, 212, 285.

9
POLITICAL, DIPLOMATIC, AND JUDICIAL LEADERS

1. Quoted in Bruce King, *Cowboy in the Roundhouse* (Santa Fe: Sunstone Press, 1998): 352.

2. For a list of all Spanish colonial governors in New Mexico, see Twitchell, *Leading Facts*, I:481-82. Lists of Spanish, Mexican, and U.S. era governors are regularly included in the *New Mexico Blue Book*, published annually by the New Mexico Secretary of State.

3. Marc Simmons, *The Last Conquistador: Juan de Oñate and the Settling of the Far Southwest* (Norman: University of Oklahoma Press, 1991): 32-4, 193-94; Eric Beerman, "The Death of an Old Conquistador: New Light on Juan de Oñate," *New Mexico Historical Review*, vol. 54 (October 1979): 311.

4. *Albuquerque Journal*, January 8, February 1 and 19, 1998; Marc Simmons, "Oñate and All That," *Journal of the West*, vol. 37 (July 1998): 5-6. For a similar controversy regarding a new statue of Oñate to be dedicated in El Paso, see Y. Leyva, "Monuments of Conformity," *New Mexico Historical Review*, vol.82 (Summer 2007):343-67.

5. Kessell, *Remote Beyond Compare*, 11, 82-90, 96, 100; interview with John L. Kessell

(Vargas biographer), February 21, 2004. Also see Marc Simmons, "The Death of New Mexico Governor Diego de Vargas," *Santa Fe New Mexican*, April 5, 2003.

6. Alfred Barnaby Thomas, *Forgotten Frontiers: A Study of the Spanish Indian Policy of Don Juan Bautista de Anza, Governor of New Mexico, 1778-1787* (Norman: University of Oklahoma Press, 1932): 373-75; Donald T. Garate, *Juan Bautista de Anza [the elder]* (Reno: University of Nevada Press, 2003): 153-55, 254n.

7. For a list of all governors of the Mexican period in New Mexico, see Twitchell, *Leading Facts*, II:25n.

8. Quoted in Ibid., II:208n. For other opinions of Armijo, see Daniel Tyler, "Gringo Views of Governor Manuel Armijo," *New Mexico Historical Review*, vol. 45 (January 1970): 23-46; Bryan, *Albuquerque Remembered*, 43-9. For Armijo's disputed genealogy, see Janet Lecompte, "Manuel Armijo's Family History," *New Mexico Historical Review*, vol. 48 (July 1973): 252-58. Also see Perrigo, *Hispanos*, 36-8; Bullis, *Pasaron por Aquí*, 20-22.

9. Janet Lecompte, *Rebellion in the Rio Arriba* (Albuquerque: University of New Mexico Press, 1985): 34. Also see Philip Reno, "Rebellion in New Mexico, 1837," *New Mexico Historical Review*, vol. 40 (July 1965): 197-213.

10. Gregg, *Commerce*, 93.

11. Quentin, *Eternal New Mexicans*, 58; Lecompte, *Rebellion in the Rio Arriba*, 11-16, 31-4, with a photo of the D.A.R.'s rock in its original location on page 30. For a "True Account of the Effects Belonging to Señor Colonel Don Albino Pérez, Showing the Distribution Made of those that Could be Recovered after His Death and the Whereabouts of the Rest, as Far as Could Be Ascertained" see Ibid., 80-3.

12. Fray Angélico Chávez, "José Gonzalez, Genízaro Governor," *New Mexico Historical Review*, vol. 30 (July 1955): 190-94; Lecompte, *Rebellion in the Rio Arriba*, 36-40, 72-4, 177n-78n; Simmons, *Yesterday in Santa Fe*, 40.

13. Max L. Moorhead's note in Gregg, *Commerce*, 94n.

14. McGuyre, "Bent Family"; *Albuquerque Journal North*, June 8, 1985; Marc Simmons, "The Day Tragedy Befell the Family of Charles Bent," *Santa Fe New Mexican*, May 18, 2002, and "Kearney Road Cemetery Sprung from First Army Post in Southwest," October 4, 2003; Lavender, *Bent's Fort*, 20, 281-83, 294; James A. Crutchfield, *Tragedy at Taos: The Revolt of 1847* (Plano: Republic of Texas Press, 1995): 103, 104.

15. Gardner and Simmons, *Mexican War Correspondence*, 175.

16. Marc Simmons, "The Forgotten Donaciano Vigil," *Santa Fe Reporter*, June 16-22, 1999; Twitchell, *Military Occupation*, 207, 226; F. Stanley, *Giant In Lillipet: The Story of Donaciano Vigil* (Pampa, Texas: n.p., 1963): 201-3; Mondragón and Stapleton, *Public Education in New Mexico*, 13, 19; Perrigo, *Hispanos*, 42-4; Archdiocese Collection, roll photo16901, Archives of the Archdiocese of Santa Fe, Santa Fe, New Mexico.

17. The house's restoration is described in Corinne P. Sze, ed., *Within Adobe Walls: Selections from the Charlotte White Journals* (Santa Fe: Historic Santa Fe Foundation, 2001).

18. Thomas A. McMullin and David Walker, *Biographical Directory of American Territorial Governors* (Westport, Connecticut: Meckler Publishing, 1984): 235-36; Calvin Horn, *New Mexico's Troubled Years: The Story of the Early Territorial Governors*

(Albuquerque: Horn and Wallace, 1963): 33; Leo E. Oliva, *Soldiers On the Santa Fe Trail* (Norman: University of Oklahoma Press, 1967): 107; Fletcher M. Green, "James S. Calhoun: Pioneer Georgia Leader and First Governor of New Mexico," *Georgia Historical Quarterly*, vol. 39 (December 1955): 310n, 311n, 347.

19. Horn, *Troubled Years*, 37-51; McMullin and Walker, *Territorial Governors*, 236-37.

20. Robert A. Griffen, ed., *My Life in the Mountains and on the Plains: The Autobiography of David Meriwether* (Norman: University of Oklahoma Press, 1965): 3; Horn, *Troubled Years*, 53-71; McMullin and Walker, *Territorial Governors*, 237-38.

21. Robert D. Hepler, "William Watts Hart Davis in New Mexico" (Unpublished Masters thesis, University of New Mexico, 1941): 1, 9; Meléndez, *Spanish-Language Newspapers*, 134-35; Beth Lander (Director of Library Services, Mercer Museum, Doylestown, Pennsylvania) to the author, April 20, 2004.

22. Horn, *Troubled Years*, 73-91; McMullin and Walker, *Territorial Governors*, 239-40.

23. Ibid, 241-42; William Frederick Milton Arny, *Indian Agent in New Mexico: The Journal of Special Agent W.F.M. Arny, 1870* (Santa Fe: Stagecoach Press, 1967); Marc Simmons, "Lincoln Appointee Helped Form the Republican Party in New Mexico," *Santa Fe New Mexican*, November 6, 2004.

24. *Santa Fe New Mexican*, September 20 and 21, 1881, with a commemorative editorial on September 23, 1881; Lawrence R. Murphy, *Frontier Crusader: William F.M. Arny* (Tucson: University of Arizona Press, 1972): 3, 244-45.

25. Horn, *Troubled Years*, 93-113; Twitchell, *Leading Facts*, V:5, 293n; McMullin and Walker, *Territorial Governors*, 240-41, Marc Simmons, "Governor Connelly's Homes," *Santa Fe New Mexican*, August 21, 2004.

26. Horn, *Troubled Years*, 115-33; Twitchell, *Leading Facts*, II:410n-11n; McMullin and Walker, *Territorial Governors*, 241-42.

27. The Pile family's original German name was Poyle.

28. *Monrovia (California) News-Post*, October 8, 1988; Horn, *Troubled Years*, 135-49; McMullin and Walker, *Territorial Governors*, 242-43.

29. *Santa Fe New Mexican*, June 4 and 5, 1875; Horn, *Troubled Years*, 151-71; McMullin and Walker, *Territorial Governors*, 244-45.

30. *Santa Fe New Mexican*, September 15, 16, 17, 19, and October 5, 1904; Coan, *History of New Mexico*, II:39-40. The phrase "Crescit Eundo" came from Book VI of the Roman poet Lucretius's epic *De Rerum Natura* (*On the Nature of Things*). The phrase was later included on the New Mexico state seal, following statehood in 1912.

31. *Santa Fe New Mexican*, August 7, 1891; Poldervaart, *Black-Robed Justice*, 121-30; Horn, *Troubled Years*, 173-97; McMullin and Walker, *Territorial Governors*, 245-47.

32. *Santa Fe New Mexican*, December 22, 1880; Wallace's autobiography was published posthumously as *Lew Wallace: An Autobiography*, 2 vols. (New York: Harper and Brothers, 1905): I:8, II:1003; Robert E. and Katherine M. Morsberger, *Lew Wallace: Militant Romantic* (New York: McGraw-Hill, 1980): 3-4, 441-43; Horn, *Troubled Years*, 199-221; Amy Passmore Hurt, "The Man Who Wrote Ben Hur," *New Mexico Magazine*, vol. 26 (June 1948): 14, 31, 33; Marc Simmons, "Lew Wallace Found the Frontier in Santa Fe," *Santa Fe New Mexican*, January 20, 2002; Julyan, *Place Names*, 203.

33. Quoted in Morsberger, *Wallace*, 442.

34. Quoted in Ibid.

35. Wallace, *Autobiography*, II:796.

36. Oakah L. Jones, "Lew Wallace: Hoosier Governor of Territorial New Mexico," *New Mexico Historical Review*, vol. 60 (April 1985): 152.

37. McMullin and Walker, *Territorial Governors*, 249-50.

38. Quotes from Arthur E. Harrington, *Edmund G. Ross: A Man of Courage* (Franklin, Tennessee: Providence House, 1997): 19, 98, 105; Edward Bumgardner, *The Life of Edmund G. Ross* (Kansas City: Fielding-Turner Press, 1949): 15, 110; Howard R. Lamar, "Edmund G. Ross as Governor of New Mexico: A Reappraisal," *New Mexico Historical Review*, vol. 36 (July 1961): 179-209; Bullis, *Pasaron por Aquí*, 270-72; *Albuquerque Morning Journal*, May 9 and 10, 1907; *Albuquerque Journal*, September 15, 1968; *Albuquerque Tribune*, July 5, 1974.

39. John F. Kennedy, *Profiles in Courage* (New York: Perennial Classics, 2000): 115; *Albuquerque Journal*, January 8, 2005; interview with the Reverend Ned Ross (great-, great-grandson), January 9, 2006.

40. *Santa Fe New Mexican*, December 9, 1922, with a commemorative editorial on that same date; *Albuquerque Journal*, December 10, 1922; *New York Times*, December 10, 1922; *Taos Valley News*, December 12, 1922; *Alamogordo News*, December 14, 1922; María E. Montoya, "L. Bradford Prince: The Education of a Gilded Age Politician," *New Mexico Historical Review*, vol. 66 (April 1991): 181; McMullin and Walker, *Territorial Governors*, 252-53; Walter J. Donlon, "LeBaron Bradford Prince: Chief Justice and Governor New Mexico Territory, 1879-1893" (Unpublished Ph.D. dissertation, University of New Mexico, 1967): 7, 341-42.

41. *Santa Fe New Mexican*, March 17, 1916, with a commemorative editorial on that same date; McMullin and Walker, *Territorial Governors*, 253-55.

42. Certificate of Death, New Mexico Department of Public Health, Santa Fe County, August 7, 1944.

43. *Santa Fe New Mexican*, August 7, 1944, with a commemorative editorial on August 8, 1944; Quentin, *Eternal New Mexicans*, 55; McMullin and Walker, *Territorial Governors*, 255-56; Perrigo, *Hispanos*, 65-8; Miguel Otero, *My Life on the Frontier, 1864-1882* (New York: Press of the Pioneers, 1935): Miguel Otero, *My Life on the Frontier, 1882-1897* (Albuquerque: University of New Mexico Press, 1939); Miguel A. Otero, *My Nine Years as Governor of the Territory of New Mexico* (Albuquerque: University of New Mexico Press, 1940) ; Julyan, *Place Names*, 253. A special Miguel Otero edition of the *New Mexico Historical Review*, with articles by Jolane Culhane, María E. Montoya, Gerald D. Nash, and Cynthia Secor Welsh, appeared in January 1992 (vol. 67).

44. Certificate of Death, New Mexico State Department of Public Health, Santa Fe County, January 28, 1935; *Santa Fe New Mexican*, January 29 and 30, 1935, with a commemorative editorial on January 29, 1935; McMullin & Walker, *Territorial Governors*, 257-58.

45. Julyan, *Place Names*, 104.

46. Quoted in the *Alamogordo News*, April 14, 1932.

47. Keleher, *Fabulous Frontier*, 252n-53n.

48. *Ruidoso News*, April 11, 1947

49. Necrology, *New Mexico Historical Review*, vol. 23 (January 1948): 80; H.B. Hening, ed., *George Curry, 1861-1947: An Autobiography* (Albuquerque: University of New Mexico Press, 1958): vii, 317; Bullis, *Pasaron por Aquí*, 75-9.

50. *Las Vegas Optic*, December 27, 1915; *Santa Fe New Mexican*, December 27, 1915; McMullin and Walker, *Territorial Governors*, 259-60; Quentin, *Eternal New Mexicans*, 97.

51. www.bioguide.congress.gov

52. *Santa Fe New Mexican*, April 21 and 23, 1875

53. Fray Angélico Chávez, *Tres Macho—He Said: Padre Gallegos of Albuquerque, New Mexico's First Congressman* (Santa Fe: William Gannon, 1985): 3-6, 44, 94, 104; Maurilio E. Vigil, *Hispanics in Congress: A Historical and Political Survey* (Lanham, Maryland: University Press of America, 1996): 6-8; Perrigo, *Hispanos*, 45-6; Bryan, *Albuquerque Remembered*, 59-61.

54. Otero, *My Life on the Frontier*, II:180; commemorative editorial in the *Las Vegas Daily Optic*, June 21, 1882; Vigil, *Hispanics in Congress*, 8-9; Julyan, *Place Names*, 252-53.

55. www.bioguide.congress.gov

56. Vigil, *Hispanics in Congress*, 9-10.

57. *Santa Fe New Mexican*, November 28, 1904; Mondragón and Stapleton, *Public Education in New Mexico*, 223; Perrigo, *Hispanos*, 53-5; Tórrez, *UFOs Over Galisteo*, 128-31; Richard Melzer, "Still A Mystery," *Valencia County News-Bulletin*, September 18, 1999; Stern and Chávez, "From Clerk to Professional," 205-07; Vigil, *Hispanics in Congress*, 10-11; Julyan, *Place Names*, 78.

58. *Santa Fe Daily New Mexican*, July 10, 1874; Floyd S. Fierman, "The Frontier Career of Charles Clever, New Mexico Territory, 1830-74," *Western Studies in Jewish History*, vol. 35 (Fall 2002): 83-4, 95n; Jaehn, *Germans in the Southwest*, 60-2, 108.

59. *Albuquerque Journal*, January 5, 6, and 7, 1911; *New York Times*, January 6, 1911; Oscar Doane Lambert, *Stephen Benton Elkins* (Pittsburgh: University of Pittsburgh Press, 1955): 2, 324-28; Bullis, *Pasaron por Aquí*, 86-7; Julyan, *Place Names*, 122.

60. *Santa Fe New Mexican*, August 29, 1918; Vigil, *Hispanics in Congress*, 11-12.

61. *Santa Fe New Mexican*, February 1, 1904; Vigil, *Hispanics in Congress*, 12.

62. *Santa Fe New Mexican*, November 21, 1892; Vigil, *Hispanics in Congress*, 12-13.

63. *Santa Fe New Mexican*, September 16, 1904; *Las Vegas Optic*, September 17, 1904; Vigil, *Hispanics in Congress*, 13.

64. *Albuquerque Journal*, April 19 and 20, 1910

65. William Jennings Bryan to Mrs. H.B. Fergusson, Washington, D.C., June 10, 1915, Box 2, Folder 10, Huning-Fergusson Collection, Center for Southwest Research, University of New Mexico, Albuquerque, New Mexico; *Albuquerque Morning Journal*, June 11, 1915, with a commemorative editorial on that same date; Calvin A. Roberts, "Harvey B. Fergusson, 1848-1915: New Mexico Spokesman for Political Reform," *New Mexico*

Historical Review, vol. 57 (July 1982): 238, 252; Ferguson, *Home In the West*, 48-79; Gish, *Frontier's End*, 92-6. For an unexplained reason, Fergusson added a second "s" to his surname.

66. *Albuquerque Journal*, January 12 and 13, 1906; Vigil, *Hispanics in Congress*, 14.

67. Certificate of Death, New Mexico State Department of Public Health, Bernalillo County, March 10, 1927; *Albuquerque Journal*, March 11, 1927, and January 14, 2006; Robert W. Larson, *New Mexico's Quest for Statehood, 1846-1912* (Albuquerque: University of New Mexico Press, 1968): 201; García and McCord, *Albuquerque*, 184; Julyan, *Place Names*, 302. Rodey's death certificate lists his date of birth as March 4, 1866. For a typical expression of his support for New Mexico statehood, see Rodey's letter to the editor of December 22, 1887, reprinted in the *Santa Fe New Mexican*, July 13, 1904.

68. *Albuquerque Morning Journal*, January 17, 1919

69. All one hundred delegates to the State Constitutional Convention are listed in Dorothy I. Cline, *New Mexico's 1910 Constitution* (Santa Fe: Lightning Tree Press, 1985): 59-61.

70. *Santa Fe New Mexican*, June 21, 1904, and August 30, 1912; *Albuquerque Morning Journal*, July 4, 1914; *Belen News*, July 9, 1914; Richard Melzer, "King Solomon's Mysterious Demise," *La Crónica de Nuevo México*, no. 54 (April 2001): 2-3; Marc Simmons, "Sheep Baron Transformed New Mexico Politics," *Santa Fe New Mexican*, March 9, 2002; Perrigo, *Hispanos*, 56-8; Julyan, *Place Names*, 215.

71. Carmack, *Cemetery Research*, 215.

72. *Santa Fe New Mexican*, April 11, 1918; Julyan, *Place Names*, 223.

73. *Santa Fe New Mexican*, February 19-21, 1917, with a commemorative editorial on February 19, 1917; Meléndez, *Spanish-Language Newspapers*, 84-6, 185; Perrigo, *Hispanos*, 72-4; Kalloch and Hall, *First Ladies*, 24; Julyan, *Place Names*, 106.

74. Certificate of Death, New Mexico State Department of Public Health, Roosevelt County, April 5, 1926; *Santa Fe New Mexican*, February 22, 1917, and April 5, 1926, with a commemorative editorial on April 6, 1926; *Alamogordo News*, April 8, 1926; Ira C. Ihde, "Washington Ellsworth Lindsey," *New Mexico Historical Review*, vol. 26 (July 1951): 177-96.

75. Certificate of Death, New Mexico State Department of Public Health, Bernalillo County, April 7, 1930; *Albuquerque Journal*, editorial, April 9, 1930, and November 16, 1952; Alfred C. Córdova and Charles B. Judah, *Octaviano Larrazolo: A Political Portrait* (Albuquerque: Division of Research, Department of Government, University of New Mexico, 1952): 1, 31; Perrigo, *Hispanos*, 78-81; Vigil, *Hispanics in Congress*, 24-26

76. Quoted in Paul F. Larrazolo, *Octaviano A. Larrazolo: A Moment in New Mexico History* (New York: Carlton Press, 1986): 13, 185-89.

77. Certificate of Death, New Mexico State Department of Public Health, Bernalillo County, May 24, 1946; *Albuquerque Journal*, May 25, 1946; *Albuquerque Tribune*, May 25, 1946, with a commemorative editorial on the same date; Quentin, *Eternal New Mexicans*, 18-19.

78. Certificate of Death, New Mexico State Department of Health, Chaves County, March 26, 1951; *Santa Fe New Mexican*, March 27, 1951; Quentin, *Eternal New Mexicans*, 182; Kalloch and Hall, *First Ladies*, 48-9.

79. Certificate of Death, New Mexico State Department of Public Health, Bernalillo County, August 4, 1936; *Albuquerque Journal*, August 5, 1936; Dan D. Chávez, *Soledad Chávez de Chacón: A New Mexico Political Pioneer, 1890-1936* (Albuquerque: n.p., 1996): vii; Salas, "Soledad Chávez de Chacón," 161-64.

80. Editorial, *Alamogordo News*, June 26, 1924. Inaugurated on January 5, 1925, Nellie Tayloe Ross of Wyoming was the first woman to be elected as a state governor in the United States. A Democrat, Ross served one two-year term, but was not reelected.

81. *Albuquerque Journal*, March 19, 1966

82. Arthur Hannett, *Sagebrush Lawyer* (New York: Pageant Press, 1964): 255.

83. *New Mexico Sentinel*, August 10, 1937; *Albuquerque Journal*, January 5 and 6, 1966, with a commemorative editorial on January 6, 1966; *Albuquerque Tribune*, January 5, 6, and 8, 1966; Charles B. Judah, *Governor Richard C. Dillon: A Study in New Mexico Politics* (Albuquerque: Division of Research, Department of Government, University of New Mexico, 1948); Kalloch and Hall, *First Ladies*, 65; Julyan, *Place Names*, 110.

84. *Santa Fe New Mexican*, September 25, 1933. Also see Kalloch and Hall, *First Ladies*, 74. On the threats against Seligman's granddaughter and his bank, see the *Albuquerque Journal*, August 16, 1933.

85. *Santa Fe New Mexican*, June 21, 1974; *Albuquerque Journal*, July 8, 1973, and June 22, 1974

86. Quoted in the *Albuquerque Tribune*, January 13, 1971.

87. Quoted in the *Albuquerque Journal*, December 25, 1960. Also see the *Albuquerque Journal*, December 28, 1960; *Albuquerque Tribune*, December 24, 1960, with a commemorative editorial on that same date, plus December 27 and 28, 1960, and October 24, 1968; Bryan, *Albuquerque Remembered*, 215-22.

88. *Santa Fe New Mexican*, October 7 and 8, 1971, with a commemorative editorial on October 8, 1971; Keleher, *New Mexicans I Knew*, 148; interview with Lloyd Miles (son), January 18, 2003.

89. *Albuquerque Journal*, March 12, 1958, with a commemorative editorial on March 13, 1958; *Albuquerque Tribune*, March 12 and 13, 1958; Kalloch and Hall, *First Ladies*, 99.

90. *Albuquerque Journal*, December 24, 1962; *Albuquerque Tribune*, December 27, 1962; Quentin, *Eternal New Mexicans*, 16.

91. *Albuquerque Journal*, December 1 and 4, 2002

92. *Albuquerque Journal*, April 12, 1975

93. *Albuquerque Journal*, editorial, April 12, 1975

94. *Portales News-Tribune*, May 22, 1978

95. Quoted in Jean Burroughs, "My Husband, the Governor," *Impact Magazine*, October 5, 1982.

96. Jerri Antunes, *Two Fists Full: The Story of Tom Bolack* (Farmington: privately published, 1999): 19, 175, 219-47, 300, 307-10; Quentin, *Eternal New Mexicans*, 84-5; *Albuquerque*

Tribune, June 4, 1993; *Albuquerque Journal*, January 2, 1963, May 21, 1998, and June 29, 1999. Bolack's wife, Alice's, ashes had also been scattered over their ranch after her death on October 6, 1978.

97. *Albuquerque Journal*, June 16 and 22, 1999, with a commemorative editorial on June 16, 1999; *Santa Fe New Mexican*, June 16, 18, and 19, 1999, with a commemorative editorial on June 17, 1999; *Roswell Daily Record*, June 16 and 25, 1999, with a commemorative editorial on June 16, 1999; interview with Michael Campbell (son), September 15, 2003.

98. *Santa Fe New Mexican*, May 16 and 18, 1921, with a commemorative editorial on May 16, 1921; *Albuquerque Morning Journal*, May 16, 1921; *Alamogordo News*, May 19, 1921; Etulain, *New Mexican Lives*, 216. Catron signed his name "Thos. B." until he was 31. He signed it "T.B." thereafter. Victor Westphall, *Thomas Benton Catron and His Era* (Tucson: University of Arizona, 1973): 9; Julyan, *Place Names*, 68.

99. Quoted in the *Santa Fe New Mexican*, May 16, 1921.

100. Quoted in Westphall, *Catron*, 391-93. Catron's political and legal careers are defended in Victor Westphall, "Thomas Benton Catron: A Historical Defense," *New Mexico Historical Review*, vol. 63 (January 1988): 43-57, and Westphall, *Catron*.

101. Certificate of Death, El Paso County Clerk's Office, El Paso, Texas, November 30, 1944.

102. *Albuquerque Journal*, December 1, 1944; *Santa Fe New Mexican*, December 1, 1944; *Las Cruces Sun-News*, December 1, 1944; *New York Times*, December 2, 1944; Martha Fall Bethune, *Race With the Wind: The Personal Life of Albert B. Fall* (El Paso: Novio Books, 1989): 148; David H. Stratton, ed., *The Memoirs of Albert Bacon Fall* (El Paso: Texas Western Press, 1966); Burl Noggle, *Teapot Dome* (New York: W.W. Norton and Company, 1965): 9, 215; Owen, *Two Alberts*, 234, 460.

103. David H. Stratton, *Tempest Over Teapot Dome: The Story of Albert B. Fall* (Norman: University of Oklahoma Press, 1998): 278, 342.

104. Sonnichsen, *Tularosa*, 269.

105. *New Mexico State Tribune*, December 21, 1927, with a commemorative editorial on that same date; Lynn Perrigo, *Gateway to Glorieta: A History of Las Vegas, New Mexico* (Boulder: Pruett Publishing Company, 1982): 92, 138.

106. *Albuquerque Journal*, August 8 and 9, 1953; *Socorro Chieftain*, August 13, 1953; Coan, *History of New Mexico*, II:16; Julyan, *Place Names*, 53.

107. *Albuquerque Tribune*, September 23, 1963, with a commemorative editorial on that same date; *Albuquerque Journal*, September 25, 1963; Coan, *History of New Mexico*, III:295-97.

108. *Santa Fe New Mexican*, May 6-11, 1935, with commemorative editorials on May 10 and 11, 1935; *Raton Range*, June 3, 1935; Richard Lowitt, *Bronson M. Cutting: Progressive Politician* (Albuquerque: University of New Mexico Press, 1992): 1, 308-09.

109. Cutting had paid for Luna's legal education before the young man joined the National Guard and was assigned to the U.S.-Mexican border. In 1916 Luna contracted endocarditis and, despite the efforts of a specialist hired by Cutting, died in El Paso. Cutting also paid for Luna's funeral in Santa Fe. Keleher, *New Mexicans I Knew*, 171-74; Lowitt, *Cutting*, 56-7, 61, 61, 343-43n.

110. Ibid., 310-11.

111. F. Romero, "Al Senador Cutting," *Hispano Americano*, May 16, 1935. The terms of Cutting's will were described in the *Belen News*, June 27, 1935, and, in more detail, in Lowitt, *Cutting*, 313-15.

112. "Senator Bronson M. Cutting: A Memorial," *University of New Mexico Bulletin*, vol. 50 (May 1, 1937): 24. Cutting's will was praised because, until like other millionaires, "He turned it [his wealth] over to men to whom it will be of some honest to God use…. It will really do somebody some good, which is so much more than we can say for the wills of most rich men." *Farmington Times Hustler*, July 19, 1935.

113. *Albuquerque Journal*, November 19-21, 1962, with a commemorative editorial on November 19, 1962; María Martinez, "Dennis Chavez and the Making of Modern New Mexico" in Etulain, *New Mexican Lives,* 242-64; Perrigo, *Hispanos*, 85-7.

114. Arthur R. Gomez and Cissie Coy, *Chavez: El Senador* (n.c.: n.p., 1988): 1.

115. "Solemn Rites Mark Burial of Senator Chavez," news clipping, Vertical Files Collection, University of New Mexico-Valencia Campus Library, Tomé, New Mexico.

116. *Acceptance of the Statue of Dennis Chavez, Presented by the State of New Mexico, Proceedings in the Rotunda, United States Capitol, March 31, 1966* (Washington, D.C.: U.S. Government Printing Office, 1966); Vigil, *Hispanics in Congress*, 29. On Popé's seven-foot tall, three-and-a-half ton marble statue by Jemez Pueblo sculptor Cliff Fragua, see the *Albuquerque Journal*, May 22, 2005.

117. *Albuquerque Journal*, September 16 and 17, 1963, with a commemorative editorial on September 16, 1963; David Porter, "Senator Carl Hatch and the Hatch Act of 1939," *New Mexico Historical Review*, vol. 48 (April 1973): 151-64; Quentin, *Eternal New Mexicans*, 12-13.

118. *Albuquerque Journal*, November 12 and 14, 1975, with a commemorative editorial on November 12, 1975; *Albuquerque Tribune*, November 12, 1975; *Santa Fe New Mexican*, November 12 and 13, 1975; Clinton P. Anderson, *Outsider in the Senate* (New York: New World Publishing Company, 1970): 4; Richard A. Baker, *Conservation Politics: The Senate Career of Clinton P. Anderson* (Albuquerque: University of New Mexico Press, 1985): ix, 12.

119. *Albuquerque Journal*, June 6, 1978, with a commemorative editorial on that same date; Vigil, *Hispanics in Congress*, 29-37.

120. Certificate of Death, New Mexico State Department of Public Health, Grant County, April 14, 1939; *Silver City Daily Press and Independent*, April 17, 1939; Coan, *History of New Mexico*, II:38.

121. *Albuquerque Journal*, October 20, 1954; Vigil, *Hispanics in Congress*, 18-19; Julyan, *Place Names*, 165.

122. *Santa Fe New Mexican*, January 13, 1923; Doris Meyer, *Speaking for Themselves: Neomexico Cultural Identity and the Spanish-Language Press, 1880-1920* (Albuquerque: University of New Mexico Press, 1996): 215; Meléndez, *Spanish-Language Newspapers*, 97-8.

123. Certificate of Death, New Mexico State Department of Public Health, Santa Fe County, February 25, 1935; *Raton Range*, February 25, 26, and 28, 1935, with a commemorative editorial on February 26, 1935.

124. *Albuquerque Journal*, August 18, 1963, December 30, 1964, and January 1, 1965; *Albuquerque Tribune*, December 29-31, 1964, and January 2, 1965; Miller, *McCormick*, 236-38; García and McCord, *Albuquerque*, 152.

125. *Albuquerque Journal*, November 7-10, 1956, with a commemorative editorial on November 8, 1956; Vigil, *Hispanics in Congress*, 21-22.

126. *Albuquerque Journal*, January 6, 1971; Roger D. Hardaway, "New Mexico Elects a Congresswoman," *Red River Historical Review*, vol. 4 (Fall 1979): 75-89; Mondragón and Stapleton, *Public Education in New Mexico*, 223. Lusk was one of six women to serve in the 80th U.S. Congress; collectively they were known as the "Petticoat Front."

127. *Albuquerque Tribune*, October 11, 2000. According to his daughter, Janet Steele, Walker's buddies during World War II gave him the nickname "Johnny" after the famous Johnny Walker whiskey. When he returned from the war and entered politics, he officially changed his name to Johnny so that his war friends would remember him and help support his political career. Interview with Janet Steele, September 19, 2003.

128. *Albuquerque Tribune*, August 5, 1980, with a commemorative editorial on August 6, 1980; *Albuquerque Journal,* August 6, 1980. Runnels's nickname was derived from his business, the Runnels Mud Company, which sold solid drilling mud for oil rigs.

129. *Albuquerque Tribune*, March 25, 1998

130. *Alamogordo Daily News*, December 8, 2003; *Albuquerque Journal*, December 8, 2003; *Washington Post*, December 9, 2003

131. *Santa Fe New Mexican*, February 28, 2005, with a commemorative editorial on February 29, 2005; *Albuquerque Journal*, June 18, 2004, and February 28, 2005; Frank V. Ortiz, Jr., with Don J. Usner, ed., *Ambassador Ortiz: Lessons From a Life of Service* (Albuquerque: University of New Mexico Press, 2005): 4.

132. Quoted in the *Albuquerque Journal*, June 18, 2004

133. Ortiz, *Ambassador*, 208. The New Testament verses are from 2 Timothy 4:6-7.

134. *Roswell Daily Record*, March 15, 1985; Louise Holland Coe, *Lady and the Law Books: Sixteen Years [as] the First and Only Woman Member of the New Mexico Senate* (Albuquerque: n.p., 1981); Louise Holland Coe, "Lady Rancher on the Ruidoso," *New Mexico Magazine*, vol. 52 (January/February 1974): 30.

135. *Santa Fe New Mexican*, October 1 and 7, 2006, with a commemorative editorial on October 3, 2006; *Albuquerque Journal*, October 1, 2006, with a commemorative editorial on October 3, 2006; Kathryn M. Córdova, *Concha: Matriarch of a 300-Year-Old New Mexico Legacy* (Santa Fe: La Herencia, 2004): 21-3; Perrigo, *Hispanos*, 82-4; Salas, "Soledad Chávez de Chacón, Adelina Otero-Warren, and Concha Ortiz y Pino"; interview with Ana Pacheco (publisher, La Herencia), October 4, 2006. A copy of Concha's baptismal certificate appears in Córdova, *Concha*, 21. Concha was christened Mabel Concepción, but disliked her first name and changed it to María.

136. Elvis E. Fleming, "'Shoeless' Jerry Simpson: The New Mexico Years, 1902-05" in Fleming and Williams, *Treasures of History*, III:114, 132-34; Karel Denis Bicha, "Jerry Simpson: Populist Without Principle," *Journal of American History*, vol. 54 (September 1967): 291-306.

137. Homer F. Cunningham, *The Presidents' Last Years* (Jefferson, N.C.: McFarland and

Co., 1989): 197; Brian Lamb, *Who's Buried in Grant's Tomb?: A Tour of Presidential Gravesites* (New York: Public Affairs, 2003): 114-17.

138. *Santa Fe New Mexican*, June 3, 1940; *The Independent of Valencia County*, December 19 and 26, 1940; Patricia Burke Guggino, "Pablo Abeita" (Unpublished M.A. thesis, University of New Mexico, 1995; Sando, *Pueblo Profiles*, 41-9.

139. *Albuquerque Journal*, November 5, 6, 10, 1998, with a commemorative editorial on November 6, 1998; *Albuquerque Tribune*, November 5, 1998

140. *Gallup Independent*, January 7 and 10, 1947, and May 27, 1949; David M. Brugge, "Henry Chee Dodge" in L.G. Moses and Raymond Wilson, eds., *Indian Lives* (Albuquerque: University of New Mexico Press, 1985): 93, 107; David M. Brugge, "Henry Chee Dodge, From the Long Walk to Self Determination," *New Mexico Historical Review*, vol. 23 (April 1948): 81-93; Virginia Hoffman and Broderick H. Johnson, *Navajo Biographies* (Chinle, Arizona: Rough Rock Demonstration School, 1970): 186-212.

141. Mabel spelled Lujan with an "h" (as it is pronounced), while Tony spelled it with the more traditional "j."

142. *Taos News*, January 31, 1963

143. Waters, *Of Time and Change*, 45-69.

144. Pedro Pino's Spanish name was used in honor of Don Pedro Bautista Pino, who had ransomed Pedro Pino from the Navajos after he had spent about two years in captivity when he was about fourteen years old. E. Richard Hart, *Pedro Pino: Governor of Zuni Pueblo, 1830-78* (Logan: Utah State University Press, 2003): 132.

145. Hart, *Pino*, 2-3, 119, 121, 127.

146. *Albuquerque Journal*, June 28, 2004; *Pueblo (Colorado) Journal*, July 1-16, 2004; *Santa Fe New Mexican*, July 21, 2004

147. *Santa Fe New Mexican*, March 2, 1874. Also see the *Santa Fe New Mexican*, February 28, 1874; *(Silver City) Mining Life*, March 7, 1874; Aurora Hunt, *Kirby Benedict: Frontier Federal Judge* (Glendale, California: Arthur H. Clark, 1961): 15, 224; Al Regensberg (Senior Archivist, New Mexico Record Center and Archives) to the author, December 3, 2003; Poldervaart, *Black-Robed Justice*, 49-66; Bullis, *Pasaron por Aquí*, 34-6.

148. *Valencia County News-Bulletin*, January 21, 1974, January 9, 1975, November 27 and 30, 1991, with a commemorative editorial on the latter date, and March 12, 2005; *Albuquerque Journal*, November 27, 1991; Daniel Gibson, "Tibo Chavez," *Del Sol New Mexico*, May 1983.

149. *Valencia County News-Bulletin*, November 30, 1991

150. Ibid.

151. Certificate of Death, New Mexico State Department of Public Health, Santa Fe County, July 19, 1930; *Albuquerque Journal*, July 21, 1930; Obituary, *New Mexico Historical Review*, vol. 5 (October 1930): 411-18; Price, *Mesilla Valley Pioneers*, 267-69; Twitchell, *Old Santa Fe*, 472-73; Kropp, *That All May Learn*, 6-22, 208. For a ringing endorsement of McFie, on his reappointment to the New Mexico Territorial Supreme Court, see the editorial, *Santa Fe New Mexican*, November 8, 2005.

152. *Santa Fe New Mexican*, September 13 and 18, 1916; Quentin, *Eternal New Mexicans*, 56.

10
RELIGIOUS LEADERS

1. On religion in nineteenth and twentieth century New Mexico see Ferenc M. Szasz and Richard W. Etulain, eds., *Religion in Modern New Mexico* (Albuquerque: University of New Mexico Press, 1997).

2. *Santa Fe New Mexican*, February 13, 1888, with a commemorative editorial on February 16, 1888; Bruce Ellis, *Bishop Lamy's Santa Fe Cathedral* (Albuquerque: University of New Mexico Press): 18, 45-6; Nancy Hanks, *Lamy's Legion* (Santa Fe: HRM Books, 2000); Julyan, *Place Names*, 196-7. As Julyan points out, Lamy's French surname is properly pronounced lah-MEE, although it is usually pronounced LAME-ee in New Mexico.

3. Simmons, "Lamy's 1867 Caravan," B1.

4. Quoted in Paul Horgan, *Lamy of Santa Fe: His Life and Times* (New York: Farrar, Straus and Giroux, 1975): 12, 437-40.

5. *Santa Fe New Mexican*, February 14 and 15, 1888

6. *Santa Fe New Mexican*, February 15, 1888. For a photoof Lamy lying in state, see John Sherman, *Santa Fe: A Pictorial History* (Virginia Beach: Donning Company, 1983): 60.

7. *Santa Fe New Mexican*, February 16, 1888. Archbishop Jean Baptiste Salpointe's official record of Lamy's funeral, with a long list of priests from across the territory in attendance, can be found in the Archdiocese Collection, roll photo16901, Archives of the Archdiocese of Santa Fe, Santa Fe, New Mexico.

8. Sister Edward Mary Zerwekh, "John Baptist Salpointe, 1825-1894 [sic]," *New Mexico Historical Review*, vol. 37 (January 1962): 1-19; (April 1962): 132-54; (July 1962): 214-29; Hanks, *Lamy's Legion*, 107-09; Archbishop Michael J. Sheehan, ed., *Four Hundred Years of Faith: A History of the Catholic Church in New Mexico* (Santa Fe: Archdiocese of Santa Fe, 1998): 20-1; Kris A. White (research librarian, Pima Community College, Tucson, Arizona) to the author, November 20, 2003.

9. Hanks, *Lamy's Legion*, 32-4; Sheehan, *Four Hundred Years*, 28-9.

10. Hanks, *Lamy's Legion*, 24-6; Sheehan, *Four Hundred Years*, 34-5.

11. *Santa Fe New Mexican*, May 23, 23, 28, 31, 1928; Sheehan, *Four Hundred Years*, 40-1.

12. Certificate of Death, New Mexico State Department of Public Health, Santa Fe County, December 2, 1932; *Santa Fe New Mexican*, December 2, 3, 5, and 6, 1932, with a commemorative editorial on December 3, 1932; Sheehan, *Four Hundred Years*, 60-1.

13. Certificate of Death, New Mexico State Department of Public Health, Santa Fe County, March 2, 1943; *Santa Fe New Mexican*, March 2 and 6, 1943; Sheehan, *Four Hundred Years*, 72-3.

14. *Albuquerque Journal*, July 26, 27, 30, 31, 1963; *Santa Fe New Mexican*, July 26, 28, 1963; Sheehan, *Four Hundred Years*, 100-01.

15. *Santa Fe New Mexican*, March 6, 1988; *Albuquerque Journal*, March 9, 1988; Sheehan, *Four Hundred Years*, 116-17.

16. *Albuquerque Journal*, August 13, 1990, with a commemorative editorial on August 14, 1990; Carol N. Lovato, *Brother Mathias: Founder of the Little Brothers of the Good Shepherd* (Huntington, Indiana: Our Sunday Visitor, 1987): 22.

17. *Albuquerque Journal*, March 12, 2001

18. Fellow American soldiers called Father Al "Al Capone" "for his skill in stealing food for his starving men" in a Japanese POW camp in the Philippines during World War II. Dorothy Cave Aldrich (Father Braun's biographer) to the author, December 30, 2004.

19. Dorothy Cave Aldrich, "Restoring Faith: Franciscan Priest Poured Heart Into 'Apache Cathedral,'" *New Mexico Magazine,* vol. 78 (December 2000): 76-80; Dorothy Emerson, *Among the Mescaleros: The Story of Fr. Albert Braun, OFM* (Tucson: University of Arizona, 1973): 2. The single grave outside St. Joseph's Church belongs to Brother Salesius Kraft, O.F.M. (better known as Brother Sales), who was killed in July 1928 after attempting to unload a massive stone from a truck during the church's construction. The stone slipped, crushing Brother Salesius. The Franciscan somehow survived several days before succumbing to his injuries. Historical literature distributed at the St. Joseph's Mission Church, Mescalero, New Mexico; Dorothy Cave Aldrich to the author, December 30, 2004.

20. Dorothy Cave Aldrich, "Father Albert Braun: Last of the Frontier Priests," Paper read at the Historical Society of New Mexico Conference, Las Cruces, New Mexico, April 12, 2002.

21. Tom Drake, "Mescalero Apache and Friars Restore Massive Stone Church," *Preservation New Mexico*, vol. 19 (August 2004): 4-5.

22. *Chicago Tribune*, July 26, 1996; *Albuquerque Journal*, with a commemorative editorial on July 23, 1996; Richard Melzer, "A Profile in Faith and Courage," *Valencia County News-Bulletin*, April 21-22, 2001.

23. Lynn Bridgers, *Death's Deceiver: The Life of Joseph P. Machebeuf* (Albuquerque: University of New Mexico Press, 1997): 15-17, 232-33; Hanks, *Lamy's Legion*, 76-8; Wommack, *From the Grave*, 115.

24. E.A. Mares, "Padre Martínez and Mexican New Mexico" in Etulain, *New Mexico Lives*, 127; E.A. Mares, *I Returned and Saw Under the Sun: Padre Martínez of Taos* (Albuquerque: University of New Mexico, 1989): 2, 7; E.A. Mares (Martinez biographer) to the author, July 24, 2003; *Santa Fe New Mexican*, August 3, 1867; Perrigo, *Hispanos*, 39-41.

25. John M. Taylor, *Dejad a los Niños Venir a Mi: A History of the Parish of Our Lady of Guadalupe in Peralta* (Albuquerque: LPD Press, 2005): 8-9; Florence Hawley Ellis, "Tomé and Father J.B.R.," *New Mexico Historical Review*, vol. 30 (1955): 195-220; Florence Hawley Ellis and Edwin Baca, "The *Apuntes* of Father J.B Rallière," *New Mexico Historical Review*, vol. 32 (1957): 10-35, 259-73; Hanks, *Lamy's Legion*, 100-01; Richard Melzer, "Father Rallière of Tomé," *Valencia County News-Bulletin*, November 18-19 and December 16-17, 2000.

26. See Phyllis Burch Rapagnani, "A Tradition of Service: Roman Catholic Sisters in New Mexico, 1852-1927" (Unpublished M.A. thesis, University of New Mexico, 1988). Nuns also taught in many public schools in New Mexico until the famous state court ruling, popularly known as the Dixon Case (*Zeller v. Huff*), banned such teaching in the

interest of separating church and state. Jacobo Baca, "The Dixon Case, 1947-1951," *La Crónica de Nuevo México*, no. 65 (July 2005): 3-7; Mondragón and Stapleton, *Public Education in New Mexico*, 37, 139.

27. *New York Times*, March 4 and April 5, 1955; *Albuquerque Journal North*, November 17, 1988; *Albuquerque Journal*, November 21, 1988, and October 2, 2000; Anne M. Butler, "Mother Katharine Drexel: Spiritual Visionary for the West" in Riley and Etulain, eds., *By Grit and Grace*, 198-220.

28. *Santa Fe New Mexican*, October 29, 1906; Thomas Richter, ed., "Sister Catherine Mallon's Journal," *New Mexico Historical Review*, vol. 52 (April 1977): 135-55, and vol. 52 (July 1977): 237-50; Sytha Motto, "The Sisters of Charity and St. Vincent Hospital: An Amplification of Sister Mallon's Journal," *New Mexico Historical Review*, vol. 52 (July 1977): 229-36; Quentin, *Eternal New Mexicans*, 40.

29. Sytha Motto, *No Banners Waving* (New York: Vantage Press, 1966): 71.

30. *Santa Fe New Mexican*, October 29, 1906

31. Ibid.

32. Sister Therese Martin, "Life Sketch of Sister Blandina Segale" in Sister Blandina Segale, *At the End of the Santa Fe Trail* (Cincinnati: Sisters of Charity, 1996): 1, 9-10; Motto, *No Banners Waving*, 83-103.

33. Julyan, *Place Names*, 164.

34. Quoted in Quentin, *Eternal New Mexicans*, 152-53.

35. *New Mexican Sentinel*, January 12, 1938

36. *New Mexican Sentinel*, January 12, 1938; Mary Daniels Taylor, *A Place as Wild as the West Ever War: Mesilla, New Mexico, 1848-1872* (Las Cruces: New Mexico State University Museum, 2004): 129-37.

37. Julyan, *Place Names*, 164; Archuletta and Holden, *Traveling New Mexico*, 285. For Augustini's great impact on the people of Las Vegas, see the *Las Vegas Optic and Livestock Grower*, May 16, 1908.

38. Translated in Taylor, *Mesilla*, 136.

39. Quoted in Cleaveland, *No Life for a Lady*, 225. Also see Chauvenet, *Hewett and Friends*, 34-5, 57-8; Ferenc Szasz, "Francis Schlatter: The Healer of the Southwest," *New Mexico Historical Review*, vol. 54 (April 1979): 89, 95; Richard Melzer, "The Healer in Valencia County," *Valencia County News-Bulletin*, December 25-26, 1999; Norman Cleaveland, *Healer: The Story of Francis Schlatter* (Santa Fe: Sunstone Press, 1989).

40. Quoted in Hewett, *Campfire and Trail*, 69.

41. Ibid., 70-5.

42. *Albuquerque Tribune*, January 30, 1970; *Albuquerque Journal*, January 31, 1970; *Silver City Daily Press*, January 31, 1970

43. Quoted in Harriet S. Kellogg, *Life of Emily Harwood* (Albuquerque: El Abogado Press, 1903): 146.

44. Motto, *No Banners Waving*, 112-18; García and McCord, *Albuquerque*, 172. Many of these letters and telegrams of condolence are included in Kellogg, *Emily Harwood*, 169-249.

45. Marc Simmons, "The Lone Missionary," *Prime Time*, March 1998; Quentin, *Eternal New Mexicans*, 11.

46. *Albuquerque Citizen*, March 15, 1897; *Albuquerque Journal*, October 31, 1971; Mark T. Banker, "Presbyterian Missionary Activity in the Southwest: The Careers of John and James Menaul," *Journal of the West*, vol. 23 (January 1984): 55-61; Reverend James Allen Menaul File, Menaul Historical Library, Menaul School, Albuquerque, New Mexico.

47. Quentin, *Eternal New Mexicans*, 78.

48. *Albuquerque Journal*, October 20 and 24, 1998

49. *Albuquerque Journal*, October 8 and 24 and November 19, 2004. He had changed his name to Harbhajan Singh Khalsa Jogiji when he became a U.S. citizen in 1976.

50. Lee Priestley, *Shalam: Utopia on the Rio Grande, 1881-1907* (El Paso: Texas Western Press, 1988): 5, 34; Elnora W. Wiley, *Inside the Shalam Colony* (Los Alamos: The Document Shop, 1991); Price, *Mesilla Valley Pioneers*, 226-28; Quentin, *Eternal New Mexicans*, 146-47.

51. Priestly, *Shalam Utopia*, 34.

52. Interview with LesLee Alexander (Director, Shalam Colony and Oahspe Mystery Museum), February 5, 2005; LesLee Alexander to the author, March 8, 2005.

53. Mike Cook, "New Mesilla Museum Gets to the 'Spirit' of the Matter," *New Mexico Magazine*, vol. 83 (February 2005): 29.

54. Interview with LesLee Alexander (Director, Shalam Colony and Oahspe Mystery Museum), February 5 and November 28, 2005; LesLee Alexander to the author, March 8, 2005.

11
SCIENTISTS AND MEDICAL PERSONNEL

1. Stefan Rozental, ed., *Niels Bohr: His Life and Work as Seen by His Friends and Colleagues* (Amsterdam: North-Holland, 1967); Richard Rhodes, *The Making of the Atomic Bomb* (New York: Simon and Shuster, 1986): 53-77, 759-61.

2. *Los Alamos Monitor*, August 21, 1997; *New York Times*, August 22, 1997; Ginny Ebinger, ed., *Norris Bradbury, 1909-1997* (Los Alamos: Los Alamos Historical Society, 2006); Craig Martin, *Los Alamos Place Names* (Los Alamos: Los Alamos Historical Society, 1998): 28.

3. Laura Fermi, *Atoms in the Family* (Chicago: University of Chicago Press, 1954); Emilio Segre, *Enrico Fermi: Physicist* (Chicago: University of Chicago, 1970).

4. Quoted in the *New York Times*, February 17, 1988. Also see Richard P. Feynman, *"Surely You're Joking, Mr. Feynman!": Adventures of a Curious Character* (New York: W.W. Norton, 1985): 11; James Gleick, *Genius: The Life and Science of Richard Feynman* (New York: Pantheon Books, 1992).

5. *New York Times*, January 29, 1988; Robert C. Williams, *Klaus Fuchs: Atom Spy* (Cambridge: Harvard University Press, 1988). Julius Rosenberg (1918-53) and Esther Ethel Greenglass Rosenberg (1917-53), the most famous Soviet spies in U.S. history and the only spies ever executed for their involvement in disclosing the secret of the atomic bomb to the Soviet Union, are buried at Wellwood Cemetery in Farmingdale, New York.

6. *Las Cruces Bulletin*, April 27, 1995; *Valencia County News-Bulletin*, November 2, 2005; Kropp, *That All May Learn*, 20, 46, 128, 179, 217, 289, 311; Owen, *Las Cruces*, 164-65; Dennis Daily (archivist, Rio Grande Historical Collection, New Mexico State University) to the author, November 7 and 8, 2005.

7. *Alamogordo News*, December 25, 1930, and July 16, 1931; *New York Times*, August 11 and 12, 1945; *Roswell Morning Dispatch*, August 15 and 16, 1945.

8. David A. Clary, *Rocket Man: Robert H. Goddard and the Birth of the Space Age* (New York: Hyperion, 2003): xix, xxi, 6, 230-32.

9. Joseph Albright and Marcia Kunstel, *Bombshell: The Secret Story of America's Unknown Atomic Spy Conspiracy* (New York: Random House, 1997): 6, 13, 17; Nancy E. Shockley (Hall biographer) to the author, October 4, 2004. Also see Albright and Kunstel's interview in Matt Kelly, *The Best of "From the Plaza": Interviews and Opinions from the Plaza of Santa Fe* (Santa Fe: Lone Butte Press, 1998): 133-45.

10. Quoted in the *New York Times*, November 10, 1999.

11. *Albuquerque Tribune*, February 24, 1963; interview with Bill Jette (son), February 10, 2005.

12. *Las Cruces Sun-News*, July 12 and 13, 1988; *Albuquerque Journal*, July 13, 1988; John Crenshaw, "Chile Man: Roy Nakayama," *New Mexico Magazine*, vol. 54 (May 1976): 37; Owen, *Las Cruces*, 165-68.

13. Quoted in the *Las Cruces Sun-News*, July 12, 1988.

14. *Alamogordo Daily News*, December 7, 1987; *(Holloman Air Force Base) Sunburst*, November 19, 1999; interview with John P. Stapp by George M. House for the Space Center Oral History Program, New Mexico State University-Alamogordo Branch, July 2, 1986, Aerospace Research Collection, New Mexico Museum of Space History, Alamogordo, New Mexico; Shirley Thomas, *Men of Space: Profiles of the Leaders in Space Research, Development, and Exploration* (Philadelphia: Chilton Company, 1960): 66-89; Thomas Hedglen (aerospace historian) to the author, October 16, 2004.

15. Quoted in Todd Copeland, "Rocket Man: Colonel John Paul Stapp, A Trailblazer in Space Research," *New Mexico Magazine*, vol. 81 (June 2003): 36-9.

16. Quoted in the *Seattle Times*, September 10, 2003.

17. Quoted in the *Mercury News*, September 10, 2003. Also see the *Albuquerque Journal*, September 10, 2003; Edward Teller, *Memoirs: A Twentieth Century Journey in Science and Politics* (Cambridge, Massachusetts: Perseus Publishing, 2001); Stanley A. Blumberg and Louis G. Panos, *Edward Teller: Giant of the Golden Age of Physics* (New York: Charles Scribner's Sons, 1990): 15; Gregg Herken, *Brotherhood of the Bomb: The Tangled Lives and Loyalties of Robert Oppenheimer, Ernest Lawrence, and Edward Teller* (New York: Henry Holt and Company, 2002).

18. *Las Cruces Sun-News*, January 18, 21, and 24, 1997, with a commemorative editorial on

January 18, 1997; *New York Times*, January 20, 1997, and January 19 and 20, 2006.

19. NMSU students first began their tradition of painting an "A" (for Aggie) on Tortugas Mountain on April 1, 1920. Kropp, *That All May Learn*, 160.

20. *New York Times*, May 15, 1984; *Santa Fe New Mexican*, May 15, 1984; Stanislaw M. Ulam, *Adventures of a Mathematician* (New York: Scribner, 1976): 9, 315; Necia Grant Cooper, ed., *From Cardinals to Chaos: Reflections on the Life and Legacy of Stanislaw Ulam* (New York: Cambridge University Press, 1988): 9-22.

21. Quoted in Cooper, *From Cardinals to Chaos*, 21.

22. Françlise Ulam's Postscript to Ulam, *Adventures of a Mathematician*, 315.

23. *Los Alamos Monitor*, May 16, 1984

24. *New York Times*, June 18, 1977

25. Quoted in Ernst Stuhlinger and Frederick I. Ordway III, *Wernher Von Braun: Crusader for Space* (Malabar, Florida: Krieger, 1994): 328.

26. Quoted in Dorothy Simpson Beimer, *Hovels, Haciendas, and House Calls* (Santa Fe: Sunstone Press, 1986): 43, 293; emphasis in the original. Also see Jake W. Spidle, Jr., *Doctors of Medicine in New Mexico* (Albuquerque: University of New Mexico Press, 1986): 155-56, 228; Henry and Georgia Greenberg, "Carl Gellenthien's World," *Impact Magazine*, December 4, 1984: 4-10; Donita Ross, "Oldest Doctor Still Makes House Calls," *New Mexico Magazine*, vol. 66 (January 1988): 22-5. Dr. Gellenthien's name was so often misspelled by telephone operators in Las Vegas, New Mexico, that they were allowed to simply write "Dr. G" on their routing tickets. Ruby Lee Gibson to the editor, *New Mexico Magazine*, vol. 83 (December 2005): 8.

27. Beimer, *House Calls*, 285.

28. *Albuquerque Journal*, December 5, 1968, and November 30, 2005; Jake W. Spidle, Jr., *The Lovelace Medical Center* (Albuquerque: University of New Mexico Press, 1987): 2; Spidle, *Doctors*, 77, 298-303.

29. *Albuquerque Tribune*, December 15 and 16, 1965, with a commemorative editorial on December 16, 1965; *Albuquerque Journal*, November 30, 2005; Robert G. Elliott, "'On a Comet, Always': A Biography of Dr. W. Randolph Lovelace II," *New Mexico Quarterly*, 36 (Winter 1966-67): 351-52, 382-83; Spidle, *Lovelace*, 31, 139-40; Spidle, *Doctors*, 303-07. Lovelace had been involved in high altitude flight testing as early as 1938. See the *Albuquerque Tribune*, July 27, 1938.

30. *Santa Fe New Mexican*, November 6, 1952, November 16, 1959, August 18, 1965, and March 9, 1969

31. Quoted in the *Santa Fe New Mexican*, March 9, 1969.

32. *Santa Fe New Mexican*, August 20, 1970; Spidle, *Doctors*, 147. Sunmount, at the corner of Camino del Monte Sol and Old Santa Fe Trail, was sold to the Archdiocese of Santa Fe. It currently serves as a Carmelite Monastery and the Immaculate Heart of Mary Retreat and Conference Center. *New Mexican Sentinel*, January 12, 1938.

33. Certificate of Death, New Mexico State Department of Public Health, Bernalillo County, May 22, 1922; *Albuquerque Morning Journal*, May 27, 1922; Spidle, *Doctors*, 133, 145, 148, 155, 159.

34. *Gallup Independent*, November 11, 12, 14, 1997; *Albuquerque Journal*, November 12, 1997; *New York Times*, November 16, 1997; Carolyn Hiethammer, *I'll Go and Do More: Annie Dodge Wauneka, Navajo Leader and Activist* (Lincoln: University of Nebraska, 2001): 3-4, 215, 241, 248-49.

35. Historical literature distributed at the Mother Whiteside Memorial Library, Grants, New Mexico.

12
WARTIME LEADERS AND VICTIMS TO THE END OF THE INDIAN WARS IN NEW MEXICO, 1886

1. Álvar Nuñez Cabeza de Vaca, *Adventures in the Unknown Interior of America* (Albuquerque: University of New Mexico Press, 1983): 8; Barbara A. Tenenbaum, ed., *Encyclopedia of Latin American History and Culture* (New York: Charles Scribner's Sons, 1996): I:499.

2. John Upton Terrell, *Estevanico the Black* (Los Angeles: Westernlore Press, 1968): 19, 138-39, 145.

3. Rick Hendricks, "Marcos de Niza," in Tenenbaum, ed., *Encyclopedia of Latin American History*, IV:194; Cleve Hallenbeck, *The Journey of Fray Marcos de Niza* (Dallas: Southern Methodist University Press, 1989).

4. Herbert E. Bolton, *Coronado: Knight of Pueblos and Plains* (Albuquerque: University of New Mexico Press, 1949): 19, 330, 404-05; Richard Flint and Shirley Cushing Flint, eds., *The Coronado Expedition* (Albuquerque: University of New Mexico Press, 2003): 291.

5. Quoted in W. Eugene Hollon, *The Lost Pathfinder: Zebulon Montgomery Pike* (Norman: University of Oklahoma Press, 1949): 8-9, 212-14.

6. Sacketts Harbor mayor quoted in Ibid., 215. Also see clippings from the *Watertown (NewYork) Daily Times*, December 3, 1909, April 23, 1926, July 9, 1934, and July 3, 1962, enclosed in Robert E. Brennan (local historian) to the author, January 29, 2000.

7. Noel M. Loomis, *The Texan-Santa Fe Pioneers* (Norman: University of Oklahoma Press, 1958).

8. Fayette Copeland, *Kendall of the Picayune* (Norman: University of Oklahoma Press, 1997): 4, 320.

9. www.geocities.com/kendall_dar/gwk.html

10. Handbook of Texas Online: www.tsha.utexas.edu/handbook/online/articles/MM/fmc90

11. On the U.S.-Mexican War in New Mexico, see Howard R. Lamar, *The Far Southwest, 1846-1912* (New York: W.W. Norton, 1970): 56-82. On the Revolt of 1847, see Michael McNierney, ed., *Taos, 1847: The Revolt in Contemporary Accounts* (Boulder, Colorado: Johnson Publishing Company, 1980). On the Treaty of Guadalupe-Hidalgo, see Richard Griswold del Castillo, *The Treaty of Guadalupe Hidalgo: A Legacy of Conflict* (Norman: University of Oklahoma Press, 1990).

12. Lamar, *The Far Southwest*, 58-61, 97, 415-16; Julyan, *Place Names*, 94.

13. Quoted in Roger D. Launius, *Alexander William Doniphan: Portrait of a Missouri*

Moderate (Columbia: University of Missouri Press, 1997): 1, 278-82.

14. Joseph G. Dawson III, *Doniphan's Epic March: The 1st Missouri Volunteers in the Mexican War* (Lawrence: University of Kansas, 1999): 320.

15. The Kearney family name was originally O'Kearny, meaning "warrior" or "victorious" in the ancient Irish language. Kearney is sometimes misspelled "Karney," a mistake attributed to a careless clerk in the War Department, according to historian Robert M. Utley. *Santa Fe New Mexican*, June 7, 1964.

16. Amsler, *Final Resting Place*, 43-4; Julyan, *Place Names*, 183.

17. Amsler, *Final Resting Place*, 44.

18. Robert E. Shalhope, *Sterling Price: Portrait of a Southerner* (Columbia: University of Missouri Press, 1971): 4, 288-91.

19. One of the best summaries of the Confederate invasion and retreat is provided in Donald S. Frazier, *Blood and Treasure: Confederate Empire in the Southwest* (College Station: Texas A&M Press, 1995).

20. *Canby (Oregon) Herald*, June 29, 1983

21. Doug Foster, "Imperfect Justice: The Modoc War Crimes Trial of 1873," *Oregon Historical Quarterly*, vol. 100 (Fall 1999): 251.

22. Quoted in Max L. Heyman, Jr., *Prudent Soldier: A Biography of Major General E.R.S. Canby, 1817-1873* (Glendale, California: Arthur H. Clark Company, 1959): 383.

23. Foster, "Imperfect Justice," 278-82.

24. *Santa Fe New Mexican*, February 5, 7, and 10, 1873; Aurora Hunt, *Major General James Henry Carleton: Western Frontier Dragoon* (Glendale, California: Arthur H. Clark, 1958): 26, 348. For a rare defense of Carleton's service in New Mexico, see Allan Holmes, "Major General James H. Carleton: New Mexico's Controversial Civil War Commander," *Southern New Mexico Historical Review*, vol. 1 (January 1994): 47-61.

25. Jacqueline Dorgan Meketa, ed., *Legacy of Honor: The Life of Rafael Chacon* (Albuquerque: University of New Mexico Press, 1986): 219, 334-35.

26. Charles Lummis affirmed that Amado Chaves had told Lummis of the removal "of my venerated old friends your parents and your sisters from the little chappel by the oak trees…to the Campo Santo at San Mateo" in Lummis to Chaves, Los Angeles, June 12, 1924, Amado Chaves Papers, Box 3, Folder 33, New Mexico State Records Center and Archives, Santa Fe, New Mexico; Simmons, *Little Lion*, 11, 215, 219-20, 247n-48n.

27. Quoted in Reginald S. Craig, *The Fighting Parson: The Biography of Colonel John M. Chivington* (Los Angeles: Westernlore Press, 1959): 24, 236-37; Wommack, *From the Grave*, 99-101.

28. Jacqueline Dorgan Meketa, *Louis Felsenthal: Citizen-Soldier of Territorial New Mexico* (Albuquerque: University of New Mexico Press, 1982): 6, 33, 124-25.

29. Jerry D. Thompson, *Desert Tiger: Captain Paddy Graydon and the Civil War in the Far Southwest* (El Paso: Texas Western Press, 1992): 2, 58-63; Marc Simmons, "Paddy's Misfortunes," *Santa Fe Reporter*, September 1-7, 1999.

30. Thomas S. Edrington and John Taylor, *The Battle of Glorieta Pass* (Albuquerque: University of New Mexico Press, 1998): 98-100; Don E. Alberts, *The Battle of Glorieta* (College Station: Texas A&M Press, 1998): 203n; Hanks, *Lamy's Legion*, 61; Francis C. Kajencki, "Alexander Grzelachowski: Pioneer Merchant of Puerto de Luna, New Mexico," *Arizona and the West*, vol. 26 (Autumn 1984): 243-60; Francis C. Kajencki, "The Battle of Glorieta Pass: Was the Guide Ortiz or Grzelachowski?" *New Mexico Historical Review*, vol. 62 (January 1987): 47-54; Quentin, *Eternal New Mexicans*, 122.

31. *Las Vegas Optic*, May 28, 1896. Also see the *Las Vegas Examiner*, May 26, 1896.

32. Quoted in Marion Cox Grinstead, *Destiny at Valverde: The Life and Death of Alexander McRae* (Socorro: Socorro Historical Society, 1992): 1, 35-7; John Taylor, *Bloody Valverde: A Civil War Battle on the Rio Grande, February 21, 1862* (Albuquerque: University of New Mexico Press, 1995): 90-1, 163n. Taylor doubts the validity of this often-told version of McRae's death.

33. Daniel C.B. Rathbun and David V. Alexander, *New Mexico Frontier Military Place Names* (Las Cruces: Yucca Tree Press, 2003): 188-19; Dusenberry, "New Mexico Hometown Heroes Committee."

34. Darlis A. Miller, "William Logan Rynerson in New Mexico, 1862-93," *New Mexico Historical Review*, vol. 48 (April 1973): 102, 125; Gary L. Roberts, *Death Comes for the Chief Justice* (Niwot: University Press of Colorado, 1990): 57, 125; Nolan, *West*, 90.

35. Meketa, *Martyrs to Murderers*, 52-63; Nita Murphy (reference librarian, Taos Historic Museums) to the author, November 6, 2003; *Taos News*, May 29, 1969; Julyan, *Place Names*, 335.

36. Ferroll Clark Hanlon, *Life on the Range and Other Memoirs: The Early Years in the Estancia Valley and Taos* (Grand Junction, Colorado: C&M Enterprises, 1995): 167.

37. *Taos News*, June 6, 1968

38. *Taos News*, January 13 and 27, 1971

39. *Taos News*, March 24 and November 17, 1971

40. Quoted in Roberts, *Death Comes for the Chief Justice*, 20, 67-70.

41. Jerry D. Thompson, *Colonel John Robert Baylor: Texas Indian Fighter and Confederate Soldier* (Hillsboro, Texas: Hill Junior College Monograph, 1971).

42. Jerry D. Thompson, ed., *Westward the Texans* (El Paso: Texas Western Press, 1990): 146n.

43. Odie Faulk, *General Tom Green: Fightin' Texan* (Waco: Texian Press, 1963): 2, 62, 67.

44. Jerry D. Thompson, *Henry Hopkins Sibley: Confederate General of the West* (Natchitoches: Northwestern State University Press, 1987): 4, 193, 358, 368-69; Jerry Thompson to the author, June 30, 1998; Julyan, *Place Names*, 334.

45. *Albuquerque Tribune*, November 7, 1988. For a description of the original burial of these men, see Alberts, *Battle of Glorieta*, 143-44. A total of forty-two Confederates were killed or mortally wounded at the battle. Forty-seven Union soldiers were killed in the action. Edrington and Taylor, *The Battle of Glorieta Pass*, 131, 137. In 1985 a heavy equipment operator discovered a similarly mysterious single grave outside the

walls of Fort Craig, near the first battle of the Civil War in New Mexico. Anthropologists determined that the body in this grave probably belonged to a young Indian or *mestizo* woman who probably died "shortly after receiving a hard blow to the upper jaw that dislodged a central incisor tooth." Unlike the bodies found at Glorieta, this woman's identity, her role at Fort Craig, and the time of her death will undoubtedly remain a mystery. George A. Agogino, "A Lonely Lady" in Charles Carroll and Lynne Sebastian, eds., *Fort Craig: The United States Fort on the Camino Real* (Socorro: U.S. Bureau of Land Management, 2000): 231-37.

46. *Santa Fe New Mexican*, April 26, 1993; *Albuquerque Journal*, April 26, 1993, and March 31, 2002; *San Antonio Express-News*, June 6, 1993; Edrington and Taylor, *Glorieta Pass*, 119-20; Alberts, *Battle of Glorieta*, 205n; Museum of New Mexico Press Release, February 1, 1993; *Socorro Defensor Chieftain*, March 3, 2004.

47. Carmack, *Cemetery Research*, 105.

48. Taylor, *Bloody Valverde*, 100, 164n. Only Lieutenant Colonel John S. Sutton, who died of his leg wounds on February 22, 1862, was given a solemn, separate funeral with full honors near the battlefield. Taylor, *Bloody Valverde*, 100-01.

49. *Socorro Defensor Chieftain*, March 6, 2004. This newspaper story includes a list of the twenty-six dead Confederates, their names, ages, regiments, dates of death, and causes of death.

50. Julyan, *Place Names*, 52.

51. Quoted in Quentin, *Eternal New Mexicans*, 131.

52. Quoted in Henderson and Henderson, "Directory of the Silver City Memory Lane Cemetery."

53. Quoted in Marc Simmons, "The Death of John Bullard," *Santa Fe Reporter*, May 2-8, 1990.

54. Henderson and Henderson, "Memory Lane."

55. Tom Dunlay, *Kit Carson and the Indians* (Lincoln: University of Nebraska Press, 2000): 412-15; Lamar, *Reader's Encyclopedia of the West*, 166; Wommack, *From the Grave*, 262, 284, 309; Woolley et. al., *Final Destinations*, 125; Marc Simmons, "Remembering Santa Fe's Forgotten Monument," *Santa Fe New Mexican*, January 26, 2002; Julyan, *Place Names*, 66, 185-86; *Santa Fe New Mexican*, May 31, 1892.

56. Arbeiter and Cirino, *Permanent Addresses*, 139.

57. Twitchell, *Military Occupation*, 282.

58. Meketa, *Martyrs to Murderers*, 61.

59. *Santa Fe New Mexican*, January 2, 1885

60. See, for example, the *Taos News*, August 30, 1990.

61. Dean S. Michelson to the editor, *Taos News*, September 6, 1990.

62. Quoted in the *Albuquerque Journal North*, July 24, 1998.

63. *Taos News*, January 25, May 23 and 30, June 6, 1968

64. Marc Simmons, *Massacre on the Lordsburg Road: A Tragedy of the Apache Wars* (College Station: Texas A&M Press, 1997): xi, 22; Shirley Hurd (local Fort Scott, Kansas, historian) to the author, December 10, 2000.

65. Simmons, *Massacre*, 184-87.
66. Archuletta and Holden, *Traveling New Mexico*, 147.

67. Martin Hardwick Hall, "Captain Thomas J. Mastin's Arizona Guards, C.S.A.," *New Mexico Historical Review*, vol. 49 (April 1974): 143-51. Hall lists Maeston's date of death as October 7, 1861.

68. According to one estimate, Buffalo Soldiers represented about ten percent of all U.S. soldiers in the post-Civil War late nineteenth century era. Almost four thousand served in New Mexico from 1866 to 1900. Frank N. Schubert, *Black Valor: Buffalo Soldiers and the Medal of Honor, 1870-1898* (Wilmington, Delaware: Scholarly Resources, 1997): 5; William H. Leckie, *The Buffalo Soldiers* (Norman: University of Oklahoma Press, 1967); Monroe Lee Billington, *New Mexico's Buffalo Soldiers, 1866-1900* (Niwot: University Press of Colorado, 1991); Marc Simmons, "Buffalo Soldiers, A Famous Black Regiment, Fought Apaches, Comanches," *Santa Fe New Mexican*, April 24, 2004.

69. *Silver City Daily Press and Independent*, September 20, 2003; Billington, *New Mexico's Buffalo Soldiers*, 53-4; William A. Aleshire's September 20, 2003, eulogy for Corporal James Betters, enclosed in correspondence from Cecilia Jensen Bell (Fort Bayard Historic Preservation Society) to the author, June 28, 2006.

70. Maisha Baton, "New Mexico's Black Women" in n.a., *History of Hope*, 41; Phillip Thomas Tucker, *Cathy Williams: From Slave to Female Buffalo Soldier* (Mechanicsburg, Pennsylvania: Stackpole Books, 2002): 3, 219.

71. Frank N. Schubert, *Voices of the Buffalo Soldier: Records, Reports, and Recollections of Military Life and Service in the West* (Albuquerque: University of New Mexico Press, 2003): 34. Schubert discovered Williams's original discharge and pension application papers in the National Archives and included copies of them in Ibid., 35. In the latter document each reference on the form that referred to "he" was carefully altered to read "she."

72. George Lang, Raymond L. Collins, and Gerard F. White, *Medal of Honor Recipients, 1863-1994* (New York: Facts On File, Inc., 1995): II:851.

73. Ibid., I:257.

74. Frank N. Schubert, *On the Trail of the Buffalo Soldier: Biographies of African Americans in the U.S. Army, 1866-1917* (Wilmington, Delaware: Scholarly Resources, 1995): 49; Schubert, *Black Valor*, 49-53, 57-9, 171; Billington, *Buffalo Soldiers*, 89; Lang, Collins, and White, *Medal of Honor*, I:257.

75. Ibid., I:258.

76. *Albuquerque Tribune*, April 7, 2003, Dusenberry, "New Mexico Hometown Heroes Committee." Bratling is sometimes spelled with two t's, although most military records show just one.

77. Schubert, *Black Valor*, 79-83; Billington, *Buffalo Soldiers*, 106; Lang, Collins, and White, *Medal of Honor*, I:260.

78. Schubert, *Black Valor*, 54-6; Billington, *Buffalo Soldiers*, 91, 132; Lang, Collins, and White, *Medal of Honor*, I: 265.

79. Lang, Collins, and White, *Medal of Honor*, I:266.

80. Schubert, *On the Trail*, 119; Schubert, *Black Valor*, 54-7, 83-6, 117, 171; Billington, *Buffalo Soldiers*, 91.

81. Lang, Collins, and White, *Medal of Honor*, I:267-68.

82. Ibid., I:268.

83. Schubert, *On the Trail*, 171; Schubert, *Black Valor*, 45-8, 169; Billington, *Buffalo Soldiers*, 51; Lang, Collins, and White, *Medal of Honor*, I:272-73; Cecilia Jensen Bell (Fort Bayard Historic Preservation Society) to the author, September 1, 2005.

84. Lang, Collins, and White, *Medal of Honor*, I:273.

85. *Santa Fe New Mexican*, May 28, 1991; Dusenberry, "New Mexico Hometown Heroes Committee."

86. Lang, Collins, and White, *Medal of Honor*, I:280.

87. Schubert, *On the Trail*, 249; Schubert, *Black Valor*, 74-5, 77-9, 87-9; Billington, *Buffalo Soldiers*, 95-6.

88. Lang, Collins, and White, *Medal of Honor*, I:285-86.

89. Ibid., I:289.

90. Dusenberry, "New Mexico Hometown Heroes Committee."

91. Lang, Collins, and White, *Medal of Honor*, I:292.

92. *Albuquerque Journal*, July 4, 1989; Ed Boles (Albuquerque Historic Preservation Planner) to the author, August 25, 2004.

93. Dusenberry, "New Mexico Hometown Heroes Committee."

94. Lang, Collins, and White, *Medal of Honor*, I:300; Thomas W. Dunlay, *Wolves for the Blue Soldiers: Indian Scouts and Auxiliaries with the United States Army, 1860-90* (Lincoln: University of Nebraska Press, 1982): 105; http://gravelocator.cem.va.gov.

95. *Santa Fe New Mexican*, May 28, 1991

96. Lang, Collins, and White, *Medal of Honor*, I:300.

97. Kent Kool (historical photographer) to the author, June 15, 2003.

98. Lang, Collins, and White, *Medal of Honor*, I:300.

99. Ibid., I:301.

100. Dusenberry, "New Mexico Hometown Heroes Committee."

101. Schubert, *On the Trail*, 377; Schubert, *Black Valor*, 69, 77-9, 87-8, 117; Billington, *Buffalo Soldiers*, 105; Lang, Collins, and White, *Medal of Honor*, I:302. Frank Schubert used *Edge of the Storm* for the cover of his book, *Black Valor*.

102. Lang, Collins, and White, *Medal of Honor*, I:302.

103. Ibid., I:304.

104. Dusenberry, "New Mexico Hometown Heroes Committee."

105. Schubert, *On the Trail*, 448; Schubert, *Black Valor*, 81-3, 87, 117, 166-67, 170; Billington, *Buffalo Soldiers*, 106; Lang, Collins, and White, *Medal of Honor*, I:309-10.

106. Ibid., I:312.

107. Schubert, *Black Valor*, 79-83, 87-8; Billington, *Buffalo Soldiers*, 106; Lang, Collins, and White, *Medal of Honor*, I:312.

108. Schubert, *On the Trail*, 473.

109. Quoted in Meketa, *Martyrs to Murderers*, 172. Max Evans's historical novel, *Faraway Blue* (Albuquerque: University of New Mexico Press, 2005), is based on Williams's life as a Buffalo Soldier.

110. Lang, Collins, and White, *Medal of Honor*, I:312.

111. Ibid., I:314.

112. Schubert, *On the Trail*, 483; Schubert, *Black Valor*, 84-8; Billington, *Buffalo Soldiers*, 106-7.

113. Lamar, *Reader's Encyclopedia of the West*, 192; Simmons, *Massacre*, 191.

114. Edwin R. Sweeney, *Cochise: Chiricahua Apache Chief* (Norman: University of Oklahoma Press, 1991): 6-7, 395.

115. Quoted in Ibid., 395.

116. Indian agent Thomas J. Jeffords quoted in Ibid., 396-97.

117. Angie Debo, *Geronimo: The Man, His Time, His Place* (Norman: University of Oklahoma Press, 1976): 7, 440-44; John Anthony Turcheneske, Jr., *The Chiricahua Apache Prisoners of War: Fort Sill, 1894-1914* (Niwot: University Press of Colorado, 1997): 106; Julyan, *Place Names*, 146. Also see Ruffo, *At Geronimo's Grave*, 6-7, 43, 78.

118. *Albuquerque Journal*, September 5, 2000; *Oklahoma City Oklahoman*, May 11, 2006; L.G. Moses, "Geronimo: The 'Last Renegade'" in Richard W. Etulain and Glenda Riley, eds., *Chiefs and Generals: Nine Men Who Shaped the American West* (Golden, Colorado: Fulcrum, 2004): 87, 102-03.

119. Dee Brown, *Bury My Heart at Wounded Knee: An Indian History of the American West* (New York: Holt, Rinehart, and Winston, 1970): 413.

120. Wooley et. al., *Final Destinations*, 139-41; Moses, "Geronimo," 102. Also see Johnny D. Boggs, "Fort Sill's Indian Graves," *Persimmon Hill*, vol. 28 (Autumn 2000): 65-6; Kent Ruth and Jim Argo, *Here We Rest: Historic Cemeteries of Oklahoma* (Oklahoma City: Oklahoma Historical Society, 1986): 63.

121. *Albuquerque Journal*, September 11 and October 10, 2004

122. Kimberly Moore Buchanan, *Apache Women Warriors* (El Paso: Texas Western Press, 1986): 27-32.

123. Lee Myers, "Mangas Coloradas's Death," *New Mexico Historical Review*, vol. 41 (October 1966): 287-304; Marc Simmons, "The Assassination of Mangas Coloradas," *Socorro Defensor Chieftain*, September 18, 1989.

124. C.L. Sonnichsen, *The Mescalero Apaches* (Norman: University of Oklahoma Press, 1973): 111-12. Historian Jerry D. Thompson reported that "a human skull with what appeared to be a bullet hole in the frontal cranium was found at Cement Spring in the late 1950s." Thompson, *Desert Tiger*, 53-4, 81n.

125. Hoffman and Johnson, *Navajo Biographies*, 88-110.

126. Stephen H. Lekson, *Nana's Raid: Apache Warfare in Southern New Mexico, 1881* (El Paso: Texas Western Press, 1987): 3-5, 39n; Boggs, "Fort Sill's Indian Graves," 66.

127. Alfonso Ortiz, "Popay's Leadership: A Pueblo Perspective," *El Palacio*, vol. 86 (Winter 1980-81): 18-22; Joe S. Sando and Herman Agoyo, eds., *Po'Pay: Leader of the First American Revolution* (Santa Fe: Clear Light Press, 2005): 82-91; Joe S. Sando, " Popé, the Pueblo Revolt, and Native Americans in Early New Mexico" in Etulain, ed., *New Mexican Lives*, 19-44.

128. Rick Romancito, "Cliff Fragua," *New Mexico Magazine*, vol. 83 (March 2005): 26-7; *Albuquerque Journal*, May 22, 2005. The controversy surrounding Popé's selection for New Mexico's second statue is review in Sando and Agoyo, *Po'Pay*, 133-40.

129. Dan L. Thrapp, *Victorio and the Mimbres Apaches* (Norman: University of Oklahoma Press, 1974): 4, 304-7; Glenda Riley, "Apache Chief Victorio" in Etulain and Riley, eds., *Chiefs and Generals*, 38-9; Julyan, *Place Names*, 373.

13
WARTIME LEADERS AND VICTIMS SINCE THE SPANISH-AMERICAN WAR, 1898

1. *St. Anthony Messenger*, vol. 53 (July 1945): 20.

2. Dale L. Walker, *The Boys of '98: Theodore Roosevelt and the Rough Riders* (New York: Tom Doherty Associates, 1998); Richard Melzer and Phyllis A. Mingus, "Wild to Fight: The New Mexico Rough Riders in the Spanish-American War," *New Mexico Historical Review*, vol. 59 (April 1984): 109-36. For a complete list of New Mexico's Rough Riders, see the Muster-In Rolls of Troops E, F, G, and H, First Volunteer Cavalry, Adjunct General Files, State Records Center and Archives, Santa Fe, New Mexico. For all New Mexican Spanish-American War soldiers and their burial sites, see www.spanamwar.com/NewMexico.

3. *Las Vegas Daily Optic*, December 13, 1972; *Las Cruces Sun-News*, April 23, 1973; Jim Brito (grandson) interview, Las Cruces, April 12, 2002.

4. *Alamogordo News*, June 16, 1927, with a commemorative editorial on that same day; Necrology, *New Mexico Historical Review*, vol. 2 (July 1927): 306; Price, *Mesilla Valley Pioneers*, 294-98.

5. Quoted in the *Santa Fe New Mexican*, June 13, 1927. Also see the *Santa Fe New Mexican*, November 26, 1900; Walker, *The Boys of '98*, 93, 216; Browning, *Violence Was No Stranger*, 145.

6. *Santa Fe New Mexican*, March 15, 1899, and November 18, 1900; *Roswell Record*, November 24, 1899; Walker, *The Boys of '98*, 216; Perrigo, *Hispanos*, 56-8; Richard

Melzer, "Governor Miguel Otero's War: Statehood and New Mexican Loyalty in the Spanish-American War of 1898," *Colonial Latin American Historical Review*, vol. 8 (Winter 1999): 91-2; Julyan, *Place Names*, 57.

7. *Albuquerque Weekly News*, June 25, 1898

8. *Santa Fe New Mexican*, August 17, 1929

9. *Santa Fe New Mexican*, January 23, 1901

10. Certificate of Death, New Mexico State Department of Public Health, Santa Fe County, September 16, 1934; *Santa Fe New Mexican*, October 26, 1922; *Carlsbad Argus*, November 2, 1922; Walker, *The Boys of '98*, 216; Wilson, *Myth of Santa Fe*, 193. Mueller's death certificate identifies January 26, 1863, as his date of birth. Mueller's surname was sometimes spelled as Muller.

11. Julyan, *Place Names*, 303. For an example of a Roosevelt visit to New Mexico, see the *Santa Fe New Mexican*, May 5, 1903; Bryan, *Albuquerque Remembered*, 176-78.

12. Edmund Morris, *The Rise of Theodore Roosevelt* (New York: Modern Library, 2001): 3-4; David McCullough, *Mornings on Horseback* (New York: Simon and Shuster, 2003): 19-20, 53-4, 367-68; Lamb, *Who's Buried*, 108-13.

13. Historical literature distributed at Sagamore Hill, Home of Theodore Roosevelt, National Historic Site, Oyster Bay, New York.

14. Certificate of Death, New Mexico State Department of Public Health, Santa Fe County, April 30, 1939; *Santa Fe New Mexican*, May 1, 1939; *Albuquerque Journal*, May 1, 1939; Lang, Collins, and White, *Medal of Honor*, II:570.

15. A good recent survey of the revolution is Michael J. Gonzales, *The Mexican Revolution, 1910-1940* (Albuquerque: University of New Mexico Press, 2002). Also see Charles H. Harris III and Louis R. Sadler, *The Border and the Revolution* (Silver City: High-Lonesome Books, 1988).

16. Gerald G. Raun, "Refugees or Prisoners of War?: The Internment of a Mexican Federal Army after the Battle of Ojinaga, December 1913-January 1914," *Journal of Big Bend Studies*, vol. 12 (2000): 133-65; interview with Gerald G. Raun, August 13, 2004. The interned Mexican soldiers were finally released from Fort Wingate in September 1914, two months following Romero's death. *El Paso Morning Times*, September 11, 1914.

17. Viljoen family friend Katharine Brown Lawrence quoted in Michael Morris, "South Africa to Southern New Mexico: Boer War General Buried in Las Cruces," *Southern New Mexico Historical Review*, vol. 3 (January 1996): 55; Dale C. Maluy, "Boer Colonization in the Southwest," *New Mexico Historical Review*, vol. 52 (April 1977): 93-110; Ben J. Viljoen, *An Exiled General* (St. Louis: n.p., 1906); *Albuquerque Journal*, January 15, 1917; *El Paso Times*, May 31, 1963.

18. Harris and Sadler, *Border and the Revolution*, 101-12; James W. Hurst, *The Villista Prisoners of 1916-1917* (Las Cruces: Yucca Tree Press, 2000): 1-4; Friedrich Katz, "Pancho Villa and the Attack on Columbus," *American Historical Review*, vol. 83 (February 1983): 101-30; Richard Melzer, "On Villa's Trail in Mexico: The Experiences of a Black Cavalryman and a White Infantry Officer, 1916-19," *Military History of the Southwest*, vol. 21 (Fall 1991): 173-90.

19. *Deming Headlight*, March 6, 11, and 12, 1991

20. *Albuquerque Tribune*, February 28, 2002; *Deming Headlight*, March 12, 1991; interview with Richard R. Dean (grandson), October 10, 2003. Richard Dean is the foremost resident expert on the Columbus raid.

21. Ibid.

22. *Albuquerque Journal*, July 28, 1981; Bryan, *True Tales*, 249-50; interviews with Bill Parks (son), September 2 and October 22, 2004.

23. *Valencia County News-Bulletin*, January 1, 1981; Gerry Hawk, "Nine Days to Columbus," *True West*, vol. 45 (January 1998): 35-9; Bryan, *True Tales*, 246-49.

24. Interview with Oscar Medders (grandson), January 7, 2005. Armando Martinez, manager of the Pancho Villa State Park, readily admits that naming the park after Villa was a "commercial ploy" to help draw tourists to the area. Interview with Armando Martinez, September 16, 2005.

25. Herrman, *Mountainair*, 116-19.

26. *Albuquerque Tribune*, July 15, 1948

27. Gene Smith, *Until the Last Trumpet Sounds: The Life of General of the Armies John J. Pershing* (New York: Wiley, 1998): vii-xi, 4, 313-14; Donald Smyth, *Pershing: General of the Armies* (Bloomington: Indiana University Press, 1986).

28. Arbeiter and Cirino, *Permanent Addresses*, 53.

29. Jaehn, *Jewish Pioneers*, 29, 59.

30. Arthur Ravel quoted in Bryan, *True Tales*, 253.

31. Esther N. Shir (Library Director, University of New Mexico-Valencia Campus) to the author, June 14, 2004. To read Hebrew tombstones, see www.jewishgen.org/infofiles/tombstones.html. On tombstone images and customs in Jewish cemeteries, see Brown, *Soul in the Stone*, 27-9.

32. Bryan, *True Tales*, 244-45.

33. Hurst, *Villista Prisoners*, 2, 33, 93, 96.

34. *New York Times*, July 24, 1923; Friedrich Katz, *The Life and Times of Pancho Villa* (Stanford: Stanford University Press, 1998); 1, 3, 732, 765-68, 788-90.

35. Harris and Sadler, *Border and the Revolution*, 7-23.

36. Samuel Brunk, "The Mortal Remains of Emiliano Zapata" in Lyman L. Johnson, ed., *Death, Dismemberment, and Memory in Latin America* (Albuquerque: University of New Mexico Press, 2004): 163. Others buried at the Monument to the Mexican Revolution were Francisco Madero, Venustiano Carranza, Plutarco Elías Calles, and Lázaro Cárdenas. For a discussion of the fate of the bodies of controversial political leaders, especially Porfirio Díaz but including Villa, see David Merchant and Paul Rich, "A Policy Toward the Dead: Repatriating Controversial Political Leaders," *Review of Policy Research*, vol. 21 (January 2004): 129-35. Also see the *Albuquerque Journal*, March 29, 1998.

37. Quoted in Katz, *Villa*, 770.

38. Translated by Beth Pollock (Chair, Department of Language and Linguistics, New

Mexico State University, Las Cruces, New Mexico) as enclosed in correspondence from Louis R. Sadler (Borderlands historian) to the author, November 16, 2004; Katz, *Villa*, 267-68.

39. Lansing B. Bloom *et. al.*, "New Mexico in the Great War," *New Mexico Historical Review*, vol. 2 (October 1926): 425-28; Lansing B. Bloom, *New Mexico in the Great War* (Santa Fe: El Palacio Press, 1927); Barron Oder, "From Western Frontier to the Space Frontier: The Military in New Mexico, 1900-1940" in Judith Boyce DeMark, *Essays in Twentieth Century New Mexico History* (Albuquerque: University of New Mexico Press, 1994): 108; Marc Simmons, "Effects of World War I Felt in New Mexico," *Santa Fe New Mexican*, September 14, 2002. A list of thirteen New Mexico Military Institute alumni who died in World War I is including in Gibbs and Jackman, *New Mexico Military Institute*, 405.

40. Quoted in Bonnie Ball O'Brien, *Harry P. Stagg, Christian Statesman* (Nashville: Broadman Press, 1976): 41.

41. Quoted in the *Albuquerque Journal*, September 19, 1999. Also see Daniel R. Carnett, *Contending for the Faith: Southern Baptists in New Mexico, 1938-1995* (Albuquerque: University of New Mexico Press, 2002): 30-52.

42. A list of these 1,242 men can be found on www.media.nara.gov/media/images/27/24/27-2314a.gif and www.media.nara.gov/media/images/28/34/28-3372a.gif. About a tenth of the New Mexicans who died in World War II were alumni of New Mexico State University killed on the Pacific front. For a list of these 126 NMSU casualties, see Walter Hines, *Aggies of the Pacific War: New Mexico College of A&M and the War with Japan* (Las Cruces: Yucca Tree Press, 1999): 155-59. One hundred and seventy-nine of the New Mexicans killed in World War II were alumni of the New Mexico Military Institute. Gibbs and Jackman, *New Mexico Military Institute*, 406-16.

43. Gerald W. Thomas, Monroe L. Billington, and Roger D. Walker, eds., *Victory in World War II: The New Mexico Story* (Las Cruces: New Mexico State University, 1994).

44. For the individual fates of members of the New Mexico National Guard captured by the Japanese with the surrender of Bataan, see Eva Jane Matson, *It Tolled for New Mexico: New Mexicans Captured by the Japanese, 1941-45* (Las Cruces: Yucca Tree Press, 1994). Also see Dorothy Cave, *Beyond Courage: One Regiment Against Japan, 1941-45* (Las Cruces: Yucca Tree Press, 1992). For a list of the fifty-five New Mexico State University alumni captured on Bataan, including twenty-six who later died in captivity, see Hines, *Aggies of the Pacific War*, 153-54.

45. Matson, *It Tolled for New Mexico*, 55-100.

46. *Silver City Daily Press*, March 8, 1997; *Carlsbad Current-Argus*, March 9, 1997; Melissa Masterson, *Ride the Waves to Freedom: Calvin Graef's Survival Story of the Bataan Death March and His Escape from a Sinking Hellship* (Hobbs, New Mexico: Southwest Freelance, 2000); Melissa Masterson to the author, November 15, 2000; Matson, *It Tolled for New Mexico*, 294-95.

47. *Santa Fe New Mexican*, February 5 and 8, 1967; *Albuquerque Journal*, February 5 and 8, 1967; *Albuquerque Tribune*, June 18, 1966, and February 6 and 7, 1967; Matson, *It Tolled for New Mexico*, 356-57.

48. Ibid., 384-85.

49. Doris A. Paul, *The Navajo Code Talkers* (Bryn Mawr, Pennsylvania: Dorrance and Company, 1973); Everett M. Rogers and Nancy R. Bartlit, *Silent Voices of World War II* (Santa Fe: Sunstone Press, 2005): 83-138; interview with Roy Hawthorne (Navajo Code

Talker), May 29, 2005. The entire code is included in www.history.navy.mil/faqs/faq61-4.htm and in Paul, *Navajo Code Talkers*, 24-9. On the Native American role in World War II as a whole, see Kenneth William Townsend, *World War II and the American Indian* (Albuquerque: University of New Mexico Press, 2000).

50. *Farmington Daily Times*, June 25 and 26, 1997; Sally McClain, *Navajo Weapon: The Navajo Code Talkers* (Tucson: Rio Nuevo Publications, 2001): 39, 290; Paul, *Navajo Code Talkers*, 12-13.

51. *Farmington Daily Times*, January 10, 1996; McClain, *Navajo Weapon*, 290.

52. Quoted in the *Gallup Independent*, February 3, 1998. Also see the *Gallup Independent*, January 30 and 31, 1998; *New York Times*, February 1, 1998; Henry and Georgia Greenberg, *Power of a Navajo: Carl Gorman, The Man and His Life* (Santa Fe: Clear Light, 1996): 11; interview with Zonnie Gorman (daughter).

53. See the "Profile of Harrison Lapahie, Sr., Navajo Code Talker" prepared by his son, Harrison Lapahie, Jr.: www.lapahie.com/Dad.cfm.

54. *Santa Fe New Mexican*, July 31, 1963, with a commemorative editorial, August 1, 1963; Don Lohbeck, *Patrick J. Hurley* (Chicago: Henry Regnery Company, 1956): 22.

55. Lang, Collins, and White, *Medal of Honor*, II:851.

56. Ibid., II:453.

57. Ibid., II:530.

58. Ibid., II:544.

59. Dusenberry, "New Mexico Hometown Heroes Committee."

60. Lang, Collins, and White, *Medal of Honor*, II:544-45; Gibbs and Jackman, *New Mexico Military Institute*, 148, 429; J. Donald Morfe (Field Researcher, Medal of Honor Historical Society) to the author, March 26, 2005.

61. *Santa Fe New Mexican*, February 7, 1999; Lang, Collins, and White, *Medal of Honor*, II:572.

62. Quoted in James Abarr, "New Mexico's Special Heroes," *Impact Magazine*, January 11, 1983.

63. Quoted in the *Santa Fe New Mexican*, November 11, 1997, and February 7, 1999.

64. Lang, Collins, and White, *Medal of Honor*, II:587-88.

65. Martha Byrd, *Kenneth N. Walker: Airpower's Untempered Crusader* (Maxwell Air Force Base, Alabama: Air University Press, 1997): 1, 107-23; Lang, Collins, and White, *Medal of Honor*, II:592.

66. For a chronology of the Manhattan Project's history, see Richard Melzer, *Breakdown: How the Secret of the Atomic Bomb Was Stolen During World War II* (Santa Fe: Sunstone Press, 2000): 107-11. The best source on the Manhattan Project remains Richard Rhodes's prize-winning *Making of the Atomic Bomb*.

67. *Santa Fe New Mexican*, December 6, 2005; *Albuquerque Journal*, December 7, 2005; *New York Times*, December 8, 2005; Rhodes, *Making of the Atomic Bomb*, 739-40.

68. *New York Times*, July 15, 1970; Robert S. Norris, *Racing for the Bomb: General Leslie R. Groves, The Manhattan Project's Indispensable Man* (South Royalton, Vermont: Steerforth Press, 2002): 19, 26, 537-39.

69. Quoted in Melzer, *Breakdown*, 17. Groves described his work on the Manhattan Project in his *Now It Can Be Told: The Story of the Manhattan Project* (New York: Da Capa, 1962).

70. Quoted in Jennet Conant, *109 East Palace: Robert Oppenheimer and the Secret City of Los Alamos* (New York: Simon and Shuster, 2005): 398. Also see Nancy Cook Steeper, *Dorothy Scarritt McKibbin: Gatekeeper to Los Alamos* (Los Alamos: Los Alamos Historical Society, 2003): 5, 147. McKibbin's former home is now a New Mexico Registered Cultural Property.

71. *New York Times*, February 19, 1967; *Albuquerque Journal*, February 19, 1967; *Los Alamos Monitor*, February 21, 1967; Abraham Pais, *J. Robert Oppenheimer: A Life* (New York: Oxford University Press, 2006): 5, 302-09; Kai Bird and Martin J. Sherwin, *American Prometheus: The Triumph and Tragedy of J. Robert Oppenheimer* (New York: Knopf, 2005); Conant, *109 East Palace*, 395-96; Martin, *Los Alamos Place Names*, 64, 85. According to some sources, including the *New York Times*, the "J" in Oppenheimer's name was just a letter, not an initial for an actual first name.

72. Al Christman, *Target Hiroshima: Deak Parsons and the Creation of the Atomic Bomb* (Annapolis, Maryland: Naval Institute Press, 1998): 7, 14, 249-53. Parsons's fellow midshipmen at the U.S. Naval Academy gave him his nickname, in reference to his pious-sounding surname.

73. *Santa Fe New Mexican*, January 23, 2003, with a commemorative editorial on January 24, 2003; Bill Mauldin, *A Sort of a Saga* (New York: William Sloane Associates, 1949); Bill Mauldin, *The Brass Ring* (New York: W.W. Norton and Company, 1971); Marc Simmons, "Cartoonist Bill Mauldin Had Role that Helped Define the Twentieth Century," *Santa Fe New Mexican*, March 8, 2003.

74. *Santa Fe New Mexican*, April 18, 1945; *Albuquerque Tribune*, April 18, 19, and 28, 1945; *Albuquerque Journal*, April 19, 1945; *New York Times*, April 19, 1945; Richard Melzer, *Ernie Pyle in the American Southwest* (Santa Fe: Sunstone Press, 1996): 11, 18, 77, 114, 120.

75. Richard Melzer, " Casualties of Caution and Fear: Life in Santa Fe's Japanese Internment Camp, 1942-1946" in DeMark, *Essays in Twentieth Century New Mexico History*, 213-40.

76. Certificate of Death, New Mexico State Department of Public Health, Hidalgo County, July 27, 1942; John J. Culley, "Trouble at the Lordsburg Internment Camp," *New Mexico Historical Review*, vol. 60 (July 1985): 225-48. Sergeant Beckham was acquitted in a court-martial held at Fort Bliss on September 10, 1942.

77. Certificate of Death, New Mexico State Department of Public Health, Hidalgo County, July 27, 1942; Culley, "Trouble at the Lordsburg Internment Camp," 225-48.

78. Melzer, " Casualties," 237n.

79. Ibid.; Sherman, *Santa Fe*, 166; *Santa Fe New Mexican*, September 26, 1999.

80. Jake W. Spidle, Jr., "Axis Invasion of the American West: POWs in New Mexico, 1942-46," *New Mexico Historical Review*, vol. 49 (April 1974): 93-122; Susan Badger Doyle, "German and Italian Prisoners of War in Albuquerque, 1943-46," *New Mexico Historical*

Review, vol. 66 (July 1991): 327-40; Prisoners of War in New Mexico Agriculture Oral History Project and Exhibit, New Mexico Farm and Ranch Heritage Museum, Las Cruces, New Mexico; www.archives.nmsu.edu/rghc/index/pow/categories.Walter Schmid, a POW in Las Cruces, mentioned two escape attempts from his camp, but no killings. Walter Schmid, *A German POW in New Mexico* (Albuquerque: University of New Mexico Press, 2005): 66-7, 134, 136.

81. Certificate of Death, New Mexico State Department of Public Health, Eddy County, January 13, 1943; *Artesia Advocate*, January 14, 21, and 28, 1943; *Roswell Daily Record*, January 14, 22, and 31, 1943; *Carlsbad Current Argus*, January 14 and 20, 1943; Cameron Saffell (New Mexico Farm and Ranch Heritage Museum, Las Cruces, New Mexico) to the author, March 23, 2004. Jaeger's death certificate incorrectly spelled his surname Jager. In addition to Jaeger and Schlegel, there are twenty-four German and Austrian POWs and fourteen Italian POWs buried at the Fort Bliss National Cemetery. Spidle, "Axis Invasion," 106-7; Holt, *Military Cemeteries*, 118. For a discussion of German POW burials in the United States, see Arnold Krammer, *Nazi Prisoners of War in America* (Lanham, Maryland: Scarborough House, 1996): 154-57.

82. Memo to the Commanding General, 8th Service Command, January 25, 1943; "383.6 Roswell Int Camp A/E"; Camp Roswell, NM (Projects File—POW Camps and Forts); General Correspondence, 1941-1962; General Records, Records of the Administrative Division; Records of the Office of the Provost Marshal General, Record Group 389, National Archives, College Park, Maryland; accessed in the New Mexico Farm and Ranch Heritage Museum archives, Las Cruces, New Mexico.

83. *Roswell Daily Record*, January 24, 1943

84. Quoted in the *Roswell Daily Record*, February 4, 1943.

85. *Las Cruces Sun-News*, February 8, 1945; Cameron Saffell (New Mexico Farm and Ranch Heritage Museum, Las Cruces, New Mexico) to the author, March 23, 2004; Holt, *American Military Cemeteries*, 118. German POWs buried at the Fort Bliss National Cemetery are honored with a ceremony on the German Day of National Mourning (the second Sunday of November) conducted by soldiers from the German Air Force Command. A photoof a similar ceremony at the German War Memorial Cemetery at Fort McClellan, Alabama, is including in Krammer, *Nazi Prisoners*, 264-65.

86. *Roswell Morning Dispatch*, May 24, 1941; James J. McBride (*SS Columbus* historian) to the author, January 5, 2004. Also see James J. McBride, *Interned: Internment of the SS Columbus Crew at Fort Stanton, New Mexico, 1941-45* (Santa Fe: n.p., 2003): 87, 99; William E. Anderson, Jr., "Guests for the Duration: World War II and the Crew of the *SS Columbus*" (Unpublished Masters thesis, Eastern New Mexico University, 1993); Ann Buffington, "The *SS Columbus* Incident," *Southern New Mexico Historical Review*, vol. 3 (January 1996): 64.

87. Certificate of Death, New Mexico State Department of Public Health, Lincoln County, March 18, 1944.

88. Certificate of Death, New Mexico State Department of Public Health, Lincoln County, February 20, 1942.

89. Certificate of Death, New Mexico State Department of Public Health, Lincoln County, February 11, 1942.

90. Certificate of Death, New Mexico State Department of Public Health, Lincoln County, May 13, 1944.

91. Photos of Steffens and Zeitsch's graves with their original gravestones are included in McBride, *Interned*, 99.

92. A list of these 184 men can be found on www.archives.gov/research_topics/korean_war_casualty_lists/nm. Ten of the 184 New Mexicans killed in the Korean War were alumni of the New Mexico Military Institute. Gibbs and Jackman, *New Mexico Military Institute*, 416-17. On Hiroshi Miyamura's brave action in the Korean War see Allen Mikaelian, *Medal of Honor: Profiles of America's Military Heroes from the Civil War to the Present* (New York: Hyperion, 2002):193-218. On Raymond G. Murphy's bravery, see Angie S. Lopez, *Blessed Are the Soldiers: Oral Histories of This Century's American War Veterans* (Albuquerque: Sandia Publishing Company, 1990): 270-72. A list of the forty-six MIA's can be found on http://lestyouforget.tripod.com/newmexicok.htm.

93. A list of the 399 New Mexicans who died in Vietnam can be found on www.archives.gov/research_topics/vietnam_war_casualty_lists/nm_a. Twenty-nine of the 399 New Mexicans killed in the Vietnam War were alumni of the New Mexico Military Institute. Gibbs and Jackman, *New Mexico Military Institute*, 417-19. On Glenna Goodacre's Vietnam Women's Memorial see www.vietnamwomensmemorial.org.

94. Lang, Collins, and White, *Medal of Honor*, II:851.

95. Ibid., II:682-83; *Valencia County News-Bulletin*, March 23, 1967.

96. Quoted in the *Albuquerque Tribune*, February 19, 1966. Also see the *Albuquerque Journal*, February 19, 1966; *Valencia County News-Bulletin*, February 22 and 24, March 1 and 3, 1966, and March 23, April 3, 6, 10, 1967; Lopez, *Blessed Are the Soldiers*, 304-08.

97. *Valencia County News-Bulletin*, March 1, 1966

98. *Valencia County News-Bulletin*, April 6 and 10, 1967; Marc Simmons, "These Men Prove Heroism Exists," *Santa Fe New Mexican*, February 9, 2002.

99. *Honolulu Star-Bulletin*, April 1, 2003; Lang, Collins, and White, *Medal of Honor*, II:699.

100. Ibid., II:721.

101. *Albuquerque Journal*, November 1, 2002; Lopez, *Blessed Are the Soldiers*, 298-303; Lang, Collins, and White, *Medal of Honor*, II:737-38.

102. Ibid., II:756-57.

103. *Albuquerque Journal*, July 9, 2005

104. Darrel D. Whitcomb, *The Rescue of BAT 21* (Annapolis, Maryland: Naval Institute Press, 1998): 36.

105. Air America's overt and covert operations in Southeast Asia were described in the *New York Times*, April 5, 1970.

106. www.pow-miafamilies.org/states/newmexico

107. *Albuquerque Journal*, December 26, 2005, and May 29, 2006

108. *Albuquerque Journal*, March 24 and 25 and April 2, 2003; *Albuquerque Tribune*, March 25, 2003; *Valencia County News-Bulletin*, March 26, April 2 and 5, 2003, and February

26, 2005; *University of New Mexico Daily Lobo*, March 27, 2003; *USA Today*, April 11, 2003; interviews with Richard and Cindy Long (parents), August 10, 2004, and June 2, 2005.

109. Newspaper clipping, Long Family Album, Goju Ryu Karate School, Belen, New Mexico.

110. Interview with Richard and Cindy Long (parents), June 2, 2005.

14
UNUSUAL GRAVES

1. Brown, *Soul in the Stone*, 123.

2. Ibid., 138-39, 168.

3. Interview with Karen Kilgore (daughter), April 4, 2005.

4. Family members of Pedro Baptista (or Bautista) Pino (circa 1752-April 19, 1829) believe that his body rests in the oratory seen in the background of this photograph. Pino represented New Mexico in the Cadíz Cortes of 1812. His fifty-one page report to the Cortes, *Exposición sucinta y sencilla de la Provincia del Nuevo México* (1812), is perhaps the best description of the region and its problems in the early nineteenth century. When nothing resulted from don Pedro's journey and detailed report, New Mexicans declared, *"Don Pedro Pino fue, don Pedro Pino vino."* ("Don Pedro Pino went, don Pedro Pino came back.") Kathryn M. Córdova, "Faith, Tradition Alive in Galisteo," *La Herencia*, vol. 47 (Fall 2005): 25; Adrian Bustamante and Marc Simmons's preface to Don Pedro Baptista Pino, *The Exposition on the Province of New Mexico, 1812* (Albuquerque: University of New Mexico Press, 1995): xii-xiii; John L. Kessell, *Spain in the Southwest* (Norman: University of Oklahoma Press, 2002): 358-61.

5. Photos of three such gravestones are included in Hordes, *To the End of the Earth*, 255. Other photos are in Cary Herz, "Culture and Memory: A Sephardic Photo Journey," *La Herencia*, vol. 40 (Winter 2003): 24.

6. Hordes, *To the End of the Earth*, 251-52; Brown, *Soul in the Stone*, 228.

7. Richard Melzer, "A Death in Dawson: The Demise of a Southwestern Company Town," *New Mexico Historical Review*, vol. 55 (October 1980): 309-30; Toby Smith, *Coal Town: The Life and Times of Dawson, New Mexico* (Santa Fe: Ancient City Press, 1993): 57-74; Albuquerque *Journal*, September 11, 1988. A list of the miners who died in the disasters of 1913 and 1923 can be found on ttp.rootsweb.com/pub/usgenweb/nm/colfax/cemeteries/dawson.

8. C.L. Sonnichsen, ed., *Morris B. Parker's White Oaks: Life in a New Mexico Gold Camp, 1880-1900* (Tucson: University of Arizona Press, 1971): 96-9.

9. Bryan, *True Tales*, 49-50; Quentin, *Eternal New Mexicans*, 132-33; Browning, *Violence Was No Stranger*, 57; Julyan, *Place Names*, 95. Michael Cooney also died as a miner in the wilderness. At the age of 76 he went searching for gold, disappeared, and was discovered dead, having perished from exposure to winter weather in mid November 1914. Unlike his brother, who was buried in a remote locale, Michael was buried in his hometown cemetery in Socorro, New Mexico. Bryan, *True Tales*, 50-1.

10. *Santa Fe New Mexican*, November 11, 1990

11. Holt, *Military Cemeteries*, 338; Woolley et. al., *Final Destinations*, 116-17; historical literature distributed at the National Cemetery, Santa Fe, New Mexico; *Carlsbad Current-Argus*, March 13, 1949. Soldier's Farewell, a station on the Butterfield Trail, was said to be named for a broken hearted private who committed suicide there in the 1850s. Julyan, *Place Names*, 338.

12. Interview with Robert R. White (New Mexico historian), December 14, 2003.

13. According to one count, there are as many as eight thousand traditional religious and secular gravestone symbols. For a listing of over 250 of these icons, see Carmack, *Cemetery Research*, 128-29, 215-23. For the story of an engraver who specialized in unique gravestone icons, creating as many as 150 in a single year, see the *Santa Fe New Mexican*, February 11, 1979.

14. *Albuquerque Journal*, October 26, 1994

15. Daniel Davis (music historian) to the author, February 26, 2004.

16. Interview with Robert Lenberg, October 7, 2004.

17. See Louis S. Schafer, *Best of Gravestone Humor* (New York: Sterling Publishing Company, 1990).

18. *Albuquerque Journal's Mature Life*, March 2003

19. Ferroll Clark Hanlon, *Life on the Range* (Grand Junction, Colorado: C&M Enterprises, 1995): 181.

20. Interview with Craig Newbill (Executive Director, New Mexico Endowment for the Humanities), August 23, 2002. When the cowboy E.L. "Slim" Pond lost his dog "Boy" he declared that it was "the saddest thing that ever happened to me," quite a statement since Pond had lost his right arm in a shooting accident when he was only sixteen. Burying Boy on a high hill on the High Lonesome Ranch in southern New Mexico, Slim placed a cross over the gravesite with the epitaph, "Best Cowboy in the States of New Mexico and Texas." E.L. Pond, *One-Armed Cowboy: The Amazing Life of E.L. "Slim" Pond* (Frisco, Texas: Bob Kinsbery, 2004): 31-35, 232-33.

21. Albuquerque Monument Company promotional literature

22. *Albuquerque Journal*, November 14, 16, and 21, 1929

23. Certificate of Death, New Mexico State Department of Public Health, San Miguel County, November 11, 1929. The movement to place a bronze statue to honor Fido was described in an editorial in the *Alamogordo News*, November 28, 1929. In another pet-related story, vandals stole the headstone of Tom, the part-St. Bernard owned by Raton's first photographer, W.A. White. The town's children had loved Tom so much that school was dismissed so they could carry the pet's coffin to the foot of Goat Hill for burial when he died in March 1885. White erected a tombstone with Tom's image and the words, "in memory of his faithful canine friend." Only a photo of the pilfered stone remains. F. Stanley, *Raton Chronicle* (Denver, World Press, 1948): 71, with a photo of the stone on page 72. For the story of Shot, a dog in England who kept vigil at his deceased master's grave each day until nightfall, see the *Belen News*, March 17, 1932.

24. *Albuquerque Tribune*, January 31, 1953; Melzer, *Pyle*, 60 and 157n.

25. *Santa Fe New Mexican*, August 29, 1972

26. Wooley et. al., *Final Destinations*, 129-30.

27. Quoted in the *Alamogordo News*, March 29, 1983

28. Leslie Bergloff, "The Capitan Gap Fire and the Making of Smokey Bear," *Southern New Mexico Historical Review*, vol. 8 (January 2001): 32-40; Julyan, *Place Names*, 337. Ray Bell, the game officer who cared for Smokey Bear for two months after his rescue and flew the cub to Santa Fe for additional medical attention, died at his home in Truth of Consequences, New Mexico, in December 2000. Bell was buried at the National Cemetery in Santa Fe. *Albuquerque Journal*, December 23, 2000. The young Smokey was also cared for by Elliott Speer Barker, New Mexico's first Game Warden. See Barker's entry in Chapter 7, No. 114. The Smokey Bear balloon crashed at the Albuquerque International Balloon Fiesta on October 10, 2004. A new version of the balloon, costing $94,000, flew in the 2005 fiesta. *Albuquerque Journal*, October 2, 2005

29. *Albuquerque Journal*, July 1, 2000

APPENDIX C:
FAMOUS NEW MEXICANS WHO HAVE BEEN CREMATED

1. Nasario García, *Tiempos Lejanos: Poetic Images from the Past* (Albuquerque: University of New Mexico Press, 2004): 20. Used with permission of the University of New Mexico Press.

APPENDIX D:
FAMOUS NEW MEXICANS WHO ORIGINALLY CAME TO NEW MEXICO TO RECOVER THEIR HEALTH OR TO ACCOMPANY SOMEONE ELSE WHO WAS ILL

1. Memoirs, Kenneth M. Chapman Papers, School of American Research, Santa Fe, New Mexico.

2. Karen D. Shane, "New Mexico: Salubrious El Dorado," *New Mexico Historical Review*, vol. 56 (October 1981): 387-99. Other illnesses have included gout, arthritis, mental exhaustion, paralysis, liver disorder, diabetes, female "disorders", asthma, the aftereffects of being gassed in World War I, and even acne.

3. Spidle, *Doctors of Medicine in New Mexico*, 97-99; Jake W. Spidle, Jr., "'An Army of Tubercular Invalids': New Mexico and the Birth of a Tuberculosis Industry," *New Mexico Historical Review*, vol. 61 (July 1986): 189-91; Wilson, *Myth of Santa Fe*, 352n.

4. The two who died of TB were Catherine Antrim and D.H. Lawrence, both, coincidentally, at age 45. For a list and brief descriptions of TB healthseekers who regained their health and made major contributions in Albuquerque history, see García and McCord, *Albuquerque*, 141-55.

Suggested Readings

Adams, Randy. *Eternal Prairie: Exploring Rural Cemeteries of the West.* Calgary: Fifth House Publishers, 1999.

Ariès, Philippe. *The Hour of Our Death.* Translated by Helen Weaver. New York: Oxford University Press, 1991.

Brooks, Patricia. *Where the Bodies Are: Final Visits to the Rich, Famous, and Interesting.* Guilford, Connecticut: Globe Pequot Press, 2002.

Brown, John Gary. *Soul in the Stone: Cemetery Art from America's Heartland.* Lawrence: University Press of Kansas, 1994.

Browning, James A. *Violence Was No Stranger: A Guide to the Grave Sites of Famous Westerners.* Stillwater, Oklahoma: Barbed Wire Press, 1993.

Carmack, Sharon Debartolo. *Your Guide to Cemetery Research.* Cincinnati: Betterway Publications, 2002.

Condie, Carol J. *The Cemeteries of Albuquerque, Bernalillo County, and Parts of Sandoval and Valencia Counties.* Albuquerque: City of Albuquerque, 1999.

Del Re, Gerard and Patricia. *History's Last Stand: The Last Gasps, Fatal Falls, and Final Gambles of Heroes, Despots, and Civilizations.* New York: Dorset Press, 1993.

Denrimo, Dorothy. *Camposantos: A Photographic Essay.* Fort Worth: Amon Carter Museum of Western Art, 1966.

Dickey, Roland. *New Mexico Village Arts.* Albuquerque: University of New Mexico Press, 1949.

Enss, Chris. *Tales Behind the Tombstones: The Deaths and Burials of the Old West's Most Nefarious Outlaws, Notorious Women and Celebrated Lawmen.* Helena, Montana: TwoDot Press, 2007.

Farrell, James J. *Inventing the American Way of Death.* Philadelphia: Temple University Press, 1980.

Felsen, Gregg. *Tombstones: Seventy-Five Famous People and Their Final Resting Places.* Berkeley: Ten Speed Press, 1996.

Holt, Dean W. *American Military Cemeteries: A Comprehensive Illustrated Guide to the Hallowed Grounds of the United States, Including Cemeteries Overseas.* Jefferson, North Carolina: McFarland and Company, 1992.

Hume, Janice. *Obituaries in American Culture*. Jackson: University of Mississippi Press, 2000.

Jackson, Kenneth T. and Camilo José Vergara. *Silent Cities: The Evolution of the American Cemetery*. New York: Princeton Architectural Press, 1989.

Johnson, Lyman, editor. *Death, Dismemberment, and Memory: Body Politics in Latin America*. Albuquerque: University of New Mexico Press, 2004.

Jones, Mary-Ellen. *Photographing Tombstones: Equipment and Techniques*. Technical Leaflet 92. Nashville: American Association for State and Local History, 1977.

Meyer, Richard E., editor. *Ethnicity and the American Cemetery*. Bowling Green, Ohio: Bowling Green University Popular Press, 1993.

Mitchell, Douglas R. and Judy L. Brunson-Hadley, editors. *Ancient Burial Practices in the American Southwest*. Albuquerque: University of New Mexico Press, 2004.

Mollan, Mark C. "Honoring Our War Dead." *Prologue*, vol. 35 (Spring 2003): 56-65.

Murphy, Edwin. *After the Funeral: The Posthumous Adventures of Famous Corpses*. Secaucus, New Jersey: Carol Publishing Group. 1995.

Nava, Margaret. *Remembering: A Guide to New Mexico Cemeteries, Monuments, and Memorials*. Santa Fe: Sunstone Press, 2006.

Quentin. *Eternal New Mexicans: A Guide to the Final Resting Places of 350 Noteworthy Persons of the Land of Enchantment*. Oakland: n.p., 1994.

Roach, Mary. *Stiff: The Curious Lives of Human Cadavers*. New York: W.W. Norton, 2003.

Robinson, Ray. *Famous Last Words, Fond Farewells, Deathbed Diatribes, and Exclamations Upon Expiration*. New York: Workman, 2003.

Sanborn, Laura Sue. "*Camposantos*: Sacred Places of the Southwest." *Markers*, vol. 6 (1989): 159-80.

Schafer, Louis S. *Best of Gravestone Humor*. New York: Sterling Publishing Company, 1990.

Siegel, Marvin, editor. *The Last Word: The New York Times Book of Obituaries and Farewells*. New York: William Morrow, 1997.

Skansie, Juli Ellen. *Death Is For All: Death and Death-Related Beliefs of Rural Spanish-Americans*. New York: AMS Press, 1985.

Sloane, David Charles. *The Last Great Necessity: Cemeteries in American History*. Baltimore: Johns Hopkins University Press, 1991.

Spencer, Thomas E. *Where They're Buried: A Directory Containing More than 29,000 Names of Notable Persons Buried in American Cemeteries*. Baltimore: Clearfield Company, 1999.

Stark, Peter. *Last Breath: Cautionary Tales From the Limits of Human Endurance*. New York: Ballantine Books, 2001.

Warren, Nancy Hunter. "New Mexico Village *Camposantos*." *Markers*, vol. 4 (1987): 115-29.

Will de Chaparro, Martina. *Death and Dying in New Mexico.* Albuquerque: University of New Mexico Press, 2007.

Wooley, Bryan *et. al. Final Destinations: A Travel Guide for Remarkable Cemeteries.* Denton: University of North Texas Press, 2000.

Yarrow, H.C. and V. Lamonte Smith. *North American Indians Burial Customs.* Ogden, Utah: Eagles' View Publishing, 1988.

Useful Web-Sites:
Association for Gravesite Studies: *www.grastonestudies.org*
Cemetery Transcriptions: www.interment.net
Find-A-Grave: www.findagrave.com
New Mexico Cemetery and Graveyard Listings: New Mexico Tombstones: freepages.genealogy.rootsweb.com/~nmtombstones/
Old West Gravesites: www.fpcc.not/~sgrimm/oldwest
Political Graveyard: *www.politicalgraveyard.com*
www.dagonbytes.com/graveyards/listings/statepage/newmexico

INDEX

Abbey, Edward P., 63, 140
Abbott, Bob, 34
Abeita, Pablo, 142, 232
Able, Joseph G.H., 275, 355
Abruzzo, Benjamin L. "Ben", 116, 146, 333, 348
Abruzzo, Patty, 146
Adams, Ansel E., 19, 53, 52, 93, 372, 379n, 392n
Adams, Kenneth M., 32, 372
Adlesperger, Christopher S., 326
Agnew, Spiro T., 324
Alarid, "Chino", 172
Alday, Richard, 275, 355
Aldrich, Dorothy Cave, 241
Alencaster, Joaquin Real, 262
Aleshire, William A., 279
Alexander, Ruth B.L., 64, 88, 168, 355, 396n
Alexander the Great, 382n
Alfange, Dean, 146
Allison, Robert Clay, 18, 157-58, 181, 274, 369
Alvarez, Francisco, Jr., 303, 350
Alvarez, Manuel, 97, 103
Amos, James, 298
Anderson, Clinton P., 77, 114, 116, 153, 225, 347, 376
Anderson, Max L. "Maxie", 116, 146, 339, 348
Andrews, William H., 116, 211, 367
Angel, Francisco "Frank", Jr., 122, 313, 373
Angel, Frank Warner, 192, 423n
Angel, Juan, 168
Angel, Paula, 168, 416n
Anthony, Susan B., 39
Antrim, Catherine, 19, 181-82, 358, 376, 382n, 420n, 421n, 457n
Antrim, Joseph, 182, 420n
Antrim, William H.H. "Bill", 181
Anza, Juan Bautista de, 196, 263
Apache Kid, 158
Applegate, Alta, 81
Applegate, Frank G., 36, 55, 61, 64, 81, 355
Aragón, José Rafael, 47
Archuleta, Tamara Long, 134, 326, 327, 337, 349
Armijo, Manuel, 23, 100, 103, 196-97, 198, 263, 264, 424n
Armstrong, Neil, 257
Arnaz, Desi, 61
Arny, William F.M., 200, 355
Arquette, Kaitlyn C., 175-76, 349
Arquette, Lois, 175, 176
Arthur, Chester A., 233
Asplund, Julia B., 126-27, 231, 355
Ashworth, Frederick L., 314, 355
Atwood, J.D., 223
Aubry, Francis X., 103, 146-47

Augustini, Giovanni María, 175, 245, 354
Austin, Aaron, 326
Austin, Mary H., 64, 81, 88, 93, 142, 372
Axtell, Samuel B., 181, 192, 193, 202, 236, 366

Baca, Elfego, 18, 153, 349, 413n
Baca, Herman, 222, 223
Baca, Jesus, 222
Baca, José A., 214
Baca, Juanita, 153
Bach, Johann Sebastian, 339
Baker, John W., 128, 148, 348
Bakos, Jozef G., 34, 36, 128, 357
Ball, Lucille, 61
Ballard, Charles L., 153, 298, 368
Bandelier, Adolph F., 18, 19, 81-82, 373
Bandelier, Fanny R., 82
Banister, Ivan A., 332
Barber, George B., 186
Barbera, Joseph, 57
Barceló, María Gertrudes "Doña Tules", 116, 168-69
Barela, Patrocinio, 47, 49, 349, 391n
Barela, Saturnino, 173
Barker, Elliott S., 65, 106, 135, 355, 376, 456n
Barker, Elsa M., 65
Barker, Ethel, 135
Barker, Roy, 135
Barker, Squire Omar, 64-65, 135, 355, 376
Barraza, Jesús Salas, 304
Barrett, Mathias "Brother Mathias", 240, 333
Baumann, Ann, 37
Baumann, Gustave, 36-37, 88, 145, 372
Baxter, George W., 334
Bayliss, J.H., 267
Baylor, John Robert, 273, 278, 367
Beacham, Howard, 18, 112, 154, 236, 347
Beardsley, Isaac, 269
Beaubien, Charles, 107
Beckham, John A., 318, 319, 452n
Becknell, William, 97
Beethoven, Ludwig van, 382n
Begay, Charley T., 308
Begay, Harrison, 127
Begay, Roy L., 308
Begay, Samuel H., 308
Bell, James W., 175, 183, 192-93, 359
Bell, Ray, 456n
Benally, John A., 308
Benedict, Kirby, 114, 168, 234
Benrino, Thomas, 33

Bent, Charles, 18, 97, 98, 103, 198, 266, 355
Bent, George, 97-98, 198, 365
Bent, John, 97, 98, 198
Bent, Robert, 97, 98, 198
Bent, William W., 97, 98, 198, 363
Bentley, Reuben P., 275, 355
Berg, Margaret, 271, 277
Berninghaus, Oscar E., 29, 30, 359
Betters, James, 279, 351
Beyer, Charles D., 279
Bhajan, Yogi, 77, 249, 374
Bingham, Harrieta, 248
Bingham, Lucy Ann, 248
Bitsie, Wilsie H., 308
Blaine, James, 104
Blumenschein, Ernest, 30, 31, 32, 36, 372
Boas, Franz, 87
Boggs, Tom, 271, 277
Bohr, Niels H.D., 251, 370
Bolack, Alice, 430n
Bolack, Thomas F., 106, 116, 219, 374
Bolack, Tommy, 219
Bolsinger, Bob, 340
Bonaparte, Napoleon, 382n
Bond, Frank, 103, 347
Bonneau, Kay, 340
Bonney, William H. "Billy the Kid", 17, 18, 19, 154, 156, 165, 181, 182, 187, 188, 189, 192, 193, 351, 420n, 421n, 422n
Bonnyman, Alexander, Jr., 310, 355
Booker, William, 275, 356
Bourgade, Pierre, 238-39
Bowdre, Charles, 181, 184, 185, 421n
Bowman, Alonzo, 280-81, 351
Bowman, Everett, 106, 148, 157, 361
Boyd, E., 15, 16, 44, 82, 373, 398n
Boyer, Francis M. "Frank", 128, 142, 359
Boyne, Thomas, 272, 280, 281, 370
Bradbury, Norris, 251, 254
Braden, John, 131-32, 347
Bradford, Richard, 69
Brady, Nadine, 422
Brady, William, 182-83, 188, 189-90
Bratling, Frank, 281, 364, 368, 444n
Bratton, Sam G., 222, 236, 347
Braun, Albert, 241, 306, 313
Brazel, Jesse W., 158
Brazel, Wayne, 154
Brazel, William W. "Mack", 135, 359, 408n
Brett, Dorothy E., 40-41, 73, 74, 93, 94, 372
Brewer, Richard M. "Dick", 181, 186, 188, 192, 353
Brito, Frank C., 157, 296, 303, 353
Brito, Martin, 330
Brown, Cosey S., 308
Brown, Henry, 181
Brown, John, Jr., 308
Brown, Joseph, 98
Brown, Milton, 258-59
Bryan, William Jennings, 210
Buchanan, William, 148
Bullard, John M., 276, 358
Bunche, Ralph J., 136, 366, 376, 409n
Bunting, Bainbridge, 82-83, 128
Burg, John B., 341
Burnett, George R., 281-82, 369
Burnett, Jim, 166

Burns, Robert, 212, 213
Burroughs, John, 106, 114, 218-19, 354
Burrowes, Edward T., 275, 356
Bursum, Holm O., Sr., 212, 221, 358, 376
Bush, George H.W., 255
Butler, Nicholas Murray, 223
Butler, Thomas F., 303
Bynner, Harold Witter, 39, 65-66, 71, 93, 333, 372, 376, 396n
Byrd, Charles A., 340
Byrne, Edwin V., 239-40
Byrne, Verne, 334

C de Baca, Ezequiel, 114, 212-13, 215, 353
C de Baca, Fabiola, 83, 128, 354
Cabeza de Vaca, Álvar Nuñez, 261
Cabot, Bruce, 55, 349
Calhoun, James S., 199, 266, 365
Calles, Plutarco Elías, 449n
Calvin, Ross R., 77, 247, 347, 377
Cambridge, Lyle, 326
Campbell, Charles, 167
Campbell, John M., 157, 219-20, 313, 374
Campbell, Michael, 219
Canby, Edward R.S., 266-67, 278, 364
Cárdenas, Lázaro, 449n
Cargo, David, 271
Carleton, James H., 266, 267-68, 278, 365, 441n
Carmack, Sharon D., 26
Carman, Rob, 172
Carmichael, Mack Rubert, 156, 157, 170-71, 368
Carpenter, Harriet S., 86
Carr, Loraine, 386n
Carranza, Venustiano, 449n
Carrillo, Sarah, 332
Carson, Christopher H. "Kit", 18, 19, 27, 93, 191, 263, 271, 272, 276-77, 358, 377, 421n
Carson, Josefa, 277
Cassidy, Gerald, 39, 66, 339, 355, 376
Cassidy, Perlina "Ina", 39, 66, 88, 145, 355, 372
Castillo, Juan, 303, 350
Cather, Willa S., 66-67, 110, 237, 242, 366, 395n
Catron, Thomas B., 109, 191, 204, 211, 212, 222-23 430n
Cervántez, Pedro "Pete", 48-49, 368
Chacon, Ed, 417n
Chacón, Juan R. "Johnny", 136, 350, 409n
Chacon, Philip "Phil", 134, 157, 171, 348
Chacon, Rafael, 268, 278, 363
Chacon, Ted, 171
Chacón, Virginia, 136
Chapelle, Placid L., 238
Chapman, Kenneth M., 44, 55, 83, 128, 373, 375, 376
Chato, Alfred, 289
Chaves, Amado, 119, 268, 355, 441n
Chaves, J. Francisco, 93, 119, 175, 208, 272, 278, 356
Chaves, Manuel Antonio, 134, 268, 278
Chávez, Angélico, 15, 44, 50, 77, 82, 89, 243, 295, 313, 322, 358, 400
Chávez, Antonio José, 21, 98, 175
Chavez, Dionisio "Dennis", 222, 223-24, 293, 337, 348
Chávez, Francisco "Frank", 171-72, 358
Chávez, José Felipe, 98-99, 106, 333, 349
Chávez, Josefa, 99
Chávez, Manuela, 99
Chavez, Tibo J., Sr., 88, 93, 230, 235, 337, 349
Chávez de Chacón, Soledad, 214, 348
Chee, John, 308

Chick, Jack, 335
Chick, Milo R., 336
Childs, Marquis W., 174
Chino, Wendell, 142, 232-33
Chis-chilling-begay, 175
Chisum, John S., 104, 193
Chivington, John M., 248, 268-69, 279, 362
Christensen, Jeremy E., 326
Christian, William T. "Black Jack", 158-59, 414n
Christy, E.B., 125
Church, Fermor Spencer, 67
Church, Margaret "Peggy" Pond, 37, 67-68, 119, 315, 372
Clanton, Mary Elsie, 287
Clark, Ann Nolan, 68, 88, 128
Clark, Iain, 132-33
Clark, Jon, 132-33
Clark, Laurel Blair S., 132-33, 260
Clark, Meriwether Lewis, 265
Clark, Terry D., 177, 178
Clary, Edward A., 157, 298, 356
Cleaveland, Agnes Morley, 20, 68-69, 106, 180, 246, 372
Cleaveland, Norman, 180
Clemens, Olivia S., 176
Clements, Bill, 274
Cleveland, Benjamin, 308
Clever, Charles P., 114, 116, 208, 356
Cochise, 278, 289-90
Cockerell, T.D.A., 179
Coe, Frank, 106, 116, 188, 191
Coe, George W., 181, 188
Coe, Louise H., 88, 128, 230, 374
Collier, John, 93, 136-37, 354
Colter, Mary E. J., 50, 365
Columbus, Christopher, 382n
Connell, Albert J., 120, 348
Connelly, Henry, 103, 196, 200-1, 260, 358
Conover, G.L., 334
Conrad, Joseph, 34
Conyea, Gwen Parks, 301
Coogler, Ovida "Cricket", 176-77, 352, 419n
Cooke, Philip St. George, 263, 264, 272, 365
Cooney, James C., 134, 279, 335
Cooney, Michael, 335, 455n
Cordova, Helen Q., 44
Cordova, Robert Harold, 329
Corfield, Stan L., 325
Coronado, Francisco Vázquez de, 262-63
Cotton, J.S.L., 274-75, 356
Couse, E. Irving, 29, 30-31, 333, 359, 386n
Cox, Mrs., 134
Cox, Theler, 134
Cravens, Melanie M., 172-73, 349
Cravens, Paul, 172-73
Crawford, Eugene R., 308
Crawford, John W. "Captain Jack", 55, 77, 279, 366
Cree, James E., 20, 382n
Creighton, Lucy, 134
Crenshaw, Frank D., 337
Crenshaw, Frank H., 337
Crenshaw, Mattie M., 337
Critcher, Catharine Carter, 29, 32-33, 128, 369
Crittenden, Tom, 159
Crosby, John O., 56, 356, 376
Crosby, Robert A. "Wild Horse", 149, 313, 354
Cunningham, Jason, 326

Curley, David, 308
Curry, George, 93, 205-6, 226, 298, 356
Curtis, Edward S., 53, 362
Curtis, Sidney H., 182
Cusey, James W., 169
Cusey, Mildred C. "Madame Millie", 169, 351
Custer, George Armstrong, 270
Cutting, Bronson M., 114, 222-23, 306, 366, 376, 430n, 431n
Cutting, Olivia Peyton, 222
Cutting, William Bayard, 222

Daeger, Albert T., 239
Da Fiesole, Angélico, 400n
Damon, Lowell S., 308
Daniels, Marguerite A., 341
Dasburg, Andrew, 41, 93, 372
Davey, Isabel Holt, 37
Davey, Randall V., 36, 37, 388n
Davidson, W.A., 303
Davis, Harry, 303
Davis, James P., 240
Davis, John, 334
Davis, Ricardo G., 325
Davis, William W.H., 199-200, 367
Dawson, Joseph G. III, 265
Day, Matthias W., 280, 282, 283, 362
Dean, Edwin, 300
Dean, James T., 116, 300, 350
Dean, Richard, 448n
de la Llana, Gerónimo, 240, 381n
Dempsey, John J., 217, 358
Dennison, George H., 308
Denny, John, 280, 282, 283, 370
Denver, John, 56, 79, 372
Desmarais, M.F., 162
Díaz, Porfirio, 449n
Dillinger, John, 156
Dillon, Richard C., 215, 347
Dixon, James, 308, 309, 351
Dobbs, Mark A., 303
Dodge, Henry Chee, 233, 260, 352, 361
Dodge, Jerome C., 309
Dolan, James J., 190, 272
Domenici, Pete V., 232
Doniphan, Alexander W., 265, 272, 365
Donnelly, Thomas C., 122, 126, 373
Donoho, Mary W.D., 109, 368
Donoho, William, 109
Dorman, H.H., 222
Dorsey, Stephen W., 104, 231, 272, 363
Drexel, Mary Katharine, 126, 243
Dudley, Nathan A.M., 193, 272, 279, 369
Dunn, Francis M., 128
Dunn, John H. "Long John", 114-15, 359
Dunne, Brian B., 70-71, 222, 223, 358
Dunton, William Herbert "Buck", 29, 31, 150, 359
Durán y Chaves, Fernando, 195
Durio, R.A., 177
Dwyer, Joseph, 101

Ebsen, Buddy, 410n
Echeverria, Luis, 304
Eddy, Charles B., 107, 366
Edwards, Barbara, 57
Edwards, Ralph L., 56-57, 362

Ehrlichman, John Daniel, 44, 77, 159, 231, 373
Eiseler, Richard, 20
Elkins, Stephen B., 208, 272, 370
Ellis, Florence Hawley, 83, 128, 373
Ellis, Fremont F., 34-35, 358
Elwood, Edwin L., 282-83, 356
Eminger, Michael J.L., 338
Emmet, Robert T., 282, 283, 366
Emmons, Frank, 190
Epps, Margaret, 300
Errett, H.H., 164
Espinosa, Antonio Gilberto, 89-90, 348, 373
Espinosa, Marcelo, 89
Estéban, 261
Evans, John, 93, 94
Evans, Tom, 115

Fall, Albert B., 106, 113, 114, 212, 220-21, 236, 298, 368
Fanning, Mart, 319-20
Faulkner, William, 63, 394n
Fechin, Nicolai, 93
Felipe IV, 195
Felsenthal, Louis, 269, 362
Ferdinand, 92
Fergusson, Erna M., 70-71, 88, 100, 110, 210, 372
Fergusson, Harvey, 70-71, 100, 210, 372
Fergusson, Harvey Butler, 70, 100, 210, 212, 226, 374, 428n
Fermer, Ann, 37
Fermi, Enrico, 251-52, 316, 364
Fernandez, Antonio M., 227, 358
Fernández, Daniel, 322-23, 356
Fernandez, Troy, 383n
Feynman, Richard P., 128, 252, 362
Fitzpatrick, George M., 77, 112, 355
Flanagan, L., 20
Flynn, Jim, 199
Foley, Everett C., 275, 356
Ford, Gerald, 324
Ford, Henry, 254
Ford, P.E., 320
Ford, Robert Newton "Bob", 159-60, 365
Foreman, Larry R., 340
Fornoff, Frederick "Fred", 154, 298, 356
Foster, J.B., 135
Fountain, Albert J., 19, 114, 157, 160-61, 164, 173, 231, 272, 279, 352, 418n
Fountain, Albert J., Jr., 173, 352, 418n
Fountain, Edward, 418n
Fountain, Henry, 19, 160-61, 164, 173, 179
Fountain, Jack, 418n
Fountain, Margaret, 418n
Fountain, Tom, 418n
Fowler, Joel A., 160
Fraker, Charles L., 103, 334
Fragua, Cliff, 293, 431n
Frémont, John C., 276, 277
French, Jim, 181
Fresques, Jeremy, 326
Frey, Evelyn L.C., 110, 349
Frink, John W., 325, 356
Frost, Max E., 112, 113, 172, 355
Fuchs, Emil J.K., 128, 252, 316
Fugate, Dody, 342
Fuzita, K., 304

Gallegos, José M., 206-7, 243, 358
Galli, Clarence, 26
Garcia, Fabian, 121, 252-53, 352
Garcia, Nasario, 371
Garcia, Orencio, 338
Garcia, Salome, 163
Garcia, Taurino, 303, 350
Garde, C.M., 213
Garfield, James A., 200
Garrett, Apolinaria, 154
Garrett, Elizabeth, 61, 77-78, 142, 154, 354, 398n, 413n
Garrett, Jarvis, 184
Garrett, Patrick F.J. "Pat", 18, 78, 106, 154-55, 188, 193, 353, 421n
Garson, Greer F., 57, 95, 106, 368
Garza, Damian, 326
Gaskill, Marylee, 300
Gauny, Samuel L., 162
Gellenthien, Alice Brown, 258
Gellenthien, Carl H., 257-58, 374, 377, 439n
George III, 382n
Gerken, Rudolph Aloysius, 239
Geronimo, 158, 290-91, 304, 331, 367, 421n
Geronimo, Harlyn, 219
Giddings, Marsh, 201, 365
Gililland, James R., 106, 160-61, 164, 173, 359
Gilmer, Jimmy, 78
Gilpin, Laura, 53, 362, 372
Giraud, Joseph, 271
Gish, Robert F., 70
Gleick, James, 55
Goddard, Kennet, 120n
Goddard, Ralph W., 120, 257, 353, 406n
Goddard, Robert H., 128, 253, 365, 377
Goebel, Arthur "Art", 147, 362
Gollmer, Christopher, 275, 356
Gonzales, Ignacio, 181
Gonzales, Irma Flores, 137, 373
Gonzales, Yolanda I., 341
Gonzales y Borrego, Antonio, 172
Gonzales y Borrego, Francisco, 172
Gonzalez, José A., 197-98
Goodacre, Glenna, 322, 454n
Goodnight, Charles, 104-5, 368
Goodnight, Mary Ann, 105
Gore, Dena Lynn, 177-78, 333, 359
Gorman, Carl N., 15, 44, 47, 88, 128, 308, 309, 374
Gorman, R.C., 44, 309
Goss, Robert S., 123, 363
Graef, Calvin R., 306-7, 356
Grant, Jonathan, 326
Grant, Ulysses S., 112
Gray, Tommy L., 326
Graydon, James "Paddy", 269, 279, 292, 356
Greaves, Clinton, 280, 283, 367
Greely, Benjamin G., 275, 356
Green, Thomas, 273, 369
Gregg, Andy, 167
Gregg, Josiah, 99, 197, 263, 376
Griego, Juan Francisco "Pancho", 179-80, 358
Griffin, Fred A., 303
Grossetete, Clotilde, 24
Groves, Leslie R., Jr., 314-15, 369
Grueber, Franz, 339
Grzelachowski, Alexander, 116, 243, 269-70, 354
Guenther, Jacob, 283, 356

Guerin, Demetrio, 134
Guerin, Mrs. Demetrio, 134
Guest, Orville, 189
Gunter, Archibald Clavering, 156
Gunter, Billy, 17
Gurulé, José, 21
Guyer, John R., 164

Habermann, August, 275, 356
Hadley, Hiram, 119, 121, 179, 353
Hagerman, Herbert J., 108, 205, 230, 374
Hagerman, James J., 108, 124, 203
Hagerman, Percy, 108
Hahn, Emily, 94
Hail, Peter, 275, 356
Haley, J. Evetts, 410n
Hall, Theodore A., 128, 253-54, 316
HAM, 344
Hamilton, Juan, 43
Hamilton, Rev., 134
Hanna, Ebineezer, 274-75, 356
Hanna, Marcus Alonzo "Mark", 124
Hanna, William, 57, 362
Hannett, Arthur T., 215, 347
Hanold, Fred H., 400n
Haozous, Bob, 45
Hardin, Charles, 75
Hardin, Helen, 47
Hardin, John W., 155
Harris, Jim, 383n
Harrison, Benjamin, 208
Hart, Bill, 156
Hart, H.M., 303
Harvey, Frederick "Fred", 110, 364
Harwood, Emily Jane, 126, 248
Harwood, Thomas, 126, 247-48, 272, 347
Hatch, Carl A., 224, 236, 347
Hatch, Edward, 279
Hatton, John, 339
Haut, Walter G., 137, 313, 354
Hawkins, W.A., 107
Hayes, Helen, 41
Heat-Moon, William Least, 9
Heinz, Miss, 124
Henderson, Alice C., 37, 71, 75, 142, 259, 355, 376
Henderson, William P., 36, 37-38, 51, 71, 81, 142, 343, 355, 376
Hendricks, H.W., Jr., 408n
Hennings, Ernest M., 33, 363
Henson, Jacob, 275, 356
Hernández, Benigno C., 157, 226, 362
Herrera, Antonio, 168
Herrera, Frederick D., 325
Herrera, Joe Hilario, 127
Herz, Cary, 333
Hewett, Edgar Lee, 19, 29, 81, 84, 85, 123, 125, 128, 246, 373
Higgins, William Victor, 29, 33, 36, 333, 359
Hignett, Sean, 41
Hildebrandt, Chad R., 326
Hill, Frank, 90
Hill, Opal K.S., 111, 347
Hill, Rita, 90
Hillerman, Tony, 25
Hilton, Conrad N., 111, 231, 306, 368
Hindman, George W., 189
Hinkle, James F., 106, 113, 214, 354

Hinkle, Lillie Roberts, 214
Hitler, Adolf, 301
Hockenhull, Andrew W., 116, 216, 350
Holliday, John Henry "Doc", 161, 260, 363
Holly, Charles H. "Buddy", 57-58, 337, 368, 393n
Hooker, Van Dorn, 50
Hopkins, F.J., 275, 356
Hoppes, Alice Faye Kent, 137, 349
Hordes, Stanley, 333
Horgan, Paul G., 41, 71-72, 93, 124, 313, 366, 376
Hough, Janaloo Hill, 61, 77, 90, 106, 142, 373
Hough, Manny, 90
House, Edwin, 223
House, Gordon, 173
Houser, Allan, 45, 127, 128, 129, 355
Howard, Edward Lee, 161, 373
Howard, Ron, 410n
Hubbard, Elbert, 110
Hubbell, James Lawrence "Santiago", 105, 272, 347
Humphrey, Hubert H., 224
Huning, Elly, 100
Huning, Franz, 70, 100, 210, 348, 373
Huning, Lina, 100
Hunt, Robert, 65-66, 395n
Hurd, Henriette Wyeth, 41, 390n
Hurd, Peter, 41, 42, 124, 373
Hurley, Patrick J., 230, 231, 310, 356
Hutton, Paul, 185

Ilfeld, Charles, 115, 353
Ilthma, Oscar B., 308
Ingersoll, Robert G., 155
Isabella, 92
Isaiah, 237
Isomura, Hirota, 318, 319, 368

Jack, Captain, 267
Jackson, Joseph, 341
Jacome, Carlos, 165
Jaeger, Walter, 319-20, 368, 453n
James, Bessy, 300, 350
James, Bill, 30
James, Jesse, 159-60, 414n
James, Milton, 300
Jaramillo, Angelina E.B., 84, 178, 358
Jaramillo, Cleofas Martinez, 84, 178, 358
Jaramillo, Julian, 26
Jaramillo, Venceslao, 178
Jeffers, Robinson, 93
Jefferson, Lemon, 26
Jeffords, Thomas J., 446
Jencks, Clinton, 138, 313, 373
Jencks, Virginia, 138
Jenco, Lawrence Martin, 134, 241, 364
Jenkins, Myra Ellen, 23, 90-91, 363, 416n
Jennings, Delbert O., 323, 363
Jennings, Waylon   , 78
Jette, Eleanor, 254
Jette, Eric R., 254, 316, 353, 374
Jimémez, Luis Alfonso, Jr., 48
Jimémez, Susan, 48
Joe, Oreland, 308
John, Schonchin, 267
Johnson, Andrew, 203
Johnson, Bill "Kid", 166

Johnson, Donald B., 339
Johnson, Edward Dana, 75, 113, 223, 355
Johnson, Gary, 232
Johnson, John A. "Jack", 149, 154, 363
Johnson, Lady Bird, 390
Johnson, Lyndon B., 42, 224, 323, 389n
Johnson, Roy W., 127, 151, 306, 313, 356
Johnson, Thomas, 178
Johnson, Walter W. "Spud", 72, 88, 94, 114, 396n
Jones, Addison D., 142, 354
Jones, Andrieus A., 129, 221, 353
Jones, George, 23
Jonson, Carl Raymond, 19, 42, 129, 373, 390n
Jordon, George, 284, 280, 366
Joseph, Antonio, 116, 210, 355
Juhl, August, 275, 356
Julyan, Robert, 20, 21, 383n, 434n
June, Alan D., 308
Jung, Carl, 93

Katz, Fenton S., 338
Kearny, Mary, 266
Kearny, Stephen Watts, 197, 264, 265-66, 365, 441n
Keene, Billy, 158
Keleher, William A., 75, 160, 348
Kelliher, Michael, 167
Kelly, George "Machine Gun", 154
Kendall, George W., 114, 263-64, 367
Kendrick, Susan "Susie" Parks, 134, 300-1, 369, 374
Kennedy, Charles, 106, 161-62
Kennedy, John F., 136, 203, 224
Kenney, Bergere, 140
Kenney, Jack, 140
Kessell, John, 16
Ketchum, Berry, 162
Ketchum, Samuel W. "Sam", 162, 163, 355
Ketchum, Thomas E. "Black Jack", 162-64, 173, 349
Kidder, Alfred V., 15, 85, 129
Kilgore, Mary D.M., 332
Kindval, Frank T., 303
King, Bruce, 184
King, Martin Luther, Jr., 137
King, Norman L., 297
King, Oliver J.B., 338
King, Robert Lee "Bob", 127, 151, 356
King, Sandy, 166
Kinney, John W.Y., 27, 116, 190, 279, 361
Kluckhohn, Clyde, 85, 129, 373
Knight, Kenneth Ray, 335
Kobata, Toshiro, 318-19
Kopecky, Arthur, 131
Kraft, Salesius, 435n
Kramer, Dorothy Dunn, 46, 88, 127-28, 362, 373

LaFarge, Oliver H.P., 71, 72, 88, 142, 313, 356, 396n
Lafranc, Margaret, 393n
LaGrone, Oliver, 43, 77, 129, 142, 376
Lambert, Charles F., 112, 155, 349
Lambert, Henry, 106, 112, 349
L'Amour, Louis, 72-73, 362
Lamy, Jean B., 116, 172, 201, 207, 237-38, 242, 243, 269, 405n, 434n
Lane, Mitchell S., 325
Lane, William Carr, 199, 260, 365
Lange, Dorothea, 54, 373, 393n
Lange, John, 54

Langston, William, 275, 356
Lapahie, Harrison, 301, 351
Larrazolo, Octaviano A., 213, 225, 348
Lasseter, John B., 113
Lawrence, David H., 18, 19, 40, 73, 93, 372, 376, 457n
Lawrence, Frieda R., 41, 73-74, 376
Lawrence, Katharine Brown, 448n
Lawton, Henry W., 297
Lea, Joseph C., 108, 124, 274, 355
Leahy, D.H., 113
Lee, Oliver M., Jr., 51, 106, 160, 164-65, 173, 231, 347
Lee, Russell W., 54
Lenberg, Robert, 339-40
Leonard, Alfred, 308
Leopold, Aldo, 135, 138, 364
Lewis, Alfred H., 170
Lewis, Bob, 173
Lewis, Edith, 66, 67, 395n
Lewis, Lucy M., 45, 129, 390n
Lewis, Thomas Halver, 337
Leyba, Marino, 165
Lillie, Gordon W., 421n
Lilly, Benjamin V., 149-50, 358
Lincoln, Abraham, 207
Lindsey, Washington E., 212, 213, 354
Lippmann, Walter, 223
Llewellyn, William H.H., 232, 296, 353
Loeffler, Jack, 63
Longworth, Alice Roosevelt, 223
Loomis, John, 271-72
López, George, 48
López, José D., 48, 350
López, Raymond, 185
López, Ricardo, 48
Lopez, Robert C., 325, 369
Lovelace, Mary, 258-59
Lovelace, William R. I, 223, 258, 348, 377
Lovelace, William R. II, 258-59, 348, 439n
Loving, Oliver, 104, 105-6, 368
Lozen, 291, 361
Luhan, Mabel Dodge, 40, 73, 74, 77, 93-94, 233, 359, 401n, 433n
Lujan, Antonio "Tony", 93, 94, 142, 233, 433n
Lujan, Manuel, 72
Lummis, Charles F., 19, 55, 77, 85-86, 110, 373, 376, 441n
Luna, Antonio J., 223, 430n
Luna, Maximiliano, 20, 157, 209, 211, 232, 296-97
Luna, Solomon, 106, 140, 209, 211, 348
Luna, Ted, 144
Luna, Tranquilino, 106, 157, 209, 211, 253
Lusk, Georgia L.W., 106, 119, 129, 227-28, 349, 432n
Lyon, Edward W., 20
Lytle, Leonidas S., 284, 358

Mabry, Thomas J., 78, 187, 212, 217-18, 236, 348
Machebeuf, Joseph P., 238, 242, 363
Madero, Francisco, 299, 449n
Maeston, Thomas J., 106, 116, 274, 278, 340, 354
Magee, Carlton C., 113, 367
Magoffin, James W., 100-1, 264, 266
Magoffin, Samuel, 100, 101
Magoffin, Susan H.S., 100, 101, 109, 365
Major, Duncan K., 336
Mallon, Catherine, 244, 358
Manby, Arthur R., 174, 359
Manderfield, William H.,113-14, 358

Mangas Coloradas, 291
Manilius, Marcus, 211
Mann, Herbert "Herbie", 58-59, 79, 372
Mann, Horace, 171
Mann, John, 23
Manuelito (Apache), 292
Manuelito (Navajo), 292
Manuelito, James C., 308
Manus, James, 275, 356
Manzanares, Francisco A., 116, 209, 353
Marbach, Stephen, 275, 356
Marin, John, 93
Martin, John R., 275, 357
Martín, Juan Miguel, 168
Martin, T.P., 418n
Martínez, Antonio José, 197, 242, 243, 359
Martinez, Armando, 449n
Martinez, Dennis, 277
Martinez, Joseph P., 311, 362
Martinez, Julian, 45-46
Martinez, Maria A.M., 45, 46, 390n
Martinez, Patricio "Paddy", 106, 115, 142, 352
Maschhoff, Martha R., 339
Mason, William, 98
Mathews, Jacob B. "Billy", 106, 190-91, 272, 355
Mauldin, William "Bill", 43, 145, 316-17, 369
Maxwell, Calvin W., 325
Maxwell, Lucien B., 108-9, 193, 339, 351
Maxwell, Peter, 183, 193, 351
McAfee, Horace, 331
McBride, James J., 320
McBride, John, 184
McCabe, William, 308
McCarthy, Dermott F., 341
McComas, Charles W., 179, 277-78
McComas, H.C., 277, 278, 364
McComas, Juanita, 277, 278, 364
McCord, James, 275, 357,
McCormick, John Medill, 407n
McCormick, Ruth "Bazy", 124
McCormick, William, 275, 357
McCullough, David, 71-72
McDonald, David, 98
McDonald, John, 98
McDonald, William C., 18, 212, 359
McFie, John R., 88, 121, 178, 235, 272, 357, 433n
McIntire, Scott W., 326
McJunkin, George, 106, 138-39, 351, 409n
McKibbin, Dorothy S., 145, 259, 377, 452n
McKinley, William, 39
McKinney, Robert, 69
McKnight, John N., 275, 357
McLaughlin, Bernice W., 106, 150, 349
McLean, Don, 58
McLeod, Hugh, 264, 274, 369
McMains, Oscar P., 114, 180, 232, 248, 363
McNab, Frank, 181
McNally, James, 272, 284, 352
McRae, Alexander, 270-71, 366, 442n
McRae, John, 270
McRee, Kathleen, 383n
McSween, Alexander A., 104, 116, 186, 188
McSween, Susanna E.H., 106, 186-87, 359, 422n
Mechem, Edwin L., 157, 213-14, 218, 225, 236, 348
Mechem, Merritt C., 213-14, 218, 236, 348, 376

Medders, Maud, 106, 134, 301, 328, 354
Medders, Will, 301
Medina, Juan N., 305
Meem, John Gaw, 19, 42, 50-51, 61, 88, 259, 372, 376
Menaul, James A., 126, 248, 348
Mera, Frank E., 86, 88, 259, 260, 306, 355
Mera, Harry P., Jr., 86, 259, 355
Mera, Reba, 86
Meriwether, David W., 116, 199, 364
Merville, Christopher A., 326
Meyers, Ralph, 93
Middleton, David, 296
Middleton, John, 181
Miles, John E., 114, 217, 355
Milford, Nadine, 173
Miller, C.C., 303
Miller, C.D., 303
Miller, Franklin D., 324, 374
Miller, John, 185, 187, 261, 361, 422n
Miller, Roger, 59, 79, 372
Mills, Ernest T. "Ernie", 77, 133, 373
Mills, William J., 206, 236, 333
Milton, Hugh, 120-21
Mirabal, Jim, 33, 34
Miranda, Guadalupe, 107
Mitchell, Robert B., 201, 272, 369
Mitchell, William B., 334
Mix, Thomas H. "Tom", 59-60, 362
Miyamura, Hiroshi "Hershey", 322, 453n
Mohr, Joseph, 339
Monroe, Harriet, 71
Monte Bill, 170
Montgomery, Alexander, 275, 357
Montoya, Geronima Cruz, 128
Montoya, Joaquin, 165
Montoya, Joseph M., 225, 358
Montoya, Nestor, 114, 212, 226, 348
Moody, 415n
Moon, Harold H., Jr., 311, 348
Moore, Charles, 20
Moore, J.J., 303
Morgan, J.P., 223
Morgan, John Cary, 124, 311-12, 369
Morley, Ada, 246
Morley, William R., Sr., 180
Morris, James L., 285
Morrison, James D. "Jim", 60, 79, 348, 370
Morrissey, Robert D., 326
Morrow, John F., 226-27, 354
Morton, Michael Ray, 335
Motz, John T., 341
Mruk, Wladyslaw "Walter", 34, 35, 366, 388n
Mueller, Frederick "Fritz", 116, 297, 357
Murphy, Lawrence G., 181, 188, 190, 272
Murphy, Raymond G., 322, 453n
Murray, Olivia Payton, 222
Musgraves, George, 153

Nakayama, Roy, 129, 254, 313, 374
Nana, 286, 288, 289, 291, 292, 367
Naráez, Pánfilo de, 261
Nash, Willard A., 34, 35, 372, 388n
Neary, D.J., 286
Neeld, Bobby G., 326.
Neuhoff, Hermann, 321, 351

Newbrough, John B., 77, 126, 249-50, 260, 339, 353
Newbrough, Justine B., 250
Newman, Larry, 146
Nez, Chester, 308
Nez, Jack, 308
Nievergelt, John G., 301-2, 368
Nightingale, Florence, 382n
Nixon, Pat, 41
Nixon, Richard M., 159, 225, 324
Niza, Marcos de, 243, 261, 262
Nolan, Frederick, 188, 183, 185, 193, 420n, 423n
Nordfeldt, Bror Julius Olsson, 36, 38, 369
Noss, Milton Ernest "Doc", 20, 139, 175, 409n
Noss, Ova B., 139

Ochoa, Marina, 89
O'Connor, Kathryn K., 61, 145, 337, 348, 376
O'Fallon, John, 265
O'Folliard, Thomas "Tom", 184, 185, 421n
O'Hara, Theodore, 261
O'Keeffe, Georgia T., 19, 43, 93, 372, 390n
O'Kelley, Edward, 159
Oldham, John S., 326
O'Leary, Dennis, 333, 335-36, 357
Olinger, Ameridth Robert B. "Bob", 183, 192, 193
Oliver, Lloyd, 308
Oñate, Juan de, 89, 91, 195, 235, 263
Oppenheimer, J. Robert, 19, 255, 257, 315, 316, 374, 452n
Oppenheimer, Kitty, 315
Orbison, Roy, 78
Orchard, Sarah J.C. "Sadie", 18, 112, 169, 359, 417n
Ortiz, Alcaria, 229
Ortiz, Alfonso, 86-87, 129, 373
Ortiz, Francis "Frank" V., Jr., 88, 229-30, 313, 358
Ortiz y Pino, Concha, 88, 106, 129, 230-31, 432n
Otero, Mariano S., 106, 116, 140, 204, 207, 209, 348
Otero, Miguel A., Jr., 51, 140, 204, 207, 209, 210, 223, 355
Otero, Miguel A., Sr., 117, 140, 204, 207, 209, 363
Otero-Warren, Maria Adelina "Nina", 77, 119, 129, 204, 207, 211, 358

Padilla, Juan José, 16, 240, 381n
Palmer, Joe, 309
Parker, George, 153
Parks, G.E., 300
Parks, Steve, 174
Parsons, Elsie Clews, 87, 373
Parsons, Martha, 316
Parsons, Orrin Sheldon, 39, 372, 376
Parsons, William S. "Deak", 315, 369, 452n
Parsons, William T., 275, 357
Partridge, John, 189
Peacock, Douglas   , 63
Peppin, George W., 191-92, 273, 353
Perea, Dolores, 200
Perea, Francisco, 106, 117, 207, 273, 348
Perea, Francisco "Pedro", 210
Perea, José Leandro, 23, 98, 101, 106, 349
Pereyra, José, 303
Pérez, Albino, 197
Pérez de Villagrá, Gaspar, 89, 91, 195, 263
Perry, John, 279
Pershing, John J. "Black Jack", 280, 302, 306, 369
Pershing, John W., 302
Pershing, Richard, 302
Pete, Frank D., 309

Peterson, Roger, 58
Pettit, Christopher S., 338
Petty, Norman, 57, 78, 114, 117, 350
Phillips, Bert Geer, 29, 30, 31, 32, 359
Picard, Juan, 99
Pike, Zebulon M., 18, 262-63, 294, 331, 366
Pile, Forrest, 201
Pile, William A., 201, 273, 230, 362, 425n
Pino, Pedro, 233, 433n
Pino, Pedro Bautista, 119, 433n, 455n
Pipkin, Daniel M., 166
Pirtle, James, 326
Pitaval, Jean B., 239, 363
Plestewa, Lori, 326
Plumhoff, Steven, 326
Poe, Edgar Allan, 382n
Pollock, S. Ernest   , 182
Pond, Ashley, Jr., 67, 119-20, 373
Pond, E.L. "Slim", 456n
Popé, 224, 234, 292-93, 431n, 447n
Pope, William H., 236, 355
Popejoy, Thomas L., 125-26, 151, 373
Porter, Eliot F., 54-55
Potter, Charles, 165
Powell, Lawrence C., 70
Powell, Ray, 158
Prather, John Albert, 140-41
Price, Sterling, 232, 265, 274, 365
Prichard, George W., 220
Prince, L. Bradford, 93, 121, 172, 204, 236, 366
Prince, Mrs. L. Bradford, 92
Puccini, 56
Pyle, Ernest T. "Ernie", 77, 317, 343, 363
Pyle, Jerry, 343

Quintana, Santiago, 44

Radcliffe, William D., 99
Rallière, Jean Baptiste, 242-43
Ramos, Christopher, 326
Rangel, José, 303, 350
Rapp, Isaac H., 51, 363
Ravagli, Angelo, 73, 74
Ravel, Arthur, 302
Ravel, Luis, 302
Ravel, Samuel "Sam", 117, 302-3, 367
Ray, Joyce, 177
Read, Benjamin, 91-92, 119, 232, 358
Reagan, Ronald, 308
Reams, Narsise, 341
Reeves, Pete, 189
Rencher, Abraham, 367
Renken, Heinrich, 321
Renteria, Eusevio, 303, 350
Revueltas, Rosaura, 409n
Reyes, Mario A., 326
Rhodes, Eugene M., 74-75, 106, 153, 164
Rhodes, May, 75
Rice, Demetrius L., 326
Richardson, Bill, 44, 137
Richardson, J.P., 58
Richardson, Robert, 176
Ritch, William G., 126, 202, 273, 357, 376
Ritchie, William T., 303
Rivera, Diego, 49

Robb, John D., 79, 87, 123, 373
Roberts, Andrew L. "Buckshot", 186, 192, 353
Roberts, Don, 176
Roberts, Ollie P. "Brushy Bill", 187-88, 368
Robledo, Damaso, 97, 401n
Rocco, Louis R., 145, 324, 368
Rocha, Moses D., 326
Rochas, François-Jean "Frenchy", 51-52, 164, 175, 352, 392n
Rodey, Bernard S., 126, 210-11, 348, 428n
Rodriguez, Eliseo , 387n
Rodriguez, José, 303
Rodriguez, Joseph E., 326
Rogers, Mary Millicent, 94-95, 359
Rogers, Will, 110, 156
Romero, Cayetano, 299, 333, 351
Romero, Ruben, 277
Romero, Trinidad, 106, 117, 157, 209, 353
Romero de Romero, Esquípula, 49, 117, 372
Rooke, Sarah J. "Sallie", 133-34, 351
Roosevelt, Franklin D., 313, 318
Roosevelt, Theodore, 205, 232, 295, 297-98, 367
Roper, John A., 178, 419n
Rosenberg, Ethel, 438n
Rosenberg, Julius, 438n
Ross, Edmund G., 121, 123, 126, 203-4, 273, 348
Ross, Nellie T., 429n
Rossin, Alice, 94
Rowdy, Y.B., 285, 357
Rudebaugh, David "Dirty Dave", 157, 165
Runnels, Harold L., 117, 228, 353, 432n
Rush, Olive, 40, 364, 372
Russell, Hattie Eliza, 102
Russell, Marion S., 101-2, 363
Russell, Richard, 102
Ryan, Charles, 139
Rynerson, William L., 106, 193, 271, 272, 353

Sage, Charles G., 114, 307, 357
St. Vrain, Cerán, 97, 102, 266, 271, 273
Salas, Antonio, 134
Salas, Rick, Jr., 326
Salazar, Leo, 49, 349
Sale, Albert D., 285-86, 364
Salpointe, Jean B., 237, 238, 361, 434n
Sánchez, George I., 128, 368, 373
Sanchez, Juan, 303, 350
Sandburg, Carl, 396
Scarborough, George, 155, 350
Schaefer, Fritz, 275, 357
Scheurich, Aloys, 277
Schiff, Steven H. "Steve", 228-29, 348
Schlatter, Francis, 246
Schlegel, Wolfgang, 320, 453n
Schmid, Walter, 452n
Schnitzer, John P., 286, 351
Scholes, Frances V., 92, 129, 306, 357
Schroeder, Otto, 275, 357
Schubert, Frank, 445n
Schwachheim, Carl, 138
Scott, Robert S., 151, 312, 322, 326, 357
Scroggins, John, 181
Scurlock, Doc, 181
Sedillo, Alfonso, 342
Segale, Rosaister Maria, 21, 129, 244-45, 260
Seligman, Arthur, 117, 215-16, 355

Selman, John H., 155
Seton, Ernest Thompson, 44, 77, 88, 129, 143, 257
Shakespeare, William, 164, 215
Sharp, Joseph Henry, 32, 88, 362
Sharpless, Edward C., 286, 287, 354
Shaw, Thomas, 273, 280, 286, 292
Sheerin, John, 287
Sheldon, Lionel A, 203, 273
Sheridan, Phil, 267
Sherman, William Tecumseh, 267
Sherrick, Charles H., 334
Shield, G.W., 162
Shor, David D., 249, 313, 348
Shortle, Abraham G., 259-60, 348
Shropshire, John, 274
Shufelt, Loren S., 330
Shuster, Don, 36
Shuster, William H., Jr., 29, 34, 36, 72, 306, 357
Sibley, Henry H., 230, 266, 274, 279
Sickels, William, 170
Siler, Kip, 274
Silva, Vicente, 165-66
Simmons, Marc, 102, 182, 184, 278, 416n
Simms, Albert G., 107, 124, 218, 227, 348
Simms, John F., Jr., 218, 348
Simms, John F., Sr., 218, 227
Simms, Ruth H. McCormick, 124, 227, 348
Simon, Paul, 303
Simpson, Jeremiah "Shoeless Jerry", 109, 117, 231
Simpson, Max C., 326
Simpson, Smith H., 135, 271-72, 277, 279
Sinclair, John L., 69, 75
Siringo, Charles, 77, 107, 155-56, 362
Sisneros, Federico, 89, 143
Skeen, Joseph R., 107, 229
Slaughter, E.R., 275, 357
Slinkard, Burt, 287
Slinkard, Joe, 287
Sloan, Dolly, 38
Sloan, Helen, 38
Sloan, John F., 36, 37, 38-39, 372
Slough, John P., 175, 236, 271, 272, 367
Smith, Chester French, 172
Smith, Sam, 181
Smith, Sam, 206
Smith, Sandra F., 339
Smokey Bear, 135, 344-45, 456n
Smokey Joe, 170
Snyder, Jake, 180
Soelen, Theodore, 36
Sonnichsen, C.L., 221, 392n
Spatts, Milton A., 418n
Speer, Christopher J., 326
Speers, Daisy, 140-41
Spiegelberg, Abraham, 103
Spiegelberg, Elias, 103
Spiegelberg, Emanual, 103
Spiegelberg, Lehman, 103
Spiegelberg, Levi, 103
Spiegelberg, Solomon, 103
Spiegelberg, Willi, 103
Spradley, Berry, 164
Springer, Frank, 89, 114, 121-22, 181, 232, 353, 373
Staab, Abraham, 116, 355, 405n
Staab, Zodoc, 116

Stagg, Harry P., 248, 305, 349, 377
Stamm, Raymond, 147
Stamm, Roy A., 412n
Stanley, Ebin, 107, 112, 287, 352
Stanley, Mary Elsie, 287
Stapp, John P., 135, 254-55, 260, 313, 322, 326, 344, 368, 373
Steel, Samuel A., Jr., 178-79, 352
Steele, Thomas J., 23
Steffens, Friedrich, 321, 351
Stegner, Wallace, 72
Stein, Leo, 93
Steiner, Stan, 135
Steinke, Becina, 272
Stephens, Steve, 181
Stevens, James R., 275, 357
Stevens, Montague F.S., 107, 150, 348
Stevenson, Philip, 76, 81
Stieglitz, Alfred, 390n
Stinson-Otero, Katherine, 52, 129, 148, 357, 372, 376
Stone, Burton R., 275, 357
Strand, Paul, 93
Straughn, William, 275, 357
Stuart, Gary L., 156
Stuart, J.E.B., 264
Suazo, John, 332
Sudo, N., 319, 358
Sullivan, Tom, 193
Sutton, John S., 443n
Sutton, Raymond "Ray", Sr., 107, 157, 174-75, 349
Suzuki, T., 304

Taeger, Mary Nell, 206
Tafoya, Maria M., 46
Taft, William Howard, 231, 298, 369
Tahoma, Quincy, 46, 127, 313
Tanner, Anna Mae, 335
Taylor, G.N., 275, 357
Taylor, Jessie P., 303
Taylor, John, 442n
Taylor, Robert, 184
Teller, Edward, 255, 256, 316
Temple, Byrnes W., 338
Tettenborn, William R. "Russian Bill", 166, 358
Thomas, Norman, 223
Thompson, Sister Alphonsa, 21, 382n
Thompson, Jerry D., 447n
Thompson, Nelson S., 309
Thornton, William T., 204, 355
Thorp, N. Howard, 77, 79, 87-88, 355
Thurmond, Charlotte J. "Lottie", 27, 170, 350
Thurmond, Frank, 170
Tight, Mabel, 125
Tight, William G., 89, 125, 373
Tingley, Carrie W., 70, 143-44, 216, 348, 376
Tingley, Clyde K., 70, 143, 144, 216-17, 348, 376
Todacheene, Lee, 326
Tolby, Franklin J., 181, 248, 349
Tombaugh, Annette, 256
Tombaugh, Clyde W., 129, 256, 374
Townley, Roy F., 325, 357
Townsend, C.H. Tyler, 179
Towson, Thomas, 98
Truchard, Augustine, 207
Truesday, Clara, 182
Trujillo, Michael H., 141

Trujillo, Miguel H., 129, 141, 357, 410n
Trujillo, Robert S., 326
Tsosie, Harry, 309
Tullio, Angelo de, 99
Tunstall, Emily, 189
Tunstall, John H., 104, 181, 188-89
Twain, Mark, 176
Twitchell, Ralph E., 86, 92, 172, 355

Ufer, Walter, 33-34, 36, 372
Ulam, Stanislaw "Stan", 255, 256-57, 374
Ulibarri, Sabine R., 76, 89, 129, 313, 348
Unser, Al, Jr., 151
Unser, Al, Sr., 151
Unser, Bobby, 151
Unser, Jeremy "Jerry", Jr., 151, 322, 349
Unser, Johnny, 151
Utley, Robert, 420n

Valdez, Antonio, 166
Valdez, Horacio E., 49-50, 350
Valdez, José F., 312, 357
Valencia, Patricio, 172
Valens, Richie, 58
Valerio, Anselmo, 26
Vance, Vivian, 61, 372
Vanderpool, Harry, 176
Van Dyne, S.S., 174
Van Stone, Mrs. George, 39
Vargas, Diego de, 15-16, 195-96, 263
Vaught, Jethro S., Jr., 167
Velarde, Ignacio, 156, 170
Velarde, Pablita, 46-47, 127
Verne, Jules, 256
Viarrial, Jacob, 234, 326
Victorio, 281, 291, 293, 335
Vidor, King, 184
Vierra, Carlos, 40, 50, 51, 55, 89, 355, 376, 389n
Vigil, Donaciano, 198, 266, 279, 358
Viljoen, Benjamin J., 77, 107, 299, 333, 353
Viljoen, Myrtle, 299
Villa, Francisco "Pancho", 14, 303-5, 296, 299, 300, 301, 302, 370
Von Braun, Werner, 257, 337, 369
Von Spiegelberg, Baron, 403n

Waconda, Josephine, 141
Waite, Fred, 181
Walker, David V., 337
Walker, Elver S. "Johnny", 228, 313, 357, 374, 432n
Walker, J. Waton, 303
Walker, Kenneth N., 306, 313, 369
Walker, Robert P., 275, 357
Wallace, Lewis "Lew", 76, 77, 192, 193, 202-3, 230, 267, 273, 364
Wallace, Susan A.E., 76, 364
Walley, Augustus, 280, 287-88, 292, 298, 365
Walsh, Charles F., 147-48, 362
Walters, William H. "Bronco Bill", 17, 155, 166-67, 352, 416n
Walton, William B. "Billy", 114, 117, 212, 226, 358
Warner, Edith, 316
Warren, Earl, 224
Waters, Frank, 76-77, 93, 142, 233, 372
Watts, Isaac, 339
Watts, John S., 207, 236, 364
Wauneka, Annie Dodge, 129, 233, 234, 260
Webb, John Joshua, 167

Weightman, Richard H., 114, 147, 206, 266, 274, 365
Weldon, Felix W. de, 224
Welker, Loyce Lee Hammett, 338
Wells, H.G., 256
Wenger, Daisy, 134
Wenger, Dan, 134
Wenger, Mrs. Dan B., 134
Westbrook, Marshall A., 326
Westphall, Victor D. III, 144
Westphall, Victor Walter, 51, 93, 117, 144-45, 313
Westphall, Walter, 144
Wetherill, Marietta, 175
Wetherill, Richard, 117, 175, 381n
Wheeler, Dan, 134
Wheeler, Harriet Adeltha, 134
Wheeler (infant son), 134
Wheeler, Jim, 68
Wheeler, Joseph Edward, 117, 248, 352
Wheeler, Lucy Ann, 134
Wheeler, Lula C., 134
Wheeler, Thomas W., 134
Wheeler, Vera, 134
Wheeler, Walter, 134
Wheeler, Willie C., 134
Whipple, Greg, 283
White, Amelia Elizabeth, 37, 343
White, Fannie, 145
White, Frank, 334
White, Horace, 343
White, James L., 145, 349
White, Martha, 37, 343
White, Robert R., 336
White, W.A., 456n
White, William Allen, 110
Whitehill, Harvey, 107, 156, 273, 358
Whiteside, Lucy J.R., 112, 260, 352, 377
Whitlock, John M., 269
Whitman, Walt, 137
Widner, Vernon, 326
Wilcoxson, John J., 307, 348
Wilder, Thorton, 93
Wilder, Wilber E., 288, 298, 303, 306, 363
Will de Chaparro, Martina, 15
Williams, Cathy, 280, 444n
Williams, Clara Belle, 129, 141-42
Williams, James II, 141
Williams, Moses, 280, 288, 292, 370
Williams, Richard B., 189, 350
Williams, W.J., 334
Willie, John W., Jr., 309
Wills, Henry, 288-89
Wilson, B. Frank, 334
Wilson, Edmund, 93
Wilson, Francis C.
Wilson, L. Edison "Bobcat", Sr., 156, 175, 352
Wilson, Thomas D., 275, 357
Wilson, William D., 309
Wilson, Woodrow, 147
Winstead, Charles B., 156-57, 316, 373
Wiseman, Bain W., Jr., 326
Wister, Marina, 41
Wiswell, Harry E., 303
Wolfe, Thomas, 93
Wood, Charles, 271, 277
Wood, Leonard, 297

Woodard, Erin L., 172, 179
Woodard, Kacee D., 172, 179
Woodard, Kandyce M.N., 172, 179
Woods, Brent, 280, 289, 292, 364
Woods, Phil, 59
Woolley, Robert, 337
Wootton, Richens L. "Uncle Dick", 103, 363
Workman, Everly John "Jack", 123, 126, 257, 316, 373
Worley, Kenneth L., 324, 362
Wright, Johnnie, 301
Wroth, William, 54

Yarberry, Milton J., 167, 348, 416n
Yazzie, Clifton, 327
Yoshikawa, D., 319, 358

Zamora, Jesse Maria, 327
Zárate, Asencio de, 240, 381n
Zafón, Carlos Ruiz, 13
Zeitsch, Otto, 321, 351
Zimmerman, James F., 125, 348

www.ingramcontent.com/pod-product-compliance
Lightning Source LLC
Chambersburg PA
CBHW080721300426
44114CB00019B/2450